Fair Trade
and Harmonization

The American Society of International Law
2223 Massachusetts Avenue, N.W.   Washington, DC   20008-2864
(202) 936-6000   Fax (202) 797-7133

Fair Trade
and Harmonization

Prerequisites for Free
Trade?

Volume 1
Economic Analysis

Edited by
Jagdish Bhagwati
Robert E. Hudec

The MIT Press
Cambridge, Massachusetts
London, England

This book was set in Palatino by Asco Trade Typesetting Ltd., Hong Kong and was printed and bound in the United States of America.

Library of Congress Cataloging-in-Publication Data

Fair trade and harmonization : prerequisites for free trade? / edited
  by Jagdish Bhagwati, Robert E. Hudec.
    v. ⟨1,   ⟩; cm.
    Includes bibliographical references and index.
    Contents: v. 1. Economic analysis. v. 2. Legal analysis.
    ISBN 0-262-02401-2 (v. 1)
    ISBN 0-262-02402-0 (v. 2)
      1. International trade. 2. Competition, Unfair. 3. International
  economic relations. 4. Foreign trade regulation. 5. Environmental
  policy. 6. Free trade. 7. Competition, Unfair—Japan.
  I. Bhagwati, Jagdish, 1934–   . II. Hudec, Robert E.
  HF1379.F34   1996
  382—dc20   95-46605

Contents

Preface

These two volumes are the final results of a research project codirected by us over the last three years. The research was supported by a grant from the Ford Foundation and the project was managed by the American Society of International Law. Our thanks go to both institutions for their invaluable support, without which a project of this magnitude could not have been started or brought to a successful conclusion.

The project involved bringing together a large number of outstanding international economists and lawyers with different political persuasions but with uniformly high professional standards. This political diversity was essential since a considered judgment on the questions to be addressed in the project required, not merely economic or legal expertise, but the ability to consider the issues of fair trade and harmonization within a wider context that would draw on fields as diverse as political philosophy and ethics.

The interaction among the project participants was productive in that regard. Two conferences, an early one at Minnesota Law School and the other toward the end in Washington DC, were most helpful in producing the needed interaction and improving the quality of virtually every paper.

While we finally decided to divide the papers into a volume addressed to economic analysis (volume 1) and another addressed to legal analysis (volume 2), the papers in each volume reflect insights obtained through the papers and the comments of the contributors to the other volume. The two volumes are nonetheless divided along the lines of economics and law—though the lawyer David Leebron's contribution is in the economics volume and the economist Brian Hindley's essay is in the legal volume—simply because economists and lawyers generally address similar questions with different tools of analysis, and at times even consider different questions within each issue area.

Since, broadly speaking, the three problem areas discussed, by issue, are the trade-environment, the trade-labor, and the trade-competition inter-faces, the economics and legal papers are conveniently read in tandem. For instance, on the questions of fair trade and harmonization involving the trade-environment interface, the economics contribution of Bhagwati (chapter 1 in volume 1) and Bhagwati and Srinivasan (chapter 4 in volume 1) should be read alongside the contributions of Hudec (chapter 3 in volume 2) and of Farber and Hudec (chapter 2 in volume 2).

Similarly, there are "pairwise" papers on labor standards in both vol-umes: Drusilla Brown, Alan Deardorff, and Robert Stern (chapter 5 in volume 1) and Virginia Leary (chapter 4 in volume 2) and Brian Langille (chapter 5 in volume 2). Equally, competition policy is analyzed in comple-mentary papers by Christopher Bliss, James Levinsohn, and Richard Clarida (in chapters 7, 8, and 9 respectively in volume 1) and by Daniel Gifford and Mitsuo Matsushita and Brian Hindley (in chapters 6 and 7 respectively in volume 2).

Chapters that deal with these issues by regions and countries are also to be found in both volumes. Thus, André Sapir (chapter 15 in volume 1) deals with the evolution of the question of harmonization in the EU from the time of the formation of the Common Market in 1957, while Gary Saxonhouse (chapter 13 in volume 1) and John McMillan (chapter 14 in volume 1) address the questions of fair trade that have afflicted Japan. Analysis of some aspects of these questions can also be found in Ken Abbott's (chapter 9 in volume 2) treatment of the fair trade questions related to foreign markets.

Then again, there are papers in both volumes that address the more theoretical, non–issue-specifc, nonregional questions that underlie much of the argumentation in regard to fair trade and harmonization. In volume 1, these include the essays by Jagdish Bhagwati, David Leebron, and Alessandra Cassella on the sources of the demands for harmonization and fair trade and the factors affecting their evolution (chapters 1, 2, and 3 respectively), and the essays on the "race to the bottom" question relating to the competitive lowering of standards to attract investment by John Wilson, Arik Levinson, and Alvin Klevorick (chapters 10, 11, and 12 respectively). In volume 2, they include the essays by Frieder Roessler (chapter 1) and the essays on "fairness" concepts in trade policy by Ronald Cass and Richard Boltuck (chapter 8) and Ken Abbott (chapter 9).

A caveat is in order. We have deliberately decided not to root out all duplications of ideas between the different chapters. Partly, this is because it is rare in the analyses of the kind found in these volumes for the treatment of any proposition to be totally identical in two different hands. The context—the nuances—provide sufficient diversity to add to the reader's understanding of the proposition being put forward. Then also, several of the chapters are quite substantial treatments of a topic and have a coherence of their own, inviting the reader to study them by themselves rather than as an integral component of a volume to be read from cover to cover. This requires that an argument that is central to a chapter's analysis not be deleted or simply be cross-referenced to another chapter whose main theme is not within the reader's realm of interest.

In conclusion, we would like to thank several economists, lawyers, philosophers, and political scientists who gave us the benefit of their advice through conversations or comments during the project. In particular, we must mention Claude Barfield, Steve Charnowitz, John Dunn, Dan Esty, Eleanor Fox, Gene Grossman, Koichi Hamada, Douglas Irwin, Karl-Göran Mäler, Fred Morrison, William Nordhaus, John Odell, Seamus O'cleireacain, Sylvia Ostry, Arvind Panagariya, Dani Rodrik, John Ruggie, Susan Rose-Ackerman, Robert Solow, and John Whalley.

Jagdish Bhagwati
Robert E. Hudec
June 1995

Fair Trade
and Harmonization

Introduction

Jagdish Bhagwati

The question of the legitimacy of diversity of domestic institutions and policies among trading nations, and its compatibility with free trade among them, has been steadily coming to dominate the trade agenda.[1]

Often, the phrase "deep integration" is used to describe the widespread demands today for a reduction or even elimination of such diversity. This is, of course, an emotive choice of words that, combining the two pleasurable words "deep" and "integration", lulls one into thinking that the demands must themselves be legitimate. For the free traders among us, the phrase is further disturbing because the simple elimination of trade barriers among the trading nation then becomes "shallow integration"—a phrase that I have actually heard and whose negative connotation is unmistakable.

In fact, the deep question facing economists, lawyers, politicians, and policymakers today is whether the demands being made to reduce diversity of domestic institutions and policies before free trade is indulged among different nations, make sense.

This is the key question before us today: Is a move toward harmonization, or what is sometimes called "fair trade" or "level playing fields", a prerequisite for free trade? Indeed, the answer to this question is the subject matter of these two volumes of economic and legal analysis that are co-edited by me and Professor Robert Hudec.

This volume, the first of the two, contains essays by several prominent economists and one distinguished legal scholar (Leebron), addressing this question from several different perspectives. Part I explores the alternative reasons why these demands for harmonization of domestic institutions and policies have arisen, since this understanding is critical to assessing the merits of these demands.

For example, if the demands to raise the labor standards in the less developed countries reflect transborder moral concerns—that we are obligated to secure for Mexicans the standards which we consider to be their right—then their probity and acceptability would require scrutiny of the moral soundness of these standards. Then a skeptic could well argue that several of the proposed standards are culture-specific and may actually harm, rather than help, the poor in the developing countries.

For instance, requiring a minimum wage in an overpopulated, developing country, as is done in a developed country, may actually be morally wicked. A minimum wage might help the unionized, industrial proletariat, while limiting the ability to save and invest rapidly which is necessary to draw more of the unemployed and nonunionized rural poor into gainful employment and income. Besides, one may well wonder whether the moral underpinning of such transborder concerns for the poor in the less developed countries is truly believable when the same groups want to tighten immigration controls on the legal and illegal influx from these countries. Such border restrictions also should make little sense to those who think in terms of concerns that transcend borders![2]

On the other hand, moral concerns do not appear to be as important in many of the environmental arguments for raising standards in other countries. Of course, to some environmentalists, the issue is not simply clean water and clean air as "goods". To them, there are deepseated moral-philosophical differences between environmental concerns and economic interests. Those concerned with economic interests typically assume that nature is in the service of humanity, whereas environmentalists typically believe in the autonomy of nature. Some environmentalists share the anguish of the poet Gerard Manley Hopkins when, in *Binsey Poplars*, he writes:

O if we but knew what we do
　　When we delve or hew—
Hack and rack the growing green!
　　Since country is so tender
To touch, her being so slender,
That, like this sleek and seeing ball
But a prick will make no eye at all,
Where we, even where we mean
　　To mend her we end her,
　　When we hew or delve:
After-comers cannot guess the beauty been,
　　Ten or twelve, only ten or twelve
　　Strokes of havoc unselve
　　　The sweet especial scene,
　　Rural scene, a rural scene,
　　Sweet especial rural scene.

There are also environmentalists who, in urging the preservation of bio-diversity, think in biblical terms of Noah's ark and the injunction to preserve two of each species. But the politically compelling arguments in favor of environmental upgrading and harmonization of standards owe far more to arguments that emphasize the "unfairness" of placing environmental burdens on a firm that hinder its ability to compete with firms that do not have to bear those burdens.

Then again, moral concerns hardly arise when questions of competition policy are being discussed. For example, if U.S. corporations feel that the Japanese government tolerates *keiretsu* that impair the negotiated access to Japan's markets (because the *keiretsu* buy from themselves rather than more cheaply from outsiders, including alien American firms) the U.S. demand will be to get the Japanese government to adopt antitrust policies. This will, in effect, harmonize Japanese antitrust policy with American policy: the harmonization will simply follow from demands for appropriate antitrust policies.

This volume of essays therefore properly starts with a substantial analysis of the numerous factors that underlie the current demands for harmonization of domestic institutions and policies. Chapter 1 by me, and Chapter 2 by David Leebron, complement each other in their intensive analysis of these factors. The focus of my analysis is on the moral, economic, structural, and political factors that drive such demands. Leebron focuses more directly on the forces that actually lead toward harmonization (such as the advantages from coordination when railway gauges are made uniform among contiguous countries).

In Chapter 3, Alessandra Casella makes the point, on the other hand, that standards will evolve with the freeing of trade. This conclusion is immediately obvious from the analysis of Srinivasan and myself in Chapter 4. We show that there will generally be a legitimate diversity of standards (such as the pollution tax rates for physically identical discharges of pollutants under the polluter-pay principle, across countries), reflecting differences in fundamentals across countries. This implies of course that any change in these fundamentals brought about by policy changes—such as the freeing of trade or parametric changes such as capital accumulation or changed tastes—will affect the standards and may lead to the convergence (i.e., toward harmonization) or the divergence thereof.[3]

This backdrop provides sufficient input for a systematic discussion of the three major harmonization issues that most analysts agree are the main issues on the world trade agenda today—environmental standards, labor standards, and competition policy. The volume extends the treatment of these and related subjects in Parts II–V.

Part VI addresses a general analytical issue that also encompasses all these issues. This is the issue of the so-called "race to the bottom" or, as John Wilson reminds us in Chapter 10, "race toward the bottom." The problem is that the use of lower environmental standards to attract investment may lead to a noncooperative Nash equilibrium that is Pareto inferior in income and environmental protection. Wilson provides a splendid theoretical review and synthesis of the vast literature that has grown up on this problem. Arik Levinson, in Chapter 11, provides a masterly synthesis of the empirical literature on whether firms do in fact let their locational and technological decisions be influenced by lower standards. (He concludes that, currently, for several plausible reasons, they do not.) Alvin Klevorick's essay in Chapter 12 provides a set of persuasive judgments on the entire question.

Complementing these general essays, Part VII of this volume contains perceptive new insights into the experience of two major trading areas with questions of "fair trade" and harmonization: Japan and the European Community. In Chapter 13, Gary Saxonhouse provides a fascinating historical analysis of the "unfair trade" complaints against Japan since the interwar period. These historical insights add to the elegant analysis of the course of the "fair trade" disputes between Japan and the United States on the issues of the *keiretsu* and the procurement system by John McMillan in Chapter 14. André Sapir, in Chapter 15, concentrates more directly on the question of harmonization policies within the EC with regard to the social policies. Sapir utilizes fresh archival research to illuminate how, starting from an eclectic position indulgent toward diversity among the member countries, this policy has moved in favor of harmonization as regional unemployment has increased. Sapir's essay shows clearly why the demand for a Social Clause (which would harmonize labor standards in member countries) at the World Trade Organization has acquired political salience in recent years.

The issues of environmental and labor standards and competition policy provide the central focus for the application of the insights gained from these general analyses. The environmental question is analyzed extensively in Chapter 4 by Srinivasan and myself; the labor standards issues are discussed in depth by Drusilla Brown, Alan Deardorff, and Robert Stern in Chapter 5; and different aspects of competition policy are treated in Chapters 7, 8, and 9 by Christopher Bliss, James Levinsohn, and Richard Clarida, respectively.

In both the former cases, demands have arisen to introduce "eco-dumping" and "social dumping" tariffs to countervail the presence of lower standards in other trading nations. In the environmental case, even when the environmental impact is strictly domestic and does not create externalities for other countries (as in the case of global warming, the fall of acid rain and the depletion of the ozone layer), these demands are typically made on the ground that the pollution tax burdens should be identical or else alien firms with lower tax rates will have an "unfair" advantage. The analysis of that issue in Chapter 4 underlines the basic perspective that diversity of cross-country intra-industry (CCII) standards is legitimate. This perspective is explored there most thoroughly, taking into account objections such as those relating to the nature of governance and associated political market failure. It also follows that if the standards are legitimately different, for example, in the poor countries, and if they are "harmonized up" by force of sanctions, including trade sanctions, by the rich countries, that will ipso facto harm the poor countries. Thus, one might argue that the presumption of (voluntary) trade being mutually beneficial is reversed with (forced) harmonization. The presumption with forced harmonization is that it will harm the countries muscled into the harmonization. The analytical treatment in Chapter 5, focuses on labor standards, underlining a different but complementary proposition: If such harmonization occurs elsewhere, there is no presumption that one will benefit either. One's economic welfare, conventionally defined, will be determined by what happens to the trade opportunity available from others after their changed standards.[4] In short, the idea of forced harmonization could well be harmful all around!

Of course, that is not the end of the story. Objectives other than economic welfare can be brought into the picture, as indeed implied by the discussion in Chapter 1 of the numerous reasons for seeking harmonization. These essays also consider, in context, the issues raised by the fear of losing one's (endogenous) standards due to a race to the bottom.

The usual complaints concern the fears of unfair loss of competitiveness to "low-standard" countries and of possible loss of one's own "high standards" due to loss of industry to these countries. This volume also analyzes the reverse issue raised by the "low-standard" countries: The high-standard countries may deliberately set their standards selectively and at high levels to impose excessive costs on their rivals in the lower-standard countries. These analyses take us directly into the question of current GATT and WTO rules concerning the setting of these standards and the advisability of changing them. In answering this question, economist readers will find it most profitable to turn to the complementary legal chapters in Volume Two as well.

Much else in the essays here bears, in one way or another, on the desirability of harmonization, whether in general or in the specific issue areas addressed. The reader will be able to infer from individual essays where an author stands on the issue. But, exactly in the spirit of skepticism that led me and Hudec to begin and see through this important project, we decided not to impose the straitjacket of harmonization on the project. Instead, we encourage the reader to reach a judgment for herself on these issues whose complexity, richness, and challenge should become apparent once these essays are read.

At minimum, we trust that these two volumes will inform and improve the current trade debate that suffers from the self-serving assertions of lobbyists and the politicians they support, the shallow arguments of the economists who advocate deep integration as manifestly desirable, the moralists who take their demands as necessarily worthy of execution simply because they proclaim their righteousness, and many among the public who stumble as they walk through the resulting fog. At maximum, we hope that the essays will play a decisive role in the debate leading up to the WTO's new trade agenda.

NOTES

1. Among the academic writings to have pinpointed sharply the emergence of this set of issues as among the principal modern challenges to free trade is my 1990 Harry Johnson Lecture, published as *The World Trading System at Risk*, (1991). Princeton, NJ: Princeton University Press. I had been working on different aspects of "fair trade" questions for some years before that, however, especially in relation to the U.S. Section 301 and the growing clamor in the United States against Japan's trade situation and policies. Quite independently, Robert Hudec was writing about "fair trade" issues as well. The present research project then grew out of the discovery of our mutual interest in similar questions. The collaboration also seemed suitable since we had collaborated beneficially in our earlier work on Section 301, published with back-to-back essays in Bhagwati, J. and H. Patrick, eds. 1991. *Aggressive unilateralism*. Ann Arbor: Michigan University Press.

2. This point has been made forcefully by T. N. Srinivasan in several recent writings.

3. Whereas Casella writes about standards as "public goods", there is no reason to confine the notion of standards to that specific format, of course. Thus, for example, the polluter-pay principle may be addressed to a simple externality.

4. In jargon, the answer depends on whether the foreign offer curve facing one shifts out or in.

I

Harmonization: General
Analytical Issues

1   The Demands to Reduce Domestic Diversity among Trading Nations

Jagdish Bhagwati

That free trade requires the harmonization of the *domestic* institutions (e.g., the retail distribution system), policies (e.g., environmental and labor standards), and practices (e.g., corporate relationships as in Japanese *keiretsu*) across trading nations is an idea that has now assumed center stage. The resulting demands to reduce, even eliminate, such domestic diversity among nations that seek freer trade among themselves raise three central questions:

- What has led to these demands to reduce diversity?
- What, in economic logic, are the virtues and vices of diversity?
- Where diversity is beneficial, how can it be sustained despite the demands for harmonization that threaten it?

In this paper, I address the first of these questions. The factors that produce harmonization and demands for it can be divided, for analytical convenience, into *philosophical* (section 1.1), economic, and political. The *economic* arguments, in turn, divide into those resulting from changes in the world economy, which may be called *structural* (section 1.2), and those that derive from the notion that without harmonization the conventional case for mutuality of the gains from free trade is invalid, which may be called *welfare-theoretic* (section 1.3). The *political* arguments (section 1.4) relate primarily to the use of "fair trade" arguments to extract protection and also to the fear that, in the absence of harmonization, the higher-standard countries will face political pressures, under free trade with lower-standard countries, to lower their own standards.

1.1   Philosophical Arguments against Diversity

The philosophical arguments for harmonization arise in regard to environmental and labor standards in particular, and can be traced to three sorts of reasoning, described in the following paragraphs.

A sense of *transborder obligation* owed to others leads those interested in environmental and labor rights (and human rights in general) to demand that the nation-states where these others are citizens should sustain those rights, and to use the threat of denial of existing and prospective trading opportunities to prod or coerce these nations into scaling up of their environmental and labor standards.

Questions of *distributive justice* also arise when it is feared that freer trade with poor countries that have abundant unskilled labor and lower environmental and labor standards will result in the immiserization of one's proletariat. Gains from trade will certainly arise, but the distribution of income will be adversely affected: trading with poor countries will produce paupers at home. Some maintain paradoxically that free trade will immiserize workers even in the poor countries.

Then, there is simply the fact that firms in higher-standard countries feel that *fairness* in competition requires that the burdens put on costs by environmental and labor standards ought not to differ across countries in free trade. Fairness, like beauty, is in the eye of the beholder, and the fact that this view is now increasingly held among business groups and labor unions makes it a potent force, in addition to all others, driving the demands for harmonization of such standards.

1.1.1   The Question of Obligation beyond Borders

In matters of social policy, relating to environment and labor standards, there is at work a sense of the obligation that we as human beings owe one another. This sense of obligation prompts and legitimates the use of the power and instrumentalities of the politically stronger nations to cajole and, if necessary, coerce the weaker nations into implementing policies that conform to the moral behavior that the obligation defines and requires of all nations in the discharge of their authority over their subjects, thus producing upward harmonization of their environmental and labor standards with one's own.

The sense of transborder moral obligation is of course ancient, long predating the modern nation-state, as John Dunn, the Cambridge political theorist, has reminded us eloquently in tracing the origins of the notion of a "human community" and the consequent answer to the question of what human beings owe one another:

An old answer [to the question of what we owe to others] with deep Greek and Christian roots, is that there is just one human community, "that great and natural community" (Locke 1988 [1960], Second Treatise, para 128), as John Locke called it, of all human beings as natural creatures, whose habitat is the whole globe and whose obligations to one another do not stop at any humanly created—any artificial—boundary. Locke had a very powerful explanation of why this was so, an explanation which tied human obligations immediately to the purposes of God himself (Dunn 1984). A pale shadow of Locke's conception, with God tactfully edited out, still lives on in modern secular understandings of human rights ... and, even more diffusely, in anthropocentric interpretations of the collective ecological imperative to save a habitat for the human species as a whole.[1]

The weakness of this obligation in reality and its strength in moral philosophy have preoccupied many over the years. Thus David Hume, who attributed such obligation to sentiment rather than reason, argued that "it is not contrary to reason to prefer the destruction of the whole world to the scratching of my finger."[2] In a similar vein, Adam Smith argued:

Let us suppose that the great empire of China, with all its myriads of inhabitants, was suddenly swallowed up by an earthquake and let us consider how a man of humanity in Europe, who had no sort of connexion with that part of the world, would be affected upon receiving intelligence of this dreadful calamity. He would, I imagine, first of all express very strongly his sorrow for the misfortune of that unhappy people, he would make many melancholy reflections upon the precariousness of human life and the vanity of all the labours of man which could thus be annihilated in a moment. He would too, perhaps, if he was a man of speculation, enter into many reasonings concerning the effects which this disaster might produce upon the commerce of Europe and the trade and business of the world in general. And when all this fine philosophy was over, when all these humane sentiments had been once fairly expressed, he would pursue his business or pleasure, take his repose or his diversion, with the same ease and tranquility as if no such accident had happened.

The most frivolous disaster which could befall himself would occasion a more real disturbance. If he was to lose his little finger to-morrow, he would not sleep to-night; but, provided he never saw them, he would snore with the most profound security over the ruin of a hundred million of his brethren. The destruction of that immense multitude seems plainly an object less interesting to him than this paltry misfortune of his own. To prevent, therefore, this paltry misfortune to himself would a man of humanity be willing to sacrifice the lives of a hundred million of his brethren, provided he had never seen them?[3]

Moral philosophers have considered how to deduce such obligation, and political theorists have speculated why the sense of such obligation varies over time and across communities, but what concerns us here is to see why and how it has prompted environmental concerns to transcend borders and indeed weaken the autonomy of nation-states within their conventionally domestic jurisdictions.

To see this issue with necessary nuance, one must understand that obligation implies rights. If then transborder obligations to others elsewhere are accepted, so must the notion that these others have rights that we are expected to sustain.

It follows then that the assumption in international relations since the Treaty of Wesphalia—that nation-states have exclusive domain over their subjects such that their treatment of these subjects is a matter of domestic sovereignty and that international relations therefore must respect moral pluralism—is no longer acceptable. As Raymond Plant (1993) has put it succinctly: "The principle of *cuius regio, eius religio* may have been central to the Treaty of Westphalia but the principle of *cuius regio, eius jus* is not compatible with the idea that there are basic human rights the moral authority of which crosses frontiers."

However, once such intervention is considered legitimate and the exclusive sovereignty of nation-states over their subjects has lost its legitimacy (in regard to these subjects' rights that our obligations extend to), intervention on behalf of the subjects of other nation-states runs into the very same difficulty that the question of rights runs into in the domestic domain. In particular, the problem of sustaining "positive" rights becomes pertinent and difficult.

Thus "negative" rights such as the right to liberty create obligations that could be described as consisting in refraining from actions harmful to others. As such, they are considered to involve indirect costs in the sense of forgone gains (e.g., if I do not enslave you, I do not get to exploit you and get rich), but they generally do not involve direct costs (e.g., I can simply refrain from enslaving you). However, even this statement is not quite accurate because I may have to incur direct costs to ensure that someone else does not deny you your negative right, say, to liberty (e.g., I may have to finance an army or a police force to deter those who would otherwise force you into slavery).

But these costs pale into insignificance when we consider the enforcement of obligation to sustain positive rights, such as to shelter, education, clean air, clean water, good health, and indeed much else.

This (relative) asymmetry has prompted many rights advocates to attach greater significance to negative rights: habeas corpus outweighs clean air, by this logic. Equally, it is widely thought that while negative rights can all be demanded of every nation-state, this cannot be the case with positive rights: the problem of costs means that we have to choose between clean air and clean water.

These choices are resolved within the nation-state in one way or another. In pluralistic nations, they are resolved through debate and politics; in authoritarian states, by fiat and possibly by neglect. But, in either case, the problem of cost is implicitly or explicitly recognized. By contrast, when the positive rights of others in the jurisdiction of foreign nation-states are defended, and these are pursued by demanding that these foreign nations (not one's own) find the resources to sustain them, it does not take much ingenuity to understand that the demands will tend to overreach and even to be "captured" politically by interests in one's own state that have their own agendas. Thus overarching environmental demands on resource-strapped nations, backed by a threat of punitive trade sanctions, may be made not just by environmental groups, but also by protectionist lobbies who see the resulting possibility of trade sanctions as a benefit to themselves.

Next, we must distinguish between the obligation that we feel we owe others because they are part of humankind and the obligation that we consider we owe to humanity itself. Thus, if environmental obligations are at stake, we may regard Mexican citizens to be entitled to clean air and clean water because they are human, as we in the United States are, and hence we may consider it our obligation to ensure their access to such amenities. But then we may consider that the depletion of the ozone layer imperils humanity itself and that we must therefore ensure that Mexicans contribute, through environmental measures, toward that survival. Interestingly, both kinds of obligation can lead to the use by environmentalists of the power of their own nation-state to coerce other nation-states, through measures such as trade sanctions, into acceptance of policies demanded of them.

What We Owe Others
It was precisely the sense of obligation to others that led the great developmental economists in the postwar period, Paul Rosenstein-Rodan and Gunnar Myrdal among them, to seek foreign aid commitments by the rich nations (even though, confronted by the realities of politics, they were reconciled to "selling" foreign aid programs as good for the givers too— not as yielding the pleasure of having done one's duty and discharged one's obligation to others, but as enlightened self-interest in the shape of "containing communism" during the Cold War). Obligation to others then led to the imposition of obligation and sacrifice on one's own government in the form of aid programs.

By contrast, in environmental matters, one's obligation to others prompts demands on *their* government: The obligation to others in Mexico, for their life chances as well as the environmental quality of their habitat, is seen as requiring that we in the United States must use instrumentalities of various kinds to force the Mexican government to ensure that its citizens enjoy a better habitat.

Where, therefore, the aid question strengthened the legitimacy of the nation-state by getting one's own government to give aid (while imposing greater demands on it and hence possibly weakening its eventual legitimacy as an agency that could deliver efficaciously what is required of it by those who are subject to its authority and whose interests it advances), the environmental question weakens it by delegitimating the notion that foreign nation-states, uncoerced and by autonomous choice, will do well by their citizens.

Then again, we must recall that demands on one's own nation-state are different in important ways from demands on others' nation-states. Where, for instance, these demands need resources to be spent, the former impose these burdens on oneself, whereas the latter impose them on others. Therefore, where the former will be moderated by the presence of resource constraints, the latter will generally tend to assume larger proportions.

What We Owe to Humanity
But the question of our obligation to humanity, to others of our species, appears to raise different issues. The overriding obligation is evidently Hobbesian and one of survival (Hobbes, 1983, 1991). Environmental questions such as the depletion of the ozone layer and global warming clearly relate to obligation *maximorum* of this variety. Even here, however, one must make room for scientific opinion that suggests that the problems are slow to intensify, leaving ample room for scientific innovation to countervail the danger (much as Malthus has been held at bay to date).

But, even if these environmental questions raise for us compelling obligations to ensure the survival of humankind, the issues that were considered earlier will resurrect themselves. For as soon as costs must be incurred to reach environmental targets (setting these targets raises, in turn, its own host of issues), the question cannot be evaded: which nation-state must incur what costs? "Efficient" solutions, as sophisticated economists know, are not ethically appropriate solutions: being paid a market wage that reflects an efficient economic system, for instance, is not to be paid the just wage.[4]

Thus, an efficient solution (which minimizes the world cost of reducing a unit of CO_2) to the global warming problem may require that Brazil's rain forests not be cut down but may not demand a reduction in the use of gas-guzzlers on U.S. roads because the latter is a more expensive solution. But then asking Brazil to take the entire burden of reducing global warming is to stick it with the bill: a most unjust outcome when you consider that the United States is a rich country and Brazil is less so. But the use of U.S. economic muscle and the relative efficacy of U.S.-based environmental groups in demanding compliance from the poor nations elsewhere rather than from their own country, where they must fight with powerful groups that oppose them (witness the inability of President Bill Clinton to adopt the BTU tax), mean that the sense of obligation to humanity's survival could translate into effective demands on others and their nation-states that are unfair or unjust in relation to demands on oneself and on one's own nation-state. Indeed, it does.

Trade Suspension and Refusal to Liberalize Trade
The assertion of transborder obligation by environmentalists, labor unions, and others can take two alternative forms in regard to trade with other nations. Either existing trade with, and the trading rights of, other nations can be suspended, *or* extension of trade through further trade liberalization (as in the North American Free Trade Agreement, or NAFTA, for Mexico) can be denied, unless these nations bring their policies into conformity with one's demands.

Evidently, the former is the more difficult, partly because it involves the suspension of a right already conceded by treaty or of a transaction already in place, and partly because it will result in direct and noticeable impact on the economic interests of producers who may be users of imported components who can then become effective adversaries of the proposed sanctions. By contrast, forgone trade liberalization denies benefits that are only potential.

The Question of Consequential Ethics
In using either trade sanctions or denial of trade liberalization to secure for others their environmental and labor standards and other rights, the moral motive remains the sense of (transborder) obligation. This, in turn, implies that the use of these methods presupposes, on the part of those who use them, a presumption that they will be effective in securing the stated objectives.

However, that presumption itself cannot be assumed to be always justified. If Mexico is forced to spend more on clean air than it can currently afford, simply to be allowed to join NAFTA, then this demand could compromise its ability to grow faster and then spend more on clean air later. Or, getting Mexico to forgo the use of the productive purse seines to catch tuna could save dolphins but reduce productivity in the tuna industry and adversely affect Mexico's growth and its capacity to generate resources to spend more on other environmental problems.

Then again, even the implementation of the threat to deny old and new trading rights may not force Mexico into submission, thus imposing costs on Mexico and indeed on oneself, while yielding no gains in terms of the desired (environmental or other) objectives. A consequentialist will then abandon the proposed trade measures.

But then, some people might feel that one should not sup with the devil even though the only consequence of such denial is that one misses a free meal. Duty, not consequentialism, then drives such environmentalists into rejecting NAFTA with Mexico if Mexico fails to fix its environmental standards as desired. But then one is saying: My obligation to Mexicans requires that I seek to advance their corresponding rights; but if I cannot do so effectively in reality (through trade measures), I nonetheless will refuse to engage with their government in freer trade, expressing my distaste and moral disapproval.[5]

1.1.2   The Question of Distributive Justice

An important motivation for harmonization, however, is not concern for others elsewhere but concern for the poor among us. Thus, if free trade with poor countries with lower environmental and labor standards will, via competitive pressures, drive down the real wages of the unskilled in one's own country, then this pressure on wages may be cause for making upward harmonization of these standards a precondition for freeing of trade. This is evidently an argument for distributive justice. Three different arguments of this type can be distinguished in the public domain at the present time.

Immiserization of One's Own Unskilled
The fear has certainly grown in the countries of the (richer) North that free trade with the (poorer) countries of the South will drive down the real wages of the unskilled in their midst. The growth in unemployment in Europe in the 1980s and the decline in real wages of the unskilled in the

United States during the same period have fueled these fears, with glob-alization of the world economy through North-South trade liberalization considered a villain and also a danger for the future.[6] (Note that this is *not* the long-standing "pauper labor" argument against free trade, which re-lates to the notion that there will be no gains from trade if you trade with poor countries with numerous paupers. Instead, the present argument says, free trade will increase overall income, but it will hurt income distribution, harming our unskilled poor. Some may fear for both gains from trade and for real wages, of course, and probably do!)

This fear has led to demands from several labor unions, as well as from politicians, to make the raising of wages in the South a precondition for expanded free trade. The most dramatic example of these demands was the debate during the passage of NAFTA through the U.S. Congress, when both the unions and Ross Perot focused on low wages in Mexico as a reason to reject NAFTA, and President Carlos Salinas de Gortari of Mexico was constrained in fact to advertise his commitment to raise minimum wages in Mexico to smooth the passage of NAFTA.

Equally, this fear has contributed to the demands for harmonization of environmental and labor standards because this also is seen as raising the costs of foreign competitors. This happens also to be the way in which President Clinton, and certainly U.S. Trade Representative Mickey Kantor, presented the supplemental agreements on these matters with Mexico: as measures that would prevent "unfair trade" with Mexico under NAFTA.[7] They legitimated, in consequence, the notion that free trade with the countries of the South required such agreements as "fair trade" preconditions.

Capital Mobility's Consequences
When capital mobility is introduced, the fear about distributive justice is accentuated. As the NAFTA debate made clear, the fear then extends to capital flowing out to where the wages and the labor and environmental standards are lower, thus leaving less capital to work with labor at home and thus reducing the real wages of labor (even if the outflow of capital enriches the country overall).[8]

Distributive Justice Abroad
Strange as it may seem, some anti-free-trade critics also fear that real wages at both ends will fall as a result of free trade. In that case, the distributive-justice argument blends into moral obligation toward others. Thus, in the NAFTA debate, it was customary to allege that even the Mexican workers would suffer from free trade.

Was this total nonsense? I would have to say, almost certainly. While freer trade, without induced capital flows, would help improve Mexican wages, the outcome would be even better with induced capital flows into Mexico. For the same reason that capital outflows from the United States to Mexico could hurt U.S. workers, they would benefit the Mexican workers.[9] (In the end, both countries could gain capital from the creation of NAFTA. Non-NAFTA capital, from the European Union and Japan in particular, would likely flow in greater magnitude to the region once NAFTA was formed. The European Community experience with the entry of Spain fits this pattern: both Spain and the United Kingdom benefited, the former from EC and the latter from non-EC sources.[10] So, even U.S. real wages could benefit from the induced capital flows resulting from NAFTA.)

One needs to probe further the fear that free trade will lead erstwhile peasants into industrial employment where their interests will be sacrificed and workers immiserized unless protections are provided by means of enforced, superior labor standards. Underlying this view, I believe, is the notion that peasants will have regret but be unable to move back to the land if immiserization occurs—as in Franco Brusati's celebrated film *Bread and Chocolate*, where the immigrant *gastarbeiter* from Italy is trapped into his miserable condition in Switzerland and unable to return home. In none of the developing countries that I know in some depth, however, can I consider this to be a likely occurrence. To deny freer trade and its advantages to the poor nations of the South without upward harmonization of their labor standards for this reason appears to me to be unwarranted.

1.1.3   The Question of Fairness

Another compelling argument for harmonization proceeds from the altogether different philosophical notion of "fairness."[11] It might fairly be said that "fairness"—and legitimacy in terms of fairness of the process within which competition for economic success takes place—is a central American value, whereas "justice" and legitimacy in terms of the distribution of success is a central European value. In turn, perhaps, this contrast reflects the uniquely different, egalitarian nature of the American society built on free immigration as opposed to the traditional, hierarchical nature of European society. Equality of access matters in the United States, equality of success in Europe.

The use of fairness is thus a central feature of the demands in the United States for harmonization. Naturally enough, since the United States is a

major player in trade negotiations whether multilateral or bilateral, it follows that the American demands also tend to seek to remake the world in
its own image. As Suzanne Berger has said well:

Americans believe that productivity growth must be based upon legitimate practices in production. . . . The gains that accrue to producers are legitimate only if
they come from legitimate economic arrangements. Gains from sweated or prison
labor are seen as illegitimate gains. I think that in the American debate, the
argument over the legitimacy of the *keiretsu* is essentially one about whether they
should be seen as a form of network organization, in which case they are legitimate and perhaps to be imitated. Or whether the *keiretsu* are organizations in
which large firms beat up on their subcontractors who, in turn, beat up on their
workers, in which case they ought to be reformed or eliminated through international pressures. Gains in trade are thus seen as fair to the extent that they are
based on national practices which are themselves fair and legitimate. Such debates
propel other nations' practices into the center of the international agenda.[12]

The demands for harmonization that ensue from notions of fairness
extend to competition in one's own markets (i.e., they relate to one's
imports) or in others' markets (i.e., they relate to one's exports), the latter,
in turn, dividing into one's exports to another country's own market or to
third markets. Thus the United States may make fairness claims, and indeed does make them, about Japan's exports to the U.S. market, U.S.
exports to Japan's market, and shares of the United States and Japan in
exports to third markets.

Thus the fairness claims about imports have conventionally related to
unfair uses of subsidies and the unfair private practice of (allegedly predatory) dumping. Uses of countervailing duties (CVDs) against unfair subsidies and of antidumping (AD) duties have long been sanctioned by
national and GATT-legitimated practice. These unfairness claims are
now being extended, especially to environmental and labor standards. The
argument is that it is unfair competition if one's rival in an industry faces
lower burdens than one does oneself, because of differential standards.
The implied norm of fairness seems to be simply that, no matter what
the economic and other justifications for the existence of such differential
standards may be (and, as I shall note later, there certainly are compelling
ones), they evidently constitute a lack of *symmetry* in the environment
faced by competing firms in the industry in different nations and hence
ipso facto are unacceptable.

In a penetrating analysis of the norms of fairness underlying the claims
regarding unfairness in exports to others' markets, as reflected in the
legislative debates and content of successive versions of Section 301 of
U.S. trade law, which authorizes retaliatory action by the United States

against unfair foreign trade practices affecting U.S. exports, Ken Abbott (1993) has distinguished among (1) the norm of adherence to international commitments and law,[13] (2) the norm of nullification or impairment of previous trade concessions or agreements,[14] (3) the norm of nondiscrimination,[15] (4) the norm of reciprocity,[16] and (5) the norm of the free market.[17] There is little doubt that the panoply of these norms, legitimating in the eyes of the U.S. complainants in industry and in the Congress the view of foreign practices as unfair and hence actionable, has fueled significantly the growth in demands for harmonization, that is, demands to remove those practices and thus harmonize other countries' domestic policies and practices in a variety of areas more closely to those of the United States.

1.2   Structural Arguments against Diversity

The economic (as distinct from the philosophical) arguments for harmonization have arisen from a variety of reasons. Among the principal ones, we must consider structural changes in the world economy. These can be divided into (1) those that are specific to the United States and arise from a sense of relative decline in the world economy, which I have called the diminished giant syndrome, and (2) those that are more general and afflict several economies simultaneously, producing similar reactions internationally. These structural changes have produced a sensitivity to domestic differences, lending an edge to the other arguments advanced for harmonization of these domestic differences.

1.2.1   The Diminished Giant Syndrome

The two decades of the 1970s and 1980s witnessed in the United States the rise of the "diminished giant syndrome," reflecting a relative decline in the U.S. share of world GNP and trade as the nations of the Pacific, especially Japan, became major players in the world economy.[18]

This trend set a historical parallel with events in Britain at the end of the 19th century, when the rise of Germany and the United States as major players in the world economy had also disconcerted many.

In both countries, the reaction was similar. Free trade without reciprocity was decried. In Britain, fair trade leagues and reciprocity associations grew up, just as the U.S. Congress was seized with similar concerns with nonreciprocal and unfair access to U.S. markets by rivals.[19] In the British case, of course, this nonreciprocity was indeed a reality, as Britain had been a *unilateral* free trader in ideology and in policy since the repeal of the

Corn Laws by Prime Minister Robert Peel in 1846. In the case of the United States, which had never accepted unilateral free trade, the belief in its own openness while the markets of others were closed was held with great conviction, even though the reality did not quite match the belief.

Declinism has thus fed the ethos in the United States in favor of reciprocal openness. In turn, it has also legitimized demands for fair trade or "level playing fields," prompting great concerns in policy making with whether the newly successful trading rivals are "cheating" or gaining advantage in unfair competition.[20] The willingness to play by the rules of free trade has always been easier, as economic historians have observed, for countries that expect to win from Darwinian competition. Declinism cuts into that optimism and sets up roadblocks such as demands for fair trade that will, in the guise of demands for level playing fields, in fact gain oneself the higher ground. Then again, the fact that the foreign nations which emerged as strong rivals were in the Far East has been a contributory factor (though Lester Thurow would have us confront the European Community and Germany as even more fearsome rivals, a diagnosis that looks increasingly unpersuasive).

Now, the British were not exactly sympathetic toward the Germans, and the rise of the United States, a former colony that had chosen the way of war and independence, may have been grating too. But, in the case of the United States today, with its generosity toward rebuilding Japan after the Second World War and its support for Japan's entry into the GATT in the teeth of European objections, resentment of Japan's success does not appear to have been a problem.

Rather, the fact that Japan's internal economic and social culture made the penetration of the Japanese market difficult relative to others because of its long history of "controlled openness," and the view since the 1930s that Japan was a predatory exporter that could not be allowed to play by the rules but had to be continually restrained by quotas on its exports, have combined to give credence to the perception that trade with Japan could not be left to the rules of free trade. Instead, fair trade and reciprocity, carried to the length of guaranteed results in terms of expanded imports (voluntary import expansions) and reduced exports (voluntary export restraints), had to be imposed on Japan.

1.2.2 Globalization of the World Economy

The demands for fair trade have also come from structural changes in the world economy that afflict several nations simultaneously and in similar fashion.

Kaleidoscopic Comparative Advantage
Chief among these structural changes is the fact that, increasingly, the integration of the world economy has made several more industries footloose than ever before, all facing fierce competition with a much-reduced cushion for their competitive edge vis-à-vis their rivals abroad. Let me explain why.

The research of the economists Will Baumol, Sue Anne Blackman, and Ed Wolff (1989) has shown that technological know-how has converged significantly among the OECD countries in the postwar period through the 1970s. Economist Richard Nelson has argued persuasively that today much technology can be easily accessed simply by having skilled personnel with the necessary scientific training—hence some of the frantic search for patent rights (to secure royalties, not to prevent dissemination). Multinationals have also become ubiquitous: they mutually penetrate each others' turf, so that Servan-Schreiber's (1968) American challenge (to Europe) yesterday could be the Tolchins' (1988) Japanese challenge (to the United States) today.[21] At the same time, the developed world's capital markets are more closely integrated than before, though the tendency of domestic savings to mimic domestic investment has not been greatly dented.[22]

The net result is that several industries can be readily competed for by many developed countries, with comparative advantage rather fragile, so that the advantage anyone enjoys in any such industry is of a knife-edge variety. Comparative advantage in these industries then is *kaleidoscopic*: it will move across countries almost randomly. In the old jargon, these industries are "footloose."[23]

In this situation, you can fairly expect those who are investing in and managing these industries to be extremely sensitive to any possibility of an "unfair" advantage gained by their foreign rivals: the slightest advantage enjoyed by them becomes suspect because it can be fatal. This situation implies then that demands will be made, both for zero-tariff or mutually identical tariff options and for the matching of nontariff barriers (NTBs) among countries, as well as for harmonization of any elements of domestic policies and institutions that might be considered to give one's rivals an edge in competition.

Exchange Rates
Yet another reason why sensitivity to differences in domestic policies and institutions by trading rivals has increased might appear to be the shift to a regime of exchange rate flexibility. However, the shift is to a dirty float,

and exchange rate volatility is not as pronounced as had been feared by the proponents of fixed exchange rates. Nor is there any evidence that the shift to flexible exchanges rates, in any event, has significantly reduced the volume of trade transactions.[24]

A more persuasive case instead might be made for the argument that serious overvaluation of a currency could, by making the tradable sectors highly uncompetitive, fuel their demands for harmonization to moderate the winds of competition in open economies. It may be no coincidence that the rise of fair trade concerns and associated demands for harmonization reached a higher level of political viability during the 1980s when the dollar was substantially overvalued and protectionism was rampant in the Congress. On the other hand, now that the yen is experiencing what the Japanese regard as an intolerable overvaluation, we do not see a commensurate rise of Japanese concerns with fair trade and harmonization, perhaps because this discourse is seen by them as available only to their critics.

1.3   Economic Arguments against Diversity

The economic arguments against diversity arise principally from concern with the following question: Does the case for mutually gainful trade between voluntarily trading nations, which is at the heart of the case for free trade, survive if there is diversity in domestic policies and institutions among them? In short, instead of mutual gains from trade, could we get predation against (i.e., immiserization from trade for) a trading nation if such diversity persists under free trade? Or, since relative gains from trade can also be an issue, one may also ask the related question: Even if predation is not inflicted on oneself, does diversity reduce one's absolute or relative gains from trade?[25]

1.3.1   The Nullification Idea and Problem

But prior to discussing this range of problems, I should mention that the analysis and institutional organization of free trade (as at the GATT) have always reflected a concern with the domestic policies of the trading nations (though not with harmonization thereof, except in a fundamental sense that I spell out later). Economists have recognized that the effects of trade policies can be nullified or impaired (to use GATT phraseology) by domestic actions.

The Idea of Equivalence
Thus economists are aware that imposing a tariff on a commodity is equivalent to imposing instead a consumption tax on it and giving a subsidy to domestic producers of it, for the tariff raises prices to consumers and for producers: both effects can be directly achieved by the mix of a consumption tax and a producer subsidy. This is just one of many "equivalence" propositions that the students of international economics are alerted to by their teachers.[26]

It immediately follows that any trade concessions can be nullified by imposing an offsetting set of domestic policies. No institutional arrangement that oversees and then monitors trade liberalization can afford, therefore, to confine its rules and attention to "border" measures. It follows then that an institution such as the GATT must have a nullification or impairment clause, as indeed Article XXIII is, to examine complaints that trade concessions have been offset by domestic policies. I should imagine that the inclusion of Article XXIII into the GATT at the very outset was approved, perhaps even suggested, by the distinguished economists associated with its design, chief among them the British Nobel laureate James Meade.

The "Systemic" Problem: Markets Matter
But the question of nullification or impairment turns into a "systemic" question of far more overarching range when we confront the fact that, given the way an economy is organized, it simply cannot be expected to offer trade concessions that can be translated into meaningful commitments of market access. Let me raise four specific areas where this question has become significant, inside and outside the GATT: (1) state trading; (2) trade with the former centrally planned economies (CPEs); (3) trade with the developing countries; and (4) trade with Japan.

In each case, the main burden of the concerns voiced by contracting parties, and of the demands for corrective action, has related to the presumption that markets matter. If markets do not function adequately because of specific domestic institutions (such as state trading) or the entire domestic economic system (such as that characterizing a CPE), then free trade by rules as contemplated by the GATT system would fail to produce the desired gains from trade.

State Trading   GATT, like economists supporting free trade, presumes that "trading enterprises will act on commercial considerations and that the economic theories of comparative advantage will lead these enterprises to extend their international trade in order to reap its benefits."[27]

The architects of the International Trade Organization (ITO) had been concerned with the fact that state trading needed to be regulated in some fashion if it was to be made tolerably compatible with a rules-based system of free trade that would let firms compete meaningfully for markets where access had been obtained by tariff concessions. Article XVII of the GATT eventually carried over two of the original three provisions in the U.S. ITO proposals, including the requirement that state trading organizations be operated in a nondiscriminatory manner.

Eventually, a 1955 working party recommended amendments to Article XVII that were adopted in 1955 and made effective in 1957. As noted by Jackson (1969), other provisions of the GATT also address the issues raised by state trading organizations: among them, Article II, paragraph 4, and interpretative notes relating to Articles XI through XIV and Article XVIII. Provisions relating to all other governmental activity also bear on the GATT obligations imposed on state trading organizations.[28] The exemptions to the state trading obligation, originally permitted for "imports of products for immediate or ultimate consumption in governmental use and not otherwise for resale or use in the production of goods for sale," have subsequently been brought under discipline in the Tokyo Round Procurement Code and subsequent negotiations.

Centrally Planned Economies   Jackson (1969, p. 361) has well said, "If the existence of state enterprises in an economy that generally follows a free enterprise system poses ... problems [for the GATT], consider the problem posed by an economy that is entirely or largely operated by state enterprises!" In fact, the accommodation of the erstwhile socialist countries into the GATT system posed considerable difficulty that surfaced again when the Soviet Union, under Mikhail Gorbachev, sought GATT entry and have appeared also in the matter of China's reentry into the GATT.

From the beginning, however, the contracting parties were torn between the desire to make the GATT as inclusive in membership as possible and the difficulty of accommodating (into a rules-based markets-presupposing international organization) countries whose economic and political organization was clearly based on nonmarket principles. France, with its attachment to *dirigisme*, expressed the inclusive principle best through its delegate at the drafting session in 1946:[29]

France wishes to see that the organization which we are planning here extends to the rest of the world.... There does not exist, in our opinion, any necessary connection between the form of the productive regime and the internal exchanges in one nation, on the one hand, and on her foreign economic policy on the other.

The United States may very well continue to follow the principle, the more orthodox principle, of private initiative. France and other European countries may turn towards planned economy. The USSR may uphold and maintain the Marxist ideals of collectivism without our having to refuse to be in favor of a policy of international organization based on liberty and equality.

Given the triumphalism that attends market-based capitalism today, the French characterization of the American preference for private initiative as "orthodox" and the indulgence toward the U.S.S.R. for its Marxist ideals seem ironic indeed. But the French statement captures pretty well the general feeling that the world was and would continue to be diverse in the methods chosen to organize national economies, and that the GATT should try to accommodate the socialist nations somehow.

Indeed, the U.S. position at the discussions on the ITO and at the GATT was precisely to find formulas to do so. The solution to the problem of defining market access obligations meaningfully, when markets did not exist in socialist countries, was to go for what we call today results-oriented, managed-trade, quantitative import obligations in the context of the "Japan problem." Thus the United States, in its suggested draft of the ITO charter, suggested that a country with a "complete or substantially complete monopoly of its import trade" (which would include all socialist countries, of course) should conclude agreements undertaking "to import in the aggregate over a period products of the other Members valued at not less than an amount to be agreed upon … subject to periodic adjustment."

As it happened, this technique was used subsequently in defining the obligations of socialist countries acceding to the GATT. Thus when Poland entered the GATT in 1967, having negotiated its entry during the Kennedy Round, the schedule for Poland carried the obligation "to increase the total value of its imports from the territories of contracting parties by not less than 7 percent per annum."

Of course, the early socialist states in the GATT were Czechoslovakia (which had joined the GATT long *before* it fell to communism), Yugoslavia (which joined in 1966), and Poland. The last two were unimportant in world trade. With the Soviet Union and China, the issue was far more potent, given the enormous size and trade potential of the two countries, raising the question of their GATT entry into a qualitatively different phenomenon. The condition of entry would then shift from quantitative import obligations (whose desirability has been challenged effectively in the Japan context by several economists) to a demonstrated commitment to, even successful transition to, markets by these countries.

Developing Countries   The special and differential (S&D) treatment accorded to the developing countries at the GATT amounted to a virtual exemption of these countries from many of the disciplines and norms of the GATT. Such treatment followed from the postwar theoretical presumption that developing countries were subject to modified economic principles, subsumed under the title of development economics, such that they had to be treated differently as a class in international economic arrangements.

Thus it was not that these countries were not working with markets. It was that the market principles did not apply effectively, given the institutional structures characterizing these countries. Thus, for instance, they had endemic balance-of-payments problems that required them to work without even current account convertibility, so that import restrictions for balance-of-payments reasons were necessary. But these restrictions meant in turn that the developing countries could not be expected to offer real market access to other contracting parties at the GATT: the use of Article XVIII(b), permitting the use of trade restrictions for payments reasons temporarily, became in effect a permanent matter, constituting an open door through which all developing countries could walk out.

Aside from this economic-theoretic legitimation of S&D treatment of the developing countries, S&D also made political sense in much the same way as the permitted entry into the GATT of the socialist countries did. Developing countries were just not important enough to make much difference to the developed countries, leading them to concede demands for S&D, including lack of reciprocity in trade concessions, without much fuss.

Evidently, in both regards, views have changed dramatically in recent years. Developing countries are much bigger players in world trade today, and few developed countries are willing to grant S&D today, except to the countries truly at the bottom of the pecking order, the so-called least-developed countries. But, more importantly, economic theory no longer considers developing countries to be "off the curve," requiring a different kind of economics to understand them and to prescribe suitable policies for them. In particular, it is now thought that current account convertibility can be achieved far more quickly than was thought to be the case earlier. Witness, for instance, the recommendations being made toward this end to the former socialist countries in light of the new thinking: where war-ravaged Europe was guided to convertibility over a decade by economists such as Robert Triffin and developing countries remained on inconvertible currencies for decades in the postwar period, Poland, Russia, and others have been successfully advised to go convertible overnight.

Modern economic thinking does not admit any longer that developing countries have a unique inability to shift to macro policies that can restore convertibility to the current account. Trade policy in developing countries, just as in developed countries, can then be expected legitimately to be "assigned" GATT-style, not to address balance-of-payments concerns, but to offer rules-based market access and thus to generate the resulting gains from trade both for themselves and for their trading partners.

In fact, today, if the NAFTA negotiations by the United States are any guide, we may well be entering a new era of "reverse S&D" because of the fear (discussed in section 1.1) that trade with the poor countries could hurt the real wages of the unskilled in the rich countries. This fear led to attempts at enforcing minimum wage increases and upgrading of environmental standards (and hence costs) in Mexico that had no parallel in the earlier negotiations with Canada (except that it was in Canada that certain groups had unsuccessfully worried about differences in social legislation between Canada and the United States as yielding "unfair" advantage to the United States); and Mexico had to accept trade sanctions as the ultimate recourse by the United States in case of violations of environmental standards, whereas Canada successfully rejected this provision. This asymmetry of obligations, tougher in principle for Mexico than for Canada, may set a pattern that is indeed tantamount to seeking greater obligations for free trade from the developing countries than from the developed.

The "Japan Problem"   The question of nullification or impairment because markets do not function as required to make trade concessions meaningful has emerged most dramatically in regard to trade with Japan.

The belief that the Japanese market is closed because of "informal" trade barriers that reduce effective market access is held with sufficient conviction to have led the EC to initiate an unsuccessful GATT complaint under Article XXIII against Japan (as distinct from a complaint against a specific Japanese industry or sector). It has also led the Clinton administration to attempt a politically supercharged shift in its Japan policy to impose managed-trade quantitative import targets, now called voluntary import expansions (VIEs), in several sectors such as autos and auto parts.

These VIEs are possibly a substitute for the earlier attempts by the administrations of George Bush and previous presidents to use the Structural Impediments Initiative (SII) to impose changes in Japan's domestic institutions and policies, bringing them more in line with those of the United States, in the expectation that such harmonization would make Japan's markets more accessible, indeed as accessible as those of the United

States. But the demands for VIEs may also be seen as a tactical device to extract such harmonization as a more acceptable option for Japan to seize in negotiations. That differences in Japan's domestic institutions and policies amount to making Japan an "unfair" trader is, of course, an assertion that is commonly made in the U.S. Congress and by industrial lobbies.

Of course, the critics of Japan consider the problem with Japan to arise not merely in regard to access to its markets. More traditionally, they have focused also on its exports, considering Japanese business practices to be predatory (and hence a natural target for antidumping actions). This view is further reinforced by the view that Japan's government, through the Ministry of International Trade and Industry (MITI), unfairly targets specific foreign industries for massive onslaught. Moreover, modern theory has provided greater legitimacy for the view that, by keeping its markets closed, Japan gives unfair advantage to its producers in high-tech sectors where scale economies are important, since Japanese producers enjoy access to both their own and others' markets while others are kept confined to their own markets. Thus import protection can lead to export promotion: comparative advantage is shifted unfairly toward Japan in such industries.[30] Of course, these beliefs are not necessarily justified simply because many hold them. Indeed, serious examination of these questions throws considerable doubt on the probity of such accusations.

1.3.2 Gains from Trade

Whereas the demands for harmonization come from the sense that otherwise the trade concessions granted by others will be nullified or impaired, the economist must recognize a different kind of argument that also drives such demands.

This argument comes from the sense that, whereas the conventional economic view is that free trade between nations is to their mutual advantage, amounting to a positive-sum game, this belief need not be so when these nations have different domestic institutions and policies behind their borders. That is, predation could, and often would, follow instead.

Alternatively, even if mutuality of gain is conceded, the fear is that the absence of harmonization will create an unfavorable distribution of the gains from trade. This is a less stark view of the matter; but, as political scientists continually remind economists, relative gains are arguably the more important bone of contention in international conflict and cooperation.

If we examine the earliest debates on harmonization, in the context of policy making and among international economists, these arose in the case of the European Community and in relation to the question of tax harmonization, as one would expect.[31] Interestingly, the dominant view among the economists who led the discussion at the time—and these included the future Nobel laureates Jan Tinbergen of the Netherlands and Bertil Ohlin of Sweden—was that diversity of tax policy among the member states of the EC was compatible with mutual gains from trade. Thus, Reddaway (1958, pp. 72–73) argued, citing the difficulty of proving things theoretically but resorting to "some simple facts, which at least give the general presumption that harmonization of taxation and social charges [as demanded by the French] is not indispensable":

This country [U.K.] had a regime of free trade for many years, the Benelux countries are not so very far away from it now—they are much nearer to free trade, for example, than to the position of France. Under each of these sets of circumstances—and it is the ones when barriers were low that are most relevant—tax systems and tax levels have differed greatly from one country to another, but this has not prevented international trade from flourishing and bringing great benefits to participants. One might indeed press this argument further, and say that the European countries have, in the last eight years or so, taken very important steps through the OEEC liberalization program to reduce the barriers to European trade: few would deny that the expansion of this trade has been very beneficial, despite the extremely varied taxes which the countries impose. In a sense the onus of proof is on those who would argue that further reductions of barriers require an elaborate harmonization of taxes....

Secondly, let us note that in cases [e.g., Benelux] which are broadly analogous to the [European] Free Trade Area tax systems have *not* been harmonised.... Similarly, in Federal countries like Australia, Canada or the U.S.A., the various States or Provinces show significant differences in their taxes, but trade between them is universally regarded as beneficial.

Similarly, Ohlin (1965, p. 83) challenged the "firm belief" in some quarters that "it is not possible to eliminate duties on trade among a large number of countries if one does not at the same time bring about a real economic integration, by means of a harmonization of economic and social policy in general":

It is not possible to "harmonize" the climate; yet international trade can run smoothly.... Trade will adapt itself to differences in the social and financial milieu in the same way it does to differences in climate ... there is no prima facie case for harmonization of the tax system in general.[32]

But if these economists were assertive about domestic diversity being compatible with mutual gains from trade, I detect signs of their admitting that more harmonization could *increase* the total gains from trade. The question of the distribution of the increased gains from trade was left unraised.[33] Later analyses, as in Shoup (1967), were sharper and did focus better on the theoretical aspects of tax harmonization in the context of trade liberalization such as in the EC; their analysis went so far as to discuss the problem as being symmetric to the question of removal of tariffs themselves, with the concepts of trade diversion and trade creation applied to the effects of domestic tax differences and changes.

Today, of course, the skepticism about the possibility of mutual gains from trade despite diversity in many domestic policies, tax and otherwise, has vastly increased. The presumption of predation from free trade in the absence of harmonization is sufficiently widespread to mark a radical change in attitudes on the question. It has become, therefore, a key question for economists to analyze in regard to different areas of domestic policy, such as environmental, labor, and competition policies.

Thus the questions I distinguished, about predation and about the relative gains from trade, need to be analytically addressed, so that the virtues and vices of diversity are understood better by economists in terms of their own methods of evaluating the social desirability of alternative policies.[34]

1.4 Political Arguments against Diversity

Finally, there is a class of arguments against diversity that can be described as belonging conventionally to the political domain. They come from protection seeking; the protectionist demands are more effectively made when unfair competition, based on (unreasonable) diversity abroad, is alleged. Equally, environmentalist and labor groups are agitated that free trade, given domestic political economy, will pull down domestic standards when lower foreign standards are claimed to be putting one's industry at disadvantage, producing a "race to the bottom." Then again, harmonization demands arise in the context of political integration such as that desired in the European Community. Just as in federal nation-states such as India, Canada, and the United States, demands are then made for a common set of social standards, not because they are essential for economic reasons but because it is felt that a key ingredient of political integration must be that each state should have at least a minimum set of standards, as in a social charter, in common among themselves.

1.4.1   Protection Seeking

Two arguments concerning protection seeking may be distinguished, one based on eased supply of protection, the other on the law of constant protection.

Eased Supply of Protection
If one thinks of actual protection as emerging from the interaction of those who demand protection (e.g., unions and firms in import-competing industries) and those who supply it (i.e., the administration and the congress or parliament), then it is manifest that the supply would be eased if, instead of simply saying that you are under pressure from foreign competition and that you need protection, you said that the foreigners are succeeding because they compete unfairly.[35]

The use of traditional "unfair trade" mechanisms, the antidumping and countervailing duties (offsetting foreign subsidies) processes, has obviously increased through the 1980s, for this among other reasons. But the objection to all sorts of differences in domestic policies and institutions in foreign countries has also been fueled by this protectionist ploy. For example, the large numbers of complaints against Japan, a successful trading rival, under the SII are to be explained, partly at least, in this fashion. Either these complaints lead to capitulation and consequent hoped-for increase in the production costs of one's rivals, or else these demands are rejected, or informally accommodated in negotiations but without being seriously implemented, in which case the ethos that foreigners are indeed wickedly unfair and untrustworthy is intensified, making the support of protection correspondingly easier for congressmen who otherwise espouse free trade.

The Law of Constant Protection
In addition, the use of unfair trade complaints as a way of securing protection may be simply a substitute for the old-fashioned use of tariff and quota barriers that came down with successive multilateral barrier reductions under GATT auspices in several rounds such as the recently concluded Uruguay Round. Economists have thus speculated that there may be a law of constant protection: You stop protection in one form and it pops up in some other form elsewhere.[36]

1.4.2   Standards at Bay: "Race to the Bottom"

But the most potent political argument leading to demands for upward harmonization has been in regard to environmental and labor standards as a precondition for free trade. This argument is often characterized as a "race to the bottom" where different jurisdictions, either local in federal nations or different countries, wind up competing with one another for industry that would otherwise be feared to gravitate to where the standards are the lowest at the outset.[37] Put differently, free trade is supposed to lead to harmonization downward from below. To prevent this outcome, harmonization upward from the top is demanded by the environmentalists and the labor groups before trade is liberalized with developing countries.

The problem of harmonization downward can arise from trade alone, but it is usually considered in the context of international capital mobility. It is feared then that entrepreneurs will close existing plants in the developed countries and move to the poor countries where the standards are lower. The latter problem is the more difficult politically. For, when factories close and the workers and their communities know where the factory has been transplanted abroad, the negative psychological reaction is more focused than when a job is lost to general competition from trade with many different countries. The "hiding hand" of the market, which prevents you from knowing *who* and *presumably what* caused your loss of a job in your factory, tends to diffuse the resentment, I think; and this advantage disappears when a furniture factory closes in San Diego and reopens in Tijuana, south of the Rio Grande, especially when Mexican environmental requirements on furniture makers are far less demanding than the tough ones in California.

While my own view, developed fully in Chapter 4, is that diversity in environmental standards, within an industry across countries, is reasonable and is even compatible with equal concern with the environment in these countries, I feel that this extra concern that obtains with international movement of direct investment in an industry to lower-standard developing countries may justify resorting to a policy in developed countries (with higher standards in an industry) which requires that their (say, U.S.) firms, when they go abroad (say, to Mexico), work with the higher standards (of the United States) than with the lower standards (of Mexico). That is, in Rome do, not as Romans do, but as Bostonians do.

Since firms are legal persons, American firms can be treated (as indeed they are in many matters already) as American citizens, subject to U.S. laws wherever they operate. The conflict of interest that often follows when a country so exercises its jurisdiction on firms operating abroad—as when the United States sought to enforce the embargo against Cuba on American firms in Canada—is most unlikely to obtain here. It is hard to see Mexico, for instance, objecting to U.S. firms adopting higher environmental and labor standards in their Mexican plants. In fact, when I recently advanced this proposal at a few international conferences and in an op-ed article in the *New York Times* (Bhagwati, 1993), the reaction from several Mexicans was favorable, as was that initially from several Americans, including members of Congress. In the end, it did not take off, partly because the different approach of the supplemental agreements for NAFTA was more or less set in cement by that time, and largely because U.S. businesses—which were definitely interested in investing in Mexico, contrary to their coached denials of such intentions once they began to be burned on the issue in the public domain—were reportedly unhappy at the thought that they would be subjected to any restrictions on their freedom to work with whatever local environmental and labor standards Mexico required of all firms, whether Mexican or foreign.

There is admittedly a problem of "horizontal equity" among different foreign firms in Mexico: U.S. firms could abide by tougher U.S. standards in Mexico whereas Japanese and European firms would not, thus putting American firms at a disadvantage. But if you believe that your standards reflect *your* valuation of environmental damage of a certain variety, you will want to stick by them even when others who do not share that valuation do not. Moreover, we ignore the dynamic of the proposal: if U.S. firms operate at U.S. standards, that fact itself is likely to put pressure on other foreign firms to shift to the U.S. standards in Mexico or face adverse political reactions, including some from Mexican nongovernmental organizations (NGOs). Studies of the larger multinationals operating in the Mexican *maquiladoras* suggest that some of them already behave in the manner I recommend they be forced to by legislation.

The race-to-the-bottom issue itself is highly contentious. Both in terms of economic logic[38] and in empirical terms as to whether lower environmental and labor standards have actually pulled in capital flows as suggested and whether, in that event, standards have actually gravitated downward in reality in federal nations or across countries, the fears of harmonization downward from below are disputed vigorously today. Nonetheless, it must be said that these fears certainly drive the demands for harmonization upward as preconditions for trade liberalization with developing countries.

1.4.3   Political Integration versus Simply Free Trade

In contrast to arm's-length free trade, nations that are integrating politically, as in the European Union, are observed to supplement elimination of

trade barriers with attempts at imposing a minimum set of common standards, especially in the social sphere, on member states. While the EU
(originally the Common Market or European Community, the EC) began
its discussions of harmonization from the strictly economic viewpoint (as
in the matter of taxation that I discussed earlier) and the demands of the
French were certainly made in this fashion at the time, it seems that the
political rationale for these demands complemented the economic ones
as the EC moved ahead. This was definitely the case with demands for
labor policy harmonization, a subject that André Sapir has investigated
in Chapter 15, showing the historic interplay of economic and political
factors leading up to the eventual adoption of the Community Charter
of Fundamental Social Rights, as modified at the Strasbourg European
Council in December 1989.

Interestingly, while the NAFTA began originally as a simple free trade
arrangement, closely approximating an arm's-length free trade negotiation,
the dynamic was such that it wound up much closer to the EC model of
closer integration, with the supplemental agreements on environment and
labor standards becoming critical components of the treaty. The explanation lies partly in several of the factors I discussed earlier, such as the fear
of decline in real wages of the unskilled in the United States and the fear of
harmonization downward from below. But the notion that the EC provided the correct model to think of NAFTA instead became dominant
among the NGOs: the Mexican sociologist Jorge Castañeda has particularly emphasized this dynamic of "unanticipated" transformation of the
NAFTA negotiations.[39]

NOTES

My thanks are due to Ken Abbott, Robert Hudec, David Leebron, and Martin Wolf for
helpful conversations on the subject of this chapter.

1. Dunn (1993a, pp. 37–38).

2. Hume (1911, vol. 2, p. 128); quoted in Dunn (1993b).

3. Adam Smith (1976, pp. 136–137).

4. It was for this reason that the Cambridge economist Joan Robinson moved away in her
later years from her celebrated definition of "exploitation" as the payment of a wage less
than a worker's marginal product: to do so would be to concede implicitly that the market
wage was the just wage. Interestingly, the Nobel laureate Robert Fogel and Stanley Enger-
man, in their monumental study of slavery, appeared to share the Robinsonian definition of
exploitation in examining the question whether slavery led to (economic) exploitation of its
victims.

5. I suspect, however, that some of those who would profess this moral point of view are likely, if you probe deeper, to be closet consequentialists. For they would still hope that the mere act of disapproval in a visible fashion, while producing immediate intransigence by the targeted country, would prompt it eventually to consider concessions instead.

6. There is now a voluminous and growing literature on this subject. It has been reviewed in depth and extended in Jagdish Bhagwati and Vivek Dehejia (1993). The fear outlined in the text is shown in this paper to be seriously exaggerated, possibly unfounded, if existing theories and evidence are considered. However, new hypotheses are suggested as to how globalization of the world economy through trade and diffusion of technology may exert a downward pressure on real wages.

7. The agreements are, as it happens, quite innocuous; I am talking about how they were actually presented and thought of by the Clinton administration.

8. This form of argumentation leads also to an alternative scenario, that the effect of such pressures, along with the competitive pressures on our industries, will be to cut away at one's own environmental and labor standards, producing a "race to the bottom." This argument is considered later in this chapter and fully in Chapters 4 and 10.

9. It is hard to understand why the anti-NAFTA critics thought that Mexican workers would be harmed. They were focusing on the "exploitation" and "low wages" that were supposedly "not reflecting productivity," inferring incorrectly that this fact implied that the *change* in wages following NAFTA would be adverse.

10. My Columbia student Rupa Chanda (1993) has shown this pattern fairly persuasively in her dissertation.

11. Cf. Bhagwati (1991a) where the rise of fair trade demands, as a threat to the world trading system, was first discussed and some of the explanatory factors analyzed.

12. Berger (1993, p. 2).

13. Abbott means by this the claim that a foreign practice violates an accepted commitment, whether at the GATT multilaterally or in bilateral and plurilateral treaties. Evidently, this is the fairest norm! The only, and critical, question it raises is, What procedure is used to establish that a commitment has been violated?

14. This differs from violation of agreements in the sense that it is not a direct, explicit violation but an indirect de facto violation. Thus, if I sell you a house and deny you possession, that is a violation. But if I build a moat around it, over which I have control and you do not, that is tantamount to nullifying my contract and your rights indirectly. Article 23 of the GATT addresses both types of denial of a contracting party's rights.

15. This norm is prominent in the GATT, of course. Abbott considers several cases where the U.S. complainants to the U.S. trade representative's office cited discriminatory practices, whether covered by treaty or not, as inherently unfair. These practices discriminated against U.S. firms in favor of domestic firms (the so-called national treatment being denied) or in favor of other foreign firms.

16. This simply matches what we face with what you face. Nondiscrimination is clearly compatible with lack of reciprocity. Abbott distinguishes among different notions of reciprocity as revealed by the legislative debates.

17. By this, Abbott means that a practice is considered unfair because it distorts market outcomes. As I argued earlier in my book *Protectionism* (Bhagwati, 1988), the economic-

philosophical basis for free trade is the Darwinian process: markets should determine outcomes. If trade practices distort that process, then their legitimacy is at a discount; unfairness ensues. Abbott discusses practices such as foreign targeting of industries for support as one such unfair practice in the U.S. debates and in the 1988 legislation.

18. See, in particular, Bhagwati (1988).

19. The parallels and contrasts between the British and the American cases have been developed at length in Bhagwati and Irwin (1987).

20. Since cheating or unfair trade in foreign countries' practices, including many domestic practices, cannot be alleged if they do what we do, evidently a great number of these objections translate into demands for the foreign nations to do what we do, i.e., into demands for them to harmonize their domestic practices with ours.

21. That there could be mutual, direct foreign investment (DFI) in two advanced countries was first noted by Stephen Hymer (1976). That such mutually penetrating investment (MPI) would increasingly take place within the *same* industry, as it has amply done since, was noted and theorized about in Bhagwati's (1972) review of Raymond Vernon's (1971) *Sovereignty at Bay*.

22. On this issue, see the fine survey by Jeffrey Frenkel (1992).

23. The concept and phrase "kaleidoscopic comparative advantage" were developed in Bhagwati (1991b) and have been elaborated further in Bhagwati and Dehejia (1993).

24. See the work of Alexander Swoboda, for instance, on this subject.

25. These questions were raised in Bhagwati (1991c) in a paper that provided the analytical guidelines for the economist participants for the Bhagwati-Hudec Ford Foundation project.

26. See, for instance, the graduate-level textbook by Bhagwati and Srinivasan (1983, Chapter 15). Equivalences on one dimension, however, do not always translate into equivalence on other dimensions.

27. Cf. Jackson (1969, p. 330).

28. See the detailed discussion in Jackson (1969, Chapter 14), especially section 14.3, pp. 336–339.

29. The following discussion, and quotes, come from Jackson (1969, pp. 361–364).

30. This is an old argument, made well by Richard Pomfret (1975), for example. It has been made more forcefully, and with considerable policy impact, in the context of modern developments in the theory of imperfect competition, by Paul Krugman (1984). Both authors use the phrasing that import protection leads to export promotion. For an alternative way in which this may happen, even when scale economies are not present, see Bhagwati (1986).

31. See, for instance, the excellent discussion in Johnson, Wonnacott, and Shibata (1968).

32. Ohlin's analysis is richer than these quotes indicate, also extending to questions of international capital mobility.

33. I base this conclusion on reading Reddaway (1958) and Ohlin (1965), in particular. Reddaway was also a member of the Tinbergen Committee which reported on this question to the EC.

34. Therefore, these are the "core" questions being addressed by the economists in this volume.

35. See the discussion in Bhagwati (1991a).

36. See the formulation of this law in Bhagwati (1988). Recent, unpublished research by Ed Mansfield of Columbia University, using a mass of cross-country data, provides some support for this law.

37. There is a vast literature in both economics and in law on this problem by now. See, in particular, the legal writings of Stewart (1977a, 1977b) and Revesz (1992), and the economic writings of Tiebout (1956), Buchanan and Goetz (1972), Oates and Schwab (1988), and Wilson (Chapter 10 of this volume).

38. If "race to the bottom" means that nations reach a Nash equilibrium that is characterized by lower standards than in a superior cooperative equilibrium, then there must be unfixed market failures. See the analysis of this question in Chapters 4 and 10.

39. In some of my writings on NAFTA, I took the similar but essentially different position, not shared by any economist that I know of, that NAFTA was a *preferential* trade arrangement being undertaken for, and with, Mexico (and not for others) by the United States, and therefore making demands on Mexico for a minimum set of democratic and social standards was thoroughly reasonable as a price to be paid by Mexico. One would not want to make preferential deals for the benefit of countries that did not adhere to some minimum set of such standards.

REFERENCES

Abbott, Kenneth W. 1993. "Defensive unfairness: The normative structure of section 301," mimeographed. Preliminary draft presented to the Conference on Fairness/Harmonization at Minneapolis, July 29–31; Northwestern University School of Law.

Baumol, William, Sue Anne B. Blackman, and Edward N. Wolff. 1989. *Productivity and American leadership: The long view*. Cambridge, MA: MIT Press.

Berger, Suzanne. 1993. "Domestic institutions, trade, and the pressures for national convergence: US, Europe, Japan," mimeographed. MIT Political Science Department.

Bhagwati, Jagdish. 1972. "Review of *Sovereignty at bay* by Raymond Vernon." *Journal of International Economics*, 2:455–459. Reprinted in Jagdish Bhagwati, *International Factor Mobility* (vol. 2 of his *Essays in International Economic Theory*, ed. Robert Feenstra). Cambridge, MA: MIT Press, 1983.

Bhagwati, Jagdish. 1986. "Export promoting protection: Endogenous monopoly and price disparity." *Pakistan Development Review*. Reprinted in Jagdish Bhagwati, *Political economy and international economics*, ed. Douglas Irwin. Cambridge, MA: MIT Press, 1992.

Bhagwati, Jagdish. 1988. *Protectionism*. Cambridge, MA: MIT Press.

Bhagwati, Jagdish. 1991a. *The world trading system at risk*. Princeton, NJ: Princeton University Press.

Bhagwati, Jagdish. 1991b. "Free traders and free immigrationists: Friends or foes?" mimeographed. Russell Sage Foundation, New York.

Bhagwati, Jagdish. 1991c. "Fair trade, reciprocity and harmonization: The new challenges to the theory and policy of free trade." Columbia University, Economics Department Working Paper. Chapter 13 in Alan Deardorff and Robert Stern, eds., *Analytical and negotiating issues in the global trading system.* Ann Arbor: Michigan University Press, 1994.

Bhagwati, Jagdish. 1993. "American rules, Mexican jobs," *New York Times,* Op-Ed Page, March 24.

Bhagwati, Jagdish, and Vivek Dehejia. 1993. "Freeing trade and the wages of the unskilled: Is Marx striking again?" mimeographed. Paper presented at the American Enterprise Institute Workshop on Trade and Wages, September; American Enterprise Institute. In J. Bhagwati and M. Kosters eds., *Trade and Wages.* Washington D.C.: American Enterprise Institute, 1994.

Bhagwati, Jagdish, and Douglas Irwin. 1987. "The return of the reciprocitarians: U.S. trade policy today." *The World Economy,* 10:109–130.

Bhagwati, Jagdish, and T. N. Srinivasan. 1983. *Lectures on International Trade.* Cambridge, MA: MIT Press.

Buchanan, James, and Charles Goetz. 1972. "Efficiency limits of fiscal mobility: An assessment of the Tiebout model." *Journal of Public Economics,* 1.

Chanda, Rupa. 1993. "Trade liberalization and direct foreign investment." Ph.D. dissertation, Economics Department, Columbia University.

Dunn, John. 1984. *Locke.* Oxford: Oxford University Press.

Dunn, John. 1993a. "The nation-state and human community: Life chances, obligation and the boundaries of society," mimeographed. King's College, Cambridge.

Dunn, John. 1993b. "Crisis of the nation-state," mimeographed. Paper presented to the Political Studies Conference, King's College, Cambridge, September 10 and 11.

Frenkel, Jeffrey. 1992. "Measuring international capital mobility: A review," *American Economic Review (Papers & Proceedings),* May.

Hobbes, Thomas. 1983. *De cive: The English version,* ed. Howard Warrender. Oxford: Clarenden Press.

Hobbes, Thomas. 1991. *Leviathan,* ed. Richard Tuck. Cambridge: Cambridge University Press.

Hume, David. 1911. *A treatise of human nature,* 2 vols. London: J. M. Dent.

Hymer, Stephen. 1976. *The International Operations of National Firms: A Study of Direct Foreign Investment.* Cambridge, MA: MIT Press.

Jackson, John. 1969. *World trade and the law of GATT.* New York: Bobbs-Merrill.

Johnson, Harry, Paul Wonnacott, and Hirofumi Shibata. 1968. *Harmonization of national economic policies under free trade,* Private Planning Association of Canada. Toronto: University of Toronto Press.

Krugman, Paul. 1984. "Import protection as export promotion." In H. Kierzkowski, ed., *Monopolistic competition and international trade.* Oxford University Press.

Locke, John. 1960.*Two treatises of government,* ed. P. Laslett. Cambridge University Press.

Oates, Wallace, and Robert Schwab. 1988, "Economic competition among jurisdictions: Efficiency enhancing or distortion inducing?" *Journal of Public Economics*, 35.

Ohlin, Bertil. 1965. "Some aspects of policies for freer trade." In R. E. Baldwin et al., eds., *Trade, growth and the balance of payments: Essays in honour of Gottfried Haberler*. Amsterdam: North Holland.

Plant, Raymond. 1993. "Rights, rules and world order," mimeographed. University of Southampton.

Pomfret, Richard. 1975. "Some interrelationships between import substitution and export promotion in a small open economy." *Weltwirtschaftliches Archiv* 111:714–727.

Reddaway, Brian. 1958. "The implications of a free trade area for British taxation." *British Tax Review*, March, pp. 71–79.

Revesz, Richard. 1992. "Rehabilitating interstate competition: Rethinking the 'race-to-the-bottom' rationale for federal environmental regulation." *New York University Law Review*, December, pp. 1210–1254.

Servan-Schreiber, Jean-Jacques. 1968. *The American challenge*. London: Hamish Hamilton.

Shoup, Carl, ed. 1967. *Fiscal harmonization in common markets*, vol. 1: *Theory*. New York: Columbia University Press.

Smith, Adam. 1976. *The theory of moral sentiments*, ed. D. Raphael and A. L. Macfie. Oxford: Clarendon Press (first published 1760).

Stewart, Richard. 1977a. "Pyramids of sacrifice? Problems of federalism in mandating state implementation of national environmental policy." *Yale Law Journal*, 86:1196–1212.

Stewart, Richard. 1977b. "The development of administrative and quasi-constitutional law in judicial review of environmental decisionmaking: Lessons from the Clean Air Act." *Iowa Law Review*, 62:713–747.

Tiebout, Charles. 1956. "A pure theory of local expenditures." *Journal of Political Economy*, 64.

Tolchin, Martin, and Susan Tolchin. 1988. *Buying into America: How foreign money is changing the face of our nation*. New York: Times Books.

Vernon, Raymond. 1971. *Sovereignty at Bay*. New York: Basic Books.

2　Lying Down with Procrustes: An Analysis of Harmonization Claims

David W. Leebron

Recently, claims for harmonization of national laws and policies have been closely linked to claims for "fair trade." The scholarly literature has begun to embrace the notion that harmonization is the mechanism by which unfair differences in legal and other regimes are eliminated, and the level playing field, the metaphoric symbol of fairness, is restored. Harmonization in this sense is the procrustean[1] response to international trade, a response fundamentally at odds with the theory of comparative advantage that has justified liberal trading policies since the early 19th century.[2] The "fair trade" idea is undoubtedly one source of harmonization claims, but it would be misleading, and ultimately damaging to the cause of free trade, to characterize harmonization claims generally in this way. Harmonization was pursued long before fair trade was the vogue in trade policy, although it may well be that the first efforts at international harmonization over a century ago were also driven, at least in part, by rationales closely akin to the fairness claim.[3] In the intervening span, however, harmonization has been pursued for a host of reasons, both internationally and within federal systems. The purpose of this paper is to elaborate a more or less complete set of justifications for harmonization efforts, and to evaluate those claims in the context of the international trading system.[4]

The increasing importance of harmonization in international relations is illustrated by the results of the recently completed Uruguay Round trade negotiations. For the first time, harmonization is incorporated in GATT agreements as a norm of international economic relations.[5] Harmonization has of course for some time been an important process in the European Community,[6] and it is undoubtedly that context in which it is most famil- iar and accepted. But harmonization has been pursued in a variety of political situations: among constituent territories of a political unit, as in federal systems; by nations that share some common political authority, as in the European Community; among nations comprising, at least for some purposes, a single economic unit with institutional structures, such as a customs union; and among nations that share no political linkages.[7] My focus in this paper is on this last category: truly "international" harmonization among independent nations sharing no common political or economic authority. Some of the issues raised by international harmonization are familiar from discussions of federalism[8] or "subsidiarity,"[9] but the context of claims for international harmonization and the process for its realization are substantially different.

The debate over harmonization and trade will be improved if we make more explicit the underlying assumptions and fundamental issues. We ought to ask a number of questions regarding any harmonization claim. What is the basis of the claim that the laws of two or more jurisdictions should be the same? Why do the laws differ in the first place, and do the reasons for difference suggest additional costs to the process of harmonization? What other costs might harmonization entail? What kind of harmonization is needed and to what degree must the laws be harmonized? What should the scope of the harmonization effort be in order to realize any goals without unnecessary costs or distortions? Are there alternatives to harmonization that might serve the goals of the proposed harmonization without entailing some of its costs?

Harmonization is not an end in itself. Rather, it is a means of achieving goals such as greater efficiency or fairness. Both the validity of the harmonization claim and the effectiveness of its implementation must be judged in terms of some asserted purpose,[10] and it is the purpose that determines whether the form of harmonization adopted is suitable. Before examining the various justifications that underlie claims for harmonization, I first try to unpack the idea of harmonization by examining abstract ways in which harmonization claims can be characterized. Then, in section 2.2, the different purposes that harmonization could serve are explored. Harmonization, of course, assumes the prior existence of differing legal regimes or policies. Section 2.3 considers the sources of such differences, and how they affect the normative claims for harmonization. These three sections comprise the primary focus of this essay, but do not completely frame the relevant issues for evaluating harmonization claims. Section 2.4 proceeds to examine briefly the processes and institutions of harmonization. Section 2.5 notes some of the costs of harmonization, and in particular the costs of enforcing "sameness" on jurisdictions that might differ in significant ways. Section 2.6 sets forth several alternatives to harmonization that should be considered before determining that harmonization is an appropriate solution to problems created by regulatory differences.

2.1   What Is Harmonization?

Harmonization can be loosely defined as making the regulatory requirements or governmental policies of different jurisdictions identical, or at
least more similar.[11] It is one response to the problems arising from regulatory differences among political units, and potentially one form of intergovernmental cooperation.[12] The term "harmonization" is often used not
only to refer to this result, but also to the process for achieving greater
similarity. A "harmonization claim," as used here, is a normative assertion
that the differences in the laws and policies of two jurisdictions should be
reduced. Although one way to eliminate differences is to assign decisions
to a common political authority, a harmonization claim in the international
context is more often a claim that nations should adopt similar laws and
policies even in the absence of such a common authority.

The term "harmonization" is something of a misnomer insofar as it
might be regarded as deriving from the musical notion of harmony, for it
is difference, not sameness, that makes for musical harmony. In the context
of international trade relations, harmony in the musical sense is provided
by the variations that lead to different comparative advantages among
nations. The claim for the harmonization of laws has come to mean something quite different—indeed almost the exact opposite of the musical
notion of harmony—namely, that international economic relations will
not function smoothly, or properly, unless the laws and policies of different jurisdictions are made more similar. Of course, it is not every difference
that makes for musical harmony; one must distinguish between harmony
and cacophony. As with music, the difficult question is which aspects
should be similar, and which different, in order to create a pleasing or
appropriate relationship. That the laws and policies of nations differ does
not mean they conflict. Very few harmonization claims are based on conflicting policies in the sense that primary actors are subjected to the incompatible commands of two sovereigns.[13]

2.1.1   Types of Harmonization: Rules, Policy Goals, Principles, and Institutions

What exactly does it mean to harmonize laws and governmental policies?
Legal regimes and the broader societal choices in which they are embedded can differ in numerous aspects. Some of these differences are
reflected in formal legal rules and institutions, and others are not. International harmonization has been pursued in a vast array of diverse fields:

monetary and fiscal policy, contract law, banking law, securities regulation, intellectual property law, labor law, environmental law, food safety, product standards and liability law, and trade law, to name only a few. Despite this variety, it is useful to distinguish several broad types of harmonization.

First, fairly specific rules that regulate the outcome, characteristics, or performance of economic goods, actors, transactions, institutions, and productive facilities could be harmonized. Performance in this context refers not merely to characteristics of output, but also the constraints under which such output is produced.[14] For example, pollution regulations for steel factories can be made more similar in various countries. Harmonized rules might impose common limitations on emissions or even mandate the use of particular pollution-control technologies. In the labor area, some early agreements and International Labor Organization (ILO) conventions adopted specific requirements regarding workplace safety or the terms of employment. This type of harmonization raises significant resource allocation and efficiency questions, since resources must be devoted to achieving the required outcomes. Some rules directly address the quality of a good or service or the performance of a productive facility. Other rules attempt to improve on the decision making involved in an economic transaction. Rules regulating the disclosure requirements in securities transactions arguably fall in this category. Rule or performance harmonization does not necessarily mean the harmonized rules are mandatory. While one approach is the adoption by governments (or intergovernmental organizations) of mandatory rules for the relevant economic actors, some harmonization goals could be attained through nonmandatory rules adopted by nongovernmental organizations, such as recognized standard-setting bodies.

Second, more general governmental policy objectives can be harmonized. For example, nations could agree that inflation ought to be kept within specified limits, that ambient air quality be maintained, or that threatened species be preserved. In the labor area, policy objectives would include the attainment of a certain level of organization by labor, or setting a standard for the *average* workweek. This type of harmonization provides only a guideline for governmental action or a standard by which national actions will be judged. Unlike the harmonization of performance requirements, states retain broad leeway to determine how to meet the policy objectives.[15] The requirements imposed by the harmonization of policy objectives are generally addressed only to the governments of the states involved. For example, a requirement that the air contain no more than a specified amount of a certain pollutant, or that an overall maximum amount of that pollutant be emitted by a nation's industries, cannot be applied directly by a polluting firm. Rule harmonization, by contrast, generally addresses the behavior of private-sector actors, although each of the participating governments might implement the law through mandatory domestic legal measures. The political consequences of the two types of harmonization differ substantially. For rule harmonization, detailed policy trade-offs must be made within the harmonization process or institution, which might be an international forum. Under policy harmonization, it remains with the domestic political process to make those choices. If, for example, only average workweek requirements are harmonized, then the government could still exempt certain industries from maximum-working-hour requirements. Similarly, if only overall goals regarding pollution are harmonized, governmental policies could still be very lax for particular industries.

Third, harmonization sometimes aims at adopting certain agreed principles that are intended to influence or constrain the factors that are taken into account in making policies and rules. In some instances, these principles limit the structure or implementation of policies. One important issue that has been implicated in some harmonization efforts is distributive principles, that is, how the costs and benefits of economic activity or governmental policies are imposed on individuals and groups. For example, the "polluter pays" principle, adopted by the European Community and the OECD,[16] does not directly address the amount of pollution that is allowed (either by individual enterprises or in the aggregate), but rather who should bear the cost of pollution reduction.[17] Whatever limits on industrial pollution a society chooses, the costs must be borne by the polluting enterprises. A similar function is served by international rules that regulate subsidies, as well as rules that mandate certain legal liabilities. Regulatory principles are not limited to distributive issues. They might suggest particular regulatory approaches. In the environmental area, for example, it might be agreed that pollution control ought to be achieved through a market in permits to emit specified amounts of pollutants. The United States sought international recognition of the principle that food standards be based only on scientific evidence.[18] In the labor area, a central principle would be the recognition of a right to organize and bargain collectively. But the recognition of that principle might result in very different levels of union organization and activity, and also different rules regarding working conditions and wages. Of course, in some instances the principles are so vaguely couched and flexible that they do not constrain processes or choices at all, amounting to little more than platitudes applicable to virtually any governmental decision.[19]

Fourth, harmonization of institutional structures and procedures, both private and public, is often sought. Such harmonization primarily serves to reinforce other types of harmonization. If the aim is to harmonize decisional outcomes by various private and institutional actors, both the substantive criteria and decisional processes are implicated. Rules, policies, and principles will generally not be truly harmonized unless the procedures and institutions for implementing them are made similarly effective, and doing so may mean making them more similar. For example, some of the North American Free Trade Agreement (NAFTA) provisions require certain procedures for enforcement of domestic laws, including appellate review.[20]

These are at best fuzzy categorizations. Yet they are helpful in thinking about the problems of harmonization. As we will discuss later, a particular harmonization claim might require one or more of these forms of harmonization, or be addressed by alternative forms. These forms entail different types of compromise at different governmental or intergovernmental levels. They vary in their continued tolerance of difference, and hence in allowing societies to reflect their own social choices. Just as important, they pose very different problems of supervising and enforcing their implementation. Adoption and enforcement of a harmonized rule or even policy objective will in many instances be fairly easy to observe; implementation of a principle will usually not be.

These forms of harmonization do not bear any fixed relationship to law. Although we often think of laws as primarily setting rules and standards or establishing institutions and procedures, they can also be used more generally to adopt policies and principles. Statutory provisions sometimes set forth policy goals or principles for the guidance of the executive or the courts, leaving it to them to implement those policies either through rule promulgation or discretionary actions. When such actions are undertaken by the executive, they may or may not be subject to direct judicial or legislative review. The harmonization of certain policy goals might result in very little harmonization of the legal regime. Some countries might respond by the adoption of detailed statutory requirements, and others might rely on private actors to respond to policy goals, perhaps with "guidance" from an administrative bureaucracy. In short, the harmonization of law often entails an additional element of harmonization and further narrows the range of options available to nations attempting to harmonize their policies.

2.1.2   Degree and Scope

Beyond these categorizations, there are two aspects that characterize all harmonization efforts: degree and scope. Harmonization entails both a qualitative directional objective (making laws or policies more similar) and a degree to which that objective is pursued, namely, how similar the laws (or small the difference) should be following harmonization. Depending on the purpose of harmonization, making very different regulatory requirements even slightly more similar could bring substantial benefits. In other cases, no benefit will be realized unless the requirements are made essentially the same. The degree to which a harmonization requirement continues to tolerate difference is the harmonization "margin." The "unification" of law, or the adoption of uniform laws, is harmonization with a zero margin.

The degree or margin of harmonization can range from a zero margin (complete harmonization), which provides for no deviation from the specified standard, to quite broad ranges of tolerance. This margin, however, is defined within the context of a particular type of harmonization, which may in turn allow for many implementation alternatives. For example, adoption of a requirement that states achieve an inflation rate of 3 percent provides for no margin, but this policy objective could be achieved through a variety of fiscal and monetary measures. The "polluter pays" rule, as a principle of distribution, could be implemented through measures requiring the polluter to pay damages, to pay effluent taxes, to pay for pollution permits, or to adopt measures of pollution control.

Zero-margin harmonization has been adopted only in certain regulatory and political contexts. Even uniform laws, if they are not accompanied by harmonization of institutions, effectively allow differences in implementation and effects. One can reject the idea that all countries must adopt the same standards while still seeking to narrow the differences. Thus in many instances margins of tolerance are implicitly or explicitly allowed. In the latter case both a "ceiling" and "floor" might be set, but more often harmonization programs only require that all countries accept some minimum.[21] The European Community, for example, adopted this approach with respect to environmental regulation, allowing each nation to impose more rigorous requirements than those mandated by Community directives.[22] In a similar vein, the Community abandoned its effort to adopt community-wide VAT rates, and instead established only the minimum VAT rates.[23] Although these programs limit the "race to the bottom" problem that will be discussed subsequently, they do raise the possibility that political forces will respond to competitive pressures, with the result that the minimum standard becomes the de facto standard for all.[24]

The second aspect is the breadth or scope of the harmonization effort. Harmonization can be pursued for isolated products or industries, or across a broad policy area. For example, in the environmental context separate harmonization efforts might be undertaken regarding the output of pollution by specific types of enterprises. Or a comprehensive set of requirements for all types of productive facilities or types of pollution could be adopted. Or even more broadly, the requirements regarding all sources of pollution (not just productive facilities) could be harmonized.

The scope of a harmonization claim in many instances determines the coherence, and hence normative validity, of that claim. If a country insists on harmonization only in certain economic sectors in a context where other sectors pose the same problems, then the harmonization claim is somewhat suspect. Furthermore, narrow harmonization efforts have the potential to create significant trade distortions. The type of harmonization does not necessarily determine its scope. Although we would ordinarily expect policy harmonization to be broader in scope than rule harmonization, the latter could be pursued comprehensively across a wide policy range. The breadth of the harmonization effort is closely linked to the harmonization procedure and the institutions involved. International institutions serving as the forum for harmonization sometimes have narrow competencies or mandates.

2.1.3   Harmonization and Integration

The broadest harmonization would result from the creation of a single economic and political space that vested all regulatory authority in the larger political unit. The formation of a single market is a decision to create a single "policy space" out of a number of distinct entities.[25] Lesser forms of economic integration, such as the formation of a common market or customs union, are also often accompanied by substantial harmonization efforts.[26]

Although harmonization might form part of the mechanism to achieve economic integration, it does not occur only within such a framework. The harmonization process is also pursued in comparatively narrow policy spheres. Underlying any harmonization claim is an implicit assertion that over some segment of governmental activity, the policies carried out by several governments, and reflected in their laws, ought to be made identical or very similar. Within the sphere of policy subjected to a harmonization effort, harmonization can be thought of as a decision to create a larger but limited-purpose policy space. Harmonization is in this sense "pick-and-choose" integration. It is an alternative to more comprehensive political and economic amalgamation, much as the formation of a free trade area is an alternative to a customs union. Unlike decisions to politically or economically integrate independent nations, international harmonization preserves the general political independence of the states participating in the harmonization effort.

Harmonization thus presents a variation on the problem of optimal policy areas. The notion of an optimal policy area applies most clearly to public goods, including the legal regime and other governmental policies.[27] Such optimal policy areas are usually defined in fairly broad terms, such as monetary policy. The normative and theoretical nature of any attempt to define an optimal policy area suggests that all closely related policies will be included. Harmonization, by contrast, tends to be more narrowly focused. For example, harmonization of food safety rules creates a single policy space for food safety. It does not, however, establish the same policy space for either product safety (let alone the broader question of human safety) or food production.[28] Harmonization among nations attempting broad-based policy integration, such as the European Community, is thus quite different from pursuing harmonization among nations not forming parts of an economically or politically integrated group.

Certainly not all governmental policies, or even more narrowly those governmental policies directly related to the production and consumption of traded goods, have the same optimal policy area.[29] Nonetheless, one of the dangers of harmonization is the arbitrariness of the sectors in which harmonization is pursued, which creates a potential for economic distortions and welfare losses.[30] Of course, domestic rules often lack coherence even apart from any international efforts or obligations that might influence the adoption of those rules. But efforts to harmonize certain rules and not others could provide an additional source of policy incoherence. Suppose, for example, harmonization is required for bacteria levels and other contaminants in poultry products but not meat or fish. If, as a result, the price of poultry is raised, consumption will potentially be skewed away from chicken (assuming some inefficiencies in the market's assessment of food safety), possibly resulting in increased rather than decreased risk levels. Similarly, harmonization of greenhouse gas emission restrictions, but not other pollutants, would potentially distort choices regarding energy sources and industrial plant design. One might expect that harmonization would be pursued across whatever policy area the arguments favoring harmonization support, and if the arguments justify harmonization of poultry requirements they are likely to justify meat and fish requirements as well. But the decision to pursue harmonization is a political decision and entails a political process, at the domestic as well as international level.[31] Nothing compels a country to pursue a broad-based or coherent harmonization program.[32] It might be that international harmonization will have a "trickle-down" effect in which domestic policies beyond the harmonized sector are then reconsidered to produce a more coherent regulatory policy, but this is not a necessary consequence.

2.1.4   The Normative Aspect of Harmonization Claims

Harmonization claims have both a normative and a nonnormative component. The normative component consists not in the assertion that two political entities should adopt the same policies or laws (that is inherent in any harmonization claim), but rather in any accompanying claim that the laws of at least one society should be conformed to a *better* standard. The nonnormative component is the claim that the laws of the two societies should be made the same, apart from any normative judgment as to either of the society's laws. Harmonization of some technical standards, such as whether parts should be designed to metric or English standards, is nonnormative.[33] Of course, those involved in such harmonization efforts may still have a strong preference for one outcome or another. States or enterprises with sunk costs will naturally prefer that the harmonized rule closely resemble the rule in which they have already invested.[34] Americans will prefer English measurement standards, and the rest of the world will prefer metric ones. But any normative claims about which standard should be adopted depend on the relative costs of conforming, not on the independent merits of the rule.

I want to be clear about my use of "normative" here. Saying that a harmonization claim is nonnormative does not mean that there is not a normative claim that the laws of two jurisdictions should be harmonized. Quite the contrary. It means only that the claim is neutral with regard to which rule should be chosen as the basis of harmonized rule. In other words, the claim consists only of the assertion that the rules that govern that the two societies should be the same. A claim that the law of all jurisdictions should be conformed to a particular standard, if it contains no nonnormative component, is in some sense not really a *harmonization* claim at all. The apparent harmonization claim results only from a truism: every nation should have law or policy *x*; therefore, all nations should have the same policy. But here the only claim for harmonization is that all nations adopt policy x; there is no claim independent of policy x that all nations should have the same policy. I will refer to this type of harmonization claim as pure normative harmonization. It is in fact a claim for the universality of a given rule.[35] Consider, for example, the claim that all nations should prohibit slave labor. That each and every nation should prohibit slave labor does not depend on any value attached to or benefit deriving from all nations having the same policy. Indeed, the claim would exist even if no nation prohibited slave labor, or if two nations had no interaction at all.[36]

Most harmonization claims are not of the pure sort (either normative or nonnormative); they contain both a normative and nonnormative element. In other words, the claim consists in part of an assertion that the law of both nations should be conform to some standard, and in part of an independent claim that the law of both nations should be the same. Much of the recent harmonization debate in the United States, during the discussion of NAFTA was strongly normative, as evidenced by the insistence on "upward" harmonization as opposed to "downward" harmonization. The existence of a nonnormative component of the harmonization claim (i.e., that the law of both nations should be the same) usually implies that some aspect of the normative view would be sacrificed in order to achieve harmonization. That is, it is better that the law of both nations be the same, even if the standard adopted is not the ideal one. A nation might, for example, hold the view that every nation should provide very strong protection to its environment, but most nations holding that view would be willing to sacrifice at least a small measure of the normatively desired level of protection if doing so would result in all nations adopting the same laws (particularly if such an outcome is thought to result in greater protection of the environment).

2.2   The Justifications for Harmonization

In this section I set forth the various purposes that harmonization might serve. I do not mean to imply here that harmonization is the best or the only means to pursue these goals, or that the goals identified are necessarily legitimate. Some of these critical questions are addressed in subsequent sections. Here I outline the reasons that might make harmonization of differing national rules desirable and a few of the principal objections.

At the outset, it is important to note that the occurrence of international transactions, and in particular trading relationships, does not in itself create any need or claim for harmonization. If a U.S. firm desires to export goods to Japan as well as sell them domestically, it can (at least in theory) manufacture goods to meet the requirements of the Japanese market as well as manufacture goods for the American market. If the export market requires airbags in automobiles and the domestic market does not, the manufacturer can produce some cars with airbags for export, and others without for domestic consumption. This point was recently illustrated during the controversy over the European Community's ban on hormone-treated beef. Despite vehement American objections to the ban and its effects on American exports, several Texas cattle ranchers expressed their willingness to meet the European requirements. Similarly, apple growers in Washington state have been specially raising apples to meet Japanese requirements, although securing Japan's approval of those apples was a tortuous process. Of course, the fact that harmonization is not *necessary* for international trade does not rule out claims for it.

2.2.1   Jurisdictional Interface

One of the most important functions of harmonization is to enable participants or systems from different jurisdictions to interact or communicate. This interface claim for harmonization is limited to cases in which transactions occur directly between two jurisdictions. In some instances, harmonization might appear necessary to make certain transnational activities possible, but in most cases it will simply be more efficient. The benefits of such harmonization are well illustrated by the difference in railroad track gauge between the Iberian Peninsula (Spain and Portugal) and the rest of continental Europe. Passengers on most trains from France to Spain must disembark at the border and change to a Spanish train that cannot run on other European train tracks.[37] Similarly, unless telecommunications protocols are harmonized, it is not possible to engage in such communications between countries. If aircraft from different countries had completely different navigation systems, a plane taking off from one country might not be able to land (at least using its navigation system) at an airport in another country. Generally, interface harmonization is nonnormative rule harmonization.

As these examples illustrate, interface problems occur most often in international services that cross borders, namely transportation and communication. However, the adoption of similar or identical *domestic* rules is rarely required. In many cases, a special interface (or international) regime will sufficiently serve the purpose.[38] For example, all countries need not adopt the same protocols for electronic data exchange; they need only adopt a common special protocol that allows data to be exported or imported across borders.

Even where harmonization of the legal regime is not necessary to overcome interface barriers, it does avoid uncertainty and transaction costs in international transactions.[39] For example, the adoption of uniform terms for the international sale of goods makes international contracting, and hence international sales, much easier.[40] This, however, is an example of the harmonization of interface rules rather than domestic rules. Most international harmonization efforts have addressed transactional interfaces.[41] These include the various efforts under the auspices of the United Nations Commission on International Trade Law (UNCITRAL) and Unidroit.

Multilateral interface regimes reduce the costs of international transactions in many cases by achieving economies of scale for all such transactions. A manufacturer or service provider who desires to export goods or services potentially faces a distinct transactional regime for every country to which goods or services are exported. Since the parties to the transactions will be accustomed to different legal regimes, transacting will be especially costly. The adoption of multilateral rules for all such international transactions means the exporter need be familiar with only two regimes: the domestic regime and the international (export) regime. Thus, once an industry engages in some export transactions, export business can be expanded to different destinations without large costs for entering each new export destination.

An alternative to (or perhaps special case of) interface harmonization in this last sense is the harmonization of rules for deciding which jurisdiction's regulatory requirements apply. In many cases, the parties can choose the substantive rule, and the only rule that must be harmonized is that the parties' choice will be respected. In a contract for the sale of goods, for example, parties from two different jurisdictions can specify which of their jurisdiction's rules apply, or in some instances even the rules of a third jurisdiction (to which the transaction has only a minimal relationship, if any). In other words, it is not necessary that the two jurisdictions generally apply the same rules to specified types of transactions, only that they apply the same rules to a particular transaction. Since harmonization of choice-of-law rules alone eliminates any need to favor one jurisdiction's substantive policies over another's, it is not surprising that most early legal harmonization was in the choice-of-law field.[42] Still, harmonization of substantive rules (or the adoption of a special uniform rule for international transactions) reduces information and negotiation costs between parties who are ordinarily subject to the rules of different jurisdictions. In the absence of clear choice-of-law rules, harmonization eliminates any need to decide which of the affected jurisdiction's rules apply,[43] itself often a significant problem both in the negotiation of transactions and in the settlement of disputes.

The ability of private ordering to solve many interface problems suggests that the interface claim for harmonization is often overstated (and may in fact be a claim based on leakage or economies of scale, discussed in sections 2.2.3 and 2.2.5). The overstated interface claim is sometimes presented, either descriptively or normatively, as the "globalization" of law.[44] It is claimed that because there are more international transactions, there is a greater need for uniformity of law. This conclusion simply does not follow. Indeed, certain claims for harmonization, such as economies of scale could decline with an increase in transnational transactions. Whereas interface problems are acute in connecting certain natural monopolies or utilizing public goods across international boundaries, many interface problems are created by government regulation that demands domestic uniformity, including government regulation that unnecessarily mandates monopolies.

2.2.2   Externalities

A second argument for harmonization is the presence of externalities.[45] Rules adopted by one jurisdiction can result in costs imposed on other jurisdictions. There are three types of externalities that might result from a nation's regulatory policies. First, domestic activity in one nation can directly impose transborder costs on another, usually neighboring, nation, resulting in an overall welfare loss to that nation. Second, those policies might adversely affect some individuals in another nation, but not result in any overall loss in welfare (distributional externalities). Third, as a result of one nation's policies, another nation might make political choices that result in a loss of welfare (politically mediated externalities). Here I address only the first type of externality, namely, the infliction by one jurisdiction of net social costs on another.[46]

A familiar example is transborder pollution. The rules on emissions in one country will directly affect the amount of pollution that spills across its borders to the detriment of neighboring nations. A less physical example of externalities that might flow from a nation's legal regime is in banking. Because banks are interlinked all over the world, the failure of a substantial bank can trigger consequences across national borders.[47]

Where jurisdictions can obtain advantages by imposing such externalities, the problem will be especially great.[48] Thus the harmonization of bank solvency requirements, as adopted by the Bank for International Settlements,[49] can be justified on this basis.[50]

Harmonization typically does not (and in some instances can not) directly negate such externalities. Unless emissions of pollutants in border areas are reduced to zero, or bank collapse completely insured against, transborder spillovers will continue to exist, albeit perhaps at a reduced level. Indeed, the fact that externalities exist whether jurisdictions have the same or different regulatory policies suggests that as a general matter this harmonization claim rests on a dubious foundation. In the international context, the objection to externalities is not so much that another jurisdiction has adopted policies that, seen from a collective perspective, are not optimal, but more often that no nation has a right to inflict injury on another nation.[51] But externalities are unavoidable in a balkanized world, and harmonization may be seen as a way to insure a certain reciprocity of such effects, so that jurisdictions will indirectly bear the costs of their externalities.[52] Harmonization also prevents a jurisdiction from deliberately taking advantage of externalities by lowering its standards to impose costs on others while reaping benefits. The harmonization argument is perhaps strongest in the context of protecting international public goods, such as the ozone layer, and it is in that area that the most aggressive international agreements have been reached.[53]

2.2.3　Leakage and the Nonefficacy of Unilateral Rules

A second kind of externality is the "leakage" into (or out of) a jurisdiction of goods or transactions that do not conform to a jurisdiction's rules, resulting in the diminished efficacy of those rules ("nonefficacy").[54] Government regulation often attempts to impose a protective envelope around a jurisdiction's territory and its inhabitants. Goods and services that enter this envelope are expected to conform with all requirements imposed by that jurisdiction's government for the protection of its citizens and residents. For example, securities sold outside the United States may leak back into the country in violation of U.S. securities laws that specify in considerable detail the requirements that must be met in order to sell or distribute securities in the United States. Similarly, intellectual property protection is often undermined by the importation of infringing goods manufactured in other jurisdictions. In these situations, there are usually rules to prevent and deter (through criminal or civil sanctions) such leakage. Thus the U.S. government has the power, under Section 337 of the Tariff Act of 1930, to confiscate infringing goods at the border.[55] But borders are hard to police, especially for invisible transactions such as securities. Even for physical goods such as cigarettes, weapons, and narcotics, border and domestic enforcement have proven inadequate in meeting regulatory goals.

An alternative to policing borders and cross-border transactions is to harmonize the rules of all jurisdictions concerned. If all jurisdictions forbid the manufacture as well as sale of infringing goods and fully enforce those laws, leakage of such goods will be less of a problem. Similarly, if the securities law of all major securities markets are the same, the possible benefit of evading U.S. laws will be substantially diminished, and the United States will need to worry little about leakage of nonconforming securities into its jurisdiction (assuming no other country's comparable laws can be evaded). In light of the increasing interrelationship and interpenetration of national markets, countries may be more willing to compromise on regulatory standards in order to achieve harmonization. The "losses" from a compromise that accepts a lower regulatory standard are compensated by the increased efficacy of the regime, as well as the reduction of border enforcement costs. Indeed, the elimination of these costs is itself an important reason for harmonization, as the European Community's move to a single market illustrates.[56]

Analytically, leakage and externalities are quite similar problems. A complaint against a neighboring country's polluting industries will not be very compelling if the complaining country's own industries are also subject to little environmental regulation and causing just as much pollution. But the articulation of the two justifications differs substantially. In the case of leakage, the claim is that one nation's laws or policies are rendered ineffective because of the policies adopted by other jurisdictions. This claim ultimately rests on the proposition that each nation is entitled to make certain effective policy choices for its own territory or citizens, and the baseline for determining harm is that set of policy choices. For externalities the claim is that the actions or laws of other jurisdictions are causing harm (without reference to the injured nation's own policies). Transborder pollution is on this basis objectionable even if it comes from a country with more stringent environmental regulation. Perhaps the major difference between these two types of justifications is the burden of proof. For leakage, the policy goals and reach of a jurisdiction's own laws must be justified. Is it really entitled to regulate those transactions that are escaping its regulatory reach? For example, is a nation entitled to protect its citizens (wherever they may be) against all harms?[57] In the case of externalities, the foreign jurisdiction must justify causing harm to the interests of the jurisdiction affected.

The basic complaint underlying the leakage/nonefficacy claim is that a jurisdiction's laws and policies are, because of another nation's policies, rendered ineffective with respect to goals or transactions they are intended to regulate.[58] In a sense, this harmonization claim is a jurisdiction claim that has been effectively nullified by the nation's inability to enforce its rules. A nation asserts jurisdiction, that is, some right to regulate certain conduct, but is unable to do so effectively. The evaluation of such claims requires a normative basis for determining the legitimate reach of a nation's laws. For example, if a government wishes to protect its citizens from entering into certain securities transactions no matter where they occur, unilaterally adopted laws will probably be ineffective in achieving the intended regulatory scope. If a citizen enters into a transaction in a foreign jurisdiction, that jurisdiction will probably apply its own laws, following the widely accepted territorial principle of jurisdiction. A jurisdiction can achieve "extraterritorial" protection of its citizens in some circumstances by aggressively applying and enforcing its own laws, and refusing to enforce foreign laws and judgments that violate its own policies. If a citizen enters into a contract in a foreign jurisdiction that violates a policy of the citizen's own country, that country can refuse to enforce the foreign contract or any judgment based on that contract, and might perhaps go so far as to enjoin others (including foreign actors) from enforcing such a contract. But the other jurisdiction will also use whatever legal means it has to enforce its laws and policy choices. One way for a nation to fully protect its own citizens will be to persuade other jurisdictions to adopt the same protections.

Alternatively, a nation in this position might assert that other jurisdictions are required to assist it through the recognition of its law, either through the application of that law in legal proceedings or the recognition and enforcement of judgments rendered in its courts.[59] But the problem posed by extensive claims of jurisdiction (and recognition) is that such claims by several countries will conflict, leaving the difficult question of which nation's claims should prevail and which should yield. Such regulatory conflict results not only in uncertainty for economic actors, but also increases enforcement costs for governments, which must either resolve the conflict or deal with hostile and uncooperative counterparts. Because of this potential for conflict, the reach of a nation's jurisdiction to prescribe and enforce laws must be circumscribed within limits that will be mutually recognized. Harmonization avoids this problem by requiring all nations to adopt the same, or at least similar, laws. Thus rather than having to resolve the conflicting interests of nations, their collective interests can be pursued while avoiding conflict.[60]

In certain regulatory areas where much activity takes place outside the physical jurisdiction of a country, nonefficacy will be a pervasive problem. Consider, for example, protecting dolphins endangered by certain methods of fishing. A nation adopts a law forbidding its fishing fleet from using those methods. Its unilateral adoption will have little or no effect if other countries' fleets do not adopt those methods and therefore can catch fish at a lower cost. Also, since jurisdiction over ships on the high seas is traditionally based on the flag of registry, the result of unilateral regulation might be that owners switch their ship registration to other countries. If the legitimate interest of the regulating government is only to prevent its citizens from engaging in conduct it regards as wrongful, then there is no nonefficacy problem. On the other hand, if it has even a partial interest in diminishing the number of dolphins killed (because dolphins, or at least those on the high seas, are regarded as worthy of protection), unilateral action of this type will not serve its goal at all.[61] More broadly, noncoercive unilateral efforts for the protection and maintenance of international public goods, such as fishing stocks in international waters, will generally not be effective.

Similar problems exist for the protection of privacy. Suppose a nation desires to protect the privacy of its citizens and stringently regulates credit bureaus, medical and insurance databases, and others who collect and sell individualized information. If information providers simply move offshore to a "data haven" jurisdiction, then those protective laws will have had little effect. Indeed, unlike most harmonization efforts, if there exists a haven that can absorb virtually limitless amounts of service providers (e.g., flags of convenience and possibly financial havens), nations may not be able to achieve their goals unless there is full compliance by all jurisdictions.

As trade and investment barriers are reduced among all nations, and as enterprises enjoy increasing flexibility to respond to regulatory differences, a slightly different problem of nonefficacy arises. It is not so much that a particular regulatory policy is threatened by the differing policies of other nations as that the domestic understandings that led to the adoption of the policy are changed. Policy choices invariably involve trade-offs. A nation does not simply choose a level of pollution control, but rather evaluates the benefits of such control against its costs, including lower wages or levels of employment. In other words, a nation adopts a particular regulatory policy in light of all of its perceived costs and benefits. If, for example, enterprises relocate to jurisdictions with less stringent regulatory requirements and imports substitute for domestic production, these trade-offs will be altered at least in the short run. Even if a nation's total welfare is not harmed, some groups will be. The only "externality" created is distributional; no net costs have been inflicted. It is in this distributional sense that the nation's policy choices have been rendered ineffective. Assuming the resulting set of trade-offs is unacceptable, four choices are available: compensate those harmed by the imports, protect the domestic industry so it is not harmed, eliminate the stringent domestic regulatory policies, and persuade the exporting nation to harmonize its regulatory policies (assuming that if such regulations are adopted, exports from that jurisdiction will no longer be able to displace the products of domestic producers).

The normative foundation of the last policy choice, the harmonization claim, is extremely weak. Unless it can be demonstrated that overall employment levels will decline as a result of comparative regulatory choices, the claim is reduced to some right to maintain employment in the affected sector. Such an asserted right suffers from two defects. First, it is irreconcilably in conflict with the fundamental precepts of a liberal trading system based on comparative advantage. Second, it rests on a false notion of cause and effect. There are many marginal changes, not just the asserted regulatory difference, that might eliminate the competitive advantage of the other jurisdiction. The existence of difference is not enough to support the claim; it must be shown that the difference is in some sense *wrong*.[62] The nonefficacy claim, however, includes no such assertion.[63]

From an overall welfare point of view, the best alternative is to compensate those harmed by the imports. To do so, however, requires a direct allocation of resources, which might not be politically possible. If the trading regime prohibits protective action, the remaining choices are to accept the injury to the domestic industry or to eliminate the stringent regulatory policies. Although the first choice is by hypothesis more efficient, the political process might adopt the second. This is the so-called race to the bottom. I do not wish here to enter the debate whether, as a theoretical matter, a welfare-maximizing government would in fact adopt such a policy.[64] But as a realistic political question, it seems indisputable that it might. This is a politically mediated externality, and any harmonization claim to avoid such an "externality" boils down to this: because we are unable to make optimal domestic political choices in the face of trade competition, you must change your laws (even if doing so is not welfare enhancing for you). Since there is no assertion that the regulatory policies of the exporting nation are wrong, the normative foundation for insisting on costly regulatory change is no stronger than if an importing nation asked an exporting nation to compensate injured domestic industry for no reason other than that the exports had caused that injury.

As leakage and nonefficacy claims are ultimately based on the notion that a nation has some right to make its policy choices effective, these harmonization claims are virtually always strongly normative. As noted previously, nations may be willing to accept the trade-off of increased efficacy for a standard they would otherwise regard as suboptimal.

2.2.4   Fair Competition

A prevalent argument in support of harmonization is fairness in trade competition.[65] The central idea is that lesser regulatory burdens will give producers an *unfair* advantage in international trade. A steel manufacturer that faces no pollution-control requirements is able to sell steel cheaper than a manufacturer located in a jurisdiction that imposes severe limitations on emissions. This claim attempts to supply the argument, missing in the nonefficacy claim discussed earlier, that there is something inherently wrong about the difference in regulatory policies.

The "unfairness" claim seems at odds with traditional theories of comparative advantage, since it is by hypothesis some difference that makes for such advantage. That is, if the exporting nation believes it is better off by imposing lax requirements, the importing nation is better off by being able to obtain cheaper goods. The latter nation's labor and capital can then be deployed in other industries, and at least in theory the gains from such redeployment could compensate losses incurred as a result of the transition. Of course, political choices may not result in actually granting full compensation. As suggested previously, the unfairness claim may be coupled with a further claim about political institutions, namely that the probable response (supported by both managers and labor) will be to lower domestic political standards to meet the foreign competition. But this additional consequence, if it does occur, adds nothing to the initial claim that the competition is in some sense unfair.

The fairness claim for harmonization usually comprises both an economic claim and an argument about justice. The underlying economic claim is that the differences in policies or regimes *distort* conditions of competition. In other words, the comparative advantage that results from regulatory differences is asserted not to be a "real" comparative advantage.

Another nation's comparatively lax regulatory policies are regarded as no different from a subsidy.[66] We will return to this question later when we examine the potential sources of difference. The point here is that the proponents of fairness claims usually support the notion of economic competition, so long as such competition is "fair." In so doing, they also accept certain aspects of the idea of comparative advantage, albeit not in any form that would be recognized by most economists.[67] On the other hand, the notion that government policies might unfairly distort the conditions of competition is a familiar one in international economic law.[68]

Even if one accepts the notion that competition is distorted and economic resources inefficiently allocated, a further question arises, as it does with the more traditional unfair trade claims of subsidization and dumping, of why a nation should object to a foreign country selling its products at below their true cost.[69] It is in answer to this question that the argument shifts from an economic basis to one about justice or fairness. Although a number of reasons have been advanced in support of such unfair trade actions, two primary types of claims are relevant here. First are claims of "justice" that are individualized (in the sense of individuals, groups, or firms, and not the national interest as a whole). The competition from cheaper imports will certainly cause losses to identifiable individuals or groups. Since that competition is "unfair," it is also regarded as unfair that the costs of that competition are borne by those individuals. This might be an argument based on notions of either distributive or corrective justice. The distributive objection is that it is unfair for those in the injured domestic industry to suffer while the rest of the country happily benefits from buying cheap imports.[70] This objection could be addressed, and probably to a nation's net benefit, by accepting the cheaper imports and compensating the individuals adversely affected. Since such solutions are rarely politically feasible, actions against imports is a "second-best" political (but not economic) solution. This solution also has a superficial corrective justice appeal, in that the benefit (i.e., sales of goods) that would have accrued to the foreign competitor as a result of its unfair actions is reclaimed for the unfairly injured domestic producer.

Some fairness claims focus not on particular competitors in international trade, but rather more generally on economic relations between nations.[71] The political consequence of such an argument is to shift the claim of harm from individuals and firms to the nation as a whole, making it perhaps more acceptable as the basis of national action. The question here is whether harmonization claims based on this broader fairness concept make sense. For example, it could be asserted generally that a foreign nation's lax pollution laws give a systemic advantage to its producers, and that its environmental laws should be harmonized upward to eliminate this unfair advantage. Similarly, weak antitrust laws might generally allow a nation's domestic producers to form cartels with distributors to block competitive imports. These unfairness claims, however, rest on an overall imbalance in trade relations, which most probably results from macroeconomic factors. Harmonization is at best a crude tool (if indeed of any use at all) to deal with such systemic or structural trade imbalances.[72]

2.2.5 Economies of Scale

A fifth argument for harmonization is economies of scale. If a manufacturer faces significantly different requirements in each jurisdiction for which it manufactures, it will not be able to achieve economies of scale beyond its market share for one jurisdiction. If further economies could be achieved by increasing the scale of production, harmonization of the regulatory requirements will make that possible. Possible gains from this type of harmonization apply not only to product specifications that affect manufacturing, but also to many other firm activities, such as advertising and raising capital on securities markets. Thus, if one registration statement and prospectus will meet the requirements of a number of markets, it may be possible to access markets that otherwise would be too expensive to enter.

Even where the marginal compliance costs for different jurisdictional requirements are low (i.e., the compliance costs are mostly variable rather than fixed), legal information costs represent an additional fixed cost for each jurisdiction that must be recovered from the sales of products in that jurisdiction. In the face of ignorance and uncertainty, a producer might be unwilling to undertake the effort to engage in a small number of international transactions.[73] In short, every separate legal system to some extent creates a barrier to trade. Harmonization substantially reduces information costs, enabling market entrance even for relatively small sales.

The economies-of-scale argument can also be cast as a fairness argument insofar as harmonization can be said to remove an "artificial" source of comparative advantage enjoyed by domestic producers. Companies established within a jurisdiction will generally have some advantage in meeting the technical requirements of that jurisdiction for their products. They may already have made the investments necessary to meet those requirements; their market share may be much greater; or they may be able to meet changing requirements more efficiently (perhaps because they can exert greater influence on the political and administrative processes). Technical harmonization under these circumstances (which very likely constitutes the majority of cases) will be politically difficult because the outcome of the harmonization process will favor the producers in the jurisdiction whose present rules come closest to that outcome. A recent example is the attempt to formulate standards for high-definition television.

2.2.6   Political Economies of Scale

A somewhat different argument for harmonization could be termed "political economies of scale."[74] Regulatory requirements generally result from a political process. The political forces and institutions involved in that process might realize certain economies, or greater effectiveness, if decisions were made or influenced by a more encompassing forum. Some institutions of harmonization shift the process to a different political forum, with different resources and political forces.

In some instances, the argument for shifting the forum to the integrated level is that resources can be better marshalled and coordinated. If there is one optimal standard for all jurisdictions, then determining that standard jointly rather than separately reduces costs. Even if the optimal standard is not precisely the same, there may be economies of scale available in applying common aspects of the standards or in adopting a common compromise. Testing new drugs, for example, is an expensive process. If several governments cooperate, perhaps by assigning responsibility to only one of them for testing each drug, citizens of all will benefit.[75] This is a governmental economy of scale, but the claim depends on the initial assumption that the optimal standards for the various jurisdictions are at least very similar. It is in this sense not truly a claim for harmonization (since it takes that as a given), but rather a claim for a certain process when it is thought that separate processes would, or should, produce similar standards or results.

Some participants in the regulatory process, however, want harmonization shifted to a different forum because their political power in the alternative forum is greater (or the costs of exercising that power are less).[76] In a sense, the economies of scale are private economies for particular political constituencies. For example, labor unions might be able to exert more influence in the International Labor Organization than in national bodies.[77] Forum shifts may be vertical, horizontal, or both. A vertical forum shift is a shift to a larger or smaller geographic jurisdiction, such as from a state to a federal level, or from national to international. For example, lawyers representing plaintiffs in tort liability suits tend to have greater political power in state than in national legislatures, and major manufacturers of consumer goods have greater power in Congress. Thus for many years product liability reform was pursued more in Congress than in many state legislatures. Vertical shifts usually, but not always, imply a hierarchical relationship between the forums. At the international level, many institutions of harmonization enjoy no hierarchical power at all over national institutions, which then make independent political decisions whether to accept the harmonization.

A horizontal forum shift is to a different political organ or regulatory bureau at the same level of government. Administrative agencies are often captured to some extent by those they are intended to regulate, so the regulation they produce will depend on their general area of substantive jurisdiction. In the context of trade, Congress made a deliberate decision to shift certain aspects of antidumping and countervailing duty cases from the Treasury Department to Commerce, believing that the Treasury Department was insufficiently sensitive to the concerns of American manufacturers.

Harmonization necessitates at least a partial vertical forum shift, insofar as the decision making of different jurisdictions must be coordinated. It is partial because the more comprehensive institution or process may provide no more than a coordination mechanism to produce proposals (e.g., model laws) or nonmandatory standards. Political authority and accountability are not changed, because the ordinary domestic institutions must decide whether to implement the outcome of the harmonization process.[78] In many instances a vertical forum shift will also entail a horizontal forum shift. Indeed, this will typically be the case when the shift is to the international level, as there is no comprehensive international political authority.[79] The narrowing of competence affects not only the substantive policy trade-offs that will be considered, but also representation and institutional expertise. For example, in many countries the state department or foreign ministry will exercise influence over all international agreements and negotiations, whereas they would have no role to play in domestic considerations of the same matter.[80] Even if the organization that represents a particular country in the international harmonization process reflects the political, economic, and social forces that would be represented in the domestic process, the representatives of other countries might have different constituencies.[81]

This second political economy argument for harmonization is also not a justification for harmonization itself, but rather a claim for a different process or institution for adopting laws or policies. And those who seek a different process do so to achieve not the harmonization of rules, but rather specific substantive outcomes. It is in this sense normative harmonization, but its normative goals are directed more at the domestic policy than the foreign one.

2.2.7   Transparency

As discussed more fully in the following section, nations can legitimately arrive at quite different policy choices. In many instances, a given policy choice might result from either legitimate or illegitimate reasons (judging from the standpoint of internationally applicable norms). Assume, for example, that a jurisdiction prohibits the use of a certain food additive. It might do so either because in its judgment that additive presents some risk to the health and safety of its people (a legitimate basis under international norms) or because many foreign competitors use the additive and the domestic industry does not. The domestic industry would achieve a measure of protection by forbidding the additive, while claiming the regulation is justified by health and safety concerns.[82]

The inability to determine whether another nation's policy choices are made on legitimate or illegitimate grounds is a serious problem for the international trading system, especially insofar as one of the prevailing norms is "reciprocity" in trading relationships. If trade liberalization commitments can be neutralized by disguised regulatory measures, then the multilateral trade negotiation process would be undermined. Requiring jurisdictions to adopt harmonized rules (e.g., international standards) eliminates their ability to choose alternative rules because of their protective effect. Of course, it also eliminates their ability to choose rules for reasons other than protective effect (such as a greater desire to protect human health and the environment), and for this reason harmonization based solely on the concern to assure trade transparency is controversial. A compromise between these two concerns is evident in the Uruguay Round Agreement on the Application of Sanitary and Phytosanitary Measures, which adopts a presumption that sanitary and phytosanitary measures that conform to international standards are not a disguised restriction on trade, and deems them "necessary to protect human, animal or plant life or health."

Two factors greatly limit the potential for harmonization to achieve transparency. First, harmonization of a substantive rule or policy will still leave many opportunities for opaqueness in the application of that policy.

Rules and policies must be interpreted, facts must be determined, and interpreted rules must then be applied to the determined facts. Second, the very process of harmonization, which generally involves compromise, has a tendency to result in both incoherence and vagueness.[83] In the absence of unified institutions for interpretation and enforcement, such vagueness enlarges the opportunities to continue implementing disfavored policies.

These categories are not separated by crisp definitional lines. A harmonization claim might be supported by arguments from several categories, as well as normative universalist claims. These seven basic arguments for harmonization—interface, externalities, leakage/nonefficacy, fair competition, economies of scale, political economies, and transparency—differ in their underlying attributes and in the type and degree of harmonization that is necessary to achieve their goal. Harmonization for the purpose of achieving fair competition in international trade, for example, would typically entail the harmonization both of performance standards (rules) and distributive principles. It does not require identical regulatory substance, although transparency concerns might lead some to advocate such complete harmonization. Interface harmonization, on the other hand, generally requires identical regulatory substance but not the harmonization of distributive principles. Harmonization to address nonefficacy and externalities could, depending on the context, be implemented either through performance or policy harmonization. Economy-of-scale harmonization will generally entail only performance harmonization, but with comparatively small margins of tolerance.

2.3   The Sources and Legitimacy of Difference

Harmonization claims cannot be evaluated solely with respect to the goals that harmonization is designed to achieve, such as economies of scale or fairness. Differences between nations may also have value, and harmonization can only be achieved at the cost of eliminating or reducing differences. Thus before evaluating claims that laws should be harmonized, we must ask why nations adopt different laws. Ultimately, the question of harmonization, particularly where the justification is fairness, is one of the legitimacy of difference.[84] If differences are legitimate, then a harmonization claim could not be based solely on the existence of difference, as the fairness claim appears to be. As discussed previously, other harmonization claims are based at least in part on the cost of difference. If differences have *value* in addition to legitimacy, then even harmonization claims based on these other arguments must take that value into account in determining whether harmonization should be pursued.

Differences between national regulatory policies could be regarded either as substantively legitimate or procedurally legitimate. They are substantively legitimate if the differences in policy are justified by differences in the substantive concerns and values that inform policy. They are procedurally legitimate if we regard the process by which they were adopted as establishing their legitimacy, whether or not the differences could be justified by reference to differing values.

2.3.1   Substantive Legitimacy

The question of why nations adopt different laws is an extraordinarily complex and difficult inquiry, one that would require all the tools and insights of the sociology of law, public-choice theory, and more to address.[85] I want to adopt here a more limited and abstract (some might say naive) approach, which I think nevertheless yields useful insights. Nations can be said to differ in five attributes that affect the laws and policies they adopt: endowments, technologies, preferences, institutions, and coalition formation. In addition, at least some differences in laws are probably stochastic.[86]

"Endowments" as used here does not refer solely to the economists' "factor endowments," but to all differences in resources (other than technologies) that might affect a nation's productive capacity. Endowments for these purposes are a construct that applies to any given decision. Policy decisions both affect and are affected by national endowments. For example, nations differ in the educational level of the population, but that education is in turn a function of the political processes that determine the resources allocated to education, which in part will reflect the extent to which the population prefers education to other uses of their resources. Endowments also encompass societal wealth, including the standard of living and health of the population. Endowments have both an aggregate aspect (e.g., gross capital formation) and an individual or distributive aspect. Both can affect the choices nations make.

Technologies determine the ways in which endowments are used to produce goods and services. Like some endowments, most technologies are transferable.[87] Developing countries have long disputed the legitimacy of the existing distribution of technologies. But given the availability of certain technologies, it is clear these will influence regulatory policies.

Identity of endowments and technologies alone does not necessarily result in identical social choices. Individuals differ in their preferences (even given identical endowments), and we cannot assume that the distribution of varying preferences is the same in all nations. I do not here inquire into the sources of differing preferences—for example, whether there are cultural differences that might cause one population to value physical fitness more highly than intellectual attainment. But it seems likely that some national differences in preferences exist and affect the social policies that individuals and groups prefer. Furthermore, endowment and preference are interactive. Changes in endowments may alter preferences, and the choices that result from differing preferences can in the longer run affect endowments. Some preferences might increase monotonically with national wealth (as has been suggested of the taste for a clean environment), but I do not assume here such a simple relationship.

Preferences are an opaque notion. The basic idea of a preference is the desire for, and preferred trade-offs among, consumption of various goods and services. There may also be differences in preference for present as opposed to future consumption (i.e., saving). These preferences are all endogenous in that they do not ordinarily depend on the consumption or wealth of others. But individuals can also have preferences regarding things other than their own consumption, such as fairness and justice. For example, individuals can have strong views regarding the distribution of goods and costs, or how political and social interactions should be structured. Such preferences are no longer autonomous, and perhaps are less likely to be endogenous.

That preferences will affect consumption is axiomatic. But it is differences in production patterns, not consumption, that are generally regarded as determining international trade. For the most part, economists have modeled trade as being determined by differences in endowments and technologies. Some preferences will directly affect the scarcity of endowments. For example, if in one society people strongly preferred to live in isolated single houses on large tracts of land and in another were perfectly content to live in smaller apartments in concentrated urban environments, land for productive use in the former society would be scarcer even if both societies had the same land and population. Similarly, if the workers in one society preferred more leisure time to more income (which would enable them to purchase more goods and services), this preference might be reflected in either lesser productivity or an effectively smaller labor supply, both resulting in greater labor costs per unit of output. Differing preferences could affect more, however, than such traditional factors of production. Many productive activities impose costs on the environment, and thus the environment can be regarded as a resource consumed in the production process. As with land, competing demands for that resource will determine its comparative cost. If the population strongly values the environment, the resource will be more costly. In each of these cases, laws and policies might be adopted reflecting the difference in preferences. Those policies, in turn, affect an enterprise's costs of production.

Even in the absence of any external effects of a nation's policies, there may be some limits on our willingness to accept as legitimate the preferences of other nations. The prohibition on slave labor, for example, could be seen in this light. Similarly, other human rights abuses that somehow convey certain productive advantages would not be regarded as a legitimate source of difference. If this approach were narrowly confined to widely recognized fundamental human rights that could be said to influence trade directly, it would provide little basis for questioning national differences. But the approach is hard to cabin. Any universalist claim rejects the substantive legitimacy of difference on that particular issue, and those who make normative claims for their societies are often inclined to believe such claims are applicable to other societies as well.

These three sources of difference (endowments, technologies, and preferences) in the laws and policies nations adopt are also commonly identified sources of a nation's comparative advantage. This observation suggests a complex relationship between differences in laws and comparative advantage in international trade. In some cases, the legal regime mediates the differences in these factors into differences in production costs. For example, a difference in environmental resources might be reflected in more stringent pollution controls, greater fines for polluting, or more frequent imposition of liability.[88] In many instances, unregulated markets will do the necessary work of translating comparative advantages into comparative costs. But where markets do not work or are perceived as generating unsatisfactory outcomes (e.g., providing public goods or solving certain coordination problems), the assistance of governmental policy and law will be needed.

If preferences, endowments, and technologies were the only differences between nations, we could perhaps assume that differences in governmental regulation and policy were (with a human rights caveat) legitimate determinants of comparative advantage. This conclusion would have two important implications for harmonization claims. First, it would be difficult to argue that the differences were "unfair."[89] Law and other governmental policies cannot be cleanly sliced away from any free market notion of comparative advantage.[90] In the modern regulatory state, virtually every aspect of production, including the terms on which labor is employed and resources are used, is subject to some measure of regulation. Second, except for stochastic differences,[91] any harmonization would come at the expense of a decline in economic welfare of the citizens of at least one of the jurisdictions, and perhaps both.

But once we take into account differences in institutions and coalition formation, the presumptive legitimacy of differences in policy choices is less clear. Assume that two societies are identically blessed with technologies and endowments, and that the distribution of individual preferences is also the same. How can we explain that the two societies make different policy choices and adopt differing regulatory regimes? It might be that there are two or more Pareto optimal policy sets, and the societies have made different choices from among those sets. To give a simple example, suppose there are only two sources of pollution, automobiles and factories. Both societies choose to invest the same amount of resources in pollution control and to achieve the same level of environmental cleanliness. But one society adopts stringent limitations on automobile exhausts, and the other adopts restrictions on factory emissions. The different choices are perhaps stochastic, particularly if the two societies are neutral between the two choices. On the other hand, if in one society the automobile drivers are well organized, whereas in the other, factory owners are, that fact will determine the choice made. Or perhaps campaign contributions are limited in one society, giving greater power to organizations that consist of many members, such as automobile associations. Now we become mired in the myriad problems of public choice. Here we need only point out that the solutions adopted by one or both societies might or might not be Pareto optimal solutions. From a "fairness" point of view these two possibilities have slightly different implications, and I address them separately.

If the two societies have made different Pareto optimal choices, it is again unclear what the basis of any fairness claim would be. The two choices, being equally beneficial from a social-welfare point of view, should both be legitimate. The consequences of those choices become part of each society's endowments. Of course, individual producers might be at a disadvantage in trade competition, but that would be the case for any producer of a good that was not within a society's comparative advantage. To use a sports metaphor, one society may invest in training basketball players and another rugby players, but if the basketball players decide to play rugby, they cannot claim unfairness when they lose.

Now suppose that the societies differ not in having chosen alternative
Pareto optimal policy sets, but in that one society has achieved the optimal
policy set, which is a potentially Pareto optimal policy set for the other
society, but the latter society is unable to adopt it. The necessary coalitions are unable to form, or institutional structures prevent change.
Assume, for example, that the optimal policy set includes both auto and
factory emission controls; one society adopts both, and the other society
adopts only auto emission restrictions. Preferences, technologies, and endowments, as well as choices among equally good policy sets, are ruled
out as potential sources of difference. Is the illegitimacy or unfairness claim
any stronger in this context?

Differences in legal and policy regimes that result from differences in
preferences, endowments, or technologies reflect differences in the optimal
regime. Any claim of unfairness would seem fundamentally at odds not
only with the theory of comparative advantage, but also a minimalist
notion of sovereignty that allowed each nation to adopt policies that are
best for it. Harmonization in such a case would require one or both nations
to adopt a less than optimal legal regime. Differences in institutions and
coalition formation, on the other hand, result only in differences in the
regime actually adopted, which might be the best politically attainable
regime for any given society. In this event, differences between societies
cannot be adequately defended on a normative basis, but only on a prag-
matic basis or on the basis of legitimacy conferred by process.

2.3.2   Process-Based Legitimacy

The simplest, and in some ways most traditional, approach would be
to regard national sovereignty as shielding from external scrutiny any
question about the legitimacy of national choices that affect comparative advantage. This would apply to differences resulting not only from
endowments, technologies, and consumption preferences, but also from
distributional preferences, institutions, and coalition formation. Recent international practice, however, suggests that not all internal choices are
regarded as "legitimate" for this purpose.

First, since World War II the idea of internationally recognized human
rights has seriously eroded this notion of national sovereignty.[92] Not all
internally made choices are regarded as legitimate. In the earlier phase of
the postwar human rights movement, the emphasis was on substantive
rights of protection from the abuse of governmental power, with ambiguity

if not agnosticism on the issue of political processes. More recently, human rights have incorporated distributional concerns[93] and a right to a democratic process.[94] There may be good reason for excluding these concerns from international trade law, but one cannot start with the idea that "national sovereignty" prevents all inquiry into the legitimacy of a nation's trading advantages.

Second, international trade law itself contains significant limitations on the notion that all differences that emerge from the exercise of national sovereignty are to be regarded as part of a nation's comparative advantage. The GATT includes an exception for prison labor that would permit a nation to exclude the products of foreign prison and slave labor.[95] The GATT also permits a nation to respond, through the imposition of countervailing duties, to foreign subsidies.[96] Arguably, the international law of subsidies is based partly on the notion that certain national choices do not confer legitimate comparative advantage.[97]

The question is whether we can let just a few things out of this Pandora's box (or as many lawyers would phrase it, whether we can stop our slide down this slippery slope). If some human rights questions (e.g., slave labor) are legitimate subjects of inquiry in the context of trade relations, why aren't all human rights questions, and how can we then limit the notion of human rights? Would it include workers' rights, and extend to such issues as a fair minimum wage as well as basic rights of bargaining? Or could we exclude inquiry into most questions of substantive legitimacy if certain requirements of procedural legitimacy were met, such as democratic government?[98]

We might think that all nations should have democratic governments, and even that economic sanctions should be used to enforce this norm. But that is not the question here. The issue is whether certain processes provide greater assurance that a nation's policy choices reflect its endowments, technologies, and preferences, and hence do not "distort" its comparative advantage. Most of the world now apparently subscribes to the view that democracy is a superior system of government and that it leads to governmental actions that better reflect the will of the people. But the unhappy truth of the matter is that from the point of view of determining some theoretical "true" comparative advantage, no process can tell us for sure whether difference is legitimate in a substantive sense. As numerous theoreticians and empiricists have demonstrated, democracy in general and bureaucratic governments in particular are often incapable of making ideal social choices.[99] If we are not willing to travel the road of directly imposing sanctions for inadequate protection of human rights, including democracy, casting the issue as one of trade distortion might turn out to be a disingenuous substitute open to protectionist abuse.

There are certainly strong arguments for not inquiring into the legitimacy of a nation's productive advantages. First, it will rarely be the case that an outside observer is able to determine whether a policy difference derives from differences in endowments, technologies, or preferences, or from a difference that is not regarded as a legitimate source of comparative advantage. Societal choices are path dependent and historically contingent, and small differences in choice probably produce chaotic results over the longer term. Harmonization could quickly become (some would say it has already become), like antidumping, just another tool of protectionism.

Second, even if the difference in laws could not be defended, a difference in institutions that produced the difference in laws might be. Regulatory differences are then a second-order phenomenon that flows from different preferences regarding institutional structures. Suppose, for example, that one nation values freedom of speech extremely highly and is unwilling to put any constraints on that freedom even though this policy results in wealthier individuals and entities enjoying relatively more speech. Another nation values free speech, but also places great emphasis on equality in the context of its democratic processes. It therefore imposes spending limits on the purchase of broadcast media for political purposes. Both nations have similar democratic processes, but as a result of the difference in spending on public speech, the first nation adopts less stringent environmental protection than the second. Now suppose it could be conclusively shown that the citizens of the first nation would in fact overwhelmingly prefer greater environmental protection. But when asked if they would be willing to change the rules of their political process to achieve it, the emphatic answer is no. This is not an argument against harmonization, but it is an argument against inquiring into the legitimacy or unfairness of difference. Perhaps we should return to the ever-popular sports analogy. Suppose team A values democracy and makes most important decisions by a vote. Team B, by contrast, values strong leadership and therefore empowers its coach to make most decisions. Team A decides to practice only four days a week; team B's coach requires six days. No doubt team B will have an advantage on the field even if it is level. But even if nearly all the team B players said they would prefer to practice only four days a week, it does not mean their advantage is unfair.

Despite these difficulties, institutional approaches to legitimacy might still be preferable to substantive approaches. Requiring nations to alter their institutional processes at least allows those nations to continue to adopt different regulatory choices. Those choices then need only be defended on the basis of fair and open processes, not their substantive legitimacy. The difficulty is in agreeing on the minimal institutional arrangements for procedurally conferring legitimacy. Must certain choices be consigned to democratically elected legislatures rather than appointed bureaucrats? And must the decisions of bureaucrats be subject to certain kinds of review? More to the point, what should be the consequence of determining that a nation's choices cannot be justified by process? In theory, such a determination would call into question not merely different regulatory policies, but all regulatory policies of any state that failed to pass procedural muster.

One approach is found in the NAFTA side agreement on environmental protection. The primary obligation imposed on Mexico was not to change its standards, but rather to enforce the standards that its legislature had adopted.[100] The other parties thus could not for the most part challenge the substantive standards, only their enforcement. One interpretation of this approach is that when a nation has democratic institutions, the choices formally expressed by those institutions will be regarded as legitimate and must be enforced. A more permissive interpretation would be that no matter what institutions are responsible for substantive policy making through law, the choices those institutions make must be implemented if they are to be treated as legitimate for trade purposes.

Both these interpretations are open to a fundamental objection. Policy choices, including the adoption of substantive laws, are made against the background of a society's institutions and cultural norms. The separation of substantive rule formulation from the mechanisms of enforcement is artificial. Nonetheless, this approach comports with an overarching norm of international economic relations: transparency. The obligation to make trade rules transparent serves both an international and domestic function. The international purpose is to make the rules visible to potential exporters to the market, and thus reduce uncertainty and transaction costs, as well as to identify the subjects of international trade negotiation. The domestic purpose is to subject those rules to domestic political constraints.

A final word of caution is in order. There is no empirical evidence that differing national preferences and regulatory policies have any effect on international trade patterns. If most interindustry international trade can be explained by differences in factor endowments and technologies,[101] other sources of difference that might be viewed as illegitimate are more likely to be scapegoats. In addition, if the impetus of claims of illegitimate advantage is that a particular domestic industry is harmed, it is likely that both corrective (i.e., harmonization) and protectionist measures will result in both domestic and international distortions.

The conclusion from this analysis is that harmonization claims that are based on the illegitimacy of difference, or that assume that difference has no value, are deeply problematic. Substantive differences alone, even among quite similar societies, convey little information about whether those differences reflect differences in some "ideal" comparative advantage based solely on differences on technologies, preferences, and endowments. Unfortunately, process-based approaches provide little more assurance. All political institutions suffer from problems in making optimal social choices. Two minimalist approaches might be worthy of consideration. One is the NAFTA solution of requiring each society to abide by the substantive choices of its own institutions. A more stringent approach is to insist that those institutions meet certain basic requirements, such as open and democratic process.

These elements—the purpose of harmonization and the sources of difference—provide the basis for a theoretical evaluation of harmonization claims. That a difference is legitimate, whether on the basis of process or substance, does not defeat a harmonization claim. Rather, it alerts us to some competing considerations and invites a more critical analysis of the claim. Furthermore, the basis of a harmonization claim does not bear any particular relationship to the source of difference, although some sources of difference undermine particular claims for harmonization. Economies of scale, more efficient interface, and transparency, for example, can be achieved whether the source of difference is preferences, endowments, technologies, institutions, or coordination structures, or whether the difference is stochastic. Hence the source of difference is irrelevant to the legitimacy of these claims. On the other hand, the costs of harmonization, and hence whether it is justified and how it should be achieved, might very well depend on the source of difference.

Suppose, for example, that the difference in legal regime derives from differences in preferences. Harmonization will entail a potential loss of welfare for at least one of the jurisdictions. This loss of welfare will be in addition to any one-time costs for implementation of the new standard. On the other hand, there will be gains to both nations from the economies of scale achieved. These gains may come both from the nation being able to produce goods at lower average costs, and from trading with the other nation. If the differences in regime stem solely from choice processes (institutions and coordination) or are stochastic, then harmonization entails no loss in welfare other than the short-run costs of adaptation.[102] In that event, an appropriate approach to harmonization might be the adoption of whatever standard entails the lowest adaptation costs, perhaps providing for some compensation by the nonadapting country (or the country that faces lower adaptation costs) to the adapting country. A similar analysis applies to claims based on jurisdictional interface and transparency.

Careful consideration of the sources of difference suggests that harmonization is often not a very good solution to the problem of externalities. If the normative claim is that another nation has no right to inflict costs outside its jurisdiction, the reasons for inflicting those costs are irrelevant. A nation injured by transborder pollution or destruction of the commons is not less injured because the difference stems from preferences rather than institutions. But, as I have argued, harmonization is not a response to this claim. If, on the other hand, the concern with externalities is only with the inefficiency that results from failing to take into account the full costs of activities, and not the distribution of those costs, harmonization might be a suitable response. Harmonized rules, unlike unilaterally determined domestic rules, would take into account the external costs that are inflicted on those in other jurisdictions.[103] Requiring each jurisdiction to adopt the policy that would be optimal for the combined jurisdiction internalizes jurisdictionally external costs. But at least in theory such rules are an appropriate solution to such inefficiencies only if we assume that the jurisdictions are similar with respect to preferences, technologies, and endowments.

If, however, jurisdictions differ in the preferences of their inhabitants, harmonization will not be welfare maximizing. Harmonization is the theoretically appropriate response to externalities only if we assume that both jurisdictions, when faced with both the costs and benefits of the activity, would adopt the same policy. But suppose the two jurisdictions would adopt very different policies. If the external costs result from the other jurisdiction applying its optimal policy (taking into account such external costs), the injured jurisdiction could make two claims. First, it could claim that the other jurisdiction has no right to inflict any such external costs at all. Harmonization is not a direct response to this claim, but it might in some circumstances be a better response than demanding that no external costs at all be imposed outside a nation's territory. If every jurisdiction insisted that other jurisdictions inflict no costs on it, this insistence might result in an inefficiently stringent policy regime (assuming positive transaction costs). Second, a nation might claim that since its citizens are being injured, the appropriate policy regime is the one that best takes the injuries into account, namely, the one that its citizens have chosen.

For example, suppose that a jurisdiction that strongly prefers the protection of the environment is located next to one with weaker preferences for environmental protection. In theory, we would want the first jurisdiction to weigh cross-border pollution externalities less than the second jurisdiction. In other words, in making its decisions we would want the jurisdiction to incorporate the preferences of those on whom the externality is inflicted.[104] A further objection to harmonization is that jurisdictions differ in the costs of controlling externalities. It might be relatively cheap for one jurisdiction to reduce or eliminate the externality and very expensive for another. In that event, harmonization would mean undertaking measures that might not be justified from an efficiency point of view.

If the harmonization claim is based on fair competition, then, as argued previously, certain sources of difference, such as preferences or endowments, undermine the claim. Where differences are the result of other factors, such as institutions and coalition formation, the fairness claim has more appeal as the difference in law is the source, rather than a reflection, of comparative advantage. It is in this sense that the comparative advantage could be thought of as "artificial" and unfair—a distortion created by unlegitimated governmental policy. Even if the harmonized regime would be welfare enhancing for the society of which harmonization is demanded, this fact will not always justify a harmonization claim made by others. In such cases, the legitimacy of the claim will depend as well on whether the domestic process establishes the legitimacy of policy choices. External judgments, even if correct, about the policy choices of a nation should not prevail over those choices when they are the result of a legitimate process.

Nonefficacy claims raise the kinds of issues long familiar to choice-of-law theorists. The force of the harmonization claim depends on the legitimacy of the interest that underlies application of a nation's laws to certain transactions, and that interest may ultimately depend on the source of difference. Suppose, for example, the difference was stochastic in the sense that neither regulatory scheme was regarded as potentially Pareto superior to the other. In that case, it would seem that there was neither a good claim to harmonization (based solely on nonefficacy) nor any reason to prefer the application of one society's rules or the other. These conclusions, however, would not prevail if primary behavior would be affected by the assumption that one regulatory scheme or the other would apply.

This framework, focusing on the benefits of harmonization and the sources of difference, provides only an initial basis for evaluating harmonization claims. Three additional factors must be taken into account. First, the process for achieving harmonization will affect the realization of its goals. Second, even apart from the elimination of differences that reflect a society's preferences, endowments, and technologies, enforcing sameness imposes costs. Third, there may be alternatives to harmonization that achieve its goals at less cost than harmonization. We will examine each of these in turn.

2.4   The Process and Institutions of Harmonization

Harmonization refers both to a substantive claim (that the laws of different jurisdictions should be more similar) and a process for accomplishing that result. Whatever the substantive merits of a harmonization claim, the process adopted will greatly influence its realization. Two aspects of the harmonization process must be considered. First is the process and institutions that lead to a harmonization "text," the substantive standards that participants (and in some instances, nonparticipants) are expected to implement. Second is the implementation and enforcement of that text. It is primarily in this second aspect that most international harmonization efforts differ fundamentally from harmonization within existing political systems. In federal systems, for example, harmonization often consists of allocating regulatory authority to a higher and more comprehensive level of government. Even when harmonization in federal systems is carried out without moving regulatory activity to the common political authority,[105] the process of coordination and adoption takes place against the background potential for such action. In the international context, harmonization can be pursued either through unilateral harmonizing actions or through multilateral processes.

2.4.1   Spontaneous and Unilateral Harmonization

Insofar as harmonization bespeaks a result—the convergence of legal and policy regimes—it will occur even in the absence of formal international efforts. Much harmonization is exogenous to the legal system,[106] and the critical inquiry is whether international legal efforts at harmonization should lead rather than follow the forces that produce harmonization. These forces include not only the convergence of the factors, such as technology and preferences, that produce differences in legal regimes, but also the internationalization of the political forces that influence domestic decision making. Those forces are being internationalized in two respects.

First, domestic economic actors are increasingly participants in international transactions. As a result, their interests extend beyond the borders of their home country. Difficulties faced by foreign enterprises in transacting with domestic actors become the latter's own difficulties. Producers who face inconsistent regulatory regimes at home and abroad may come to see reform of their own domestic regime as the solution to problems of interface and economies of scale. If a nation's industry has no vested interest in a particular rule or standard, it may be in their interest to accept more widely adopted standards unilaterally. Suppose, for example, that two different pesticides would adequately protect a farmer's crops. For one the government has adopted extremely stringent standards for residues, and for the other comparatively lax standards. Most countries, however, permit only the first pesticide. Farmers engaged both in domestic and export sales might exert political influence to have the domestic standards changed in order to make their products more marketable, or at least avoid the expense of segregating crops and using two different pesticides.

We would particularly expect to see such unilateral harmonization by small countries whose economies are heavily dependent on international trade. This effect will be pronounced when a single large market (or group of markets with harmonized rules) is the primary export destination. For example, small European nations that were not members of the European Community often conformed their legislation to Community rules. Such harmonization often represents a potentially Pareto superior move judged from a national viewpoint, but the changes required will not always be to the benefit of all groups within a society. If there is an industry that would not be internationally competitive, the retention or adoption of standards incompatible with those in other countries could serve as a protective barrier in lieu of a tariff. For example, in the case of the farmer, domestic producers might have been afforded protection by the fact that the products of most countries were prohibited on the domestic market because they contained residues of the less favored pesticide.

Second, international economic actors, such as multinational corporations, increasingly participate in the domestic policy formulation of multiple jurisdictions.[107] They may demand, as a condition of local manufacturing or other activity, that local law conform with certain familiar principles. For example, a foreign investor interested in building a manufacturing facility might want to assure that its output can be sold in both home and host countries as well as third markets. Not only does this assurance help achieve economies of scale, but it also diversifies the risks faced by the manufacturer in its product markets. In other contexts, multinational corporations might be unwilling to change certain production techniques that they have long used in their home country, or want to assure that their industrial secrets will be protected. In effect, international economic actors such as multinational corporations provide the international coordination necessary to move toward harmonization.

In the absence of such actions, harmonization does present a coordination problem: how can two or more independent political entities achieve greater similarity in applicable rules and policies? One approach is to negotiate the adoption of a common regulatory framework, but countries also sometimes attempt to offensively achieve harmonization by imposing sanctions on other countries that do not adopt their standards. Many countries are in effect taking such an approach when they refuse to allow the importation of products that do not meet particular standards. Indeed, it is implicitly this type of penalty that provides the incentive for the unilateral harmonization discussed previously. Assuming the products are exported by and to parties to the GATT, unilateral actions are limited to instances where the product itself, rather than some aspect of the production process, fails to conform with the rules of the importing country.[108] The importing country cannot insist that the laws of the exporting country conform to its own, only that the product itself conforms.

Where the method of production might affect the product, however, countries are entitled to insist that such methods conform to their own rules. Such is typically the case with many agricultural products, especially meat and poultry. Not surprisingly, such regulations have become the source of bitter disputes.[109] Furthermore, the recent Uruguay Round agreements suggest two other instances in which failure to harmonize rules in the exporting country would allow the importing country to impose differential restrictions. First, because of certain characteristics of services, most countries regulate services by regulating service providers rather than their product.[110] Under the General Agreement on Trade in Services, countries can insist to some degree on harmonization of the producer's home laws as a condition to entry into its market.[111] Second, under the Agreement on Technical Barriers to Trade, parties are encouraged to accept determinations of conformity by other jurisdictions if their rules and procedures substantially conform to their own.[112]

This type of unilateral requirement does not go beyond well-recognized principles of national jurisdiction. Such measures discriminate against the products or services of nonharmonizing jurisdictions and hence encourage their harmonization,[113] but they do rest on a claim that other countries should conform their laws. In some instances, countries have gone a step further in adopting unilateral measures to encourage other countries to harmonize laws that do not so directly affect the regulatory interests of the importing country. The United States, for example, has insisted that countries benefiting from certain preferential trade regimes recognize workers' rights.[114] And in the legislation that led to the much-ballyhooed GATT tuna decision, the United States attempted, through trade sanctions, to unilaterally impose standards regarding fishing techniques that endangered dolphins.[115] Section 301, and Special 301, also aim occasionally at harmonization through the threat of unilateral trade sanctions.[116] To the extent such efforts are tied to trade benefits or sanctions, they violate the most-favored-nation obligation under the GATT.

2.4.2   Multilateral Harmonization

Unilateral efforts, whether through "spontaneous" adoption of common standards or the application of offensive sanctions, have a limited ability to achieve harmonization, and they are sometimes of dubious legality under the GATT. For the most part, they are necessarily aimed at bilateral rather than multilateral harmonization.[117] More structured, formal arrangements are needed for broad-based harmonization. This is not the place to fully analyze the various modes of multilateral cooperation and forms of international organization.[118] The important point here is that organizational structures fundamentally affect both the harmonization process and its outcome.

Formal international harmonization processes are either mandatory or nonmandatory.[119] A mandatory process entails an international commitment to adopt (and maintain) the harmonized regime. Such a commitment might be made either before the harmonization text is formulated ("delegation") or after a nonbinding text is put forward for agreement. The latter is the case where the harmonized rules are part of an international treaty. It is only after the treaty text is promulgated that a nation must decide whether to sign and ratify the treaty.[120] Nonmandatory harmonization limits itself to the formulation of harmonized rules. In some cases, each nation must formally indicate whether or not it accepts the rules, but such acceptance does not necessarily entail an international commitment. In other instances, each nation simply adopts the rules or not. Nonmandatory processes may be particularly appropriate where the degree of harmonization required is comparatively low (that is, there is a relatively large margin of tolerance).[121]

Perhaps the most straightforward solution to harmonizing the laws of different jurisdictions is to assign responsibility for policy formulation, implementation, and enforcement to a common centralized authority.[122] This is often, but not always, the approach adopted within federal systems, and increasingly in the European Community. Even within federal systems, such harmonization processes sometimes result in incoherent allocations of responsibility.[123] International regimes with such extensive powers (formulation of policy, legislative implementation, and enforcement) simply do not exist. There are, however international organizations with fairly extensive lawmaking and dispute-settlement powers, and somewhat more limited enforcement powers.[124] The most comprehensive international harmonization regime would replace national lawmaking authority by international machinery whose promulgations are directly applicable in national law, although national institutions would be relied on for enforcement. An alternative mandatory structure is a treaty mechanism that obligates nations to implement the harmonized legal regime, with some international supervision through dispute settlement.[125]

Most international harmonization efforts have taken place without international legal obligation. A common methodology is the drafting of model or uniform laws and standards.[126] Because the regime will not be mandatory, it may be easier to reach agreement on the substantive terms. Nonetheless, the formulation of a single international regime significantly alters the incentives to harmonize national rules, and thus parties will pursue their interests vigorously even when the result is in this sense nonbinding.[127]

Once a text is formulated, the problem is how to encourage adoption of the harmonized regime, since the participating, as well as nonparticipating, states will be under no obligation to do so.[128] In some cases, solving the coordination problem and identifying the harmonized regime will be sufficient; no additional incentive will be needed to encourage adoption.[129] This will often be the case where the claim for harmonization is based on interface or economies of scale. Any nation desiring to participate in the benefits of harmonization will have to follow the agreed form.[130] Where, however, a nation perceives substantial costs to conforming and limited benefits, adoption without incentives is less likely. Furthermore, if the harmonization regime is intended to address barriers to international trade, or even incidentally does so, domestic producers may use their influence to prevent implementation, as it would in effect remove a measure of protection. Countries insisting on harmonization might, as with unilateral harmonization, adopt incentives to encourage other nations to harmonize their laws. These incentives could take the form either of punishing nonharmonizing nations or withholding benefits extended to harmonizing nations.[131] Such sanctions could be unilateral or imposed collectively by nations agreeing to harmonization. In either case, they might violate the most-favored-nation obligation under the GATT and other World Trade Organization agreements.

2.4.3   Getting to Harmonization: Substance

Whether harmonization is pursued on a mandatory or nonmandatory basis, the initial problem is the formulation of substantive harmonization terms. Consider first the more limited problem of bilateral harmonization. Given two different rules, there are four basic substantive ways in which they could be harmonized. The laws of nation A can be made the same as nation B, or the laws of B can be conformed to those of A. Alternatively, nations A and B can agree on some compromise law. Here I use compromise in the sense of an outcome that lies at a point between the two positions of A and B that is in some sense fair to both given the costs of adopting the compromise. Of course, such a compromise does not necessarily result in an overall minimization of adaptation costs. Ordinarily, we would expect to minimize adaptation costs by accepting the status quo in at least one of the harmonizing countries as the harmonized text.[132]

A final alternative is that A and B agree on the best harmonized regime independent of their present positions. This approach, independent agreement, might be similar to a compromise result, but in fact could also be the same as A's rules, B's rules, or some other outcome. We ought to distinguish between harmonization proposals that are collectively and individually optimal, and those that are only collectively optimal. A harmonization proposal is individually optimal if for each participant in the harmonization it is the best-harmonized rule.[133] The proposal would only be collectively optimal if, somehow taking into account the interests of all participants, it is optimal but for some individual participants there are other rules that would be better. If there is general agreement that the independently proposed harmonized regime is individually optimal, this might undercut any claim for compensation by nations with greater adaptation costs.

Multilateral harmonization presents a corresponding but more complex set of alternatives. When a larger number of nations is involved in the harmonization effort, compromise or optimal solutions are more likely also to be the current regime of one or more of the parties. Coordination difficulties and the incidence of strategic behavior are increased. Governments will be reluctant to agree to a harmonization proposal that differs from their current regime for a number of reasons. First, the change will entail one-time adaptation costs. These will include the costs to the government of adopting the new regime and taking whatever measures are necessary to implement it (including, for example, publication and the training of bureaucracy). In addition, producers will also encounter costs that will be very difficult to recover, particularly if there is competition from countries that do not have such adaptation costs. Second, if the harmonization regime is not the optimal regime from a country's point of view, harmonization will entail continuing welfare losses. Third, harmonization will sometimes result in the removal of a measure of protection for domestic industry. And fourth, the international distribution of the costs and benefits of harmonization may be regarded as unfair.

A comparison with the more usual trade negotiations on tariffs and nontariff barriers illustrates the difficulties of harmonization. The underlying theory of trade liberalization is that all nations benefit from freer trade. This might be true of a harmonization effort, but there is no general theoretical proposition that all nations will benefit from harmonization. In addition, trade negotiations are structured around a norm of reciprocity which assures that "losses" (measured in terms of increased access of foreign exporters to one's domestic markets) are offset by "gains" (measured in terms of access to other markets). It is very difficult to structure harmonization in this way. Harmonization is generally pursued on a cluster of related issues. Within a regulatory area, it will not make sense to adopt one rule from nation A and another from B; the rules must work together as a coherent regulatory framework. As a result, the costs and benefits of the proposed harmonization are likely to be quite skewed. Consider the case of harmonization of technical standards to achieve economies of scale. If a country with a large market but comparatively small exports joins the harmonized scheme, it is in effect granting a good deal of market access and gaining little. Its decision to adopt the harmonization program in effect creates a positive externality for all other countries adopting the harmonization. International bargaining over harmonization will be greatly complicated by these asymmetries in the costs and benefits harmonization is expected to bring, particularly if mercantilist approaches to trade negotiations are adopted.[134] Even when harmonization is in the interest of all nations, the inability to distribute the costs and benefits in a manner perceived as equitable will stand as an obstacle.

Compromise solutions are also difficult because the gains and losses are often incommensurable. Concessions and benefits in most trade negotiations are measured in monetary terms, such as expected increases in the value of imports and exports or foregone tariff revenues. Consider in contrast the case of negotiating a compromise on environmental standards. A country with a lower standard that must harmonize "up" might look primarily at the costs of pollution control, or possibly lost jobs. The high-standard country that contemplates harmonizing "down" must evaluate lower environmental quality and potential health effects. Both countries will also realize some benefits from the harmonization, but in many situations it will be perceived as a "lose-lose" exchange.

These difficulties are exacerbated if the harmonization claim has a strong normative component. If nation A takes a normative view of harmonization, its own law will probably be regarded as setting the appropriate standard. In that case, it will be unwilling to conform its laws to those of nation B solely in order to achieve harmonization. If the claim is overwhelmingly or purely normative, nation A will be willing to make few if any compromises. Nation B might accept the view that harmonization would be beneficial, but reject the normative aspect of A's harmonization claim. Both countries would benefit from the harmonization, but nation B would bear all the costs of any agreement A would accept. Unless the other jurisdiction is willing to offer compensation (rare in such international negotiations),[135] agreement will be difficult to reach. We should, therefore, expect to see greater resort to unilateral processes of harmonization particularly in two situations: a strongly normative component to the harmonization claim or great disparities in adaptation costs.

Given this array of difficulties, it is not surprising that international harmonization, other than interface harmonization, has met with very limited success.[136] Furthermore, this analysis is naive in that it assumes that the representatives of each nation in the harmonization process will represent that nation's interests. As mentioned previously, harmonization inevitably involves forum shifts. These shifts will often result in different forces being represented and influential in the bargaining.[137] In international forums, "experts" who are often allied to particular constituencies play a greater role than in domestic political processes.[138] Thus the goal each nation attempts to achieve within the harmonization process might be quite different from the goal it would adopt domestically, even where the harmonization is strongly normative.

For these reasons, the structure of the harmonization process is often contentious not only internationally, but domestically as well. Important questions include these: Who will be able to participate in the process? Should the process be one of governmental representation, or conducted by nongovernmental organizations? If a nongovernmental process, should it be subject to a multilateral approval mechanism, or should each nation make its own decision whether or not to adopt the harmonization proposal? As these questions suggest, there are numerous permutations. I examine here very briefly several alternatives and some of the implications of the process.

International Bargaining through Representation of Nations
The most common structure for reaching international agreements is negotiation by official national representatives, who most often report to the chief executive of the nation. Critical to the outcome is the perspective such representatives bring to the negotiations, as well as the constituencies they most represent. On the issue of food standards, for example, negotiation among national trade representatives would probably reach different results than negotiation among the heads of national agricultural agencies or the agencies responsible for consumer safety. If the process is nonmandatory, the choice of representative agency will be less important, since the outcome must satisfy every constituency able to exercise an effective veto in the domestic political process. Still, by the time any proposal is presented for domestic ratification, the choice will usually be between harmonization on the basis of that proposal or no harmonization at all. Under these circumstances, proposals that would not ordinarily be viable in the domestic political process might be adopted.

Even if negotiation is through officially designated national representatives, other organizations might be granted some role in the process. Nongovernmental organizations, whether domestic or international, are sometimes granted observer or participant status. Observer status gives them a greater ability to maintain domestic debate during the course of the international process and to generate political pressures on that process. Participant status in addition allows them to express their views within the negotiation process.

International Group of Experts
The formulation of a harmonization text is sometimes assigned to a group of experts who are instructed that they are not to represent their home countries in the process.[139] The Codex Alimentarius Commission, which promulgates international food standards, incorporates this model. Priorities for the formulation of standards are set by a representative body.

The formulation of the standards, however, is assigned to a group of experts. Once they have proposed a standard, the representative body can obtain comments from participating nations, approve the standard, or send it back to the group of experts for further work.[140] The expert commission structure would seem well suited where the goal is the identification and adoption of the "ideal" international standard, but the complicated Codex process has been criticized as tending toward political compromise.[141]

The attraction of the expert model of harmonization is also its weakness: isolation from political forces and, to some extent, from self-interested economic forces. If these groups are excluded from a significant role in the process, they are more likely to exercise their political power in the domestic process to prevent the adoption of harmonization proposals they regard as contrary to their interests.

Constituency Representation at the International Level: The ILO
One approach to harmonization is to move the bargaining among various constituencies to the international level. This is the basic structure of the ILO, in which representatives of workers' and employers' organizations, as well as governments, participate directly in the formulation of ILO conventions.[142] Each delegation to the ILO consists of four members: two nominated and instructed by their national government, one representative of labor, and one of industry. Other than the double representation granted to governments, the three "constituencies" participate equally in most aspects of the ILO's work, including the formulation and adoption of international labor standards. Even the executive organ of the ILO is structured along similar representative lines. Trade-offs are thus not necessarily resolved, either before or after the harmonization process, within nations. Of course, not all constituencies that would play a role in the domestic process are likely to have a role in the international forum. Consumer organizations, for example, are not represented in the ILO.

Although the international representational model remains unusual, it may very well be the wave of the future—particularly in trade negotiations. As the scope of the international trade agenda has expanded, and as the linkages between trade and other areas, such as investment, labor, consumer interests, and environmental protection, have become more salient, more groups are clamoring for a place at the international table. In part, this trend reflects the reality that once the harmonization process is complete at the international level and presented for domestic approval, there will often be little possibility for change to accommodate interests not represented in the earlier phases of the process.

The complexities of process—political, institutional, and strategic—
suggest that international harmonization will generally be cumbersome
and contentious. Four factors in particular contribute to these problems:
disputed normative content of harmonization; the presence of domestic
conflict over harmonization; the skewed distribution (among nations) of
the costs and benefits of harmonization; and the importance of the choice
of the institution and procedural structure for harmonization. These factors
will be present even where there is substantial agreement on the desirability
of harmonization and little variation in the potential sources of difference.

2.5   The Costs of Sameness

In a number of contexts, we find expressions of the idea that policy
decisions ought to be made by the smallest appropriate political unit. In
the international sphere, it is the jealous protection of sovereignty; in the
United States, incantations of the value of federalism; in the European
Union, the talisman of subsidiarity;[143] and even below these levels the
general value of "localism."[144] Making decisions on a more local basis has
both substantive and procedural value. The substantive value derives from
the ability of a more local population to implement choices which, as
suggested earlier, better reflect its preferences, resources, and technologies.
If the optimal policies for national populations do differ, then harmonization requires that some measure of local welfare be sacrificed (assuming
local policies could be made effective). The procedural value of localism is
one of participation, of having a more meaningful say over the policies
that affect one's life, and of maintaining a more direct influence over one's
government and governmental officials.

There are important differences between harmonization (or at least
some processes of harmonization) and centralization. Harmonization, unlike centralization, is not inconsistent with localism to the extent the local
unit retains final authority over whether to adopt the harmonization proposal. Insofar as it continues to respect the distinct sovereignty of its
adherents, harmonization maintains the potential for competition and difference. Unlike federal systems, harmonization does not entail the adoption of a "common legal order."[145] Moving policy making within a sector
to a common superior political authority is not, like international harmonization, merely the creation of a cartel; it is the establishment of a monopoly. Cartels have an inherent instability. If the policies adopted through
harmonization are not perceived by local populations, or their political
representatives, as the best policies for their needs, their government has

the option to withdraw. In the international context at least, the harmonizing institution or process has limited hierarchical authority.

It is useful to separate two slightly different purposes served by locating policy-making authority at a more local (in this case national) level. One is the value of responding to difference. Here the assertion is that populations differ in the laws and policies that best serve their needs, and harmonization limits their ability to adopt what would be the "best" laws.[146] The other is the value of independence. Regardless of whether populations differ, there are benefits to giving them independence. Harmonization is the establishment of a policy cartel that restrains (but does not necessarily forbid) competition among the adherents of the harmonized regime. The basic premise of the "race to the top" theorists is that policy cartels, like industrial cartels, are economically bad; competition among governmental units will in their view lead to the optimal policies.

Independence has additional value if there are differences in responsiveness to change at the national level and by the institutions of harmonization. Once the harmonized rule is agreed upon, it may be very difficult to change. International representatives and bureaucrats might be less responsive to changing views and circumstances. National legislative organs are now typically in nearly constant session; international institutions often meet only periodically and are not as fully staffed. Implementing change through a multilateral process is a cumbersome endeavor, and thus harmonization has the potential to stifle regulatory innovation. Although harmonization is often intended to achieve regulatory simplification, the process can instead result in the opposite. If, for example, the goal of the harmonization is to achieve economies of scale or more efficient interface, those benefits might be undermined by the increased rigidity and complexity of the harmonized regulatory regime.[147] However, it is far from axiomatic that international institutions of harmonization will be less responsive than domestic political institutions. It depends on how those institutions are structured, and who participates. Domestic changes may be forestalled by the very comprehensive nature of the political institutions; changes in one context must be traded for changes in another. It is at least possible that the more limited institutions of international harmonization will be able to focus on relevant concerns and hence be more responsive to them.

Many of the costs of harmonization can be avoided by adopting non-mandatory, flexible regimes that provide a readily identifiable common framework.[148] One could still make "cartel" type objections to even such loose harmonization processes, but policy-making cartels are quite different from industrial cartels in that within each participant (nation) in the policy-making cartel, conflicting forces will continue to exercise their influence.

Harmonization also introduces costs not found in comprehensive regulatory systems. Because harmonization is invariably selective in some sense, it has the potential not only to introduce new distortions in both domestic and international policy,[149] but also to result in greater rather than less divergence in the actual effects of regulatory policy. Consider, for example, the problem of harmonizing product liability law. If one jurisdiction allows no recovery for purely economic loss and has a jury determine damages in all cases where they are recoverable, and another jurisdiction allows recovery for economic loss but has a judge determine the amount of damages, harmonization of the substantive rule alone might result in greater divergence in terms of expected liabilities. This is a sort of legal version of the theory of the second best: when legal regimes are not completely unified (i.e., all relevant differences eliminated), harmonizing selected elements might in fact produce greater distortions and divergences.[150] Indeed, some recent harmonization efforts seem to recognize that procedures, and in particular enforcement, are more important than the substantive rules applied.

2.6   Alternatives to Harmonization

In cases in which harmonization is not justified despite a worthwhile objective, there may be means short of harmonization that would at least partially obtain that objective.[151] Even if harmonization would appear warranted when measured against the existing regime, the question is whether harmonization is the best solution to the problems posed by differing legal regimes. Alternatives that at least in part address the claims underlying harmonization must be considered as well. Although in some cases harmonization would be preferable to maintaining the existing differences in policy and law, an alternative measure could be preferable to both. In other words, the inquiry should be whether the marginal benefits of harmonization are worth the costs when measured against alternative solutions that might realize some of the benefits of harmonization without entailing some of the costs. Harmonization is but one form of intergovernmental cooperation. I very briefly outline here five common alternatives to harmonization: mutual recognition, cooperation in enforcement, unilateral measures, "private" harmonization, and circumvention.

2.6.1   Mutual Recognition

The principle of mutual recognition requires that jurisdictions accept for domestic purposes certain regulatory determinations of other jurisdictions, even though those determinations and the criteria on which they are based are not harmonized. For example, products of a foreign producer approved for sale in its home jurisdiction would, solely on that basis, be permitted for sale in the importing country.[152] Similarly, the registration of securities in one jurisdiction or the approval of a prospectus might be accepted for access to another country's capital markets.[153] In some instances, mutual recognition is applied to the substantive rules; in others, only to determinations of conformity with harmonized rules.

Mutual recognition is most clearly an alternative to harmonization when the underlying purpose is to enable firms to realize economies of scale across international markets. Particularly where the harmonization has little in the way of a normative component, mutual recognition achieves most of the benefits of harmonization with few of its costs. Indeed, the European Community, after grappling with the immense difficulties posed by its ambitious harmonization program, retreated back into the mutual recognition solution.[154] Mutual recognition also fully addresses transparency concerns, as it forbids the erection of domestic regulatory barriers to imported products. On the other hand, mutual recognition is not a solution to claims based on externalities, nonefficacy, or fair competition. Obviously, mutual recognition is unlikely to be the alternative solution when the harmonization claim is strongly normative. Such a claim asserts that the exporting nation's policies are inappropriate not only for the potential importing nation, but for the exporting nation as well.

In theory, mutual recognition allows two jurisdictions to maintain policy independence, but at the same time it exacerbates problems of leakage and nonefficacy, depending in part on the mobility of the regulated providers or entities. Consider, for example, the problem of regulating professional qualifications. If jurisdictions mutually recognize professional certification but the standards are regarded as being substantially different, then the jurisdiction applying the least onerous standards will become the favored place of entry. Indeed, one story, perhaps apocryphal, has it that some Germans decided that the easier path to the practice of law in Germany was to gain entrance to the practice of law first in Spain, and then through mutual recognition in Germany, as required by European directives and decisions of the Court of Justice. Mutual recognition creates the internal regulatory equivalent of a free trade area. As with free trade areas, entry will generally be through the component territory imposing the lowest barriers. This effect can be dampened by the same kind of mechanism used in free trade areas: rules of origin. Producers would only be allowed to use regulatory approval by their home country as the basis for mutual recognition.

In most contexts, mutual recognition is not so much an alternative as a complement to harmonization. Many efforts at harmonization require some mutual recognition if they are to achieve their purpose. Regulatory coordination ranges from substantial harmonization in scope and degree, accompanied by correspondingly minimal requirements of mutual recognition, to modest efforts at harmonization accompanied by a very broad notion of mutual recognition.

2.6.2   Recognition of Greater Jurisdictional Authority and Enforcement Assistance

Some claims to harmonization could be addressed by providing the affected jurisdiction greater ability to enforce its chosen rules. (Mutual recognition, by contrast, entails a reduction in enforcement authority.) The problem of nonefficacy, for example, could be solved by giving the harmed jurisdiction the necessary lawmaking and enforcement powers. The force of national rules can be further extended if other jurisdictions agree to enforce them. This was to some extent the intention of Article VIII(2)(b) of the IMF agreement, which required all member states of the IMF to provide some assistance in the enforcement of exchange controls of other jurisdictions.[155] This solution requires cooperation among states, but not the harmonization of substantive rules.[156]

Making a jurisdiction's rules more effective entails a number of elements. First is the choice of law to govern particular actors or transactions. This is often approached as a problem of harmonization, that is, on the assumption that the jurisdictional reach of each nation should be determined by the same neutral principles. Nothing requires such neutrality with respect to either the substance of its regulatory policies or the importance that a nation attaches to them. It might, for example, be more important to one jurisdiction than another that certain of its rules be applied more broadly and effectively. Such was undoubtedly the case with rules against insider training. A second element is the recognition and enforcement of judgments and other penalties. A third is assistance in the gathering of information.

This type of solution has also been advocated with regard to claims that implicate both fairness and nonefficacy concerns, namely, the flight of industries to take advantage of less stringent foreign labor and environmental standards. One recent proposal that found support in some perhaps surprising quarters was that U.S. firms operating abroad be subject to U.S. labor and environmental standards. There are good reasons to criticize this approach, but again it might be preferable to the pursuit of broader harmonization.

Giving a state greater power to enforce its rules will also, in some circumstances, address externality problems, and probably more appropriately than harmonization. For example, subjecting a polluter to liability for damage from cross-border pollution requires that the polluter take that externality into account without requiring the other country to adopt harmonized rules that might not be appropriate for it.

2.6.3   Greater Unilateral Efforts

Other states will not always be willing to cooperate in addressing the problems of nonefficacy and externalities. An alternative to both harmonization and greater cooperation in enforcement is stronger unilateral measures to prevent leakage, including border enforcement. Such measures may be more costly than harmonization not only to the jurisdiction seeking greater effectiveness of its laws, but to other jurisdictions as well. Greater border enforcement measures, for example, almost invariably impose costs on trade, and thus constitute a nontariff barrier. This could produce welfare losses to all trade partners. But unilateral efforts aimed directly at achieving more effective enforcement might again be preferable to unilateral efforts aimed at achieving harmonization.

2.6.4   "Private" Harmonization

If by harmonization one has in mind mandatory or nonmandatory regimes arrived at by an intergovernmental process or institution, an alternative is to allow nongovernmental actors to formulate, and decide whether to adhere to, harmonization proposals or otherwise achieve harmonization. Government policies can play an important role in determining the extent of opportunities for such private harmonization. For example, labor standards might be harmonized by the internationalization of labor organizations. The requirements and structure of each nation's labor laws will determine whether labor relations can be internationalized in this way.

Similarly, organizations of firms in particular industries often formulate technical standards. There may be good reasons to object to industry autonomy in some contexts, but private harmonization avoids some of the costs and difficulties of governmental harmonization efforts.

2.6.5 Circumvention

I use the term "circumvention" here to refer to measures taken by private actors to reduce or eliminate the consequences of differing legal regimes. For example, the problem of economies of scale can be eliminated if a competitive product can be designed that meets the requirements of both jurisdictions.[157] It is largely for this reason that the Standards Code requires, where possible, that product specifications be in terms of performance rather than design.[158] Similarly, interface problems can be circumvented if the supplier can provide its own international delivery network. In such circumstances, governments should seek the elimination of barriers to circumvention rather than harmonization.

These alternatives to harmonization can be implemented along with certain less burdensome forms of harmonization. For example, suppose the basic problem sought to be addressed is economies of scale. These can be accomplished either through harmonization or mutual recognition. But as outlined earlier, mutual recognition creates problems of leakage. The optimal solution might be harmonization with a substantial margin accompanied by mutual recognition.

2.7 Conclusion

The evaluation of harmonization claims is a complex and difficult endeavor. It requires first that we understand the nature of the claim and the extent to which it is normative (in the sense it asserts that certain substantive outcomes other than harmonization alone must be achieved). Then we must identify the basis of the harmonization claim: what is objectionable or unduly costly about the existence of different legal regimes? Before harmonization is pursued, we need to understand the sources and value of the difference that is the predicate to harmonization. With all this in mind, we must determine what harmonization processes would be most suitable, and whether some alternative to harmonization would better serve our goals.

Many of these questions are admittedly unanswerable in the context of actual claims for the harmonization of national laws and policies. More dubious harmonization claims (e.g., fairness) will sometimes have more political appeal than sounder harmonization claims (e.g., economies of scale). Nonetheless, requiring those engaged in a debate over harmonization to make explicit their underlying arguments and assumptions should benefit the process.

NOTES

I thank Jagdish Bhagwati, Mark Barenberg, George Bermann, Alice Hammerli, Gerald Neuman, Richard Pierce, and the participants in the NYU International Jurisprudence Colloquium for comments on an earlier draft. Bartolomeo Migone, Vinit Bharara, and Regina Lee provided valuable research assistance.

1. It is perhaps worthwhile to recall the myth of Procrustes, who tied all travelers to his iron bed. "If they were shorter than the bed, he stretched their limbs to make them fit it; if they were longer than the bed, he lopped off a portion" (Bulfinch, p. 151).

2. The theory of comparative advantage is generally attributed to David Ricardo's publication in 1817 of *The Principles of Political Economy and Taxation*.

3. See Hansson (1983) and Leary (Chapter 5 in Volume 2 of this work).

4. For a brief and insightful analysis of harmonization, see Fox (1991).

5. See Final Act Embodying the Results of the Uruguay Round of Multilateral Trade Negotiations (Version of 15 December 1993), General Agreement on Trade in Services, Doc. MFN/FA II-A1B, Art. VII.1, Annex on Financial Services, Sec. 3.1; and Agreement on the Application of Sanitary and Phytosanitary Measures, Paras. 9–13, 38, 41. The latter agreement defines "harmonization" as "the establishment, recognition and application of common sanitary and phytosanitary measures by different Members" (Annex A [Definitions], Para. 2).

6. See generally "Harmonization in the European Community" (1991); Hurwitz (1983).

7. In his recent writings, Jagdish Bhagwati has argued that the rationales for harmonization in the context of arm's-length free trade, free trade areas, and politically integrated common markets should be different. See, e.g., Bhagwati, "Challenges to the Doctrine of Free Trade" (1993a).

8. See, e.g., Rose-Ackerman (1992), Rubin and Feeley (1994), Gray (1983), Foote (1984), and Pierce (1985, pp. 645–661).

9. See, e.g., Bermann (1994b), Wilke and Wallace (1990), and Trachtman (1992).

10. Prof. Martin Boodman (1991) put the point in the following way:

The harmonization of law as it relates to inter-jurisdictional and international transactions is value neutral and cannot be justified in and of itself. Thus, the international and inter-jurisdictional harmonization of any legal domain particularly through legislative reform requires specific justification as to the desirability of harmonization and model upon which it is based. The justification cannot be found in any attribute of harmonization.

11. Cf. Hansson (1990, p. 1): "Harmonization . . . is defined as the coordination of economic policy actions and measures in order to reduce international differences in such actions." My interest, unlike Hansson's, is primarily in the harmonization of legal rules and regimes

rather than economic policy actions. As elaborated in section 2.5 coordination may or may not be part of the procedural basis of harmonization.

See also, Zweigert and Kötz (1992):

The political aim behind [the international unification of law] is to reduce or eliminate, so far as desirable and possible, the discrepancies between the national legal systems by inducing them to adopt common principles of law.

12. As discussed on pp. 78 et seq. harmonization can also result "spontaneously" or from unilateral actions intended to encourage other nations to harmonize their laws. It thus does not require cooperation in its more limited sense.

13. Such a conflict can arise either if two nations assert jurisdiction over a particular transaction and their regulatory requirements for that transaction conflict, or if only one nation asserts jurisdiction over the transaction, but its regulatory requirements for that transaction would cause the actor to violate the rules of another state even though the latter state does not assert jurisdiction over the transaction. An example of the first type of conflict occurs if two nations assert jurisdiction over a securities offering, and one nation requires disclosure of earnings predictions whereas the other nation forbids the use of such information in the sale of securities. In such a case, the conflict can be eliminated either by agreeing on a jurisdictional rule that would assign the transaction only to one of the jurisdictions (which might be accomplished through the harmonization of jurisdictional rules), or by harmonizing the substantive rules. An example of the second type of regulatory conflict occurs if the second nation does not assert jurisdiction over the transaction, but the first nation requires disclosure of certain information that the second nation requires be kept secret under all circumstances. This second type of conflict results not from any jurisdictional conflict, but only from specifically conflicting substantive obligations.

14. International trade law regarding goods currently draws a distinction between regulations aimed at the product as such (i.e., physical characteristics of the product) and production or processing methods. See p. 109.

15. One way in which policy objective harmonization is coupled with more specific rules is through a "menu approach" that requires the state to adopt one or more of several alternatives. For example, the Social Security (Minimum Standards) Convention of 1952 (No. 102) allows a signatory to implement three out of nine types of benefits. See also European Social Charter, Article 20.

16. Treaty on European Union, Article 130r; OECD Council Recommendation on the Implementation of the Polluter-Pays Principle (1974), reprinted in 14 I.L.M. 234 (1975).

17. Insofar as the "polluter pays" principle aims at the internalization of pollution costs, it could also be regarded as aimed at achieving allocational efficiency.

18. See Hamilton (1993). The U.S. proposal, aimed largely at the European ban on meat from livestock treated with growth hormone, was defeated in the Codex Alimentarius by a 28 to 13 vote (with 9 abstentions). More recently, a paper prepared by the Codex Secretariat seems to lend support to the U.S. position; see "Science should be predominant factor" (1994). The position seemed fueled in part by the Codex's new role in the Uruguay Round trade agreements (ibid.). Under the Agreement on the Application of Sanitary and Phytosanitary Measures, signatories must, subject to significant exceptions, base sanitary and phytosanitary measures on international standards, which are defined to be Codex standards in the case of food safety (Paragraph 11 and Annex A, para. 3).

19. For example, the World Economic Conference held in 1976 adopted a Declaration of Principles and Program for Action "which called for strategies and national development plans and policies to 'include explicitly as a priority objective the promotion of employment and the satisfaction of the basic needs of each country's population'" (Galenson, 1981).

20. See, e.g., North American Agreement on Environmental Cooperation between the Government of Canada, the Government of the United Mexican States, and the Government of the United States of America (1993) (the NAFTA "side agreement" on the environment), reprinted 32 I.L.M. 1480 (1993).

21. Of course, there may be some disagreement about what is the ceiling and what is the floor. A recent example of "floor-only" harmonization was the agreement on European Community VAT rates. Initially, it was proposed that both a floor of 14 percent and a ceiling of 20 percent would be set (4 and 9 percent for essential products such as food); see Pinkerton (1993). It was ultimately agreed, however, to establish only a floor of 15 percent. Of course, countries adopting higher VAT rates would face a nonefficacy problem as their citizens sought to purchase goods in other countries. The pressure to reduce comparatively high VAT rates will increase once the Community switches from a "destination" to an "origin" principle of indirect taxation.

22. EC Treaty, Article 130t. The treaty also allows member states to adopt more stringent measures in the area of worker health and safety—Article 118a(3).

23. Hart (1994).

24. But see Revesz (1992), showing that in some instances units of a federal system will raise pollution-control requirements above a federally mandated minimum, even if in the absence of such a federal minimum a race to the bottom might occur.

25. The basic form of customs union does not require the elimination of barriers to trade other than border controls, such as different standards and the use of domestic subsidies. A single or internal market goes beyond a customs union in its attempt to eliminate all such nonborder impediments to trade.

26. A customs union, by definition, entails the harmonization of external trade rules and policies. They are often accompanied by additional harmonization, for example, on governmental subsidies to private enterprises. The abolition of internal border controls in a customs union or common market greatly exacerbates leakage and nonefficacy problems, discussed later. Initially, the European Community maintained internal border controls, in part to enable enforcement of each country's fiscal policies. The decision to abolish internal borders required some harmonization of those policies in light of the recognition that policy independence was no longer viable. Free trade areas do not require harmonization, but several concerns make it unsurprising that harmonization often accompanies their formation. The most important include the difficulty of unilaterally adopting effective policies in light of greatly reduced trade barriers (see discussion p. 55) and the desire to prevent surreptitious trade barriers (see p. 65). Both of these factors are important in international harmonization, but are even more salient among states that have adopted more aggressive measures to eliminate trade and other economic barriers.

27. See Cooper (1986, p. 127), Tiebout (1956).

28. This is the case at present, as international food safety is largely harmonized by Codex standards, whereas product safety and food production generally are subject to much less international coordination, if any.

29. See Cooper (1986, p. 127).

30. This is an application of the theory of the second best. Suppose, for example, that countries A and B together would be an optimal policy area for related policies X, Y, and Z, but can agree only to harmonize policies X and Y. The theory of the second best tells us that it is not necessarily an improvement to harmonize those two policies and not Z, and that we might be better off without any harmonization at all.

31. See, e.g., Puchala (1984).

32. The harmonization of domestic regulatory policies can be contrasted with the decision of two or more countries to remove trade barriers. In the latter case, the GATT requires that such barriers be removed on "substantially all" the trade between the countries as part of the formation of a free trade area or customs union. Selective removal of trade barriers such as tariffs (unless extended to all countries that are parties to the GATT) would not comply with Article XXIV of the GATT, and hence be in violation of the most-favored-nation provision of Article I. To the extent that technical barriers remain significant barriers to trade, harmonization efforts threaten to undermine the most-favored-nation obligation. The problems are particularly acute with regard to trade in services, and the proposed General Agreement on Trade in Services (GATS) imposes relatively weak obligations to extend harmonization programs to third-country GATT members. See Article VII of the GATS.

33. Nevertheless, one might make the claim that the metric system, as a system, is superior to the English system of weights and measures. Certainly a decimal-based system has advantages over a system that lacks a simple numerical principle. A better example of a case in which a little or no normative claim could be made would be the choice between the Fahrenheit and Celsius temperature systems, or between driving on the left or right side of the road.

34. Perhaps the best recent example of the intensity of feeling on even nonnormative standards is the effort to establish international standards for high-definition television (HDTV). Although one aspect of the standards setting, the "redraw" rate, was arguably related to the frequency of home electric current, other aspects, including the number of lines, were largely without independent substantive importance. Thus the parties tended to favor standards on which they had already made investments. Indeed, the United States was behind on the development of HDTV, and thus favored even more advanced digital technology on which it might be able to "leapfrog" Japan and European countries (see Snyder, 1992). Of course, in most instances countries will be able to articulate some normative basis for the standards they favor. In the context of HDTV, for example, the United States argued that the Japanese and European analog system was "wasteful of spectrum and bandwidth" and not optimal for nonbroadcast signal delivery (i.e., cable) (ibid.).

35. Technically, a purely normative harmonization need not be universal in the sense that the claim applies to all nations. The United States might assert, for example, that Canada should have the same level of environmental protection because any society with some-what similar geographic resources and state of development should have a certain level of environmental protection. The assertion does not depend on the rule in force in the United States. This nonnormative but not quite universalist claim could be described as a conditional universalist claim.

36. However, even in the context of pure normative harmonization, the existence of policy differences might serve an important role. If those policy differences result in consequences

adverse to the country adopting the normatively preferred rule, those consequences might confer upon the complaining country some justification (in addition to moral altruism) for insisting that the other country conform its policy to the preferred standard. This is one kind of externality that serves as a basis for harmonization claims. (See discussion beginning on p. 55).

37. Although this is an example of interface harmonization that would be extremely advantageous, it demonstrates that such harmonization is rarely absolutely required. Rather than laying down new railroad tracks of the same gauge as the rest of Europe, Spain requires virtually all passengers going to and from France (except to and from Barcelona) to disembark at border points. In the case of one special night train, sleeping compartments (i.e., the upper parts of the sleeping cars) are silently shifted to narrower-gauge rail cars at the border crossing in the middle of the night. In both cases, the international transport of passengers proceeds, albeit at a cost. As Spain has laid new railway tracks for high-speed trains, it has chosen to adopt the same gauge as the rest of Europe (*Fortune* magazine, November 20, 1989, p. 131).

38. Of course, adoption of a special rule for international transactions creates problems of its own; see David, "International unification of private law."

39. See Zweigert and Kötz (1992, p. 23). The "lex mercatoria" for international commercial transactions has long constituted a special interface regime.

40. See, e.g., United Nations Convention on Contracts for the International Sale of Goods, reprinted at 19 I.L.M. 671 (1980).

41. For a good overview of the international unification of private law, see David, note 38. One example of the limitation of harmonization to interfaces is the work of UNCITRAL. (See Vis, 1986: "It is a common feature of UNCITRAL texts that uniform rules formulated by it do not abolish or overrule existing national law, but are intended to be applicable to international transactions only.") Unidroit also initially limited its efforts to interface harmonization. See Matteucci (1976, pp. xvii, xix).

42. See David, "International unification," pp. 141–150.

43. See Zweigert and Kötz (1992, p. 27: "Unification of substantive law excludes the application of private international law").

44. See generally "Symposium: The globalization of law" (1993).

45. My analysis here is addressed primarily to negative externalities, that is, costs imposed on other jurisdictions. Pierce (1985) argues that positive externalities justify regulation at the federal rather than state level. Harmonization for the purpose of encouraging positive externalities would face the same basic objections as harmonization for negative externalities, namely, that one cannot assume that the affected populations will evaluate the costs and benefits in the same way. Imposing costs, through harmonization, on other jurisdictions so that they will provide a benefit to those outside the jurisdiction rests on a weaker normative foundation than insisting that other jurisdictions do not impose costs. One current dispute that arguably fits in this framework is over the preservation of the tropical rain forests. Particularly where those being asked to provide the positive spillover are less well-off, some compensation would seem in order.

46. Distributional and politically mediated externalities are addressed on page 59.

47. See Scott (1982); Worth (1992).

48. In this event, the potential to exploit externalities creates a prisoner's dilemma.

49. Bank for International Settlements, Committee on Banking Regulations and Supervisory Practices Consultation Paper on International Convergence of Capital Measurement and Capital Standards (July 1988), reprinted 30 I.L.M. 967 (1991).

50. See Alford (1992); "Cooperative efforts" (1982).

51. As the arbitral tribunal put it in a well-known arbitration involving transborder air pollution from Canada into the United States:

Under the principles of international law, ... no State has the right to use or permit the use of its territory in such a manner as to cause injury by fumes in or to the territory of another or the properties or persons therein, when the case is of serious consequence and the injury is established by clear and convincing evidence. (Trail Smelter Arbitration [United States v. Canada], 3 R.I.A.A. 1905, 1965 [1941])

52. Of course, if the transborder pollution results from downwind or downstream flows that go in only one direction, harmonization would not result in such reciprocity.

53. See, e.g., Montreal Protocol on Substances that Deplete the Ozone Layer, reprinted in 26 I.L.M. 1541 (1987).

54. The phenomena described here as leakage and nonefficacy are sometimes explored under the rubric of "regulatory arbitrage" (see Trachtman, 1993). I eschew this term because the broader claim is not directed solely toward deliberate attempts to avoid one jurisdiction's more stringent rules in favor of another jurisdiction with weaker rules.

In some instances, the consequences of different regulatory regimes might be worse than mere nonefficacy, resulting in greater costs than the adoption of the other jurisdiction's regulatory policies. Richard Pierce (1985) gives the example of different regulation of the drinking age. In that case, many of those who are under the legal age in one jurisdiction will travel by automobile to another jurisdiction with a lower minimum age. The increased incidence of driving while intoxicated might more than offset the benefits of the higher drinking age.

Similarly, if another jurisdiction adopts more lax regulatory policies, firms that operate out of the jurisdiction might not only escape the substantive regulatory policies of other jurisdictions, but also more generally not be subject to legal process even on matters that have nothing to do with those regulatory policies.

55. But see GATT Dispute Settlement Panel Report: United States—Section 337 of the Tariff Act of 1930, 36S BISD 345 (1989).

56. In the European Community, for example, the decision to harmonize VAT rates was largely the result of the decision to eliminate internal border controls.

57. The relationship between nonefficacy and extraterritoriality is well illustrated by recent U.S. regulatory activity to protect American citizens who are "sprayed" with pesticide on certain outbound international flights. In order to protect themselves against disease-bearing or crop-harming insects, some countries require that airplane cabins be sprayed with pesticide before landing. Two congressmen have suggested regulatory or legislative action to protect Americans from such spraying (see Tolchin, 1994, p. 34). Certainly the United States has some interest in protecting its citizens, particularly on flights originating in the United States. But should it be able to tell other countries what measures they may take within their airspace to protect their health and crops?

58. Lea Brilmayer has examined the nonefficacy problem in its relationship to choice of law; see Brilmayer (1991, pp. 172–177).

59. A somewhat unusual international agreement that pursues harmonization, but allows extraterritorial effect of protective rules that are not harmonized, is the IMF Agreement. That agreement attempts to eliminate exchange controls for all member nations but allows such controls for certain purposes and under certain circumstances. Where exchange controls are permissible, all nations must refuse to enforce contracts that violate them (International Monetary Fund Agreement, Article VIII.2.b). See note 155.

60. Cf. Brilmayer (1991, pp. 161–167, comparing reciprocity in recognition with the adoption of uniform laws); Trachtman (1993, p. 70: harmonization "results in any jurisdictional overlap or conflict of laws becoming a false conflict because the competing substantive rules are the same").

61. The recent GATT panel decision on the Marine Mammal Protection Act implicitly regarded the United States' only legitimate interest as the regulation of the conduct of its own citizens. It did not address the international public good aspects of the problem, except to suggest that a less restrictive alternative to the United States' unilateral action would be to pursue international agreement on the subject. United States—Restrictions on Imports of Tuna, reprinted in 30 I.L.M. 1598 (1991) (not yet adopted by the GATT Council). The panel in a more recent decision on a complaint by the European Community regarding the same act took a broader approach regarding the United States' environmental interests outside its borders, but determined that the United States could not adopt measures the efficacy of which was dependent on the coercive effect on other governments. See United States—Restrictions on Imports of Tuna, reprinted in 33 I.L.M. 839 (1994).

62. Perhaps it is helpful to analogize to the problem of causation in tort law. Many causes and factors combine to produce an injury. Two cars collide at an intersection. A multiplicity of actions by either one driver or the other might have avoided the injury. We assign as the cause of the accident the wrongful behavior of one of the drivers, but only if its hypothetical elimination would have prevented the accident from occurring.

63. In contrast, the fairness claim discussed in section 2.2.4 rests directly on such an assertion.

64. The literature on the race to the bottom debate is immense, and spans several substantive areas. See, e.g., Bebchuk (1992); Revesz (1992); Shaviro (1992).

65. This idea of the "level playing field" is not the only fairness notion incorporated into U.S. trade policy. For a comprehensive analysis, see Abbott (Chapter 10 in Volume 2 of this work).

66. See, e.g., Gore (1992, p. 343).

67. Consider the following statement by an AFL-CIO representative:

We spend a great deal of time talking about free trade and comparative advantages, and so forth, and I'm sure these are important concepts and certainly we in the U.S. labor movement subscribe to them. Labor has benefitted greatly from freeness and free trade, not only internationally but domestically, from the comparative advantages that result from having a productive society as large and as diverse as we do in the United States, but the American labor movement has always taken the position that, to the maximum extent possible, labor costs should be removed from that equation, because labor is more than just a cost of production. Labor involves human dignity; it involves another whole dimension than does capital or interest or the other factors of production, and it therefore has to be treated very differently from them. (In Park, 1987, panel discussion)

68. For example, the IMF agreement provides that "each member shall ... avoid manipulating exchange rates or the international monetary system in order to prevent effective balance of payments adjustment or to gain an *unfair competitive advantage* over other members" (IMF Articles of Agreement, Article IV:1[iii]). And the long-standing practice of imposing duties to nullify the subsidies of foreign governments is also based on a notion that government policies might distort the conditions of fair competition. Of course, the implementation of countervailing duty law has not been fully consistent with this underlying idea; see Roessler (Chapter 2 in Volume 2 of this work).

The theoretical foundation for fairness-based harmonization claims is also flawed in that such claims implicitly confuse (or substitute) a theory of absolute advantage for comparative advantage. It is not the absolute costs of production that determine whether a nation will import or export particular goods, but rather the opportunity costs in terms of the various factors of production. Of course, changes in the relationship of factor costs between nations could very well affect their relative opportunity costs as well.

69. As Adam Smith put it simply more than 200 years ago,

What is prudence in the conduct of every private family, can scarcely be folly in that of a great kingdom. If a foreign country can supply us with a commodity cheaper than we ourselves can make it, better buy it of them with some part of the produce of our own industry, employed in a way in which we have some advantage. (Smith, 1776, bk. 4, ch. 2)

70. Cf. the following remarks of an AFL-CIO economist:

The overriding issue in discussions of trade and development is not free trade versus protection, more trade versus less trade, open markets versus closed markets, more investment versus less. Rather, it is how economic ties among nations, each with its own set of rules and practices governing production and trade, affect the lives of working people. To the extent that these relationships among nations play a role in distributing the fruits of economic growth, the AFL-CIO is concerned with who will benefit—the tiny number of people on the top rungs of the economic ladder, or the vast numbers on the bottom and middle rungs. The issue is not whether the U.S. should be engaged in economic activity internationally. Rather, the issue is how to be engaged so that it is beneficial to American workers and that such benefits are equitably distributed. (statement of Dr. Gregory Woodhead, Task Force on Trade American Federation of Labor and Congress of Industrial Organizations, Before the House Committee on Small Business on the Uruguay Round of Multilateral Trade Negotiations, April 26, 1994)

Or more specifically regarding the Uruguay Round agreement on textiles:

This agreement clearly means sharp increases in unemployment among the more than two million workers in apparel, textiles, and supporting industries in the early years after the agreement goes into effect. There are no effective alternative Administration employment plans in sight. Here, the price for "liberalized trade" will be paid by those who can least afford it. (ibid.)

71. This type of fairness claim is often supported by reference to persistent trade imbalances. See, e.g., testimony of Dr. Gregory Woodhead, Task Force on Trade American Federation of Labor and Congress of Industrial Organizations, Before the House Committee on Small Business on the Uruguay Round of Multilateral Trade Negotiations (April 26, 1994):

The persistent U.S. trade deficits have been matched by corresponding bilateral trade surpluses of a small number of America's major trading partners. For example, Japan's global merchandise trade surplus for 1993 was a record $120 billion. The asymmetry of world trade is further highlighted by the fact that the U.S., by itself, absorbs more than half of all less developed countries' manufactured exports. These persistent patterns of trade clearly indicate that the benefits and costs of the "open trading system" are not being borne equally, and that major reforms are urgently needed to bring about some measure of equity and balance.

An alternative argument for not accepting the cheap imports is an economic argument based on perceived positive externalities of the threatened industry. But this is an argument that, to the extent it is true about a given industry, does not depend on the presence of unfair trade.

72. Harmonization might, however, be an appropriate measure for reinforcing trade liberalization commitments. This claim for harmonization is included under the rubric of "transparency" discussed in section 2.2.7.

73. See Lando (1992) for the dispiriting answer to the hypothetical question posed by a potential German exporter to his lawyer: "Is it legally too risky for us to attempt to export our services and supplies to other countries in the European Community." Lando points out that harmonization for these reasons is more necessary among jurisdictions with different languages and cultures, since the transaction costs are much higher than among jurisdictions with similar language and cultures (e.g., the states of the United States).

74. Cf. Keohane (1984), discussing the benefits of economies of scale from international regimes.

75. Sweden, Canada, and Australia have apparently reached an agreement to "share the burdens of testing new drugs" (Jacobs, 1994, p. 13).

76. Cf. Macey 1990 (suggesting in part that federal deference to states can be explained as a response to certain interest groups that will fare better in the state political process).

77. In addition to whatever influence labor would have over its own national government, in the ILO it would have its own representative. Even if the governmental representatives were not prolabor, the labor representatives would gain the support of other governments that were. In addition, some employer representatives from countries that have stringent labor standards might also support harmonization as better from their perspective than allowing other nations to operate under lax labor standards.

78. This is not to imply that the outcome of such a nonbinding harmonization process is without significance. First, international agreement alone will exert some suasive force. Second, the existence of a harmonized proposal that other nations are adopting creates some incentives for all nations to adopt it.

79. Perhaps a good example of the importance of forum shifting is the regulation of food safety standards. Domestically, this is primarily the responsibility of the Food and Drug Administration, an independent agency that identifies its mission primarily as the protection of the consumers. International harmonization is through the Codex Alimentarius (see p. 86), where the U.S. Department of Agriculture coordinates all participation of the United States. The Agriculture Department has generally emphasized the interests of U.S. producers, in marketing exports and protecting domestic markets, among other things. Furthermore, agricultural and food manufacturing interests are well represented in Codex institutions, whereas consumer interests are not. See Rogaly (1993, p. 9, reporting that 445 nongovernmental participants in Codex proceedings represented industry, and eight represented public interest groups); Goldman (1992, pp. 1287–88). This imbalance in part has formed the basis for strong objections from Ralph Nader and others regarding the Uruguay Round Agreement on the Application of Sanitary and Phytosanitary Measures, which

provides that standards that conform to Codex standards presumptively comply with the agreement, whereas other standards may not.

For an interesting account of a standards battle waged in both domestic and international forums, see articles by Gasperello (1994), describing the efforts of traditional producers of carrageenan, a food additive, to prevent PNG (Philippine Natural Grade) carrageenan from being included within the standard for carrageenan.

80. One recent example of a turf war in international standards setting was between the Commerce and State departments over standards for high-definition television (see "New turf war," 1989, p. 2; "Markey bills put HDTV work," 1990, p. 34). In the context of the European Community, it has been noted that harmonization generally shifts regulatory power away from the legislature to the executive (Majone, 1994, p. 81).

81. For example, participants in the International Organization for Standardization include representatives of the national standards group for each participating nation. The United States is represented by the American National Standards Institute, which encompasses "firms, trade associations, technological societies, consumer organizations, and government agencies" (Carlton and Klamer, 1983, pp. 448–449). The standards organizations of other nations might not be so broadly based.

82. Such situations have produced numerous trade disputes, including the European Community's ban on hormones in beef and Taiwan's ban of certain additives in soft drinks (see Leebron, 1992).

83. Rosett (1992, p. 688). One source of incoherence is the choice of the subjects and scope of harmonization (see p. 48). One official of the state department expressed some frustration at finding a satisfactory answer to the question "How does the international community, through these organizations, or through countries working through these organizations, choose the subjects that become the subjects of conventions?" (Taft, 1986, pp. 233, 247). An additional source of incoherence, as well as deliberate vagueness, is the political nature of the international harmonization process, which often requires compromise (ibid., p. 236, remarks of Willem Vis).

84. There are also arguments against harmonization that derive not from the legitimacy of difference, but rather from the benefits of independence (see p. 89). This view has been the central claim of theorists who, disputing the race-to-the-bottom claim, suggest that there is a race to the top; see, e.g., Winter (1978).

85. Zweigert and Kötz (1992, pp. 10–11):

[The comparative lawyer] knows, of course, that causal factors [of legal differences] may exist anywhere throughout the fabric of social life, but often he will have to go to the sociology of law to learn just how far he must cast his net, so as to include, for example, the distribution of political power, the economic system, religious and ethical values, family structure, the basis of agriculture and the degree of industrialization, the organization of authorities and groups, and much else besides.

86. Cf. David, "International unification," p. 27. David identifies three reasons for the "variety of legal systems": natural factors, "different ideas entertained in various places of what is just or good for society," and "purely accidental" differences, or more briefly, "natural, ethical or accidental" (p. 28).

87. Some technologies resemble ideologies, in that they directly affect how individuals subjectively assess the world around them. (I thank Gerry Neuman for this insight.) Such technologies are closely related to preferences, and are not easily transferable. Furthermore,

some technologies might depend on institutional arrangements and behavioral approaches that differ among nations and are not easily transferred. For example, some claimed in the wake of the 1984 Bhopal disaster that Union Carbide's dangerous technologies (which were the same as those used in an American plant) were not appropriate for a developing country.

88. The political boundary, which ordinarily determines the reach of governmental policy, is itself an artificiality that distorts the conditions of comparative advantage. Even assuming that governments adopt optimal policies, and that the only differences between nations are endowments, technologies, and preferences, those policies will not necessarily be optimal for all regions. Thus it might very well be that there are no significant differences across a somewhat arbitrary political boundary, but because the populations on either side of the boundary are part of different nations, they will be subject to different rules based on some aggregate view of their respective nation's optimal policies. Unless nations are assumed to be optimal policy areas, distortions will result. To the extent that the optimal policy area is less than the nation, optimal policies (and in this sense undistorted comparative advantage as mediated by law) can be achieved by assigning to regional or local governments the relevant policy-making authority. If the optimal policy region spans a border, such subnational areas should in theory be given authority to enter into a harmonization process.

89. One could still argue that the source of the difference, such as less wealth or access to technologies, is unfair. This is a claim of international distributive justice. A difference in laws will also be unfair only if harmonization of the laws would reduce the distributive imbalance. Recent harmonization claims in trade negotiations have suggested just the opposite: reducing trade gains accruing to poorer countries because of lower labor costs. Thus the United States has advocated "upward" harmonization in labor and environmental regulation against the objections of developing countries.

90. See Bhagwati (1993b): "If fair traders are to be confronted, we need a revolution in the way we think about the theory of commercial policy and the gains from trade, divorcing it altogether from (untenable) notions of 'market determined' comparative advantage."

91. For example, the choice whether automobiles should be driven on the left or right side of the road.

92. See generally Henkin (1978).

93. See International Covenant on Economic, Social, and Cultural Rights, Articles 7, 9, and 11.

94. See Franck (1992).

95. General Agreement on Tariffs and Trade, Article XX(e). The United States has banned the import of goods produced by convict labor since 1890 (see "Worker rights," 1990). See also Dunkel (1987): "There is not disagreement that countries do not have to accept the products of slave or prison labor."

96. General Agreement on Tariffs and Trade, Article VI.

97. The linkage between subsidies and human rights on the one hand and "legitimate" comparative advantage on the other, was well illustrated in the recent testimony of an AFL-CIO representative:

Regrettably, the Uruguay Round did nothing to address the cruelest and most prevalent trade subsidy of all—the suppression of human and worker rights by governments seeking a low-wage, low-standard "comparative advantage" on the world market. (Testimony of

Dr. Gregory Woodhead before the House Committee on Small Business on the Uruguay Round of Multilateral Trade Negotiations, April 26, 1994)

98. As Senator Daniel Patrick Moynihan remarked in the context of the NAFTA debate, "I'm a free trader with free countries" (Moynihan, 1993). Secretary of Labor Robert Reich put the point in the following way regarding labor standards:

Labor conditions are determined by both economic and political factors, and it is difficult to disentangle the effects of each. But the existence of democratic institutions—multiple parties, freedom of speech and the press, clean elections—makes it more likely that low wages and poor working conditions are caused by unfortunate but legitimate economic constraints. The less democratic is the country, conversely, the greater the grounds for suspicion that labor standards are being suppressed to serve narrow commercial interests or a misguided mercantilist impulse on the part of elites, at the expense not just of mass living standards but also of global economic efficiency.

Where there are reasonably robust democratic institutions, then, we can presume that labor conditions reflect what the country can afford, given its level of development. (Reich, 1994).

99. See, e.g., Wilson (1989, pp. 316 et seq.); Mashaw (1983, pp. 49 et seq.). See generally Pildes and Anderson (1990).

100. See North American Agreement on Environmental Cooperation Between the Government of Canada, the Government of the United Mexican States and the Government of the United States of America (1993), Articles 22, 24, and 28 (inter alia).

101. A number of empirical studies have confirmed the importance of factor endowments in international trade patterns; see Forstner and Ballance (1990).

102. I assume here that harmonization could be achieved without cost to any institutional preferences that resulted in the adoption of different rules.

103. The presence of mutual externalities results in a prisoner's dilemma, producing a "race to the bottom." Regardless of what the other countries do, each country is better off if it chooses not to prevent the externality. If, however, the countries can coordinate their strategies through binding harmonization, they will choose to adopt the optimal standard. As noted in text, this reasoning assumes both that the externalities are fully reciprocal and that the costs and benefits relating to eliminating the externality are the same in all jurisdictions.

104. Externalities can result either from the failure of the decision maker to take account of costs imposed by its activities or from failure to take account of the preferences of those on whom the costs are inflicted.

105. As would be the case when harmonization is accomplished through the adoption of uniform or model laws.

106. See Rosett (1992).

107. This naturally remains a matter of controversy, especially in developing countries, as reflected in the United Nations Code on Transnational Corporations, but also in developed countries. The United States, for example, requires special registration of any who represent foreign interests (Foreign Agents Registration Act of 1938, as amended, 12 U.S.C. 511 et seq.). This is in essence a process of the homogenization of nations, which leads in turn to harmonization. Increasing immigration, as well as trade and investment, might also decrease heterogeneity among nations.

108. GATT Dispute Settlement Panel Report on United States Restrictions on Imports of Tuna, 39S BISD 155 (1993), also reported in 30 I.L.M. 1598 (1991) (decision not yet adopted by the GATT Council); Report of the Panel on Complaints on Belgian Family Allowances, 1S BISD 59 (1953).

109. One recent example was the dispute between the United States and European Community regarding hormone-treated cattle; see Rothberg (1990); Froman (1989); Halpern (1989).

110. See Leebron (1994).

111. See General Agreement on Trade in Services, Article VII.

112. Agreement on Technical Barriers to Trade, Article 6.

113. If harmonization is driven by potential economies of scale, then the incentive of the exporting country to harmonize will primarily depend on three factors: the size of the importing country's market, the exporting country's actual or potential share of that market, and the degree to which the domestic market of the exporting country is protected by tariffs or regulatory barriers. If the exports are large enough to provide sufficient economies of scale, then harmonization will not be required if either (1) the domestic market is also large enough to provide economies of scale or (2) the domestic market is protected, whether by tariffs or regulatory barriers. In those cases, the manufacturer can comply separately with the requirements of the foreign and domestic markets and remain competitive on both markets. If the protection is provided by nonharmonized regulatory barriers that would be removed through harmonization, then the cost of access to the export market will be the loss of protection of the domestic market. In these contexts, harmonization can exercise a trade-liberalizing influence.

114. These include both the U.S. Generalized System of Preferences, 19 U.S.C. 2462(a)(4), (c)(7), and the Caribbean Basin Economic Recovery Act, 19 U.S.C. 2702(b)(7), (c)(8). The United States also conditions the grant of OPIC investment insurance on the recognition by the host country of workers' rights. In all of these cases, the insistence is on internationally recognized workers' rights, not on conformity with U.S. law. The president retains discretion under the CBERA and OPIC provisions, whereas the GSP provision is mandatory.

115. Marine Mammal Protection Act of 1972, 86 Stat 1027, as amended. The United States has taken a similar approach with the harvesting of undersized lobsters. A panel established pursuant to the United States Canada Free Trade Agreement found that this provision did not violate Article III of the GATT. Lobsters from Canada, USA 89-1807-01, 1990 WL 299945 (U.S.Can.F.T.A.Binat.Panel). Unlike tuna harvested through methods dangerous to dolphins, undersized lobsters are physically different from full-sized lobsters. But in both cases the United States was insisting that other countries play by the same rules even though its interests (other than in "fair competition") were not directly affected. See Leebron (1992).

116. See generally Bhagwati and Patrick (1990).

117. A country that enjoys economic hegemony as a market for other country's exports might be able effectively to force multilateral harmonization. But since the incentive to harmonize depends both on market share and whether the domestic market is protected, that incentive will vary substantially among nations.

If the harmonization is embedded in relations that are subject to a most-favored-nation obligation, bilateral harmonization may be "multilateralized" through the operation of that obligation. For example, if the United States were to condition entry of certain agricultural products from the European Community on the harmonization of its sanitary and phyto-sanitary regulations, other countries could arguably benefit from that regime by invoking the United States' most-favored-nation obligation. See GATT Panel Report, 28S BISD 92 (1982).

118. For an extremely insightful collection of essays, see Ruggie (1993).

119. See Bermann (1994a, p. 75). Many organizations use both mandatory and non-mandatory processes. The International Labor Organization, for example, formulates both "conventions," which are intended to become mandatory after ratification as treaties, and "recommendations," which are intended only to provide guidance for national policies; see generally Osieke (1985). In some cases, binding conventions are used to adopt policy or principle harmonization and nonbinding recommendations for rule harmonization (ibid., p. 147, citing example of Employment Policy Convention [No. 122] and Recommendation [No. 122] of 1964). Similarly, the Codex Alimentarius Commission promulgates both "standards" and "guidelines"; see Codex Alimentarius Commission Procedural Manual (4th ed. 1975). Standards, however, are not of themselves mandatory, but rather subject to "acceptance" by participating governments. Such acceptance may also specify target dates for compliance or deviations from the standard; see Hui (1986); Lister (1987).

120. The Constitution of the International Labor Organization requires its members to submit conventions and recommendations adopted by the International Labor Conference to the appropriate authority for adoption within 12 or 18 months; ILO Constitution, Article 19(5) and 19(6). Thus, for example, the president of the United States would be required to submit any such convention to the Senate for ratification, or to the Congress for adoption of implementing legislation. But in so doing, the president could recommend against ratification; see Osieke (1985, pp. 158–159).

121. Compare the following statement by UNCITRAL:

The Commission has sometimes cast its uniform rules in the form of multilateral convention where, for example, it has considered it desirable and possible to deal comprehensively with an area and to achieve complete uniformity of law through the elaboration of rules in a mandatory form. This technique was adopted in the international sale of goods and the carriage of goods by sea. In other cases, however, it has cast its uniform rules in different, non-mandatory, forms. For example, in the area covered by the UNCITRAL Model Law on International Commercial Arbitration, the Commission considered that complete uniformity was desirable but not absolutely necessary. Moreover, it considered that the objective of harmonization of law in this area could be achieved most effectively and efficiently by enabling States to agree on a set of uniform rules that was a model and that their legislatures could, if necessary, adapt to the circumstances and requirements of their countries in implementing the rules. (UNCITRAL 12, 1985)

122. This approach does not necessarily require harmonization. Nothing in U.S. constitutional law prohibits the federal government from applying different legal rules to different states, so long as there is a mere rational basis for the distinction; see Neuman (1987). Even where the constitutive document forbids enacting formally different regimes for the units, relying on formally neutral criteria might still result in effectively nonharmonized regimes.

123. For example, securities law and many aspects of share voting are regulated by federal law in the United States, whereas internal corporate relations (including those between the corporation and its shareholders) are governed by state law. Much regulation of the banking industry and pension funds is at the federal level, but insurance regulation is

primarily a matter of state law. The federal government is responsible for many aspects of consumer protection against dangerous products, but product liability is exclusively determined by state law.

124. It was debated at the Paris Peace Conference of 1919 whether the International Labor Organization should have the power to adopt rules that would be binding under international law, but no provision was adopted giving the organization that power to adopt legislation binding on its members; see Osieke (1985, pp. 143–144); Advisory Opinion on the Competence of the ILO to Regulate Incidentally the Personal Work of the Employer, PCIJ, Series B, No. 13 (1926). The International Convention for the Regulation of Whaling provides for a one-nation one-vote commission that is granted significant powers to adopt regulations by a majority vote; see Majone (1994, p. 156).

125. A critical question in dispute settlement is who is authorized to initiate proceedings. The most common model in international agreements is to reserve such power to the signatory states. This tends to make the initiation of proceedings a political and diplomatic question, and generally to weaken the comprehensiveness of the regime, particularly when all parties are committing violations. Alternatives include giving the international organization enforcement powers (as in the IMF, but not the GATT) and giving private individuals the right to raise complaints (as in certain human rights instruments).

126. UNCITRAL, the United Nations Commission on International Trade Law, has used the following techniques "to further the harmonization and unification of the law of international trade": international conventions, model treaty provisions, model laws, uniform rules for the use of parties to private transactions, legal guides (suggesting approaches to problematic legal issues), and recommendations (UNCITRAL 11, 1985).

127. It is therefore not at all so surprising that the establishment of one harmonization effort, even if nonmandatory, will lead to the establishment of competing regimes in order to diminish the natural attraction of a single harmonization program.

128. The ILO partially addresses the problem by requiring its members to submit labor standards adopted either in conventions or recommendations to the appropriate national authorities; see Osieke (1985).

129. The ILO, for example, has maintained that its standards have exercised considerable influence on national legislation, even of members who have not ratified the relevant convention; see, e.g., ILO, *International Labor Standards* (1978); ILO, *The Impact of International Labor Standards* (1976).

130. This depends, however, on the type of harmonization and whether the benefits of the harmonization are somehow conditioned on compliance. If they are not so conditioned, harmonization might result in free-rider opportunities. Consider, for example, product standards. A small nation that does not cooperate would benefit from harmonization by other nations by taking advantage of the economies of scale that result from all its export markets adopting the same standards. At the same time, however, it could restrict access to its market by maintaining its own inconsistent standard.

131. The most notable recent example of an agreement imposing sanctions for failure to adhere is the so-called Montreal Protocol on Substances that Deplete the Ozone Layer, reprinted in 26 I.L.M. 1541 (1987), which requires signatory countries to prohibit trade in certain controlled substances (and potentially in products produced with those substances) with nonsignatory countries.

132. There are certainly some situations where compromise will be the cost minimization approach. This is more likely to be the case when the costs of production adaptation are small or nonexistent.

133. In some circumstances, the individually optimal harmonized rule will be the same as the optimal rule in the absence of harmonization. This would typically be the case where the harmonization claim is based on economies of scale or interface. In other circumstances, however, the optimal harmonized rule for one nation will not be the same as the optimal rule for that nation in the absence of harmonization. This is, for example, likely to be the case when the basis of harmonization is externalities or nonefficacy.

134. Even the GATT, with its emphasis on reciprocity in trade negotiations and concessions, contains a strongly mercantilist element.

135. Such side payments or the establishment of "harmonization funds" has been a feature of environmental harmonization proposals (see "The multilateral fund of the Montreal Protocol," 1992).

136. In 1982, for example, countries that responded to a Codex Alementarius proposal accepted less than 60 percent of the proposed maximum residue levels for pesticides. In 1988, the United States accepted only 35 percent of 2,784 Codex maximum residue levels; see Markus (1992).

An apparent exception to the general lack of success in harmonization (other than international interface harmonization) is intellectual property. But those conventions had little in the way of teeth, and a number of important nations, including the United States, for a long time refused to become parties. Indeed, it was really only as a result of including intellectual property on the Uruguay Round agenda that widespread harmonization of intellectual property regimes now seems likely. Arguably, the Uruguay Round success illustrates the point in text that harmonization is difficult to negotiate because it is hard to structure it as reciprocal trade-offs. In the Uruguay Round, however, not only could trade-offs be made across previously unconnected intellectual property regimes (e.g., patents and copyright), but also between intellectual property and a vast array of traditional trade issues, including access for textiles and agriculture (of particular interest to developing countries that had traditionally opposed international enforcement of intellectual property rights).

137. See, e.g., Moy (1993, p. 461, nn. 17–18); Moy (1992).

138. For a criticism of the Codex Alimentarius Commission on the basis that certain interest groups are represented and others not, see "Public participation" (1993).

139. A distinction should be drawn between the use of independent experts for rule formulation on the one hand and dispute settlement and enforcement on the other. A number of organizations use independent experts in some capacity for the latter function, even if they play no formal role in rule formulation. These include both the International Labor Organization (see Galenson, 1981, pp. 173–174) and the proposed World Trade Organization.

140. See Hui (1986, pp. 346–349); Modderman (1989).

141. See Kay (1976).

142. On "tripartism" within the ILO, see generally Osieke (1985); Galenson (1981). Such representation in international organizations, particularly where it is endowed with voting power, raises difficult problems in determining who is entitled to represent particular

interests such as "employers" and "employees." Such representation cannot completely be left to the government of the participating countries, as doing so would defeat the basic notion that such constituencies are entitled to independent representation. Within the context of the ILO, it became a matter of some controversy whether the managers of state-owned enterprises were, for purposes of tripartism, employers. See Galenson, (1981, pp. 13–14, 35–47).

143. See Bermann (1994b).

144. See Briffault (1990).

145. Lanaerts (1990): Federalism is "umpired by the supreme court of the common legal order."

146. I have assumed in this paper that the value of difference comes from the effect of domestic laws on the resident population. But the regulatory regime can also be a product, or a constituent element of a product, that is traded; cf. Trachtman (1993, p. 79). One example is the law of contracts, under which parties are often free to choose the law that governs their contractual relations. Of course, since law is typically structured as a public good, the exporting state receives no payment for its export. But this is not so unusual. Tourism is one of the most important sectors in the international trade in services. What drives this trade, however, is also largely public goods, such as beautiful natural scenery or historic buildings. Yet in order to enjoy those public goods, foreigners must purchase other services, including transportation, lodging, and food. Similarly, the "export" of law is often accompanied by the export of legal services. An example of the role of law as a component of a product is gambling services, whether traded through travel to casinos or the export of lottery tickets. The potential for such trade exists even if gambling is forbidden to local residents.

The potential role of law as product suggests an additional cost of sameness. In this case the loss of welfare is not directly to the jurisdiction's residents, but rather to the nonresident purchasers of a product that might no longer be available in a harmonized world.

147. See Jacobs (1994, p. 13).

148. Arthur Rosett put the point elegantly: "The wonderful virtue of seeking to achieve harmonization without resorting to unification or codification is that we are betting on a sure winner. Harmonization will occur for reasons exogenous to the law" (Rosett, 1992, p. 684).

149. See p. 48.

150. Conversely, harmonization claims that isolate aspects of difference without considering the larger contexts of policy implementation are suspect; see p. 48. Cf. Rosett (1992, p. 684): "Theoretical differences often are offset in practice by a countervailing rule that usually brings the result back in general harmony."

151. It should also be kept in mind that the costs of one type of harmonization that would partially realize the harmonization benefits might be less than the costs of another form of harmonization. For example, if economies of scale are sought, interface harmonization will achieve some of those benefits; see discussion p. 53. Similarly, harmonization of policies or principles is often less costly, in terms of the values of difference and independence, than harmonization of rules; see pp. 44–45.

152. This has been the basic rule of the European Community since the Court of Justice's decision in the "Cassis de Dijon" case, Judgment of the court of 20 February 1979, Rewe-zentral AG v Bundesmonopolver-waltung fuer Branntwein; see Porges (1995). The

Cassis de Dijon rule has not been applied with equal force to all contexts. For example, it has been somewhat inconsistently applied to services, and barely at all to the problem of pesticide residues; see, e.g., Judgment of the Court of 19 September 1984, Officier van Justitie v. Albert Heijn B.V. Australia also applies mutual recognition between its states; Mutual Recognition Act of 1992, 1992 Aust. Act 198.

153. Canada and the United States have entered into a variant of such an arrangement; see 23 *Securities Regulation & Law Report* (BNA) 829 (May 31, 1991); Greene (1991, p. 1583, n. 175). The U.S.-Canada Multijurisdictional Disclosure System (MJDS) is a hybrid between the "common prospectus" and "reciprocal prospectus" approaches; see Trachtman (1991): MJDS is "limited mutual recognition based on limited harmony of legal standards."

154. See Pelmans and Sun (1994, p. 179).

155. Article VIII.2.b rejects, at least for exchange controls, the long-established rule that penal and tax (including exchange-control) laws would not be given recognition outside the territory of the state that promulgated them. Less clear is whether Article VIII.2.b requires member states affirmatively to aid a state in the enforcement of its exchange controls (by providing, for example, a cause of action for damages) as opposed to merely recognizing a defense against enforcement that would violate those rules. Compare Banco Frances e Brasiliero S.A. v. Doe, 36 N.Y.2d 592, 370 N.Y.S.2d 534, 331 N.E.2d 502 (1975) (court recognized recovery in tort for private bank injured by violation of exchange controls), *with* Banco do Brasil v. A.C. Israel Commodity Co., 12 N.Y.2d 371, 239 N.Y.S.2d 872, 190 N.E.2d 235 (1963) (court denied governmental instrumentality recovery in tort for violation of exchange controls), cert. denied, 376 U.S. 906 (1964). See Restatement Third, Foreign Relations Law of the United States, 822, Reporters' Note 3.

156. See also Trachtman (1993, p. 102): "Horizontal cooperation is always required, not necessarily in regulation, but in allocating regulatory jurisdiction."

157. Some emphasis should be placed on the word *competitive*. In many instances, particularly where two jurisdictions impose minimum requirements but one is more burdensome than the other, there will be no difficulty in designing a product that meets the requirements of both, namely, the more burdensome ones. However, this solution would result in most cases in the product's being more expensive (unless the increased costs of compliance are offset by economies of scale) and hence not competitive if there is no demand for goods that conform to the higher standard.

High-definition television presents an opportunity for circumvention. Instead of harmonizing HDTV production and reception standards, television sets can be designed to accommodate multiple standards. Of course, such multiple compliance is not costless. See Butler (1992, p. 173).

158. Agreement on Technical Barriers to Trade (Uruguay Round), Art. 2.8 and Annex 3, para. I.

REFERENCES

Abbott, K. 1995. "Defensive unfairness: The normative structure of Section 301" (Chapter 9 in Volume 2 of this work).

Alford, D. 1992. "Basle Committee minimum standards: International regulatory response to the failure of BCCI." *George Washington Journal of International Law and Economics*, 26:241.

Bebchuk, L. 1992. "Federalism and the corporation: The desirable limits on state competition in corporate law." *Harvard Law Review*, 105:1435.

Bermann, G. 1994a. "Managing regulatory rapprochement: Institutional and procedural approaches." In *Regulatory cooperation for an interdependent world*. Paris: Organization for Economic Cooperation and Development.

Bermann, G. 1994b. "Taking subsidiarity seriously." *Columbia Law Review*, 94:331.

Bhagwati, J. 1993a. "Challenges to the doctrine of free trade." *New York University Journal of International Law and Politics*, 25:219.

Bhagwati, J. 1993b. "Fair trade, reciprocity, and harmonization: The novel challenge to the theory and policy of free trade." In *Protectionism and world welfare*, pp. 17–53, ed. D. Salvatore. Cambridge: Cambridge University Press.

Bhagwati, J., and H. Patrick, eds. 1990. *Aggressive unilateralism: America's 301 trade policy and the world trading system*. Ann Arbor: University of Michigan Press.

Boodman, M. 1991. "The myth of harmonization of laws." *American Journal of Comparative Law*, 39:699.

Briffault, R. 1990. "Our localism: Part I—The structure of local government law." *Columbia Law Review*, 90:1.

Brilmayer, L. 1991. *Conflict of laws: Foundations and future directions*. Boston: Little Brown.

Bulfinch, T. (1979 edition). *Mythology*. New York: Grammercy.

Butler, J. 1992. "HDTV demystified: History, regulatory options, and the role of telephone companies." *Harvard Journal of Law and Technology*, 6:155.

Carlton, D., and J. Klamer. 1983. "The need for coordination among firms, with special reference to network industries." *University of Chicago Law Review*, 50:446.

Cooper, R. 1986. *Economic policy in an interdependent world*. Cambridge, MA: MIT Press.

"Cooperative efforts in international banking regulation: A panel." 1982. *American Society of International Law Proceedings*, 76:352.

David, R. 1971. "International unification of private law." In *International Encyclopedia of Comparative Law*, vol. 2. New York: Oceana.

Dunkel, A., ed. 1987. *Trade policies for a better future: The Leutwiler report, the GATT, and the Uruguay Round*. Boston: Kluwer Academic.

Foote, S. 1984. "Beyond the politics of federalism: An alternative model." *Yale Journal of Regulation*, 1:217.

Forstner, H., and R. Ballance. 1990. *Competing in a global economy*. London: Unwin Hyman.

Fox, E. 1991. "Harmonization of law and procedures in a globalized world: Why, what, and how?" *Antitrust Law Journal*, 60:593.

Franck, T. 1992. "The emerging right to democratic governance." *American Journal of International Law*, 86:46.

Froman, M. B. 1989. "The United States–European Community hormone treated beef conflict." *Harvard International Law Journal*, 30:549.

Galenson, W. 1981. *The International Labor Organization: An American view*. Madison: University of Wisconsin Press.

Gasperello, L. 1994. "A tale of two seaweeds"; "Politics, Science Tangled in Seaweed Controversy"; "Free Trade winds are blowing for PNG carrageenan." *Food & Drink Daily*, vol. 4 (February 8; March 21; March 31).

Goldman, P. 1992. "Resolving the trade and environment debate: In search of a neutral forum and neutral principles." *Washington and Lee Law Review*, 49:1279.

Gore, A. 1992. *Earth in the balance: Ecology and the human spirit*. Boston: Houghton Mifflin.

Gray, C. Boyden. 1983. "Regulation and federalism." *Yale Journal of Regulation*, 1:93.

Greene, E. F. 1991. "Regulatory and legislative responses to takeover activity in the 1980s: The United States and Europe." *Texas Law Review*, 69:1539.

Halpern, A. R. 1989. "The U.S.–EC beef controversy and the standards code: Implications for the application of health regulations to agricultural trade." *North Carolina Journal of International Law and Commercial Regulation*, 14:135.

Hamilton, N. 1993. "Feeding our future: Six philosophical issues shaping agricultural law." *Nebraska Law Review*, 72:210.

Hansson, G. 1983. *Social clauses and international trade: An economic analysis of labor standards in trade policy*. New York: St. Martin's Press.

Hansson, G. 1990. *Harmonization and International Trade*. London: Routledge.

"Harmonization in the European Community." 1991. *Columbia Journal of Transnational Law*, 29:1–214.

Hart, C. 1994. "The European Community's value added tax system: Analysis of the new transitional regime and prospects for further harmonization." *International Tax and Business Law*, 12:1.

Henkin, L. 1978. *The rights of man today*. Boulder, CO: Westview Press.

Hui, Y. H. 1986. *United States food laws, regulations and standards*. New York: Wiley.

Hurwitz, L., ed. 1983. *The harmonization of European public policy*. Westport, CT: Greenwood Press.

Jacobs, S. 1994. "Why governments must work together: Interdependence of international regulations." *OECD Observer*, February.

Kay, D. A. 1976. *The international regulation of pesticide residues in food*. St. Paul: West Publishing.

Keohane, R. 1984. *After hegemony: Cooperation and discord in the world political economy*. Princeton: Princeton University Press.

Lanaerts, K. 1990. "Constitutionalism and the many faces of federalism." *American Journal of Comparative Law*, 38:205.

Lando, O. 1992. "Principles of European contract law: An alternative to or a precursor of European legislation." *American Journal of Comparative Law*, 40:573.

Leary, V. "Workers' rights and international trade: The social clause (GATT, ILO, NAFTA, US Laws)" (Chapter 5 in Volume 2 of this work).

Leebron, D. 1992. "Non-tariff trade barriers: Technical barriers to trade," in Workshop on the Multilateral Trade Negotiations of GATT: Issues and Policy Implications for the ROC on Taiwan. Taipei: Chung-hua Institution for Economic Research.

Leebron, D. 1994. "Trade in services" (unpublished manuscript).

Lister, B. A. 1987. "Comparison of the U.S. laws and regulations concerning labeling of prepackaged foods with the Codex Alimentarius draft General Standard for Labeling of Prepackaged Foods." *Food, Drug, and Cosmetic Law Journal*, 42:174.

Macey, J. 1990. "Federal deference to local regulators and the economic theory of regulation: Toward a public-choice explanation of federalism." *Virginia Law Review*, 76:265.

Majone, G. 1994. "Comparing strategies of regulatory rapprochement." *OECD, Regulatory cooperation for an interdependent world*. Paris: Organization for Economic Cooperation and Development.

"Markey bills put HDTV work under Commerce roof." 1990. *Broadcasting*, March 12, p. 34.

Markus, C. 1992. "International harmonization of pesticide tolerances—Legal, procedural, and policy issues." *Food and Drug Law Journal*, 47:701.

Mashaw, J. L. 1983. *Bureaucratic justice: Managing social security disability claims*. New Haven, CT: Yale University Press.

Matteucci, M. 1976. "Unidroit: The first fifty years." In *UNIDROIT, New directions in international trade law*. Dobbs Ferry, NY: Oceana.

Modderman, J. P. 1989. "Specifications." In *International food regulation handbook: Policy, science, law*, ed. Roger Middlekauff and Philippe Shubik. New York: M. Dekker.

Moy, R. C. 1992. "Essay: Patent harmonization, protectionism, and legislation." *Journal of the Patent and Trademark Office Society*, 74:777.

Moy, R. C. 1993. "The history of the patent harmonization treaty: Economic self-interest as an influence." *John Marshall Law Review*, 26:457.

Moynihan, D. P. 1993. Remarks on "Meet the Press," NBC, September 19, 1993, as quoted in *BNA International Trade Daily*, September 21, 1993.

"The multilateral fund of the Montreal Protocol: A prototype for financial mechanisms in protecting the global environment." 1992. *Cornell International Law Journal*, 25:181.

Neuman, G. 1987. "Territorial discrimination, equal protection, and self-determination." *University of Pennsylvania Law Review*, 135:261.

"New turf war: Dingell and Markey attack State Dept. HDTV activities." 1989. *Communications Daily*, March 13, p. 2.

Osieke, E. 1985. *Constitutional Law and Practice in the International Labor Organization*. Dordrecht: Martinus Nijhoff.

Osieke, E., and F. Kirgis. 1986. "Constitutional law and practice in the International Labor Organization." *American Journal of International Law*, 80:417.

Park, F. 1987. "Worker rights and international trade." *American Society of International Law Proceedings*, 81:59.

116   References

Pelmans, J., and J. Sun. 1994. "Towards a European Community regulatory strategy: Lessons from 'learning-by-doing.'" *OECD, Regulatory Cooperation for an Interdependent World.* Paris: Organization for Economic Cooperation and Development.

Pierce, R. 1985. "Regulation, deregulation, federalism, and administrative law: Agency power to preempt state regulation." *University of Pittsburgh Law Review,* 46:607.

Pildes, R. H., and E. S. Anderson. 1990. "Slinging arrows at democracy: Social choice theory, value pluralism, and democratic politics." *Columbia Law Review,* 90:2121.

Pinkerton, R. 1993. "The European Community—'EC 92.'" *International Journal of Purchasing and Materials Management,* 29:18.

"Public participation in international pesticide regulation: When the Codex Commission decides, who will listen?" 1993. *Virginia Environmental Law Journal,* 12:329.

Puchala, D. J. 1984. *Fiscal harmonization in the European Communities: National politics and international cooperation.* London: F. Pinter.

Reich, R. B. 1994. Keynote address to Symposium on International Labor Standards and Global Economic Integration, April 25, 1994, reprinted in *BNA Daily Labor Report,* April 29, 1994.

Revesz, R. 1992. "Rehabilitating interstate competition: Rethinking the 'race-to-the-bottom' rationale for federal environmental regulation." *New York University Law Review,* 67:1210.

Ricardo, D. 1817. *The principles of political economy and taxation.* London: J. M. Dent & Sons.

Roessler, F. 1995. [Volume 2, Chapter 1].

Rogaly, J. 1993. "The deal: Sour milk or apple pie?" *The Financial Post,* December 10, p. 9.

Rose-Ackerman, S. 1992. "Rethinking the progressive agenda: The reform of the American regulatory state." *Harvard Law Review,* 105:1402.

Rosett, A. 1992. "Unification, harmonization, restatement, codification, and reform in international commercial law." *American Journal of Comparative Law,* 40:683.

Rothberg, S. 1990. "From beer to BST: Circumventing the GATT standards code's prohibition on unnecessary obstacles to trade." *Minnesota Law Review,* 75:505.

Rubin, E., and M. Feeley. 1994. "Federalism: Some notes on a national neurosis." *UCLA Law Review,* 41:903.

Ruggie, J., ed. 1993. *Multilateralism matters: The theory and praxis of an institutional form.* New York: Columbia University Press.

"Science should be predominant factor in Codex decision making, paper says." 1994. *Food Chemical News,* February 28.

Scott, H. 1982. "Supervision of international banking post-BCCI." *Georgia State University Law Review,* 8:487.

Shaviro, D. 1992. "An economic and political look at federalism in taxation." *Michigan Law Review,* 90:895.

Smith, A. 1776. *The Wealth of Nations.*

Snyder, G. 1992. "Setting standards for high-definition television: Federal policy must promote more than just a better picture." *Buffalo Law Review,* 40:613.

"Symposium: The globalization of law, politics, and markets: Implications for domestic law reform." 1993. *Indiana Journal of Global Legal Studies*, 1:1.

Taft, G. 1986. "International unification of private law: The multilateral approach" (speech). Reprinted in *Proceedings of the American Society of International Law*, 80:233.

Tiebout, C. 1956. "A pure theory of local expenditures." *Journal of Political Economy*, 64:416.

Tolchin, M. 1994. "Panels in Congress to act on improving air quality on aircraft." *New York Times*, April 24, p. 34.

Trachtman, J. 1992. "L'etat, c'est nous: Sovereignty, economic integration and subsidiarity." *Harvard International Law Journal*, 33:459.

Trachtman, J. 1993. "International regulatory competition, externalization, and jurisdiction." *Harvard International Law Review*, 34:47.

Trachtman, J. 1991. "Recent initiatives in international financial regulation and goals of competitiveness, effectiveness, consistency and cooperation." *Journal of International Law and Business*, 12:241.

Vis, W. A. 1986. "International unification of private law: The multilateral approach" (speech). Reprinted in *Proceedings of the American Society of International Law*, 80:233.

Wilke, M., and H. Wallace. 1990. *Subsidiarity: Approaches to power-sharing in the European Community*. London: Royal Institute of International Affairs.

Wilson, J. Q. 1989. *Bureaucracy: What government agencies do and why they do it*. New York: Basic Books.

Winter, R. 1978. *Government and the corporation*. Washington, DC: American Enterprise Institute for Public Policy Research.

"Worker rights and international trade." 1990. *American Society of International Law Proceedings*, 81:59.

Worth, N. 1992. "Harmonizing capital adequacy rules for international banks and securities firms." *North Carolina Journal of International Law and Commercial Regulation*, 18:133.

Zweigert, K., and H. Kötz. 1992. *An introduction to comparative law*. Oxford: Clarendon Press.

3   Free Trade and Evolving Standards

Alessandra Casella

3.1   Introduction

As markets continue to integrate and tariff barriers are progressively eliminated, the political debate has shifted to differences in standards and regulations as possible instruments of markets protection and of trade distortion. In the United States, the public discussion accompanying the ratification of the North American Free Trade Agreement (NAFTA) has provided a good example. Trade unions feared that firms would move to Mexico, attracted by the lower production costs that result from laxer regulation. At the same time, environmental groups worried that competition with Mexican cheap labor and looser environmental regulations would lead unions to exercise pressure toward lower environmental standards domestically. There was concern that the final effect of the trade agreement could be both more unemployment and a less protected environment.

One response to these misgivings has been to call for some form of standards harmonization as precondition for the opening of trade. In this perspective, outstanding differences in regulations could be invoked as sufficient reason for market protection. To trade economists, used to the general idea that gains from exchange stem from differences between individuals and countries, not from uniformity, the demand for harmonization sounds suspicious. In addition, the implicit assumption that standards can be taken as given, ignoring the effect that trade per se would have on their determination, seems unsatisfactory.

The purpose of this chapter is to look at these questions with the help of simple results from economic theory. The point of departure is very simple: standards are regulations aimed at attaining public goods that a community deems desirable: healthy working conditions, a clean environment, safe food, reliable and compatible machines. But if standards fulfill a well-defined function in the economy, then they also respond to a well-defined demand; to the extent that this demand depends on economic fundamentals—endowments, preferences, information, technology—we expect it to be different across societies or groups that differ in terms of these fundamentals. We have no a priori reason to think that efficiency requires standards and regulations to be equal everywhere. These conclusions echo the analyses of Bhagwati and Srinivasan (Chapter 4 in this volume) and Brown, Deardorff, and Stern (Chapter 5).

Having established this initial point, the main contribution of this chapter is to study the effect that trade per se exercises on the standards that an economy chooses. If standards are shaped by society's demands, then we must acknowledge that in each economy these demands will be modified by changes in economic fundamentals: standards evolve with economic conditions and change as allocations change.

It becomes natural to ask then whether harmonization can be the spontaneous result of opening trade. Without setting preconditions for free trade, without formal treaties between governments, would trade itself lead individuals to establish similar standards? If some convergence occurs, does it need to be inefficient, as in many "race to the bottom" arguments, or can it be the appropriate response to the changed allocations caused by trade flows?

The first part of the chapter studies these questions with the help of a very stylized model of international trade. With NAFTA in mind, I have modeled two economies with different relative factors endowments and such that in equilibrium the demand for standards depends on the level of income. The model shows that uniformity of standards, either before or after trade is opened, has no necessary correlation with gains from trade. In addition, trade causes standards convergence if its effect is to reduce international differences in national income. This conclusion is reinforced if we assume that the two economies have different productivities, or if we allow for increasing returns to scale and imperfect competition. The convergence in standards is not caused by self-defeating efforts to gain competitiveness at the expense of the other country, but simply by more similar demands for the public goods that the standards provide.

Although this conclusion relies on several specific assumptions, the main mechanism responsible for the tendency toward harmonization is the convergence in national incomes brought by trade. Failing this convergence, the convergence in standards will also fail. Thus the main role of the model is not to predict that harmonization will always occur spontaneously, but to emphasize that standards will change with trade, and that the direction of their change is likely to depend on the fundamental effects of trade on the well-being of a society.

In this traditional model, standards are treated as national policies, expressed by national governments and extending over the territory of the country. All citizens of a country are subject to homogeneous standards and have access to the same national public good. But a different perspective is also possible. If standards are either adopted voluntarily by groups of producers, or if the government regulations that impose them refer to specifications developed by private industry groups, then the appropriate unit of analysis may not be the country any longer, but the freely formed coalitions of private agents that propose and adopt the standards. In this approach, standards are not necessarily defined geographically, but according to product types, and the coalitions of producers can be physically located anywhere. More to the point, they can be located across national borders.

Although standards are often sanctioned by national governments, the evidence discussed in this chapter suggests that a shift is taking place toward an increasing role for private voluntary organizations. These coalitions have flexible borders, and they contract or expand as industries contract or expand. Their composition is endogenous: in the same way as the standards themselves respond to the opening of trade, so the composition of the group expressing the standards is modified.

The second part of the chapter discusses this alternative approach to the determination of standards. It describes two simple general equilibrium models of coalition formation, where a standard is needed for efficient trading but agents' preferences over the standard depend on the type of their endowment (Casella and Feinstein, 1990; Casella, 1994a). Think of the standard as a restriction on production that guarantees the quality of the good that each individual brings to the market. A coalition shares the choice and the cost of the standard, and the guaranteed quality obtained through its use is available exclusively to coalition members (and, in one of the two models, to their partners). Since it is important to have access to the appropriate standard and since individuals are heterogeneous, in general several coalitions will form in equilibrium. What is the effect of changes in market size on the partition in groups and on the choice of the standards expressed by these groups?

The models reach two main results. First, an increase in market size is consistent with an increase in the optimal number of coalitions. Individuals that shared the same standard when the market was small find it desirable to divide into new coalitions when the market becomes larger. Second, the reorganization of the coalitions is not simply a secession by a subgroup, but a wider rearrangement where previous coalitions' borders are crossed and new alliances are formed.

The conclusions of the models lead to the following conjecture. Could it be that larger markets, larger in a geographical sense and larger in the range of economic goods that can be exchanged, will be associated with a shift from national alliances expressing generic standards to international partnerships organized along finer and finer industry lines? Could international harmonization take place "from the bottom," through the voluntary agreements of international groups adopting a common standard or independently lobbying their governments for the same standard? It is with this suggestion that the chapter concludes.

The chapter proceeds as follows. Section 3.2 discusses the interpretation of standards as public goods. Section 3.3 presents a simple, traditional model of international trade, shows how differences in standards need not have implications for gains from trade, and discusses the potential role of trade in fostering standards convergence. Section 3.4 discusses how the theory is modified when the coalitions expressing the standards are allowed to change in response to market changes and concludes with an empirical discussion of the importance of private voluntary standards. Section 3.5 concludes. The Appendix describes the solution of the model in section 3.2 in the presence of increasing returns.

3.2   Standards as Public Goods

The general term "standards" has many meanings. In their original definition, standards are units of measure: weight, time, length, temperature, value. By immediate extension, standards are also conventions about goods' characteristics that facilitate exchange and compatibility: the shape and size of a plug, the thread of a screw, the distance between two rails and their width, a certain type of keyboard, an operating system for a computer. If standards define the technical properties of a good, then they apply also to those characteristics of the good's production that are not readily observable in the final product but that guarantee its quality. So French champagne is produced in a specific region following precise rules, Italian pasta is made of durum wheat, and silver 925 is different from silver 800. Following the same logic, if the quality of the final product is what matters, then standards may refer not so much to characteristics of production as to guaranteed performance. In each country where there are safety regulations for children's clothes and toys, the terms "fire resistant," "nontoxic," and "appropriate for children of age x" have specific technical meanings. But then, by extension, standards may refer to regulations that affect certain aspects of the performance of a product even when these aspects are not immediately linked to the intended use of the product but are valued in themselves. So, for example, environmental standards specify emission requirements for cars, regulations on the emissions from smoke-stacks, or maximum pollution allowances for factories. Similarly, standards may be linked to regulations that specify procedures of production, again not because they affect the quality of the final product but because they are deemed desirable per se: labor standards defining prohibitions against child labor, or specifying working conditions and working hours, or estab-lishing the right to strike.

Diverse as the meanings of the term appear, all the standards we have described have one characteristic in common: they derive their value from being shared by a community. They may have become established through convention and historical attrition, or through the explicit formu-lation of the law, or through the initiative of few entrepreneurs, but in all cases their role depends on their adoption by a group. An individual adopting a rule alone does not, by definition, establish a standard. He can differentiate his product and his factory, he can build a reputation for quality, reliability, and good management, but he cannot rely on a shared agreement that extends beyond the sphere of his personal reputation. The original purpose of standards—facilitating exchange and contractual rela-tions—requires that standards be public goods. Or more precisely, it requires that standards be common rules or regulations through which a society achieves a public goal: guaranteed product quality, predictability of contracts, safety of the workplace, clean air and water.

The observation that standards are public goods does not imply that they must always be established by government fiat. As described by Kindleberger (1983), historically standards have had their origins in gov-ernment actions at times, but most often in the coordinated initiative of groups of merchants, and in more rare cases in the success of a single firm so far ahead of its competitors to be able to establish the direction of the industry. I use the term "public good" to refer to joint consumption—the common reference to the same standard and the common enjoyment of the public goal it makes possible—not to the impossibility of appropri-ating privately the surplus generated by the standard. In other words, property rights over standards can in general be defined, and therefore the return from establishing the standard can be appropriated and the standard itself privately provided (think for example of wine's *appellation contrôlée*).

On the other hand, the value of the standard depends on its being shared by a group that is not too small for the standard to emerge as indeed a standard. In the terminology of public finance theory, a standard is excludable but not rival; it is, properly speaking, a "club good" (Buchanan, 1965).[1]

Once we recognize that standards are public goods fulfilling specific functions deemed desirable by the community that shares them, it becomes clear that they must reflect the characteristics of the community: preferences, endowments, and technological possibilities and constraints. Two conclusions follow. First, we expect different communities to need and have different standards. There is no presumption that in general standards should be the same across economies, even when they fulfill the same function, since other characteristics of the economies will differ. Even in economies with similar cultures—and therefore similar preferences—the amount of resources devoted to a clean environment, to the prevention of child labor, and to the safety of working conditions will be affected by the technologies each society has access to and by the total resources it commands.

Second, standards should change as these characteristics change: standards are endogenous. As we do not expect them to be constant over time, so we should not expect them to be constant when the structure of the economy is altered. In particular, because free trade modifies the national income of an economy, its production pattern, and the distribution of its resources, we should expect standards to react to the opening of markets.

These observations do not imply that standards cannot or will not be used to distort trade. If an economy stands to gain relative to its competitors from the strategic use of standards, it will do so, and the resulting market allocations, trade flows, and standards may be inefficient. As in traditional analyses on the provision of public goods in competing jurisdictions, the outcome may be excessive or insufficient supply of public goods.[2] However, there is no logical connection between the inefficiencies that can be created by the strategic use of standards and the existence of *different* standards: the observation that standards differ across economies does not imply in any way that they are distortionary, exactly as the observation that they are equal does not imply that they are not distortionary and suboptimal. The two questions are logically distinct.

To show more precisely the meaning of these statements, in the next section I describe a very simple model of international trade with endogenous standards. Some conclusions of the model will recall the results of Bhagwati and Srinivasan (Chapter 4) and Brown, Deardorff, and Stern (Chapter 5). However, here the main focus is on the evolution of standards in response to trade, a different perspective from the one taken in the other works.

3.3 Harmonization of Standards through Trade

3.3.1 A Simple Model of International Trade

Imagine two countries that do not trade with each other and decide in isolation the level of standards they want in their economy. Suppose conditions are such that one country chooses higher standards than the other. If the two countries then decide to open trade, will the country that starts out with the higher standards be hurt by free trade? Would the gains from trade to this country be higher if standards abroad were forced up? These questions summarize one of the concerns expressed by supporters of standards harmonization. But initial difference in standards need not distort trade: in the model described here, the standards chosen abroad have no effect either on the direction of trade or on the welfare gains that result from opening borders.

In addition, since standards respond to the opening of trade, in the model it is trade itself that leads to their convergence. Calling for standards harmonization as a precondition for free trade would be mistaken, since foreign standards do not affect gains from trade, and useless, since some convergence would eventually come on its own. If ex ante harmonization were prohibitively expensive for the country with initially lower standards, then requiring it as precondition for free trade could also be counterproductive, since it may prevent profitable free exchanges.

The model is special and is meant only as an example of the more general logic underlying the observations just made. Nevertheless, with NAFTA in mind, I have tried to choose assumptions that appear appropriate to exchanges between Mexico and the United States. In particular, the model assumes that trade is driven by differences in factors' endowments, with one country (Mexico) relatively abundant in low-skill labor and the other country (United States) in high-skill labor (see the discussion in Lustig, Bosworth, and Lawrence, 1992, and Leamer and Medberry, 1993). In addition, building on empirical results obtained by Grossman and Krueger (1991), the model is such that in equilibrium income will be the determinant of desired standards. It follows that traditional results on the effect of trade on national income and its distribution can be applied directly to the question of standards.

At first, let us ignore standards and describe the basic structure on which additional features will be added later. There are two countries, 1 and 2, two factors of production, H and L, and two final goods, X and Z. We can think of H and L as high-skill and low-skill labor, and of X and Z as low-tech and high-tech goods. Country 1 is relatively abundant in low-skill labor L, and country 2 in high-skill labor H:

$$\frac{L_1}{H_1} > \frac{L}{H} > \frac{L_2}{H_2} \tag{1}$$

where L is the total supply of factor L, and L_1 is the amount of L in country 1 (and similarly for H). The difference in factors' endowments will be the engine of trade.

The production of the low-tech good X requires only low-skill labor, and the production of the high-tech good Z only high-skill labor. Both final goods are produced with constant returns to scale technologies, and the technologies are equal in the two countries and are given by

$$X_1 = aL_1 \qquad Z_1 = bH_1$$
$$X_2 = aL_2 \qquad Z_2 = bH_2 \tag{2}$$

implying that the two goods will be priced according to

$$p_{X1} = w_{L1}/a \qquad p_{Z1} = w_{H1}/b$$
$$p_{X2} = w_{L2}/a \qquad p_{Z2} = w_{H2}/b \tag{3}$$

where p_{X1} is the price of good X in country 1, and w_{L1} is the wage of factor L in country 1.

In both countries, individuals have the same tastes and derive utility from the consumption of the two goods, according to the utility function

$$U = xz \tag{4}$$

where x and z are individual consumptions of good X and good Z.

If the two countries do not trade, the demand for each good must equal its supply within each country. In equilibrium, relative wages in the two countries are then

$$\frac{w_{L1}}{w_{H1}} = \frac{H_1}{L_1} \qquad \frac{w_{L2}}{w_{H2}} = \frac{H_2}{L_2} \tag{5}$$

And relative prices are

$$\frac{p_{X1}}{p_{Z1}} = \frac{bH_1}{aL_1} \qquad \frac{p_{X2}}{p_{Z2}} = \frac{bH_2}{aL_2} \tag{6}$$

The relative wages of the two factors depend only on their relative supply in each country. Because country 1 is abundant in factor L, employed in the production of good X, in autarky the relative price of the low-tech good X will be lower in 1 than in 2 (or the relative price of the high-tech good Z will be lower in 2 than in 1).

When trade is opened, each good must be sold at the same price by both countries, and with equal technologies wages must be equalized across borders. In equilibrium, the relative wage for the two factors will now be such that total demand for each good equals total supply. This condition yields

$$\frac{w_L}{w_H} = \frac{H}{L} \tag{7}$$

In both countries the relative price of the two goods is

$$\frac{p_X}{p_Z} = \frac{bH}{aL} \tag{8}$$

When trade is opened, the relative wage is determined by the relative supply of the two factors worldwide; therefore, it falls for factors that within each country are disproportionately scarce, and it rises for factors that are disproportionately abundant. It follows that trade increases the relative price of good X in country 1, and lowers it in country 2. As expected, country 1 exports good X and imports good Z.

If we use as deflator the price index[3]

$$P = (p_X p_Z)^{1/2} \tag{9}$$

then factors' real incomes are a measure of utility, and by comparing incomes before and after trade we see immediately who gains and who loses from trade. Call real income y. In autarky,

$$y_{L1}^A = (abH_1/L_1)^{1/2} \qquad y_{H1}^A = (abL_1/H_1)^{1/2}$$
$$y_{L2}^A = (abH_2/L_2)^{1/2} \qquad y_{H2}^A = (abL_2/H_2)^{1/2} \tag{10}$$

When trade is opened,

$$y_L^T = (abH/L)^{1/2} \qquad y_H^T = (abL/H)^{1/2} \tag{11}$$

Trade has caused a rise in real income for low-skill labor in country 1 and high-skill labor in country 2, and a decline in real income for high-skill labor in country 1 and low-skill labor in country 2. This is a simple version of familiar results on the effects of trade on income distribution.

At the same time, trade is beneficial for each country as a whole. In this model, the ratio of real national income with trade to real national income in autarky is a measure of aggregate gains from trade:[4]

$$\frac{GNP_1^T}{GNP_1^A} = \frac{1}{2}\left[\left(\frac{HL_1}{H_1 L}\right)^{1/2} + \left(\frac{LH_1}{L_1 H}\right)^{1/2}\right]$$

$$\frac{GNP_2^T}{GNP_2^A} = \frac{1}{2}\left[\left(\frac{HL_2}{H_2 L}\right)^{1/2} + \left(\frac{LH_2}{L_2 H}\right)^{1/2}\right] \tag{12}$$

The right-hand side of equations 12 is larger than 1 in both countries as long as relative factors' endowments in 1 and 2 are different, that is, as long as $L_1/H_1 \neq L/H$, which is the assumption of equation 1.

Finally, it is easy to show that the relative increase in real national income—and therefore aggregate gains from trade—is larger in country 1 than in country 2 if the distribution of low-skill labor between the two countries is more balanced than the distribution of high-skill labor, that is, if

$$\frac{|L_1 - L_2|}{L} < \frac{|H_2 - H_1|}{H} \tag{13}$$

Notice that one implication of equation 13 is that the economy of country 1 is smaller than the economy of country 2.

3.3.2 Public Goods and Standards

Assume now that in both countries individuals' utility depends not only on consumption of the two private goods, but also on the availability of a public good, representing, for example, a clean environment or a safe workplace:

$$U_1 = xzG_1^g \qquad U_2 = xzG_2^g \tag{14}$$

where G_1 is the amount of public good available to a citizen of country 1, and g is a parameter representing the relative importance of the public good.[5]

The standards are the regulations that individuals impose on themselves to achieve the level of public good they desire. These regulations cost resources, either directly (the higher cost of "clean" technologies) or indirectly, when constraining the set of possible activities (only specific production procedures are allowed). A simple way of modeling the standards, therefore, is to see them as taxes collecting resources from producers, resources that are then transformed into the public good. More precisely, assume that the public good is produced from the two private goods X and Z, and the taxes required to finance this production are sustained by firms. For example, suppose that firms must support the cost of employing clean or safe production processes, processes requiring new machines that are themselves produced by combining the low-tech and the high-tech goods in the appropriate proportions. In this formulation, the standards are the taxes faced by producers.

To keep matters as transparent as possible, I assume that each firm has to pay a nominal tax t per worker employed.[6] All firms in one country face the same tax. Total tax revenues in each country are then proportional to total employment:

$$T_1 = t_1(L_1 + H_1) \qquad T_2 = t_2(L_2 + H_2) \tag{15}$$

where T_1 are total taxes in country 1, and t_1 is the nominal tax per worker imposed on all firms in country 1 (the standard).

In both countries, the public good is produced from the two private goods according to the technology:

$$G = X_G Z_G \tag{16}$$

This formulation implies that total tax revenues are equally spent on purchases of each of the two final goods, and therefore that the presence of the public good does not increase the relative demand for one good and for the services of one factor. This is the crucial assumption that guarantees that the public good does not distort allocations and trade flows. It is certainly special, but the important point is that, as we will see, this condition is independent of whether standards do or do not differ between the two economies.

Since firms are taxed per worker, the two final goods are now priced according to

$$p_{X1} = (w_{L1} + t_1)/a \qquad p_{Z1} = (w_{H1} + t_1)/b$$

$$p_{X2} = (w_{L2} + t_2)/a \qquad p_{Z2} = (w_{H2} + t_2)/b \tag{17}$$

Because tax revenues are spent equally on the two goods, relative prices do not depend on the standards: as before they are determined by the relative supplies of the two factors. Once again, equilibrium prices are given by equations 6 in autarky, and by equation 8 when trade is opened. *Because relative prices do not depend on the standards, the level of the standard in one country has no effect on the other country.* Although it is financed through taxes on firms that affect the absolute level of prices, the standard has no influence on trade, and therefore on the welfare effects from opening the borders.

Within each country, equation 14 is such that each individual finds optimal a tax on firms equal to a fraction g of his income. In the case of low-skill workers in country 1, for example,

$$t_{L1}^* = g w_{L1} \tag{18}$$

where the asterisk denotes the preferred choice.

The same result holds for all other groups. Notice that nothing has been said about international trade: the statement remains true whether trade is open or not. Of course, the trade regime determines relative prices; therefore, real incomes and the physical amount of resources that individuals want to devote to the public good are affected by international trade. But the proportionality between income and desired taxes remains constant. It implies that the effect of trade on the standard can be traced simply and exactly by looking at the effect of trade on real incomes.

In real terms, using as deflator the price index P, we obtain

$$\tau_{L1}^A = g'(abH_1/L_1)^{1/2} \qquad \tau_{H1}^A = g'(abL_1/H_1)^{1/2}$$
$$\tau_{L2}^A = g'(abH_2/L_2)^{1/2} \qquad \tau_{H2}^A = g'(abL_2/H_2)^{1/2} \tag{19}$$

in autarky, and

$$\tau_L^T = g'(abH/L)^{1/2} \qquad \tau_H^T = g'(abL/H)^{1/2} \tag{20}$$

with trade, where τ_{L1} is the real tax per worker that low-skill labor in country 1 wants domestic firms to face, and g' equals $g/(1+g)$.[7]

3.3.3 First Results

Although the setup is extremely simplified, several interesting results follow immediately from the observations we have just made.

(1) Since desired standards are proportional to income, there is in general no agreement about optimal standards not only across countries, but also within each country. This statement is true whether in autarky or with

free trade. The sector that commands higher income also desires higher standards. If we assume that in both countries there are fewer high-skill workers than low-skill workers (although more so in country 1 than in country 2), then it is always true that the two groups consistently disagree, with low-skill workers pressing for lower standards, and high-skill workers pressing for higher standards.[8]

(2) However, in country 1 the disagreement is reduced by opening trade: trade increases the level of standards desired by low-skill workers, while reducing that desired by high-skill workers. On the contrary, trade increases the disagreement in country 2, where low-skill workers will now press for lower standards, and high-skill workers for higher ones.

Since the two groups disagree, it is not clear which view will prevail, and we cannot say whether trade will necessarily act to increase or reduce standards. We can, however, make a few more limited statements.

(3) Suppose first that standards are decided democratically (i.e., following the preferences of the majority). Then, if high-skill workers are everywhere fewer than low-skill workers, the latter will decide in both countries. In this case, standards in autarky are higher in country 2 than in country 1, and they become identical when trade is opened: trade raises standards in country 1 and lowers them in country 2. On the other hand, if high-skill workers are the majority in country 2, then trade will increase standards in both countries. In this case, standards are higher in country 2 than in country 1 both in autarky and in free trade. However trade decreases the disparity between the two national standards if country 1's national income is smaller than country 2's.

(4) Because desired standards depend on income alone, we can use directly traditional welfare results from trade theory. In particular: (a) Although in each country trade raises desired standards for one group and lowers them for the other, there exists a feasible transfer of income between the two groups such that when trade is opened, everybody desires standards that are at least as high as those he desired in autarky. (b) Suppose that standards must be decided unanimously, with the two groups within each country exchanging income transfers to influence each other's preferences. Then in both countries unanimity will be reached around higher standards when trade is open than in autarky. In addition, if country 1's national income is smaller than country 2's, then unanimity standards are always higher in country 2, but the disparity is reduced by trade.[9]

(5) Because standards do not affect relative prices, in this model countries do not have any (economic) interest in the standards adopted abroad.

Nevertheless, suppose that country 2 insisted on its own standards being adopted everywhere as precondition for opening trade. Even this simple model shows the fundamental problems: First, it is possible that country 1 would find the required standards too unpopular to be able to adopt them. In this case trade would not take place and both countries would be worse off than they could have been. Second, and more interesting, country 2 would lock itself into standards that it will then find undesirable once trade is open. I expect that in general both conclusions will continue to hold in more realistic and richer models.

(6) Suppose now that together with the opening of trade, migration becomes a possibility. If we assume that the number of individuals is sufficiently large, then each of them can ignore the effect of his move on the chosen standard. Suppose that the standard is decided by low-skill workers everywhere. Then when trade is open, prices, incomes, and standards are equalized in the two countries: the only difference between the two economies is the size of their populations, and therefore the amount of public good available to their citizens. Let us assume that the population of country 2 is larger than the population of country 1. Then citizens of country 1 will continue to migrate to country 2, until the difference disappears. Suppose now that the public good is decided by low-skill workers in country 1 and high-skill workers in country 2. Then high-skill workers from country 1 will certainly migrate, since by doing so they benefit both from preferred higher taxes per worker and from the economies of scale inherent in the production of the public good. The only equilibrium where two separate countries continue to exist and where they are not identical is provided by the case of complete segregation: all low-skill workers are concentrated in one country, and all high-skill workers in the other. And in this model even this equilibrium requires some congestion in the enjoyment of the public good. Of course, the specific conclusion depends on the model studied in this paper. But its flavor is more general: as long as the economic size of two countries is very different, if there are economies of scale in the provision of the public good, migration toward the richer country is likely to continue. In the short run at least, the opening of trade per se will not be sufficient to modify this fact.[10]

While I find most of the preceding results compelling, some of them are implausible if the analysis is applied to countries at different stages of development. The conclusion that trade alone will suffice to equalize incomes (and therefore standards) across the two countries seems much too strong. The statement that in autarky income is highest (and so are desired standards) for the high-skill workers in country 1 is empirically false. Finally, the prediction that once trade is opened, higher standards in one country necessarily imply lower disposable incomes for its citizens seems unconvincing. These three features of the model all depend on a single assumption: we have stated that technologies are identical in the two countries, which implies that factors productivity is identical. But if the two economies differ quite radically in their development, the assumption is inappropriate: even if technologies can be replicated, other elements ignored by the model—infrastructure, ease of communication, predictability of the legal regime—are likely to create a more productive environment in the more developed country. In the next section I study the implications of different productivities.

3.3.4 Different Productivities

Suppose now that productivity of both factors is higher in country 2 than in country 1. Technologies in the two countries are described by

$$X_1 = aL_1 \qquad Z_1 = bH_1$$
$$X_2 = \phi aL_2 \qquad Z_2 = \phi bH_2 \tag{21}$$

where ϕ is larger than 1. For simplicity, I have assumed that productivity in country 2 is higher by the same proportion in both sectors, but the important point is only that productivity differences do not alter the comparative advantage of the two countries. It is still the case that country 2 is relatively more efficient in the production of good Z, and country 1 in the production of good X.

Relative prices of the two goods in autarky are again given by equations 6, but when trade is opened the relative price in both countries becomes

$$\frac{p_X}{p_Z} = \frac{b(H_1 + \phi H_2)}{a(L_1 + \phi L_2)} \tag{22}$$

Since

$$\frac{H_1 + \phi H_2}{L_1 + \phi L_2} > \frac{H}{L} \tag{23}$$

the relative price of good X with free trade is higher now than it was when the two countries had equal productivities: in other words, trade causes a larger decline in the price of good Z in country 1, and a smaller decline in the price of good X in country 2. The larger is ϕ, the productivity advantage of country 2, the closer the after-trade price approaches country 2's autarky price.

It remains true that each factor considers optimal a nominal tax on firms equal to a fraction g of his income, but incomes are now higher for the more productive factors located in country 2. In autarky, desired real standards are

$$\tau_{L1}^A = g'(abH_1/L_1)^{1/2} \qquad \tau_{H1}^A = g'(abL_1/H_1)^{1/2}$$

$$\tau_{L2}^A = \phi g'(abH_2/L_2)^{1/2} \qquad \tau_{H2}^A = \phi g'(abL_2/H_2)^{1/2}$$

(24)

And with trade

$$\tau_{L1} = g'\left(ab\frac{H_1 + \phi H_2}{L_1 + \phi L_2}\right)^{1/2} \qquad \tau_{H1} = g'\left(ab\frac{L_1 + \phi L_2}{H_1 + \phi H_2}\right)^{1/2}$$

$$\tau_{L2} = \phi g'\left(ab\frac{H_1 + \phi H_2}{L_1 + \phi L_2}\right)^{1/2} \qquad \tau_{H2} = \phi g'\left(ab\frac{L_1 + \phi L_2}{H_1 + \phi H_2}\right)^{1/2}$$

(25)

All the results discussed before remain true in this case. The most important new aspect is that, as mentioned previously, the trade equilibrium is closer to country 2's autarky equilibrium. This fact has two main implications. First, aggregate gains from trade are now smaller in country 2 and larger in country 1. If we require unanimous agreement over standards in each country, then standards will increase with trade everywhere, but they will do so more than before in country 1, and less than before in country 2. Therefore, the difference in productivity gives trade a larger role in reducing disparities in standards.

Second, because the effects of trade are now smaller in country 2 than in country 1, the changes in each group's preferences over standards are also less pronounced in 2 than in 1. If standards are decided democratically and low-skill workers are everywhere more numerous than high-skill workers, then, as before, standards will rise in 1 and fall in 2, but they will rise by more than before in 1, and fall by less than before in 2: standards now converge toward a higher level. Finally, although standards do not become identical in the two countries, it can be shown that trade reduces the absolute distance between them by more now than in the case of equal productivities.

3.3.5   Increasing Returns

It has been argued that a more realistic picture of the effects of trade requires the recognition that markets are not competitive, and technologies are not characterized by constant returns to scale (see, for example, Helpman and Krugman, 1985). In the specific case of NAFTA, researchers have found that ignoring scale economies leads to underestimating the benefits from the agreement (see the review by Brown in Lustig, Bosworth, and Lawrence, 1992). Our framework can be generalized to allow for increasing returns to scale and imperfect competition.

In particular, a plausible assumption is that the high-skill sector consists of a number of differentiated products, each of which is produced in a regime of monopolistic competition by firms whose technology presents increasing returns to scale. Different varieties of the good are imperfect substitutes for one another, creating some scope for monopolistic behavior on the part of each producer. Products in the low-skill sector, on the other hand, are homogeneous and compete directly with one another.

The solution of the model is described in the Appendix, but the results can be easily summarized. Imperfect competition increases the price of high-tech goods and reduces the value of real incomes and the amount of real resources that consumers want to devote to the public good. However, from the point of view of the effect of trade on desired standards, we reach exactly the same results discussed in section 3.3.4. The only difference emerges if the economies of scale are steeper in the more productive country, country 2. In this case, it becomes possible for both factors to see their real incomes rise in response to trade in country 1 and fall in country 2, and therefore for everybody to want higher standards in country 1 and lower standards in country 2.[11] For our purposes, the important result is that for any decision-making mechanism, standards' convergence is enhanced. If different productivities lead to steeper economies to scale in country 2, and if imperfect competition affects primarily the high-skill labor sector and results in the existence of differentiated products, then trade will lead to larger convergence of standards.

3.4   Harmonization of Standards through Coalition Formation

3.4.1   Standards and the Theory of Clubs

In the model described so far, standards are expressed by national coalitions, and they are instrumental in providing public goods that are enjoyed strictly within the borders of each country. This formulation is in line with the traditional view of standards as government regulations, homogeneous within a country, but not extending beyond its boundaries.

If standards are identified with public goods that extend over a specific geographical area, then they can be analyzed with the tools of local public goods theory. As in the study by Wilson in this volume (Chapter 10), the "country" assumes a precise geographical meaning, and the value of the standards should then be capitalized in the price of land. The approach is appropriate to the study of public goods that must be physically located near the consumers—environmental regulations, for example.

However, there are other standards that directly affect individuals that are distant from the place of production. Standards for children's toys, for example, or restrictions on content and labeling for foodstuffs, are important to consumers of these goods, independently of their location. The knowledge that a given product has not been produced employing child labor may increase a consumer's utility even if the consumer does not live in the community directly affected by the regulation. In these cases, the price of land at the place of production may capitalize only very imperfectly the value of the standard, and the best characterization of the public good need not be geographical.

In fact, if standards take the form of specialized regulations, each targeting a specific good in a large spectrum of different products, then we can suggest a different perspective. Standards may be linked to public goods that are defined not in physical space, but in economic space: the standards we consume may depend more on the products that we buy than on the place where we live. If this assumption is correct, the natural unit of analysis ceases to be the geographical region with its physical borders and becomes the coalition of producers of similar goods sharing the same standard. If the standard is adopted voluntarily or if government regulation relies on private agents and industry representatives for the development of the standard, then we can think of these coalitions as voluntary. At least in principle, their members can be scattered in different places: the identification of the country as the natural realm of the standard is not automatic any longer, and we must allow for the possibility of voluntary coalitions forming within or across national borders.

A natural implication follows. If the coalitions have flexible borders, then in general their composition will change in response to changes in economic structure—for example, in response to the opening of markets. Section 3.3 stressed that standards are endogenous and are likely to respond to the expansion of trade. The rest of the chapter studies the statement that the coalitions that demand the standards are themselves affected by trade.

The distinction between geographical space and economic space is at the heart of the distinction between the theory of local public goods and the theory of clubs (see, for example, Scotchmer, 1993). When regulations and standards are appropriately described as lacking an inherent geographical character, then the theory of clubs gives us the most relevant conceptual tools. In sections 3.4.2 and 3.4.3, I describe two simple models that use principles from the theory of clubs to study more rigorously the intuitive observations made here.

3.4.2   A Model with Endogenous Markets and Clubs

Many discussions about harmonization begin from an unfocused feeling that firms competing in the same market should share the same rules. If firms belong to a unique market, they should also be members of a unique club. Casella and Feinstein (1990) address the question through a model where the conceptual difference between market and club is kept rigorously clean and agents are free to choose which market and which club they want to join.

The economy is formed by a continuum of individuals of different types distributed uniformly along a line. Each individual belongs to two institutions: a market, where he is matched with a partner, and a club, where a public good is chosen, financed, and provided to all members. Think of the public good as a standard guaranteeing the quality of the individual's endowment (for example, the minimum required education level if the endowment is human capital; or restrictions on a prior production process, if the endowment is a physical good). In the market, the return from each match depends on the distance between the two partners—a stylized representation of the difference between them and thus of traditional gains from trade—and on the public good the partners have access to. Because a larger public good implies higher quality for the two endowments, it raises the pretax return from all matches. But in addition the level of the public good determines the optimal distance between partners: a higher standard makes the endowments more flexible (as in the case of education) or more reliable (as in the case of production standards), allowing matches between more distant partners—partners too dissimilar to monitor each other effectively. When two partners from two different clubs are matched in the market, they can choose which of the two standards available to them they want to use, but suffer a fixed transaction cost. The transaction cost represents the cost of learning about the other trader's standards. Notice that while the partnership is most easily thought of as a joint venture in production, it can represent a more general transaction, including a simple exchange between a buyer and a seller. The main deviation from traditional assumptions is in representing the exchange as bilateral and decentralized (as for example in Diamond, 1982) instead of being mediated through a centralized market and a price system.

In the club, all members vote on the choice of the standard, which is decided through majority rule, and all members sustain the same lump-sum cost necessary to finance its adoption. The standard is available only to the members of the club or to their partners in production, and every individual must belong to a club. There is free entry in both markets and clubs.

Both a market and a club are sets of traders who willingly group themselves for the specific purposes of the two institutions. Each is represented by a segment, or a collection of disjointed segments, of the line. The model puts no restriction on the composition of markets and clubs; in addition, any number of markets is allowed, while clubs are restricted, for simplicity, to be either two or one. In this model, standards are harmonized within a market when all members of the market choose to belong to a single club. The paper asks two questions: (1) Will harmonization occur in equilibrium, or will markets and clubs differ, so that individuals who plan to trade together still prefer different standards? (2) How do markets and clubs react to exogenous shocks to the productivity of the partnerships?

When matched to a partner with a cheaper standard, belonging to a club whose standard is more expensive is costly because of the higher taxes, because of the transaction costs, and because it provides to the partner a chance to free ride. Therefore, we would expect that individuals who belong to the same market will find it advantageous to belong also to the same club. The first result of the Casella and Feinstein paper is that such a conclusion does not necessarily happen. The main force against harmonization in this paper is the heterogeneity among the traders. Because traders have different endowments—because they occupy different position on the line—they have different preferences over the standard. So, for example, individuals specializing in more innovative activities may be willing to spend more time or more money in devising standards that are up-to-date and that insure compatibility. Or countries that specialize in activities that make intensive use of human capital and generate high value added may put a premium on—and be able to afford—a high level of education for their citizens.

Notice that the heterogeneity among the traders does not disappear as markets integrate. Even when all traders belong to a single market, their endowments differ; indeed their difference is exactly the reason they want to trade with one another. And as long as they differ, their demand for the standard will differ. There is no presumption that harmonization *must* occur. To see under what conditions it will occur, we turn to the second question.

One of the characteristics of economic development is a shift from small, local, personalized markets to markets that are larger and anonymous: the harvest ceases to be sold or exchanged among members of the same small village community and reaches the town; credit moves from being a form of coinsurance among relatives to a transaction with a bank operating on a much larger scale. In the model we are discussing, a simple way to capture development is through increases in an exogenous parameter that represents productivity and that, ceteris paribus, makes advantageous matches with more distant partners. As this process occurs, in equilibrium markets expand.

The change in clubs is more complex: for low or high values of the productivity parameter, traders who belong to the same market may choose to form either one or two different clubs; but for intermediate values of the productivity parameter the second club disappears. The reason can be found in the transaction costs: when productivity is low, transaction costs are important, and most traders (though not all) are willing to adopt the more expensive standard if a majority of the market does so. The lower likelihood of facing transaction costs compensates for the higher cost of the standard. When productivity is high, transaction costs become a minor issue, and individuals sort themselves between the two clubs according to their economic characteristics. Harmonization, however, *must* occur when productivity is in an intermediate range: transaction costs are not sufficiently important to compensate for the cost of the more expensive standard, but are still sufficiently high to prevent the optimal partition into two clubs.

When productivity is high, the partition into two clubs reflects different preferences over the standard. As can be expected, such a partition is optimal: although not everybody is better off than in the case of a single club, a majority of the traders are, and those who gain, gain enough to more than compensate the losers. On the other hand, at low productivity values the division into two clubs is wasteful. Although traders disagree on their preferred choice for the standard, the transaction costs are large, and these costs overshadow individuals' fundamental economic characteristics in determining the size and the composition of the two clubs.

Summarizing, the Casella and Feinstein paper studies the contemporaneous evolution of markets and clubs, in response to exogenous increases in productivity. It finds that markets respond by integrating, and as markets integrate, clubs initially integrate too. At still higher productivity levels, however, clubs divide again to accommodate the different preferences over the standard that still persist in a single market. The two main forces driving the results are heterogeneity among the economic agents and transaction costs. Harmonization is the unique equilibrium when transaction costs are high enough, relative to gross returns, to prevent a partition into two clubs that correctly reflects the needs of the traders, but not so high as to compensate the users of the more expensive standard for the difference in costs. Harmonization occurs in response to market integration, but possibly only for an intermediate range of productivity.

This model has two main strengths. First, it distinguishes clearly between the market and the club and allows both to form endogenously. Second, it begins a rigorous discussion of the interaction between them in a framework that recognizes the role of heterogeneity. It also has, in my opinion, three main weaknesses. Since it ignores the role of the price system in market allocations, the cost of having different standards is captured by the transaction costs, but not by the possible loss of competitiveness. The standard itself is not modeled in detail, and in particular the different tastes over *types* of standards are captured only roughly by disagreement over *levels*. Finally, the model allows each individual to choose the market and the club he wants to join, but it does not allow for the formation of coalitions who together decide to deviate. Since a club is a coalition that acts in a coordinated fashion, it is natural to allow groups of individuals to coordinate not only on the choice of standard but also on the preliminary decision of whether or not to form a separate coalition. In the next section, I discuss a second model that addresses these issues.

3.4.3   A Monopolistically Competitive Model with Endogenous Clubs

Imagine an economy where a continuum of individuals is distributed uniformly around a circle.[12] Each individual is endowed with one unit of a differentiated good, and his location on the circle represents the specific type of his endowment. All individuals have the same tastes and put a premium on being able to diversify their consumption (as in Dixit and

Stiglitz, 1977). They will consume all varieties of the good available on the market, each according to its own price.

As in an Italian town, all exchanges take place in the piazza, located at the center of the circle. To arrive there, consumers need roads, which are costly to build but can be shared by as many users as desired. However, individuals face transport costs in moving from their specific location to the entrance of the road. Since building a road is costly, it is not desirable for each agent to build his own, but since using a road that is too far away is also costly, in general more than one road will be built. Individuals will form clubs: all members of the club will share the cost of the road and will be allowed its use, and all members will vote over the location of the road. As in the previous model, the decision is taken through majority rule. The model addresses the following two questions: (1) What is the number and the location of the clubs formed in equilibrium, as a function of the size of the circle? (2) Is the equilibrium optimal; that is, does it replicate the choice of a social planner?

Before discussing the answers to these questions, notice that although the story just told uses spatial terms—roads, location, transport costs—it is meant as a simple concrete representation of a more general problem. As discussed earlier, space in these models should be interpreted as economic space: the road, necessary to reach the market and located as close as possible to an individual's position on the circle, stands for a public good that is necessary for completing market transactions but that should be tailored to the specific variety of the private good—a technical standard, for example. The tax cost of building one's own road is the cost of creating too many different standards, a cost that includes the resources devoted to developing the standards but also the loss of compatibility and of learning about the other standards present in the market.

Second, contrary to the previous model, the market now is exogenous. As before, its size is represented by the mass of different varieties of private goods that are exchanged in private transactions, but such mass is now given: it is the circumference of the circle, and there is always a unique market. The model studies the impact of market size on the formation of clubs, but ignores the reverse effect, from the formation of clubs to the size and composition of markets.

The only stable partition into clubs that can emerge in equilibrium is given by identical, continuous segments of the circumference. Within each club, the road will be located exactly in the middle. Since all clubs have identical size, per capita taxes are the same in all of them. Since the roads are located in the middle of each club, individuals at the border between two clubs are equidistant from the clubs' roads and thus indifferent between joining either one, while all individuals in the interior of a club are strictly closer to that club's road than to any other and thus strictly prefer that club to any other.

For a single individual, deviation is not profitable independently of the number of clubs. It is natural to ask, however, what number of clubs would be chosen by a central planner and what number would be chosen in the decentralized equilibrium if individuals could communicate and agree on joint deviations.

The main result of the model is that under reasonable assumptions about the public good technology, the number of clubs should increase as the size of the market increases. The two elements whose trade-off determines the result are taxes, on one side, and the costs of an inappropriate standard, on the other. For given market size, an increase in the number of clubs means that each club is smaller and therefore that per capita taxes are higher, but the standard is better tailored, on average, to the needs of the club members. Consider now an increase in the size of the market—that is, in the size of the circle—for given number of clubs. Since the radius of the circle is larger, the road is longer and thus, in general, more expensive: the standards required for transactions in a more diverse market are likely to be more sophisticated and costly. At the same time, each club's size is also larger, and thus the standard in each club is on average less precisely tuned to the needs of the members. Because each club's size rises, the higher cost of the standard is shared over more taxpayers, and the first effect is mitigated. But not so the second: for a sufficiently large increase in market size the optimal number of clubs must increase. The very fact that the standard is a public good implies that its costs are shared, but the loss from an inappropriate standard is borne separately by each individual trader.

Notice that in this model a standard that is not well tailored to the needs of a trader reduces his supply to the market and his purchasing power. But the decreased supply is also reflected in the higher relative price, which negatively affects everyone else too: everybody has an interest in the appropriate standards being available. This is a general point: if standards play a positive role in market transactions, if they respond to a well-defined demand, then suboptimal choices that economize on the costs will be reflected in market inefficiencies.

In the absence of a central planner, the decentralized equilibrium with coordinated deviations yields similar but not identical results. While it remains true that an increase in market size eventually triggers an increase in the number of clubs, the range of market sizes for which a given number of clubs is an equilibrium is larger than in the case of a central planner. This statement implies that there may be too many or too few clubs. The possible suboptimality of decentralized choices is a recurrent preoccupation of the literature on technical standards (see, for example, Dybvig and Spatt, 1983; Farrell and Saloner, 1985). For our purposes, the suboptimality implies that there may be a role for centralized, mandated action, but still in this diverse world there is no case for harmonization unless the market is sufficiently small.[13]

In the previous model, we found that harmonization could be an intermediate stage between two regimes with multiple clubs. However, multiple clubs were suboptimal when productivity was low and the optimal size of the market was small. These conclusions reappear in the present model. As the central planner's results make clear, harmonization is again desirable only when the market is small and relatively homogeneous. The results of the decentralized equilibrium, however, also show that multiple clubs can emerge too early and be followed by a phase of harmonization. Although the two models are quite different, they reach similar conclusions because both take as their starting points the same main assumptions: standards play a role in insuring the good functioning of private markets; individuals trade because they are heterogeneous; and heterogeneous individuals have different opinions over ideal standards, opinions that are shaped by their different roles in the market.

An important final comment: Notice that in this model an increase in the number of clubs is not a simple subdivision of the previous coalitions. It is a change in all borders across clubs: groups previously belonging to two different clubs are joined in a new coalition, and the composition of all others adjusts in response. The evolution of trade associations, the jurisdictional disputes among trade unions, and the changing formation of associations developing voluntary technical standards are examples of the type of phenomena studied by the model, and indeed they follow the pattern of combinations and breakups suggested by the theory. An analysis that takes as given the composition and the size of the group sharing the standard misses the possibilities for recombination that the model suggests and that reality appears to bear out. The important question at this stage becomes the empirical relevance of these changing, flexible alliances, and I discuss it in the next section.

3.4.4   The Empirical Relevance of Voluntary Standards

Most discussions on the importance of standards as barriers to trade assume implicitly that standards are imposed through government laws.

Agreements on harmonization or on mutual recognition can then come only in the form of international accords among governments. The models we have just discussed propose an alternative: suppose standards were developed voluntarily by private groups—for example, to insure the advantages of compatibility, or to benefit from a uniform system of certification. Could increased trade lead to the development of voluntary standards by international coalitions of producers, fostering harmonization not through a policy imposed from the top, but simply through the recognition of similar needs for producers in the same industry? If we accept the description of standards as public goods provided by voluntary clubs, we are led to the conclusion that clubs will change composition in response to the expansion of trade. Since the new clubs will include members of different previous coalitions, it is tempting to think of the new clubs as international.[14]

In this section, I focus on technical standards and discuss the extent to which these standards are developed by private groups of industry representatives and the weight these voluntary standards are given in government regulations. Finding that private groups play a large role in issuing standards would certainly not mean that standards are used efficiently, or that they do not fulfill protectionist purposes. However, it would mean that the assumption of flexible coalitions made in the two models just discussed is appropriate, and that the scope for a reshuffling of these coalitions as economic conditions change—as trade increases, for example— exists in reality.

The organization of process of standardization varies widely across countries. In general, regulations concerning safety, health, and the environment are issued by the government. Often, however, technical standards, including at times the specific measures that satisfy the objectives of the government regulations, are left to private organizations and publicized as voluntary standards. One important innovation occurring everywhere in recent years is the increased relative importance of voluntary standards: "Recent trends in all [OECD] countries seem to converge towards a greater emphasis on self-regulation and non-mandatory standards.... [This] introduces an element of flexibility into national safety systems which may become more open to international harmonization" (OECD, 1991, p. 55).

The United States is remarkable for the high decentralization of its system of standards. In 1984 a census of organizations involved in the development of standards counted 750 different organizations, of which 420 were nongovernmental (Global Engineering Documents, 1986). In 1991 the number of voluntary organizations had risen to 600 (UNIDO,

1991). According to the OECD, in 1991 the number of standards developed by voluntary organizations in the United States was about 35,000, compared to approximately 55,000 to 60,000 standards developed by governmental bodies (OECD, 1991). The American National Standards Institute (ANSI) coordinates private standards, approves standards as American National Standards and represents the United States in international standards organization. In practice, however, only about one-half of all private standards developers participate in the ANSI system, and several who do not participate are as well-known internationally as ANSI. The largest private standards organization is the American Society of Testing, which has issued about 8,500 widely recognized standards, roughly the same number as those recognized by ANSI (OECD, 1991).

In the United States as everywhere the importance of private standards developers is rising: between 1973 and 1984, for example, "the number of non-government standards has been increasing at an average rate of about 3.5 percent per year; at the same time [the main standards-setting government agencies] are canceling as many standards as they are creating" (Global Engineering Documents, 1986). The pattern has prevailed since the inception of the U.S. system of standards: "Although the government provided at the turn of the century the first impetus for national standards, it gradually relinquished much of this responsibility to private standards setting organizations" (U.S. Congress, 1992). The federal government itself has been encouraged to rely on private standards, both domestic and international, in its procurement and regulatory activities (Office of Management and Budget, 1982).

The large role played by private standards developers has predictably raised concerns of antitrust violations. In 1983 the Federal Trade Commission noted that private firms provide the bulk of the funds necessary for the development of private standards (FTC, 1983). These funds are not negligible: in 1977, for example, it was estimated that they amounted to roughly half a billion dollars annually (U.S. Department of Commerce, 1977). The FTC discussed the potential to use standards and certification procedures to control the market and expressed its concerns in view of the likelihood that "the use of private standards as a substitute for federal government regulation [will] become even more extensive in the future" (FTC, 1983, p. 35). The report described various examples of standards decisions deemed illegal by the courts[15] and concluded with recommendations for improving procedural practices in standards organizations. I have found no evidence, however, that the potential for antitrust litigation has significantly slowed the trend toward private standards.

Even in those areas where government regulation is considered necessary to guarantee consumers' protection, the role of private standards
developers has been important and is expanding. For example, since 1973
issues involving product safety have been the responsibility of the United
States Consumer Product Safety Commission (CPSC).[16] But the CPSC has
consistently encouraged the development of voluntary standards: by 1991
it had issued 36 mandatory standards and participated in the development
of more than 100 voluntary standards (OECD, 1991). In 1981, amendments introduced by Congress in the Consumer Product Safety Act required the commission to defer to a voluntary standard if such a standard
is being developed by industry. The commission has the authority to
convert a voluntary standard into a mandatory one if it deems that compliance is unsatisfactory.

Although the extent of decentralization of the United States system is
unique, the trend toward voluntary standards is not. In Germany, for
example, the Deutsches Institut für Normung (DIN) coordinates all standards activity not developed by the government. Its activity has been
steadily increasing in recent years: DIN standards in progress have risen
from 12,000 in 1984 to 17,000 in 1988, and they have been mostly
concentrated in new technologies, food and health, and safety rules, exactly the fields where standards have traditionally been provided by the
government (UNIDO, 1991).

Similarly, increased cooperation between government bodies and private organizations is particularly striking in the United States, but is becoming the dominant model through which regulation is developed in
other parts of the world as well. In Sweden and in Australia, for example,
the government issues general guidelines but relies on the voluntary
adoption of appropriate product specifications by industry. In a more formalized approach, in Germany, France, and the United Kingdom, the government has concluded an agreement with the main private organization
and refers to the privately developed standards in regulations (OECD,
1991). This line is also followed in the "New Approach" described by the
1985 EC Council resolution "Technical Harmonization of Standards": products with potential health, safety, or environmental implications are to be
regulated by the Commission. The Commission provides general directives, while the European standardization bodies (CEN, CENELEC, and
ETSI) develop the detailed technical standards. Although the technical
standards are not mandatory, national authorities are obliged to recognize
products developed according to these standards as satisfying national
requirements, until there is proof to the contrary.

Notice that while the agreement is still between national states—it is an EC Council resolution—the new standards are developed by international technical committees organized by industry. Coupled with the principle of "mutual recognition" for products not regulated by the Commission, the "New Approach" creates the conditions that could lead to the development of standards through voluntary international coalitions following industry lines. In Germany, for example, in 1991, only 30 percent of DIN resources were spent on the development of national standards (compared to 60 percent in 1984 and 40 percent in 1988); 35 percent of resources were spent on work within CEN and CENELEC (compared to 10 percent in 1984 and 25 percent in 1988), and 30 percent on international non-European standards (compared to 25 percent in 1984 and 30 percent in 1988) (UNIDO, 1991). Germany has a leading role in the development of European standards, but a similar trend toward internationalization can be seen in the other major European countries.[17]

In the model described in the previous section, clubs are purely voluntary, and their number multiplies as the market expands because the increase in the variety of goods makes necessary a more finely tuned targeting of the public good. In the real world, the institutions that more closely resembles the assumptions of the model are the International Organization for Standardization (ISO) and its affiliate, the International Electrotechnical Commission (IEC). They are private, voluntary, non-governmental organizations whose members are the national standards institutes of different countries and whose support comes from contributions by private industry and national standards organizations.

The two institutions are organized in technical committees devoted to specific areas. Over time, the number of technical committees has been increasing, reflecting the need for new standards as technology progresses: in 1967, ISO had 122 technical committees; in 1973, 135; in 1989, 164. A similar increase has taken place in IEC. However, the reorganization of the committees is more complex than a pure increase in number: as new technologies arise and evolve, the committees expand, split, and merge as in the theoretical model. The evolution of the committee devoted to computer standards is instructive. In 1960, Technical Committee 97 was created, in charge of standardization for computers and computer systems. In 1981, TC95 (office machinery) merged with TC97. In 1983, two TC97 subcommittees (SC8, numerical control of machines, and SC9, programming languages for numerical control) merged to create a new technical committee, TC184 (industrial automation systems). In 1984, the scope of TC97 was expanded to "information processing systems," and three new groups of subcommittees were formed (application elements, equipment and media, and systems). In 1987, TC97 was merged with two IEC committees, to become Joint Technical Committee 1 (JTC1). A fourth group of subcommittees (systems support) was added to the existing three. While these developments were taking place, the number of members of the two institutions was also growing: in 1973, ISO counted 67 member countries; in 1989, ISO had 91 members, and IEC 42.

The two organizations issue recommendations, but no member country is obliged to enforce them. How much weight do they exert on national standards? It is easy to find quotations stating, for example, that "with the expansion of international trade, the actions of ISO and IEC are becoming increasingly influential" (Crane, 1979, p. 29), but more difficult to find precise information. In 1990 the OECD concluded three case studies of international safety requirements in toys, child-resistant closures, and flammability requirements for upholstered furniture (OECD, 1991). For upholstered furniture, it found that, out of 18 countries participating in the study, only the United Kingdom and the state of California had mandatory requirements. Among the other countries, if a standard was referred to at all it was the ISO standard on textile flammability. In the case of child-resistant containers, the elaboration of the ISO standard was found to have had a very large impact, with 13 countries having adopted it or being on the verge of doing so. In the case of toys, work on an ISO standard was still not concluded, but the OECD appeared to believe that it would fulfill the role of common reference in the maze of national standards that had developed.[18]

In conclusion, the trend seems to be moving increasingly toward voluntary private standards, at least in the case of Western industrialized countries. There is also a parallel trend toward internationalization of standards, led by the European Union and confirmed by the expansion of international organizations like ISO and IEC. It is more difficult to say to what extent the two trends overlap, yielding increased influence to international voluntary organizations. It seems likely that such an influence is still limited, compared to the role of formal treaties among governments, but rapidly increasing.

3.5   Conclusions

This chapter has provided a survey of simple theoretical results on the interaction between free trade and the provision of standards. Its first, general conclusion is that, although standards can be used to distort trade, if policy makers are concerned about economic efficiency, then insistence on harmonization as precondition for free trade is incorrect on two grounds. The first reason is that there is no logical link between the efficiency of standards and their being equal or different across countries: identical standards may well be the inefficient result of a game between countries, just as different standards may simply reflect fundamental differences across economies that should be reflected in different regulations. The second reason is that standards are not fixed but evolve with economic conditions and change as allocations change. In particular, standards will be modified by the opening of trade. The chapter has studied in detail a plausible scenario where desired standards depend on the level of income, and it has shown how free trade is likely to lead standards to converge.

These observations derive directly from well-established results in international trade theory. Although we may debate how robust the results are to changes in assumptions, they are reasonably noncontroversial and constitute in my opinion the appropriate point of departure for understanding the economic relationship between standards and trade.

The second part of the chapter is less orthodox. Although we typically think of standards as national policies, in most industrialized countries there is a strong and growing trend toward voluntary, privately developed standards. If countries are not too dissimilar and coalitions expressing common interests can be formed across borders, there is no reason to think that these coalitions should be strictly national. The point is independent of whether standards developed by private groups are efficient or are used to insure and protect collusive behavior within an industry. Simply, if a group is formed in a world of open international markets, why wouldn't the group be international? The evidence supports the hypothesis that international private standards organizations are becoming more common and playing a larger role, although it is hard to tell how much real influence they have at this point.

If we can think of standards as developed by private coalitions, then opening trade will modify not only the standards but also the coalitions that express them. As markets change, groups will form and reorganize; as markets expand and become more heterogeneous, different coalitions will form across national borders, and their number will rise. Far from bringing uniformity, trade brings diversity, a diversity based not on political frontiers, but on economic variables, on technologies, on market roles.

APPENDIX

Increasing Returns

This appendix describes the solution of the simple model of section 3.3 when the high-tech sector Z is characterized by increasing returns to scale and monopolistic competition.

Following Dixit and Stiglitz (1977), utility functions are modified to capture the existence of differentiated products in sector Z:

$$U_1 = x\left(\sum_{i=1}^{n} z_{ic}^{\theta}\right)^{1/\theta} G_1^q \qquad U_2 = x\left(\sum_{i=1}^{n} z_{ic}^{\theta}\right)^{1/\theta} G_2^q \tag{26}$$

where z_{ic} is individual consumption of variety i of good Z. The parameter θ is assumed smaller than 1, representing the imperfect substitutability of the different varieties; the closer θ is to 1, the closer we return to the previous assumption of one homogeneous variety.

Similarly, the public good is now given by

$$G = X_G\left(\sum_{i=1}^{n} z_{iG}^{\theta}\right)^{1/\theta} \tag{27}$$

Technologies in sector X continue to be described by equation 21, reproduced here for convenience:

$$X_1 = aL_1 \qquad X_2 = \phi aL_2 \tag{21a}$$

while technologies in sector Z present increasing returns to scale. Call h_{1i} the amount of high-skill labor employed in the production of variety i in country 1. Production in sector Z is described by

$$z_{1i} = b(h_{1i} - F_1) \qquad z_{2i} = \phi b(h_{2i} - F_2) \tag{28}$$

where z_{1i} is the production of variety i in country 1, and F_1 are units of labor that must be employed in country 1 before any production can begin. In other words, the term F is meant to capture the existence of fixed costs and is the origin of the increasing returns. This general equilibrium model of imperfect competition is common in the literature and in particular has been used repeatedly by Paul Krugman (see, for example, Krugman, 1981).

Although competition in sector Z will not be perfect, free entry into the sector will insure zero profits in equilibrium.

As before, prices in sector X are given by

$$p_{X1} = (w_{L1} + t_1)/a \qquad p_{X2} = (w_{L2} + t_2)/(\phi a) \tag{17a}$$

In sector Z, the presence of the fixed costs insures that each firm specializes in one single variety. Firms choose prices so as to equate marginal revenues to marginal costs. For all varieties,

$$p_{Z1} = (w_{H1} + t_1)/(b\theta) \qquad p_{Z2} = (w_{H2} + t_2)/(\phi b\theta) \tag{29}$$

Since each firm makes zero profits, its scale of production is given by

$$z_{1i} = b\theta F_1/(1 - \theta) \qquad z_{2i} = \phi b\theta F_2/(1 - \theta) \tag{30}$$

Differences in the size of the high-skill labor force between the two countries are reflected in differences in the number of varieties produced:

$$n_1 = H_1(1 - \theta)/F_1 \qquad n_2 = H_2(1 - \theta)/F_2 \tag{31}$$

Finally, it remains true that each consumer considers optimal a tax per worker equal to a share g of his own income.

In autarky, we can look at an equilibrium where all varieties of the Z good produced within each country have the same price. Relative prices are given by

$$\frac{p_{X1}}{p_{Z1}} = \theta \frac{bH_1}{aL_1} \qquad \frac{p_{X2}}{p_{Z2}} = \theta \frac{bH_2}{aL_2} \tag{32}$$

and real taxes per worker deemed optimal by the various groups are

$$\tau_{L1}^A = g'(\theta abH_1/L_1)^{1/2} \qquad \tau_{H1}^A = g'(\theta abL_1/H_1)^{1/2}$$
$$\tau_{L2}^A = \phi g'(\theta abH_2/L_2)^{1/2} \qquad \tau_{H2}^A = \phi g'(\theta abL_2/H_2)^{1/2} \tag{33}$$

When trade is opened, the equilibrium depends on the assumption we want to make about fixed costs in sector Z in the two countries. Two alternatives seem plausible. The first one is to assume

$$F_2 = F_1/\phi \tag{34a}$$

In this case, reflecting the different productivity of the labor force, the amount of labor that must be employed before production can take place is proportionately smaller in country 2: all costs, fixed and variable, are smaller in country 2. If we make this assumption, equation 30 shows that the quantity of each variety produced in equilibrium is the same for all firms, whether located in country 1 or country 2. Therefore, there is an equilibrium with trade such that all varieties sell at the same price. The relative price between the two goods is given by

$$\frac{p_X}{p_Z} = \theta \frac{bH}{aL} \tag{35}$$

and real taxes per worker deemed optimal by the various groups are

$$\tau_{L1}^T = g'(\theta abH/L)^{1/2} \qquad \tau_{H1}^T = g'(\theta abL/H)^{1/2}$$
$$\tau_{L2}^T = \phi g'(\theta abH/L)^{1/2} \qquad \tau_{H2}^T = \phi g'(\theta abL/H)^{1/2} \tag{36}$$

Although imperfect competition in sector Z reduces the relative price of good X and the value of real incomes, from the point of view of the effect of trade on desired standards we reach exactly the same results discussed in section 3.3.4. Trade increases real incomes of low-skill workers in country 1 and high-skill workers in country 2, and therefore their desired standards increase. The opposite is true for low-skill workers in country 2 and high-skill workers in country 1. The larger is ϕ, the difference in productivity between country 2 and country 1, the closer the equilibrium with trade approaches country 2's autarky equilibrium. In both countries, trade raises national income, and therefore the standards around which unanimity could form also rise. Finally, under most decision-making mechanisms, trade will lead to convergence of standards. The more balanced is the distribution of low-skill labor between the two countries compared to the distribution of high-skill labor, and the more productive country 2 is compared to country 1, the greater will be the convergence of standards. As discussed in the text, the only important difference between the case of perfect competition and the scenario studied here is that now gains from trade are not summarized simply by real incomes. The presence of a larger number of varieties of good Z when trade is opened has an independent positive effect on utility.

A second possibility is to assume

$$F_2 = F_1 \tag{34b}$$

In this case, fixed costs are the same between the two countries, while variable costs are not. As shown in equation 30, the implication is that country 2 will produce a larger quantity of each variety in equilibrium and therefore will sell all its varieties at a lower price.

While good X will sell at the same price in both countries, the relative price of varieties of good Z is given by

$$p_{Z1}/p_{Z2} = \phi^{1-\theta} \tag{37}$$

implying

$$z_{2c} = \phi z_{1c} \tag{38}$$

and

$$w_{H2} + t_2 = \phi^\theta (w_{H1} + t_1) \tag{39}$$

The extent to which the higher productivity of country 2 is reflected in higher labor costs depends on the importance of scale economies in sector Z, as captured by the parameter θ. The closer θ is to 1, the closer we are to the equilibrium with perfect competition: labor costs reflect exactly the higher productivity, and all Z goods sell at the same price. However, the more important are economies of scale, and the closer θ is to 0, the cheaper are the varieties of good Z produced in country 2, the larger is the relative consumption of these varieties for all consumers, and the smaller is the difference in the total costs of high-skill workers in the two countries. In other words, the smaller is θ, the more protected high-skill workers in country 1 are from the competition of the more productive workers in country 2. Therefore, we can expect that the closer θ is to 0, the smaller will be the decline in their real incomes in response to the opening to trade.

With different prices for different varieties, the correct price deflator for sector Z is now given by

$$p_Z = \left(\frac{n_1 p_{Z1}^{-\theta/(1-\theta)} + n_2 p_{Z2}^{-\theta/(1-\theta)}}{n_1 + n_2} \right)^{-(1-\theta)/\theta} \tag{40}$$

When trade is open, the relative price is then

$$\frac{p_X}{p_Z} = \theta \frac{bH}{a(L_1 + \phi L_2)} \left(\frac{H_1 + \phi^\theta H_2}{H} \right)^{1/\theta} \tag{41}$$

and desired real taxes per worker are

$$\tau_{L1}^T = g' \left[\theta ab \frac{H}{L_1 + \phi L_2} \left(\frac{H_1 + \phi^\theta H_2}{H} \right)^{1/\theta} \right]^{1/2}$$

$$\tau_{H1}^T = g' \left[\theta ab \frac{H(L_1 + \phi L_2)}{(H_1 + \phi^\theta H_2)^2} \left(\frac{H_1 + \phi^\theta H_2}{H} \right)^{1/\theta} \right]^{1/2} \tag{42}$$

$$\tau_{L2}^T = \phi g' \left[\theta ab \frac{H}{L_1 + \phi L_2} \left(\frac{H_1 + \phi^\theta H_2}{H} \right)^{1/\theta} \right]^{1/2}$$

$$\tau_{H2}^T = \phi^\theta g' \left[\theta ab \frac{H(L_1 + \phi L_2)}{(H_1 + \phi^\theta H_2)^2} \left(\frac{H_1 + \phi^\theta H_2}{H} \right)^{1/\theta} \right]^{1/2}$$

It is easy to check that all equations tend to the solutions of section 3.3.4 as θ goes to 1. In addition, the effects of trade on desired standards also reduce to what we have found earlier if ϕ equals 1.

For θ and ϕ different from 1, however, the results are more complex. If θ is sufficiently low and ϕ sufficiently high, increasing returns provide relative protection from competition to sector Z in country 1. If θ is very low, trade offers country 1 the availability of new varieties of good Z produced relatively cheaply in country 2, without the need to make substantial cuts in domestic prices, and thus in incomes for domestic high-skill workers. The smaller decline in sector Z prices in country 2 negatively affects real incomes of all other groups, but the effect is too small to counterbalance the positive impact on low-skill workers in country 1 of larger relative demand for their services. Both high- and low-skill workers in country 1 may have higher incomes, while citizens of country 2 may face a decline in their real incomes. Therefore it is now possible for everybody to want higher standards in country 1, and lower standards in country 2. Standards convergence is enhanced.

NOTES

This chapter was prepared for the project on "Fairness Claims and Gains from Trade." I thank Jagdish Bhagwati for his careful comments and for the invitation to participate in the project; the participants in the meetings in Minneapolis (July 29–31, 1993) and in Washington (September 30–October 1, 1994), in particular Alvin Klevorick and T. N. Srinivasan, for their suggestions; Dani Rodrik for several interesting conversations; and Adriana Kugler at U.C. Berkeley for research assistance.

1. This interpretation is consistent with the one offered by Kindleberger (1983), although he calls "private" standards that were jointly consumed but privately provided. Within the literature on standards, North (1979) discusses the role of the state in promulgating standards, and Dybvig and Spatt (1983), Katz and Shapiro (1985), and Farrell and Saloner (1985) discuss the economic rationale for viewing standards as public goods that are often privately provided.

2. See Wilson (Chapter 10 in this volume).

3. Given the utility function in equation 4, the price index corresponds to the minimum cost of a bundle of goods yielding one unit of utility.

4. In this model, a country's GNP is a measure of the sum of utilities of its residents. Comparing real national incomes before and after trade is analogous to showing the existence of a feasible transfer from winners to losers that would compensate the latter for any loss from trade, while leaving the former still strictly better off.

5. An interesting model on the interaction between public goods provision and trade is studied in Clarida and Findlay (1991).

6. Taxing firms per worker employed is exactly identical to collecting lump-sum transfers on individuals.

7. Although it is always the case that the desired tax rate is a share g of income, since nominal prices depend on the tax, real incomes are now smaller than they were in the absence of public goods. Indeed, if a group obtains its optimal tax, then its realized real income equals a fraction $1/(1 + g)$ of its real return with zero taxes (equations 10 and 11). This explains the term g' in equations 19 and 20.

8. If firms were taxed in proportion to their total labor costs, rather than per worker employed, the disagreement would disappear. Taxing firms per worker seems more faithful to real-world practices, and of course the general point that trade affects the desired amount of resources devoted to the public good remains true in either case.

9. In this simple linear model, "unanimity" standards are equal to the average of the standards desired in a country, and to the choice of a central planner maximizing the weighted sum of (the square root of) individual utilities, using the size of each group as weight.

10. This conclusion has the same flavor as a more general result derived by Wilson (1987a, 1987b). Wilson has studied the effect of opening trade between identical regions that provide a public good to their residents, and where private goods are produced using land and labor in different intensities. While land is immobile, labor can migrate across regions. He finds that each region will specialize in the production of one of the private goods, and wages and the provision of the public good will differ across regions. Contrary to the conclusions derived earlier in the absence of factors mobility, when labor is allowed to migrate, trade leads regions to diverge. Notice, however, that the result does not depend on the movement of a small minority of workers, but on the possibility of massive migration until differences in well-being have been erased. In the case of countries with very large differences in per capita income, such as the United States and Mexico, migration is likely to be constrained, and the analysis in the text retains its validity. (Different estimates set Mexican GDP per capita between 12 and 25 percent of the U.S. level, depending on the choice of price deflator [Hufbauer and Schott, 1992; Summers and Heston, 1991], and provisions on free migration of labor between the two countries are conspicuously absent from the free-trade agreement.)

11. When the model is modified to allow for imperfect competition, gains from trade are not summarized simply by real incomes, and all consumers experience higher utility with trade than in autarky even when their incomes decline.

12. This section draws on Casella (1994a).

13. Two observations: First, the expansion of the market is represented in the model by an increase in the size of the circle and thus by an increase in the variety of goods present in the market. This approach is in line with much thinking on economic growth (among recent contributions see, for example, Romer, 1990; Lucas, 1993; Grossman and Helpman, 1991) and captures the intuition that growth—or market expansion through trade—is likely to be expansion not only in the scale but also in the range of products. In any case, the results of the model would remain identical if the exogenous change were an increase in each agent's endowment, for a given number of varieties. Second, note that coordination alone, in the usual sense of letting all agents plan their actions together, does not achieve the central planner's allocation in the absence of compensating transfers.

14. Since the models do not specify national borders (only club borders are defined), the conjecture cannot be phrased rigorously within the frameworks discussed here. For an effort in this direction, see Casella (1994b).

15. See for example, *Hydrolevel Corporation* v. *American Society of Mechanical Engineers*, 102 S.Ct. 1935, [1945 n.8], 1982.

16. With the exception of food, drugs and cosmetics, pesticides, tobacco, guns and ammunition, and means of transportation.

17. For example, between 1989 and 1990, the number of man-days devoted by the British Standards Institute to European work increased by more than 30 percent (U.S. Congress, 1992). In France in 1991 more than 60 percent of the standards endorsed by the Association Française de la Normalisation had international or European origin (UNIDO, 1991).

18. It is interesting to note that even in the presence of different national standards, the OECD was unable to find evidence of impediments to trade.

REFERENCES

Buchanan, J. M. 1965. "An economic theory of clubs." *Economica*, 32:1–14.

Casella, Alessandra. 1994a. "The role of market size in the formation of clubs" (mimeo). Columbia University, December.

Casella, Alessandra. 1994b. "Trading on a sphere." May, in progress.

Casella, Alessandra, and Jonathan Feinstein. 1990. "Public goods in trade: On the formation of markets and political jurisdictions." NBER W.P. no. 3554, December.

Clarida, Richard, and Ronald Findlay. 1991, "Endogenous comparative advantage, government and the pattern of trade." NBER W.P. no. 3813, August.

Crane, Rhonda. J. 1979. *Politics of international standards: France and the color TV War*. Ablex.

Diamond, Peter. 1982. "Aggregate demand in a search economy." *Journal of Political Economy*, 90:881–94.

Dixit, Avinash, and Joseph Stiglitz. 1977. "Monopolistic competition and optimum product diversity." *American Economic Review*, 67, June: 297–308.

Dybvig, Philip, and Chester Spatt. 1983. "Adoption externalities as public goods." *Journal of Public Economics*, 20:231–247.

Farrell, Joseph, and Garth Saloner. 1985. "Standardization, compatibility, and innovation." *Rand Journal of Economics*, 16 (Spring): 70–83.

Federal Trade Commission (FTC). 1983. *Standards and certification: Final staff report*, April.

Global Engineering Documents (ed.), 1986. *Directory of Engineering Documents Sources*, Santa Ana, CA: Global Engineering Documents.

Grossman, Gene, and Elhanan Helpman. 1991. *Innovations and growth in the global economy*. Cambridge, MA: MIT Press.

Grossman, Gene, and Alan Krueger. 1991. "Environmental impacts of a North American free trade agreement." NBER Working Paper no. 3914, November.

Helpman, Elhanan, and Paul Krugman. 1985. *Market structure and foreign trade*. Cambridge, MA: MIT Press.

Hufbauer, Gary, and Jeffrey Schott. 1992. *North American free trade: Issues and recommendations.* Washington, DC: Institute for International Economics.

Katz, Michael, and Carl Shapiro. 1985. "Network externalities, competition and compatibility." *American Economic Review,* 75:424–440.

Kindleberger, Charles. 1983. "Standards as public, collective and private goods." *Kyklos,* 36:377–396.

Krugman, Paul. 1981. "Intraindustry specialization and the gains from trade." *Journal of Political Economy,* 89, no. 5 (October). pp. 959–973.

Leamer, Edward, and Chauncey Medberry. 1993. "U.S. manufacturing and an emerging Mexico." NBER Working Paper no. 4331, April.

Lucas, Robert. 1993. "Making a miracle." *Econometrica,* 61:251–272.

Lustig, Nora, Barry Bosworth, and Robert Lawrence, eds. 1992. *North American free trade: Assessing the impact.* Washington, DC: Brookings Institution.

North, Douglass. 1979. "A framework for analyzing the state in economic history." *Explorations in Economic History,* 16:249–259.

OECD. 1991. *Consumers, product safety standards and international trade.* Paris.

Office of Management and Budget. 1982. *Federal participation in the development and use of voluntary standards.* Circular A-119, October 26.

Romer, Paul. 1990. "Endogenous technological change." *Journal of Political Economy,* 98 (October): S71–S102.

Scotchmer, Suzanne. 1993. "Public goods and the invisible hand." In John Quigley and Eugene Smolensky, eds., *Modern Public Finance.* Cambridge, MA: Harvard University Press.

Summers, Robert, and Alan Heston. 1991. "The Penn world table (Mark 5): An expanded set of international comparisons, 1950–1988." *Quarterly Journal of Economics,* 106, no. 425 (May).

UNIDO. 1991. *International product standards: Trends and issues.*

U.S. Congress, Office of Technology Assessment. 1992. *Global standards: Building blocks for the future,* TCT-512. Washington, DC: U.S. Government Printing Office, March.

U.S. Department of Commerce. 1977. *Voluntary standards: Problems, issues and alternatives for federal action.* July.

Wilson, John Douglas. 1987a. "Trade in a Tiebout economy." *American Economic Review,* 77 (June): 431–441.

Wilson, John Douglas. 1987b. "Trade, capital mobility and tax competition." *Journal of Political Economy,* 95:835–856.

II
Environmental Standards

4

Trade and the Environment: Does Environmental Diversity Detract from the Case for Free Trade?

Jagdish Bhagwati
T. N. Srinivasan

The potency of the contention that fair trade or level playing fields consti-tute a precondition for free trade and that, therefore, harmonization of domestic policies across trading countries is necessary before free trade can be embraced to one's advantage, should not be underestimated today. It is nowhere more manifest or more compelling in its policy appeal than in the area of environmental standards.

Both the *general* view that cross-country intra-industry (CCII) harmoni-zation of environmental standards is required if free trade is to be imple-mented and the *specific* proposals currently in vogue to implement this view are therefore in need of analytical scrutiny.[1] This is the task that we undertake primarily in the present chapter.

Section 4.1 briefly reviews the factors that drive the demands for cross-country intra-industry harmonization of environmental standards and the specific proposals, in particular the countervailing of so-called "social dumping" when harmonization does not obtain but free trade does. Its main purpose, however, is to categorize the (four) main issues that arise as the "high-standard" and "low-standard" countries engage in freer trade and contemplate consequences of the differences in their environmental standards when the pollution involved is purely domestic.

Section 4.2 sets forth several basic theoretical propositions (derived from the theoretical Appendix), concerning optimal commercial and envi-ronmental policies under different circumstances when the environmental problem is purely domestic. In light thereof, the basic legitimacy and desirability of free trade with diversity of domestic environmental stan-dards is established. Also, a detailed examination of two (of the four) issues distinguished in section 4.1 is offered: relating to the objections to diver-sity under free trade, reflecting fears of unfair trade and the loss of one's high standards.

Section 4.3 considers the related but distinct problems raised by concerns with ethical preferences or "values" that result in objections to free trade with diverse standards.

Section 4.4 addresses the concern that current institutional mechanisms for overseeing free trade, chiefly the GATT and its successor the World Trade Organization (WTO), threaten high standards by permitting successful challenges by low-standard countries on diverse grounds reflecting mainly their market-disruption potential.

While these analyses concern the issues arising from purely domestic environmental problems, section 4.5 concludes by sketching the trade problems that differentially arise when the environmental problems are international (or "global"), that is, when they involve transborder externalities.

4.1   Demands for Cross-Country Intra-Industry Harmonization of Environmental Standards: Categorizing the Issues for Purely Domestic Environmental Problems

In reviewing and assessing the demands for CCII harmonization of environmental standards, it is customary now to make a distinction of analytical importance between (1) environmental problems that are intrinsically *domestic* in nature (though they may be "internationalized" for reasons we will discuss); and (2) those that are intrinsically *international* in nature because they inherently involve "physical" spillovers across national borders.

Thus, if India pollutes a lake that is wholly within its borders, the pollution is an intrinsically domestic question. If, however, India pollutes a river that flows into Bangladesh, the pollution is an intrinsically international question. So are the well-known problems of acid rain, ozone-layer depletion, and global warming. These intrinsically international problems of the environment raise questions that interface with the trade questions both in common and in different ways from the intrinsically domestic problems.

It has become commonplace among some environmentalists to assert that this distinction is of no consequence because the intrinsically domestic environmental problems are increasingly seen to have transnational impacts. Science has shown, for instance, that aerosol sprays are not just an environmental nuisance where used; they endanger the planet! But the fact that science seems occasionally to turn local (and partial-equilibrium) environmental impacts into transnational (and general-equilibrium) impacts is no proof that the former are an empty set. We should not be deterred, therefore, from using this important conceptual distinction.

4.1.1   Objections to Diversity of Standards

It would seem, at first glance, that at least the intrinsically domestic environmental problems should be matters best left by governments to domestic solutions and within domestic jurisdiction (although transnational, global "educational", and lobbying activities by environmental nongovernmental organizations, the NGOs, are compatible with this solution). Why should anyone object to the conduct of free trade with any country on the ground that its preferred environmental choices and solutions (by way of setting pollution standards and taxes) to intrinsically domestic questions are unacceptable because they are incompatible with the case for (gains from) free trade? Yet, the fact is that they do.

And the objections are directed, not merely at free trade, but also at the institutional safeguards and practices, as at the GATT, which are designed to ensure the proper functioning of an open, multilateral trading system that embodies the principles of free trade. These objections take mainly four forms:

1. *Unfair Trade.* If you do something different, and especially if you do what appears to be less, concerning environment than I do in the same industry or sector, this difference is considered to be tantamount to lack of "level playing fields" and therefore amounts to "unfair trade" by you. Free trade, according to this doctrine, is then unacceptable because it requires, as a precondition, "fair trade."[2]

2. *Losing Higher Standards.* Then again, the flip side of the "fair trade" argument is the environmentalists' fear that if free trade occurs with countries having "lower" environmental standards, no matter what the justification for this situation, the effect will be to lower their own standards. This will follow from the political pressure brought to bear on governments to lower standards to ensure the survival of their industry.

An associated argument is that capital will move to countries with lower standards, so that countries will engage in a "race to the bottom," each winding up with lower standards than desired because standards are lowered to attract capital from each other.

3. *Conflicting Ethical Preferences.* Environmentalists also often worry about the compatibility of ethical preferences and free trade among trading nations who do not share the same ethical preferences. Free trade in products that offend one's moral sense (either in themselves, or because of the way in which they are produced, as in the use of purse seines in catching tuna or leghold traps in hunting for fur) is then considered

objectionable because *either* trade in such products should be withheld so
as to induce or coerce acceptance of such preferences *or* such trade should
be abandoned, even if it has no effective consequence and might even hurt
only oneself, simply because "one should have no truck with the devil,"[3]
or one's labor or industry "should not have to compete" with others who
do not uphold the ethical standards that one considers important.

The first argument presumes higher morality in one's behalf, which
should be spread to other nations with lower morality (and with corresponding lack of standards/laws therefore to reflect the higher morality).
The other arguments seek no such morally imperial outreach; one simply
wants no part in complicity with lower morality elsewhere via participating in gainful free trade with nations guilty of tolerating such lower
morality while the other rejects these gains from trade somewhat differently as imposing an "unfair" burden on one's producers who conform to
the higher ethical standards. In each case, the diversity of standards is
considered then to be incompatible with the pursuit of free trade.

4. *Institutional Vulnerability of High Standards to Countries with Low Standards Fearing Protectionism.* Then, finally, the environmentalists fear that
they will lose their high standards, not because market forces under free
trade bias the *domestic* political equilibrium in favor of lower standards or
generate a race to the bottom,[4] but because the current "institutional"
arrangements, at the GATT in particular, enable the low-standards countries to object to, and threaten, the high standards in other countries by
claiming protectionist intent or consequences, for instance.[5]

4.1.2   The Political Salience of These Objections

Thus, just consider why the first argument concerning the *unfair trade*
of lower CCII standards elsewhere has become such a politically salient
issue today. Though we will turn to this argument in greater depth
in section 4.2, it should suffice to note here that the fear is that competition will be greater if a rival abroad faces lower burdens of environmental regulations, and hence the argument follows that this competitive
advantage enjoyed by one's foreign rivals is *illegitimate* and must be
countervailed, much as dumping or subsidization is, or must be eliminated
at the source.

Thus, Senator David Boren, who introduced legislation in the U.S. Congress to countervail the "social dumping" allegedly resulting from lower
standards abroad, proposed such a measure on the ground that[6]

we can no longer stand idly by while some US manufacturers, such as the US carbon and steel alloy industry, spend as much as 250 percent more on environmental controls as a percentage of gross domestic product than do other countries.... I see the *unfair advantage enjoyed by other nations exploiting the environment* and public health for economic gain when I look at many industries important to my own state of Oklahoma.

We will argue, in section 4.2, that environmental diversity is, contrary to these statements, perfectly legitimate, that it can arise not merely because the environment is differently valued between countries in the sense that the utility function defined on income and pollution is not identical and homothetic, but also because of differences in endowments and technology across countries. Hence, the common presumption driving harmonization and (alternatively) "social-dumping"-countervailing demands, that others with different CCII standards are illegitimately and unfairly reducing their costs, is untenable.[7]

Nonetheless, these demands are part of a general shift to demands to harmonize a great, and possibly increasing, number of domestic policies: in labor standards, in technology policy, and so on. Why?[8]

With industries everywhere increasingly open to competition, thanks precisely to our postwar success in dismantling trade barriers, with multinationals spreading technology freely across countries through direct investments, and with capital more free than ever to move across countries, producers face now the prospect that their competitive advantage is fragile and that more industries than ever before are "footloose." There is, therefore, much more sensitivity to *any* advantage that one's rivals abroad may enjoy in world competition, and a propensity for the rivals to look over their shoulders to find reasons why their advantage is "unfair."

The notion of unfairness is also attractive to those who seek relief from international competition. If you go to your congresswoman and ask for protection because the competition is tough, it is going to be difficult to get it. After all, many of them have been sufficiently educated, or perhaps brainwashed (depending on your point of view), into thinking that protection, while not a four-letter word, is not something you want to embrace if you aspire to anything like statesmanship. But if you go to her and say that your successful rival is playing by "unfair" rules, you are going to do better. In the United States, in particular, the "unfairness" notion can take you really far, since the economic and social ethos reflects notions of fairness and equality of access (rather than success) more than anywhere else.

The fact that the United States also went through the "diminished giant" syndrome vis-à-vis the Pacific nations, which fed its fear of consequent deindustrialization, also made the American politicians more susceptible during the 1980s to these "unfair trade" arguments from interested lobbies. The continuing dominance of the United States in setting the world's trading agenda powerfully reinforces, in turn, the trend toward "fair trade" and "level playing fields."

While the "unfair trade" argument for rejecting free trade with countries with different environmental standards is therefore part of the generic and more general demands for harmonization and level playing fields in world trade, environment (whose protection is legitimately a virtue in itself) brings to this trend yet added arguments with perhaps even more powerful appeal. Chief among them is the fear, leading to the second argument in the list, that competition with the imports and exports in third markets from countries with lower standards will put pressure on domestic industries, triggering political action by them to lower standards *down* to the levels abroad.

Believing (possibly with justification) that U.S. Vice President Dan Quayle's Competitiveness Council was doing precisely this under the administration of President George Bush, the environmental NGOs in the United States, and their friends in the European Community and elsewhere, came to see this lowering of standards as a real threat to their goals if free trade were embraced and if harmonization *up* were not imposed simultaneously by coercion on foreign countries, especially the poor ones. As Walter Russell Mead put it in a much cited article in *Harper's Magazine*:[9]

Either the progressive systems of the advanced industrial countries will spread into the developing world or the Third World will move north. Either Mexican wages will move up or American wages will move down. Environmentalists, labor unions, consumer groups, and human-rights groups must go global—just as corporations have done.

This concern reflects at the global level the debate within the EC: the fear that the Common Market's free trade and free capital flows will lead to harmonization *down* of standards "from below" and the efforts by many in consequence to impose harmonization at a *higher* level of standards "from the top."

Finally, the demands for CCII harmonization are fed also by the feared adverse effects of free trade and capital flows on the real wages of workers: an issue that became important in the 1992 presidential election in the

United States. The Bill Clinton campaign did not just focus on the failure of the Bush administration to revive the economy. It also made much of the so-called structural problem that is defined by the stagnation of real wages of the unskilled workers during the 1980s. At least one of the candidates for explaining this phenomenon has been the integration of the world economy and the competition in consequence with poor countries with abundant unskilled labor.

We doubt the importance of this explanation,[10] but it has powerful appeal. The attempts at globalizing the higher environmental and labor standards, with the latter coming uncomfortably close to attempts at also raising wages in the industrial sectors of the poor countries on human-rights and labor-rights grounds, can be seen in fact as indirect ways of trying to reduce the perceived threat to real wages of the unskilled in rich countries from free trade with (and capital outflows to) the poor countries.

We may remark that, if the argument about the adverse effect of trade on wages of the unskilled is really bought, we are back to the old concerns that free trade with the poor countries will truly act like free immigration from them: the immigration would directly depress workers' wages; free trade would indirectly do so. Interestingly, in the animated British debate prior to the passage of the 1905 Immigration Act, the free traders were also free immigrationists, and the protectionists were also for restrictions on immigration. Immigration was even described as free trade in paupers![11]

Hence, the growing sentiment that free trade with the poor countries will increasingly depress rich countries' real wages should eventually lead to, not just palliatives like the imposition of environmental and labor standards that are harmonized upward, and attempts at restricting capital outflows (synonymous in politics with "losing jobs") to them by way of direct foreign investment. We predict that we will also witness increasing attempts at encouraging population control in these countries.[12]

4.2 The Case for Free Trade with Diversity of Environmental Standards

We now argue (based on the theoretical analysis in the Appendix) that the case for free trade, with diversity of environmental standards across countries, is essentially robust. We then proceed to address specifically the two issues distinguished at the beginning of this chapter: unfair trade and fear of loss of higher standards.

At the outset, note that "standards" may refer to general principles such as the "polluter pays" principle, or they may be defined as the precise tax rates that are levied on the polluter. In the political debate over differential standards, along with demands for CCII harmonization or for "eco-dumping" duties when harmonization does not obtain, the complaints are evidently against lower pollution tax rates or charges—for example, that widget manufacturers are taxed, for the effluents that they discharge, at lower rates in Mexico than in the United States. These definitions, therefore, indicate the sense in which we will discuss CCII harmonization in this chapter, unless otherwise specified.

4.2.1 The Basic Theoretical Presumptions

Distinguish again between the two major cases: where the pollution is domestic and where it is global (and spills over across national borders). Then the following basic theoretical conclusions follow (Appendix), defining welfare in the conventional economic sense:

Domestic Pollution

1. For a small country (with no influence on its terms of trade), free trade remains the best policy, with its own pollution being taxed as required and regardless of whether the other country fixes its own pollution.[13] Where abatement is feasible with spending, there is no case for a subsidy.[14]

2. For a small country, if its own pollution is not taxed optimally, free trade will generally cease to be optimal. Also, it follows equally from the postwar theory of commercial policy under distortions that free trade, with domestic distortions, can immiserize.[15]

3. For a large country, free trade is not an optimal policy, but an optimal tariff is (on the assumption that there is no retaliation), while its domestic pollution is directly fixed through a pollution tax. As is well known, such an optimal solution for the large country is not Pareto optimal for the world economy.[16]

4. With free trade between two countries (small or large) and optimal pollution taxes within each country, global Pareto optimality will follow.

5. However, generally speaking, the optimal pollution taxes (in a globally Pareto optimal solution) will *not* be equal across the countries: *diversity in these tax rates will be both natural and appropriate, hence also "legitimate."*

6. Imposing one country's pollution tax rates on another will then create an *inefficient*, globally Pareto suboptimal solution.

7. Such harmonization, or "straitjacketing" to be more accurate, of the other country's standards toward one's own will also necessarily harm the

other country. Thus a lower-standard country, forced to "harmonize up," will be harmed.

8. Whether such "harmonization up" will benefit the higher-standard country is, however, problematic: it may help or harm.[17] The presumption that it will necessarily help is false.

Global Pollution

1. When global pollution occurs, the globally Pareto optimal solution will be characterized by free trade and by pollution taxes in each country producing the pollution, these taxes being different except in singular circumstances.[18]

2. The globally Pareto optimal solution is not necessarily equitable. To be equitable as well, the market solution must be generally supplemented by (lump-sum) transfers.[19]

3. A small country, taking the foreign terms of trade, tariffs, and pollution abatement as given, will continue to find free trade to be its optimal policy. It will combine this with optimal pollution taxes and abatement addressed to its own pollution.[20] But such Cournot behavior makes little sense: it is more likely that each small country will "free ride" on pollution taxes and abatement and reproduce the "tragedy of the commons" in the use of the common property resource (i.e., the target of the pollution).

4. A large country, indulging in Cournot behavior with respect to the foreign tariffs and pollution abatement expenditures, will use an optimal tariff, not free trade, to maximize its welfare. The Cournot behavior, however, will yield a Nash equilibrium that is not Pareto optimal.[21]

4.2.2   Examining the Objections: Unfair Trade and Feared Loss of High Standards

In light of these propositions, we can now proceed to examine the four issues distinguished in section 4.1, especially the first one relating to "unfair trade" and the associated agitation for countervailing duties against "eco-dumping" in the absence of CCII harmonization.

Does Diversity of Environmental Standards Imply That Low-Standard Countries Are Indulging in "Unfair Trade"?
The theoretical analysis clearly shows that the basic presumption is that different countries will have *legitimate diversity of CCII environmental taxes and standards*. This diversity will arise even if they share the same "utility

function" with associated trade-offs between income and different types of pollution: the diverse tax rates can come from differences in technology and in endowments in the broadest sense (so as to include weather, demography, geography, inherited abatement policies, etc.).[22]

As it happens, there is also no compelling reason to think that every society must share the same utility function. It is perfectly appropriate, and not an indulgence of willful "sovereignty," for Mexico to value clean water higher than clean air, compared to the United States, because a dollar expended on the former instead of the latter will produce greater health gains for Mexicans, whereas the situation would be the reverse for the United States.

The overall trade-off between income and (some generalized index of) pollution will also be different between societies: income may be more valuable at the margin when societies are poor and poverty takes people close to malnutrition than when societies are rich and malnutrition results from overindulgence rather than deprivation. A clear example again is the emphasis on saving dolphins rather than increasing productivity in tuna fishing in the United States and the contrasting emphasis on ameliorating poverty instead in Mexico by using purse seines that kill dolphins while fishing for tuna.

The notion, therefore, that the diversity of CCII pollution standards and taxes is illegitimate and constitutes "unfair trade" or "unfair competition" is itself illegitimate. So is the consequent demand, following from this notion, that CCII harmonization is necessary for "free and fair trade,"[23] in the absence of which CCII differences must be treated as eco-dumping and be countervailed.

In fact, since the effect of such policies would be to force (at least some) countries to harmonize up their preferred lower CCII standards, the consequence would equally be to inflict a welfare loss on them. We might even argue that, while we advocate free trade traditionally, with diversity of domestic standards, on the presumption that voluntary trade is beneficial (relative to autarky) for every trading nation, and hence it is a mutual-gain policy prescription, the opposite is true for CCII harmonization to be superimposed on free trade:[24] it will amount to immiserization of the trading nation whose standards are being "distorted" up.

This basic case against CCII harmonization can be challenged on grounds that we now examine and mainly find unpersuasive.

Objection 1: Competing with Foreign Firms That Do Not Bear Equal Burdens Is Unfair   This competitiveness argument is common, especially on the part of some business groups and also some unions. As notions of unfairness are expressed by them, and as implied by proposed legislation to equalize burdens, this is certainly a strongly felt belief. Underlying it is the sense of outrage that one's ability to hold on to an industry is compromised by the fact that one's rivals abroad do not carry the same burdens.

The contrary arguments, which reject this competitiveness argument, are as follows:

(a) The fact that others abroad do not carry the same burdens is symmetric with the fact that these countries have different wages, capital costs, skills, infrastructure, weather, and what have you: all of which lead to differential advantages of production and trade competitiveness. Diversity of environmental tax burdens is thus no ground for complaints of unfairness.

(b) Losing competitive advantage because we put a larger negative value on a certain kind of pollution than others do is simply the flip side of the differential valuations. To object to that implication of the differential valuation is to object to the differential valuation itself, and hence to our own larger negative valuation. To see this clearly, think only of a closed economy without trade. If we were to tax pollution by an industry in such an economy, its implication would be precisely that this industry would shrink: it loses competitive advantage vis-à-vis other industries in our own country. To object to that shrinking is to object to the negative valuation being put on the pollution. There is, therefore, nothing "unfair" from this perspective, if our industry shrinks because we put higher standards on our industry and others, who mind the pollution less, choose lower standards.

(c) Besides, attributing competitive disadvantage to differential pollution tax burdens in the fashion of CCII comparisons for individual industries confuses absolute with comparative advantage. Thus, for example, in a two-industry world, if both industries abroad have lower pollution tax rates than at home, both will not contract at home. Rather, the industry with the *comparatively* higher tax rate will.

Objection 2: Others' Lower Standards Do Not Reflect Their Citizens' Preferences Correctly   In turn, some environmentalist critics argue that the foreign governments do not reflect their citizens' "true preferences," and therefore in relation to these true preferences that would lead to higher valuation of pollution, the governments have unduly low standards, implying "unfair" competition.

There are counterarguments, in turn:

(a) Similar arguments, about failure of "political markets," apply to most countries, including high-standard countries, and to many areas of governmental regulation. It is commonly argued that the earliest legislations mandated "too-high" environmental standards that went beyond the "optimal" levels because costs were ignored and virtually limitless gains were assumed from the regulations. Now, in the United States for sure, cost-benefit considerations are steadily being introduced into the legislative process; and even the judiciary seems to have turned increasingly to this type of analysis, which then tends to weaken the bite of the standards legislatively laid down.[25]

Since arguments can be made persuasively that all legislation strays from the optimal because of political market failures endemic to any political system, however democratic, objecting only to lower environmental standards as reflecting such political market failure is to be arbitrary. It is also to open a Pandora's box, in favor of the more powerful countries that can then throw stones at others' glass houses while building a fortress around their own.

(b) Again, even if one argues that the decisions made undemocratically by a dictatorship or an oligarchy are vitiated, there is no reason to believe that the higher standards being pursued by a foreign country representing the competitive interests of a foreign industry or labor union in an industry are what a more democratic process would yield. The correct approach should rather be to encourage a shift to more democratic procedures in arriving at social and economic legislation, including environmental policy. Process, not outcomes (especially outcomes sought by self-serving groups elsewhere), is what we should aim at in countries that lack democratic ways.[26]

Should High-Standards Countries Force Low-Standards Countries into Upward Harmonization to Preserve Their High Standards?

In political-economy theory there are two forms of argument for CCII harmonization that take the high standards themselves to be at risk under free trade. Consider each, in turn.

(1) The less common argument is simply that, under pressure of competition from the low-standard countries, the political equilibrium will shift in favor of those who oppose high standards.

But this argument suffers from the fallacy of misplaced concreteness. Intensified international competition, *no matter why it arises*, will put such pressure on governments to reduce business costs. Why pick on lower standards elsewhere, even assuming that they are contributing to the problem?

(2) Far more worrisome to environmentalists than the simple effects of trade competition are the fears that "capital and jobs" will move to countries with lower standards, triggering a "race to the bottom" (or, as John Wilson has remarked, more accurately a race *toward* the bottom) where countries lower their standards in an interjurisdictional contest, below a level that some or all would like, in order to attract capital and jobs. So, a cooperative solution that would *coordinate* the setting of standards would, generally speaking, be a better solution. This coordinated solution, however, need not be characterized by harmonization at the level of the standards in the high-standard country or, in fact, by harmonization at all.

What we have here is a valid theoretical argument.[27] It is stated with analytical rigor as follows: independent governments (or jurisdictions), setting public policy for environmental protection (via taxes and abatement) and competing for investment by reducing environmental standards in a world of mobile and scarce capital, will set these standards at levels that are "too low," that is, that are inefficient for the world economy (composed of the nations whose governments compete in this way). The inefficiency is to be construed as usual: alternative policies exist that make at least one jurisdiction better off and no other jurisdiction worse off. In short, we have nonPareto-optimal Cournot-Nash equilibria (as we have already stated in earlier analysis in this chapter), characterized by lower environmental standards than in the cooperative equilibrium.

To see the matter more clearly, consider the following analysis based on arbitrarily specified, conventional payoff matrices reflecting the incomes yielded (in brackets) when different pollution abatement expenditures are undertaken at levels 0 and A (i.e., zero and a finite amount) by the two countries, home and foreign. The abatement expenditures are assumed to be a monotonic and increasing function of environmental standards.

There are thus four possible combinations of home and foreign expenditures on abatement. The payoffs associated with each combination with the first (resp. second) component being the payoff of the home (resp. foreign) jurisdiction are given by the following payoff matrix:

Foreign expenditure

		0	A
Home expenditure	0	$(-2, -2)$	$(2, -3)$
	A	$(-3, \; 2)$	$(1, \; 1)$

It is easily seen that each jurisdiction has a *dominant* strategy, namely, to spend nothing, because by doing so it maximizes its payoff whether the other jurisdiction spends nothing or A. Yet, compared to this *individually* rational dominant-strategy Nash equilibrium with both jurisdictions spending nothing on abatement, the *collectively* rational strategy of each spending A will yield a *higher* payoff for *both*.

Of course jurisdictional competition need not necessarily lead to such a "prisoner's dilemma" type of Nash equilibrium. For example, if the payoff matrix is as follows,

$(-4, -4)$ $(2, -3)$

$(-3, 2)$ $(1, 1)$

so that one jurisdiction spends nothing while the other spends A, $(0, A)$ and $(A, 0)$ are "pure strategy" Nash equilibria.

In both these cases the Nash equilibrium is characterized by a "race to the bottom" in the sense that the pollution abatement expenditure is zero for at least one jurisdiction. But this result need not occur, as consideration of the following payoff matrix shows. Thus, consider

$(-2, -2)$ $(2, -3)$

$(-3, 2)$ $(3, 3)$

and it is readily seen that we have a unique Nash equilibrium where each jurisdiction spends A on abatement.

Of course, these are arbitrarily constructed payoff matrices, and we need to ground them in underlying models of economies to see whether such outcomes are sensible within them. As argued by John Wilson, this can indeed be done to show that the "race to the bottom" need not occur, and that even a "race to the top" might.[28]

The question that now arises is whether this theoretical possibility of the "race to the bottom" is an empirical possibility of any significance. Leaving out the question as to whether the parametric evidence shows that the noncooperative Nash equilibrium, including the special case of the prisoner's dilemma, will be characterized by significantly lower environmental standards relative to the cooperative equilibrium, we may ask whether there is any empirical support anyway for the propositions that (1) capital is in fact responsive to the differences in environmental standards and (2) different countries and jurisdictions actually play the game then of competitive lowering of standards to attract capital. Without both these phenomena holding in a significant fashion in reality, the "race to the bottom" could be a theoretical curiosity.

As it happens, systematic evidence is available for the former proposition alone, but the finding is that the proposition is not supported by the studies to date: at best, there is very weak evidence in favor of interjurisdictional mobility in response to CCII differences in environmental standards. Arik Levinson, who has reviewed the available evidence thoroughly, concludes:[29]

The conclusion of the literature on domestic location decisions, like that on international locations, is that there is not a lot of evidence that environmental regulations deter investment. In fact, most authors are careful to note the limitations of their research, and to place caveats on their counterintuitive conclusions that stringent regulations do not deter plants nor do lax regulations attract them. But the literature as a whole presents fairly compelling evidence that this is true.

Of course, there are many ways to interpret this finding of an extremely weak effect of CCII differences in environmental standards on industry location. There are three classes of explanation for the finding: (1) that the differences in standards are not significant and are outweighed by other factors that affect locational decisions; (2) that exploiting differences in standards is not a good strategy relative to not exploiting them; and (3) that lower standards may paradoxically even repel, instead of attracting, direct foreign investment.

Explanation 1

a. The obvious, and most cited, explanation is that the standards differences are a small factor in the location decision because they are dominated by other more important factors such as tax breaks, infrastructure facilities, and proximity to markets.[30]

b. Industry location may be seen to be more sensitive to CCII differences in standards if executive enforcement and voters-cum-NGO activism are taken into account as well. The de facto differences in standards may then be more acute than assumed in many studies.[31]

Explanation 2

c. Another (static) explanation is that when multiplant firms, such as most multinationals, invest in different locations, they tend to work uniformly with the most stringent standards they face among these locations, to reduce the transaction costs involved in making diverse choices.[32]

d. Another (dynamic) explanation is that, faced with divergent standards, firms extrapolate that all countries are on an escalator to similar higher standards and therefore decide that it is best to be "ahead of the curve" in the countries that currently have lower standards and to conform to higher standards even though not required. In this case, again, convergence of standards adhered to will emerge, as in the preceding (static) argument, and differences in (required) standards across different jurisdictions will become moot, showing little relationship in practice between such differences and industry-location choices.[33]

e. Another (dynamic) explanation is that firms may argue that the higher-standard countries are the ones that innovate, that many innovations lead to embodied technical change, that such innovations are likely to be embodied (only) in recent vintages of capital goods that already meet the higher standards, and therefore the important benefit of significant technical change will accrue to a firm only insofar as processes and capital goods using higher-standard technology at present are being used by it.

Explanation 3

f. An ingenious explanation of a different analytical variety is that multinationals are discouraged from investing in low-standard countries because local firms have comparative advantage in using pollution-intensive technology that conforms to lower standards. Hence, direct foreign investment (DFI) is likely to be less, not more, when CCII differences in standards are greater between countries![34]

A possible underlying explanation is that firms in the higher-standard countries are likely to scrap their earlier-vintage lower-standard equipment and sell it to the lower-standard countries for the local firms to use, instead of undertaking DFI themselves with such discontinued technology. In short, arm's-length sale of lower-standard equipment to local manufacturers may be preferred to DFI with such equipment, because the local firms are more likely to be able to work with this technology than the multinationals that have moved on to higher-standard, newer-vintage technology—engineering and maintenance know-how tend to be specific to the technology one is working with.

Most of these suggested explanations only reinforce the view that CCII differences in standards, as a factor prompting a "race to the bottom," should not be a source of concern.[35] And this conclusion is further reinforced when one contemplates the fact that there is almost no evidence for the proposition that, regardless of the capital-sensitivity to CCII differences in environmental standards, different countries and jurisdictions nonetheless actually compete for capital by sacrificing environmental standards[36] (as against doing so via tax breaks, infrastructure construction, tariff policy, preferential trading arrangements such as NAFTA where Mexico sought DFI-diversion toward itself through preferential access to the U.S. market, etc.).

The fuss that is made nonetheless over the "race to the bottom" in the political arena, as happened in the NAFTA negotiations, may then be explained either as a reaction to ill-founded fears or as a cynical ploy to advance environmental or protectionist lobbying interests.

Other Arguments and an Alternative Proposal
Therefore, neither the concern with "unfair trade" nor the concern with "threats to high standards," as the reason to push for CCII harmonization as a precondition for free trade or alternatively to invoke eco-dumping duties to countervail CCII differences in pollution tax burdens, is compelling. It is best to take, as a general policy, the option of *mutual recognition* of standards, recognizing the fact that diversity of CCII standards is basically a natural and appropriate phenomenon, consistent with free trade and the consequent gains from trade for all.

Protectionist Capture   The wisdom of the policy conclusion of the preceding paragraph is reinforced by contemplating the certain protectionist consequences of doing otherwise. Thus, consider what an eco-dumping procedure, supplementing our normal antidumping (AD) procedure, would do. We presume that the eco-dumping procedure would calculate the subsidy implied by lower standards and proceed to levy a countervailing duty unless the foreign costs were raised by the estimated amount, with the option that the duty would be lifted when foreign standards were suitably raised and the costs of foreign firms demonstrably raised by the calculated amount.

It is well known that AD actions have become the favored policy instrument of protectionists today. Their desirability from the viewpoint of protectionists derives form the fact that, unlike safeguard actions (under Section 201 of U.S. law and Article XIX of the GATT), AD actions are *selective*: they can target down to the level of the firm, not just a specific foreign country! Besides, compared to preset tariffs, they are also *elastic*: the duties will be set at rates that are decided during litigation and therefore are a function of litigation expenditure, impartiality of the procedures governing the litigation, and the bilateral game played between the complainants and their targets.

Furthermore, in playing the game, the rules are set in favor of litigants, relative to what the rules would be if the objective of AD actions were truly to avoid economically defined predation. In particular, the usual game of reconstructing true costs, against which prices charged are compared to determine dumping margins, has been played to the hilt to get these margins to be as high as possible in litigation. But, as was the case with the former centrally planned economies whose own prices and costs were dismissed as illegitimate, these reconstructed "true" costs can be arbitrary, leading the procedure to effective protectionist capture.

Such capture would surely be the case also with eco-dumping duties, since the eco-dumping margins would have to be *necessarily* estimated on the basis of reconstructed costs of meeting the pollution standards of the complainant country. The U.S. Environmental Protection Agency, for example, would be estimating the cost of implementing U.S. standards in Rio or in Jakarta, so as to arrive at the implicit (*not* actual and observable) subsidy that must be countervailed through an eco-dumping duty by the United States, just as the Department of Commerce does for conventional dumping. There is no reason to doubt that the inherently arbitrary outcomes would be similarly obliging to local lobbies.[37]

Infinite Shadow Prices?   Thus we conclude that the demands for eco-dumping duties to countervail CCII differences in environmental standards and pollution tax and abatement burdens are both illogical (in denying the legitimacy of such diversity) and unwise (in being inherently susceptible to protectionist capture). We have considered, at different stages of our analysis, several reasons why these demands nonetheless appear reasonable and why they have political salience. We must conclude, however, by adding one more reason, which probably has a counterpart also in the case of labor standards and which springs from the nature of our basic argument for the legitimacy of diversity in CCII standards.

Recall our argument that the different shadow prices for pollution that can, and generally will, emerge among different countries, implying differential rather than harmonized environmental taxes and standards, are "natural" for us to contemplate and accept. But suppose that we were putting an infinite price on any and every specific pollution, regardless of its level, small or large. Then these differences would disappear. We believe that

many environmentalists have tended to approach their specific environmental concerns with an implicit infinite shadow price, thus leading to
demands for harmonization, though this tendency is declining. This fact is
well-illustrated by the following remarks in Cropper and Oates' excellent
recent review of environmental economics:[38]

The economist's view had—to the dismay of the profession—little impact on the
initial surge of legislation for the control of pollution. In fact, the cornerstones of
federal environmental policy in the United States, the Amendments to the Clean
Air Act in 1970 and to the Clean Water Act in 1972, explicitly prohibited the
weighing of benefits against costs in the setting of environmental standards. The
former directed the Environmental Protection Agency to set maximum limitations
on pollutant concentrations in the atmosphere "to protect the public health": the
latter set as an objective the "elimination of the discharge of *all* [our emphasis]
pollutants into the navigable waters by 1985." [Although standards were to be
set solely on the basis of health criteria, the 1970 Amendments to the Clean Air
Act did include economic feasibility among its guidelines for setting source-
specific standards. Roger Noll has suggested that the later 1977 Amendments
were, in fact, more "antieconomic" than any that went before. See Matthew
McCubbins, Roger Noll, and Barry Weingast (1989) for a careful analysis of this
legislation.]
    The evolution of environmental policy, both in the U.S. and elsewhere, has
inevitably brought economic issues to the fore: environmental regulation has
necessarily involved costs—and the question of how far and how fast to push for
pollution control in light of these costs has entered into the public debate. Under
Executive Order 12291 issued in 1981, many proposed environmental measures
have been subjected to a benefit-cost test. In addition, some more recent pieces of
environmental legislation, notably the Toxic Substances Control Act (TSCA) and
the Federal Insecticide, Fungicide, and Rodenticide Act (FI-FRA), call for weighing
benefits against costs in the setting of standards.

Once, therefore, we get away from the limited, perhaps almost empty,
set of infinite-shadow-price environmental objectives, we are then back
also to the legitimacy of diversity of standards among trading nations as
the natural and reasonable way to look at the issue.[39]

An Alternative Proposal   We should thus reject the calls for "CCII harmonization or countervailing duties on eco-dumping." But the political salience of such calls remains a major problem. One may well ask then, Are
there any "second-best" approaches, short of the eco-dumping and CCII
harmonization proposals, that may address some of the political concerns
at least economic cost? In that spirit, we would suggest the following
proposal for consideration.

Proposal: Extend the Domestic Standards of High-Standard
Countries to Their Firms in Low-Standard Countries, Unilaterally
or through an OECD Code

In our view, the political salience of the harmful demands for eco-dumping duties and CCII harmonization is greatest when plants are closed by one's own multinationals and shifted to other countries. The actual shifting of location, and the associated loss of jobs in that plant, magnify greatly the fear of the "race to the bottom" and of the "impossibility" of competing against low-standard countries. Similarly, when investment by one's own firms is seen to go to specific countries that happen to have lower standards, resentment is readily focused against those countries and their standards. However, when jobs are lost simply because of *trade* competition, it is much harder to locate one's resentment and fear on one specific foreign country and its policies as a source of unfair competition.[40] Hence, a second-best proposal could well be to address this particular fear, however unfounded and often illogical, of outmigration of plants and investment by one's firms abroad in low-standard countries.

The proposal is to adapt the Sullivan Principles approach to the problem at hand. Under Sullivan, U.S. firms in South Africa were urged to adopt U.S. practices, not the South African apartheid ways, in their operations. If this principle that U.S. firms in Mexico be subject to U.S. environmental policies (choosing the desired ones from the many that obtain across different states in the federal United States) were adopted by U.S. legislation, it would automatically remove whatever incentive there was to move because of environmental burden differences.[41]

This proposal that one's firms abroad behave as if they were at home—do in Rome as you do in New York, not as Romans do—can be either legislated unilaterally by one high-standard country or by a multilateral binding treaty among different high-standard countries. Again, it may be reduced to an exhortation, just as the Sullivan Principles were, by single countries in isolation or by several as through a nonbinding but ethos-defining and policy-encouraging OECD Code.

The disadvantage of this proposal, of course, is that it does violate the diversity-is-legitimate rule whose desirability was discussed earlier. Investment flows, like investment of one's own funds and production and trade therefrom, should reflect this diversity. The proposal, therefore, reduces the efficiency gains from a freer flow of cross-country investments today. But if environmental tax burdens are not very different or do not figure prominently in firms' locational decisions, as the empirical literature seems to stress,[42] the efficiency costs of this proposal could also be minimal while the gains in allaying fears and therefore moderating the demand for bad proposals could be very large indeed.

Yet another objection may focus on intra-OECD differences in high standards. Since there are differences among the OECD countries in CCII environmental tax burdens in specific industries for specific pollutions, this proposal would lead to "horizontal inequity" among the OECD firms in third countries. If the British burden is higher than the French, British firms would face a bigger burden in Mexico than the French firms. But then such differences already exist among firms abroad, since tax practices among the OECD countries on taxation of firms abroad are not harmonized in many respects.[43] Interestingly, the problem of horizontal equity has come up in relation also to the demands of the poor countries (which often find it difficult to enforce import restrictions effectively) that the domestic restrictions on hazardous products be automatically extended to exports by every country. Such a practice would put firms in the countries with greater restrictions at an economic disadvantage. But agreement has now been reached to disregard the problem.

Other problems may arise: (1) monitoring of one's firms in a foreign country may be difficult; and (2) the countries with lower standards may object on grounds of "national sovereignty." Neither argument may be compelling. It is unlikely that a developing country would object to foreign firms doing better by its citizens in regard to environmental standards (which it cannot afford to impose, given its own priorities, on its own firms). Equally, it would then assist in monitoring the foreign firms.

4.3   The Question of Ethical Preferences

So far, we have considered only those demands for harmonization of cross-country intra-industry standards that arise because of considerations centered on "unfair trade" and the fear that one's standards would be endangered if competitiveness were reduced because of lower standards abroad.

However, we must recognize that, for some environmentalists, the desire to spread one's ethical values to others also leads to demands for harmonization, especially of production processes. Thus, opponents in the United States of purse-seine fishing of tuna, which cruelly kills dolphins along with the tuna, would like to see the suspension of trade in Mexican tuna so as to get the Mexicans to accept the U.S. restrictions on such fishing. Of course, some of the agitation proceeds from environmentalists who would find it morally reprehensible to trade in products whose harvesting has cruelly abused nature or a preferred species. But a main impulse is simply the old, morality-driven desire to spread the values to which one subscribes, suspension of access to one's market being justified by a consequentialist ethic rather than a categorical imperative. Consider these two arguments in reverse order.

4.3.1   Spreading Ethical Preferences to Others

We think that GATT sanctioning of the use of unilateral *state* action to suspend other countries' trade access, or (in GATT-defined parlance) their trading rights under the GATT "treaty," unless one's choice of ethical concerns is adopted by others through implicit harmonization in one's direction, is inappropriate for several reasons.[44]

(1) The values sought to be imposed are often not at the level of "human rights" violations such as the massacres perpetuated on one's population or apartheid. They are "lesser" values and are idiosyncratic in the sense of being closely culture-bound rather than reflective of basic and universal aspects of human nature. Thus Americans are particularly touched by dolphins being caught cruelly in purse seines in tuna fishing. But we wonder when we see on television an interview with the man who brought this practice to national attention by filming the dolphins in distress: he is, we think, eating fish in the wilds. If Americans have their dolphins, the Indians have their sacred cows. Animal-rights activists object to slaughterhouses. Others may see the fishing scenes in Robert Redford's *A River Runs through It*, not as magical moments of rapport with nature, but as violation of it with cruelty to a fish that twists and turns, writhing in agony.

The culture specificity of these values, and hence their lack of salience to other economically weaker nations on whom they are sought to be imposed, creates then the inevitable sense that the use of trade sanctions to impose them is simply an act of unjustified moral militancy that is itself ethically offensive. This view gains further credibility when the "values" being pushed on others are actually at the expense of more fundamental values. For example, Americans would prefer to protect dolphins at the expense of Mexican prosperity. The use of purse seines, which are more productive than other nets, would reduce Mexican poverty, but Americans put dolphins ahead of Mexicans. The Mexican reaction may then well be similar to the way American liberals would react if they had to confront the moral militancy of Pat Robertson allied with Genghis Khan.

(2) And then there is the objection that comes from the lack of symmetry in imposing one's idiosyncratic moral preferences on others, as
between the strong and the weak nations. Thus, even some NGOs in
poor countries, whose natural tendency would be to ally with NGOs
in rich countries, have expressed resentment and opposition to the "eco-
imperialism" implied when the strong nations use trade power to force
their preferred values on the weaker nations but the equally autonomous
values of the weaker nations cannot be forced upon the stronger nations in
the same way.[45] These NGOs deny that the NGOs of the strong nations
have a monopoly on virtue.

Thus we may quote the most radical of today's proenvironment NGOs
in India on this issue, in an editorial, "Trade Control Is Not a Fair Instrument," in the country's leading environmental magazine, *Down to Earth*:[46]

In the current world reality trade is used as an instrument entirely by northern
countries to discipline environmentally errant nations. Surely, if India or Kenya
were to threaten to stop trade with USA, it would hardly affect the latter. But the
fact of the matter is that it is the northern countries that have the greatest impact
on the world's environment and yet, their past record in their own countries ... is
nothing to be proud of.... the instruments that need to be devised for ... a system
of global discipline must be fair and equally accessible to all. Reinforcing [through
unilateral muscle-flexing by rich-country NGOs and their governments via trade
sanctions] the power that already flows in a northern direction cannot improve the
world.

(3) The 1991 GATT report *Trade and the Environment* drew attention,
not to this disturbing asymmetry of effective enforceability of the "values"
of the North versus the equally autonomous "values" of the South owing
to differential power. Rather, eschewing the problem of asymmetric power
and instead assuming that each nation can play the same game with equal
effectiveness, it advanced the "slippery slope" scenario: if any country
could suspend another's trading access in products produced in an "unacceptable" fashion (when no international physical spillovers could be cited
as a possible justification and only "values" were at stake), the result was
likely to be a proliferation of trade restrictions without any discipline or
restraint:[47]

It is difficult to think of a way to effectively contain the cross-border assertion of
priorities. If governments suspend the trading rights of other nations because they
unilaterally assert that their environmental priorities [i.e., "values"] are superior to
those of others, then the same approach can be employed on any number of
grounds. Protectionists would welcome such unilateralism. They could exploit it
to create embargoes, special import duties and quotas against rivals by enacting

national legislation that unilaterally defines environmental agendas that other countries [with different "values"] are likely to find unacceptable.

Changing the world trading rules so as to permit the suspension of trading rights of others by individual contracting parties, based simply on the unilateral and extra-territorial assertion of their environmental priorities, undoubtedly would be difficult because many countries would consider such a change to be a big step down a slippery slope.

(4) These views concerning unilateralism to impose one's values on others acquire yet greater cogency when we recognize that there are alternative ways in which one's values can be indulged and propagated.

(a) Most important, if your values are good, as with human rights values that are now widely shared, they will spread because of their intrinsic appeal. Mahatma Gandhi's idea of nonviolence spread far and wide, not because India had economic power to force it on others or because Western NGOs urged trade sanctions against their own nations to canvass its adoption. It spread because of its inherent and powerful moral attractiveness. The Spanish Inquisition should not be necessary to spread Christianity; quite appropriately, the pope has no troops.

Thus consider the following argument, advanced by one of the ablest advocates of environmentalist causes, Steve Charnovitz, in defense of biodiversity:

There are important medical reasons to preserve biodiversity. But there are also important moral reasons. Geopolitical boundaries should not override the word of God who directed Noah to take two of every living creature into the Ark "to keep them alive with you."[48]

We must confess that, as two Hindus among nearly 900 million on this planet, we find this moral argument culture-specific rather than universal in its appeal. It is unlikely that it can spread because of its intrinsic moral merit; should it then be forced on others anyway?

(b) Moreover, alternative private options are often available to propagate your particular ethical preferences if greater activism is desired. Nothing today proscribes NGOs in United States, for example, from financing NGOs in Mexico that bring pressure on *their* government to change its attitude on purse seines, thus changing the balance of forces in Mexico away from more productive tuna fishing that benefits Mexico economically and toward "dolphin-safe" fishing that benefits the dolphins in the Eastern Pacific instead.

(c) Then again, voluntary private boycotts can be a potent instrument as well. A long-standing tradition permits such private boycotts in pluralistic democracies. Provided that labeling requirements provide an opportunity for consumers to make choices in the marketplace between, say, "dolphin-safe" and "dolphin-unsafe" tuna, these boycotts will provide an option to "dolphin-agitated" activists.[49]

This option is not the same as proscription, of course. Environmentalists will thus note that labeling may be ineffective because "consumers may act *rationally* in calculating that their individual purchase of environmentally unfriendly products ... would have only a negligible effect" and that "consumers may act *irrationally*" by not appreciating the ecological importance of avoiding the consumption of the offending product.[50]

Then again, there are bound to be substantive disagreements about the nature and extent of labeling: "dolphin-unsafe" labeling may be objected to as too pejorative and "tuna from Mexico" may be considered too weak. The problems that have plagued the labeling issue for a variety of reasons within the United States itself, both in terms of its design and its uniformity versus diversity among the different states of the union, will not go away at the international level: if anything, they will be more fiercely debated.[51]

But, against these factors that weaken the efficacy of the voluntary-boycott prescription, we must put contrary arguments. Indeed, one might argue that, if enough people desire to attach opprobrium to "dolphin-unsafe" tuna, then "dolphin-safe" tuna producers can use their own "dolphin-safe" labels, requiring only state monitoring and prosecution of false labeling by the dolphin-unsafe tuna producers. After all, the Body Shop has done pretty well in this way.

Moreover, boycotts in rich countries with big markets, even when leaky, can carry disproportionate clout, and the funds at the disposal of some of the environmental NGOs and certainly in their aggregate (as demonstrated when they carry enormously expensive full-page ads simultaneously in newspapers such as the *New York Times*, *Washington Post*, and *The Financial Times*) are evidently large relative to what the poor countries they occasionally target can muster in defense of their own practices and preferences.[52]

One might also add that the passionate zeal with which these boycotts are advocated, and the occasional willingness to portray those that disagree as morally defective, add to their potency as weapons.

A critic may well suggest that we contradict ourselves if we allow private boycotts but would disallow governmental prohibitions, since governments are only "agents" of the citizens. Strictly speaking, this criticism is not true: there is considerable debate in the social science literature on the "principal-agent" relationship and on how poor an agent the government can be. But, that complexity aside, we do distinguish all the time in democracies between state and private actions, permitting far greater latitude to the latter. Thus, when the Harvard lawyer Alan Dershowitz agitated successfully to have the Boston Symphony Orchestra cancel Vanessa Redgrave's appearance because of her politically incorrect views, he was considered well within his rights to disgrace himself; but the U.S. government proscribing her appearance would have been a disgrace to the nation and in violation of national tradition and would surely have been struck down by our courts. And this asymmetry between what private parties and public governments may do is likely to be accepted by most democratic governments today.

(5) So far, we have proceeded on the assumption that unilateral suspension of trade access to spread one's ethical preferences is effective and have argued essentially that it is unwise and undesirable. But a legitimate critique may well be that such action is likely to be ineffective in its objective, thus disrupting trade to no advantage.

It is hard to settle this question on theoretical grounds alone. The cost imposed on the nation whose offending trade is suspended may or may not be significant enough to matter in its calculation; the cost itself will reflect the importance of the embargoed market relative to others, ability to evade, and so on. But it is surely improbable that this cost in any specific instance will be compelling.[53]

The matter becomes less problematic if the cost is greatly increased by other punishments and inducements: Mexican compliance with nonuse of purse seines, despite the favorable Tuna-Dolphin Panel ruling, was secured by convincing President Carlos Salinas de Gortari that it would be hard to pass NAFTA in Congress otherwise. These added instruments, however, will be available only to large and powerful nations, chiefly the United States, making the argument's relevance fairly negligible for most nations.

The sanctioning, as WTO-consistent, of unilateral, governmental withdrawal of market access from other nations for their offending products simply with a view to coercing them into accepting one's idiosyncratic "value" preferences seems, therefore, to be undesirable on several grounds, chiefly these:

• It is essentially intransitive, with each nation able to say its specific values are better than another's; it thus creates the potential for chaotic spread of trade restrictions based on self-righteousness, compounded by a likely encouragement of the process by protectionists.

• In its reliance on force rather than persuasion, it is inherently asymmetric toward poor nations with less economic clout, implying that the economically strong nations are also morally superior and their governments must not be constrained by multilateral rules from coercing others into conversion.

• There are alternative private options that can be used to create a multilateral consensus of shared values based not on the sword but on precept, example, and even pressure through boycotts.[54]

Even though some of the environmental NGOs in the United States, in particular, and perhaps elsewhere too, are skeptical or scornful of them, it is noteworthy that these arguments are spreading within the international community. Thus, Steve Charnovitz has recently complained:[55]

The GATT's campaign against unilateralism is having some impact. Earlier this year, the UN Conference on Trade and Development adopted a resolution stating that "Unilateral actions to deal with environmental challenges outside the jurisdiction of the importing country should be avoided." The Rio Declaration repeats this statement.

We have little doubt, however, that unilateral actions designed simply to spread "lesser values" to others through the use of suspension of trading access are unwise. We are, therefore, only delighted that this view is gaining ground.

4.3.2   Rejecting Trade in "Defiled" Products

Suppose, however, that your intention in unilaterally denying Mexico access to the U.S. market is not to change Mexican fishing of tuna in a "dolphin-safe" direction, but simply to avoid eating a "defiled" product that offends your moral values.[56] Should you then be forced into consuming Mexican tuna? That would seem a tall order to many.

But there is an answer to this objection. Nothing in current or prospective GATT rules forces you (quite correctly) into this offensive option. For, you could certainly compensate the country whose trading rights (i.e., access to your market) are being denied or suspended by *either* offering other concessions, *or* (in the odd manner of GATT procedures) having the other country withdraw some "equivalent" concessions of its own to you.

Confronted by this argument, some environmentalists are offended: why should we have to pay for our principles? The answer is that it is a small price to pay if the alternative (of unilateralism) has the many drawbacks that we have noted already. If it is right in the Christian tradition to buy indulgences to pay for one's vice, perhaps one should not object to a proposal to pay for one's virtue: at least, the former is for personal gain, the latter (if you accept our arguments) for social gain.[57] Besides, the "payment" is not in cash but in compensation in the form of reductions of other trade barriers against the foreign country to offset the enactment of the trade barrier against its offending export (or a retaliatory raising of trade barriers by the foreign country). Such payment, in fact, should work in the direction of moving resources away from the offending foreign activity, thus reinforcing the case for using such a policy option.

Charnovitz also appeals to "original intent" to argue that the original signatories to the GATT, and earlier practice in some cases, permitted exceptions to market access based on extrajurisdictional exercise of "values" in cases such as the prohibited U.S. landing and sale of U.S. sponges from the Gulf of Mexico gathered by "certain harmful methods [such as] diving or using a diving apparatus."[58] We are assured by academic legal experts on the GATT, however, that the GATT's "original intent" is not unambiguously inferred in this as in many other instances.

John Jackson, one of the leading authorities on GATT law, has thus argued:[59]

It has been argued [by Charnovitz] that the drafting history of the GATT would lead to an interpretation of Article XX that would permit governments to take a variety of environmental measures and justify them under the general exceptions of GATT. While this view is interesting, and the research is apparently thorough, it is not entirely persuasive and overlooks important issues of treaty interpretation. Under typical international law, elaborated by the Vienna Convention on the Law of Treaties, preparatory work history is an ancillary means of interpreting treaties. In the context of interpreting the GATT, we have more than forty years of practice since the origin of GATT, and we also have some very important policy questions.... Thus, unlike certain schools of thought concerning United States Supreme Court interpretation of the United States Constitution, it is this author's view that one cannot rely too heavily on the original drafting history.

In any event, the liberal environmentalists who would ordinarily oppose the appointments of "original intent" judges on the Supreme Court should not endorse this juridical approach in seeking to prevent the GATT from pursuing (what we have argued are) sensible interpretations of its laws on environmental issues.

4.3.3   Dealing with Ethical Preferences

Where does this analysis leave us? Based on it, as also on arguments in the discussion that follows immediately concerning the way GATT deals with objections by contracting parties to processes of production (as distinct from products themselves) used by other contracting parties, we think that the following recommendations have merit in case of ethics-based objections to providing market access:

Unilateralism

• Unilateral suspension of trading access for reasons based on ethical preference should not be sanctioned by the WTO.

• Such unilateral suspensions, where desired, should be "paid for" by other, equivalent trade concessions.

Plurilateralism and Multilateralism
Where the ethical preference is embodied in a plurilateral (i.e., multination) treaty signed by many nations, we need to distinguish between two major cases:

1. Plurilateral treaties concerning an ethical preference, as on preventing the production of chickens in batteries or injecting cattle with hormones, for instance, may be signed by enough nations to enable a WTO waiver; in this case, the compatibility of the plurilateral treaty and the WTO is assured.

2. When the number of nations signing the ethical-preference-embodying treaty falls short of the required WTO waiver majority, then the conflict can lead to problems. In particular:

• *Products*: Where the plurilateral treaty simply provides for *suspension of trade access* for the offending products—such as ivory or tigers or whales—there is no difficulty in enforcing such a ban as long, of course, as the ban extends in a nondiscriminatory fashion to both foreign and domestic supply.[60]

Where, however, the signatory nations seek to impose *trade sanctions* (i.e., trade disruption of products other than the one in dispute), as a punishment aimed at securing compliance, the consensus appears to be that such sanctions would be GATT-inconsistent.[61] In that case, our solution would be to treat these sanctions as indeed so and instead to encourage nations to use other instrumentalities (of the kind discussed earlier, e.g., suasion, NGO activities) to secure the necessary acceptance of the ideas by a plurality of WTO contracting parties sufficient to obtain a waiver. This is indeed the procedure that has been used to undertake trade embargoes in matters such as apartheid where South Africa, despite being a GATT member, was embargoed under multilateralism-based UN procedures that would equally have procured a GATT waiver.

• *Processes*: The GATT would appear to proscribe the suspension of market access to other contracting parties in products whose manufacture or production is objected to by the importing contracting party. In our view, as developed in the next section, this is a desirable proscription. If, therefore, it is desired that such suspension of market access be undertaken in any event—as was the case with the proscription of hormone-fed beef by the EC—then we would recommend that the suspension be "paid for" by compensatory trade concessions elsewhere, exactly as in the case of unilateral trade access suspensions discussed previously.

4.4   Institutional Vulnerability of High Standards to Objections by Low-Standard Countries: GATT's Threat to Environmental Autonomy

We turn finally to the question of the threats seen by many environmentalists to their high standards (aimed at domestic regulation) by GATT procedures that enable low-standard countries to question, and (if successful) to undermine, these high standards. We must ask, Are the environmentalists legitimately worried about the roadblocks that current and prospective GATT rules can pose for environmental regulations and standards aimed entirely at domestic production and consumption, matters that are conventionally and properly within domestic jurisdiction?

Now, as long as these rules are applied without discrimination between domestic and foreign suppliers and among different foreign suppliers, there is really little that GATT rules can do to prevent a country from doing anything that it wants to do. For domestic conservation, safety, and health reasons, a contracting party of the GATT can even undertake discriminatory, selectively targeted trade-restraining action, subject to safeguards, under Articles XX(b) and XX(g).[62]

Thus, if you insist on safety belts or air bags in cars, you can impose them on cars as long as both imports from all sources and domestic production are symmetrically treated. So also for requiring catalytic converters to reduce environmentally harmful emissions.

4.4.1   The Problem of Processes

The most significant and contentious conceptual question arises when you have a rule that says that consumption (from both domestic and foreign sources) of a product will be restricted if the product is produced, *using a process you disapprove of*. Objecting to a process used in a foreign (or, strictly, nondomestic) jurisdiction is, under GATT rulings, not acceptable. There are two types of such process-related problems that we might distinguish:

1. Where the process used is objected to because of "values": e.g., purse seines or leghold traps.

2. Where the process used is objected to because it creates cross-border physical spillovers and hence a global pollution problem: e.g., acid rain or global warming.[63]

GATT law, as currently interpreted, forbids the use of trade restrictions for *both* classes of objections. For the first class of actions, this proscription seems to us justified, in light of our discussion in section 4.3.

The presence of cross-border physical spillovers, whose analysis we sketch only briefly in section 4.5, raises more legitimate worries about altogether ruling out process-related trade restraints, and appropriate changes in GATT law will be necessary in this class of cases where it seems evidently inappropriate to prevent nations from *any* use of trade restraints to limit the physical harm being imposed on them by other nations whose trade accentuates this harm. Such use must, however, be regulated in a way that ensures symmetry of rights, equity, and efficiency. Devising appropriate procedures and rules to regulate the use of such trade restraints in the context of global environmental problems is a challenge for the architects of the new GATT system.

4.4.2   Products

It would appear, however, that the GATT rules should cause no problems for the environmentalists (except for the process-related issues) when only purely domestic environmental problems are at issue. Thus, the GATT report argues:[64]

Under GATT's rules, governments can employ many different measures to protect and improve the local environment. Thus, sales taxes on products that can create pollution (those containing chloroflurocarbons, for example), deposit refund schemes for recyclable waste (bottles, scrap cars), or favourable tax treatment of environmentally friendly products (lead-free gasoline, solar panels for home heating) and other non-discriminatory measures ensuring a pattern of domestic consumption that minimizes pollution would not normally be open to challenge.

There is also nothing in the GATT that prevents contracting parties from taxing or regulating domestic producers who engage in polluting activities—even to the extent of prohibiting the production and sale of particular goods. For instance, ceilings on air pollution levels, and levies on companies that discharge pollutants into lakes and rivers, are fully consistent with GATT rules.

In certain cases, even a measure taken for environmental protection purposes which would otherwise violate GATT obligations not to discriminate may be permitted under Article XX of the GATT. The narrowly-defined exceptions in Article XX permit a contracting party to place health, safety or domestic resource conservation goals ahead of non-discrimination, but only when certain conditions are fulfilled. In general, these conditions ensure that a trade measure is necessary for the achievement of such goals—and that these goals are not used as a pretext for reducing competition from imports.

GATT rules, therefore, place essentially no constraints on a country's right to protect its own environment against damage from either domestic production or the consumption of domestically produced or imported products. Generally speaking, a country can do anything to imports or exports that it does to its own products, and it can do anything it considers necessary to its own production processes.

Alas, that is not the end of the matter for the environmentalists. For, as the GATT report suggests, even if a regulation or a standard were set in an apparently nondiscriminatory fashion, it is perfectly possible that

• in reality, its intention is to discriminate against imports rather than to reach the stated (environmental or other) objective; and

• in practice, even if the intention is truly to reach the stated goal, the choice from different ways to reach that goal may have been in favor of a regulation or standard that effectively discriminates most, rather than least, against imports.

Then again, especially when safety and health standards are set (as with phytosanitary standards), there have been increasing demands for "scientific tests" as a precondition for the imposition of such standards, so as again to make these palatable to other trading nations who might see their resulting loss of markets as otherwise unreasonable.

These are perhaps the most contentious issues today where the trading interests see the reasonableness of current and prospective GATT procedures designed to ensure as much freedom of access to markets as possible, whereas the environmental interests see in the same procedures an unreasonable bias against themselves. In all these areas, the GATT permits challenges to be mounted by contracting parties to be mediated by dispute settlement panels and for codes and rules that define how the panels might adjudicate these disputes. We will say a little about each of these issues.[65]

The Intention Issue

Economists have long recognized the intention issue. Thus the classic instance we regale our students with relates to Gottfried Haberler's example of the provision in the German tariff, dating from 1902 and valid decades later, which was clearly meant to apply to Switzerland and Austria, relating to "brown or dappled cows reared at a level of at least 300 meters above the sea and passing at least one month in every summer at a height of at least 800 meters."[66]

Within the environmental field, a fine example where the United States was the aggrieved party is provided by the Canadian province Ontario's 10 percent tax on beer cans but not bottles, on environmental grounds. Even if the United States authorities did not challenge the objective of restricting the use of cans,[67] they could legitimately note that the law was likely to have been motivated by the desire to discriminate against foreign beer supplies who (unlike local rivals) predominantly used cans rather than bottles, combined tellingly with the fact that the use of cans for other products such as soups and juices (where Ontario producers would have been affected) was not proscribed.[68]

It is hard to see how a good, open trading system cannot permit member countries to examine the bona fides of environmental (and other) regulations in this way. Surely, given the ease with which regulations and standards can be misused for protectionist purposes, *some* mechanism must exist for grievances to be aired and adjudicated. The GATT dispute settlement mechanism, improved after the Uruguay Round and further changed in the direction of greater transparency, is sufficiently objective and neutral between contracting parties to provide a better method for dealing with the problem than national procedures that would always be suspect as having been influenced by national political considerations.

The Alternative-Measures Issue

There are more difficult issues, however, when the question of the use of alternative ways of reaching an environmental objective is raised.

It seems totally sensible that, if alternative ways of meeting an environmental objective exist, a contracting party should be asked to choose one that infringes least on another's trading rights. In fact, this view seems embodied in GATT's Article XX(b), which allows even discriminatory trade restrictions against another contracting party if the measures are deemed "necessary" to protect human, animal, or plant life or health.

Two different views of the matter, however, can be taken in interpreting what is "necessary." Thus, in the case of Thailand's restrictions on importation and internal taxes on cigarettes, the GATT panel decided that Thailand should use the "least GATT-inconsistent" measure to achieve its domestic objective. Then again, one could consider a "least-trade-restrictiveness" test which, of course, will not necessarily coincide with the "least-GATT-inconsistency" test.[69]

Aside from the greater difficulty of determining ordinally what greater and lesser GATT-consistency means, the economic superiority of the test that requires least damage to trade is manifest. In fact, the December 1991 Dunkel Draft of the proposed Uruguay Round treaty adopted the latter test: it is built into the Standards Code and also into the Sanitary and Phytosanitary Decision. It is also the test used in the GATT panel decision in 1992 on the alcoholic beverages case where the United States lost. The laws in five states that required a common carrier to enforce their tax and alcohol policies were held to be unacceptable because

the United States has not demonstrated that the common carrier requirement is the least trade restrictive enforcement measure available to the various states and that less restrictive measures, e.g. record-keeping requirements of retailers and importers, are not sufficient for tax administration purposes.[70]

This test seems reasonable, of course. The objections to it amount mainly to objections to the methods by which the Beverage Panel arrived at the judgment that less-trade-restrictive measures to achieve the same objectives were available in that instance. But there are indeed inherent difficulties in defining the set of alternative policies that, with differential trade impact, would achieve identical environmental (or other domestic) objectives. It is hard to imagine *identical* results on these objectives from alternative policies, though *similar* results can sometimes be deemed possible (though, here too, judgments will differ in many cases).

In the end, any practical enforcement of the "least-trade-restrictive" test for evaluating the acceptability of an environmental regulation or standard will likely force the adjudicating panel into evaluating, implicitly or explicitly, *trade-offs* between the cost in trade disruption and the cost in reaching the environmental objective: a phenomenon and a problem that economists, who accept free lunches but do not believe in them, have no difficulty recognizing.

The jurisprudence, by necessity if not by choice, will have to move in the direction of evaluating and deciding upon the solution to such trade-offs. Thus, in the case of EC law, in the case involving Denmark's laws concerning disposable beer cans, the European Court of Justice seems to have explicitly considered such a trade-off between the interests of "free movement of goods" (and consequent trade benefits) and "environmental protection."[71]

It is natural, therefore, that environmentalists and trade experts who seem occasionally to attach opposing weights to the environmental and the trade benefits of any regulation or standard will worry about what weights the adjudicating panels would choose in reaching their decisions. If, therefore, disputes are to arise between nations, and tests of "necessity" that imply weighing alternative policies leading to different trade-offs are to be utilized, it is certainly proper for the environmentalists to seek improvements in the dispute settlement process that would give them greater access in terms of the ability to file written friend-of-the-court briefs and also make the panel procedures more transparent than hitherto at the GATT.

A complementary policy of prevention rather than cure would also be useful as we move increasingly into this difficult and contentious area. The input of "principally affected" trading countries into the setting of domestic environmental and other regulatory standards, such that the policy alternatives are discussed and adopted in light of such input, would help to reduce conflict to an irreducible minimum that the judicial process must address and resolve. Instances of such international input into domestic setting of standards are not lacking: the United States, worried by the trade-restrictive implications of EC standards-setting procedures, has indeed gained some access to the EC processes. But clearly more institutionalized and satisfactory procedures for doing so, available to weak and not just to strong nations, would appear to be a most useful innovation.

The Scientific-Test Issue

The use of scientific tests to determine whether a product can be proscribed, even on a nondiscriminatory basis between imports and domestic production, creates yet another important source of disagreement. Suppose that the United States uses Alar to spray apples and that the EC does not. Suppose then that, faced with agitation from consumers who consider Alar-sprayed apples to be a hazard to their health, the EC bans their sale. The U.S. industry and government can then be expected to demand that the EC justify, through the use of a scientific test, its fear that Alar-sprayed apples are a hazard.

Although this case is hypothetical, the EC-U.S. conflict on the EC's proscription of hormone-fed beef is not. In this instance, the U.S. beef producers that used hormones and the biotech industry that invented and produced the hormones were pitted against what they considered to be a

wholly unscientific fear of hormone-fed beef. The United States went to
the length of trade retaliation under Section 301; the EC in the end did
not counterretaliate; and the matter was not taken to the GATT dispute
settlement process for adjudication, with both the EC ban and the U.S.
retaliation continuing in place. Given the high probability that a scientific
test criterion would have been required by a GATT dispute settlement
panel, it is likely that the EC would have lost the case.

But the case was an early warning sign of the tension between commercial and environmental interests on this issue. Admittedly, even hard science is not hard enough most of the time. The many who are convinced of
a hazard to their health, no matter what the *current* preponderance of
scientific opinion, might well turn out to be right after all. Then again,
even if scientists were agreed on measuring the risk from any event or act
of consumption or production, the subjective reaction of different people
to the objective risk may vary greatly and, in fact, does.

It is tempting then to say, Let any regulation pass, regardless of the
scientific test, no matter that it reduces another's access to one's market.
But we are back then to the "slippery slope" scenario. Without the restraining hand of current science, the itch to indulge one's fears could be
overwhelming.

The solution may then well be to institutionalize what in effect happened with the hormone-fed beef case: have the scientific test; if you lose,
"pay up" (as the EC did) if you do not wish to change your regulation or
standard; or settle by shifting your regulation or standard so as to broadly
move in the direction of achieving your objective by alternative policies
(e.g., by labeling hormone-fed beef rather than proscribing it altogether,
and then undertaking education, propaganda, and boycotts against its use).

Again, if the notion of "paying up" appears offensive to the environmentalists because science should not stand in the way of our deeply held
concerns, we would just urge them to undertake one thought experiment.
We all know from science today that AIDS does not spread through
simple contact. Suppose that our immigration policy nonetheless rules out
HIV-infected immigrants, even when refugees and family reunification are
involved, because large numbers of Americans are sure (unscientifically)
that such admissions will spread AIDS to them. Would a typically liberal,
activist environmentalist agree to such a policy?

The Circumventing-Democracy Issue
We would be remiss if we did not also note the increasing appeal to some
environmentalists of the notion that "the process of negotiating interna-

tional agreements [like the GATT's Uruguay Round] is less subject to public scrutiny, and therefore a threat to democratic accountability,"[72] and that "faceless" and unelected bureaucrats at the GATT will overrule democratically enacted environmental and other social regulations. Leaving aside the question whether such regulations will be overturned—an issue that we just discussed at length—the question regarding democratic process is far more complex than the simplistic denunciations that find their way into anti-GATT propaganda. In particular, we would argue the following:

1. It is inconsistent to hold simultaneously, as many do, that the low standards of other countries should be countervailed by foreign NGOs and governments that are "unelected" and "faceless" as far as these low-standard countries are concerned, while condemning the GATT panel members, chosen by democratic procedures multilaterally agreed among the contracting parties, as "faceless" and "unelected."

2. Is it really correct to hold that one level of governance is more "democratic" than another? After all, it is the contracting parties that have chosen the GATT panel procedures democratically.

3. Moreover, it is not necessarily correct to argue that the closer the level of governance to the ground, the better the decision. If local governance were dominant, Al Capone could flourish without the Feds, capital punishment would thrive, land reforms in developing countries (legislated and enforced from the top when grassroots activism is frustrated by the local power structure) might go slower, and so on.

4. There is no reason to think that the GATT works any worse than the national or local legislatures in these matters. Contrast the contribution of the GATT, including its panels, with the gift that the U.S. Congress gave to the world in 1934 with the Smoot-Hawley Tariff and is currently giving us with its 301 and Super 301–style championing of aggressive unilateralism.

5. The current U.S. position, opposed effectively by other contracting parties, that environmental NGOs be allowed to participate in GATT Council deliberations on panel rulings is couched in terms of transparency and democracy. But it raises compelling objections that presumably emerged during this debate:
a. The NGOs should be able to participate through their own governments, which represent them *and* other constituents in democratic governments; there is no reason to think that their added participation is any

more desirable than that of consumer groups, protectionist lobbies, unions, and the like, all of whom can and do compete for influence in national politics and hence on international policy deliberations.

b. The environmental NGOs are not necessarily handicapped financially vis-à-vis the other groups, and their organization and clout are disproportionately greater than their finances, since they can often successfully claim the higher moral ground (e.g., we are "rescuing the dolphins" from the rapacious multinationals; we are "saving the planet"), so they certainly do not need a "second voice," when others are denied it, at the GATT Council.

c. While there are indeed NGOs in the developing countries, the heavily financed ones are in the rich countries and will reflect *their* concerns, priorities, and views (e.g., protecting dolphins rather than aiding Mexico's tuna industry to help Mexico's development and removal of poverty); the rich countries would then have a double voice, when they can often drown out the voice of the poor countries with just one voice, thus undermining the notion of democracy at the *international* level.

4.5   Concluding Observations: Environmental Problems with Transborder Externalities and Trade Questions

We conclude our exhaustive analysis of the case of purely domestic environmental problems, and the associated demands for CCII harmonization and eco-dumping countervailing duties and so on, with a sketch of the policy problems that arise in the context of transborder externalities. These are generally more complex in character than the ones that arise with purely domestic pollution[73] and more compelling as well. It may be useful, from a policy viewpoint, to distinguish between two cases: (1) a special case where the problem is simplified by assuming a single country that pollutes the other, raising questions of response such as the use of trade barriers by the other; and (2) a general case where the problem is truly global in character. A good example of the former is U.S. transmission of acid rain to Canada; an excellent example of the latter is global warming, to which many countries contribute while all are affected by it (though each in a different degree, and not all negatively).

4.5.1   One-Way Transmission of Pollution and Two Countries

The case of pollution transmitted from one country to another is helpful because it illustrates in a simple way the problem raised by transborder

externalities concerning the use of second-best trade instruments by the
injured country when the offending country does not implement a first-
best solution and uses its jurisdictional autonomy in the spirit of malign
neglect. The principal question, then, is whether a country that is being
damaged by pollution from another has the right to impose a trade restraint to affect the exports, and hence production, and hence the pollution, of the other country that comes into one's area.[74]

Thus, suppose that the United States is transmitting acid rain to Canada,
thanks to its CO_2-producing processes used in producing electricity in a
CO_2-intensive way, since U.S. generation of electricity uses fossil fuel
(whereas the Canadian industry uses cleaner, hydroelectric processes). If
the United States refuses to tax its electricity producers for the SO_2
pollution they generate, or refuses to compensate Canada for the damage
that is inflicted by the acid rain that is transmitted to Canada by wind
drift, then should Canada have the right to tax its import of U.S. electricity (and even of other U.S. exports that are produced using the
electricity that produces the acid rain and then transmits a fraction of it to
Canada)?

Modifying the GATT rules to explicitly allow for such a possibility
would make sense as a "second-best" solution, since the offending party
(the United States in the example) refuses to undertake a "first-best" solution. That also seemed to be, as Charnowitz has noted, the position taken
in some early and unofficial thinking by the GATT Secretariat. Of course,
the usual caveats about satisfying scientific tests and the like would have
to be noted and codified.[75]

The problem, of course, is that this type of trade remedy is generally
likely to be so weak for problems like acid rain that one may ask, Is it
worth modifying the GATT/WTO to legitimate such trade actions? Thus,
take the example of acid rain itself. The generation of acid rain in the
United States, a fraction of which comes across to Canada, is geographically concentrated, of course, at the border whereas the import tariff would
affect all electricity generation in the United States; moreover, the effect
on SO_2 generation would be indirect, not direct through tax on the process itself; then again, only a fraction of the acid rain generation effect
would get into the transmission. The tariff instrument would then be
extremely weak, and the Canadian gain from its use in reducing the loss
from the acid rain would be outweighed by the reduced gains from trade,
that is, the gains from importing cheaper electricity from the United
States.[76]

4.5.2   Global Transborder Externalities

The chief policy questions concerning trade when global pollution problems are involved, as with ozone-layer depletion and global warming, take
a different turn related to the cooperative-solution-oriented multilateral
treaties that are sought to address them.[77] They are essentially tied into
noncompliance ("defection") by members and "free riding" by nonmem-
bers. Because any action by a member of a treaty relates to targeted
actions (such as reducing CFCs or CO_2 emissions) that are a public good
(in particular, that the benefits are nonexcludable, so that if I incur the cost
and do something, I cannot exclude you from benefiting from it), the use
of trade sanctions to secure and enforce compliance automatically turns up
on the agenda.

At the same time, the problem is compounded because the agreement
itself has to be *legitimate* in the eyes of those accused of free riding or
noncompliance. Before those pejorative epithets are applied and punishment prescribed in form of trade sanctions legitimated at the GATT/
WTO, these nations have to be satisfied that the agreement being pressed
on them is efficient and, especially, that it is equitable in burden sharing.[78]
Otherwise, nothing prevents the politically powerful (i.e., the rich nations)
from devising a treaty that puts an inequitable burden on the politically
weak (i.e., the poor nations) and then using the cloak of a "multilateral"
agreement and a new GATT/WTO legitimacy to impose that burden with
the aid of trade sanctions with a clear conscience, invoking the "white
man's burden" to secure the "white man's gain".

As a result, the policy demand, often made, to alter the GATT/WTO to
legitimate trade sanctions on contracting parties who remain outside of a
treaty, whenever a plurilateral treaty on a global environmental problem
dictates it, is unlikely to be accepted by the poor nations without safeguards to prevent unjust impositions. The spokesmen of the poor countries have been more or less explicit on this issue, with justification. These
concerns have been recognized by the rich nations.

Thus, at the Rio Conference in 1992, the Framework Convention on
Climate Change set explicit goals under which several rich nations agreed
to emission-level-reduction targets (returning, more or less, to 1990 levels),
whereas the commitments of the poor countries were contingent on the
rich nations footing the bill.

Ultimately, burden sharing by different formulas related to past emissions, current income, current population, and so on is inherently arbitrary;
such formulas also distribute burdens without regard to efficiency. Econo-

mists will argue for burden sharing dictated by cost minimization across countries, for the earth as a whole: if Brazilian rain forests must be saved to minimize the cost of a targeted reduction in CO_2 emissions in the world, while the United States keeps guzzling gas because it is too expensive to cut down, then so be it. But then this efficient "cooperative" solution must not leave Brazil footing the bill! Efficient solutions, with compensation and equitable distribution of the gains from the efficient solution, make economic sense.

A step toward them is the idea of having a market in permits again, at the world level: no country may emit CO_2 without having bought the necessary permit from a worldwide quota. That ـystem would ensure efficiency,[79] whereas the distribution of the proceeds from the sold permits would require a decision reflecting multilaterally agreed ethical or equity criteria (e.g., the proceeds may be used for refugee resettlement, UN peacekeeping operations, aid dispensed to poor nations by UNDP, the WHO fight against AIDS, and so on). This type of agreement would have the legitimacy that could then provide the legitimacy in turn for a GATT/WTO rule that permits the use of trade sanctions against free riders.

APPENDIX

We consider a sequence of models to illustrate the trade policy implications of bringing environmental considerations into contexts that differ with respect to (1) the nature of pollution (e.g., purely domestic versus global), (2) whether or not the economy is a price taker in world markets, (3) whether or not pollution can be abated through expenditure of resources, and (4) whether global welfare or national welfare is the policy objective. In much of the analysis pollution is modeled as a production externality that affects welfare. In the last section we relate our analysis to that in the literature.

A4.1   Purely Domestic Pollution

A4.1.1   Small Country, Purely Domestic Pollution, No Abatement Possible

For simplicity consider a two-commodity model with the production transformation function $X_1 = F(X_2)$ where X_i is the output of good i. Pollution $P = P(X_1, X_2) \equiv P(F, X_2)$. Clearly for any given production choice (X_1, X_2) where $X_1 = F(X_2)$, pollution P is determined regardless of trade. As such, since the economy has no market power, free trade is optimal from a consumer perspective.

This model implies in particular that, if the given production choice is fixed at the production vector associated with the autarky optimum, opening the economy to free trade in consumption cannot reduce welfare. As such, as long as appropriate policy instruments are available to ensure the separation of consumption from production, trading cannot hurt.

Now, allow instead a production response to trading opportunities. Writing $Y = X_1 + \pi X_2 = F + \pi X_2$ for income where π is the world relative price of good 2 in terms of good 1, $V(\pi, Y, P)$ for the indirect utility function, the first-order condition for the optimal choice of production is given by[80]

$$V_2(F_1 + \pi) + V_3(P_1 F_1 + P_2) = 0 \tag{1}$$

where the subscript i of a function denotes the partial derivative with respect to its ith argument.

Of course if $V_3 = 0$ so that pollution does not affect welfare, equation 1 reduces to $\pi = -F_1$, or world price = domestic marginal rate of transformation so that free trade is optimal from a producer perspective as well. In the case where $V_3 < 0$ so that pollution affects welfare adversely, equation 1 can be rewritten as

$$\pi + V_3(P_1 F_1 + P_2)/V_2 = -F_1 \tag{2}$$

Now $(P_1 F_1 + P_2)$ is the *net* marginal change in pollution as the output of good 2 increases: it is the sum of the direct marginal change P_2 from the increase in output of good 2 and the indirect marginal change $P_1 F_1$ from the fall F_1 in output of good 1 induced by the increase in the output of good 2. Thus if $P_1 F_1 + P_2$ is negative (resp. positive) so that the net change in pollution from an increase in the output of good 2 is negative (resp. positive), the domestic rate of transformation of good 2 for good 1 is larger (resp. smaller) than the world price of good 2; that is, if an increase in the output of good 2 reduces (resp. increases) pollution, since pollution is an uninternalized *domestic* externality, the output of good 2 should be subsidized (resp. taxed) relative to its world price. This optimal rate of tax or subsidy will in general be different in a trading optimum as compared to autarky. Nonetheless, welfare in a free-trading optimum will be no less than under autarky.

This is a straightforward application of the standard theory of domestic distortions to what, in the present instance, is a production externality.[81]

A4.1.2   Small Country, Purely Domestic Pollution, Abatement Possible by Spending Resources

Let K_a, L_a denote the amount of capital and labor respectively devoted to abatement. Let $\bar{K}$, $\bar{L}$ denote the aggregate endowment of capital and labor. Now the transformation function is $X_1 = F(X_2, \bar{K} - K_a, \bar{L} - L_a)$ and pollution is $P = P(X_1, X_2, K_a, L_a)$.

As before, with given X_1, X_2, K_a, and L_a, clearly free trade is optimal from a consumer perspective. As such, opening the economy to trade in consumption, while keeping production at autarky optimum levels, cannot reduce welfare. The indirect utility is as before $V(\pi, Y, P)$ where $Y = X_1 + \pi X_2$.

The first-order conditions for the optimal (interior) choice of production of X_2 and of resources K_a, L_a devoted to abatement are

$$V_2(F_1 + \pi) + V_3(P_1 F_1 + P_2) = 0 \tag{3}$$

$$V_2 F_2 + V_3 P_3 = 0 \tag{4}$$

$$V_2 F_3 + V_3 P_4 = 0 \tag{5}$$

First, equations 4 and 5 imply $F_2/F_3 = P_3/P_4$; that is, the marginal rate of substitution of capital and labor is the same in commodity production (i.e., F_2/F_3) as in pollution abatement (i.e., P_3/P_4).

Second, equation 3 is the same as equation 1 so that the conclusion that if an increase in output of 2 reduces (resp. increases) pollution it should be subsidized (resp. taxed) relative to its world price remains even with abatement possibilities. Only, now, the effect of or pollution of an increase in output of 2 is evaluated given the optimum levels of resources devoted to abatement.[82]

Finally, the result that welfare in a free-trading optimum is no less than under an autarky optimum continues to hold, though in general the optimal production tax or subsidy could be different in the two optima. Again this is a straightforward implication of the standard theory of domestic distortions.

A4.1.3   Large Country, Purely Domestic Pollution, Active Trade Policy with No Retaliation, Abatement Feasible

It should be evident from the analysis of the small-country model that, as long as pollution is a purely domestic distortion, standard theory should go through when a *purely* international distortion, namely, the ability to influence the terms of trade (which is not internalized by private domestic agents) is added. We confine ourselves to demonstrating this result for the case where abatement is possible. The same results can be easily seen to hold for the case when abatement is not possible.

Since terms of trade are now endogenous, it is more convenient to work with the direct utility function

$$U[F(X_2, \bar{K} - K_a, \bar{L} - L_a) + \pi(E_2)E_2, X_2 - E_2, P(F, X_2, K_a, L_a)]$$

where E_2 represents the net exports of good 2 and $\pi(E_2)$ the average price (in terms of good 1) per unit of good 2 exported. The choice variables are X_2, E_2, K_a, L_a. The corresponding first-order conditions for an interior maximum of U are

$$U_1 F_1 + U_2 + U_3(P_1 F_1 + P_2) = 0 \tag{6}$$

$$U_1(\pi_1 E_2 + \pi) - U_2 = 0 \tag{7}$$

$$-(U_1 + U_3 P_1)F_2 + U_3 P_3 = 0 \tag{8}$$

$$-(U_1 + U_3 P_1)F_3 + U_3 P_4 = 0 \tag{9}$$

From equation 7 it is seen that the domestic marginal rate of substitution between good 2 and good 1—that is, U_2/U_1—equals the *marginal revenue* (in terms of good 1) per unit of exports of good 2 at the optimal level of exports. Thus U_2/U_1 equals the marginal terms of trade and differs from the average terms of trade by the term $\pi_1 E_2$. The difference is the standard optimal tariff to exploit market power.

From equations 8 and 9 it is clear that the marginal rate of substitution between capital and labor in goods production—that is, F_2/F_3—equals that in pollution abatement—that is, P_3/P_4. Rewriting equation 6 as

$$-F_1 = U_2/U_1 + U_3(P_1F_1 + P_2)/U_1$$

it is seen that the domestic marginal rate of transformation between goods 1 and 2—that is, $-F_1$—differs from the domestic marginal rate of substitution U_2/U_1 by the addition of $U_3(P_1F_1 + P_2)/U_1$. By assumption, pollution hurts welfare so that U_3, the marginal utility of pollution, is negative, while U_1, the marginal utility of consumption of good 1, is positive. Thus the additional term is positive, zero, or negative according as the net addition to pollution of an increase in production of good 2—that is, $(P_1F_1 + P_2)$—is negative, zero, or positive. For example, if the net addition to pollution is positive so that the additional term is negative, it follows that, in addition to an optimal tariff (equation 7) to exploit market power in external markets, an optimum tax [of $U_3(P_1F_1 + P_2)/U_1$] on the production of good 2 is needed to allow for the *purely domestic distortion* of pollution.

It is evident that the feasibility of abatement does not affect the algebraic form of equations 6 and 7 on which the preceding result (about the need for an optimum tariff and a production tax) is based. As such the absence of the possibility of abatement does not affect the result.[83] Also, it should be obvious that welfare with trade restricted by an optimum tariff would be no less than under autarky.

The rest of the world's offer curve to the home economy—that is, $\pi(E_2)$—in the preceding analysis in principle could be viewed as a function $\pi(E_2, T^*)$ of home exports E_2 and foreign tariffs on home imports. Thus, given Cournot behavior, the home economy's optimal tariff will be a function (the home reaction function) of the given foreign tariff T^*. Similarly, there will be a foreign reaction function linking the optimal tariffs of the rest of the world to the home economy's tariff. As is well known since the work of Harry Johnson (1954), the intersection of the two reaction functions is the Cournot-Nash equilibrium of the tariff game. And such an equilibrium is not Pareto optimal from a global perspective.

A4.2   Global Pollution

A4.2.1   Small Country, Global Pollution

We begin, in this section and the next, with *national welfare* maximization, and then consider, in sections A4.2.3 through A4.2.8, questions relating to global Pareto optimality (i.e., "world welfare").

Assume now that the pollution is global; that is, its effect cuts across (some or all) national borders. In this case, the pollution function may be rewritten as $P[F(X_2, \bar{K} - K_a, \bar{L} - L_a) + X_1^*, X_2 + X_2^*, K_a + K_a^*, L_a + L_a^*]$ where the starred variables X_2^*, K_a^*, L_a^*, respectively, denote the output of good i ($i = 1, 2$) and the capital and labor devoted to abatement in the rest of the world.

Implicit in this formulation are two strong assumptions: first, only global levels of outputs, and not their distribution between countries, affect global pollution;

second, only global expenditure of resources on abatement, and not their distribution between countries, matters. The latter in effect postulates the *same technology*
of abatement among countries in the sense that at any level of *aggregate* resources
devoted to abatement, the marginal reduction in pollution achieved by a marginal
increase in *domestic* resources devoted to abatement is the same as that achieved
by a marginal increase in *foreign* resources devoted to abatement. But of course
this statement does not necessarily imply that the same amount of resources will
be devoted to abatement at home and abroad in any equilibrium. In section A4.2.7
we relax these assumptions.

Since by assumption a small country cannot affect the prices at which it trades
with the rest of the world through its trade policy, there is no channel by which it
can affect the commodity or factor prices in the rest of the world.[84] If we assume
Cournot behavior in that the small country takes the rest of the world's outputs
and pollution abatement resources as given, it is easily shown that the results of
section A4.1.2 continue to hold: free trade is optimal and the domestic marginal
rate of substitution between capital and labor should be the same in goods
production and pollution abatement.

However, the assumption of Cournot behavior is rather artificial in this case. It
is more natural to assume that if the country is "small," it will behave as if its
shares of global outputs and global resources devoted to abatement are negligible.
Thus it will treat pollution P as if it is a constant $\bar{P}$ that cannot be influenced by its
action. Clearly, it is optimal for such a country not to devote any resources to
pollution abatement; that is, it will free ride on the rest of the world's expenditure
of resources for abatement. It follows that if the trading system consisted a large
number of small countries in this sense, no country will spend any resources on
abatement: this is the analogue of the "tragedy of the commons" in the use of
common property resources.

A4.2.2   Large Country, Pollution Global, Cournot Behavior with Respect to Both Tariffs and Resource Allocation for Abatement Abroad

For simplicity consider a trading world of two countries. For any given level of
foreign tariff T^* and resource allocation for abatement K_a^*, L_a^*, the home economy's
terms of trade π depends on its own exports E_2. Thus the direct utility of the
home economy could be written as

$$U[F(X_2, \bar{K} - K_a, \bar{L} - L_a) + E_2\pi(E_2, T^*), X_2 - E_2, P]$$

where $P = P[F(X_2, \bar{K} - K_a, \bar{L} - L_a) + X_1^*, X_2 + X_2^*, K_a + K_a^*, L_a + L_a^*]$. Note that,
since the pollution is now global, the utility function is different from that in
section A4.1.2 insofar as it additionally includes *foreign outputs* that generate
pollution and *foreign inputs* that abate it (since both determine the amount of
foreign pollution).

The first-order conditions for an interior maximum of U with respect to X_2, E_2,
K_a, L_a are

$$U_1 F_1 + U_2 + U_3(P_1 F_1 + P_2) = 0 \tag{10}$$

$$U_1(\pi_1 E_2 + \pi) - U_2 = 0 \tag{11}$$

$$-(U_1 + U_3 P_1)F_2 + U_3 P_2 = 0 \qquad (12)$$

$$-(U_1 + U_3 P_1)F_3 + U_3 P_4 = 0 \qquad (13)$$

As is to be expected, given Cournot behavior (concerning both foreign tariffs and resource-abatement expenditures), these are exactly the same algebraically as equations 6 through 9. In other words, corresponding to each specified $(X_1^*, X_2^*, T^*, K_a^*, L_a^*)$, we have a home output $X_2(X_1^*, X_2^*, T^*, K_a^*, L_a^*)$, optimal tariff $T(X_1^*, X_2^*, T^*, K_a^*, L_a^*)$, and home expenditure of resources $K_a(X_1^*, X_2^*, T^*, K_a^*, L_a^*)$, $L_a(X_1^*, X_2^*, T^*, K_a^*, L_a^*)$. These three represent the *home* reaction functions to foreign outputs X_1^* and X_2^* (X_1^* and X_2^* are on the foreign transformation function, so that only one of them is independent), tariff T^*, and resources K_a^*, L_a^* allocated for abatement. It should be noted that, unless the utility function is additively separable in pollution, the domestic marginal rate of substitution (MRS) U_2/U_1 will be a function of foreign outputs and abatement resources. As such, from equation 11, it follows that the domestic optimal tariff will be a function not only of foreign tariff as usual, but also of foreign outputs and abatement resources.

Analogously one defines *foreign* reaction as a function of given values of the home outputs, tariff, and resource allocation for abatement. The "intersections" of the home and foreign reaction functions represent the Nash equilibrium values of outputs in the two countries and T^N, T^{*N}, K_a^N, K_a^{*N}, L_a^N, L_a^{*N}. As is well known, such Nash equilibria are not Pareto optimal.[85]

A4.2.3   Global Pareto Optimal Allocations

Pareto optimal allocations, on the other hand, are derived by maximizing a non-negatively weighted sum of the welfares of the two countries. It is more convenient to write the two utility functions as $U[C_1, C_2, P]$ and $U^*(C_1^*, C_2^*, P)$ where C_i, C_i^* represent the consumption of commodity i ($i = 1, 2$) and pollution

$$P = P[X_1 + X_1^*, X_2 + X_2^*, K_a + K_a^*, L_a + L_a^*] \qquad (14)$$

$$X_1 = F(X_2, \bar{K} - K_a, \bar{L} - L_a) \qquad (15)$$

$$X_1^* = F^*(X_2^*, \bar{K}^* - K_a^*, \bar{L} - L_a^*) \qquad (16)$$

Market clearance implies

$$C_1 + C_1^* = X_1 + X_1^* \qquad (17)$$

and

$$C_2 + C_2^* = X_2 + X_2^* \qquad (18)$$

Maximization of $\alpha U + (1 - \alpha)U^*$ (where $0 \le \alpha \le 1$) with respect to C_1, C_2, C_1^*, C_2^*, X_2, X_2^*, K_a, K_a^*, L_a, L_a^* subject to equations 17 and 18 after substituting equations 14, 15, and 16 into U and U^* yields the following first-order conditions for an interior maximum:[86]

$$\alpha U_1 - \lambda_1 = 0 \qquad (19)$$

$$\alpha U_2 - \lambda_2 = 0 \qquad (20)$$

$$(1 - \alpha)U_1^* - \lambda_1 = 0 \qquad (21)$$

$$(1 - \alpha)U_2^* - \lambda_2 = 0 \qquad (22)$$

$$[\alpha U_3 + (1 - \alpha)U_3^*](P_1 F_1 + P_2) + \lambda_1 F_1 + \lambda_2 = 0 \tag{23}$$

$$[\alpha U_3 + (1 - \alpha)U_3^*](P_1 F_1^* + P_2) + \lambda_1 F_1^* + \lambda_2 = 0 \tag{24}$$

$$[\alpha U_3 + (1 - \alpha)U_3^*]P_3 - (\lambda_1 + \alpha U_3 P_1)F_2 = 0 \tag{25}$$

$$[\alpha U_3 + (1 - \alpha)U_3^*]P_4 - (\lambda_1 + \alpha U_3 P_1)F_3 = 0 \tag{26}$$

$$[\alpha U_3 + (1 - \alpha)U_3^*]P_3 - [\lambda_1 + (1 - \alpha)U_3^* P_1]F_2^* = 0 \tag{27}$$

$$[\alpha U_3 + (1 - \alpha)U_3^*]P_4 - [\lambda_1 + (1 - \alpha)U_3^* P_1]F_3^* = 0 \tag{28}$$

From equations 19–22, it follows that the marginal rate of substitution (MRS) between goods 1 and 2 in consumption is the same in the two countries; that is, $U_2/U_1 = U_2^*/U_1^* = \lambda_2/\lambda_1$ regardless of the value α. Thus, from a consumer perspective, there is free trade in a Pareto optimum.

However, from equations 23 and 24, it is seen that the marginal rate of transformation (MRT) between goods 1 and 2 at home, $-F_1$, equals $\lambda_2/\lambda_1 + (1/\lambda_1)[\alpha U_3 + (1 - \alpha)U_3^*](P_1 F_1 + P_2)$; and abroad, $-F_1^*$ equals $\lambda_2/\lambda_1 + (1/\lambda_1)[\alpha U_3 + (1 - \alpha)U_3^*](P_1 F_1^* + P_2)$. Thus MRT at home (resp. abroad) differs from the common MRS by $[1/\lambda_1][\alpha U_3 + (1 - \alpha)U_3^*][P_1 F_1 + P_2]$ (resp. $[1/\lambda_1][\alpha U_3 + (1 - \alpha)U_3^*][P_1 F_1^* + P_2]$). This term is easily interpreted: $[\alpha U_3 + (1 - \alpha)U_3^*]$ is the global welfare effect of a marginal increase in pollution, that is, the shadow price of a unit of pollution again in global welfare units; λ_1 is, as noted earlier, the shadow price of good 1. Thus the ratio of these two terms represents the global shadow "price" of a marginal unit of pollution in units of good 1, and at a Pareto optimum it is the *same* in the two countries. The term $(P_1 F_1 + P_2)$ is the net pollution effect of a marginal increase in the production of good 2 at home. The product of all three terms is thus in units of good 1 per unit of good 2 and represents the trade-off between the pollution of the two goods at home through the relative global welfare effects they have through pollution. Thus, at a Pareto optimum, the home MRT between the two goods must equal the sum of their relative welfare effects through their consumption—that is, λ_2/λ_1—and their relative welfare effects through pollution, which is the second term. An analogous condition applies in the foreign country.

If we interpret the difference between MRS and MRT as a shadow production tax or subsidy on good 2 it is seen from equations 23 and 24 that this tax/subsidy would be the same in the two countries if $F_1 = F_1^*$ at an optimum, that is, if the MRT is the same in the two countries. At the same time, it is evident from equations 25–28 that the marginal rate of substitution between capital and labor is the *same* in the two countries in *all* activities, whether production or abatement. Thus, if we interpret the marginal rate of substitution as the shadow wage-rental ratio, it is the same in the two countries. With shadow commodity prices the same, factor price equalization follows. If the available technology of production of goods is the same in the two countries, then with factor price equalization the shadow production tax/subsidy rates will be the same in the two countries. The global Pareto optimal solution will require tax harmonization!

The first-order conditions relating to MRT in the two countries, taken together with the fact that MRS is the same in the two countries, imply that free trade combined with an appropriate production tax or subsidy is the appropriate policy associated with a Pareto optimum. However, in general, if the value of α is set *exogenously*, trade between the countries need not be balanced so that a lump sum income transfer from the country running the trade surplus to that running the deficit would be required to support the chosen Pareto optimum. But α can be chosen *endogenously* to ensure that no transfers are needed; that is, trade is balanced. A heuristic argument for the existence of such an α is as follows (the existence of such a unique α is shown for a special case in section A4.2.7). Set $\alpha = 1$ so that the foreign economy's welfare receives a zero weight. Clearly, at the associated Pareto optimum, the foreign economy in effect transfers its entire income to the home economy. The reverse happens when α is set at zero. Thus, by continuity, at some α between 0 and 1, the required transfer will be zero. However, the implementation of the associated Pareto optimum involves the use of information on the welfare effect of pollution in *both* countries for devising the appropriate taxes and subsidies in each.

A comparison of the first-order condition relating to home MRT with the analogous conditions in the Cournot-Nash case of section A4.2.2 makes it clear that, in the latter, each country ignores the effect of its production choice on foreign welfare through pollution so that the resulting Nash equilibrium cannot be Pareto optimal.

A4.2.4   Deviant Behavior by One Country, Global Pareto Optimality

The implementation of the global Pareto optimum with or without transfers involves the use of a set of optimal production taxes or subsidies in each country and the expenditure of appropriate levels of resources on pollution abatement. Suppose for instance, however, that one of the countries, say the home country, is required to devote a positive amount of capital and labor to abatement in supporting the Pareto optimum. If it deviates and, for example, does not spend *any resources* on abatement, we may ask whether a restricted Pareto optimum is still attainable. Will it involve the use of trade policy?

Referring back to the first-order condition (equations 19–28) characterizing a Pareto optimum, we see now that conditions 25 and 26 relating to the capital K_a and labor L_a devoted to abatement by the home country no longer apply. But the remaining conditions continue to hold. Therefore, free trade along with an appropriate set of production taxes and subsidies continues to support a restricted Pareto optimum.

Of course, the reason why a restricted Pareto optimum is achievable with free trade even though the home economy devotes no resources to abatement is obvious: since by assumption the externality of pollution arises from *production*, no deviation from free trade with respect to *consumption* is called for.

Indeed this argument goes even further. Suppose, for instance, that for whatever reason the home economy not only devotes no resources to abatement but also chooses production levels different from those associated with an unrestricted Pareto optimum. This assumption means that conditions 23, 25, and 26 no longer apply. However, equations 19–22 continue to apply so that free trade with respect to *consumption* continues to be optimal. And since equation 24 still applies, the foreign economy has to levy an optimal production tax or subsidy to sustain this further-restricted Pareto optimum. The home economy can, of course, sustain its deviant behavior through a variety of means.

It should be noted that, from the perspective of a global Pareto optimum, countries are symmetric. As such, which country, namely the home or the foreign country, deviates in its behavior is immaterial to the characterization of the restricted Pareto optimum. In the preceding analysis, if the foreign, rather than the home, country does not devote as many resources as it should in supporting an *unrestricted* Pareto optimum, conditions 27 and 28 rather than 25 and 26 no longer apply. But this difference does not affect the conclusion that free trade, along with an appropriate set of production taxes and subsidies, supports a *restricted* Pareto optimum.

A4.2.5   Shadow Factor Price Equalization

In the model of section A4.2.3, the shadow factor prices are equalized at the chosen Pareto optimum; whether or not there is international factor mobility is therefore irrelevant. However, such shadow factor price equalization need not always occur. The considerations that lead to the shadow factor price equalization in section A4.2.3 are as follows:

1. At a global welfare optimum in which a *positive* amount of each commodity is consumed in each country, the shadow commodity prices for consumers (in global welfare units) have to be the same in both countries.

2. The shadow price of pollution (in welfare units) is also the same in both countries.

3. If each country is devoting a positive amount of *each* factor to pollution abatement, then because one country's factor is a perfect substitute for the other country's in pollution abatement, and the price of pollution is the same in the two countries; the marginal value of each factor in pollution abatement must be the same in the two countries; and it follows then that the shadow price of each factor in global welfare units is equalized between countries. Also, because the consumer shadow price of each commodity in *welfare* units is the same in the two countries, we see by taking the ratio of shadow factor price to the shadow consumer price of either commodity that the equalization of shadow factor prices in *commodity* units follows.

Thus, shadow factor prices (in any commodity unit) cannot be equalized if any of the preceding considerations do not apply. For example, if consumers in the home country do not consume the first commodity while foreign consumers do, the marginal rate of substitution of the two goods in consumption at home will differ between countries. As such, factor prices in commodity units could differ between countries even if they are equalized in welfare units.

A4.2.6   Efficiency and Equity: Possible Conflicts

The Analytical Argument
A globally Pareto optimal allocation of resources is *efficient* in two senses. It is *distributionally* efficient in the sense that there is no other feasible allocation that

could make one country better off without making some other country worse off. It is also *productively* efficient in the sense that the allocation across countries of production, and hence of pollution generated by production, is such that there is no other feasible allocation that will increase the consumption of some commodity in a country without reducing the consumption of any other commodities anywhere or increasing pollution, or alternatively will reduce pollution without at the same time reducing the consumption of some commodity somewhere. The pure gain in moving to an efficient allocation from an inefficient one could be distributed among countries to make at least one country better off without hurting others.

While a Pareto optimal allocation is thus *efficient*, it need not be *equitable*. For example, an allocation that uses all of the world's resources to maximize just one country's welfare is Pareto optimal but hardly equitable. On the other hand, an equitable allocation in the sense of maximizing a *global* welfare function that incorporates equity considerations would also be Pareto optimal as long as the global welfare function is increasing in each country's welfare. Thus such an equitable allocation is necessarily Pareto optimal and hence efficient in both senses.

The preceding arguments suggest that there needs to be no conflict between equity and efficiency. Indeed this would be the case if instruments exist that would sustain an equitable Pareto optimal allocation. For example, a market mechanism for resource allocation, *supplemented* by lump sum *transfers* as needed between countries, could sustain an allocation such an allocation. However, if transfers are infeasible, then an equilibrium market allocation (without transfers) need not be equitable. Then achieving a more equitable allocation will involve in this case the sacrifice of efficiency in one or both senses.

Illustrations
A suggestive illustration of a possible conflict between efficiency and distributional equity is shown in Figure 1. The marginal cost of pollution abatement in the United States is seen to be above that in Brazil at all levels of pollution to be abated up to $\bar{P}$. As such, it will be cost efficient for only Brazil to engage in pollution abatement up to $\bar{P}$. For Brazil also to bear the full cost of such abatement would be deemed (at least by Brazilians) inequitable!

Consider also the following simple version of the model of section A4.2.3. Take two countries. The home (resp. foreign) country has $\bar{H}$ (resp. $\bar{H}^*$) hectares of virgin forest. A hectare of this forest, if cleared and planted with wheat (resp. rice), will produce 1 ton of wheat (resp. rice), and release μ (resp. μ^*) liters of pollutants into the environment. Left as forest land, on the other hand, that hectare would have removed γ (resp. γ^*) liters of pollutants from the environment.

Home utility U is given by

$$U = \theta_1 \log C_1 + \theta_2 \log C_2 + \theta_3 \log(\bar{P} - P) \qquad (29)$$

where $1 \geq \theta_i \geq 0$, $\theta_3 \equiv 1 - \theta_1 - \theta_2$, C_1 is the consumption of wheat, C_2 is the consumption of rice, P is the quantity of (net) pollutants in the economy and $\bar{P}$ is the maximum amount of pollutants consistent with survival. Analogously, foreign utility U^* is given by

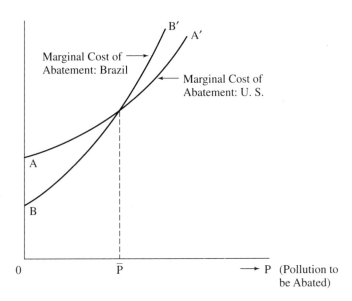

Figure 1
Efficiency and Equity with Global Pollution: Partial Equilibrium

$$U^* = \theta_1^* \log C_1^* + \theta_2^* \log C_2^* + \theta_3^* \log(\bar{P} - P) \tag{30}$$

where $1 \geq \theta_i^* \geq 0$, $\theta_3^* \equiv 1 - \theta_1^* - \theta_2^*$.

Clearly, in this model we have

$$C_1 + C_1^* = X_1 \equiv \text{Output of wheat} \tag{31}$$

$$C_2 + C_2^* = X_2^* \equiv \text{Output of rice} \tag{32}$$

$$P = \mu X_1 + \mu^* X_2^* - \gamma(\bar{H} - X_1) - \gamma^*(\bar{H}^* - X_2^*)$$

$$= (\gamma + \mu)X_1 + (\gamma^* + \mu^*)X_2^* - \gamma\bar{H} - \gamma^*\bar{H}^* \tag{33}$$

As in section A4.2.3, Pareto optimal allocations are derived by maximizing $[\alpha U + (1 - \alpha)U^*]$ for $0 \leq \alpha \leq 1$. The resulting production, pollution, consumption, and welfare levels can be characterized as follows.

In this simple model, the efficient combinations of X_1, X_2^*, and P (in the production sense) are given by equation 33 where obviously $0 \leq X_1 \leq \bar{H}$ and $0 \leq X_2^* \leq \bar{H}^*$. It can be shown that the efficient values of X_1, X_2^*, and P associated with the Pareto optimum corresponding to α are given by[87]

$$X_1 = \left[\frac{\alpha\theta_1 + (1 - \alpha)\theta_1^*}{\gamma + \mu}\right][\bar{P} + \mu\bar{H} + \mu^*\bar{H}^*] \tag{34}$$

$$X_2 = \left[\frac{\alpha\theta_2 + (1 - \alpha)\theta_2^*}{\gamma^* + \mu^*}\right][\bar{P} + \mu\bar{H} + \mu^*\bar{H}^*] \tag{35}$$

$$\bar{P} - P = [\alpha\theta_3 + (1 - \alpha)\theta_3^*][\bar{P} + \mu\bar{H} + \mu^*\bar{H}^*] \tag{36}$$

The consumption of wheat and rice in the two countries in the Pareto optimum is given by

$$C_1 = \left[\frac{\alpha\theta_1}{\alpha\theta_1 + (1 - \alpha)\theta_1^*}\right]X_1; \qquad C_1^* = \left[\frac{(1 - \alpha)\theta_2^*}{\alpha\theta_1 + (1 - \alpha)\theta_1^*}\right]X_1 \tag{37}$$

$$C_2 = \left[\frac{\alpha\theta_2}{\alpha\theta_2 + (1 - \alpha)\theta_2^*}\right]X_2^*; \qquad C_2^* = \left[\frac{(1 - \alpha)\theta_2^*}{\alpha\theta_1 + (1 - \alpha)\theta_2^*}\right]X_2^* \tag{38}$$

The welfare levels U and U^* in the Pareto optimum are given by

$$U = (\theta_1 + \theta_2)\log\alpha + \theta_3\log[\alpha\theta_3 + (1 - \alpha)\theta_3^*] + \theta_1[\log\theta_1 - \log(\gamma + \mu)]$$
$$+ \theta_2[\log\theta_2 - \log(\gamma^* + \mu^*)] + \log(\bar{P} + \mu\bar{H} + \mu^*\bar{H}^*) \tag{39}$$

$$U^* = (\theta_1^* + \theta_2^*)\log(1 - \alpha) + \theta_3^*\log[\alpha\theta_3 + (1 - \alpha)\theta_3^*] + \theta_1^*[\log\theta_1^* - \log(\gamma + \mu)]$$
$$+ \theta_2^*[\log\theta_2 - \log(\gamma^* + \mu^*)] + \log(\bar{P} + \mu\bar{H} + \mu^*\bar{H}^*) \tag{40}$$

The shadow prices (in global welfare units) of goods 1 and 2 and "clean" air (i.e., $\bar{P} - P$) for consumers are, respectively,

$$\lambda_1 = \left[\frac{(\alpha + \mu)}{\bar{P} + \mu\bar{H} + \mu^*\bar{H}^*}\right], \quad \lambda_2 = \left[\frac{\alpha^* + \mu^*}{\bar{P} + \mu\bar{H} + \mu^*\bar{H}^*}\right], \quad \lambda_3 = \frac{1}{\bar{P} + \mu\bar{H} + \mu^*\bar{H}^*} \tag{41}$$

Note that the shadow prices do not depend on α. Two further observations are in order.

First, it can be easily shown now that as α increases from zero to 1, U increases and U^* decreases. Eliminating α between equations 39 and 40 yields the utility possibility frontier of U^* as a function of U. The value of consumption at home (resp. abroad), namely, $\lambda_1 C_1 + \lambda_2 C_2$ (resp. $\lambda_1 C_1^* + \lambda_2 C_2^*$) exceeds disposable income $\lambda_1 X_1$ (resp. $\lambda_2 X_2^*\lambda$) by $\alpha\theta_2 - (1 - \alpha)\theta_1^*$ [resp. $(1 - \alpha)\theta_1^* - \alpha\theta_2$]. Thus an income transfer of $\alpha\theta_2 - (1 - \alpha)\theta_1^*$ from country 2 to country 1 is implicit in the preceding Pareto optimum. No transfer will be required only for $\alpha = \theta_1^*/(\theta_1^* + \theta_2)$. (The reason that consumer disposable income is the value of production at consumer prices is that a lump-sum tax or subsidy needed to finance the wedge between consumer and producer prices has to be subtracted [or added] to the value of production at producer prices [i.e., income at factor cost] to arrive at disposable income at market prices.)

Second, inspection of equations 34–36 also reveals that if $\theta_i = \theta_i^*$ ($i = 1, 2, 3$) so that both countries have identical tastes, efficient production and pollution levels (X_1, X_2^*, and P) are independent of α. Thus the choice of α affects only the distribution of the fixed outputs of X_1 and X_2^* between the two countries for consumption purposes. In this case, the utility possibility frontier is given by

$$U^* = (\theta_1 + \theta_2)\log[1 - e^{-(\delta - U)/(\theta_1 + \theta_2)}] + \delta, \qquad -\infty \leq U \leq \delta \tag{42}$$

where $\delta = \theta_1[\log\theta_1 - \log(\gamma + \mu)] + \theta_2[\log\theta_2 - \log(\gamma + \mu)] + \theta_3 + \log(\bar{P} + \mu\bar{H} + \mu^*\bar{H}^*)$. It can be seen from equations 39 and 40 that as $\alpha \to 0$, $U \to -\infty$ and $U^* \to \delta$, and as $\alpha \to 1$, $U \to \delta$ and $U^* \to -\infty$. In fact U^* is a concave function of U as depicted in Figure 2 for the case $\delta > 0$. It is seen that δ represents the maximal utility that *either* country would achieve if *global* resources are used to maximize only its utility—in other words, the weight placed on the other country's utility in the global welfare function is zero. With the countries being identical in tastes, this maximal utility is the same for both countries.

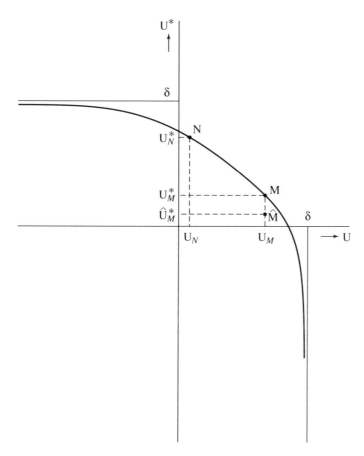

Figure 2
Efficiency and Equity in World Pollution: General Equilibrium

We may now use this simple model, with the added simplification of *identical tastes*,[88] to illustrate efficiency-equity conflicts in two different ways.

(1) Suppose first that income transfers between the countries are infeasible so that the only feasible Pareto optimal allocation is that corresponding to $\alpha = \theta_1 / (\theta_1 + \theta_2)$ (point N in Figure 2 which assumes identical tastes). If, say, the welfare U_N of the home economy at N is deemed too low and an increase of it to U_M is deemed desirable, had transfers been feasible, the point M on the utility possibility frontier would have been the optimal way (i.e., with the least loss of foreign welfare) of achieving such an increase. With transfers infeasible, the welfare of the foreign economy would have to be reduced below U_M^* (say to $\hat{U}_M^*$) for achieving such an increase. Thus the loss $(U_M^* - \hat{U}_M^*)$ is the loss from distributional inefficiency (in departing from Pareto optimality) incurred in order to achieve equity, given that transfers are infeasible.

(2) However, the no-transfer Pareto optimal allocation N might be deemed unsatisfactory for a reason other than its being inequitable; the associated global pollution levels may be viewed as "too high." This might happen if it is believed that one or both counties attach "too low" a value to clean air in their preferences. In the context of our simple model, if preferences are the same in the two countries, a natural way to express this concern is to set an upper bound $\hat{P}$ on pollution levels. Now from equation 36 it is seen that $P = \bar{P} - [\alpha\theta_3 + (1 - \alpha)\theta_3^*](\bar{P} + \mu\bar{H} + \mu^*\bar{H}^*)$. If tastes are identical so that $\theta_3 = \theta_3^*$, then recall that P is independent of α and equals $\bar{P} - \theta_3(\bar{P} + \mu\bar{H} + \mu^*\bar{H}^*)$. If this exceeds $\hat{P}$, then there is no feasible Pareto optimum with or without transfers that can achieve the upper bound $\hat{P}$. If it is less than or equal to $\hat{P}$, the upper bound is respected at all Pareto optima.

Let us consider the case where $\bar{P} - \theta_3(\bar{P} + \mu H + \mu^*\bar{H}^*) > \hat{P}$ so that the upper bound represents a binding constraint. Of course, if we give up all production and consumption, net pollution P will be negative, since the pollutant-absorbing capacity of the virgin forests will come into full play then. As such, it is feasible to meet the bound $\hat{P}$ by reducing production relative to the levels at a Pareto optimum. It can then be shown that the *efficient* way of achieving $\hat{P}$ without transfers is to *reduce* the output of X_1 and X_2^* by the same proportion so that $X_1 = \beta X_1^0$, $X_2 = \beta X_2^{*0}$ where X_1^0 *and* X_2^{*0} are the values given by equations 34 and 35, and $\beta = \left(\dfrac{\hat{P} + \bar{\mu}\bar{H} + \mu^*\bar{H}^*}{\bar{P} + \bar{\mu}\bar{H} + \mu^*\bar{H}^*}\right)(1 - \theta_3)$.[89] Clean air—that is, $\bar{P} - \hat{P}$— goes up relative to $\bar{P} - P^0$ by the factor $\left(\dfrac{1 - \beta(1 - \theta_3)}{\theta_3}\right)$. This *reduces* the welfare of each country by the *same amount* $-(\theta_1 + \theta_2)\log\beta - \theta_3[\log(1 - \beta(1 - \theta_3)) - \log\theta_3]$. While such a reduction is efficient in meeting the bound $\hat{P}$ on pollution, the incidence might be viewed as inequitable if the post-reduction welfare level of one of the countries is relatively low. Once again, meeting the bound and being equitable at the same time will then mean deviating from efficiency.

What happens in the *general case* in which the two countries do not have identical tastes so that $\theta_3 \neq \theta_3^*$? It is then seen from equation 36 that pollution P is an increasing (resp. decreasing) function of α if $\theta_3^* > \theta_3$ (resp. $\theta_3^* < \theta_3$). This observation is not surprising, since θ_3 (resp. θ_3^*) is analogous to the "share" of clean air in the home economy's spending and, as α increases, the home economy's share in world spending increases. Hence, if the "share" of clean air in the home economy's spending is less than that of the foreign economy, pollution increases as a greater share of world spending accrues to the home economy.

Now, for concreteness, assume that $\theta_3^* > \theta_3$ so that pollution increases with α. Then, as long as there exists an $\hat{\alpha}$ $(0 < \hat{\alpha} < 1)$ at which pollution equals $\hat{P}$, pollution will be less than $\hat{P}$ for *all* α in the interval $0 \leq \alpha \leq \hat{\alpha}$. Of course, unless the no-transfer value of α—that is, $\theta_1^*/(\theta_1^* + \theta_2)$—is less than $\hat{\alpha}$, the bound $\hat{P}$ cannot be met at a Pareto optimal allocation if transfers are ruled out: efficiency will have to be sacrificed again in the interest of equity.

Our analysis of this model has then illustrated the following key propositions:

(a) As long as lump-sum income transfers between countries are feasible, it is possible to achieve a resource allocation that is at the same time *distributionally efficient* in the sense that relative to it, any other allocation will make at least one country worse off in terms of consumer welfare, *productively efficient* in the sense that relative to it in any other allocation there will be less output of at least one commodity or greater pollution, and *equitable* in the sense of maximizing a global welfare function that incorporates distributional equity among countries while being an increasing function of each country's welfare.

(b) If such transfers are infeasible, at least one of the preceding three desiderata has to be given up. For example, a distributionally and productively efficient allocation without transfers was shown to exist that was not deemed equitable. Achieving equity then involves a sacrifice of efficiency in both senses.

(c) Equity was judged in propositions a and b by a global welfare function that was solely a function of the welfare of consumers in each country as perceived by them. In other words, the welfare evaluations of each country's consumers were respected. If, for example, these evaluations are deemed inappropriate because they attach too little weight to global pollution, then an efficient allocation without transfers that is equitable (in the sense of proposition a) may not be satisfactory from the perspective of a global welfare function that overrides consumer weighing of global pollution. Once again, to achieve a satisfactory allocation, either efficiency or equity, in the sense of proposition, a or both have to be given up.

A4.2.7   Country-Specific Pollution Generation and Abatement

As noted earlier, the preceding analysis of global pollution assumed that the outputs of two countries (resp. the resources devoted to pollution abatement) were perfect substitutes for each other in the generation of pollution (resp. in abatement). This assumption is easily relaxed. Consider again the case of global Pareto optimality of section A4.2.3. Let the pollution function (equation 14) be replaced by

$$P = P[F(X_2, \bar{K} - K_a, \bar{L} - L_a), X_2, K_a, L_a, F^*(X_2^*, \bar{K}^* - K_a^*, \bar{L}^* - L_a^*), X_2^*, K_a^*, L_a^*] \quad (43)$$

First-order conditions (equations 19–22) still hold, and as such free trade with respect to consumption continues to be optimal. Conditions 23, 25, and 26 still hold (recall that subscript i of P continues to denote the partial derivative with respect to its ith argument, except P now has eight, instead of four, arguments). Equation 24 is replaced by $[\alpha U_3 + (1 - \alpha) U_3^*][P_5 F_1^* + P_6] + \lambda_1 F_1^* + \lambda_2 = 0$. Equations 27 and 28 continue to hold with P_3 replaced by P_7 and P_4 by P_8.

The only significant result that is different from section A4.2.3 is that, while *within each country* the marginal rate of substitution between capital and labor is the same in goods production and pollution abatement, this common rate is not in general the same in the two countries. As such, the factor price equalization result need no longer hold. Also, with the outputs and resources devoted to pollution abatement in the two countries not being perfect substitutes for each other in pollution generation and abatement, respectively, the efficiency-equity conflict discussed in section A4.2.6 is more likely.

A4.3   Previous Contributions of Relevance to Our Analysis

There is a significant volume of scholarly literature on trade and the environment, most of it published in the last three years or so.[90] The literature is diverse in incorporating environmental considerations into economic models and in the policy questions addressed. It is beyond our scope to provide a critical survey and assessment of this literature.

Before discussing the two contributions most closely related to this Chapter, however, it is worth pointing out that we have mostly confined our analysis to "first-best" policies in a context where environmental externalities or other distortions are present. We did so primarily because it is well known that (1) when a number of distortions are present, removing or reducing a subset of them need not be welfare-improving and that whether it is or not would depend on the specific circumstances; and (2) when first-best policies are infeasible, other policies might exist that will improve welfare over laissez-faire, but in general the ranking of such policies according to the net welfare improvement they bring about is not possible (while of course in particular circumstances it might be).

In the literature, a frequently posed question is whether moving from autarky to free trade would be welfare improving in situations where trade-environment interactions are present, and, of course, answers vary depending on assumptions about other policies. This is just another illustration of the first of the two well-known results stated in the preceding paragraph. After all, the welfare superiority of free trade over autarky depends on the absence of other distortions.

The contributions that come closest to our Chapter are by Markusen (1975, 1976). Markusen (1975) models pollution much in the same way as we do except that, in his case, the production of only one of the two commodities (the same one in each country) generates global pollution and no abatement is possible. His analysis of "first-best" policies for maximizing national welfare is the same as for our case of a large country but without abatement possibilities (section A4.2.2): an optimum tariff combined with a production tax is first-best optimal.

He then considers the case when the first-best combination is infeasible and in turn examines the use of consumption taxes only, tariffs only, and production taxes only, as second-best policy instruments. He finds that the formulas for the calculation of some second-best instruments contain components of opposite algebraic signs so that taken together they lead to an ambiguous sign for the instrument. This result means, first, that whether the instrument will be a tax or subsidy or neither (i.e., laissez-faire) will depend on the numerical balance between the positive and negative components, a balance that can only be decided empirically. Second, even if a second-best instrument has an unambiguous sign, it does not mean that its use will produce a superior welfare outcome compared to another instrument whose second-best value is of ambiguous sign. This is an illustration of the second of the well-known results: second-best policy rankings are circumstance-dependent.

Markusen (1976) models pollution the same way as Markusen (1975). But now the policy issues are considered not from the perspective of a single large country that faces no retaliation or ignores it even if it is possible, but in the context of two countries that are "small" relative to the rest of the world from the perspective of commodity trade but whose production-generated pollution affects the welfare of both. Each government has production and trade taxes as policy instruments at its disposal.

Markusen first solves for the optimum tax structure for each when it takes the other's tax structure as given (Cournot behavior) thus leading to a Cournot-Nash equilibrium tax structure in the usual fashion. The Cournot-Nash equilibrium is then compared with two types of cooperative equilibria—one without transfer payments and the other with transfer payments. Three conclusions are derived. First, for any distribution of world resources, there exists some set of allocations that make both countries better off relative to some suboptimal equilibrium. Second, in the absence of transfer payments, there exists a set of cooperative solutions that achieve such an allocation. Third, if transfer payments are permitted, Pareto optimal allocations that make both countries better off relative to the Cournot equilibrium are attainable. These conclusions are clearly similar to some of ours relating to Nash equilibria and global Pareto optimality.

NOTES

We have profited from the comments on an earlier draft by several project participants, especially Ken Abbott, Christopher Bliss, Drusilla Brown, Alessandra Casella, Alan Deardorff, Robert Hudec, Al Klevorick, Brian Langille, Virginia Leary, Andre Sapir, and John Wilson, at a conference at the Minnesota Law School in July 1993 and at a Washington, DC, conference in October 1994. The comments of Claude Barfield, Steve Charnowitz, Dan Esty, William Nordhaus, Susan Rose-Ackerman, and Karl-Göran Mäler have been very helpful. While we take joint responsibility for the entire chapter, the blame for any errors in the text must be assigned to Bhagwati and in the Appendix to Srinivasan!

1. By CCII, we mean harmonization of standards within the *same* industry across different trading countries.

2. This, of course, is the central issue addressed later in this chapter.

3. The suspension of trade generally, i.e., the use of trade "sanctions" (to promote human rights, for instance) is a related but different issue that we do not discuss in this chapter in depth.

4. As in argument 2.

5. The difficulties posed by the GATT, and now the WTO, for the environmentalists extend to GATT law (i.e., Dispute Settlement Panel findings) in regard to the ethical-preference issue as well. The general issue of GATT law on the entire range of relevant questions concerning the environment is addressed by Frieder Roessler in Chapter 2 in Volume 2 of this work.

6. *International Pollution Deterrence Act of 1991*, Statement of Senator David L. Boren, Senate Finance Committee, October 25, 1991.

7. We will be considering several objections to this view, of course, before reaching this conclusion.

8. The entire range of the factors (philosophical, economic, and political) that are currently prompting the drive toward CCII harmonization is reviewed and synthesized by Bhagwati

in Chapter 1. See also the discussion in Daniel Esty, *Greening the GATT* (Washington, DC: Institute for International Economics, 1994), pp. 108–114, 156–167.

9. "Bushism, Found: A Second-Term Agenda Hidden in Trade Agreements," *Harper's Magazine*, September 1992, p. 44.

10. Cf. J. Bhagwati and M. Kosters, eds., *Trade and Wages* (Washington, DC: American Enterprise Institute, 1994). Several trade economists share this skeptical view; see the most recent review in Jagdish Bhagwati, "Trade and wages: Choosing among alternative explanations," *Federal Reserve Bank of New York Economic Policy Review*, January 1995.

11. Cf. J. Bhagwati, "Free traders and free immigrationists: Friends or foes?" (mimeo) (New York: Russell Sage Foundation, 1992).

12. The prominent U.S. role in the UN Conference on Population in Cairo in September 1994 may be explained, at least in part, in this fashion.

13. Cf. Appendix, section A4.1.1.

14. Cf. Appendix, section A4.1.2.

15. Thus, any unfixed domestic distortion, such as failure to have optimal pollution taxes or adequate institutional arrangements to prevent the overuse of commons, for instance, can lead to immiserization under free trade vis-à-vis autarky. Cf. the review in Bhagwati (1971). Also see the recent writings of Graciela Chichilinsky, Peter Lloyd, and others on this question.

16. Cf. Appendix, section A4.1.3.

17. Cf. the contribution of D. Brown, A. Deardorff, and R. Stern (Chapter 5). The answer eventually depends on how the offer curve of the lower-standard country shifts with the harmonization up.

18. The conditions under which tax harmonization will occur in a globally Pareto optimal solution are discussed in section A4.2.3 of the Appendix.

19. Cf. Appendix, section A4.2.4.

20. Cf. Appendix, section A4.2.1.

21. Cf. Appendix, section A4.2.2.

22. We should also state the related but distinct proposition that diversity of standards across countries will be observed as the norm in competitive equilibrium and, besides, will change with trade and hence income (as implicit, of course, in our preceding analysis and in the Appendix). This proposition is also derived, in the context of a model where standards are characterized as having some of the characteristics of "public goods" in each of two trading countries and enter directly the utility functions in these countries, by Alessandra Casella in Chapter 3. The focus of our analysis instead is on the issue of CCII harmonization and on the question of standards diversity when welfare maximization is being pursued (and may require departure from a laissez-faire competitive equilibrium).

23. This phrase has passed even into the latest annual report of the Council of Economic Advisers as part of a definition of "competitiveness" that Paul Krugman has castigated in a recent article in *Foreign Affairs*.

24. If the country is large, then we must substitute an optimal tariff for free trade in this sentence.

25. Thus recent judicial determinations in the United States have undermined the public law that had grown up earlier with strong support for environmentalism, not reflective of costs and benefits, for the possibility of "takings" in the public environmental interest and in regard to standing and judicial review. The earlier public law literature is well represented by Abram Chayes, "The role of the judge in public law litigation," *Harvard Law Review*, 89 (1976), and Ronald Dworkin, *Law's empire*, 1986; and it is also well developed in India, in regard to standing (for NGOs etc.) in particular, in the public interest litigation developed in the Supreme Court. The reverse movement in the United States can be seen from cases such as *Lucas v. South Carolina Coastal Council* and *Nollan v. California Coastal Commission* on takings, *Lujan v. National Wildlife Federation and Lujan v. Defenders of Wildlife* on standing, and *Competitive Enterprise Institute v. National Highway Traffic Safety Administration* and *Corrosion Proof Fittings v. EPA* on judicial review. The last area has, in particular, seen the increased judicial scrutiny of the cost-benefit aspects of executive actions implementing legislated regulation. The U.S. Congress is itself currently in the midst of an intense battle over precisely this question, with the New Democrat Clinton administration much more open to cost-benefit analysis than the older Democrats.

26. The question of democracy is addressed, from a different perspective, in section 4.4.3.

27. An in-depth review and synthesis of the theoretical literature on this question is provided by John Wilson in his chapter for the project, "Capital mobility and environmental standards: Is there a theoretical basis for a race to the bottom?" (Chapter 10 of this volume). We therefore only sketch the nature of the argument here.

28. Wilson, Chapter 10.

29. Cf. Arik Levinson's chapter for the project, "Environmental regulation and industry location: International and domestic evidence" (Chapter 11 of this volume). Levinson looks at both the international and the domestic evidence (e.g., interstate locational decisions in the United States, since states have different standards), having himself produced first-rate work in the latter genre.

30. Cf. Levinson, Chapter 11, citing, for instance, work by Baumol and Oates, Low, etc.

31. Levinson, Chapter 11, cites work by Hamilton, Baldwin, and Welles, and Walter on voter participation, in particular.

32. Levinson, Chapter 11, cites this explanation from the work of Gladwin and Welles, and Knögden. The argument requires that the transaction costs of diverse choices are large enough to offset the forgone advantage of meeting each standard only as necessary and not beyond. Besides, it does not apply to single-plant firms or to subsidiaries that act as more or less independent decision makers.

33. Again, the argument requires that the advantages of being "ahead of the curve" offset the advantages of conforming to lower standards now and adapting or retooling later when the higher standards emerge.

34. Cf. Levinson, Chapter 11, citing Pearson.

35. E.g., the (static and dynamic) arguments underlying Explanation 2 imply that CCII differences will be disregarded by multinationals in any event, with their plant-design choice gravitating toward the higher-standard technology everywhere and therefore locational choices becoming independent of CCII differences in standards.

36. Cf. Levinson, Chapter 11.

37. To our knowledge, the countervailing of *implicit* subsidies would be a novel principle in GATT law on subsidies as well, and is not to be contemplated with equanimity in view of its explosive potential; it is probably for this reason that the concept of remedy used by the proponents of harmonization of standards is that of AD rather than of CVD (countervailing duties on foreign subsidies).

38. Cropper and Oates (1992, pp. 675–676).

39. Questions raised by "values"-related differences in CCII standards are considered separately later in this chapter.

40. This statement, of course, does not apply equally to trade in highly differentiated products like autos where one can get fixated on specific countries, e.g., Japan.

41. See Bhagwati, "American Rules, Mexican Jobs," *New York Times*, March 24, 1993.

42. Recall our analysis, based on Arik Levinson's review, Chapter 11.

43. One of the important reasons for such nonharmonization (documented by Joel Slemrod in Chapter 6) is that horizontal equity among firms from different countries abroad can conflict with the desire to have horizontal equity among one's firms at home and one's firms abroad. This problem comes up quite directly in regard to personal income taxation where the U.S. practice is to tax on basis of citizenship while the practice elsewhere is to tax on basis of residence. The former ensures horizontal equity between U.S. citizens at home and abroad but, given the residence-based taxation practice of other nations, leads to lack of horizontal equity between, say, U.S. and French citizens in Manila or New Delhi where U.S. citizens must continue to pay U.S. income taxes (subject to some exemptions) while the French citizens do not have to pay French income taxes. The questions raised by the U.S. practice of exercising income tax jurisdiction on its citizens abroad, through the citizenship rather than residence nexus, have been extensively studied by modern economists cognizant of the extensive international personal mobility today. Cf. Jagdish Bhagwati and John Wilson, eds., *Income taxation and international personal mobility* (Cambridge, MA: MIT Press, 1991).

44. Insofar as it involves suspension of trade access by a country for products that are produced by processes that are disapproved of, it is also GATT-*illegal* as per the first Tuna-Dolphin Panel finding, and as discussed in section 4.4.

45. This "break in the ranks" occurs when there are diverse priorities at stake. Among single-issue NGOs, as on child labor, we can expect more international solidarity, of course.

46. August 15, 1992, p. 4. The magazine is published in New Delhi and enjoys a large circulation.

47. GATT, *Annual Report* (Geneva, Switzerland, 1991), pp. 33–34.

48. Steve Charnovitz, "GATT and the environment: Examining the issues," *International Environment Affairs*, 4(3), Summer 1992, p. 211. This is an interesting, thought-provoking, and lucidly argued but ultimately unpersuasive critique of the GATT report (note 47) and of the Dolphin-Tuna Panel Report.

49. Cf. GATT, *Annual Report* (1991), pp. 33–34.

50. Cf. Charnovitz, "GATT and the environment," p. 213.

51. The recently activated GATT Group on Environment Measures and International Trade has among its tasks the examination of the trade effects of packaging and labeling requirements intended to protect the environment. It has been examining the packaging and labeling questions in depth.

52. It is not just that the budgets of the poor countries are financially strapped. It is also that few parliaments would sanction expenditure of the huge amounts of money that are needed to take out ads in the Western papers and to hire lobbyists in Washington. The only democratic exception seems to be Mexico, which had, at the end of 1991, as many as 71 lobbying firms in the United States registered as "foreign agents" acting on behalf of NAFTA.

53. We are talking here of unilateral actions. Where a substantial plurilateral or multilateral consensus is achieved on a suspension of trade access, the cost imposed will generally be higher.

54. Jessica Matthews has argued that sometimes unilateralism has enabled the United States to provide leadership on important issues. But, even if this were true, it would not justify unilateralism. After all, just because dictatorships may sometimes be beneficial, we would not permit them and renounce our loyalty to democracy.

55. Charnovitz, "GATT and the environment," pp. 206–207.

56. So, you are not a "consequentialist" but one who has an "absolute" moral value. You may not expect to change Mexican behavior; you may even be hurting only yourself. But you may be doing what you think duty or virtue compels. It is worth noting, however, that one does not have to deny Mexico access to the U.S. market to avoid eating a "defiled product." After all, by not eating any tuna whatsoever and by directing political action at boycotts or education instead of seeking official embargoes, one can hurt the market for Mexican tuna as well. As noted earlier, the market pressure induced by such an action could also lead Mexican fishermen to abandon dolphin-unsafe fishing methods in order to regain lost markets.

57. There is, of course, a "moral hazard" problem: countries may become deliberately sinful to be bribed into virtue. But we doubt this is likely to be a serious problem, since the compensation in practice is likely to continue to be in form of other trade concessions in lieu of the one withdrawn.

58. Ibid., pp. 204–205.

59. Cf. Jackson, (1992), pp. 1241–42.

60. This point is argued in section 4.4. It may, however, be useful to clarify the matter so as to eliminate any ambiguities and doubts in the matter.

61. Section 301 actions aimed at securing new trade concessions, rather than at securing compliance with treaty-defined trade objections, fall into this class of problems, of course. On their GATT-inconsistency, see Jagdish Bhagwati and Hugh Patrick, eds., *Aggressive unilateralism* (Ann Arbor: Michigan University Press, 1991), especially the contributions by Hudec and Bhagwati.

62. These questions are addressed with far greater authority by Frieder Roessler, legal counselor to the GATT, in Chapter 1 of Volume 2 of this work. Also see Chapters 2 and 3 by Robert Hudec and Daniel Farber.

63. Nearly all cases can be fitted into one or both of these categories. Thus producing chickens in batteries may be objected to as cruel, fitting it into category 1. Overfishing in the commons to which I have access fits into category 2. If you use your forests in an "unsustainable" way, I may object to it because I think that is bad per se, i.e., category 1, or because it affects global warming and hence me, i.e., category 2, or because of both reasons.

64. GATT, *Annual Report* (1991), pp. 22–23.

65. The GATT law on this general question, and its relatively more environmentally friendly nature relative to the interstate "Dormant Clause" doctrine in the United States, are the subject of the penetrating analysis by Daniel Farber and Robert Hudec in their chapter for this project (Chapter 2 in Volume 2). They distinguish between the "facially discriminatory" and the "facially neutral" (but nonetheless discriminatory, whether "indirectly" and "incidentally" or otherwise) regulations, analyzing how GATT and U.S. jurisprudence apply to each of these in regard to their implications for trade that lead to litigation.

That the GATT law is essentially more environmentally friendly was borne out also by the GATT panel finding in the EU versus the United States case on U.S. fuel conservation measures in September 1994, which upheld much of the U.S. law as consistent with the GATT, even when the conflict seemed compelling prima facie.

66. Gottfried Haberler, *Theory of international trade* (London: William Hodge, 1936), p. 339. Haberler cited this amusing case as an instance of the manner in which countries evaded the obligation of the most favored nation clause.

67. As we will argue, a challenge to recycling and packaging requirements cannot be ruled out on the ground that alternative, less-trade-restricting measures are possible and should be undertaken.

68. From the economic perspective, a domestic firm acting strategically may also be able to persuade its government to enact higher standards whose effect is to make the cost of entry by foreign rivals, which must tool up to meet these higher standards, disproportionately higher (since the domestic firm has a significantly higher proportion of its sales in its own market). Higher standards in this case would then be in reality a protectionist technique for making market access by foreign firms more expensive.

69. Cf. Charnovitz., "GATT and the environment," pp. 213–214. For the Thailand case, see GATT, *Basic Instruments and Selected Documents*, 375/200 (Geneva, Switzerland). Also see Esty, *Greening the GATT*, p. 48.

70. Cited in Charnovitz, "GATT and the environment," p. 214.

71. Cf. ibid., p. 215. Charnovitz calls this the "proportionality" issue, but it is really a "trade-off" issue.

72. This was the issue addressed to a panel of trade and legal scholars at the Conference on the Morality of Protectionism at the New York University Law School in November 1992. It is quoted in Robert Hudec's excellent contribution, "'Circumventing' Democracy: The Political Morality of Trade Negotiations," New York University *Journal of International Law and Politics*, vol. 25. 1993, pp. 311–322.

73. Some issues are, of course, similar to those raised in the case of domestic environmental problems. Thus, we must ask again, How convincing is the science being invoked to spur action? Ironically, some of those who attack the use of science to attack environmental regulations in challenging phytosanitary standards defend the use of science in urging action on global problems. The fickle nature of science in these matters is evident from the

history of the ozone problem. Scientists in the United States were in the forefront in suggesting the link between CFCs and ozone depletion, leading in 1978 to the prohibition of the use of CFCs in aerosol spray cans. The Europeans were skeptical; so was the Reagan administration. The discovery of the big hole in the ozone layer in Antarctica in 1984 turned almost everyone around, leading to the Montreal Protocol in 1987 and the further change therein in 1990 to eliminate CFCs by A.D. 2000.

74. The theoretical analysis of this instrument is in the Appendix, section A4.1.3, and, more fully, in Markusen (1975).

75. This would clearly be a case where the process that generates the *physical* transborder externality is being objected to and a trade measure against it is being legitimated, as distinct from the *"values"* objection to a process as discussed earlier.

76. This is the conclusion reached by Aparna Guha in a dissertation at Columbia University, examining the options before Canada in relation to the acid rain from the United States. She is currently studying the possibility of a market in permits to use fossil fuels in U.S. electricity generation where Canada could bid and pay herself to reduce the acid rain being generated in the United States. This approach would require, of course, that the permits be segmented by the states that generate the acid rain that comes across to Canada, else the cost to Canada could become prohibitive. There is much excellent work on the acid rain problem, including by Karl-Göran Mäler and his associates in Stockholm.

77. Of course, the question of single-country use of a second-best tariff policy can be raised here just as well as in the preceding case, but this question has raised no interest in the global-pollution context.

78. Cf. Appendix, section A4.2.6 on this question.

79. This efficiency is only in the sense of cost minimization when pollution anywhere equally affects a single target such as CO_2. The number of permits may, however, be too small or too large, and getting it right by letting nonusers also bid (and then destroy permits) is bedeviled by free rider problems.

80. In this appendix, unless otherwise stated, we will simply *assume* that the relevant set of first-order conditions indeed characterize a unique solution to the optimization problem under consideration. We do not go into the assumptions on the production, utility, and pollution functions that will ensure that this will be the case.

81. Cf. Srinivasan (1987) and Bhagwati (1971).

82. Note also that we do not have a reason to subsidize the use of abatement technology.

83. Of course, the precise values of the optimum tariff and subsidy would in general differ depending on whether or not abatement is feasible.

84. Even though the trade flows of a small economy by definition have no influence on the terms at which the flows take place, such flows could influence the output in the rest of the world. This is best seen in a Ricardian model in which the small open economy specializes in producing its exportable good while the rest of the world (ROW) is incompletely specialized and the equilibrium world prices are the autarky prices of the ROW. With the opening of trade with the small economy, ROW still consumes its autarky consumption bundle while its production adjusts to accommodate the trade flows from the small economy. Although policy-induced changes in the trade flows of the small economy do not affect equilibrium world prices, they do affect the production in ROW and, hence, pollution, if pollution is a by-product of production.

85. Since the home (resp. foreign) country takes the foreign (resp. home) country's outputs and resources allocated for abatement as given, each country's reaction function with respect to the variables it chooses (X_2, K_a, and L_a for the home country and X_2^*, K_a^*, and L_a^* for the foreign country) are functions of the values of the variables for the other country taken as given. Nash equilibrium is a mutually consistent set in the sense that each country's choices as obtained by substituting the other country's choices in its reaction function, when substituted into the latter's reaction functions, yield the latter's choices. Thus $X_2(X_1^{*N}, X_2^{*N}, T^{*N}, K_a^{*N}, L_a^{*N})$ etc. when substituted in the reaction function $X_2^*(\ )$ will yield back X_2^{*N} and vice versa. We are assuming that such Nash equilibria exist. The existence issue is a complex one.

86. The variables λ_1 and λ_2 are the Lagrangean multipliers associated with the constraints of equations 17 and 18, respectively; these are shadow prices in global welfare units of good 1 and 2, respectively.

87. It is assumed that the parameters and endowments are such that the feasibility constraints $X_1 \leq \bar{H}$ and $X_2^* \leq \bar{H}^*$ hold.

88. The more general case of different tastes is briefly discussed on page 212, however.

89. Its efficiency can be demonstrated by showing that this solution satisfies the conditions for Pareto optimality subject to the requirements that pollution does not exceed $\hat{P}$ and there are no transfers. In particular, we can show that shadow cost of pollution in global welfare units will be the same in the two countries, though higher than its value at the no-transfer Pareto optimum without a binding upper-bound constraint on pollution.

91. Among the important contributions, aside from those reviewed in the Appendix, are Lloyd (1992), Snape (1992), and Baumol and Oates (1988). There are many others on issues such as the "race to the bottom" that are not addressed intensively in this chapter but are the foci of other authors in this project.

REFERENCES

Baumol, William, and Wallace Oates. 1988. *The theory of environmental policy*, 2nd ed. Cambridge, England: Cambridge University Press.

Bhagwati, Jagdish, N. 1971. "The generalized theory of distortions and welfare." In J. Bhagwati, R. Jones, R. Mundell, and J. Vanek, eds., *Trade, balance of payments, and growth: Papers in international economics in honor of Charles P. Kindleberger*. Amsterdam: North Holland.

Cropper, Maureen, and Wallace Oates. 1992. "Environmental economics: A survey." *Journal of Economic Literature*, 20 (June): 675–740.

Johnson, Harry. 1954. "Optimum tariffs and retaliation." *Review of Economic Studies*, 21 (55): 152–153. Reprinted in H. G. Johnson, *International trade and economic growth* (London: Allen and Unwin, 1958).

Lloyd, Peter. 1992. "The problem of optimal environmental policy choice." In Kym Anderson and Richard Blackhurst, eds., *The greening of world trade issues*. New York: Harvester/Wheatsheaf.

Markusen, James. 1975. "International externalities and optimal tax structures." *Journal of International Economics*, 5:15–29.

Markusen, James. 1976. "Cooperative control of international pollution and common property resources." *Quarterly Journal of Economics*, 90:618–631.

Snape, Richard. 1992. "The environment, international trade and competitiveness." In Kym Anderson and Richard Blackhurst, eds., *The greening of world trade issues*. New York: Harvester/Wheatsheaf.

Srinivasan, T. N. 1987. "Distortions." In J. Eatwell, M. Newgate, and P. Newman, eds., *The new Palgrave*, 865–867. London: Macmillan.

III

Labor Standards

5   International Labor Standards and Trade: A Theoretical Analysis

Drusilla K. Brown
Alan V. Deardorff
Robert M. Stern

5.1   Introduction

The interaction of labor standards and international trade policy is not, as we will note, a new issue. Nonetheless, it has assumed new importance because of the concerns of labor interests in the United States and elsewhere that labor issues were ignored in the Uruguay Round of Multilateral Trade Negotiations and therefore should be placed high on the agenda of any future negotiating round. Issues of labor standards were also at the center of the public debate surrounding the North American Free Trade Agreement (NAFTA). Prominent among the objections to the NAFTA were concerns that labor standards are not enforced at a sufficiently high level in Mexico, and therefore that the competition that will ensue from the NAFTA will place U.S. domestic industries at a disadvantage vis-à-vis their Mexican competitors. The result, it is feared, is that either U.S. firms will shut down or move production to Mexico, or that pressure will be put on the United States to lower labor standards domestically.[1] Because of these concerns, President Bill Clinton placed labor standards on his list of three issues for which side agreements had to be negotiated before bringing the NAFTA to Congress for approval.

While issues of labor standards have obviously taken on a high profile in policy discussions and negotiations, there has been comparatively little theoretical analysis of the connections between labor standards and trade. It is our purpose in this paper to explore these connections more fully. In contrast to and complementing Bhagwati and Srinivasan (1995), who examine principally whether diversity of standards is compatible with the case for free trade, our focus will be on the welfare and other effects of standards themselves, and whether it is in a country's interest to adopt common standards internationally.

After first reviewing the institutional and historical background of labor standards and trade in section 5.2, we will devote the rest of the paper to examining several theoretical approaches to the issue. In section 5.3, we begin with a partial equilibrium analysis of standards as a general problem, not limited necessarily to labor standards. Our first conclusion is that if one abstracts from effects of labor standards on a country's terms of trade, then the general economic interest of a country will determine the level of its labor standards independently of standards that exist abroad. Similarly, to the extent that countries agree internationally on the implementation of a common standard, it is not necessarily the case that each country's self-interest is in establishing an international standard most like its own. Rather, their position in international trade, as either a net exporter or net importer of those goods most affected by labor standards, will determine whether they favor international standards that are high or low.

The reason for this result turns out after all to have to do with the terms of trade, and we therefore turn in section 5.4 to several models that focus explicitly on the effects of standards on the terms of trade. The models here are all two-sector general equilibrium models. They differ in the extent to which countries are assumed to be specialized in production, and in whether the standards themselves merely divert resources from production in all sectors, or whether they instead raise production costs directly in particular sectors. In all cases, in this section of the paper, we confine attention to standards that are imposed exogenously, rather than explicitly modeling the market failure to which they may be a response.

In section 5.5 we make a first attempt at modeling the market failure, considering a case in which standards take the form of occupational health and safety regulations. Looking at a case in which workers choose among industries that differ in their inherent riskiness of illness or accident, we allow firms to select endogenously the levels of occupational safety that they provide, at some cost, and also the wage that they will pay their workers. With homogeneous preferences over safety and wages on the part of workers, or with enough competitive firms to tailor their offerings to heterogeneous worker preferences, there is no apparent market failure. If the government nonetheless intervenes, mandating a higher standard than is provided endogenously, then we work out the effects that this standard will have, in a context of international trade, both on the level of worker safety and on the trade, terms of trade, and welfare of the country as a whole. We then modify the model to allow for heterogeneous workers. With more kinds of worker preferences than there are firms to cater to those preferences, this heterogeneity causes a market failure that may plausibly be the basis for policy. We examine this case too, showing the possibly perverse effects that such standards may have in the context of international competition.

In section 5.6 we summarize the main results of our theoretical inquiries and conclude by examining the implications for the international harmonization of labor standards.

5.2 Labor Standards in Historical Perspective

5.2.1 Definition and General Principles of Labor Standards

Because labor standards are multifaceted, it is useful to begin by detailing the most important standards and by outlining the general principles involved in their interpretation and implementation.[2] For this purpose, we shall follow the definitions and principles set out by Lyle (1991, pp. 20–31). These are summarized in the Appendix. It should be noted that the definitions and principles listed in the Appendix do not cover all aspects of international worker rights. Rather, they are intended to highlight those worker rights standards that are set forth in U.S. trade law, but not to give the full legal text. The standards include (1) freedom of association, (2) the right to organize and bargain collectively, (3) freedom from forced labor, (4) a minimum age for employment, and (5) acceptable conditions of work, including a minimum wage, limitations on hours of work, and occupational safety and health rights in the workplace. We shall have more to say later in this chapter on these standards when we address issues of modeling and analysis of the presence or absence of particular standards in the context of international trade and the effects of harmonization of standards between trading countries.

5.2.2 Trade Effects of Intercountry Differences in Labor Standards

As will be noted in more detail later, there has been long-standing concern in the world economy about the absence or relatively weak official acknowledgment and enforcement of labor standards, especially in developing countries. The sources of concern have been both ethical and economic. It has been maintained on ethical grounds that there are certain basic human rights that are universal to mankind, and that governments everywhere should therefore be urged or maybe even coerced to institute measures that will insure that these rights are available to their citizens. The economic argument is that countries that do not guarantee and enforce these rights domestically may have an undue cost advantage in their export trade insofar as private costs do not fully reflect the social costs that would incorporate various standards. This argument presumes that the labor standards are defined to be absolute and universal rather than matters to be decided by sovereign nations. Of course, the issue becomes immediately ambiguous if it is recognized and granted that the choice of labor standards may depend on a country's stage of development and per capita income, and therefore that the weights attached to standards in an individual nation's social welfare function may differ. Clearly, many of the world's developing countries have found themselves in a situation historically of opting for standards lower than those that prevail in richer neighboring countries, and many continue to do so today.

In more advanced countries in which high labor standards are articulated and legally enforced, private and social costs will presumably be reconciled through policy. There may be a perceived disadvantage for the country's firms, however, as import-competing firms may argue that they cannot compete effectively against imports from countries with lower labor standards. Exporters may likewise argue that they also cannot compete effectively in third markets against foreign firms whose costs are artificially low because of the absence or weak enforcement of labor standards abroad. Import-competing and exporting firms in the high-standards country may respond to this situation by instituting measures to adjust to the domestic standards by undertaking capital-labor substitution, or, depending on their market power, by depressing wages. Exporting firms may also decide to relocate some of their production to foreign locations with lower standards. Another conceivable consequence is that efforts may be made to induce the government authorities to weaken or remove what are believed to be particularly onerous and costly standards.

To avoid all this, it seems appealing to urge or require that the foreign government raise its standards to the same levels as in the high-standard nation. If the foreign nation resists, the high-standard nation may wish to take punitive measures of some kind that are designed to bring about the desired change. Such actions could involve imposing import restrictions or some other type of sanction that will be costly to the foreign nation.

There is evidently, therefore, a range of responses that may occur in the high-standard country, and it is not always clear what the economic effects of the responses may be. As will be developed more fully in our theoretical discussion, the economic effects of certain responses may be counterintuitive and indeed counterproductive from a welfare point of view.

The preceding discussion abstracts from the political economy of protectionism and trade liberalization insofar as the focus is on the particular
issue of the presence or absence of effective labor standards. What is
missing is that both import-competing and export firms and workers may
use issues of lower foreign labor standards to further their own narrow
interests to the detriment of their nation's welfare. Thus, for example, there
may be pressure for trade restrictions or some other restrictive measures
ostensibly aimed at getting the foreign nation to raise its labor standards.
In such an event, we encounter the same problem that is found generally
when a government is requested to intervene in trade, namely, how to
separate the ostensibly genuine motive from the more purely protectionist
motive. It is also possible that forcing developing countries to adopt
cost-raising labor standards may be harmful to their economic interests
and could interfere with their efforts to pursue less interventionist and
more export-oriented economic policies.[3,4]

5.2.3   International Monitoring and Enforcement of Labor Standards

As noted by Hanson (1983, pp. 11 ff.), the call for international legislation
dealing with labor standards dates from the first half of the 19th century in
Europe.[5] These early movements were motivated in large measure by
ethical considerations and were designed especially to improve working
conditions in relation to hours of work, women's and children's labor, the
use of hazardous materials, and so on. The links between labor standards
and trade were recognized then and later. But, as Alam (1992, p. 13) points
out, the early reformers generally took free trade as a given and desirable
objective and sought to use moral suasion and international agreements to
deal with differences in labor standards. Various international meetings
were convened in the latter part of the 19th century and in the first part of
the 20th century to deal with international labor standards on ethical as
well as competitiveness grounds. By and large, however, the results of
these (and later) efforts could be characterized as "rather modest" on the
whole (Charnovitz, 1987, p. 580).

Following World War I, as Part XIII of the Treaty of Versailles of 1919,
the International Labor Organization (ILO) was founded. The methods and
principles set out in the ILO constitution deal with all conceivable aspects
of labor standards, although no explicit trade sanctions are included. As
stated in ILO (1988, p. 4), ILO action designed to promote and safeguard
human rights takes three main forms: (1) definition of rights, especially

through national adoption of ILO conventions and recommendations; (2) measures to secure the realization of rights, especially by means of international monitoring and supervision but not by imposition of trade sanctions; and (3) assistance to nations in implementing measures, particularly through technical cooperation and advisory services. Since World War II, the role and influence of the ILO regarding labor standards have been central to the declarations and efforts of the United Nations and associated regional organizations designed to protect and promote human rights.

As noted by Charnovitz (1987, pp. 566–567) and Alam (1992, p. 16), issues of alleged unfair competition involving labor standards were addressed in Article 7 of Chapter II of the 1948 (Havana) Charter of the (stillborn) International Trade Organization (ITO): "The members recognize that unfair labor conditions, particularly in the production for export, create difficulties in international trade, and accordingly, each member shall take whatever action may be appropriate and feasible to eliminate such conditions within its territory." Since the General Agreement on Tariffs and Trade (GATT) was conceived with a more narrow mandate in mind, it did not address issues of labor standards, except in Article XX(e), which provides for prohibition of goods made with prison labor.

Charnovitz (1987, p. 574) notes that as early as 1953 the United States proposed (unsuccessfully) adding a labor standards article to the GATT. The proposed standard, which was supported by organized labor, was very broad and would have empowered GATT members to take measures against other countries under GATT Article XXIII. The United States continued to push for negotiation of a GATT article on labor standards in both the Tokyo and Uruguay rounds of multilateral trade negotiations. While receiving some support from other GATT member countries, the U.S. efforts continued to be unsuccessful.[6] The issue of labor standards in the GATT is thus in a state of limbo. However, in its April 1994 statement at the Marrakesh signing of the Uruguay Round accords, the United States put the international community on notice that it intends to pursue issues of labor standards in future multilateral negotiations.

Issues of worker rights have also been given prominence in the European Community (EC) because of concern over low-wage competition from some EC member countries. It is interesting that many of the arguments that have been voiced in the United States about the potentially detrimental effects of imports from developing countries with lower labor standards have been made in the EC context as well. As De Boer and Winham (1993, p. 17) note, the issue of a Community-wide social charter was first broached in 1972. Subsequently, with the issuance in 1985 of the white paper intended to remove remaining barriers to trade and creation of a single market, the Community Charter of Fundamental Social Rights for Workers was drafted in 1988. This charter was adopted in 1989 on a voluntary basis by all EC members except the United Kingdom. It was hoped to incorporate the Social Charter into the Maastricht Treaty in December 1991, but this action was opposed once again by Britain. The Social Charter was subsequently approved by the other eleven EC members, but on a voluntary basis and not as part of the Maastricht Treaty.[7]

The issue of a social charter for North America was brought up in the context of NAFTA as a possible means of protecting the interests of workers.[8] It is interesting, accordingly, to consider what lessons, if any, the experience of the EC has for NAFTA. The answer appears to be not much. First, the EC efforts to forge a social charter have to be regarded in the broad context of the integration process that is intended to harmonize social programs and policies in the EC member countries.[9] Second, while limited in amount, the EC provides financial transfers to the less advanced and lower-income regions and countries in the Community to assist with structural adjustment and development. Being a free trade agreement, the NAFTA does not contemplate an EC type of economic and eventual political union, and, at least for now, funds have not been set aside to deal with problems of low-wage workers. This is not to say of course that there is no scope for the harmonization of labor standards in the NAFTA. In this connection, Weintraub and Gilbreath (1993) favor a tiered agreement on issues of labor standards, with the timing of the implementation of particular standards geared to increases in Mexican real wages.[10] But there is a catch to all this, as Watson (1993) points out, since a North American social charter would affect Mexico asymmetrically and have detrimental effects by trying to force up Mexican real wages. It would also constitute perhaps an unwarranted intrusion into Mexican sovereignty. Watson's conclusion, therefore, is that it would be preferable to forgo completely a North American social charter, in the expectation that the NAFTA may increase Mexican real wages, and to provide technical and financial assistance to Mexico to help them raise and maintain their standards.[11]

We have provided a brief historical overview of efforts to deal with international labor standards on a global and regional basis, and we have made some reference to the unsuccessful U.S. efforts to include labor standards on the agenda of the GATT negotiations. This should not be taken to mean, however, that U.S. policy has remained otherwise silent on these issues. Rather, the opposite is the case as, in the last decade, the

United States has introduced a number of unilateral policy measures dealing with labor standards, to which we now turn.

5.2.4   Labor Standards in U.S. Trade Policy and Law

The evolution of labor standards in U.S. trade policy and law is set forth in Table 1. The earliest prohibitions of imports were directed against imports made by prison and forced labor. A fair labor standards provision was included in the National Industrial Recovery Act (NIRA) of 1933, but the NIRA was subsequently judged by the Supreme Court to be unconstitutional. Beginning in the 1980s, it is evident that there have been a number of legislative actions establishing criteria for eligibility for trade preferences, as in the cases of the Caribbean Basin Economic Recovery Act (CBERA) of 1983 and the 1984 renewal of the Generalized System of Preferences (GSP). Adherence to worker rights was made a condition in a 1985 amendment covering the activities of the Overseas Private Investment Corporation. In 1986, U.S. firms in South Africa were required to adhere to fair labor standards, and similar conditions were attached to the 1987 U.S. participation in the Multilateral Investment Guarantee Agency of the World Bank.[12] Finally, the denial of worker rights was made actionable under Section 301 of the 1988 Omnibus Trade and Competitiveness Act. The 1988 Trade Act also expanded the requirements of the Departments of State and Labor to submit periodic reports to Congress on human rights abuses and foreign adherence to internationally recognized worker rights. It is thus evident that labor standards have become explicitly linked with U.S. trade (and investment) policy in a number of different legislative measures in the past decade.

It is noteworthy that the CBERA and GSP stipulations on labor standards are linked with U.S. preferential trade concessions. In the case of the CBERA, the stipulations were made advisory, but they are mandatory for continued GSP eligibility. As Lyle (1991, p. 9) notes, official U.S. investigations of worker rights under the GSP are carried out by an interagency subcommittee of the Trade Policy Staff Committee, which includes members from the Office of the U.S. Trade Representative and several cabinet departments. Investigations of worker rights violations are initiated in response to petitions from interested parties, using information contained in the State Department's annual country reports on human rights, reports from U.S. embassies and consulates, ILO findings, and other pertinent information, including public hearings. Recommendations are made to the president, who has the final say in determining continued GSP eligibility. If

Table 1
Evolution of Labor Standards in U.S. Trade Policy Legislation

Year	Act	Labor Standards Provisions
1890	McKinley Act	Prohibited imports made by convict labor.
1930	Tariff Act	Prohibited imports of goods made by convict labor, forced labor, or indentured labor under penal sanction.
1933	National Industrial Recovery Act (NIRA; judged unconstitutional by U.S. Supreme Court in 1935)	Imports permitted only if produced according to U.S. domestic fair labor standards, including the right to organize and bargain collectively, limits on maximum hours of work, and minimum wages.
1974	Trade Act	Directed the president to seek the adoption of fair labor standards in the Tokyo Round of GATT negotiations.
1983	Caribbean Basin Economic Recovery Act (CBERA)	Criteria for eligibility as a beneficiary country extended to include the degree to which workers are afforded reasonable workplace conditions and enjoy the right to organize and bargain collectively.
1984	Generalized System of Preferences (GSP) Renewal Act	Criteria for eligibility as a beneficiary country extended to include whether or not the country has taken, or is taking, steps to afford its workers internationally recognized worker rights defined as including freedom of association, the right to organize and bargain collectively, freedom from forced labor, minimum age for the employment of children, and acceptable conditions of work with respect to wages, hours of work, and occupational safety and health.
1985	Overseas Private Investment Corporation Amendments Act	The corporation is to insure, reinsure, guarantee, or finance a project in a country only if the country is taking steps to adopt and implement internationally recognized worker rights as defined for GSP purposes.
1986	Anti-Apartheid Act	Made it incumbent on U.S. firms employing more than 25 persons in South Africa to follow a code of conduct that includes fair labor standards.
1987	U.S. participation in Multilateral Investment and Guarantee Agency of World Bank	Made U.S. participation conditional on countries affording internationally recognized worker rights to their workers.

Table 1 (continued)

Year	Act	Labor Standards Provisions
1988	Trade Act (Omnibus Trade and Competitiveness Act)	Made the systematic denial of internationally recognized worker rights (as defined above) by foreign governments an unfair trade practice and liable for U.S. countermeasures where such denials cause a burden or restriction on U.S. commerce.

Source: Adapted from Alam (1992, p. 25)

GSP privileges are removed or suspended, a country must reapply to have the privileges reinstated.

In April 1991, GSP privileges were removed from Sudan, and in prior years similar actions were taken with respect to Burma, the Central African Republic, Chile, Liberia, Nicaragua, Paraguay, and Romania. The U.S. experience with GSP may thus provide some useful insights into the design and implementation of policies and procedures governing trade-linked labor standards in other contexts. Perhaps the most noteworthy features are that trade concessions can be withdrawn if investigation concludes that labor standards are not being upheld, and that evidence of a change in policies abroad is a condition for reinstatement of the concessions.[13]

Having set the context and discussed some of the possible consequences of intercountry differences in labor standards and experiences in the monitoring and enforcement of labor standards globally, regionally, and with reference especially to the United States, we turn now to our central task of the theoretical modeling and analysis of international labor standards.

5.3   International Standards Coordination—A Simple Model

In this section we use a partial equilibrium model to examine how standards in general may be set by countries acting individually and how these countries would be affected if instead they were to coordinate on a common standard. In a world with countries that are too small to affect their terms of trade, we will argue that if governments act in their independent national interests, then they will set possibly diverse standards that will be optimal from the point of view of the world.[14] However, it will be in the interests of particular groups of producers within these countries to press for higher standards abroad than would otherwise obtain. Also, it will be in the countries' national interests (including both producers and consumers) to press for either higher or lower standards for the world as a whole depending upon whether, as countries, they are net exporters or net importers of the good in question.

The theoretical modeling of labor standards in international trade is complicated by the fact that, in any country large enough for the world to care about it, standards that affect trade also affect the terms of trade. This statement is true not only of labor standards, but of other standards as well, and this problem is a common one for any analysis of policies and regulations that are intended to deal with externalities and other social concerns in a context of international trade. The effects of such policies on international prices are undoubtedly important, and we will explore them more fully and carefully in subsequent sections of this paper. However in almost all cases, these terms of trade effects are not the central concern of proponents of such policies, and to include them in the analysis inevitably intertwines the concerns of the policy advocates with the effects of trade in ways that cloud, rather than clarify, the issues.

Therefore, in this first theoretical section, we attempt to consider the general problem of international policy coordination in a way that will most clearly capture the concerns of the policy advocates, and thus in a way that abstracts from effects on the terms of trade. This task is not easy. For one country to have no effect on its terms of trade, it must be small. For a particular trading partner, whose policies the first country wishes to influence, also to have no effect on world prices requires that it too be small. But if that assumption is true, the first country will care about the second country's policy on only moral grounds.[15] We look here at a world of many countries, each one of which is assumed to be too small to affect world prices. Each country's interest is then in its own policy choice, plus the collective choices of the other countries. In this context, no country on economic grounds would care about the policy choices of other individual countries. They would, however, care about international agreements that might alter the policy choices of all other countries collectively.

In this context, as we will later explain more fully, we model a standard as a policy that raises the costs of firms while at the same time providing a benefit to society as a whole. At the end of section 5.4 we will discuss the mechanisms by which the particular labor standards mentioned in section 5.2 do in fact raise costs.

Consider then a partial-equilibrium, perfectly competitive model of many small countries, each of which supplies and demands a good that is traded freely by all. World supply and demand are the sums of the individual-country supplies and demands, and these interact to determine a world price that is taken as given by all. The situation of a representative

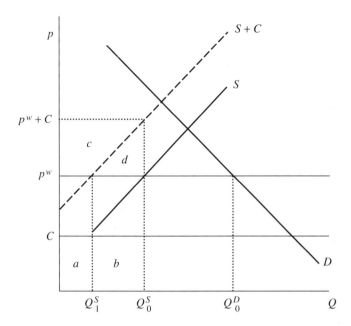

Figure 1
Partial Equilibrium Effects of a Standards Policy in a Small Country

importing country is shown in Figure 1. The world price is p^w, the country's supply and demand curves in the absence of any policy are S and D, with D intersecting p^w to the right of S because we have selected a country that imports the good.

Suppose now that the behavior of suppliers in the absence of any policy is such as to impose an additional cost on society that is not captured in the supply curve. This could be an external diseconomy of the usual sort (such as pollution), or, to accord better with our topic of labor standards, it might be a measure of the societal opprobrium associated with, say, employing children. For this section of the paper at least, it does not matter what the source of the social cost is, merely that it exist and be somehow quantifiable.

To quantify the social cost in a relevant way, however, we must also consider what will be done about it. There is one cost that is appropriate if the suppliers are allowed to continue their behavior unchanged and nothing is done about it. There is a second that is appropriate if suppliers continue their behavior but the government devotes its own resources to undo the damage. And there is a third cost that is appropriate if the suppliers are required to discontinue the offending behavior, the cost of doing so then being borne by the suppliers themselves. Presumably an optimal policy will select whichever of these alternatives, or a combination of them, imposes the lowest cost on the country as a whole. It will also clearly require that the suppliers bear this cost at the margin, either by paying a production tax equal to it, or by directly changing their means of production, since otherwise their choice of output would be higher than optimal. To capture all this, then, we include in Figure 1 a curve representing this minimum social cost per unit of output C and assume that it represents both the cost of optimally solving this problem and an addition to the costs of suppliers when the solution is implemented.

We will speak, then, of a "standards policy" as one that adds this social cost C to the costs of private firms for all levels of output, and at the same time eliminates a cost to society at least equal to C. The supply curve in the presence of the standard is then $S + C$, the private supply curve S displaced upward by the social cost C.

The effects of the standard are easily seen from the figure. Because the country is small, the world price is unchanged, as is the domestic quantity demanded Q_0^D. Quantity supplied to the domestic market by domestic suppliers falls, however, from Q_0^S to Q_1^S, and the quantity of imports increases by this same amount.

As for welfare effects, demanders are of course unaffected, since they still buy the good at the unchanged world price. Suppliers bear the increased cost C of production due to the policy, and their welfare would have been unchanged if the price had risen to $p^w + C$. Since it did not, they lose producer surplus equal to area c in the figure. Society, on the other hand, gains at least the areas $a + b$, recalling that C represented the least-cost way of dealing with the social cost, and was therefore no larger than the cost itself in the absence of the standard. The country as a whole, therefore, gains at least the triangular area d, since by construction $c + d$ is equal to $a + b$.

All of this was done taking the world price as given, which the country, as a small open economy, was bound to do. No standard was imposed in the rest of the world, and as suppliers would surely remind us, the imposition of the standard has cost them dearly. However, there is no question that the standard was a desirable policy: the country gained more from its imposition than the suppliers lost, and assuming as usual that they could somehow be compensated if it were viewed as desirable to do so, the country's welfare has gone up. The absence of a standard abroad may have altered the size of the gain, as we will soon see, but it cannot have undermined it totally.

Nor is there a case here for interfering with trade. Suppliers, of course, would welcome a tariff equal to C along with the standard, so that the domestic price would rise exactly enough to offset all cost to them. But if this were done, we would have the usual deadweight losses associated with a tariff, and welfare would fall, not rise. Thus free trade remains here the optimal policy, even though the standard was not matched by standards abroad.

Suppose, however, that the standard *were* matched by standards abroad. That is, suppose that all other countries were in exactly the same situation as this one (except that some export rather than import the good), and that they too responded by setting the standard C. In that case, at the initial world price p^w, all suppliers would supply less and the world price would have to rise. To determine how much it would change, we would need to construct the relevant curves, but that is not necessary. Given the same standard in all countries, it is clear that the world price could not rise as high as $p^w + C$, since if it did, all supplies would remain at their initial level (see Figure 1), while all demands would fall. Therefore, we can be sure that a common standard of C set by all countries would lead to a rise in world price by something less than C. Exactly how much it would rise depends, as usual, on the various supply and demand elasticities, and need not concern us here.

Figure 2, then, shows the situation with such a common standard. The suppliers' cost still rises by C, but now the world price also rises by a fraction of that amount, and the suppliers' loss in producer surplus is confined to the smaller area c (which is smaller than c in Figure 1). Society still gains at least the area $a + b$ (which still sums to $a + b$ in Figure 1), but now demanders also lose from the rise in price. The loss in consumer surplus is area $e + f + g + h + i + j$, giving a net effect on the country as a whole of $+d - (h + i + j)$. As drawn, this change in country welfare is negative, and would be so for any country that imports a significant amount of the good in comparison to its domestic production. The reason is that consumers of the imported good do not share at all in the social benefit of the standards imposed abroad, but bear part of the cost due to the rise in world price.

This outcome would be reversed if the country were an exporter of the good. In that case (and also if the country were an importer but of only a small amount), as the reader can verify, the losses of both producer and consumer surplus are more than made up for by the gain from eliminating the social cost.

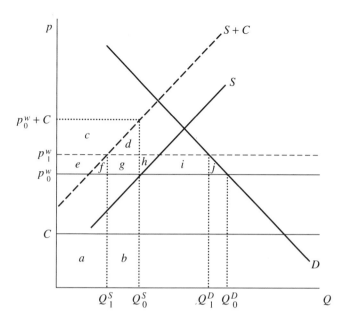

Figure 2
Partial Equilibrium Effects of a Common International Standard in a Small Country

We set out in this section to abstract from effects on the terms of trade and to focus theoretical attention only on the sorts of effects that seem to be the concern of the advocates of labor standards. The small country assumption worked well for this purpose so long as we considered only standards in one country. But as we have just seen, once multilateral standards are considered, terms-of-trade effects inevitably play a role. It is quite possible for a country to lose from imposing a standard, even when that standard is optimally configured from the point of view of undoing or correcting a social cost, simply because of the country's position in the trade of the good involved. A country that imports a good on which a standard is imposed is likely to lose from the standard because of the rising cost to its consumers. A country that exports such a good, on the other hand, has a more than normal interest in obtaining multilateral standards.

This result, especially for an importing country, is very much at variance with the stated arguments of most advocates of standards, in the labor arena and elsewhere. The reason may be that these advocates often have a point of view that is narrower than that of the country as a whole, perhaps identifying only with producers. Or they may recognize the consumers' interests but reject them as being illegitimate, on the grounds that consumers were benefiting immorally from the low price permitted by the absence of a standard previously. Whatever may be the case, it is useful here to be able to separate the several welfare effects of a standard, and this our partial equilibrium model is nicely suited to do.

That is, in comparing Figures 1 and 2, one can easily see why countries are reluctant to impose standards unilaterally, even when those standards would raise welfare in the country overall. As long as the interest of the policy makers is to give greater weight to producer interests and to social costs than they do to consumer interests, then it is quite natural to press for multilateral standards. These will achieve greater reduction in social cost worldwide, and they will lessen (though not remove) the burden on producers.

So far we have assumed that multilateral standards are set all at the same level. If the problem at hand were a social cost that was the same, per unit of production, for all countries, then that would be a natural assumption. But in fact, as we have already noted in passing, countries often disagree as to the level of cost associated with a particular market failure, sometimes for cultural reasons, sometimes because of differences in levels of development. Suppose then that the social costs C were to vary across countries.

Without a multilateral standard, countries would each have an incentive to impose standards at the level of their own social cost, as we saw in Figure 1, and this choice would indeed be optimal for the world as a whole. The collective effect of these diverse standards would be qualitatively the same as shown in Figure 2, except that there would be no assurance that the world price would rise by less than the size of a particular country's standard. High-standard countries would find the world price rising by substantially less than their own standard, and thus have their producers bear a larger proportion of the cost. Low-standard countries would, in contrast, experience price increases that would be larger in comparison to their own standards and that might even be larger absolutely than the standards themselves. In that case, their producers would gain, not lose, from the multilateral standards.

It is this possibility, presumably, that motivates demands that the standards of different countries be "harmonized," which in this case may be taken to mean set at the same level. As this model makes clear, however, there is nothing in the economics of the situation that calls for such harmonization. On the contrary, world efficiency is best served by letting each country set its standard in accordance with its own needs and perceptions of cost. To do otherwise—to require that all countries impose the same standards—will mean that some countries impose higher standards than the corresponding social costs or that others will impose lower standards than social cost. Either way, outputs will then be set inappropriately low or high, as the case may be, and welfare will not be maximized.

To conclude this section, let us return one final time to the terms-of-trade effects that we tried so hard to exclude. Suppose now that some countries are not in fact small, but instead that they can influence the terms of trade through their policies. How they will behave will of course depend on the direction of their trade in the product in question. Any standard they set, regardless of their pattern of trade, will cause the output of their own producers to fall and will then lead to a rise in the world price. If they import the good, as does the country in Figure 1, and if they attempt to maximize their entire country's welfare, then this worsening of the terms of trade will lead them to cut back on the policy, setting a standard that is lower than the social cost. Exporters, in contrast, recognizing that their standards not only correct the social cost but also improve their terms of trade, will set their standards higher than social cost.

This is exactly the kind of outcome that we sought to avoid in this section, for it means that standards are being used for purposes that have nothing to do with the problems they are ostensibly intended to solve. But the result does have an interesting and perhaps rather surprising implication. Exporting countries are presumably those with lower cost, as a result, one hopes, of comparative advantage. Since, as we have just seen, it is exporters who have the incentive to set standards too high, and importers who have the incentive to set standards too low, it follows that standards will be used to bring costs closer together across countries.

Throughout this discussion, we have confined our attention to a single industry in partial equilibrium. This approach is appropriate for problems that in fact arise in only one or a small number of industries, as long as those industries are small relative to other markets in the economy. For some kinds of standards, that may well be the case. But for labor standards, which are likely to apply across the board to all industries, it certainly is not. We used partial equilibrium here, as we said, in an effort to abstract from terms-of-trade effects, and to decompose the effects of standards into those on producers and consumers. But it is time to leave this framework and turn instead to models of general equilibrium. We begin this task in the next section.

5.3.1   Summary

Let us sum up what this partial equilibrium analysis has told us. We have modeled a standard as policy that imposes additional cost on domestic firms, the purpose being to correct an externality of some sort that imposes a cost on society that would not otherwise be borne by the firm. The first result is that, if countries are too small to affect their terms of trade and if the social cost of the externality is borne only by the country where the firm is located, then domestic policies that internalize the externality are welfare improving from the points of view of both the individual country and the world as a whole. This is the case whether or not the partner country also imposes a standard. Furthermore, trade sanctions that punish trade partners for failing to do so are not beneficial.

Pressure for international standards may nevertheless emerge, in part since separate interests within each country desire different outcomes. For obvious reasons, producers that are subject to these standards would prefer not to be. At the same time, producers would also prefer that higher standards be set abroad, since these will raise world prices to their own benefit. Therefore, for example, if optimal standards are diverse across countries, producers in the high-standard countries will press for adoption of a common standard worldwide, even though that would not be socially optimal.

National interests also diverge from the optimum when it comes to finding international agreement on the level of standards to set. Since national welfare (including both producers and consumers) rises with the world price of a net export and falls with the world price of a net import, and since standards tend to raise world prices, net exporters will press for higher-than-optimal international standards while net importers will press for lower-than-optimal ones. This observation is true even though individually, as small countries, the standards they would set for themselves would be optimal.

Finally, allowing countries to be large enough to influence world prices by their own actions, these incentives to distort standards for terms-of-trade purposes also extend to the setting of their own standards. Net exporters, for example, will set standards higher than optimal, since high standards will secure the additional benefit of a higher world price and improved terms of trade.

5.4   Effects of Imposed Labor Standards on Trade and the Terms of Trade

In this section we examine how standards alter welfare in a large country, and how this effect depends on the resources that are used by the standard itself.[16] Depending on the particular model that applies, we find that countries now have an incentive to set standards either too high or too low, and that there is a clear case for some form of coordination, if not full harmonization, to achieve the world optimum. In one case, where countries specialize completely in different traded goods, each country's standard will act like any trade restriction and thus improve its terms of trade. Such countries will set standards too high, will prefer that other countries set no standards at all, and will need to coordinate to reduce the level of standards that would be arrived at independently. In a second case, where countries produce the same tradable goods but in different proportions, the effect of a labor standard depends on the resources that it withdraws from world production of tradable goods. If the standard, say, uses primarily labor, then it will make labor more scarce, raise the world prices of both labor and labor-intensive goods, and improve the terms of trade of labor-abundant countries. Because countries now experience the same price changes from labor standards but differ in the welfare implications of these prices changes, standards will now be set too high in some countries and too low in others, making it desirable for both that the world harmonize on a level of standards somewhere in between.

In contrast to the previous section, where we tried to abstract from terms of trade effects, we begin our general equilibrium analysis by examining effects that a country's labor standards may have precisely on its trade and terms of trade. For this purpose we initially ignore whatever distortions may exist in the economy that provide the reason for the labor standards, and assume instead that they are simply imposed exogenously. This assumption does not mean that the standards are without purpose, but it does mean that their purpose is not to offset or correct a distortion in the economy that would in turn have its own effects on production and trade, and that might change with the imposition of the standard. We will consider such distortion-correcting labor standards in section 5.5.

For now, consider a generic labor standard Z that may be imposed at some level in a country and that uses resources that would otherwise be used for production. We will consider several different models of trade and of the interaction between the labor standards, production, and trade, in order to determine how the standard will alter the country's output and trade, its potential to gain from trade, and the terms of trade between it and the rest of the world. We will also consider the issue of harmonization of labor standards in these models, asking how a country's welfare will be affected by standards abroad, and how these standards, if set optimally, will interact with one another.

Once again the standard is modeled simply as a policy that raises cost of production, now being explicit about which resources are used up in this process. At the end of the section we will discuss how the particular labor standards described in section 5.2 relate to this theoretical formulation.

5.4.1   Model 1: Labor Standards in a Specialized Economy

We consider first a country that is specialized in the production of a single tradable good X, which it exports in exchange for a second tradable good that it does not produce, Y. The potential imposition of a labor standard takes the form of producing a nontraded good Z at some level, and this production withdraws resources from the production of tradable X. It is not necessary, in this model, to be specific about what these resources are. Instead we merely assume a production possibility frontier (PPF) between X and Z that summarizes the trade-off.

Figure 3 illustrates. In the top quadrant appear a family of indifference curves, indicating the welfare that the country derives from consumption of the two traded goods X and Y. The downward-sloping straight lines also indicate, for some particular world prices, the rate of exchange between the two goods.

The bottom quadrant shows the PPF between X and Z. Initially, without any labor standard, Z is set at zero and production is at point P. A portion

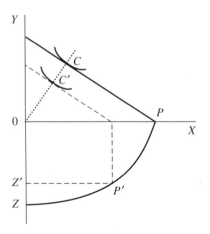

Figure 3
General Equilibrium Effects of a Standards Policy in a Specialized Economy

of the output of X is exported in exchange for Y, and the country consumes at point C.

When a labor standard is imposed at some level Z', production moves to point P', less X is produced, and less is also exported in exchange for Y. As long as both tradable goods are normal goods, consumption of both will fall, to point C', as will the quantities of trade. Assuming for simplicity that preferences are homothetic, consumption and trade all decline by the same percentage, equal to the fall in the output of X.

Clearly the country loses welfare in terms of what it derives from consuming the traded goods. That result does not mean that the standard was ill-advised, however, since we have not specified its purpose. If we assume that there is a benefit to be obtained from the standard—one that is separable from the benefits of consuming X and Y and that does not alter the economics of the X and Y industries—then presumably the standard could be set optimally, balancing the marginal benefit from the standard against the marginal cost in consumption.

If the country were small, this would be the end of the story, since the reduced trade would have no effect on equilibrium world prices, or on anything else of concern to the foreign economy. If the country were small, however, its labor standards would not be an international issue. We therefore assume for the rest of this section that the countries we consider are large enough to influence their terms of trade.

The direction of the effect is obvious. Since at initial prices the country both exports less of X and imports less of Y, the world price of good X will rise relative to Y. That is, the country's terms of trade will improve. This is a benefit to the country imposing the standard, and a cost to its trading partner.

Now, consider the issue of harmonization. At one level the question is simply whether a country will benefit more by imposing a labor standard unilaterally, or would instead do better getting its trading partner to impose the same standard. To answer that question, we need first to know how a standard imposed by the other country will affect welfare at home. In this model the answer is clear: since the other country is specialized in good Y and will withdraw resources from its production if it imposes a standard, the foreign labor standard has an effect on world prices that is opposite to that of a domestic standard. If we use a standard, it improves our terms of trade; if they use one, it improves theirs but worsens ours. Thus each country would prefer to go it alone.

At a slightly deeper level we can assume that each country's labor standard will be set optimally, given the standard of the other, and we can ask how the standards will differ depending on whether they are set noncooperatively or cooperatively (harmonization). In this model, because each country's standard imposes a negative external effect on the other by altering the terms of trade, each will have an incentive to set too high a level of the standard. If countries can cooperate, they will need to harmonize their labor standards to *lower* levels than they would set unilaterally.[17]

This result, which is quite different from the kind of harmonization that one sees called for by labor activists, arises because the effect of the labor standard that is driving the result is quite different from what labor activists are likely to have in mind. In section 5.5 we will try to consider alternative models that are closer in spirit to the views of labor. Nonetheless, the possible terms-of-trade effect of a labor standard is certainly a valid one, and also a potentially important one that can arise in general equilibrium. It should be taken into account in any complete analysis of international labor standards.

The terms-of-trade effect will not, however, always work in this direction. This first model with complete specialization is quite special in that regard, as we will now see.

5.4.2   Model 2: A Heckscher-Ohlin Model with Economy-Wide Labor Standards

Suppose now that the countries produce both of the traded goods, using two factors of production and identical, constant-returns-to-scale production functions in the manner of the Heckscher-Ohlin trade model. For this model, assume that labor standards are again imposed separately from production of the tradable goods, so that they simply withdraw a portion of the factors that would have been available for production of tradable goods. How a standard affects output and trade now depends on the factor intensity of the standard itself—that is, the ratio of the factors withdrawn from tradable production as a result of the standard—in comparison to the factor intensities of the tradable goods.[18]

Figure 4a illustrates. The outer PPF between tradable goods X and Y shows the maximum outputs of the two goods if all of the home country's (A's) resources are devoted to their production. We assume that good X is labor intensive and that the home country is labor abundant, so that in free trade equilibrium it produces at P, consumes at C, and exports good X to the world market.

If a labor standard is now imposed, this will use up some of the labor and capital that underlie the outer PPF, and will therefore shift it inward.

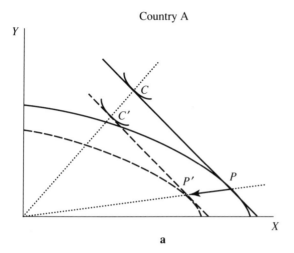

a

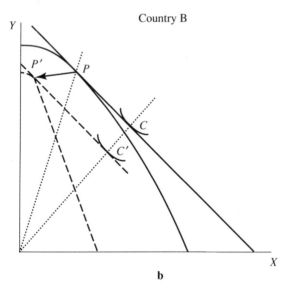

b

Figure 4
General Equilibrium Effects of Economy-Wide Labor Standards in a Heckscher-Ohlin Model

The direction of the shift depends on the factors used by the standard. An especially simple but special case is shown in the figure, where the PPF is shifted proportionally inward by the standard. This would happen if the standard withdrew the two factors in the same proportions as they exist in the endowment of country A.

In this special case, we find once again that the standard will unambiguously, at initial prices, cause a fall in the country's trade. This in turn will cause its terms of trade to improve when we allow for equilibrium on the world market.

However, the similarity with Model 1 ends here. It is not the case that the same labor standard imposed in the other country will improve *its* terms of trade. As shown in Figure 4b, the foreign PPF shifts inward, not proportionally, but rather in the same direction as that of country A, assuming that the labor standard there requires the factors in the same proportion as in the home country. But since the foreign country produces the goods in quite different proportions, because of its greater abundance of capital, this is a shift that is very much biased toward continuing to produce its export good.

In fact, since the ratio of the drops in output of the two goods is the same as the ratio of production in the home country, and since this is less than the common ratio of consumption in both, it must be the case that the foreign country's production of good X falls by more than its consumption, and it actually increases its demand for good X from the world market. Hence, a labor standard that matches in its factor requirements the factor endowments of the home country will necessarily improve the home country's terms of trade regardless of which country implements it.

More generally, what matters in this model for the effect of a labor standard on the world market and the terms of trade is how the factor requirements of the standard compare to the factor requirements of *world* production. If a standard uses, say, a higher ratio of labor to capital than is available in the world market, then it will withdraw from tradable-goods production—in either country where it is implemented—amounts of factors that will reduce the country's output of the labor-intensive good relative to its consumption of that good. As a result, such a labor standard will raise the world relative price of the labor-intensive good, regardless of who exports it.

Thus the only completely neutral labor standard will be one that uses factors in the same proportion as world endowments. Any other labor standard will tilt the world prices in favor of one country or the other. Considering the harmonization issue, this finding means that a labor-abundant country will get an extra terms-of-trade benefit from a labor-intensive standard, and will tend to overprovide it, while a capital-abundant country will experience a loss and will tend to underprovide it. Harmonization in favor of a more uniform standard will therefore be desirable from the world-efficiency perspective.

5.4.3   Model 3: A Heckscher-Ohlin Model with a Standard That Raises Production Cost

In our analysis up to now, labor standards were assumed simply to divert resources from the country as a whole. Here we allow for the standard to be implemented within an industry in a manner that raises that industry's cost. For simplicity we allow for the standard in only one of the two industries of a Heckscher-Ohlin model.

Figure 5a (on p. 252) shows the PPF for a home country exporting the labor-intensive good X prior to imposition of a labor standard. The effect of a labor standard will be to increase the factor requirements of production in X, and therefore to shift the PPF inward. The exact nature of that shift, however, depends on how factor requirements in the industry are changed by the labor standard.

A simple possibility is shown in Figure 5: the standard is Hicks neutral in the sense that it raises the required amounts of both factors in the same proportion and therefore leaves the shapes of all X isoquants unchanged. Were one to draw the Edgeworth production box for this situation, the standard would leave the efficiency locus unchanged in appearance, with only the levels of X output along it reduced by the percentage of the increased cost. Thus the PPF is shifted proportionally to the left in Figure 5a, with the level of output of X that corresponds to each level of Y being cut by a fraction.

It follows immediately that, once again, at given prices of the goods the country will trade less. This result in turn will cause an improvement in its terms of trade to clear the world market.

At the same time, in Figure 5b, the same shift in the PPF of the partner country causes it to trade more, and this outcome also will lead to a further improvement of the home country's terms of trade. As in the case of economy-wide labor standards in Model 2, it is the standard itself that favors one country or the other, and not the identity of the country that implements it.

Figure 5 shows only one very special case. A labor standard in an industry could just as easily increase the industry's factor requirements in

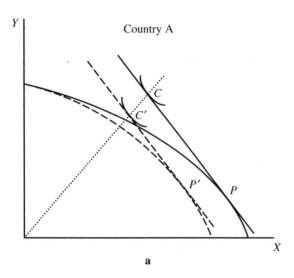

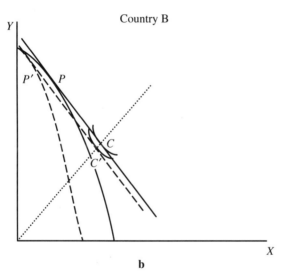

Figure 5
General Equilibrium Effects of an Industry Labor Standard in a Heckscher-Ohlin Model

ways that are biased toward one factor or the other, and this bias would change the way that the PPF shifts because of the standard.[19] We will not go through any more of these cases here, but will merely note that the result just found, of a standard that raises the world price of the industry where it is imposed, is in some sense the normal outcome but is not inevitable. One can construct a case in which a standard imposed on an industry actually leads the relative output of that industry to expand and drives down its price. That, however, is a rather skewed and unusual outcome.

5.4.4   Factor Requirements of Labor Standards

Having identified the importance of the "factor requirements" of labor standards for their effects on trade, let us pause a moment and relate our discussion to our earlier list of labor standards noted in the Appendix. In what sense can actual labor standards be accurately modeled as diverting factors from other uses, and which factors do they divert?

Freedom of Association and Right to Organize: These two standards do not, in any obviously important way, divert resources. Presumably a small amount of labor is needed to administer a labor union, for example, but this must be a negligible aspect of a union's economic effects.

Freedom from Forced Labor: If an economy is making use of forced labor, the question here must be whether that labor would continue to be available if it were not forced to work, presumably at a higher wage. If at least some of the forced workers would choose not to work, or not to work as much, then this standard will reduce the supply of labor to the economy. It is a purely labor-using standard.

Minimum Age for Employment: A standard that prohibits children from working simply removes them from the labor force. It too is a purely labor-using standard.

Minimum Wage: A minimum wage does not obviously alter the quantity of factors available, but only, supposedly, their price. However, if one believes that labor markets function well, then an effective minimum wage will price out of the market some marginal workers, and the labor force will be reduced. In this sense, a minimum wage is, again, a labor-using standard.

Hours of Work: An upper limit on hours of work, if it is effective (and not merely circumvented by workers taking second jobs), is a straightforward reduction in the labor force. It too, then, is labor using.

Occupational Safety and Health: OSH regulations are therefore the only standard we consider that may not be purely labor using. These regulations may well require investments in capital (safer machines) or land (to reduce overcrowding) in order to be implemented. Depending on the nature of the particular regulation, therefore, and the technologies available for satisfying it, OSH regulations could easily be less labor intensive than world production as a whole.

In summary, with the exception of OSH regulations, most labor standards appear to be primarily labor using. That is, they remove a portion of a country's labor force that would otherwise be available. Such standards will tend to make labor more scarce in the countries where they are implemented. This scarcity will in turn increase the world prices of labor-intensive goods, improving the terms of trade of those countries that export labor-intensive goods and worsening the terms of trade of others. Thus it would appear that the general economic interests of advanced countries, whose comparative advantage presumably is based on factors other than labor, would favor limiting the spread of these standards rather than imposing them on the less-developed world. Similar conclusions or the opposite, however, could apply to OSH regulations, depending on the factors required for their implementation.

All this, however, neglects the role of any distortions that may exist and provide the basis for having labor standards in the first place. We now turn to the modeling of such distortions and their interaction with standards and trade.

5.5   Endogenous Working Conditions and Labor Standards

In the preceding sections we have analyzed two aspects of labor standards in international trade: (1) correcting market failure due to the presence of an externality in an international trade environment, and (2) the resource costs of labor standards and their implications for the terms of trade. In the first of these cases, where we dealt with market failures, we did not identify the source of the market failure, but we did make the assumption that the government had the ability to correct the externality.

However, much of the labor literature on occupational safety and health is devoted to analyzing specific sources of market failure and the tools used by governments to address these problems.[20] Generally, it is found that establishing minimum labor standards rarely corrects, or even partly corrects, labor-market failure associated with worker safety.

In this section, we analyze legally mandated minimum safety standards using a model in which occupational safety and health are endogenously determined. First, we consider a setting in which the market is able to provide the socially optimal level of worker safety. In this case, government intervention in the form of a minimum safety requirement naturally reduces social welfare, both nationally and from a world point of view.

We then turn to evaluate a market that is not able to provide the socially optimal level of worker safety because of heterogeneity of worker preferences over working conditions and wages. The existence of a market failure raises the possibility that the government might usefully intervene. However, in the case analyzed here, we find that government-mandated working conditions will not restore Pareto optimality.

Our conclusions concerning international bargaining over labor standards depend, as in section 5.3, on whether the minimum safety requirement is imposed on the export industry or on the import-competing industry. The implications for working conditions are more surprising. A minimum safety standard always improves working conditions in the industry in which it is imposed. In addition, as long as the labor standard is applied in the capital-intensive sector, then wages and working conditions improve in all sectors of the economy. This is the case in both regulated and unregulated industries. However, if the standard is imposed in the labor-intensive sector, then workers in all sectors of the economy are made worse off. Money wages decline in all industries. Safety rises in the regulated sector, but not by enough to compensate for the fall in wages. Finally, both wages and safety actually decline in the unregulated sector.

5.5.1   Endogenous Safety without Market Failure

Generally, if labor markets are perfectly competitive and sufficiently deep, then firms and workers will choose the Pareto optimal level of safety in each plant. In this case, government intervention that establishes a minimum safety level is, of course, not defensible on efficiency grounds. Nevertheless, governments occasionally attempt to raise standards despite the absence of an identifiable market failure. Therefore, it is useful to analyze the implications of minimum standards for wages, working conditions, and international trade when labor markets are functioning efficiently.

The sufficient conditions for Pareto optimality when the safety level is endogenous are well established (see Dickens, 1984):

1. All markets are perfectly competitive.

2. Firms set safety and wage levels to maximize profits.

3. There is a large enough number of workers and firms such that for the safety level chosen by the firm there exists some wage at which the firm can hire any amount of labor it wants but can hire no labor at a lower wage.

4. Workers and firms have perfect knowledge of wage and safety levels at all other firms.

5. There are no external economies.

Obviously, Pareto optimality can fail for several reasons. One case will be discussed in this section. However, consider, first, safety setting in an economy that satisfies the efficiency conditions listed.

Suppose, as in section 5.4, that there are two goods: X the labor-intensive export good and Y the capital-intensive import-competing good. Labor and capital are taken to be freely mobile between sectors and traded in perfectly competitive markets.

For present purposes we will take technology to be Cobb-Douglas, so that

$$X = K_x^\alpha L_x^{(1-\alpha)}$$
$$Y = K_y^\beta L_y^{(1-\beta)}$$

(1)

where $\beta > \alpha$

There is some danger to workers producing both X and Y, but each firm can improve working conditions if it chooses to do so. We assume that safety is produced using the same technology required to produce a unit of X. Further, the X sector is taken to be inherently more dangerous than the Y sector, so that it takes $g_x > 1$ times as much expenditure per worker in the X sector to achieve a particular level of safety compared to what would be required for the same level of safety per worker in the Y sector. Finally, all workers are assumed to have identical preferences over safety and money wages.

There are three basic conditions that characterize firm behavior in the labor market. First, for each firm in sectors X and Y, the cost of providing the worker with a wage-safety combination must equal the worker's marginal value product. That is

$$p_x MP_L^x = p_s g_x + w_x$$

(2)

$$p_y MP_L^y = p_s + w_y$$

(3)

where p_i and w_i, $i = x, y$, are goods prices and wages in sector i, and p_s is the price of a unit of safety in sector y. Second, workers must be indifferent between the X-sector and Y-sector wage-safety combinations. This indifference implies that

$$U(s_x, w_x) = U(s_y, w_y) \qquad (4)$$

Third, cost-minimization requires that each firm choose a wage-safety combination so that the worker's marginal rate of substitution between safety and wages equals the ratio of the wage to the price of safety. That is,

$$MRS_{s,w}(s_x, w_x) = \frac{w_x}{g_x p_s} \qquad (5)$$

$$MRS_{s,w}(s_y, w_y) = \frac{w_y}{p_s} \qquad (6)$$

These labor-market conditions are depicted in Figure 6. For each industry, the worker's indifference curve is tangent to the line that depicts all combinations of safety and money wages that cost the firm the worker's marginal value product. In addition, the level of utility achieved by a worker in sector X is the same as that in sector Y.

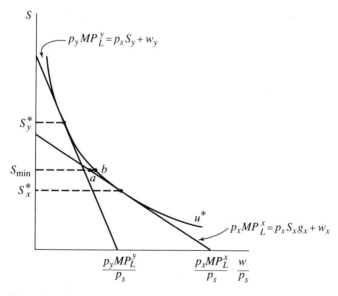

Figure 6
The Trade-off between Wages and Safety for Firms and Workers in Two Sectors

Two points are worth noting about this equilibrium. First, the marginal-value product of labor in the X sector is higher than in the Y sector. This relationship can be seen by comparing the wage-intercept of the X-iso-labor-cost line to that of the Y-iso-labor-cost line in Figure 6. The economic intuition is straightforward. Since safety in the X sector is more expensive than in the Y sector, it costs an X firm more money to provide a particular real income to one of its workers than for a firm in the Y sector. Hence, an X-sector worker must have a higher marginal value product than a Y-sector worker.

Second, suppose that we hold the world prices constant while increasing the capital intensity of production in both sectors. Then the marginal value product of labor must rise at a slower rate in the X sector than in the Y sector.

To see this point, recall that equilibrium in the capital market requires that

$$p_x MP_K^x = p_y MP_K^y \tag{7}$$

or at constant world prices

$$\hat{MP}_K^x = \hat{MP}_K^y \tag{8}$$

where the circumflex indicates percent change. For the purposes of the assumed technology, this condition can be written as

$$\hat{MP}_K^x = -(1 - \alpha)\hat{k}_x = -(1 - \beta)\hat{k}_y = \hat{MP}_K^y \tag{9}$$

where k_x and k_y are the capital-labor ratios in the X and Y sectors, respectively.

The implication for the labor market, however, is that, since $\alpha < \beta$

$$\hat{MP}_L^x = \alpha \hat{k}_x = \frac{\alpha(1 - \beta)}{1 - \alpha} \hat{k}_y < \beta \hat{k}_y = \hat{MP}_L^y \tag{10}$$

for $\hat{k}_x, \hat{k}_y > 0$. That is, there is a magnification effect on the marginal value product of labor in the Y sector.

Now, let the government impose a minimum safety standard in sector X that exceeds the equilibrium level in Figure 6, holding world prices fixed. In the new equilibrium, Y-sector firms are not constrained by the minimum standard, so that the worker's safety-wage indifference curve must still be tangent to the Y firm's labor isocost curve. However, X-sector firms are not so characterized. For these firms it is merely necessary that the worker's indifference curve pass through (or touch) the X firm's labor isocost curve at the minimum safety level. Tangency is not required, since competing firms are legally prohibited from reducing cost by trading off worker safety for higher wages.

These conditions are clearly not satisfied at the minimum safety level in Figure 6. If the firm pays the safety-wage combination at b, it can hold on to its workers, but it is then paying those workers more than their marginal value product. On the other hand, if the firm pays the safety-wage combination at a, then it will lose all of its workers to the Y sector.

The government might expect that the new standard will cause the real wage to rise. However, this is not the case. In order to satisfy the labor-market-clearing conditions, raising the real wage requires that we expand the labor-intensive sector X. All firms would become more capital intensive so that the marginal value product of labor would rise and the two labor isocost lines in Figure 6 would begin to shift out. However, as noted previously, the X-sector isocost will shift out proportionately less than the Y-sector isocost. Therefore, it will be impossible to find a pair of isocost curves that satisfies the equilibrium conditions as characterized earlier.

Contracting the labor-intensive X sector has the opposite effect. As capital intensity falls, the marginal product of labor in the X sector falls more slowly than in the Y sector. The isocost curves shift left, rendering a new equilibrium as depicted in Figure 7.

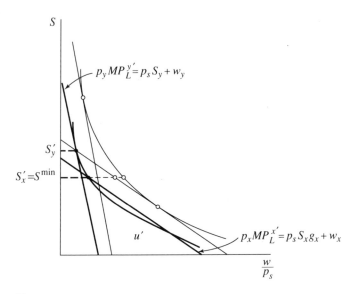

Figure 7
Effects of a Minimum Safety Requirement

Clearly, the safety in the X sector has risen. We can see, though, that as long as safety is a normal good, safety in the Y sector has fallen, since real income of workers declined.

Now consider the consequences for international trade. We can see that X production has fallen. Since X is the export good, it is likely that the terms of trade will improve with the standard. A similar standard in the partner country will also contract X supply onto the world market, further improving the home country's terms of trade. Therefore, the home country might seek an international standard if its objective is to improve its terms of trade or, more likely, if the home country is concerned with the level of employment in the X sector.

It is interesting to consider reversing the factor intensity ranking, letting X be the capital-intensive sector. In this case, increasing capital intensity in both sectors will cause the iso-labor-cost curve in the X sector to shift out faster than in the Y sector. A minimum labor standard that affects only industry X, then, would require a contraction of the X sector, thereby raising the real wage, increasing the capital intensity of production, and shifting the iso-labor-cost curve in the X sector out faster than in the Y sector.

Unlike the previous case in which the X sector is labor intensive, the standard *raises* the real wage. In addition, the safety level rises in *both* sectors even though the standard binds only on the X sector. Nevertheless, if world prices are variable, the terms of trade would still improve with the standard as long as it is imposed in the export sector. Thus an international standard would be desirable from the point of view of the home country. Conversely, a country's interest in harmonization on terms-of-trade grounds would be reversed if the standard were applied to the import-competing sector.

Our analysis of models with endogenous safety comports well with the model discussed in section 5.4. As before, the trade status (export or import) of the industry in which government intervention occurs determines the terms-of-trade effects associated with the standard. In addition, the terms of trade improve for the exporter of the relevant good no matter which country imposes the standard.

The two classes of models differ, though, in their predictions concerning worker safety. In the previous section we assumed that the standard would improve working conditions. By contrast, in models with endogenous safety, if a standard is imposed in the labor-intensive sector, then real wages fall economy-wide and the level of safety actually falls in the capital-intensive sector. We can be guaranteed that working conditions improve for all workers only if the minimum standard is imposed in the capital-intensive sector.

5.5.2   Endogenous Working Conditions and Market Failure

We turn now to consider a case in which the market does not give rise to efficient working conditions. One labor-market failure can come about even in a perfectly competitive environment if worker attitudes toward risk are highly heterogenous and nonuniformly distributed across the labor force. In this case, we find that if attitudes toward risk are normally distributed across workers, then safe plants that hire safety-conscious workers may not be safe enough. That is, workers preferring a safer plant but lower wages could compensate their coworkers preferring higher wages in a less safe plant. By contrast, the more dangerous plants may be too safe given the distribution of non-safety-conscious workers employed.

For the purposes of this model we will retain the assumption that the X sector is the labor-intensive export sector and Y is the capital-intensive import-competing sector. Worker attitude toward safety, however, will be handled somewhat differently.

We will make two assumptions concerning worker preferences. (1) no two workers have the same set of preferences over safety and money wages; and (2) near the mean of the distribution of preferences over safety and money wages, workers are more similar to each other than in the tails. We impose one final condition: there is a floor below which labor employment in a particular firm cannot fall. As we will see, without this condition, each plant would employ only one worker.

To get a sense of this model, consider the wage-safety trade-off for two industries, X and Y, with X as before requiring greater expenditure to achieve a given level of safety. Each firm must choose a safety-wage combination along its industry isocost line. Now, however, the available workers have varying preferences for safety and wage income. Rather than having to offer a safety-wage package that all workers will regard as equivalent to what is available elsewhere, each firm can target a group of workers and tailor its safety-wage package to the members of that group. Equilibrium requires that each employee like the compensation package at least as much as others available, and thus that the marginal employee be indifferent between his or her employer's package and those packages that are most similar offered by other firms. The heterogenous preferences are shown in Figure 8 by several indifference curves, each for a different worker.

Recall that there is a minimum number of workers required for each firm. In the case shown, that number of workers supports three firms, numbered 1, 2, and 3, in the safer industry Y, plus three other firms, numbered 4, 5, and 6, in the more dangerous industry X.

Firm 1 has selected the highest level of safety and the lowest wage, and employs only workers from the safe tail of the preference distribution. Firm 2 selects somewhat less safety and a higher wage, employing the next group of workers. The indifference curve connecting the safety-wage packages of firms 1 and 2 is that of the marginal worker, who would be indifferent between the two firms. Continuing down and to the right in the figure, the safety-wage choices of firms 3 through 6 are shown, together with the corresponding indifference curves of the marginal workers in each case. There are also, of course, some lucky inframarginal workers (indifference curves, not drawn) for whom their current job is unequivocally more attractive than the next best alternative.

Note a couple of points about Figure 8. First, for each marginal worker, because the indifference curve passes below the isocost line, there are many safety-wage combinations that are more attractive to the worker and cheaper for the firm. However, a new entrant who tries to locate between

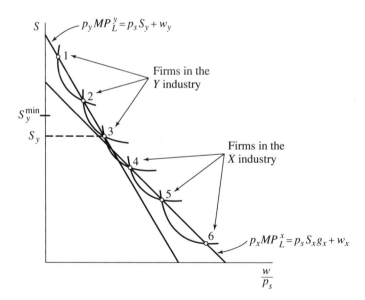

Figure 8
Two Industries with Heterogeneous Worker Preferences

two plants, to capture the marginal workers, will not be able to attract a sufficiently large number of workers to meet the minimum start-up size.

As a corollary, no firm would ever locate so as to hire more than the minimum number of workers. Otherwise, an entrant could come in, offer a cheaper wage-safety combination, and still hire enough workers to undertake production.

Second, plants toward the center of the distribution have more similar safety levels than plants out in the tails. This conclusion follows from our assumption that in the center, the safety-wage trade-off is densely populated with workers. It also implies that the marginal-worker indifference curves pass further below the isocost lines at the tails of the distribution than they do toward the center. That is, workers in the tails are less satisfied with wages and working conditions than those with preferences closer to the mean.

The safety level within a plant has properties very much like a public good. Pareto optimality is achieved if the average marginal rate of substitution between wages and safety at each plant is equal to the price of safety.[21] As long as each plant is drawing equally from workers who prefer more safety and workers who want less safety, then the condition for Pareto optimality will be satisfied. However, if the entire distribution of worker tastes has a central tendency, as we assume, then our condition for efficiency will fail to obtain.

There is much debate among labor economists as to the direction of the resulting bias in plant safety. The model described here is strongly disposed to the conclusion that plants safer than average are, in fact, not safe enough, whereas plants more dangerous than average are too safe, given the allocation of workers across plants. This result follows from the fact that each plant draws more workers from an extreme of the wage-safety distribution than from the center. As a consequence, the distribution of preferences at each plant is skewed despite the fact that the overall distribution of worker preferences is symmetric.

Take, first, the plant located at the mean of the worker distribution. If the distribution of worker preferences is symmetric, then the central plant hires half of its employees from the population of workers that prefer more wages and less safety than average, and the other half from those who prefer more safety and less wages. This one plant, therefore, is likely to meet the requirement of Pareto optimality that the average MRS is equal to the firm's relative price of safety.

Now consider the adjacent next-safer plant. The central plant and the next-safer plant are going to divide the workers lying between them on the distribution. We can see, though, that since the distribution of workers is more dense close to the central plant than the next-safer plant, the central plant will be able to attract more of these intermediate workers than the next-safer plant. In order for the next-safer plant to acquire a full complement of workers, therefore, it must hire more than half of its workers from the group that would prefer an even safer plant.

The opposite is the case for plants below the mean. We conclude then that the presence of a central tendency in worker preferences will cause plants more safe than the mean to be too dangerous for the workers that they employ, whereas the plants that are more dangerous than the mean are too safe for the workers employed.

The consequent market failure, then, requires that safe plants become even safer. The government may therefore attempt to introduce a minimum safety standard that applies only to the safer of the two industries. Such a policy is depicted in Figure 8.

Suppose that we consider a minimum safety standard in the Y sector that is between the safety levels of the two most dangerous plants in this sector. Clearly, if the most dangerous Y plant tries to move from its current position and locate at the minimum standard, it will not be able to attract enough employees to meet the start-up requirement.

Further, the most dangerous plant employed in the Y sector must shut down. The owners of the next most dangerous plant now realize that they can lower costs by offering less safety and higher wages. This is the case because they no longer have to compete with the Y sector's most dangerous plant for workers. They are bounded, of course, by the minimum safety standard.

Some of the resources released by the most dangerous Y-sector plant will find their way to the X sector. The resulting increase in production of the labor-intensive good will raise the real wage and shift both labor isocost curves outward. However, as before, the Y-sector isocost line will shift out faster than the X-sector isocost line.

A new X-sector plant will open up at a position like a in Figure 9. Such a plant could not have existed in the absence of a minimum standard in sector Y. For without the minimum standard, a Y-sector firm could have located at point b, stolen all of firm a's labor, and still broken even.

It is unclear what happens to the level of safety in the economy. The average level of safety rises in both sectors, but the more dangerous industry has expanded and the safer industry has contracted.

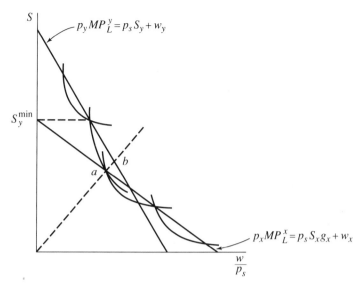

Figure 9
Minimum Safety Standard with Heterogeneous Worker Preferences

However, in any event, the market failure has not been corrected. The safe plants are still too dangerous and the dangerous plants are still too safe given the employees working at these plants.

The terms-of-trade effects are similar to those in the previous model. If the industry targeted for the minimum standard is in the import sector, then terms of trade deteriorate, and an international standard will make the home country worse off. Otherwise, the standard improves the terms of trade, and harmonization is attractive.

5.5.3 Summary

In the previous sections of this chapter we analyzed international bargaining over labor standards under the presumption that the government could usefully intervene to correct labor market failure. In this section we considered whether commonly used government policies, such as occupational safety and health regulations, do in fact have the desired effect.

We found that, under fairly reasonable assumptions, the labor market is capable of generating an efficient level of worker safety, so that no government intervention is necessary. Working conditions may vary across plants and industries, but this variability is largely a reflection of varying worker attitudes toward risk.

Nevertheless, the assumptions necessary to guarantee efficient working conditions may not apply in all industries. However, in most cases of market failure, government-mandated minimum working conditions will not restore Pareto optimality. We examined the case of heterogeneity of worker preferences over risk and money wages, and found that safety standards did little to correct the market failure.

Moreover, minimum safety standards can hurt the very workers they are intended to protect. A minimum standard applied to the labor-intensive sector will reduce money wages for workers in all sectors of the economy, and safety will decline in the unregulated sector. Safety rises in the regulated sector but not by enough to compensate for the lower money wages.

We can be certain that workers gain from the standards only if the standard is applied to the capital-intensive sector. In this case wages and safety levels rise in all sectors of the economy, whether regulated or not.

5.6   Conclusions and Implications for International Harmonization of Labor Standards

Historically, labor standards began to emerge in the middle of the 19th century for reasons that had little to do with international goods trade. Reforms were generally concerned with the welfare of disadvantaged labor groups such as women, children, and prisoners. In some cases, the objective of the reforms was to eliminate techniques of production that had such horrible health consequences for workers that the reformers could not believe that the workers would take these jobs if they were aware of the dangers. The interest in international standards turned more on the desire to eliminate certain practices worldwide than on the desire to alter the trade in goods or gain an advantage in trade.

Over time, the pursuit of international labor standards has taken on a more protectionist tone. In some cases the protectionist intent is barely disguised. In fact, it is quite commonly feared that countries with below-average labor standards are gaining unfair advantage in trade.

In analyzing the economics of international labor standards we have sometimes found support for this view. However, the consequences of harmonization depend very much on the market setting. Frequently, harmonization is not found to be in the interest of the high-standard country. Some of the results of our analysis are summarized in the following list:

Summary of Main Results

1. In a price-taking environment, standards that are least-cost methods of fixing a market failure, like internalizing an externality, are welfare improving whether or not trade partners behave similarly. Welfare gains associated with setting price equal to social marginal cost are not contingent upon correct pricing in the rest of the world. Intervention in trade to punish foreigners who do not comply would not be welfare improving, since a price-taking economy cannot affect world prices.

2. Point 1 does not imply that a small country has no interest in international labor standards. On the one hand, action by all foreign governments could raise the world price of the affected goods, a result that would be beneficial to domestic producers of the good.

Domestic consumers would, of course, be made worse off because they would suffer an increase in price but might not benefit from the improved allocation of foreign resources. However, domestic consumers could benefit despite the increase in price if the labor standard has a moral basis, such as eliminating child or forced labor.

On the other hand, if home-country consumers do not benefit from foreign standards, and if the domestic sector is small enough, a small country could actually be made worse off by an internationally coordinated attempt at correcting a market failure. But even so, such a country may still pursue harmonization if producers have a disproportionate role in policy making.

3. World welfare is best served when all countries internalize external effects. However, for cultural or economic-development reasons, the external cost of a labor-market abuse often varies by country. In such a case, harmonizing on an international standard will not produce an efficient outcome.

Pressure to harmonize may still be applied, nevertheless, particularly by countries where the externality is large. For these countries, the cost of the standard borne by their producers will exceed the increase in the world price. Governments may therefore seek relief for their producers by demanding harmonization.

4. The standards themselves may have resource costs. In most cases, such as freedom from forced labor, child labor laws, maximum hours limitation, and a minimum wage, the standard is labor using. Or, as in the case of child labor laws that increase education, they may be unskilled labor using but skilled labor augmenting. These standards can be analyzed in the same manner as a change in the endowment of labor.

However, other standards, such as occupational safety, require resources other than labor. The factor proportions of the safety industry then play a role in determining the effects of safety standards.

5. In a setting in which each economy is completely specialized in production, any standard that diverts resources away from the production of goods will contract the supply of exports to the world market. A terms-of-trade gain then results.

A partner country imposing a standard will also improve its own terms of trade, thereby hurting the home country. Thus each country should prefer to go it alone.

Because standards not only have a direct beneficial effect on labor but also improve a country's terms of trade, each country may be tempted to set a standard above the level necessary to correct any market failure that may exist. In such a setting, therefore, noncooperative behavior will leave the world with standards that are above the Pareto optimal level. International cooperation will be called for, but, as with tariffs, the treaty will call for a mutual lowering of labor standards.

6. The result under point 5 is quite fragile, however. Once we move away from a model with complete specialization to a Heckscher-Ohlin model, the outcome is quite different. Surprisingly, the terms-of-trade effect of a labor standard is entirely independent of the country that imposes the standard. The only parameter that matters is the factor proportions employed in implementing the standard relative to the world's factor endowments.

If the standard has a higher capital-labor ratio than the world's endowment of capital relative to labor, then the price of the capital-intensive good will rise on the world market. The capital-abundant country will gain, whether or not it was the source of the standard.

In such a setting, the capital-abundant country will tend to want a high labor standard, whereas a labor-abundant country will want a low standard. Harmonization would, therefore, improve world efficiency.

7. Labor standards that apply to only one industry have a similar property. Gains from the standard are determined by the country that exports the affected good, not the country that imposes the standard.

8. Finally, we explicitly modeled the market for safety. First we considered the case in which the market chooses the efficient level of safety. The results under point 7 carry over to the endogenous safety model. A standard will improve the terms of trade if applied to the export sector but worsen the terms of trade if applied to the import sector.

There are two curious features of this model. The imposition of the safety standard will raise real wages only if the regulated sector is capital intensive. Otherwise, real wages fall. This is a consequence of the Stolper-Samuelson theorem. Also, if the regulated sector is capital intensive, then the safety level will rise in both the regulated and unregulated sectors.

The gains from trade are difficult to establish in this model because government intervention introduces a distortion into the economy. However, gains are more likely if the export rather than the import sector is regulated, because increasing the price of the export good reduces the distortion caused by the regulation.

We then turned to a model in which excessive worker heterogeneity gives rise to a market failure. As in the efficient endogenous safety model, terms of trade improve if the regulated sector is also the export sector.

This model can also be used to illustrate that minimum safety standards frequently do not address the underlying market failure. Informational externalities are sometimes offered as an explanation for government regulation of working conditions. However, as in the heterogeneous worker model, a minimum safety level does not correct the market failure.

It should be evident from the foregoing summary that we have relied on a variety of models that have been designed to reflect settings in which different national characteristics may determine the outcome of the introduction of labor standards. Our intention accordingly has been to investigate the relationships between labor standards and trade primarily on a theoretical level. While our effort is by no means the final word on the subject, it appears to us that a fruitful next step would be to identify the interest groups and industries that are seeking to influence policy making in the design and implementation of international labor standards in different nations and to assess the economic effects of alternative policies.

5.6.1   Implications for International Harmonization of Labor Standards

Harmonization as a principle of negotiation in the GATT has served us well when applied to tariffs. It is established from a world-welfare point of view that harmonization on a zero tariff is best. This follows from the remarkably robust result that intervention at the border is virtually never a first-best policy.

It is natural to try to carry over the principle of harmonization to other aspects of negotiations, such as environmental and labor standards. Unfortunately, the principle that serves us so well with tariffs cannot be appropriately applied to the regulation of internal policies.

It is true that world welfare is best served by eliminating market failures where they exist, and the labor market is no exception. To the extent that labor standards are the appropriate remedy, then national governments should certainly enact them. However, there is little to suggest that such market failures are uniform across countries and, therefore, should be countered with similar measures. Hence, international harmonization of labor standards cannot be supported from a world-welfare point of view.

Furthermore, each country has a strong incentive to correct the market failures that exist within its borders. Therefore, there is not a strong case for international pressure to do so.

Our first conclusion, then, is that we should expect diversity in working conditions as the norm. As a terminological matter, it seems inappropriate to label as "unfair" the trade that follows from differences in labor standards as long as the labor standards are consistent with efficient resource use.

There is one important exception, however, to this conclusion. There are some cases in which labor standards are designed for income redistribution rather than to correct a market failure. Slave labor and child labor are two obvious examples. In the latter case, there are certainly efficient allocations that are highly inequitable, especially where children are concerned.

The international imposition of labor standards is even more difficult to defend because standards as commonly enacted rarely if ever address existent market failures. In our theoretical analysis, we offered as an example a minimum safety standard that was intended to address the market failure associated with diversity in tastes between wages and working conditions for workers within a plant. We found that the minimum standard raised real wages only if they were imposed in the capital-intensive sector. Otherwise, real wages fell economy-wide, and safety declines in the sector were not bounded by the minimum safety standard. Furthermore, the standard did not correct the market failure.

We turn now to consider the likely effect of harmonization on high- and low-income countries. First, do high-income countries gain from imposing standards on low-income countries?

On the one hand, low-income countries tend to be abundant in un-skilled labor. Minimum standards that impose restrictions on hours worked, child labor, prison labor, and the like remove some labor from the workforce. According to Heckscher-Ohlin type reasoning, the effect will be a contraction in the supply of labor-intensive production on the world market. As a consequence, the terms of trade of low-income countries will rise at the expense of high-income countries, thus making high-income countries worse off.

On the other hand, if the labor standard happens to be imposed in the capital-intensive sector, then the low-income countries will expand their export of labor-intensive goods. In this case, the terms of trade of the high-income countries will turn to their advantage.

Of course, the objective of labor standards in high-income countries may not be to raise national welfare, but rather to protect their scarce factor (unskilled labor). Labor standards in low-income countries will support this objective, but they will do so only by lowering welfare of both the high-income countries and the world as a whole.

In any event, the important point to realize here is that the gains from trade for the high-income countries do not depend on efficient resource use in low-income countries. The gains from trade stem simply from the opportunity to trade at prices other than autarky prices. Therefore, high-income countries should be willing to trade with low-income countries whether or not they have optimally configured labor markets.

This conclusion naturally raises the opposite question. Do low-income countries gain from having standards imposed upon them? There are several reasons why this might be the case.

First, for various reasons a breakdown in the political process may prevent governments from enacting legislation that corrects a market failure. An international requirement to do so, therefore, may be politically useful. However, it must be kept in mind that, for this argument to be compelling, we would have to be confident that the required policy does indeed correct the labor-market failure. This point has yet to be demonstrated, as we discussed previously.

Second, as a historical matter, the right to organize has been a precursor to the development of democratic institutions. Supporting nascent labor organizations may be a legitimate activity for existing democracies.

Third, as noted earlier, standards that withdraw labor from the market will contract the supply of labor-intensive goods. The terms of trade of the low-income countries will therefore improve as a consequence. However, again, it should be kept in mind that the reason the low-income countries are gaining stems from the fact that the standard is helping labor to collude and exercise market power by withdrawing their services from the market. This outcome may be in the interest of the workers, but it lowers world welfare.

We finally come to the question of whether it would be appropriate to countervail against low-standard countries. There are some conditions under which countervailing would be counterproductive or unjustified. For example, if all countries in the world are essentially price takers, then a countervailing action by one country against another will serve only to reduce the welfare of the countervailing country and have no effect on the exporter.

More realistically, it seems entirely likely, indeed certain, that efficient use of the world's resources will require varying labor standards across countries. These varying labor standards will probably give rise to some trade flows. However, it seems inappropriate to punish countries whose exports are stimulated by low standards as long as the trade of these countries is consistent with the efficient use of productive resources.

Countervailing may be justified if labor standards that are necessary for efficient resource allocation have not been enacted. In this case, the absence of labor standards could depress the wages of unskilled workers worldwide. However, it should be noted that a countervailing duty in this case could lower wages in the offending country, thereby further worsening working conditions in the low-income country.

Consider a duty imposed by a high-income country on the labor-intensive exports from a low-income country. Within the high-income country, the duty will have the desired effect. The price of labor-intensive goods will rise, pulling up the return to labor. In contrast, the opposite will occur in the low-income country. The duty will lower the price of exports of the labor-intensive good. As a consequence, the return to labor in the low-income country will tend to fall.

To sum up, we would have to say that the case for international harmonization of labor standards is rather weak. As genuinely motivated as such calls for international harmonization may be, the theoretical case has not been made. Furthermore, it is likely that international harmonization of labor standards will have unintended adverse consequences for the very people they are intended to protect.

APPENDIX

Worker Rights Standards

I. Freedom of Association
    A. Definition: The right of association concerns relations between unions and governments and involves the right of workers and employers
        1. to establish and join organizations of their choosing without previous authorization;

2. to draw up their own constitutions and rules, elect their representatives, and formulate their programs;

3. to join in confederations and affiliate with international organizations; and

4. to be protected against dissolution or suspension by administrative authority.

B. General principles

1. Freedom of association applies to everyone *except* military and police.

2. Unions should be independent of the government or ruling party.

3. Restrictions on the right to strike are legitimate only for government service (civil servants engaged in the administration of the state) and "essential services" (only those services whose interruption would endanger worker or public safety and health). When denied, there should be an effective alternate process for mediation, arbitration, and settlement of grievances.

4. Unions' civil liberties must be respected.

5. Unions may form and join federations, confederations, and international confederations.

II. The Right to Organize and Bargain Collectively

A. Definition: The right to organize and bargain collectively concerns relations between unions and employers and involves the right of workers

1. to be represented in negotiating the prevention and settlement of disputes with employers;

2. to protection against interference with union activities;

3. to protection against acts of antiunion discrimination; and

4. to protection against refusal of employment, dismissal, or prejudice resulting from union membership or participation.

5. Government should promote processes for voluntary negotiations between employers and workers and their organizations.

B. General principles

1. Voluntary collective bargaining should be protected by law and should be practiced.

2. Antiunion discrimination by employers should be illegal.

3. Speedy and effective processes should exist to review union/worker complaints of antiunion discrimination.

III. Forced Labor

A. Definition: Forced labor should be prohibited and suppressed in all its forms. Although there are certain exceptions, forced labor refers to work or service exacted from any person under the menace of penalty and for which the person has not volunteered. "Menace of penalty" includes loss of rights or privileges as well as penal sanctions.

B. General principles

1. Forced labor should *never* be used for the following purposes:

   a. economic development.

   b. to enforce racial, social, national, or religious discrimination.

      c. as political coercion or education, or punishment for holding or expressing political views opposed to the established political, social, or economic system.

      d. for labor discipline.

      e. as a punishment for having participated in legal strikes.

  2. The following do not constitute "forced labor" as defined under the international standards:

      a. certain forms of prison labor, *only* when imposed following conviction for a crime in a court of law.

      b. national service obligations (compulsory military service and normal civic obligations).

      c. genuine emergency, limited to a "sudden, unforeseen happening, calling for instant countermeasures, such as war, calamity or threatened calamity such as earthquakes, floods, pestilence, etc."

      d. minor communal services, defined as services performed by community members in the direct interest of the community.

IV. Minimum Age for Employment

  A. Definition: The minimum age standard aims at the effective abolition of child labor by raising the minimum age for employment to a level consistent with the fullest physical, mental, and social development of young people.

  B. General principles

    1. The minimum age for employment should be set no lower than 15, with an option for a lower minimum of 14 for developing countries with a level of economic development that makes the realization of the higher standard impossible. Countries that set the minimum age at the lower level, however, should be trying to progressively change conditions so that they can meet the higher standard.

      a. Exceptions: light work is permissible for 13−15-year-olds; minimum age of 18 for dangerous work; work in connection with education or training; participation in artistic performances.

    2. Minimum age legislation should cover all economic activity, not just employment under contract.

    3. Education should be provided for all children and should be compulsory. The minimum age for employment shall not be less than the age for completion for compulsory schooling.

    4. Minimum age legislation should have an effective enforcement system that includes an adequate number of inspectors and penalties that serve as effective deterrents. Penalties should include fines and/or imprisonment.

V. Acceptable Conditions of Work

  A. Definition: The standards for acceptable working conditions provide for the establishment and maintenance of systems, adapted to national conditions, that provide for minimum working standards: wages that provide a decent living for workers and their families; working hours that do not exceed 48 hours per week, with a full 24-hour rest day; a specified annual paid holiday; and minimum conditions for protection of the safety and health of workers.

B. Basic principles
   1. Minimum wage principles
      a. There should be a national, statutory minimum wage.
      b. It should be set realistically, preferably as a result of an open, public, or tripartite process, with certain specified criteria.
      c. Wages should be protected, that is, paid in money, and workers should be able to choose where and how they spend their wages.
   2. Hours of work
      a. Working hours should not exceed 48 hours per week, with a full 24-hour rest day. Workers should have a specified annual paid holiday.
      b. Overtime should be regulated, remunerated at a higher rate than for "normal" working hours, and prohibited from exceeding a certain number of hours in a given period.
   3. Safety and health principles
      a. Workers should have health and safety rights in the workplace, including a complaint process for hazardous conditions and the right to remove themselves from hazardous situations.
      b. The government should set health and safety standards as part of an open, public, or tripartite process.
   4. Enforcement principles
      a. There should be a legislatively mandated enforcement system for minimum wage, hours of work, and safety and health.
      b. Inspectors should have the right to enter the workplace, should have access to workers and their representatives, and have the right to issue citations for violations.
      c. Workers and unions should be protected against adverse action in filing complaints.
      d. Penalties for violations should not be limited to warnings, but should include fines and prison sentences.

Note: As stated in Lyle (1991, p. 20): "These are not intended to be legal definitions, nor to encompass the entire spectrum of internationally recognized worker rights. Rather, they represent general guidance intended merely to highlight the basic principles behind each of the five internationally recognized worker rights found in U.S. trade law."
Source: Adapted from Lyle (1991, pp. 20–31).

NOTES

We wish to thank Asad Alam, Jagdish Bhagwati, Steve Charnovitz, Robert Hudec, Greg Schoepfle, participants in the July 1993 Fairness-Harmonization Project Meeting and the September 1994 project conference, and members of the International Economics and the Labor Economics seminars at the University of Michigan for helpful comments on earlier versions of this paper.

1. For a theoretical evaluation of this "race to the bottom" problem, see Wilson (1995). An assessment of this issue, taking the empirical aspects into account, can be found in Bhagwati and Srinivasan (1995), Klevorick (1995), and Levinson (1995).

2. For additional details and perspective on the history of labor standards, see Leary (1995).

3. The view being expressed here is at variance with the view of the so-called neo-institutionalists, who argue that the imposition of labor standards may have positive welfare and growth effects. These positive effects may result from the labor-income-raising effects of capital-labor substitution, greater harmony in the workplace, more emphasis on worker training, and increased incentives for productivity-enhancing investments. For a more complete statement of this neoinstitutionalist position and a critique of the "neoclassical" view with its emphasis on comparative advantage and the gains from (free) trade, see Hanson (1983, esp. pp. 53–63), Herzenberg (1988), Kochan and Nordlund (1989), Office of Technology Assessment (1992, esp. pp. 77–78), Portes (1990), and Singh (1990).

4. Bhagwati (1995) provides further insight into the issues involved in the arguments made in support of reducing the diversity of institutions and policies among trading nations. See also Howse and Trebilcock (in process) and Schoepfle and Swinnerton (1994).

5. This section is based in large measure on Alam (1992, esp. pp. 10–44), Charnovitz (1986, 1987, 1992), Hanson (1983, esp. pp. 11–32), and ILO (1988).

6. See Marshall (1990) for a forceful argument in favor of trade-linked labor standards as part of the GATT system and Charnovitz (1992) for some recommendations on GATT actions regarding labor standards.

7. The highlights of the EC Charter of Fundamental Social rights are summarized in De Boer and Winham (1993, pp. 36–37), and the full text is to be found in Commission of the European Communities (1990). See also Campbell (1990). For an analysis of the economic effects of social protection in the EC, see Abraham (1994).

8. A useful reference is Lemco and Robson (1993).

9. Bhagwati (1995) notes that the EC can be viewed as representing a process of building a *federal* political structure, close, say, to those of the United States, Canada, and India, and therefore having a set of *minimum* labor standards makes *political* sense. See Sapir (1995) for a review of the process of social harmonization in the EC from the 1950s to the present. Sapir concludes that, while there have been noteworthy efforts to formalize the objectives of EC social policies, the implementation of explicit measures has remained limited and is not likely to change at least in the near future.

10. In connection with the NAFTA debate, Bhagwati (1995) notes that he favored asking for some minimum labor standards because the NAFTA could be construed as a *preferential* gift to Mexico for which something could be asked for in exchange. Notwithstanding this suggestion, it seems apparent that the EC model became the prototype for a number of nongovernmental organizations that were seeking to introduce explicit labor standards requirements into the NAFTA, which were reflected in the side agreements on the environment and labor that were negotiated.

11. Further support for this view is to be found in Morici (1993) and Garcia Rocha (1990). It will be interesting, accordingly, to analyze the content and potential economic effects of the side agreement on labor issues in the NAFTA that has been negotiated among the three NAFTA nations.

12. See Perez-Lopez (1993) for a discussion of voluntary codes of conduct that have been proposed for U.S. corporations operating in countries with allegedly questionable labor practices.

13. See Dorman (1989) for an evaluation of the procedures and decision-making criteria regarding worker rights in the implementation of the U.S. GSP; case studies of El Salvador, Malaysia, and Chile; and recommendations for improving the procedures and decision-making criteria in investigating alleged violations of worker rights standards. The reports prepared by the Bureau of International Labor Affairs (ILAB) are also worth noting. They include evaluations of worker rights in export processing zones (see U.S. Department of Labor, 1989–90, and Schoepfle, 1990), child labor, worker rights restrictions in East Asia, and characteristics of the informal sector in a number of developing countries (see U.S. Department of Labor, 1992, and Schoepfle and Perez-Lopez, 1993). For some background discussion of the issues involved in the renewal of the GSP in late 1994, see Lande and Dybner (1994).

14. Note that we are referring here to purely domestic externalities as compared to transborder externalities. Bhagwati and Srinivasan (1995) distinguish the two types of externalities, noting that the Pareto optimality proposition applies only to domestic externalities. Labor standards involve domestic externalities, except in cases in which one country may affect standards in another country due to a "good" or "bad" example or because there may be a "race to the bottom." We shall abstract from such possibilities.

15. For a discussion of moral considerations, see Bhagwati (1995).

16. The models of this section, as well as many of the results, draw heavily on Alam (1992).

17. Asad Alam has pointed out to us that if countries are symmetric, in the sense that the terms-of-trade gain to one is of the same magnitude as the terms-of-trade loss imposed by the other when each raises its labor standards, any cooperative solution would neutralize the terms-of-trade effects. Both countries would still gain, however, so long as the level of the standard is such that the marginal benefit exceeds the marginal cost from reduced consumption.

18. It should be clear that this problem is identical to that of the effects of accumulation of factors of production. In that sense, our results are merely applications of known results and techniques from the literature begun by Rybczynski (1955).

19. The results may also change if preferences are nonhomothetic.

20. See U.S. GAO (1993) for comparative information on the design and operation of occupational safety and health programs in the United States and Canada and references to earlier reports comparing the United States and Mexico.

21. See Dickens (1984) for a demonstration.

REFERENCES

Abraham, Filip. 1994. "Social protection and regional convergence in a EMU." *Open Economies Review* 5:89–114.

Alam, Asad. 1992. "Labor standards and comparative advantage." Unpublished doctoral dissertation, Columbia University.

Bhagwati, Jagdish. 1995. "The demands to reduce domestic diversity among trading nations." Chapter 1 in this volume.

Bhagwati, Jagdish, and T. N. Srinivasan. 1995. "Trade and the environment: Does environmental diversity detract from the case for free trade?" Chapter 4 in this volume.

Campbell, Duncan C. 1990. "EC 1992: The social dimension at issue," in Jorge F. Perez-Lopez, Gregory E. Schoepfle, and John Yochelson, eds., *EC 1992: Implications for U.S. workers*, Proceedings of a Working Roundtable, jointly sponsored by the U.S. Department of Labor and Center for Strategic and International Studies. *Significant Issues Series*, 12:97–124.

Charnovitz, Steve. 1986. "Fair labor standards and international trade," *Journal of World Trade Law* 20:61–78.

Charnovitz, Steve. 1987. "The influence of international labour standards on the world trading regime: A historical review." *International Labour Review*, 126:565–584.

Charnovitz, Steve. 1992. "Environmental and labour standards in trade." *The World Economy*, 15:335–356.

Commission of the European Communities. 1990. *The Community Charter of Fundamental Social Rights for Workers*. European File 6/90. Brussels: Commission of the European Communities.

De Boer, Elizabeth, and Gilbert R. Winham. 1993. "Trade negotiations, social charters, and the NAFTA." In Jonathan Lemco and William B. P. Robson, eds., *Ties beyond trade: Labor and environmental issues under the NAFTA*. Canadian American Committee: C. D. Howe Institute (Canada) and National Planning Association (U.S.A.).

Dickens, William T. 1984. "Occupational safety and health regulation and economic theory." In William Darity, Jr., ed., *Labor economics: Modern views*. Boston: Kluwer-Nijhoff.

Dorman, Peter. 1989. *Worker rights and U.S. trade policy: An evaluation of worker rights conditionality under the general system of preferences*. U.S. Department of Labor, Office of International Economic Affairs, Bureau of International Labor Affairs. Washington, DC: U.S. Government Printing Office.

Garcia Rocha, Adalberto. 1990. "Mexico." In Stephen A. Herzenberg, Jorge Perez-Lopez, and Stuart K. Tucker, eds., *Labor standards and development in the global economy*. Washington, DC: U.S. Department of Labor, Bureau of International Labor Affairs.

Hanson, Gote. 1983. *Social clauses and international trade: An economic analysis of labour standards in trade policy*. New York: St. Martin's Press.

Herzenberg, Stephen A. 1988. "Institutionalizing constructive competition: International labor standards and trade." Economic Discussion Paper 32, U.S. Department of Labor, Bureau of International Labor Affairs, Office of International Economic Affairs, Division of Foreign Economic Research.

Howse, Robert, and Michael J. Trebilcock. In process. "The fair trade free trade debate: Trade, labour and the environment," University of Toronto.

International Labor Organization (ILO). 1988. *Human rights: A common responsibility*. International Labor Conference, 75th Session, 1988. Geneva: ILO.

Klevorick, Alvin K. 1995. "Reflections on the race to the bottom." Chapter 12 in this volume.

Kochan, Thomas A., and Willis Nordlund. 1989. *Reconciling labor standards and economic goals: An historical perspective.* U.S. Department of Labor, Office of International Economic Affairs, Bureau of International Labor Affairs. Washington, DC: U.S. Government Printing Office.

Lande, Stephen, and Ariel Dybner. 1994. "The future of the U.S. Generalized System of Preferences," Overseas Development Council, *Policy Focus,* No. 5.

Leary, Virginia A. 1995. "Workers' rights and international trade: The social clause (GATT, ILO, NAFTA, U.S. Laws)." Chapter 5 in Volume 2 of this work.

Lemco, Jonathan, and William B. P. Robson, eds. 1993. *Ties beyond trade: Labor and environmental issues under the NAFTA.* Canadian American Committee: C. D. Howe Institute (Canada) and National Planning Association (U.S.A.).

Levinson, Arik. 1995. "Environmental regulation and industry location: International and domestic evidence." Chapter 11 in this volume.

Lyle, Faye. 1991. "Worker rights in U.S. policy." *Foreign Labor Trends,* 91–154, U.S. Department of Labor, Bureau of International Labor Affairs. Washington, DC: U.S. Government Printing Office.

Marshall, Ray. 1990. "Trade-linked labor standards." In Frank J. Macchiarola, ed., "International trade: The changing role of the United States." *Proceedings of the Academy of Political Science,* 37:67–78.

Morici, Peter. 1993. "Implications of a social charter for the North American Free Trade Agreement." In Jonathan Lemco and William B. P. Robson, eds., *Ties beyond trade: Labor and environmental issues under the NAFTA.* Canadian American Committee: C. D. Howe Institute (Canada) and National Planning Association (U.S.A.).

Office of Technology Assessment (OTA), Congress of the United States. 1992. *U.S.-Mexico trade: Pulling together or pulling apart?* Washington, DC: U.S. Government Printing Office.

Perez-Lopez, Jorge F. 1993. "Promoting international respect for worker rights through business codes of conduct." *Fordham International Law Journal,* 17:1–47.

Portes, Alejandro. 1990. "When more can be less: Labor standards, development, and the informal economy." In Stephen A. Herzenberg, Jorge Perez-Lopez, and Stuart K. Tucker, eds., *Labor standards and development in the global economy.* Washington, DC: Bureau of International Labor Affairs.

Rybczynski, T. M. 1955. "Factor endowment and relative commodity prices," *Economica,* 22:36–41.

Sapir, André. 1995. "Trade liberalization and the harmonization of social policies: Lessons from European integration." Chapter 15 in this volume.

Schoepfle, Gregory K. 1990. *Labor standards in export assembly operations in Mexico and the Caribbean.* U.S. Department of Labor, Bureau of International Labor Affairs. Washington, DC: U.S. Government Printing Office.

Schoepfle, Gregory K., and Jorge Perez-Lopez, eds. 1993. *Work without protections: Case study of the informal sector in developing countries.* Washington, DC: U.S. Department of Labor, Bureau of International Labor Affairs.

Schoepfle, Gregory K., and Kenneth A. Swinnerton, eds. 1994. *International labor standards and global economic integration: Proceedings of a symposium.* Washington, DC: U.S. Department of Labor, Bureau of International Labor Affairs.

Singh, Ajit. 1990. "Southern competition, labor standards and industrial development in the North and South." In Stephen A. Herzenberg, Jorge Perez-Lopez, and Stuart K. Tucker, eds., *Labor standards and development in the global economy.* Washington, DC: U.S. Department of Labor, Bureau of International Labor Affairs.

U.S. Department of Labor, Bureau of International Labor Affairs (ILAB). 1989–90. "Worker rights in export processing zones." *Foreign Labor Trends,* FLT 90–132, including Volume 2, "Worker rights in export processing zones: Mexico." Washington, DC: U.S. Government Printing Office.

U.S. Department of Labor, Bureau of International Labor Affairs (ILAB). 1992. *International worker rights: Child labor, special categories in East Asia, informal sector.* Biennial Report to Congress. Washington, DC: U.S. Department of Labor.

U.S. General Accounting Office (GAO). 1993. *Occupational safety and health: Differences between programs in the United States and Canada.* GAO/HRD-94-15FS (December).

Watson, William. 1993. "A skeptical view of the social charter." In Jonathan Lemco and William B. P. Robson, eds., *Ties beyond trade: Labor and environmental issues under the NAFTA.* Canadian American Committee: C. D. Howe Institute (Canada) and National Planning Association (U.S.A.).

Weintraub, Sidney, and Jan Gilbreath. 1993. "The social side to free trade." In Jonathan Lemco and William B. P. Robson, eds., *Ties Beyond Trade: Labor and environmental issues under the NAFTA.* Canadian American Committee: C. D. Howe Institute (Canada) and National Planning Association (U.S.A.).

Wilson, John Douglas. 1995. "Capital mobility and environmental standards: Is there a theoretical basis for a race to the bottom?" Chapter 10 in this volume.

IV Tax Policy

6

Tax Cacophony and the Benefits of Free Trade

Joel Slemrod

6.1   Introduction

6.1.1   Selective Review of Academic Literature and European Policy

There is wide cross-country variation both in the overall level of tax revenue, relative to national income, and in the structure of taxation that generates this revenue. Often these taxes distort the structure of production away from what a country's comparative advantage would dictate in the absence of taxes. For this reason it is natural to inquire whether the existence of tax disparities mitigates the gains to be expected from a movement toward free trade and, if so, what types of harmonization of tax systems ought to be undertaken in advance of, or in concert with, trade liberalization.

This issue has been taken up, in the context of European trade liberalization, by a host of eminent economists. In 1953 the High Authority of the European Coal and Steel Community (ECSC) appointed the Committee of Experts, chaired by Jan Tinbergen, to consider and compare the economic effects of a system of origin-based and destination-based indirect taxes. In its report, known as the Tinbergen Report (1953), the committee noted that for indirect taxes applied uniformly, there was no real difference between the two systems. Exchange-rate adjustments would eliminate any apparent competitive disadvantage or differential in production costs. As the report notes, though, "What an exchange rate *cannot* do, is to offset *unequal* additions to the costs of different commodities. The pattern of production and trade will have been distorted from the 'ideal'" (p. 24). Distortions will arise under either the destination or origin-based system if there are nonuniform taxes, but only under origin-based taxes will the locational pattern of production be disturbed.

The Tinbergen Report deals only briefly with "direct" taxes such as income tax. It remarks that income taxation "produces no distortions because it applies to all commodities alike" (p. 24). Two further points are noted. First, if one particular industry were made to pay a specially high income tax, strictly speaking the country ought to give a refund on all products of that industry that were exported, and also ought to impose a compensatory duty on imports of such products. Second, the report speculates that it would be theoretically possible to levy a general destination-based income tax, under which a refund would be granted with respect to all exports of the direct taxes paid as a result of exports, together with a compensating duty to all imports. They dismiss this alternative because it is impractical, calling the origin-based system of direct taxes "much simpler."

W. Brian Reddaway (1958), a member of the ECSC Committee of Experts, reaffirmed the conclusions of the Tinbergen Report. He concluded that

the introduction of a Free Trade Area does not raise any fundamentally new issues in relation to taxation, though it makes the old ones of rather greater importance because barriers to trade will be smaller; in particular there is no need to incorporate in the treaty any agreement for "harmonisation of tax systems and social charges". . . . The Free Trade Area can, like ordinary international trade, work with benefit to all concerned even though tax-systems and tax-rates ... vary widely between the countries." (p. 78)

One reason that Reddaway reached this sanguine conclusion was that he thought that the current practice in Europe accorded reasonably well with the requirements of a non-trade-distorting tax system—that specific taxes be destination based, and that uniform taxes could be either origin based or destination based. He noted the exception to this observation of policies deliberately designed to protect certain industries.

In 1960 the Commission of the European Community appointed the Fiscal and Financial Committee, under the chairmanship of Fritz Neumark, to study tax harmonization. Its report, known as the Neumark Report (1963), recommended the replacement of turnover taxes with the value-added tax (VAT), excluding the retail stage, levied by member countries at approximately the same rate. They favored the origin principle, under which exports are taxed and imports are free of tax, because there need be no "tax frontiers"—goods may pass without tax control.

Ohlin (1965) argues, that "there is no prima facie case for harmonization of the tax system in general" (p. 87) as a prerequisite for trade liberalization. He regarded tax differences as posing the same issues as differences in social legislation, and he came to the same conclusion in both cases—that "trade will adapt itself to differences in the social and financial milieu in the same way it does to differences in climate" (ibid.). He added, however, that "if changes in industry and trade can be proved to be the outcome of a difference in tax policy, and if these changes are considered unfavorable to one or several member countries, it will be natural to take up the matter of effecting a change in taxation through action by one or several of them" (ibid.).

Ohlin then goes beyond the standard static analysis of the gains from trade to consider how freer movement of factors might affect economic development. He considers the case where one country has very generous depreciation rules for capital. Such rules, he argues, will favor capital-intensive manufacturing industries, and these sectors will grow relatively quickly. He goes on to argue that the relative advantage of such a tax policy, and the relative handicap to other countries, may be enhanced when tariffs are eliminated. He does not view this problem as one that requires harmonization of business tax policies.

Similarly, Johnson (1968) argues that a free trade area does not in and of itself require harmonization of other policies. He does, though, emphasize the problem of tax or expenditure policies that "involve evasion of the free trade commitment by the substitution of fiscal for commercial policy discrimination" (p. 10); these cases, he suggests, will have to be resolved by negotiation among representatives of the parties affected. He surmises that "the major gains to be obtained are offered by freedom of trade *per se*, and that the gains obtainable by harmonization of policies in other areas of economic activity are of a much lower order of magnitude" (p. 14). With respect to corporate taxes, he judges the extra degree of harmonization necessitated by a move toward free trade to be "negligible, owing to the probability that a substantial degree of harmonization in this field has already been effected as a consequence of competitive pressures and the negotiation of double tax treaties" (p. 24).

Considerable attention has been paid in the European Community to achievement of some uniformity in the type and base of commodity taxes. In 1967 the EC Council of Ministers decided that all member countries should substitute the VAT for turnover taxes, in part to prevent member countries from using indirect taxation to favor domestic producers through the manipulation of border tax adjustments. In contrast to turnover taxes, for which the border tax arrangements required by the destination principle are difficult to implement, the VAT provides a precise method for eliminating the tax on exports and levying an equivalent compensating tax on imports. By 1973, nine member countries had introduced the VAT. The sixth VAT directive, adopted in 1977 and implemented by all member countries in 1979, achieved a broad harmonization of the tax base. In June 1991, after a series of proposals in the late 1980s, the EC Council of Ministers agreed on a minimum standard VAT rate of 15 percent, with one or two reduced VAT rates of at least 5 percent. The effective date of these rates—at the end of 1992—was to coincide with the elimination of border controls. To eliminate the need for border controls, the destination principle for the VAT was to be replaced by the origin principle in 1997; in the meantime, border tax adjustments were to be administered through a postponed accounting system, whereby transactions are reported to tax authorities in both the importing and exporting countries, without border declarations.

As the foregoing discussion suggests, the issue of whether tax differences would mitigate any gains from liberalized trade was raised most often in the context of indirect taxes. Often direct taxes were ignored because they were presumed to have a uniform impact across commodities, and thus create no trade distortions. These are some notable exceptions, however. The Neumark Committee proposed that a split-rate corporate tax system (with a lower tax rate on dividends compared to retained earnings) be instituted, with uniform rates among all member countries.

In contrast to this recommendation of the Neumark report, the Van den Tempel report (1970) to the Commission of the EC recommended that the European corporate tax systems should be harmonized toward a classical, unintegrated tax system, where there is no differentiation between the tax rate on retained earnings and that on dividends. In 1975 the EC commission itself issued a draft directive proposing to coordinate corporate tax systems along the lines of a "partial imputation system," under which shareholders receive partial credit against their personal taxes for taxes paid at the corporate level (Commission of the EC, 1976). The rate of tax was to be between 45 and 55 percent, but there was no requirement for a uniform definition of the tax base. The Commission repeated this proposal in 1980, with a recommendation for a harmonized base, but no action was taken.

In the academic literature, there has been considerable discussion of the economic costs of unharmonized business tax systems. Shoup (1963) discusses the correspondence between the destination-based sales tax and residence-based income tax and also between the origin-based sales tax and source-based income tax. He also notes that under a business tax, even if the definition of profits and tax rate are uniform, the average tax rates will be different across sectors, and so "the allocation of resources ... will be affected even by a uniform income tax" (p. 36).

Musgrave (1963) is the most prominent example in the early literature of a focus on the issue of direct taxes (specifically, profits taxes). She notes several points that have been prominent in the later literature. One is that, to the extent that the level and pattern of tariffs compensates for direct tax differentials, removal of tariffs may increase distortions. She also notes that differing source-based effective tax rates on profits will interfere with an efficient worldwide allocation of capital. Finally, she notes that the existence of different source-based rates of tax across countries provides incentives for profit shifting into low-tax jurisdictions and, more generally, provides opportunities for tax evasion. She concludes that harmonization of profit taxes should be given priority over harmonization of indirect taxes, because the use of the destination principle is an effective device to eliminate the trade-distorting effects of indirect taxes, but no such device for direct taxes is easily implemented. More recently, Tanzi and Bovenberg (1990) have argued for harmonization of corporate tax bases with at least partial uniformity of statutory tax rates, while both Musgrave (1987) and Cnossen (1989) advocate both tax-rate and tax-base harmonization.

Concern over the distortionary effects of nonuniform capital income taxes was heightened by the movement in the 1990s toward elimination of border controls and the liberalization of capital movements. In 1990 the European Commission established the Committee of Independent Experts, commonly referred to as the Ruding Committee, after its chairman, Onno Ruding. The committee was charged with examining whether any measures should be taken to reduce the distortions to international business activity caused by the various countries' company taxation. Its report, published on March 10, 1992, documented substantial differences among member states in both tax rates and definition of taxable income, and showed that there were higher effective tax rates overall on foreign direct investment than on domestic investment. The committee proposed to bound the statutory corporate tax rate between 30 and 40 percent and to harmonize in several ways the tax bases of member countries. For the most part, these proposals, which require a unanimous vote, were not adopted.

6.1.2 Road Map of This Chapter

Although early discussions of the efficiency cost of nonuniform tax systems discounted the importance of direct taxes, this conclusion has been disputed recently, especially in light of the liberalization of factor movements and the failure of the European Community to achieve any significant harmonization of business taxation. For these reasons there exist large differences across countries in the system and rate of business taxation—a veritable tax cacophony—differences that lead to an inefficient allocation of economic activity across countries and to an excessive amount of resources devoted to tax compliance and tax planning. They also lead to a widespread complaint that domestic companies are put at a competitive disadvantage by the onerousness of the home country's tax system.

For the most part, the discussion of the efficiency cost of nonuniform business taxation has not been closely tied to the issue of liberalization of trade in goods and services—the analysis could proceed in a one-good model and deal with how business tax differences lead to an inefficient allocation of capital across countries.

In this chapter I attempt to address this issue more directly and address the following questions: How does the presence of this tax cacophony affect the benefits of movement in the direction of free trade? Does it enhance, diminish, or leave unaffected the gains that might be expected in the absence of these tax differences? I proceed in several steps. First, in section 6.2, I present some measures of the extent of business tax cacophony now existing and then, in section 6.3, I discuss the economic costs of disharmony. Section 6.4 addresses the prospects for tax harmonization, either through multilateral coordination or tax competition. Section 6.5 draws some conclusions.

6.2   Cross-Country Differences in Business Taxation

In this section I present some basic facts about cross-country differences in the taxation of business. In order to keep the analysis from becoming too complicated too quickly, I begin by ignoring multinational investment. Thus I first present evidence about how a purely domestic business would be taxed in different countries.

6.2.1   Corporation Income Tax Rates

Not all businesses are incorporated. Furthermore the fraction of business activity that is carried out by incorporated firms varies across countries, depending on, among other things, the tax penalty to incorporation. Nevertheless, a preponderance of business activity is carried out in incorporated form, especially among large businesses. Thus looking at the variation in the taxation of corporations is a good place to start looking for evidence of tax disharmony.

Table 1 (on p. 290) presents evidence on the statutory rates of corporation income tax for OECD countries in 1992; it includes both the rate imposed by the central government and the average rate set by subfederal governments. It is clear that the total rate varies widely, from a low of 28 percent in Norway to a high of 58.1 percent on undistributed profits in Germany.

The statutory rate of tax is not necessarily a reliable indicator of the true burden imposed by business taxes. The statutory rate ignores the rules that are used to determine taxable income and credits against tax liability. Critically important are the rules governing depreciation allowances and inventory accounting, including to what extent they account for inflation, the extent of investment and other business tax credits, and a host of other tax accounting rules. These rules are emphatically not harmonized across countries, so one cannot conclude much from a comparison of tax rates about the relative burden of corporation income taxes. For example, it is well known that allowing immediate write-off of capital investment is equivalent to a zero effective tax rate on new investment, *regardless* of the statutory rate of tax. Nevertheless, these statutory rates indicate the rate of tax on a dollar of additional income and are therefore the relevant tax rates for certain decisions such as the sourcing of output among given plants and income shifting.

There are two other common procedures for assessing the magnitude of the tax burden placed on corporations. The first is to look at how much revenue is actually collected from corporation income tax as a percent of GDP (the second column of Table 1). Two striking facts are immediately apparent. First, there is even more variation in the ratio of corporate tax revenues to GDP than there is in the statutory corporate tax rate. The coefficient of variation is 0.57, compared to 0.24 for tax rates. Second, there is surprisingly little correlation (0.13) between the statutory corporation tax rate and the revenue/GDP ratio. Rather than offsetting differences in rates, the differences in the definition of taxable income exacerbate the differences. Note, though, that for either measure Japan is near the top of the list. This fact may be somewhat surprising in view of the general perception that the Japanese government has a relatively cooperative, rather than adversarial, relationship with its resident corporations.

A second approach to measuring the tax burden on business is to calculate the marginal effective tax rate on investment by deriving the difference between the pretax and posttax real rate of return required from a hypothetical but typical investment project. This procedure takes into account not only the statutory tax rate but also the depreciation allowances, inventory accounting, credits, and degree of inflation indexing. It

Table 1
Alternative Measures of the Corporate Tax Burden in OECD Countries, 1992

Country	Statutory Corporate Tax Rates (manufacturing)	Corporate Tax Revenues as a Percentage of GDP	Marginal Effective Tax Rate
Australia	39.0	4.3	30
Austria	39.0	1.4	9
Belgium	39.0	2.9	7
Canada	38.3	2.5	19
Denmark	38.0	1.6	15
Finland	40.2	2.1	11
France	34.0	2.3	7
Germany	58.1	1.8	11
Greece	40.0	2.1	0
Iceland	45.0	0.9	25
Ireland	10.0	1.8	2
Italy	47.8	3.9	15
Japan	51.0	6.7	22
Luxembourg	39.4	8.2	21
Netherlands	35.0	3.4	11
New Zealand	33.0	2.5	26
Norway	28.0	4.1	26
Portugal	39.6	2.6	12
Spain	35.3	3.0	19
Sweden	30.0	1.8	0
Switzerland	30.3	2.1	7
Turkey	49.2	1.9	31
United Kingdom	33.0	4.0	15
United States	38.3	2.2	14
Average	37.94	2.92	14.79
Standard deviation	9.21	1.67	8.95
Coefficient of variation	0.24	0.57	0.61

Source: OECD (1991).

must make assumptions about such things as the required posttax return, the rate of economic depreciation for various classes of assets, the marginal sources of financing new investment, and the rate of inflation. A multicountry calculation of marginal effective tax rates requires an enormous amount of data and information about the tax codes; for this reason few such studies have been attempted. The results of a careful recent study done by the OECD (1991) are presented in the final column of Table 1.

Note first that the correlation between the marginal effective tax rate and the statutory tax rate is 0.34, and it is 0.35 between the marginal effective tax rate and the tax-to-GDP ratio. Thus, although the three tax measures do not tell an inconsistent story about the ordering of countries' corporate tax burdens, there are certainly differences in the stories they tell. This finding is true not only for the ordering but also for the degree of divergence among the rates. The coefficient of variation is 0.61 for marginal effective tax rates, compared to 0.57 for the revenue/GDP ratio and 0.24 for statutory corporate rates.

6.2.2   Tax Integration

The United States operates a "classical" system of taxing corporate income. Under this kind of system, corporate income, with payments to debt holders deductible, is subject to an entity-level corporate income tax. Dividend payments from the corporation to the shareholder are then subject to individual income tax; capital gains on the shares of corporations may also be subject to the individual-level tax. This system subjects equity owners to two levels of tax, to the extent that dividends are paid out.

The classical system is, however, the exception rather than the rule among OECD countries; only four of 24 countries adhere to it. The other 20 countries have some form of "integration" of the corporate and individual income tax systems, with the result of alleviating the double taxation on equity-financed corporate capital. Under full or complete integration, corporate income is part of individual taxable income of the shareholders, who are given a credit for any corporate tax paid "on their behalf" by the corporation; such a system implies that corporate-source income is taxed no differently than the income earned by a partnership in a sole proprietorship; that is, it is taxed once at the tax rate of the ultimate owner.

For a number of reasons, principally its administrative impracticability, full integration has not been implemented. The 20 OECD countries with integrated tax systems all have some form of partial integration. In three countries, integration takes the form of some degree of tax relief at the corporate level for dividends paid. In the remaining 17 countries integration is achieved by providing tax relief for dividends at the shareholder level, either by granting a flat tax credit per dollar of dividends received, applying a separate flat schedule or withholding tax to dividends, or by the gross-up and credit method. Three countries have full integration for dividends only, but not for retained earnings.

Table 2 (on pp. 294–295) presents some evidence about the extent to which integration alleviates the double taxation of dividends, as well as the extent to which it affects the conclusions reached earlier about the cross-country differences in the taxation of corporate income. The first column (A) of Table 2 contains the statutory corporation tax rates of Table 1, with some slight modifications. The second column (B) gives the top personal tax rate. The third column (C) calculates what, in the absence of integration, would be the total (two-level) tax rate on corporate earnings paid out as dividends. The fourth column (D) lists what the actual tax is on corporate earnings paid out as dividends. Note that only for the four countries with no integration at all—the United States plus Luxembourg, the Netherlands, and Switzerland—is the figure in the fourth column no lower than the figure of the third column. For all the other countries it is lower, reflecting the integration relief of double taxation. For those countries with full integration for dividends—Australia, Finland, and New Zealand—the fourth column is equal to the second column, reflecting the fact that the corporate tax is effectively treated as a withholding tax, with the ultimate liability being determined by the graduated personal income tax. For certain countries—Belgium, Denmark, and Norway—the effective tax on dividends is actually lower than the top personal rate, so that not only is there not double taxation, but there is preferential tax treatment of dividends compared to other income. The net effect of integration is summarized in the final column (E) of Table 2. This "degree of dividend relief" is equal to zero for unintegrated systems and to 100 for perfectly integrated systems, and it exceeds 100 for systems that afford preferential treatment to dividends.

A comparison of the first and fourth columns of Table 2 suggests that recognizing integration does not significantly diminish the degree of divergence among rates of taxation. The standard deviation is 11.2 percent for the fourth column, compared to 6.1 percent for the first column. (Note that, among the larger countries, the United Kingdom has the lowest statutory corporate tax rate and the lowest total tax on corporate income paid out as dividends.)

6.2.3   Taxation of Multinational Enterprises' Foreign Direct Investment

There is one other important source of cross-country disharmony of taxation of business—foreign direct investment (FDI). This is an exceedingly complicated area of taxation because of the problem of overlapping tax jurisdictions and because of the difficulties—both conceptual and practical—of determining the "location" of income. A brief overview follows.[1]

Each country in the world asserts the right to tax the income that is generated within its borders, including the income earned by foreign multinational corporations. Countries differ widely, however, in the tax rate they apply, the definition of the tax base, and the special incentives they offer for investment. Nevertheless, the first and quantitatively most important tax burden on FDI comes from the government of the country (known as the "host" country) where the investment is located.

Many countries, including the United States, Japan, and the United Kingdom, also assert the right to tax the worldwide income of their residents, including resident corporations. As a rule, the income of foreign subsidiaries is recognized only upon repatriation of earnings through dividends, interest, or royalty payments. In order to avoid the potentially onerous burden of two layers of taxation, the countries that tax on a worldwide basis also offer a credit for income and withholding taxes paid to foreign governments. The total credit available in any given year is usually limited to the home country's tax liability on the foreign-source income, although credits earned in excess of the limitation may often be carried forward or backward to offset excess limitations for other years. Several other countries, including France and the Netherlands, operate a "territorial" system of taxing their resident corporations, under which foreign-source business income is completely exempt from home-country taxation.

This would be the end of the story if the geographical location of income were not a matter of dispute. In fact, even if all the information necessary to ascertain the location of income were costlessly available, the conceptual basis for locating income would be controversial (Ault and Bradford, 1990). In reality, corporations do not have the incentive to fully reveal all the information on which to base a determination of the geographical source of income. For any pattern of real investment decisions, a multinational has the incentive to shift the apparent source of income out of high-tax countries into low-tax countries. Such shifting can be accomplished through, for example, the pricing of intercompany transfers of

Table 2
Effect of Tax Integration Schemes on the Total Tax on Dividends

Country	A Corporate Tax Rate[a]	B Top Personal Tax Rate	C Total Tax on Dividends if no Integration[b] $[=A + (1 - A) \cdot B]$	D Total Tax on Dividends with Actual Integration	E Degree of Dividend Relief[b] $[=(C - D)/(C - B)]$
Australia	39	48.3	68.5	48.3	100
Austria	39	50	69.5	54.3	78
Belgium	39	58.9	74.9	54.3	129
Canada	44.3 (38.3)	49.1	71.6	64.5	31
Denmark	38	68	80.2	65.9	117
Finland	40.2	56.2	73.8	56.2	100
France	34/42	57.9	75.6	63.4	69
Germany	58.1/44.5	55	75.0	61.7	67
Greece	46 (40)	50	79.0	50	100
Iceland	45	39.8	66.9	Varies	Varies
Ireland	40 (10)	52	71.2	61.6	50
Italy	47.8	50	73.9	58.1	66
Japan	51	65	85.0	68.2	82
Luxembourg	39.4	51.3	70.5	70.5	0
Netherlands	35	60	74	74	0
New Zealand	33	33	55.1	33	100
Norway	28	41	57.5	28	179
Portugal	39.6	40	63.8	54.7	38
Spain	35.3	56	71.5	65.1	42

Sweden	30	51	65.7	Varies	Varies
Switzerland	30.3	43.8	60.8	60.8	0
Turkey	49.2	47.5	73.3	49.2	93
United Kingdom	33	40	59.8	46.4	68
United States	38.3	36	60.5	60.5	0
Average	39.5	50.0	69.9	56.7	68.6
Standard deviation	6.1	8.9	7.5	11.2	46.4
Coefficient of variation	0.15	0.18	0.11	0.20	0.68

[a] Rates in parentheses apply to special rates on manufacturing profits. Rates following slash apply to distributed profits.
[b] Calculated using rates for distributed profits, nonmanufacturing companies.
Source: Cnossen (1993).

goods and intangible assets ("transfer pricing") or borrowing through subsidiaries in high-tax countries. Note that this incentive applies regardless of whether the home country operates a territorial or worldwide system of taxation.

Much of the complexity of the taxation of foreign-source income arises from the attempt of countries to defend their revenue base against the fungibility of income tax bases. Complex rules cover standards for acceptable transfer pricing, allocation rules for interest expense and intangibles, and taxing certain types of income on an accrual basis. It is impossible to concisely summarize the variety of rules that countries employ to determine the location of income. In some countries the statutes are not as important as the outcomes of case-by-case negotiations between representatives of the multinational enterprises and the countries involved. In other cases the source rules are governed by bilateral tax treaties. What is clear, however, is that the de facto rules that govern the sourcing of income are at least as important for understanding the effective taxation of foreign direct investment as the tax rates, depreciation rules, and tax credits.

The complexity of the rules makes quantitative assessment of the current system a very difficult task. The most heroic attempt to do so, in OECD (1991), is summarized in Table 3. The first column presents, for the sake of comparison, the marginal effective tax rates on a domestic investment presented in Table 1. The second column presents the OECD's calculation of the actual average total tax burden—imposed by the host and home country—of an investment located in the country in question. Note that in all cases this tax rate is higher than the tax rate in the first column. The increase is due primarily to two factors: the additional tax levied by the home country and the "withholding" taxes levied by host countries on dividends repatriated from the foreign affiliate to the parent company in the home country.

The third column of Table 3 presents the calculated average total tax rate on investments from the country in question, where the investment is assumed to be located in a representative mix of foreign countries.

One important caveat must be attached to the calculations of Table 3, in particular to the impression it leaves that multinationals' foreign direct investment is taxed at a higher rate than purely domestic investment. This conclusion is not necessarily warranted, because the calculations of Table 3 do not take any account of the income-shifting possibilities that are available to multinationals. A recent empirical study by Harris et al. (1993)

Table 3
Marginal Effective Tax Rate on Domestic Investment and Transnational Investment

Country	Domestic Investment	Source (investment to named country from all other countries)	Residence (investment from named country into all other countries)
Australia	30	40	33
Austria	9	42	31
Belgium	7	26	25
Canada	19	35	31
Denmark	15	29	19
Finland	11	30	17
France	7	37	18
Germany	11	19	38
Greece	0	19	36
Iceland	25	38	32
Ireland	2	26	32
Italy	15	32	37
Japan	22	35	37
Luxembourg	21	30	26
Netherlands	11	28	24
New Zealand	26	44	33
Norway	26	18	30
Portugal	12	32	39
Spain	19	36	28
Sweden	0	17	24
Switzerland	7	29	25
Turkey	31	36	39
United Kingdom	15	31	23
United States	14	31	32
Average	14.8	30.8	29.5
Standard deviation	9.0	7.4	6.6
Coefficient of variation	0.61	0.24	0.22

Source: OECD (1991), Table 5.16.

concluded that U.S. multinationals reduce their tax burden between 3 and 22 percent by shifting reported taxable income out of high-tax countries and into low-tax countries. The tax-shifting opportunities that arise from operating in multiple jurisdictions are not captured by Table 3.

6.2.4   Tax Cacophony within a Country

One final caveat is in order before leaving the attempted quantification of tax cacophony and addressing the policy and welfare implications of this disharmony. The caveat is that there is tax disharmony even within any given country. In general, the effective tax rate that applies to, for example, the agriculture sector, will differ from that which applies to the manufacturing sector.

There are several reasons for the within-country tax disharmony. Some countries have explicit preferential tax rates for certain sectors, such as the 10 percent tax rate on manufacturing profits in Ireland, or for certain areas of the country, such as the enterprise zone proposals in the United States or the state tax abatements offered to attract new investments. In some countries, investment tax credits are offered, often only for machinery investment, and these are more beneficial to capital-intensive, or machinery-intensive, sectors. More generally, tax laws that are designed to apply uniformly to all activities imply different effective tax rates depending on such exogenous factors as the rate of inflation, riskiness of the sector's activity, degree of competitiveness, extent of incorporation, and other factors.

For these reasons it is not possible to assume, for example, that if a country has a lower-than-average overall corporate tax rate, then the low rate would apply uniformly to all its sectors. Nor it is possible to assume away the possibility that a country with a higher-than-average overall corporate tax rate might have a sector that receives preferential tax treatment.

There is no reliable up-to-date source for sector-by-sector cross-country tax comparisons. As an illustration of the potential magnitude of this problem, Table 4 presents evidence about U.S. sector-specific effective tax rates, both before and after the Tax Reform Act of 1986. Note that the large divergence among effective rates before 1986 occurred despite the lack of any sector-specific sections of the tax code. Note also that the base-broadening aspects of the Tax Reform Act produced a noticeable reduction in the intersector differences in effective tax rates.

Table 4
Marginal Effective Total Tax Rates by Industry, before and after the Tax Reform Act of 1986

Industry	Prior Law	Tax Reform Act of 1986
Agriculture, forestry, and fisheries	.361	.354
Mining	.310	.442
Crude petroleum and gas	.358	.399
Construction	.378	.427
Food and tobacco	.469	.469
Textiles, apparel, and leather	.400	.457
Paper and printing	.355	.454
Petroleum and refining	.429	.484
Chemicals and rubber	.346	.453
Lumber, furniture, stone, clay, and glass	.379	.458
Metals and machinery	.409	.467
Transportation equipment	.443	.473
Motor vehicles	.365	.466
Transportation, communication, and utilities	.270	.443
Trade	.422	.433
Finance and insurance	.364	.386
Real estate	.303	.314
Services	.254	.403
Average	.367	.432
Standard deviation	.058	.045
Coefficient of variation	.157	.104

Source: Fullerton, Henderson, and Mackie (1987), Table 6.6 ("New View" columns).

6.2.5   Tax Cacophony Reviewed

Although the measurements are imprecise, the preceding sections establish indisputably that corporate tax cacophony is a fact. The divergences across countries are large no matter which alternative measure is chosen. Nor is it possible to argue that the differences in corporate tax levies merely mirror differences in the services that host governments provide without charge to businesses, so that the net tax liability is much more equal than the comparison of tax rates could suggest; there is simply no evidence to support that position.

The balance of this paper addresses the implications of this tax cacophony—what its economic costs are and how these costs interact with a movement toward freer trade.

6.3   The Consequences of Tax Cacophony for Evaluating the Benefits of Freer Trade

In this section I explore the efficiency consequences of the tax cacophony detailed earlier, in particular their relationship to the benefits of freer trade. I begin by ignoring the cacophony within a country, which produces effects similar to differential production taxes, and consider the impact of different overall levels of capital income taxes across countries, first ignoring and then considering multinational enterprises. Finally I investigate the consequences of differential capital income taxes within countries.

6.3.1   Nondiscriminatory Source-Based Taxes in a World without Foreign Direct Investment

Begin with a world in which all countries levied only source-based nondiscriminatory taxes on business; that is, all income earned within country A was taxed only by country A, and the rate of tax was independent of the nationality of the corporation or the nationality of the shareholders of the corporation. The source-based effective tax rates may differ from country to country.

The equilibrium in this world would be characterized by an allocation of capital such that the pretax rate of return in each country would adjust so that the after-tax rate of return was equalized worldwide. For example, if the risk-adjusted world after-tax rate of return was 4 percent, in equilibrium a country that levied a 50 percent tax would have a capital stock such that its pretax return was 8 percent, while a country that levied a 33.3 percent tax would have a capital stock such that its pretax rate of return was 6%; an investment by an investor would yield 4 percent after tax in either case.

What are the welfare implications of this regime? From a worldwide perspective, there is an inefficient allocation of capital—too much capital goes to the low-tax-rate countries, where the pretax rate of return is lower than in the high-tax countries.[2] A given stock of capital, if shifted from a low-tax to a high-tax country, would produce a higher level of output.

What are the welfare consequences of eliminating barriers to trade in this setting? From a world welfare point of view, this problem is an example of the economics of the second best. There is a preexisting distortion in capital allocation caused by the worldwide variation in source-based capital taxes. The world efficiency gain from eliminating the barriers to trade, which would be positive if this were the only source of distortion, must now be modified with an additional term. The sign of that term depends on the direction of cross-border capital movement induced by the shift to free trade. Loosely speaking, if capital moves from countries with low tax rates (with an inefficiently high capital stock) to countries with high tax rates (with an inefficiently low capital stock), then this movement is an additional source of welfare gain. If, however, the movement of capital is in the other direction, there is an efficiency loss that must be subtracted from the gain otherwise achieved.

Which of these two scenarios will occur depends on whether countries with relatively high capital income taxes are more or less likely to have been induced by trade barriers to adopt relatively capital-intensive domestic production. If they are more likely, then the second-best consideration reduces the gains from free trade, as countries with an inefficiently low capital intensity become even less capital intensive as a result of free trade.

I know of no attempt to assess the empirical magnitude, or even the sign, of this effect. It must for now be left as a theoretical consideration.

6.3.2   Additional Considerations Attributable to the Presence of Multinational Enterprises

"Tariff-jumping" foreign direct investment is one response to tariffs. As alluded to previously, multinational enterprises pose particularly difficult tax problems because it is difficult to establish, conceptually or practically, the location of the profits of a global enterprise. This difficulty leads to the socially costly game of corporate tax planning to shift profits from high-tax to low-tax countries, to complicated rules and enforcement regimes in the high-tax countries to prevent such shifting, and to active courting of multinational enterprises by "tax haven" countries.

There are a few ways in which a movement toward free trade interacts with the tax treatment of multinationals. The principal way in which income shifting is effected is through intracorporate transfer pricing, by which sales of products to (from) affiliates in low-tax countries are given low (high) prices, thus inflating profits there and lowering profits elsewhere. However, the setting of transfer prices must also take into account the incremental tariff liability caused by adjusting prices. Lowering tariffs, therefore, means that corporate transfer pricing policy can become more focused on worldwide tax minimization, rather than tax-plus-tariff minimization.

To the extent that a reduction of tariffs reduces the incentive for tariff-jumping foreign direct investment, then the movement toward free trade

may directly reduce the tax problems associated with multinational enterprises. Whether free trade will in fact serve to reduce FDI is an empirical
question. Even though free trade makes tariff-jumping FDI less necessary,
any increase in trade generated may itself induce certain kinds of FDI—for
example, as home financial institutions expand to be close to their customers. This question brings up the ever-controversial, and still unresolved, issue of whether trade crowds out or stimulates FDI. It may also be
true that bilateral or multilateral agreements to reduce barriers to trade at
the same time reduce barriers to FDI.

6.3.3   The Differential-Production-Tax Effect of Business Taxation

The fact that the effective tax rate on business income varies sector by
sector means that, in effect, there are differential production taxes. These
raise a number of interesting issues. Recall that imposing a tariff on a
particular good is equivalent to imposing a consumption tax on that good
combined with a subsidy to domestic production, all at the same rate; in
both cases the price to domestic consumers and domestic producers rises,
but the price received by importers does not rise. Another way to state the
same equivalence is that levying a tariff and a production tax on a particular good is equivalent to a tax of the same magnitude on consumption of
the good.

   These equivalences imply that, in principle, a country can offset any
change in tariffs by the appropriate adjustment in domestic taxes. For
example, if a bilateral or multilateral free trade agreement requires that a
particular tariff be eliminated, a country could simply reduce the effective
production tax implicit in its business-tax system and increase the consumption tax rate by the amount of the original tariff. This response is
what Johnson (1968) had in mind when he referred to "evasion of the free
trade commitment by the substitution of fiscal for commercial policy discrimination." This would leave all incentives unchanged, thwarting the
presumed allocational goals of the tariff reduction. This story is reminis-
cent of the one sometimes told about nontariff barriers to trade—that a
reduction in tariffs can be offset by nontariff barriers, leaving the allocational effect unchanged but saddling the protecting countries with a more
opaque and unwieldly instrument for achieving the protection.

   It is true that Article 3 of the GATT is designed to prevent the possibility that countries that comply by reducing tariffs can achieve the same
protective effect through taxation or other fiscal instruments. In addition,
Article 231-B of the GATT allows contracting parties to withdraw conces-

sions if a binding on a tariff is offset by the use of some other instrument in a direct or deliberate way. Whalley (1990) concludes that, through these two provisions in GATT, the contracting parties have, in principle, already bound themselves to prevent changes in domestic policies that undo the effects of changes in tariffs.

This conclusion may be true in principle, but in practice it may be difficult to establish that an aspect of domestic tax policy is a direct and deliberate attempt to achieve protection, especially if the production tax adjustments are implicit in business taxation. Large cross-sector differences in the effective tax rate can be due not to differences in the statutory tax rates, but instead to more technical aspects of the tax system such as the depreciation schedules, inventory accounting rules, research and development credits, and the rate and applicability of investment tax credits. As a result, it is possible to favor or penalize a particular sector without any explicit differentiation in the tax system, such as a preferential lower tax rate for manufactured goods. This would undoubtedly complicate the application of the two GATT articles that limit this kind of offsetting fiscal policy.

This argument has two edges, though. Setting sector-specific effective production-tax rates by altering technical aspects of the tax system is an imperfect process; for this reason any particular change in the tariff structure can only be approximately offset. In fact it is the superior sectoral targeting capability of tariffs compared to taxes that Levinsohn and Slemrod (1993) rely on in their model of tariffs and taxes in the presence of multinational corporations. In that model, multinational corporations have market power and are owned entirely by nationals, so it may be in the national interest to utilize tax and/or tariff policy to shift profits from competing foreign multinationals to domestic corporations. Profit shifting can occur if the fiscal policy effectively allows the domestic corporations to commit to output plans that would, in the absence of the tax or tariff policy, not be credible. Tax policy (in this case, a tax that is uniform across countries and thus is not a source-based production tax) is superior to tariff policy because it does not cause inefficient location decisions. However, if only certain sectors are candidates for strategic, profit-shifting policy, then tariff policy can be part of the optimal policy because of its sector-specific nature.

Even if GATT prevents countries from offsetting tariff reductions with domestic tax policy, the latter must be considered in any evaluation of the welfare cost of trade barriers. As Gordon and Levinsohn (1990) stress, the prereform fiscal setup of a country may include both tariffs and domestic tax policy that to some extent offsets the allocational effects that the tariffs by themselves would create. Although the standard normative tax theory suggests that tariffs should not be part of an optimal tax structure, the lower administrative and compliance costs of tariffs, compared to income taxes, make them attractive to many countries, especially to less-developed countries whose human and bureaucratic capital inadequacies make tariffs especially attractive. Riezman and Slemrod (1987) document the empirical relationship between a country's reliance on tariffs and its demographic makeup.

To the extent that the domestic tax structure offsets the border ineffi-ciencies of the tariffs, eliminating or reducing the tariffs may make the inefficiencies worse rather than better. The preliminary empirical work reported in Gordon and Levinsohn (1990) suggests that, in LDCs, tariffs are in fact to a large extent simply offsetting the distortions of domestic production taxes and vice versa. Among richer countries, which have virtually no border distortions, their significant production taxes distort trade patterns. Given that the richer countries tend to export industrial goods that are subject to the production tax, this production tax discour-ages international trade, in the same way that a tariff on these goods would.

The underlying message of this section is that neither the level of trade distortions nor the way in which they will be affected by a dimunition of tariffs can be evaluated by looking only at the pattern of tariffs. The tax structure, including the effective production-tax pattern of business taxa-tion, must be considered. Two important elements of this consideration are to what extent production and consumption taxes can respond to changes in tariffs on a sector-specific basis and to what extent such changes are consistent with the GATT.

6.4   The Prospects for Tax Coordination and Harmonization

Up to this point I have discussed the implications of business tax dishar-mony, or cacophony, for the evaluation of freer trade. In this concluding section I discuss the prospects for multilateral coordination or harmoniza-tion of business tax systems. If one concludes that tax cacophony is a significant problem, either because it reduces the benefits of an integrated world economy or for other reasons, it is important to understand the chances of alleviating the problem through explicit or implicit coordination.

To be blunt, the prospects are not good. There is no tax analogy to the GATT although, as discussed earlier, the GATT does deal with tax policies that are designed deliberately to achieve protectionist objectives. There has been some discussion among academics about the benefits of a multilateral tax agreement (see, e.g., Tanzi, 1995) and on what such an agreement might consist of (Slemrod, 1990). But, as of yet, the academic debate has not generated any movement on the policy front.

There are two important obstacles to multilateral tax coordination. The first is that countries are unwilling to cede sovereignty over such an important element of domestic policy. For most countries tariff collections represent a small fraction of total revenue, so that downward adjustments required by multilateral agreements do not cause a major fiscal disruption (although note the controversy in the United States over making up the revenues lost as a result of the Uruguay Round of GATT). Minimal disruption cannot, though, be assured when the subject of multilateral coordination is income or consumption taxes.

The other obstacle to multilateral tax coordination is the absence of an obvious focal point. There is such a target for trade policy—zero tariffs and nontariff barriers to trade. One can dispute the optimal path to that end, but the target is, conceptually speaking, not controversial. The same cannot be said for tax policy. As discussed earlier, there is a vast cacophony of tax rates and tax systems, and no consensus on which is the best. Each country would undoubtedly prefer it if the world converged toward its own tax system, thus minimizing its own domestic disruption.

The recent attempts at business tax harmonization within the EC illustrate the difficulties, and lack of success, usually encountered. Recall the earlier discussion of the Ruding Committee, which considered what business tax harmonization, if any, would be required to maximize the benefits of trade liberalization. The committee opined that harmonization of corporate tax systems would be desirable in the long run, and recommended that all countries' corporation-income-tax statutory rates lie within a band bounded by 30 and 40 percent, thereby minimizing the private gains from shifting income from high-tax to low-tax countries. Even this suggestion was not adopted by the EC, nor was it seriously considered. Those countries whose rates currently lie below 30 percent (and which therefore are "importers" of shifted taxable income) objected, and these objections, among others, carried the day.

What coordination there is among countries on tax matters mostly occurs within the context of bilateral tax treaties, the network of which includes most developing countries. The signatories of these treaties agree not to discriminate in tax matters against foreign companies operating within their borders, agree to some dispute-resolution procedures and exchange of information, and try to establish reciprocal tax rates on cross-border payments of interest, dividends, and royalties that are less than those that apply to nonsignatories. The treaties do not, though, deal with coordination of important features of domestic tax policy that have been discussed in this paper.

It is possible that, even in the absence of an explicit multilateral agreement to harmonize taxes, tax competition among countries will accomplish the same thing. Simple theoretical models of tax competition predict that a particular kind of harmonization will prevail, one in which no country (except those with market power) will levy any source-based taxes (e.g., production taxes or corporation income taxes) on capital. This approach leads to a harmonization with no capital income tax at all. Such a system is harmonious, but certainly not necessarily optimal from a world point of view. It is also possible that a cooperative outcome could be achieved without an explicit agreement.

There is no convincing evidence that world tax systems are moving toward harmonization at a zero capital income tax rate or any other uniform rate. It is true that U.S. corporation income tax collections, as a fraction of total revenue, have been falling steadily for the last 15 years, but the same trend is not evident in other OECD countries. Nor is there evidence that the cacophony in tax systems is declining on its own through tax competition or implicit cooperation. Marginal effective tax rates on capital have converged in the EC since 1980, but much of this convergence can be traced to convergence of inflation rates and interest rates, rather than tax reform.

6.5 Conclusions

Countries have a cacophony of corporate tax rates and systems, leading to widely diverging effective tax rates. Countries also differ in how much they alleviate the double taxation of dividends by integrating their corporate and personal tax systems, although the resulting total (corporate plus personal) effective tax rates on equity-financed business capital still diverge widely across countries. Whether the differences are due to explicit sector-specific rules or not, each country also imposes differential effective tax rates on sectors within the country.

The cacophony of business taxation causes allocational distortions. It also implies that a reduction in tariffs must be treated as a problem of the second best, and consideration must be given to whether the existing pattern of tariffs offsets or exacerbates the distortions that are created by the tax system. There is, though, little empirical evidence on this matter. Whatever the conclusions about the welfare consequences of the interaction of business taxes and tariffs, the prospects for conscious multilateral harmonization or coordination of taxes are very slim. Recent efforts in this regard have not been successful. Nor is there convincing evidence that tax competition is, in the absence of explicit agreement, inducing countries to harmonize capital income taxes toward a zero level, as some simple theoretical models suggest should happen.

NOTES

This chapter was prepared for the Fairness Claims and Gains for Trade Conference, held in Washington, DC, on September 30 and October 1, 1994.

1. This overview is adapted from Slemrod (1989).

2. Note that the welfare consequences from the perspective of any one country are quite different. In simple theoretical models, a small open economy should not levy any source-based distortionary tax on capital income. Because of the mobility of capital, the burden of the tax will be borne by immobile factors such as labor and land. However, compared to a direct tax on these immobile factors, a tax on capital drives capital away so that its stock is inefficiently low; that is, its return exceeds the opportunity cost of capital to the country. This stark conclusion can be altered if the economy is large enough to alter the terms on which it can attract capital (i.e., an optimum tariff argument).

REFERENCES

Ault, Hugh, and David Bradford. 1990. "Taxing international income: An analysis of the U.S. system and its economic premises." In A. Razin and J. Slemrod, eds., *Taxation in the global economy*. Chicago: University of Chicago Press and NBER.

Cnossen, Sijbren. 1989. "On the direction of tax harmonization in the European Community" (mimeo). Erasmus University.

Cnossen, Sijbren. 1993. "What kind of corporation tax?" *Bulletin for International Fiscal Documentation*, January 1993, pp. 3–16.

Commission of the European Communities. 1976. "Proposal for a directive of the council concerning the harmonization of company taxation and of withholding taxes on dividends." *European Taxation*, Nos. 2–4.

Commission of the European Communities. 1980. "Report on the convergence of tax systems in the Community." *Bulletin of the European Communities*, Supplement 1.

Fullerton, Don, Yolanda K. Henderson, and James Mackie. 1987. "Investment allocation and growth under the Tax Reform Act of 1986." In *Compendium of tax research, 1987.* Washington, DC: Office of Tax Analysis, Department of the Treasury.

Gordon, Roger, and James Levinsohn. 1990. "The linkage between domestic taxes and border taxes." In A. Razin and J. Slemrod, eds., *Taxation in the global economy.* Chicago: University of Chicago Press and NBER.

Harris, David, Randall Morck, Joel Slemrod, and Bernard Yeung. 1993. "Income shifting in U.S. multinational corporations." In A. Giovannini, R. G. Hubbard, and J. Slemrod, eds., *Studies in international taxation.* Chicago: University of Chicago Press and NBER.

Johnson, Harry G. 1968. "The implications of free or freer trade for the harmonization of other policies." In *Harmonization of national economic policies under free trade,* 1–41. University of Toronto Press for the Private Planning Association of Canada.

Levinsohn, James, and Joel Slemrod. 1993. "Taxes, tariffs, and the global corporation." *Journal of Public Economics,* March.

Musgrave, Peggy. 1963. "The harmonization of profits taxes." In *Proceedings of the 19th conference of the International Institute of Public Finance.* Detroit: Wayne University Press.

Musgrave, Peggy. 1987. "Interjurisdictional coordination of taxes on capital income." In S. Cnossen, ed., *Tax coordination in the European Community.* Deventer, Netherlands: Kluwer.

Neumark Report. 1963. *Tax harmonization in the Common Market.* New York: Commerce Clearing House.

Ohlin, Bertil. 1965. "Some aspects of policies for freer trade." In J. Baldwin et al., eds., *Trade, growth, and the balance of payments: Essays in honor of Gottfried Haberler.* Chicago: Rand-McNally; Amsterdam: North Holland.

Organization for Economic Cooperation and Development (OECD). 1991. *Taxing profits in a global economy: Domestic and international issues.* Paris: OECD.

Reddaway, W. Brian. 1958. "The implications of a Free Trade Area for British taxation." *British Tax Review,* March, pp. 71–79.

Riezman, Raymond, and Joel Slemrod. 1987. "Tariffs and collection costs." *Review of World Economics,* pp. 545–549.

Ruding Committee. 1992. *Report of the Committee of Independent Experts on Company Taxation.* Brussels: Commission of the European Communities, 1992.

Shoup, Carl S. 1963. "The theory of harmonization of fiscal systems." In *Proceedings of the 19th conference of the International Institute of Public Finance.* Detroit: Wayne State University Press.

Slemrod, Joel. 1989. "The impact of the Tax Reform Act of 1986 on foreign direct investment to and from the United States." In J. Slemrod, ed., *Do taxes matter? The impact of the Tax Reform Act of 1986.* Cambridge, MA: MIT Press.

Slemrod, Joel. 1990. "Tax principles in an international economy." In M. Boskin and C. E. McLure, Jr., eds., *World tax reform.* San Francisco: ICS Press.

Tanzi, Vito. 1995. *Taxation in an integrating world.* Washington, DC: Brookings Institution.

Tanzi, Vito, and Lans Bovenberg. 1990. "Is there a need for harmonizing capital income taxes within EC countries?" In H. Siebert, ed., *Reforming capital income taxation*. Tübingen Germany: J.C.B. Mohr (Paul Siebeck).

Tinbergen Report. 1953. *Report on the problems raised by the different turnover tax systems applied within the Common Market*. European Coal and Steel Community.

Van den Tempel, A. J. 1970. *Corporation tax and individual income tax in the European Communities*. Brussels: Commission of the European Communities.

Whalley, John. 1990. "Comment on 'The linkage between domestic taxes and border taxes', by R. Gordon and J. Levinsohn." In A. Razin and J. Slemrod, eds., *Taxation in the global economy*. Chicago: University of Chicago Press and NBER.

V

Competition Policy

7   Trade and Competition Control

Christopher Bliss

Much attention has been devoted to commercial policy, including tariff protection, quotas, and other nontariff barriers. Yet only recently have economists begun to take into account the fact that almost any national law affecting production or consumption will have consequences for international trade and competitiveness. These implications are at their minimal level, although they still exist, in the case of the standard textbook model, with perfect competition, constant returns to scale, and often small countries. They loom larger when those assumptions are relaxed.

The chapter begins with a brief discussion of what trade laws are intended to achieve, arguing that this is not as obvious as it may at first seem to be, and establishing a taxonomy that proves useful later. After an examination of the so-called *level-playing-field* argument, the chapter turns to its chief task, which is to investigate what should be the international trade laws, if any, governing antitrust rules, merger regulation, or government promotion of mergers and monopolies, all covered by the umbrella term *competition control*.

It is argued that competition policy, conceived as antitrust and merger regulation, should be left outside trade law. True, there do exist cases in which world efficiency would be promoted by ideal fully informed antitrust legislation. However, in practice such a legislation would face insuperable problems in deciding any case. Weak antitrust control mainly harms the nation that allows it and usually antipromotes its exports.

7.1   What Are International Trade Laws Meant to Achieve?

The answer to the question of what international trade laws are meant to achieve is less obvious than it may at first seem. The issue is a general one, which is encountered whenever any trade law is considered and with all cases of harmonization, whatever may or may not be harmonized. To prove the point, consider three possible answers—there may be more:

1. Trade laws may be designed to provide injured parties (trading nations) with redress against *trade torts*, including injunctions that require parties to desist from committing torts and financial compensation for the commission of torts.

2. Trade laws may be designed to bring into effect some ideal world allocation of resources with a consequent international division of labor and specialization.

3. By subjecting particular trade issues to general, internationally agreed principles, trade laws may have the purpose of protecting nations, or rather their political processes, from themselves. Otherwise, each trade intervention would be subject to the full force of particular national political pressures.

Of course, all these points may be involved simultaneously, but they are not identical in their implications. Consider, for instance, Bhagwati and Srinivasan's argument (Chapter 4 of this volume) concerning environmental harmonization, according to which national differences in tastes and situations concerning the environment, with no cross-national external implications, should be allowed to result in divergences in practice. These authors examine the issues from the point of view of the second item on the list, arguing that divergence promotes world efficiency.[1] They could equally have argued that no material trade torts are implied by the same divergences. For the third item on the list, however, the conclusion would be different. If legislated harmonization dulls domestic political pressure, it may be desirable, even if it runs against world efficiency. Similarly, a small country may adopt a policy that moves the world (slightly) away from efficiency, but in such a way as only to harm itself. Then there is certainly no trade tort.

7.2   The Harmonization Issue

People claim to favor free trade in principle but to oppose it in the case of the import of manufactures from the sweated-labor factories of Asia or "dirty" East European steel. Businessmen claim that the relaxation of competition rules is needed to allow them to compete effectively with outside producers. Such examples raise important practical and theoretical questions and are encountered in many fields. For example, how should the

European Community regulate competition in its single market? And how should an ideal reformed GATT address competition rules and antitrust regulations?

The GATT makes some reference to the issue of monopolies and cartels but none to national competition regulations and their diversity. In general, the GATT is not concerned with establishing a level playing field, except in the specific aspect of most-favored-nation symmetry. The GATT was built on the basis of simplicity, especially the most-favored-nation principle, which in turn assumed trade in standardized and uncontroversial goods. It was probably felt that complexity would provide many covers for old-fashioned protectionism. The same can be said of objections to trade based on such arguments as a dislike of sweated labor or to poor safety standards in third-world or other factories. Intuition suggests that many such arguments are self-serving and insubstantial, but surely not all of them. But exactly how they can be subjected to economic analysis is far from clear.[2]

The GATT suggests no principles for the regulation of cartels comparable in reach to the most-favored-nation principle. Also, being a treaty rather than an analytical text, the GATT, naturally, does not distinguish between different types of monopoly or cartel, or discuss the sources of such market power in terms of natural monopolies, barriers to entry, or restriction on the movement of goods through wholesale and retail networks. This gap, which was of limited significance when the agreement was drafted, is today of singular importance. References to monopoly power are frequently invoked in arguments against free trade. European policy makes competition control a condition for the efficient function of the single market, with the implication that both national and international competition control are required, and the United States frequently charges Japan's marketing networks with being closed to outsiders. Even for the pursuit of efficiency, aside from "fairness" issues, what is the importance of these factors?

The focus of interest has shifted in the direction of *harmonization*, meaning that trading nations should have similar or congruent institutions in order to make trade efficient or acceptable. Similar ideas are embodied in the idea of the *level playing field*. Does any of this apply to competition policy? Should countries have harmonized competition policies to effect efficient trade or to avoid trade torts? Of course, if an overbearing international competition policy is applied to all countries, then some harmonization is automatically entailed.

This chapter argues that competition policy, conceived as antitrust and merger regulation, should be left outside trade law. The case is in part practical. It will be shown that there certainly exist in principle cases in which world efficiency, particularly, could be improved by an ideal fully informed antitrust regulator able to legislate the number of producers in each country. However, in practice such a regulator would face insuperable problems in deciding any case. Moreover, weak antitrust control mainly harms the nation that allows it and usually antipromotes its exports. Therefore, the institutions required might be confined to individual trading nations with results about as good as will ever be achieved. This is a controversial line to take, but as the reasoning behind it will be laid out carefully, readers will eventually be in a position to judge it for themselves.

7.3   Worldwide Monopoly and International Trade

Worldwide monopoly of a product without close substitutes is rare in the modern world, although not unknown. The Boeing company's monopoly of jumbo passenger jet production is a case in point, and is based on huge economies of scale in the production of these aircraft.[3] In the past, monopoly not based on such overwhelming scale economies has proved to be transitory and insecure. This statement is true even when monopoly is defended aggressively and ruthlessly, as was the case when John D. Rockefeller attempted defense of his monopoly of mass kerosene sales in the 19th century. Interestingly, Rockefeller's monopoly fell to international competition in world markets and to trust-busting legislation in the U.S. market.

Future historians may well put OPEC in the company of Standard Oil as a monopoly that had little long-term influence on the oil price, as opposed to affecting the timing of price changes around an unaffected trend. The only way for OPEC to have had a larger and more enduring effect would have been for Saudi Arabia to have adopted the role that it seems to have considered at times, under which it would pursue a punishment strategy, flooding the market to punish any member who overproduced. If anything, Saudi Arabia played the opposite role, backing off when others overproduced.

The most successful international cartel of modern times has been the de Beers diamond cartel. Had diamonds been more important for the world economy than they are, its effect would have been of huge importance. Here is the classic case of a cartel based on the leader-follower principle, with de Beers the leader and other producers being willing followers. This system worked particularly because the Soviet Union was glad to cooperate and because other producers were intimidated by fear of retaliation by de Beers from cheating on the implicit agreement. Again, future historians may classify this cartel as one of the many institutions that depended on the Cold War and failed to outlive its end, for without the acquiescence of Russia the cartel can hardly survive.

7.4   The Cartelization of National Markets

If a number of oligopolistic producers can in principle sell in a market, it is always an attractive idea for a subset (which could be one member) to seize control of the market and to bar access to others. To achieve this result, the cartel needs a viable strategy to keep competitors out of the market. A *direct entry barrier* might take the form of a punishment strategy under which the cartel would spoil the market for any entrant by flooding it with sales. Such strategies may or may not be credible. For details, see Tirole (1988).

This theory has implications for international trade if national cartels bar foreign sellers from access to their domestic market. They may find it easier to ban foreign sellers than it would be to bar certain national producers. If such bans are imposed and the national government does not take steps against the national cartel, then it is conniving at protection, and it is absolutely appropriate that international trade law should take an interest. In arguing that international trade law should not concern itself with national competition laws, I am not advocating the removal of legislation that prohibits the direct exclusion of foreign producers from the domestic market.

It does not make a great difference if the entry barrier is indirect. For instance, it is sometimes asserted that Japanese retail networks effectively bar access to foreign products by refusing to handle them, or by somehow being so unfriendly to them that the seller is driven away. Such claims demand further analysis. Control of the retailing network is of no use to a cartel if the competition can enter the retailing sector, but perhaps such entry is impossible. Protecting the cartel's position by sacrificing profits in retail firms that the cartel controls may not be sensible. This argument tends to resolve itself into quite a specialized discussion concerning the nature of Japanese retailing, Japanese consumers' preference for home products, and so on. Without entering this discussion, for which I am unqualified, the general principle already mentioned stands. If a cartel is a direct barrier to trade and directly discriminatory against foreign firms, then trade law should require it to be dismantled. To claim otherwise would be to permit protection via cartels while prohibiting it via tariffs or quotas, and there is no logic in that position.

7.5 National Competition Regulation and the Motives of Governments

The national competition regulation considered here is concerned with the regulation of the extent of competition in the domestic market, especially as that is affected by the number of domestic producers. If worldwide monopoly turns out to be of limited importance in practice, why can we not conclude that lax competition regulation in individual national markets will also be of limited importance? The question has special point if tariff and nontariff barriers are kept low, so that national monopolists or oligopolists have to compete with outside producers on fair terms.

The opening classification of what international trade laws are meant to achieve is helpful here. There seem to be no trade torts involved, but see the following discussion. There may well be interference with the efficiency of world resource allocation. Yet then free trade would be the answer because it would tend to limit the power of local monopolies. International competition rules could in principle protect governments from the temptation to give in to pressures from national monopolists. This kind of effect has been important in the European Union (EU), although the power of Brussels in that regard has proved to be extremely limited in practice, as the recent history of the so-called restructuring of Air France demonstrates.

The point that international rules may protect governments from pressure groups tells only part of the story. In fact, the commitment of individual governments to free trade is always partial, for rational or partly rational reasons, briefly presented here:

1. Efficiency cannot be the only consideration for a government that lacks the practical means to compensate losers from free trade in a nondistorting manner. The theoretical trade literature, with its emphasis on small countries and lump-sum transfers, tends to obscure this point.

2. In principle, departing from free trade may shift the distribution of income between factors, say, in favor of labor, in a direction favored by the government. This is the famous *Stolper-Samuelson effect*. Usually trade theorists have argued that redistributive taxation would achieve the same

outcome at lower cost. However with real feasible tax instruments the arguments become quite arcane,[4] and governments may be ignorant of such subtleties.

3. With large countries and large producers within those countries, the pattern of national production may generate favorable international rent shifting, even if it goes against strict international efficiency.[5]

Another consideration is that the world is always changing, so that a country is typically adjusting to changes which reach it, and slow adjustment may be, or seem to be, more attractive than rapid adjustment. However this is not really an independent point, but is a special case of items 1 and 2. Another reason why governments may wish to depart from free trade has traditionally been classified as irrational on the grounds that other devices apart from protection would achieve the desired outcome better. This is the case of the so-called *noneconomic objective*. An example would be the desire on the part of a government to have a certain industry operate within its borders, or to have it operate on a larger scale, not from any motive that could be classified as economic, but, say, for reasons of national prestige.[6]

With these points in mind, we can understand the role for international rules and negotiated agreements, institutions that seem hard to understand if one concentrates on small countries with perfect redistribution, when unilateral free trade is typically in the interest of the individual country acting alone. This line of argument has been developed by Krugman (1992).

7.6   The Effects of Oligopoly and Competition Policy

With the general principles in mind, we can now turn our attention to the specific case of competition control. It is not easy to model competition control. Regulations may control mergers and takeovers in such a way that more independent firms operate in the national market than would be the case without intervention. However, the total profitability of the larger number of firms may be lower than the total profitability of a smaller number. It may even be negative. In that case the government by its policy is trying to create a state of affairs that is not a sustainable equilibrium. Some of the larger number of firms would like to exit the industry. In order to prevent them from doing so, the government will need to subsidize firms to keep them operating in the sector. Governments have sometimes adopted the opposite policy, encouraging firms to merge and even subsidizing mergers (e.g., by making contracts or aid conditional on the merger). If we assume that the government intervention is doing more than just helping along a process that would tend to happen in any case, then probably the total profitability of the merged firms will be smaller than when they operate separately.[7] In general, there is no reason to suppose that the number of firms that operate in equilibrium is either the profit-maximizing number or the socially optimal number for the nation.

7.7   The Use of Competition Policy for Protection or Export Pro:notion

Traditional discussion of commercial policy sees governments using such devices as tariffs, quotas, and voluntary export restraints to achieve trade objectives. Can competition policy be applied to similar ends? The answer is that it certainly can but that the type of intervention involved is not always that which is popularly advocated. For instance, producers frequently exhort governments to go easy on domestic competition regulation to enable them to compete more effectively in foreign markets. For the purpose of considering this case, assume that domestic competition is defined in terms of the number of domestic producers serving the home market. When there is competition from foreign producers, there is nothing logical about that test. Yet it is commonly applied and is enshrined in European law.

Krugman (1984) proposed a model that became highly influential. He assumes a large producer in the home economy with a nonlinear cost function

$$C = f(y) \tag{1}$$

which exhibits diminishing *marginal* costs. That is, $\partial f(y)/\partial y$ decreases with y, and that relationship is an essential component of the argument. Krugman argues that import protection can promote exports. What happens is that tariff protection has the usual effect for this type of model. It inhibits imports and gives the home producer a larger share of the home market. With constant marginal costs these consequences would be the entire effect. Greater production for the home market would confer no advantage on the firm when it comes to exporting to external markets. With diminishing marginal costs, however, sales to the home market and to the foreign market are no longer insulated from each other and determined separately. The larger volume of production for the home market consequent upon the tariff makes the home firm more competitive in foreign markets. Import protection promotes exports.

On the other hand, competitive attempts to knock out producers in other countries are not just a theoretical possibility. We see the makings of such a battle with the EC volume car makers. Most experts agree that there is at least one too many of them to survive in the single market once national restrictions on free trade in cars are completely dismantled. This situation makes it tempting for several countries to try to ensure that someone else's industry goes to the wall. The manipulation of exit conditions will be a growing problem and one that the EC commissioners will be exercised to regulate.

Can the type of argument promoted by Krugman be translated to competition control? Is there a competition policy that promotes exports by protecting the home market? The answer broadly is no, and the reason why that is the answer is interesting and enlightening. With competition control there are two conflicting forces at work. We may think of a policy that decreases the number of producers in the home market as slack competition policy. Then slack competition policy does decrease the number of producers in the home market, hence providing the larger producer with the benefits of economies of scale. But then it cannot avoid an effect that by itself is inimical to exports. Other things being equal, *the more domestic producers there are, the higher will be the level of exports.* The reason is elucidated in the next section.

7.8   The One Good Cross-Hauling Model

Most of the results considered in this chapter are derived from the model of international trade between olipolistic producers, sometimes known as the crosshauling model because it allows for trade in identical goods in both directions—crosshauling. I provide a general discussion here, taking advantage of the fact that mathematical details are readily available elsewhere. See Brander (1981), Brander and Krugman (1983), Dixit (1984), Dixit and Grossman (1986), Eaton and Grossman (1986).

Consider a very simple oligopoly model, which we can develop to examine the effects of competition policy. In each of several countries there is one product, "food," produced by labor under constant returns to scale and by numerous competitive producers, and identical "cars," produced by one or more oligopolistic firms in each country. The model can readily incorporate tariffs, but these are ignored as they are not germane to the main issue of competition policy. By shifting sales between markets, any producer will ensure that the net marginal revenue will be the same in each market. Assume that a producer who wants to sell in a market delivers output to that market, when the price on the market is determined by an inverse demand curve. A producer is satisfied with sales in a particular market if she does not wish to change the amount she is selling in that market, given how much other producers are selling. In standard terminology, we are looking at Nash-Cournot equilibrium. Producers are treated as if they have infinite capacities and choose outputs unconstrained.

With just one market, an equally valid, and probably better, interpretation of the Cournot quantity-setting oligopoly model is to suppose that producers choose capacities in the knowledge that price competition will drive them to sell up to capacity. A similar interpretation is available with many markets. The producer chooses a capacity sufficient to provide for all the markets in the knowledge that price competition will drive production up to the total capacity when the marginal profitability of unit sales is equated across markets.

The following results may be derived:

Theorem 1   With all sellers in a market in a Nash equilibrium of sales levels, market shares are inversely related to marginal costs of producing and delivering to that market.

The theorem applies generally, whenever more than one producer sells in the same market. An immediate implication is one of those *certeris paribus* propositions of which economists are inordinately fond. Other things being equal, more producers means more sales—more sales into any market. This observation implies, for instance, that policies which increase the equilibrium number of domestic producers are import substituting and export promoting. The other-things-being-equal clause is very important here, because higher marginal costs imply a lower market share in any market, and it is possible that more firms would mean higher marginal costs for each of the firms. Meanwhile, assume that all producers in all countries have (not necessarily equal) constant marginal costs. In that case the cost function must be

$$C = \alpha + my \tag{2}$$

where C is total cost, y is the level of production, and α and m are constants. Now the more-firms-means-more-sales result applies in a straightforward way, with no other-things-being-equal subtleties.

Notice that the equilibrium condition applies to all markets into which a producer sells. This does not and could not imply that any particular producer will choose to sell into any particular market. This point is obvious when one considers that marginal revenue is finite but marginal cost could be as large as required. At some point, equality of marginal revenue and cost becomes impossible even when the level of sales into a market is tiny (when marginal revenue is equal to price). In that case the producer concerned will not sell into that market. Then it is obvious that the multiplication of producers of the same type, when one of that type does not sell into a particular market, generates no sales into that market.

These findings are summarized in the next theorem:

Theorem 2   Given an international equilibrium of many oligopolists interpenetrating the markets of various countries, replication of one type results in

1. an increase in the share of the domestic market taken by home producers of the country whose producers were affected by the replication;

2. an increase in the share of home sales into each foreign market into which the replicated producer was previously selling; and

3. a fall in the market price in each market into which the replicated producer was previously selling.

Tariffs, or equivalent selling costs, by increasing the cost to foreign sellers of selling into the home market, protect home oligopolists. Consumers, however, suffer from this protection because less crosshauling means higher car prices in the home market. Crosshauling in a symmetrical model with transport costs is wasteful from the point of view of production efficiency. Yet consumers benefit from increased competition, and this gain has to be offset against the wastes of useless trade and the loss of producers' surplus as a result of lower car prices.

7.9   Which Type of Competition Policy Promotes Exports?

We have seen that where there are increasing returns to scale resulting in falling marginal costs, there is a fundamental ambiguity concerning the effect on exports of a policy that decreases the number of firms. Where there are constant marginal costs, any policy that increases the number of firms promotes exports. Equally, to state the opposite extreme, if there are sharply falling marginal costs, a policy that promotes or allows a decrease in the number of firms promotes exports. There is an important asymmetry between the two cases. With sharply falling marginal costs, competition policy only needs to be permissive, as firms have a private incentive to merge. With constant marginal costs, firms may or may not have an incentive to merge, as total profitability of all the firms may increase or decrease when they merge.

With constant marginal costs, an increase in the number of identical producers in one country increases their sales in all markets in which that type of producer is selling and lowers the price in all those markets. Lower prices must lower the profitability of each producer, and it is possible that they will do so to such an extent that some producers will not generate enough profit to cover overheads, when exit will result. For the time being, this issue is postponed, and it is assumed that whatever number of producers we choose to consider is an equilibrium. That assumption also requires that there should be no incentive to entry—that is, not so much excess profitability that new producers are encouraged to join the sector. These issues are potentially intricate.

7.10   Profitability, Exit, and Industrial Policy

Our treatment of producer equilibrium in a model of international trading oligopolists has been extremely parsimonious, based on just equal net marginal revenue conditions for sales into different markets. That approach assumed a general equilibrium, but that assumption is usually no problem. In any case the argument derived valid necessary conditions for a pure-strategy Nash quantity-setting equilibrium in which all producers sell in all markets, and pointed to the extension to zero sales into a market in which the price is equal to, or lower than, the total marginal cost of selling into that market.

Even extended, however, the equilibrium conditions are far from being sufficient conditions for long-run general equilibrium. We also need to look at the overall equilibrium situation of the producer. To examine that in the most simple case, we stay with the linear cost function (equation 2), now renumbered 3:

$$C = \alpha + my \tag{3}$$

Think of α as large, which will explain the oligopolistic structure of the industry. The level of constant marginal cost is not directly important in itself. Yet, for given sales and prices, high marginal costs reduce the gross profit available before overhead costs have been paid for. Whether a producer will continue to operate in the industry depends on whether it can make enough gross profit to pay its overhead costs.

So far, our discussion of competition policy has been loose and unclear. We might consider a policy that enforces a divorce between two parts of a unified producer. Yet under the assumptions employed, why is this necessary? If the sector can support an extra producer, what stops another producer from entering? If it cannot support an extra producer, how will the breaking-up policy work? There is no point in breaking up producers just to see some wither for lack of profit and the sector end up with the same number of producers with which it started.

Things change spectacularly when we make the number of foreign producers endogenous by adding an exit condition for them. We have seen that a tough competition policy at home increases penetration of the foreign market. This must lower the profit of the local producers and may induce exit. If that happens, a tough competition policy will turn out to be even more export promoting, and it will be additionally probable that domestic operating profitability will be augmented. There is another more sinister way of producing a similar outcome. Extra protection for the home market is plainly bad for foreign-producer profitability and may induce exit. After exit by foreign producers, imports may well increase, in which case import protection will have promoted exports.

7.11   Conclusions for Harmonization and Trade Rules

We have seen that it is very doubtful whether the international government of trade has to be much worried where worldwide monopoly is concerned. The diabolical monopolist who seizes the world supply of fill-in-the-blank and milks the market for everything it can give is not a plausible cause for anxiety. On the other hand, it is the case that competition control can affect international trade among oligopolists. We need to apply the tests proposed at the start of this chapter to see what importance this issue may have. But to do so clearly it is useful to distinguish three types of cases (each of which includes subcases):

1. Nations with tough competition control, which results in their having many domestic producers, may enjoy an export advantage, independent of comparative cost advantage. This may confer national benefits in terms of rents shifted, being profits made on foreign sales.

2. Where increasing returns to scale are important, nations with slack competition control, which permits there to be few national producers

(including only one), may enjoy an export advantage. This again may be independent of comparative cost advantage, although notice that comparative cost is a less clear and unambiguous concept when it depends upon the scale of operation.

3. In the increasing-returns case, government subsidies are not strictly of the essence, although they may play a facilitating role, especially if the total profitability of the merged companies would be lower, despite increasing returns, although rent shifting from abroad would be larger. However, more generally, government subsidies may be used to promote sectors or exports, even if there are no increasing returns.[8]

Depending on the case, there may or may not be trade torts. With item 1 it is hard to identify a serious tort. The nation with tough competition control is doing the rest of the world a favor in terms of the pricing of the product—making it cheaper. That could still be regarded as harmful by a government itself trying to promote a sector or its exports. However, that government could retaliate by itself adopting tough competition control, to the general benefit. Where increasing returns to scale and serious rent shifting are involved, there is an obvious role for international cooperation, limiting such interventions, and hence a role for trade law. All three reasons listed apply: there may be trade torts; the efficiency of the international division of labor is involved; and governments may very well need to be saved from themselves.

Much of the ground, however, will be covered by existing trade law. For instance, Brander-Krugman import protection as export promotion, which depends upon tariff protection of the home industry, is illegal under the GATT and should remain so. It is true that one can invent examples in which allowing one country to protect its home market improves world efficiency where increasing returns to scale are important. As a result, every country could be made better off with compensatory transfers, and it is even possible that these may not be needed. Even so, on an extension of the principle that hard cases make bad law, clever economist's examples make bad trade law. Tariff protection should be prohibited because, hard cases apart, allowing it on contrived grounds would open up floodgates.

Unfortunately, national subsidies have some of the same effect as tariffs, even if they are disguised subsidies, such as favoring national producers for government contracts. They can generate trade torts, particularly where rent shifting is involved; they can distort the international division of labor; and they can involve a destructive competition between interventionist governments, which they would do well to prohibit by a cooperative solution policed by trade law.

Finally, note that our discussion of competition and oligopoly has been based on quite a static formulation of the problem. National competition laws often legislate against such things as entry-deterring dynamics. On the whole, entry in international oligopoly is a good thing and should be encouraged.[9] Hence similar laws should, in principle, be incorporated into international trade law.

NOTES

1. Bliss (1995) discusses this Bhagwati-Srinivasan argument in detail. The claim is that when countries wish to protect domestic activities, whether for good or bad reasons, international agreements should treat together environment regulation, the slackness of which may be used to promote trade, and straightforward protection.

2. The question of how trade and harmonization can be reconciled in the case of environmental problems is discussed extensively by Esty (1994).

3. The worldwide dominance of the film production industry by "Hollywood" has been cited by France, particularly, as harmful. This is a vastly more complicated example than that of Boeing. First, Hollywood is not one producer, and were it to attempt to become one it would violate U.S. antitrust law. Second, the harm claimed is not mainly that the size of the U.S. industry makes it hard for national producers to compete. Rather, a supposed cultural externality is cited to justify protection.

4. For an exposition of the relevant theory, see Bliss (1994).

5. See, for example, Brander and Spencer (1985).

6. National security is often cited as a reason for wishing to have a certain industry in the nation. However, whether this really is a noneconomic issue depends on the outcome of reductionist analysis of the particular case. Winters (1991) shows that agricultural protection fails this test.

7. In principle, if there is more total profit to distribute, the arrangements for a merger can involve side payments such that all firms gain.

8. It may be felt that sector- or export-promoting subsidies are outside the scope of this chapter. Yet where oligopolistic industries are involved, subsidies and competition control are closely interrelated because both affect the number of producers that will be possible in equilibrium, and some numbers of producers may require subsidies if they are to be in equilibrium.

9. This is not strictly a general theoretical result, as again one can construct examples in which entry is welfare reducing.

REFERENCES

Bliss, C. 1994. *Economic theory and policy for trading blocks.* Manchester: Manchester University Press.

Bliss, C. 1995. "Dirty trade: Slack environmental regulation and trade promotion." Oxford: Nuffield College Discussion Paper No. 93.

Brander, J. 1981. "Intra-industry trade in identical commodities." *Journal of International Economics,* 11:1–14.

Brander, J., and P. R. Krugman 1983. "A 'reciprocal dumping' model of international trade." *Journal of International Economics,* 15:313–321.

Brander, J., and Barbara J. Spencer. 1985. "Export subsidies and market share rivalry." *Journal of International Economics,* 18:83–100.

Dixit, A. K. 1984. "International trade policy for oligopolistic industries." *Economic Journal,* supplement, 16.

Dixit, A. K., and G. M. Grossman. 1986. "Targeted export promotion with several oligopolistic industries." *Journal of International Economics,* 21:233–250.

Eaton, J., and G. M. Grossman. 1986. "Optimal trade and industrial policy under oligopoly." *Quarterly Journal of Economics,* 101:331–344.

Esty, D. 1994. *Greening the GATT.* Washington, DC: Institute for International Economics.

Krugman, P. R. 1984. "Import protection as export promotion." In Henryk Kierzkowski, ed., *Monopolistic competition and international trade.* Oxford, Blackwell.

Krugman, P. R. 1992. "Does the new trade theory require a new trade policy?" *The World Economy,* 15(4):423–441.

Tirole, J. 1988. *The theory of industrial organization.* Cambridge, MA: MIT Press.

Venables, A. J. 1985. "Trade and trade policy with imperfect competition: The case of identical products and free entry." *Journal of International Economics,* 19:1–20.

Venables, A. J., and A. M. Smith. 1986. "Trade and industrial policy under imperfect competition." *Economic Policy,* 1:622–672.

Winters, L. A. 1991. "Digging for victory." *The World Economy,* 13:170–190.

8   Competition Policy and International Trade

James Levinsohn

8.1 Introduction

While recent advances in international trade theory have borrowed heavily from the industrial organization literature, this work has a schizophrenic
quality to it. One of the insights that motivated the new trade theory
was the observation that many markets were not perfectly competitive.
For the case of purely domestic markets, the industrial organization literature provided a foundation for policy advice, and most countries have
well-established public policy regarding competition between firms. While
trade theorists have borrowed heavily from the theory of industrial organization, they seem to have ignored the existence of competition policy
when investigating trade policy. The two interact in important ways, and
pretending that trade policy in imperfectly competitive markets takes place
in the absence of any antitrust or competition policy is akin to pretending
that standard tariff policy takes place in the absence of any domestic tax
structure. Just as a tariff is equivalent to a production subsidy coupled with
a consumption tariff at equal ad valorum rates, analogous, although less
exact, relationships surely exist between trade and competition policy.[1]
Ignoring these interactions may have important public policy consequences.

Policy makers and firms, at least in some instances, have been aware of
the interactions between trade policy and competition policy even if economic theorists mostly neglected the issue. For example, in Korea the
government blocked a merger in a chemical industry because that industry
was subject to a 30 percent tariff that limited much foreign competition.[2]
In the United States, the new Department of Justice Merger Guidelines
(1992) make explicit reference to the role import quotas might play in
determining the anticompetitive effects of horizontal mergers. In particular,
foreign competition that is restricted by quotas cannot increase their U.S.
sales when a merger between U.S. firms induces a price increase. This

constraint on competition, as a result of trade policy, is taken into consideration by the Department of Justice Antitrust Division. Firms, too, are often aware of the role international competition has on domestic oligopolies. They frequently do not enthusiastically welcome foreign competitors in these industries. In one Asian country, the oligopolistic domestic film producers used snakes to discourage consumers from attending movie theaters showing foreign films.[3] Closer to home, U.S. automakers considered an antidumping suit against all foreign competitors in late 1992. This potential international trade dispute was not pursued, and domestic antitrust concerns were said to play a role in that decision.

The purpose of this chapter is to begin to explore some of the interactions between competition and trade policy and to investigate both the role these interactions play when countries with differing policies trade with one another and the effects of policy harmonization. The approach of this chapter is to raise what I think are interesting and previously neglected questions. While some intuition into probable results is posited, this chapter intentionally does not provide much in the way of formal economic modeling. (Such modeling is the subject of ongoing research.) Before discussing how competition and trade policies interact, it is useful to summarize just what the policy landscape actually is. The next section of this paper provides an overview of the sorts of competition policies adopted by various groups of countries.[4] Section 8.3 provides a similar but more brief overview of how trade policy has been implemented in imperfectly competitive industries. In section 8.4, I discuss the interactions between these two sorts of policies, and section 8.5 surveys issues that will arise when countries with differing competition and trade policies opt to harmonize. Conclusions are gathered in section 8.6.

8.2   A Survey of Competition Policies

8.2.1   A Taxonomy of Competition Policies

Since I will later discuss issues surrounding harmonization of competition policies, it makes sense to first outline some of the policies actually used. If there were no significant differences, the issues of harmonization would of course be moot. Summarizing competition policies is tricky business, as simple taxonomies seem inadequate. Unlike trade policies that can more or less be ranked on a unidimensional scale from quite liberal to quite restrictive, competition policies are more complex. There are several ways in which competition policy is codified. Many countries use the same policy for firms that sell their products domestically and for firms that are primarily exporters. Other countries exempt exporters from domestic antitrust legislation. Not surprisingly, the countries that exempt exporters from antitrust legislation usually have small domestic markets. While policies vary across countries, the degree to which the policy on the books is enforced also varies a great deal. Many countries have laws on the books that simply are not enforced. Although a simple summary is sure to be somewhat incorrect, I will try to offer one anyway.

Competition policies generally fall into five groups. First, some countries have exceptionally lax and laissez-faire approaches in which almost anything goes in both domestic and export markets. The second approach is at the other end of the spectrum, employing exceptionally strict competition policy in both domestic and export markets. Most countries fall somewhere between these extremes. Here, a "rule of reason" is often employed. The "rule of reason" means that many actions that might decrease competition are not illegal simply because they exist, but rather courts or regulatory boards balance the effects of the anticompetitive behavior. Courts or regulators, in this case, consider the gain in profits or firm efficiency against the loss in consumer surplus that might result from anticompetitive behavior. The third group of countries employs a rule-of-reason approach for domestic markets while employing a lax policy in export markets. The fourth group of countries employs a rule-of-reason approach in both domestic and export markets. Finally, a fifth group of countries have very strict competition policies applying to purely domestic industries, while exporting firms are completely exempt from competition policy. To further cloud any taxonomy, within each group of policies, the degree of enforcement varies tremendously. In the remainder of this section, I review the policies of some particular countries. Most countries are not explicitly discussed, but an effort is made to review the policies of some of the most important economic players in world markets.

8.2.2   Examples of Lax Competition Policies

The most lax competition policies have very little antitrust legislation pertaining to both export and domestic markets. Examples of countries in this category include Hong Kong, Taiwan, Denmark, and Italy. These countries tend to rely heavily on the market to ensure competition. As will be discussed later, though, a lax competition policy does not automatically mean that prices are oligopolistically high if the country is small and has a very liberal trade policy. For example, Hong Kong is often cited as having one of the most open trading regimes in the world. International competition, in such a case, may be sufficient to make competition policy redundant. For the case of Hong Kong, the government has passed the Code on Takeovers and Mergers, but these guidelines are simply suggestions and do not carry the force of law.[5] Another Pacific Rim country, Taiwan, also has a very lax competition policy. There, most competition policy is directed at regulating the prices of several state-owned and private monopolies.

Denmark and Italy also lack comprehensive legislation concerning anticompetitive firm behavior.[6] In Denmark, monopolies are neither illegal nor regulated, and while there are government guidelines, they are enforced only through publicizing the abuses of offending firms. Italy's policy is only marginally more strict. It too has no comprehensive competition policy, and the Civil Code only restricts anticompetitive behavior that harms the national interest. Since monopoly profits are argued to be in the national interest, it is a lax policy indeed. Denmark' and Italy's lax policies are especially interesting, since they are part of the European Community. The role of competition policy within the Community is discussed in section 8.2.5.

8.2.3   Examples of Policies with Differing Standards for Domestic and Export Markets

The competition policies of the four countries discussed in the preceding section do not make distinctions between firms that produce for the domestic market or for a foreign market, but such distinctions frequently are made. Several countries are more strict with domestic-market firms, as the government recognizes the consumer's interest in low prices and a wide variety of goods. These same governments, though, also recognize that profits earned from abroad are a good thing, and exporting firms are permitted much leeway. Countries that adopt a rule-of-reason standard in assessing anticompetitive actions by firms that serve the domestic market while allowing exporting firms to pursue their own interests include the Philippines, Ireland, Germany, Greece, and Switzerland.

In Ireland, no competitively restrictive practice or trade restraint is per se illegal; rather each act is evaluated on a case-by-case basis. Mergers and acquisitions that would result in a dominant domestic market position are allowed only by consent of the minister. While domestic-market firms are generally restrained from exercising significant market power, firms that export more than 90 percent of their output are exempt from domestic standards. These firms compete in the international market free from regulation if their operation does not unfairly impair the domestic level of competition.

Of the countries with very distinct competition policies depending on whether the market is domestic or export, Germany is probably the most economically powerful. Domestically, German competition law appears on the surface to be relatively strict. It is, though, full of loopholes and exemptions.[7] One interesting exemption arises when a merger would allow small and medium-size firms to achieve scale economies. (It is in this same circumstance that an active trade policy is also sometimes proscribed.) Most domestic competition law in Germany is codified and does not allow for much judicial discretion. The law is detailed and can be determined directly from the statutes. Merger and acquisition laws are an exception, and they are handled on a case-by-case basis. German competition law allows firms to collude if their product is destined for foreign markets. In sum, German competition law for domestic firms is moderate, weighing the interests of firms and consumers. For export firms, though, the regulations are relaxed, and cartelization is permitted.

8.2.4   Japanese Competition Policy

If summarizing the competition policies of a country in a paragraph or two is tricky business, trying to summarize Japan's competition policy as briefly is plain crazy. Nonetheless, a summary of the competition policies of the world's larger economic players would be seriously incomplete without some mention of Japan.[8] Japan's competition policy is not unlike those of several other countries that enforce a fairly strict policy at home yet allow collusion in export markets. There are some distinctive features of the Japanese system, though.

Beginning in the 1960s, Japan's Antimonopoly Law, which had been around since 1947, began to be strengthened. Further amendments in 1977 increased the enforcement of domestic antitrust laws. In general, domestic antitrust law prohibits any firm activity that would "fix, maintain, or enhance prices; or limit production, technology, products, or customers or suppliers, thereby causing, contrary to the public interest, a substantial restraint of competition."[9] Cartels are illegal, and this law is apparently enforced. There are, though, some important exceptions. In particular, the Japanese government has the authority to grant exemptions for certain industries as well as for rationalized or depressed industries.[10] While the Fair Trade Commission (FTC) oversees the enforcement of antitrust law, the Ministry of International Trade and Industry (MITI) oversees industrial policy, and it is MITI which has the power to grant exceptions to the antitrust laws.

Export cartels are usually given a blanket exemption from the Anti-monopoly law. MITI has also given several other specific sectors exemptions. These include machinery, electronics, coal mining, textiles, sugar, silk yarn, fruit, fertilizer, liquor, and perishable food. Also, joint research and development ventures are often cartelized in Japan. Indeed, it is estimated that about 20 percent of all research and development projects are cartelized horizontal ventures.[11] In order to obtain MITI's permission to cartelize, a domestic industry must show that the cartel does not violate international treaties, is not contrary to the importer's interest, does not hurt export trade, is not unduly discriminative, is not unreasonably restrictive, does not unreasonably hurt domestic agriculture, and does not unreasonably hurt Japanese consumers. Clearly, these guidelines leave room for some latitude in interpretation.

The contradictions between a relatively strict domestic-firm policy and a lax export-firm policy create obvious conflicts between the FTC and MITI, and while some court cases have suggested that MITI decisions can supersede the FTC, the FTC is generally perceived as doing an effective job of ensuring a competitive domestic market (although the list of exemptions is certainly nontrivial.)

An interesting aspect of Japan's competition policy that has received recent attention is that foreign companies have a very difficult time seeking protection with the antitrust laws. This is because the FTC will only discuss Japanese firms in its rulings. Even if the foreign firm is in association with Japanese firms, it does not have standing before the FTC, so foreign firms are left without recourse.[12]

8.2.5   The European Community and Some Member-Country Policies

Several countries employ similar antitrust standards for domestic and export markets. Examples of countries that use a rule of reason to judge antitrust cases, domestic or export oriented, include Spain, France, the Netherlands, Sweden, and Belgium, as well as the European Community. In each of these countries, the government essentially considers the trade-off between profits and consumer surplus when considering merger requests. There are few blanket rules, and mergers that lead to sufficiently large gains in efficiency, technological improvement, or exports may be approved if they do not infringe too much on product choice, quality, and price to consumers.

Among EC countries, the United Kingdom has perhaps the most complex competition policy. The United Kingdom also has "a manufacturing sector which is one of the most highly concentrated (if not the most highly concentrated) in the world."[13] The British government has a long history of ignoring anticompetitive interactions. While British law has relied on the rule-of-reason approach, this has frequently led to anticompetitive behavior. Under the Thatcher government, Britain moved toward a more strict competition policy, although the law still depended on the rule of reason to determine abuses. Nonetheless, efficiency gains from mergers are usually said to offset the loss of domestic competition, and mergers are usually allowed without too much trouble. Perhaps because its competition policy is much more lax than most other EC members, the United Kingdom has been unwilling to cede authority over its competition policy to the European Economic Community. EEC policy is more restrictive, and Britain may fear such a policy would place its firms at a competitive disadvantage. There seems to be little discussion regarding the presumably positive effects EEC policy would have on U.K. consumers.

The EEC competition policy provides a nice case study in what might happen when competition policies are harmonized. EEC competition policy is based on the Treaty of Rome, and it is enforced by the European Commission and the national courts of the EEC's member states. EEC competition policy is based on a rule-of-reason approach and represents something of a compromise between the individual policies of the member states. In practice, prior to 1990, the Treaty of Rome competition statutes were rarely invoked, and enforcement was quite limited. In 1990, though, new regulations took effect that changed the way mergers were evaluated by lowering the levels at which a merger must be reported to the EEC. Mergers between small firms, however, need not be reported.[14] An interesting conflict arises when EEC competition law is contradicted by a member nation's law. A precedent has been set in the Costa/Enel case, establishing the superiority of Community law, and this precedent has generally been accepted by member states. This issue, though, is still an emerging one and is without definite resolution at this point.

8.2.6   North American Competition Policies

In North America, Canada and the United States provide contrasts in competition policy. Canada, like the United Kingdom, has a long history of lax competition law. This lax policy coupled with a small domestic market has led to a high level of firm concentration in Canada. Canada's competition law is minimal, and between 1946 and 1986, no merger cases and only one monopoly case were prosecuted.[15] In 1986, Canadian competition law was changed to become rule of reason. A tribunal weighs issues of international competitiveness, economies of scale, and technical progress against the decline in domestic competition.

If Canada is especially lax, the United States generally lies at the other extreme. The United States has one of the oldest and strictest sets of antitrust laws. The Sherman Act (1890) and Clayton Act (1914) laid the foundation for U.S. competition law. The Sherman Act was enacted as a broad policy against the emerging trusts of J. P. Morgan and J. D. Rockefeller, and it places severe restrictions on merger activity. The Clayton Act furthered competition law by outlawing more specific acts of anticompetitive behavior, including tying arrangements, exclusive-dealing agreements, and requirements contracts.[16]

One of the more controversial aspects of the U.S. law is the awarding of treble damages in antitrust suits. As a result, 95 percent of all antitrust actions in the United States have been instigated by private corporations, in contrast to other countries where the government typically initiates investigations into antitrust abuses. Because of the very large punishment for collusion under the law, most U.S. firms opt to merge instead. These mergers are evaluated using the Department of Justice Merger Guidelines.

Like many other countries, the United States allows some cartelization for export purposes, and this is covered by the Webb-Pomerene Act of 1918. This act permits firms in a given industry to export through a single sales agency.[17] Although Webb-Pomerene provides protection from antitrust laws for some export cartels, the law has not been widely exploited.

8.2.7 Summary

The basic trade-off that countries face in constructing their competition policies is that between firm profits and consumer welfare. When the consumers affected by collusion are not citizens, since the firms are exporters, the trade-off vanishes and the search for firm profits guides policy. There are obviously some potential problems, though, with allowing cartelizations for exports and enforcing competition in the domestic market, and countries have taken varying approaches to dealing with this issue. One aspect of competition policy that is apparent in most of the countries surveyed is that competition policy is set at the national level and not at the industry level. That is, while some industries may obtain various exemptions, competition policy is not written separately for every industry. This practice is in stark contrast to international trade policy, for trade policy is typically set at the industry level. The next section provides a very brief survey of the sorts of trade policies employed in imperfectly competitive industries. In section 8.4 we consider interactions between competition and trade policy, and then, in section 8.5, we discuss issues pertaining to the harmonization of competition policies.

8.3   International Trade Policies in Imperfectly Competitive Industries

The previous section outlined how competition policy is actually implemented in several countries. In this section, I outline some of the trade policy tools used throughout the world. Whereas competition policy was set nationally, trade policy is usually set at the industry level; hence, generalizations about a specific country's trade policies are difficult and potentially misleading. A country might have very free trade in high-tech sectors but border on mercantilism when it comes to agriculture. Since I will want to consider how trade and competition policy interact when discussing issues of harmonization, I concentrate on trade policy in imperfectly competitive industries. When industries are characterized by very many firms, each without market power, competition policy is irrelevant.

Some trade policies are simple, but these are more commonly found in international-trade theory papers than in the real world. Import tariffs and export taxes or subsidies are the most straightforward policies. Whereas either policy decreases economic welfare with perfect competition, the effects of even these simple policies are ambiguous with imperfect competition. When firms produce homogeneous products and simultaneously set quantities conditional on the quantities they expect other firms to produce, export subsidies may be welfare enhancing if enough output is sold abroad. The intuition behind this statement is that firms would like to produce more, since there are profits to be made, but they refrain from doing so in equilibrium, since the threat to do so would not be credible conditional on the other firms' responses. An export subsidy allows the home firm to credibly produce more, increasing home profits at the expense of foreign firms. One can make the case that there are not many examples of export subsidies in practice, but this is not necessarily so. While a simple payment to a firm for each unit exported or produced is not a common practice, there are more subtle ways to subsidize exports. These include special tax treatment of investment in a particular industry, government subsidized research and development, special financing available for export credits, and government loans to firms that plan to export.

While trade theory indicates that an export subsidy might be prudent public policy under very particular conditions, under other conditions economic welfare is enhanced with export taxes. In industries that produce similar but not identical products (differentiated products) and set prices as their strategic variable, an export tax might be welfare enhancing. The intuition here is that firms would like to raise prices but decline to do so for fear that their competitors will undercut them and steal away profitable sales. An export tax allows firms to increase prices, and, in some cases, both domestic and foreign firms reap higher profits (with the larger increase usually going to the firms whose government placed the export tax). An import tariff also allows firms to reap higher profits in some cases for similar reasoning, although if the good is purchased by domestic consumers, their welfare declines with the higher prices they must now pay. Import tariffs and export taxes are oft-employed trade policies, although there is scant evidence that they are used in industries in which they might enhance domestic economic welfare.

Nontariff barriers are prevalent and sometimes subtle trade policy instruments used in imperfectly (and perfectly) competitive industries. These may take the form of quotas, voluntary export restraints (VERs), product standards, government procurement policies, or other subtle forms of protection. Also, trade policies can typically be emulated by some combination of domestic tax policies. While the former is clearly under the realm of the GATT, the latter is less so. When considering harmonization of trade policies, it is useful to keep in mind that if a country really wants to maintain the protection it had when a tariff was in existence, it could agree to remove the tariff or subsidy only to replace it with the appropriate adjustment to the domestic tax code.

Another type of trade protection is found in antidumping law. While exact definitions of dumping vary across countries and even within a country over time, most definitions refer to selling a product in a foreign market for either less than some specified definition of cost (plus markup, in many cases) or to selling a product in a foreign market for less than it sells for in the home market. Antidumping law is used a great deal in the United States, and there is evidence that it serves as a collusion-promoting device. Many antidumping suits are dropped either before a ruling or, in some cases, before a suit is formally filed but after one is threatened. The result may be higher prices charged by both the foreign and competing domestic firm. Firms gain at the expense of domestic consumers.

8.4   Interactions between Trade and Competition Policy

Sections 8.2 and 8.3 outlined competition and international trade policy separately, but neither exists without the other, and neglecting interactions between the two types of policies may provide misleading policy guidelines. Trade and competition policies typically promote competing interests. Trade policy is typically implemented to further the interests of producers. Producers are better organized than consumers, and while more international trade furthers consumers' interests, most trade policy is directed at restricting trade. Competition policy, on the other hand, is more directly aimed at protecting (domestic) consumer interests. As such, they may have offsetting influences.

The plan of this section is to first discuss ways in which trade policy and competition policy interact, and section 8.5 discusses possible implications of policy harmonization. Whereas there are exact equivalences between trade policy and domestic tax policy, interactions between trade and competition policy are fuzzier.

8.4.1   Competition and Trade Policy for Small Countries

When a country is economically small, the interactions between trade policy and competition policy are especially simple. If a small country maintains an open trading regime, then, in the tradables sector, competition policy is redundant. That is, if borders are open, the fact that a domestic industry has a very high concentration of sales by a few firms should not be all that worrisome, as international competitors take the place of the minimal domestic competition. This notion has been termed the imports-as-market-discipline hypothesis, and it has found some validity in econometric tests.[18]

While this relationship between competition policy (or the lack thereof) and trade policy is theoretically straightforward, reality is usually messier. There are several caveats to keep in mind before abandoning a role for competition policy for a small open country. First, many services are not traded, so concentration in the service sector may be an appropriate target of domestic competition policy. Second, and relatedly, vertical relationships between importers and service sectors such as banking and finance may constrict international competition. For example, even if borders are open, importers frequently need to obtain credit to purchase goods. If the banks are owned by conglomerates that also own manufacturing firms that would compete with the imports, importers may have difficulty obtaining financing. Third, in a differentiated-products industry, domestic firms may still have enough market power to warrant concern from the competition office. If the cross-price elasticity of demand for home varieties with respect to the price of foreign varieties is not very elastic, domestic firms will still be able to exert market power.

8.4.2   Competition and Trade Policy Interactions with Constant-Returns-to-Scale Oligopolists

A general principle in considering the effects of trade policy and antitrust policy in oligopolies is that there are few generalities. The effects of policies are very dependent on the exact market conditions to which they are applied. As already noted, whether firms set prices (Bertrand competition) or quantities (Cournot competition) in markets will affect the *sign* of the optimal trade policy. In the merger literature, there is a somewhat analogous result, as the welfare implications of mergers, and hence, indirectly, of competition policy, also depend on whether firms set prices or quantities. For the case in which firms produce a homogeneous product and set quantities, it is straightforward to show that with symmetric firms, linear demand, and constant returns to scale, economic welfare falls directly as industry concentration rises. A prior question is whether individual firms would find it in their interest to merge in the absence of restraints. Salant, Switzer, and Reynolds (1993) showed that in the absence of cost savings, horizontal mergers are unprofitable so long as not too much of the industry merges. The policy implication was that horizontal mergers that are observed must then be resulting in cost savings and would necessarily be socially efficient. This evocative result has been challenged, and when one adds potential competition, learning, or returns to scale, this result may be altered.

If, in a simple quantity-setting framework, firms do not find it profitable to merge, this is certainly not the case when firms set prices. In a framework in which firms producing related but not identical products set prices, horizontal mergers are generally profitable. This conclusion has been proved in a fairly general setting by Deneckere and Davidson (1985). Hence, when considering the effects of competition policy, whether firms set prices or quantities matters. The exact same issue arises in considering the effects of trade policies. The predicted welfare consequences of trade or competition policies are not very robust to assumptions about how the market works, and this fact makes it difficult to generalize about interactions between trade and competition policy. Some particular examples, though, are provided prior to a discussion of policy harmonization.

As a first example of interactions between trade and competition policy, consider the case of a country that implements a very restrictive competition policy. Firms that might previously have colluded or merged are now forced to compete. In a standard neoclassical economic framework, the stricter policy, in the absence of returns to scale, learning, or other synergies, would increase economic welfare. Monopoly or oligopoly profits would shrink and consumer surplus rise by more than the decline in profits. How might trade policy alter this desirable outcome? If firms produce differentiated products, as is the case in most manufacturing industries, and compete with one another by setting prices, an export tax or import tariff has the effect of raising prices and profits at the expense of consumers. In an oligopoly, this trade policy has the effect of implicitly moving firms closer to a collusive equilibrium—exactly opposite the goal of the restrictive competition policy. Suppose, then, that a tariff or export tax is implemented as competition policy is strengthened. Then, if trade policy is not considered when competition policy is made more strict, the consumer gains from competition policy reform are diminished.

A related example occurs in the case of trade policy liberalization. Suppose GATT or other treaty obligations lead to the removal of export taxes/subsidies or import tariffs that had been leading to higher domestic industry profits at the expense of foreign firms (profit shifting). Recall that tariffs and subsidies can take other more subtle forms. If at the same time that countries retreat from these profit-shifting trade policies, they allow domestic firms to explicitly collude in international markets, the procompetitive effects of the trade policy liberalization would be muted. Since many of the competition policies reviewed in section 8.2 were marked by explicit permission to collude in export markets, this notion is not so far-fetched.

With constant returns to scale, trade policy is often directed at enabling home firms to exercise market power to shift profits away from foreign firms, while competition policy is typically directed at restricting the exercise of market power. The obvious exception occurs when competition policy explicitly permits export cartels. This exception aside, competition policy and trade policy frequently work in opposing directions. With increasing returns to scale, though, the story is different.

8.4.3   Competition and Trade Policy Interactions with Increasing
Returns to Scale

When perusing competition policies, most countries allow mergers when
there are significant efficiency gains. This would be the case with notable
increasing returns to scale internal to the firm. That is, if the post-merger
firm can produce the same quantity that the premerger firms produced, but
at lower cost, there are efficiency gains to the merger. Even the United
States, with one of the strictest competition policies, takes efficiency gains
into account in its Merger Guidelines. Hence, competition policy, in the
face of increasing returns to scale, tends to be less procompetitive. Trade
policy prescriptions in the presence of increasing returns to scale vary
widely.

There are multiple models that generate monopolistically competitive
industries and in which an active trade or competition policy would be
welfare decreasing. The basic idea behind this class of models is that there
are efficiency gains on the production side to having just one firm produce
each variety of good, because of the increasing returns to scale, while on
the consumer side, consumers benefit from the larger number of varieties
available with free trade and hence from an efficient domestic production
structure. In these models, tariffs or quotas are typically welfare decreasing
as they raise the prices that consumers pay while profits are not shifted,
since, because of the monopolistically competitive industry structure, competition from similar varieties drives profits to zero. A pro-competitive
competition policy would force more than one firm to produce each variety, and in the presence of increasing returns to scale or fixed costs, this is
inefficient. While an active trade or competition policy is usually welfare
decreasing in this class of models, there do not appear to be obvious links
between the two.

This is not the case for another industry structure, again with increasing
returns to scale. If industries are characterized by increasing returns to
scale and are oligopolistic, then protection may be welfare enhancing, but
the benefits of an active trade policy would be counteracted if competition
policy were not coordinated with the trade policy. Like most oligopolistic
market structures, there are many possible cases to consider, but the intuition underlying welfare-enhancing trade policies with increasing-returns-
to-scale oligopolists runs along the following lines. If an increasing-
returns-to-scale oligopolist is afforded protection against international
competition, the firm finds itself able to produce more at a lower marginal
cost. Once able to produce at this lower marginal cost, the firm may now

be competitive on international markets, whereas prior to the protection, it was not. As shown by Paul Krugman, the result of the import protection is export promotion. A key element to this scenario is that once given protection, the domestic firm is allowed to expand and reap the benefits of increased efficiency. If, on the other hand, there are competition policies that place limits on the market share of the domestic firm or firms in an industry, the domestic firm will not be permitted to reap the efficiency gains, and import protection will not become export promotion. Hence, competition policy that is not coordinated with trade policy would lessen the efficacy of the trade policy.

8.4.4   Price Discrimination and Antidumping Law

A discussion of interactions between competition policy and international trade policy would not be complete without at least some mention of the relationships between price discrimination, which is typically the domain of competition policy, and antidumping law, which is typically the domain of international trade policy. Further, price discrimination is only possible with market power in a domestic setting or segmented markets in a international setting.

Competition policy addresses price discrimination in various ways. In the United States, the key piece of legislation is the Robinson-Patman Act, which amended section 2 of the Clayton Act. Passed originally to protect small independent stores from the large chain grocery stores, the act was designed to control the large powerful buyers who could exercise monopsony power.[19] The law makes it illegal to "discriminate in price between purchasers of commodities of like grade and quality ... where the effect of such discrimination may be substantially to lessen competition or tend to create a monopoly." As such, the law addresses predatory pricing more directly than run-of-the-mill price discrimination.

With the creation of a single market, Europeans may be more acutely aware of price discrimination. Nonetheless, in Europe, the gist of competition policy regarding price discrimination is similar to that in the United States, but one must generally show that price discrimination is being practiced by a dominant producer.

In its extreme form, what competition policy calls price discrimination, trade policy might call dumping. Again, the definitions of dumping vary across countries (and even within a country over time), but the basic idea is that it is illegal for an exporter to sell a product in a foreign market for either less than some construed cost or less than it is sold for in the home market. The parallels between price discrimination and dumping are clear. If every country had strong prohibitions on price discrimination, antidumping law would be redundant. Further, if domestic price discrimination policy applied to exports, and if antidumping law were really used to address price discrimination, then the two policies would be very related, and it would be natural to attempt to coordinate them. In practice, though, it is difficult to make the case that antidumping law is really used to address price discrimination.

As an economic point, prohibiting price discrimination seldom makes a great deal of sense unless the price discrimination is predatory pricing in disguise. Forcing producers to sell for one price, either domestically or internationally, may lead a profit-maximizing firm to avoid servicing some markets entirely, and such a response may entail a net welfare loss. Further, alleged dumping, if it does not lead to predatory behavior, provides consumers with inexpensive goods, and this result is typically welfare enhancing. The punch line here is that laws prohibiting dumping and price discrimination in simple static economic models are often hard to justify on economic grounds. Here, trade and competition policy are alike in that they are both often misguided policies.

8.5   Harmonization of Competition Policies: Issues and Questions

The previous sections have outlined which competition and trade policies dominate the economic landscape and how these policies interact. In this section, I investigate some issues that arise when one considers harmonization of competition policies. In particular, as countries with different competition policies consider harmonization, what happens to the gains from trade between these countries? As the previous section suggests, there are few general answers. Rather, the particulars of the markets under consideration will matter, as well as the trade policies that coexist with the to-be-harmonized competition policies. By discussing two examples and the concerns these stylized examples raise, the salient issues will be highlighted and, hopefully, the relevant questions posed.

The practical importance of understanding the forces at work when harmonizing competition policies is clear. As trade policies become more integrated and coordinated, other aspects of economic policy that are not harmonized naturally receive more attention. Competition policy is no exception, and indeed in 1992, the EC Commissioner for External Economic Affairs and Commercial Policy, Sir Leon Britain, argued that GATT ought to consider setting explicit rules for competition policy.[20]

The potential list of cases one might investigate is quite large. A general taxonomy is as follows. Countries may trade a differentiated product, or they may trade homogeneous products. The former appears as intra-industry trade, while the latter is more traditional Heckscher-Ohlin trade. Within a country, a good may be produced by either a perfectly competitive industry or an oligopoly. The degree of collusiveness within an oligopoly may vary, with monopoly as a limiting case. The oligopolists might act simultaneously (in a Nash fashion) or one country might follow the other(s) (in a Stackelberg fashion). Also, oligopolists might set price or quantity. Competition policy might apply the same or different standards for export markets. This taxonomy, while still very incomplete, suggests dozens of permutations in which one could investigate the interactions between trade and competition policy. In most of these cases, careful analysis would require straightforward mathematical modeling. As this chapter is decidedly nontechnical, I model two of the very simplest cases using diagrammatic analysis.

The first case looks at international trade in a market in which one country has a very lax competition policy while another has a very strict one. I consider the case of trade in homogeneous goods, although most of the lessons will also pertain to markets in which goods are differentiated. In this context, I investigate two types of harmonization, which I label "us-like-them" and "them-like-us." The second case looks at a market in which one firm has significant market power both at home and in an export market, and considers issues that arise when competition policy adopts different standards for home and export markets.

8.5.1   Homogeneous Goods with Strict Competition Policy at Home and Law Competition Policy Abroad

Suppose that two countries trade homogeneous goods. To make the example concrete, suppose the United States produces televisions *and* imports them from Korea.[21] Suppose the United States enforces a strict competition policy so that economic behavior of the television industry approximates perfect competition while the Korean television industry, because of lax competition policy, is approximating a monopolist. Under these circumstances, I pose the following questions. Should the United States trade with Korea? Within Korea and the United States, are consumer and producer interests coincident or opposite? Across the countries, are producer and consumer interests the same or different? If the countries decide to harmonize their policies, should the United States adopt an "us-like-them" approach or a "them-like-us" approach, and what happens to the gains from international trade under each approach?

The triptych in Figure 1 illustrates the television market in this setup. While quite simple, it conveys many of the considerations that dominate more complicated models. The right panel illustrates the Korean demand for televisions. In this example, Korea's demand for televisions is assumed to be small relative to the U.S. demand for televisions. The middle panel illustrates the U.S. market for televisions. Since the United States is assumed to enforce competition policy, the supply of domestically produced televisions is given by a supply function that approximates marginal cost. Korea, which is assumed to have a very lax competition policy, faces a demand for televisions that consists of the U.S. excess demand (U.S. demand less U.S. supply) plus Korean demand. Since Korea is assumed in this example to not enforce a competition policy, the marginal revenue perceived by Korean manufacturers lies below the total demand they face. One could loosely parameterize the strictness of Korea's competition policy by altering how steep this perceived marginal revenue curve is. With cartelization of the industry, it would be twice as steep, while with perfect competition it would coincide with the (linear) demand curve. With free trade, the price of televisions in Korea must equal the price in the United States (given the assumption of homogeneous products and abstracting from transport costs). The price chosen by Korean producers to maximize profits must be such that total Korean production equals U.S. imports plus Korean domestic demand. This price is given by P_{ft}, the free trade price. At this price, the U.S. imports amount to BC, and the gains from trade to the U.S. are ABC. Korean welfare is given by consumer surplus, DEF in panel 1 plus pure profits $GHIJ$ in panel 3. Of the pure profits $GHIJ$, a fraction $(FENM/GHIJ)$ are earned in Korea with the rest being earned in the export market, where $FENM$ is seen in panel 1 and is the same height as $GHIJ$ in panel 3 but of smaller width.

Korea's gains from trade are obtained by first drawing the marginal revenue associated with the Korean domestic demand as seen in panel 1 and superimposing the marginal cost curve from panel 3. The difference between the consumer surplus plus profits $(DKLM)$ in panel 1 and the much larger areas of DEF and $GHIJ$ from Figure 1 represent the gains from trade to Korea.

Note that Korea faces a trade-off between the welfare of its consumers and that of its producers. With international trade, Korean producers gain while Korean consumers are made worse off. This example has considered the case of free trade, and hence the same price to consumers in the United

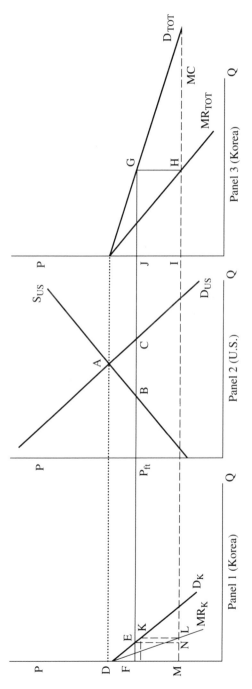

Figure 1

States and Korea, but Korea could increase its welfare if the price to the small domestic market were made lower while maintaining the higher price in the U.S. market. Free trade prevents this divergence.

Now consider the effects of harmonization of competition policies on the gains from trade and on economic welfare of each country. There are two possibilities: the "us-like-them" or "them-like-us" harmonization strategies. Suppose the United States adopts a lax competition policy itself in the television industry, hence allowing its domestic producers to themselves collude or at least compete less vigorously. In this case, the television market is oligopolistic as U.S. and Korean firms each recognize their ability to impact the market outcome. The outcome will depend on particulars of the TV market. Since we are assuming TVs are a homogeneous good, I will assume firms set quantities, for if instead they competed in prices, price would be driven to marginal cost. At this point, the simple partial equilibrium diagrams are insufficient. Nonetheless, some general lessons emerge.

If the U.S. law allowed the U.S. industry to become cartelized, the television market would be characterized by a duopoly in which the United States was the high-cost producer. (Recall, the United States imports TVs.) The equilibrium would be one in which the United States would produce fewer TVs than Korea, since market shares vary inversely with marginal cost. In general, the oligopolistic equilibrium price would exceed the price that cleared the market when the U.S. market was competitive while the Korean was not. U.S. profits would increase, U.S. consumer surplus would decrease, and the United States would on net be hurt by an "us-like-them" policy. Due to the oligopolistic nature of the market, Korean producers would also be affected by the U.S. policy change. Korean profits would also increase. If the Korean domestic market is not too large relative to the amount of exports to the United States, Korean welfare would actually increase with the U.S. policy change. The effect of an "us-like-them" harmonization has the (presumably unintended) effect of benefiting the United States' trading partner while harming U.S. interests. It is worth remembering, though, that U.S. producers *are* helped by this harmonization, and producer interests often appear to dominate consumer interests in the political arena in which trade policy is formed.

Next consider the alternative approach to harmonization of competition policies—a "them-like-us" approach. This would entail either regulating Korean TV manufacturers to price more procompetitively or, if the industry was quite concentrated, breaking up the large firms. In this case, the market-clearing price falls, and Korean profits fall while consumer surplus there rises. The net effect on Korean welfare will depend on how large the export market was relative to the domestic market. If the export market was very large, the lost profits earned from American consumers would not make up for the increased Korean consumer surplus, and Korean welfare would fall. On the other hand, if the export market was not too large, the net effect would be a welfare increase for Korea.

In the United States, as the price of TVs falls because of strict Korean competition policy, imports rise. U.S. producers are hurt, but consumers gain even more and the gains from trade are now *higher*. The net effect is that both the United States and Korea might benefit from such a harmonization. That such a policy shift might not actually take place bears testament to the political clout of firms, as firms in both countries are harmed by the harmonization.

There are a few lessons from this simple example of harmonization. First, producer interests coincide. What is good for producers in one country proves to be beneficial to producers in the other country. This observation would imply that producers might agree on harmonization. Second, consumer interests also coincide. As is often the case, producer and consumer interests, while coincident across countries, differ within countries for both the harmonization schemes discussed. Third, when considering which competition policy to adopt from a global viewpoint, the intuition imparted by an intermediate microeconomics course provides a decent guide: harmonize to the policy that is less distorting. In this case, adopt strict competition standards, not lax ones. Put another way, two wrongs, in this case, do not make a right.

It remains to be seen whether these lessons are robust to some simple modifications of the assumptions. I next discuss some such modifications.

Suppose the United States had a lax competition policy, but Korea a strict policy. Then, in the television industry, Korean imports would act as market discipline to U.S. firms, preventing them from exerting much market power. (Again, recall Korea is the low-cost producer of TVs in this example.) This is a case in which a lax competition policy does not make much difference, since free trade prevents U.S. firms from exploiting the lax policy. If harmonization led the U.S. to adopt a stringent policy, there would be very little effect. If harmonization led Korea to adopt the lax U.S. competition policy, we would be back in the duopolistic situation discussed previously. Korean and U.S. firm profits increase as prices rise, Korea is made better off so long as its domestic market is small relative to exports, and U.S. welfare falls. Again, firms agree on harmonization, as do consumers, with the former benefiting and the latter suffering. From a global welfare perspective, one would again opt for a policy that led to harmonization toward the more strict competition policy.

8.5.2   The Case of Different Competition Policies for Export Markets

Here, I consider the case of an exporting country that must set competition policy. As illustrated by the discussion of actual policies in section 8.2, some countries have explicitly separate policies for domestic and export markets. The economic welfare implications of issues that arise in this context are considered in this subsection. The situation I consider is one in which the exporting home country sells to a foreign country that does not produce the exported good itself. So that competition policy might play a role, the market under consideration, lacking regulation, is imperfectly competitive. Again to fix ideas, consider the hypothetical example of the home country (Canada) selling lumber to the foreign country (Japan). What are the economic effects of the policy options facing Canada?

Simplifying a complex world, Canada faces the following four options:

1. Regulate the domestic firm to price "competitively" at home while allowing it to operate unfettered abroad.

2. Enforce competition both at home and abroad.

3. Allow the industry to be completely unregulated both at home and abroad.

4. Enforce a single price, but beyond that, do not regulate.

In terms of harmonization, options 2 and 4 might be considered harmonized while 1 and 3 are not.

Figures 2a and 2b present a diagrammatic analysis of these options for the simplified case of a home monopolist. Most of the results, though, are robust to the case of multiple home oligopolistic firms, although with multiple home firms, the home government will sometimes want to discourage "wasteful" competition abroad. This issue obviously does not arise with a monopolist. Another simplification in Figures 2a and 2b is the assumption of constant marginal costs. This assumption allows one to consider the markets independently, for with upward-sloping marginal costs, output decisions in one market affect costs (and prices) in the other market. This is an important simplification. First consider option 1: regulation at home and not abroad. This is given at the top of Figure 2a. In the home market, price is set equal to marginal cost, while in the foreign market, the home firm exercises its market power and reduces exports

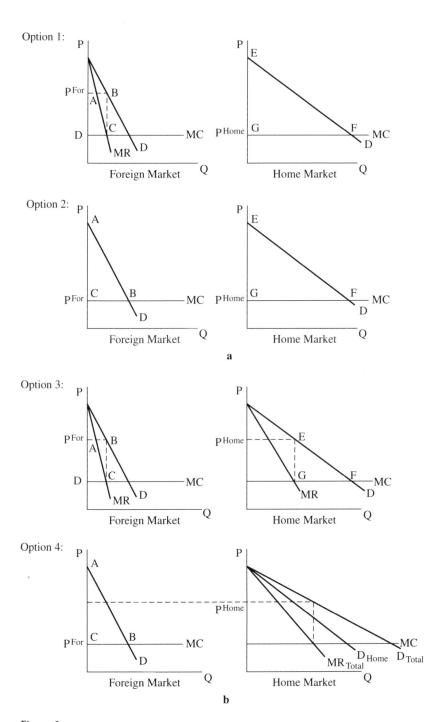

Figure 2

while raising the price of those exports. Home welfare is given by consumer surplus *EFG* and profits from the export market *ABCD*. As this is the policy adopted by many countries, consider it the benchmark case for this analysis.

If instead the home country enforces competition policy at home *and* abroad, the situation is given by the bottom two panels in Figure 2a. Here, price is the same at home and abroad. Global welfare is higher, as the foreign consumer surplus is now *ABC*, but the home country is worse off, as it has forfeited the profits it was previously earning. Hence, while this option is in the two countries' additive best interest, the home country is worse off but by less than the foreign country gains. Why, then, do some countries enforce competition policy at home and abroad when the latter is not in their own clear interest? There are at least two possibilities, both relating the oversimplification of the diagrammatic examples. First, countries do not set a competition policy for just one market and only one time. Rather, these policies are set in a repeated fashion and in multiple markets. Hence, there may be gains from policy coordination. (That is, if you enforce competition policy for exports to my country, I will do so for firms exporting to your country. Or, if you are "nice" to me this year, I will respond in kind next year.) Furthermore, it may be difficult to segment markets effectively. That is, it may be difficult to allow collusion abroad but not at home. If the home country government has very good information on the costs of a firm or firms, this problem is not very large. Often, though, the government does not know a firm's marginal costs. (Often the firm does not know the firm's marginal costs.) Also, it may not be in the firm's interest to truthfully reveal its costs. With imperfect information, regulation is imperfect, and collusion in the foreign market may facilitate collusion at home.

Under option 3—no competition policy enforced at home *or* abroad—the home firm acts like a price-discriminating monopolist and charges the price that maximizes its profits in each market. Unless the home and foreign demands have the same elasticity, the price charged will differ across markets with the higher being charged in the market where demand is more inelastic. The firm earns profits *ABCD* in the foreign country as in option 1, but it now earns profits at home also. Consumers in the home country pay a higher price than in option 1, and relative to that benchmark, the home country is worse off by *EFG*, the deadweight loss due to monopoly at home.

The final option considers harmonization of a different sort. Here the home-country firm is forced to charge the same price in both markets, but it is not hindered by competition policy in setting that uniform price. This might be the case if the foreign country had an appropriately defined antidumping law or if the home country prohibited price discrimination. The former seems much more likely. This option is diagrammed at the bottom of Figure 2b. Total demand is the sum of each country's individual demands and is given in the right panel. The marginal revenue perceived by the firm corresponding to this demand schedule is given in this panel by MR_{Total}. The price, in both markets, is given by P. This price will necessarily lie between the two prices that would obtain with price discrimination (option 3). Whether this policy results in a higher or lower domestic price, relative to price discrimination, depends on demand elasticities and is in general indeterminate. Home-country welfare with this policy option may be lower than allowing the home firm to price discriminate. Again, it depends on relative demand elasticities. If foreign demand is more inelastic relative to home demand, then the profits forgone by forcing the firm to harmonize to one price will be larger. If, on the other hand, domestic demand is more inelastic, forcing harmonization could help the home country as the home market outcome moves closer to the welfare-maximizing competitive outcome. From the firm's perspective, removing the option to price discriminate will never, in this setup, increase profits. Hence, firms are likely to oppose this option.

The case for harmonization, either with option 2 or option 4, is not a strong one in this simple world. With option 2, the home country forgoes the pure profits it could have earned abroad, while with option 4 welfare might rise or might fall, but it will not exceed the home welfare under option 1. Option 2, though, has the beneficial property that if all countries adopted this policy in all markets, global welfare would rise even though some individual players in this economy might be worse off.

8.5.3   Caveats

These examples are intentionally very simple. There are plenty of ways in which one might make the models more realistic and, at the same time, more complex. Almost surely, the policy implications will change with these alterations. For this reason, it is important to advertise truthfully the many ways one could amend the examples presented here. One of the most important aspects of reality ignored is the possibility of increasing returns to scale. By imposing constant returns to scale, the examples did not allow consideration of the efficiency effects of harmonization. Still, with increasing returns to scale, efficiency effects will matter to the harmonization debate much as they are important in the debate about how to set competition policy. Also, the examples were constructed around linear demand schedules and constant marginal costs. Altering the former can change results, especially in oligopoly models, while altering the latter will introduce a potentially important linkage between the home and foreign markets. Finally, the models did not consider the more reasonable alternative of oligopoly. When one considers oligopoly models, past experience suggests that the particular equilibrium outcome is quite sensitive to the mode of market conduct (i.e., Cournot versus Bertrand, as in the merger literature discussed in section 8.4.2) and whether the product is homogeneous or differentiated. The issues of increasing returns to scale and linearity of demands will also matter in oligopoly models. All of these cases suggest that the specific cases discussed here should be viewed as informative examples, but no more.

8.6   Summary and Conclusions

This chapter has provided a brief international survey of countries' competition policies. It also discussed several issues that arise when competition policy is set in a world in which international trade takes place. It contends that in a global economy, what were once purely domestic policy realms have international implications. Just as domestic tax policy can play an important role in international trade patterns, competition policy also has important international implications. Some issues only arise in an international context. For example, should governments enforce competition policy in export markets? Other issues have traditionally arisen in a domestic context but also have implications for international trade. For example, does a strict competition policy that is sound economic policy in a closed economy still make for good policy when a country's trading partners have a very lax competition policy? There are few general issues, but one message is clear. There are important linkages between competition policy and international trade, and ignoring one or the other may result in misguided policy. There are many unanswered questions, and it is hoped that this chapter will motivate others to begin to examine these important linkages.

NOTES

This chapter was prepared for the Fairness Claims and Gains from Trade project. I am grateful to Daniel Laytin for background research assistance and W. James Adams and Ennio Stachetti for helpful discussions. I am grateful to Jagdish Bhagwati for getting me to think about the issues covered in this chapter and suggesting the general topic.

1. For expositional ease, I will refer to what in the United States is commonly called antitrust policy as competition policy.

2. See Boner and Krueger (1991), p. 13.

3. See Feketekuty (1993), p. 5.

4. This section relies heavily on background work by Daniel Laytin in "National antitrust laws" (mimeo). University of Michigan. (1993). I am grateful for his superb research assistance.

5. See Fook-Lun Leung (1991) for details.

6. See Von Kalinowski (1987) for details.

7. See Boner and Krueger (1991) for a categorization of these loopholes and exemptions.

8. For a more detailed discussion, also see Gifford and Matshusita (Chapter 6 in Volume 2 of this work).

9. See Matsushita and Schoenbaum (1989) for details.

10. A more detailed explanation of these exceptions is found in Boner and Krueger (1991).

11. See Boner and Krueger (1991), p. 96.

12. See Matsushita and Schoenbaum (1989), beginning p. 142, for a discussion of how foreign firms are treated under Japan's competition laws.

13. See Grant for details.

14. See Boner and Krueger (1991), pp. 39–42, for details.

15. See Grant (1989), pp. 152–153, for a discussion of the Canadian law.

16. See Von Kalinowski (1987) and Grant (1989) for a summary of U.S. competition policy.

17. See Larson (1970) and Dick (1990) for economic analyses of the Webb-Pomerene Act.

18. See "Testing the Imports-as-Market-Discipline Hypothesis" by Levinsohn (1993).

19. See Neale and Goyder (1982) for a discussion of U.S. law and price discrimination.

20. Cited in Feketekuty (1993).

21. The countries, policies, and goods in this example are not intended to reflect reality. They are chosen only to help with exposition.

REFERENCES

Boner, Roger, and Reinald Krueger. 1991. "The basics of antitrust policy." World Bank Technical Paper Number 160. Washington, DC: World Bank.

Deneckere, Raymond, and Carl Davidson. 1985. "Incentives to form coalitions with Bertrand competition." Rand Journal of Economics, 16:473–486.

Dick, Andrew. 1991. "Are export cartels efficiency enhancing or monopoly promoting?" UCLA Working Paper No. 610.2.

Feketekuty, Geza. 1993. "Reflections on the interactions between trade policy and competition policy" (mimeo). OECD Trade Committee.

Fook-Lun Leung, Frankie. 1991. "Hong Kong." In *Competition laws of the Pacific Rim countries*, ed. Julian Von Kalinowski. New York: Bender.

Grant, Wyn. 1989. *Government and industry: A comparative analysis of the U.S., Canada, and the UK.* Hampshire: Elger.

Larson, David. 1970. "An economic analysis of the Webb-Pomerene Act." *Journal of Law and Economics*, 13:461–500.

Laytin, Daniel. 1993. "National antitrust laws" (mimeo). University of Michigan.

Levinsohn, James. 1993. "Testing the imports-as-market-discipline hypothesis." *Journal of International Economics*, 35, 1–22.

Matsushita, Mitsuo, and T. Schoenbaum. 1989. *Japanese international trade and investment law.* Tokyo: University of Tokyo Press.

Neale, A. D., and D. G. Goyder. 1982. *The antitrust laws of the U.S.A.* Cambridge: Cambridge University Press.

Salant, Stephen, S. Switzer, and R. Reynolds. 1983. "Losses from horizontal mergers: The effects of an exogenous change in industry structure on Cournot Nash equilibrium." *Quarterly Journal of Economics*, 97:185–199.

U.S. Department of Justice. 1992. Merger Guidelines, 1992 version.

Von Kalinowski, Julian. 1987. *Overview: World competition law.* New York: Matthew Bender.

9

Dumping: In Theory, in Policy, and in Practice

Richard H. Clarida

Dumping [is] a predatory pricing practice condemned under U.S. law.
U.S. Trade Representative Clayton Yeutter (1987) as quoted in Bovard (1991),
p. 156

9.1 Introduction, Overview, and Executive Summary

This chapter surveys and evaluates the policies that have been used in the United States to bring sanctions against dumping in light of the modern economic theory of dumping. Until 1974, U.S. statutes defined dumping as an act of international price discrimination: the export of goods to the United States at a price that falls below the price charged in the home market.[1] With the Trade Reform Act of 1974, the definition of dumping was expanded to include the export of goods to the United States at a price that falls below "constructed value"—the average cost of production in the home country, plus imputed administrative overhead, plus a "reasonable" profit. In addition, the 1974 act mandated that, to the extent that some portion of home-country sales are at prices that fall below constructed value, those sales must be excluded in calculating the home-country price that is used as the basis for determinations of "sales at less than fair value."

There are two basic antidumping laws in the Unites States.[2] The first U.S. statute to explicitly prohibit dumping was the Revenue Act of 1916, sometimes referred to as the Antidumping Duty Act of 1916. The 1916 Antidumping Duty Act—still on the books—makes it a crime for a foreign producer or a group of foreign producers to conspire to engage in systematic dumping with the intent to monopolize trade and commerce in a particular industry or to destroy or materially injure a U.S. industry. The 1916 act punishes a foreign producer found guilty of dumping—the sale of goods in the United States at a price substantially less than the home market value or wholesale price of such goods—with a fine and imprisonment for up to one year. Moreover, U.S. firms that are injured by any violation of the 1916 act may bring a civil suit in U.S. district court to recover treble damages and reasonable attorney's fees.

The 1916 act has only very rarely been employed as a basis for a criminal or civil prosecution of dumping. Indeed, "for more than half a century [following the passage of the 1916 Antidumping Duty Act] there was not a single reported government prosecution under the Act, and only one civil action … was reported under the law" (Victor, 1983, p. 340). Over the past 20 years, several cases have been brought under the 1916 act, most famously *Zenith v. Matsushita*, which was decided by the U.S. Supreme Court in favor of the defendants, seven major Japanese television producers, in 1986. Very few, if any, of the other cases brought under the 1916 act have culminated in verdicts favorable to the plaintiffs. Indeed, according to Victor (1983), "no indication of a successful government prosecution under the 1916 Act, or of a civil judgement rendered thereunder, can be found" (p. 346).

The Antidumping Act, enacted in 1921, is the second basic antidumping law in the United States. It was passed in response to the realization that dumping was difficult to prove under the 1916 act because of that act's requirement that an intent to monopolize or injure a U.S. industry be established. The 1921 act provides administrative relief from sales at less than fair value that injure a domestic industry. In contrast to the 1916 act, the Antidumping Act of 1921 is not a criminal statute, nor does it provide for a private cause of action. Instead, a finding of dumping carries with it the sanction of a duty imposed on the imported merchandise equal to the difference between the U.S. price and the "fair value" of the imports as determined by the department charged by Congress with administering the 1921 act.

Applebaum (1974) provides an illuminating interpretation of the legislative history of the two basic antidumping laws. He argues:

It does seem relatively clear and uncontroverted that the 1916 Act was based upon antitrust considerations, as reflected in its concern for destruction of a U.S. industry. The basis of the more important 1921 Act, however, is not at all clear. Scholars and advocates, as well as members of the [International Trade] Commission, have been able to find aspects of the legislative history going both ways. There are, for example, references in the legislative history to the Sherman Act and to the need to protect competitors from unfair trade practices. However, there are also suggestions that the injury requirement was inserted to guard against frivolous complaints or over-zealous enforcement, rather than to reflect antitrust considerations. Two factors support this view. First, the injury requirement was added in the senate to a house-passed version of the bill which contained no such requirement. Second, the U.S. law was in large part patterned after the then existing Canadian dumping law, which required no showing of injury. (Applebaum, 1974, pp. 592–593)

Historically, the U.S. Treasury administered the antidumping laws as set forth originally in the Antidumping Act of 1921 and as amended in successor statutes (The Tariff Act of 1930 and The Trade Reform Act of 1974).[3] This provision was changed by the Trade Agreements Act of 1979. In exchange for passing the 1979 act and approving the Tokyo Round trade accords, Congress "pressured the president into taking the responsibility for the administration of the antidumping and countervailing duty laws away from the Treasury Department ... [and shifting] responsibility for these matters to the Department of Commerce" (Baldwin and Moore, 1991, pp. 257–258).

Following these changes in the U.S. trade laws, the 1980s witnessed an explosion in the number of dumping cases brought by U.S. producers against foreign exporters. According to the data compiled by Baldwin and Steagall (1993), 494 dumping investigations were initiated in the eleven years 1980–1990, an average of 45 per year. One hundred sixty of these investigations were initiated during the U.S. recession years 1980, 1981, 1982, and 1990. This represents an average of 40 investigations per recession year, actually fewer investigations per year of recession than were initiated during an average year of the 1980s.

A second noteworthy fact about the dumping cases initiated since 1979 is that a great number of formal dumping complaints, and ultimate findings, have been based not on allegations of international price discrimination—the traditional definition of dumping—but rather on allegations of pricing below the constructed value or average cost of production.[4] According to results presented in Murray (1991), more than 30 percent of the dumping cases investigated by the Department of Commerce between 1979 and 1986 were decided on the basis of a constructed-value calculation and not on the basis of international price discrimination. Murray (1991) also finds that, of all the cases that were decided on the basis of a constructed-value calculation, a full *89 percent* resulted in a finding of dumping. Of the 56 percent of cases that were decided on an international-price-discrimination calculation, 82 percent resulted in a finding of dumping. Interestingly, of the remaining 14 percent of the cases that were decided on the basis of prices charged in a third market, only 59 percent resulted in a finding of dumping. Horlick (1989), using a somewhat different sample and broader definition, reports that 60 percent of all dumping cases decided since 1980 have been based, at least in part, on a constructed-value calculation of selling below average cost. Kaplan, Kamarck, and Parker (1988) estimate that 66 percent, a full two-thirds, of dumping cases decided in recent years have been based, at least in part, on a constructed-value calculation.

Regardless of whether the constructed-value basis for the determination of dumping is a factor in 30 percent or 66 percent of all investigations, the apparent prevalence since 1979 of the production-cost standard for dumping is truly striking in light of statutes that guide a Commerce Department dumping investigation. For, according to Cass and Narkin (1991):

Under U.S. law ... the Commerce Department is directed to rely on the foreign market value of the imported merchandise, as reflected in the ... [home country] prices. However, when the merchandise in question is not sold in sufficient quantities in the home market, Commerce is directed to establish fair market value by looking at the prices ... [charged] in third-country markets by the exporting country, or by calculating the constructed value of the merchandise.... In the ordinary case, when the home market is too small (or nonexistent), Commerce is expected to use data on sales to third countries ... if such data are available; constructed value as the measure of fair market value is, in theory at least, a last resort.... Formerly, this was made explicit in the statute. Now Congress's intent on this issue is evident only from a reading of the legislative history. (Cass and Narkin, 1991, pp. 212–213)

In light of this stated policy that the constructed-value method of determining dumping is to be used only as "a last resort," it will be recalled that the Commerce Department ignores all home-market sales that are made at less than constructed value. It is not an exaggeration to assert that the use of the cost-of-production standard for dumping has "become the centerpiece of U.S. antidumping law and policy without any serious consideration being given to the phenomenon" (Horlick, 1989, p. 133).

The plan of the chapter is as follows. Section 9.2 provides an overview of Commerce Department dumping findings for finished-manufactures imports over the years 1979–1990—that is, since the last major change in the U.S. dumping laws, the Trade Agreements Act of 1979. A look at the data since the 1979 transfer of dumping determinations to the Commerce Department (which incorporated the 1974 addition by Congress of the constructed-value, cost-of-production standard for dumping) reveals that the current reality of U.S. antidumping administration is at variance with the widely held—and at one time no doubt accurate—view that dumping is primarily an act of international price discrimination by producers in "heavy" basic industries (such as steel and chemicals) that is especially prevalent during downturns in the trade cycle (Viner, 1923). We show the facts are consistent with the views of Ethier (1982), Bhagwati (1986), and other scholars that (1) for a wide variety of finished manufactured products, the antidumping statutes have become the battleground for the "new protectionism"; (2) the antidumping statutes are regularly employed by U.S. manufacturers seeking relief from imports that are not found to be priced below home-country prices but, rather, that are found to be priced below the Commerce Department's estimate of average cost; and (3) if anything, dumping cases for finished manufactures since 1979 have been more numerous during years of economic expansion than during years of recession.

Section 9.3 of the chapter surveys methodology and findings of six of the leading theoretical contributions to the international trade literature on dumping that have appeared since 1980. Three of these papers, by Brander and Krugman (1983), Staiger and Wolak (1991), and Hartigan (1994) present models of dumping as international price discrimination between segmented markets. The other three papers, by Ethier (1982), Gruenspecht (1988), and Clarida (1993) present models of dumping as selling below the cost of production in a world in which the law of one price holds. In five of these six papers, market structure is exogenous—no firm takes into account that its actions may influence the number of its competitors. This statement is true of the oligopolistic models of Brander and Krugman (1981), Staiger and Wolak (1991), and Gruenspecht (1988), and it is also true of the competitive models of Ethier (1982) and Clarida (1993). While these papers have a great deal to say about dumping, they—and the bulk of the theoretical trade literature on dumping—have nothing to say about the phenomenon of "predatory" dumping. By "predatory dumping," we refer to actions that would, under the Supreme Court's 1986 ruling in *Zenith v. Matsushita*, be in violation of the Antidumping Duty Act of 1916. That is, predatory dumping is an act of setting prices in the home market by a foreign rival that drives home firms out of business, leaving all of the home market to the foreign rival and allowing the rival to recoup its losses, from the monopoly profits that will be earned after the home firms have exited, and thus injure competition—not just competitors.

Drawing upon the theoretical industrial organization literature on predatory pricing, Hartigan (1994) presents one of the very few examples in the theoretical trade literature—indeed the only one I can find—of truly predatory dumping. In Hartigan's paper, dumping is modeled as the outcome of a rivalry between an incumbent foreign "predator" and a home-market "prey" producer in which the foreign "predator" takes into account the entry and exit decision of the "prey," and thus chooses whether or not the market structure will be duopolistic or monopolistic in the future. If the predator foreign firm chooses to price so as to drive the home firm out of business, profits will be low initially but will be high in the future when the predator has the home market to himself. As we shall see, in Hartigan's model, this strategy may not be possible, and if it is possible, it may not be optimal. When it is both possible and optimal, the effects of antidumping policies on welfare and industry structure can be evaluated, yielding interesting insights.

Section 9.4 examines the current practice of implementing the antidumping statutes, taking into account whether or not a lack of access to the dumper's own market by U.S. firms is a factor for inferring a predatory intent to monopolize a U.S. industry and thus ultimately to injure competition. We argue that, since in the vast majority of dumping cases, those brought under the Antidumping Act of 1921, it is not necessary that predatory intent or the likely success of a predatory strategy be established, it is not surprising that the administration of the 1921 act by the Commerce Department and the International Trade Commission does not require, nor does it typically rely upon, evidence of or investigation into whether or not a lack of access by a U.S. firm to the alleged dumper's home market has made sales at less than fair value possible (Murray, 1991, p. 30). Indeed, if anything, the chain of reasoning employed in dumping investigations is more typically just the reverse: based upon rather mechanical and conceptually flawed accounting studies that use imperfect and often misleading data on prices and costs, the Commerce Department first determines that goods are exported to the United States at "less than fair value" and then, based upon such a finding, bureaucrats, domestic producers, and politicians merely *infer* that foreign exporters must be engaging in predatory pricing (Palmeter, 1991, pp. 65–66).

In section 9.5, we evaluate this inference and find it to be without any substantial basis in either economics or law. As a matter of economics, dumping—defined either as international price discrimination or pricing below cost by the Antidumping Act of 1921 and its successor statutes the Trade Reform Act of 1974 and the Trade Agreements Act of 1979—is easily understood within the context of a variety of modern theoretical models (Brander and Krugman, 1983; Ethier, 1982; Gruenspecht, 1988; Staiger and Wolak, 1991; Clarida, 1993) in which neither predation nor predatory intent plays any role by assumption. Of course, it is possible that foreign firms, as in the model of Hartigan (1994), do dump as part of a long-term predation strategy aimed at eliminating competitors in the United States. If so, a U.S. firm can petition the Department of Commerce and the International Trade Commission to investigate the allegation of dumping and to impose dumping duties if dumping is found. The point is that a finding of dumping consistent with the Antidumping Act of 1921 and its successor statutes conveys no information about the presence or absence of predatory behavior on the part of the dumping firms. Moreover, the theoretical models imply that the absence of predatory behavior on the part of a firm that exports to the United States at a price that is less than the Commerce Department's definition of fair value is perfectly consistent with both (1) international price discrimination by oligopolistic rivals across segmented national markets, as in Brander and Krugman (1983) and Weinstein (1992), and (2) sales at less than average cost in an industry in which the law of one price holds, as in the competitive models of Ethier (1982) and Clarida (1993) and the duopolistic model of forward pricing by Gruenspecht (1988). Thus the basis upon which the Commerce Department determines that sales at less than fair value have occurred—either international price discrimination or sales at less than constructed value—is not informative about the presence or absence of predatory dumping.

Section 9.6 provides some concluding thoughts on how the administration of the antidumping laws in the United States might be revised. We conclude that the antidumping laws have indeed become the battleground of the new protectionism, inflicting a not insubstantial cost on U.S. consumers and downstream producers. Moreover, it is difficult to make either an economic or an equity case in favor of the continuation of the current antidumping laws as administered by the Commerce Department and the International Trade Commission. If the Commerce Department is put out of the business of imposing dumping duties, predation by foreign firms selling in the United States can be deterred by either civil or criminal action brought under the 1916 Antidumping Duty Act. Concerns that U.S. industries will be destroyed by a flood of dumped imports can be addressed by providing relief under the Section 201 Escape Clause.

9.2   The Dumping of Finished Manufactures: A Look at the Data

Historically, a great number of dumping cases have been brought by the steel, chemical, cement, and other raw materials industries (Wares, 1977). These are industries in which dumping "is particularly likely [when] there is surplus capacity in large plants [brought about by a] cyclical reduction in demand" (Lloyd, 1977). A great deal of policy discussion has focused on cyclical dumping. Indeed Viner conjectured that "it is probable that [trade cycle dumping] is the most prevalent form of dumping" (Viner, 1923).

In this section of the chapter, we provide an overview of Commerce Department dumping findings for finished-manufactures imports over the years 1979–1990, that is, since the last major change in the U.S. dumping laws, the Trade Agreements Act of 1979. A look at the dumping cases involving finished manufactures since 1979 reveals that the current reality of U.S. antidumping administration is at variance with the widely held— and at one time no doubt accurate—view that dumping is primarily an act of international price discrimination by producers in "heavy" basic industries that is especially prevalent during downturns in the trade cycle. In fact, we shall argue that the facts are consistent with the views of Ethier (1982), Bhagwati (1986), and other scholars that (1) the antidumping statutes have become the battleground for the "new protectionism" for a wide variety of finished manufactured products and not just steel, chemicals, and the products of other heavy industries; (2) the antidumping statutes are regularly employed by U.S. manufacturers seeking relief from imports that are not found to be priced below home country prices but, rather, that are found to be priced below the Commerce Department's estimate of average cost; and (3) dumping cases for finished manufactures since 1979 have, if anything, been more numerous during years of economic expansion than during years of recession.

9.2.1 Data Sources and Methods

Data covering the years 1979–1990 were collected from issues of the *Federal Register* on all dumping cases in which the Department of Commerce issued a preliminary determination of the dumping of finished manufactures.[5] The Department of Commerce issues a preliminary determination of dumping only after a positive preliminary determination of injury has been issued by the International Trade Commission. If the ITC issues a negative preliminary determination of injury, the investigation is terminated without a Commerce determination of dumping. If both the International Trade Commission and the Commerce Department reach positive preliminary determinations, imports of the dumped product are assessed, *from the date of the Commerce Department's preliminary determination*, a tariff in the amount of the dumping margin reported by the Commerce Department in its preliminary determination. According to Murray (1991):

It is no small matter to suspend liquidation on the basis of the preliminary investigation. When liquidation is suspended, imports are cleared through customs ... subject to the posting of a bond or otherwise guaranteeing that tariffs and ... antidumping duties will be paid upon assessment.... [I]mporters are at risk for the payment of antidumping duties beginning on the date of a positive preliminary determination by the DOC and continuing throughout the period of the investigation, which can last an additional six to nine months. As a consequence, it is common for importers to begin shifting orders from the alleged unfair trading partners to domestic and other foreign suppliers of competing goods. Thus, [following a preliminary determination] alleged dumpers will lose sales even if they are subsequently judged to be innocent of the allegation. (Murray, 1991, pp. 31–32)

The choice of collecting data on Commerce Department preliminary dumping determinations was based on the much more extensive and detailed information provided in the preliminary determination reports as compared with the terse summary statements often provided with reports on the final determinations. If our interest was in studying the dumping margins themselves, our use of the margins reported in the preliminary determinations could be misleading. However, we are interested not in the dumping margins, but rather in the basis employed by the Commerce Department to reach each determination. Typically, the Commerce Department report on a final determination of dumping does not discuss in sufficient detail the basis for the determination, but instead refers to the preliminary determination for such details.

9.2.2   A Look at the Data

Table 1 (on p. 366) presents the data set that will be investigated throughout the remainder of this section of the chapter. The first column of the table contains the calendar year during which dumping is alleged to have taken place, the period of investigation. Many investigations carry over two calender years. In such instances, the year chosen was the calender year in which the investigation ended. As is traditional in the literature, we shall define one Department of Commerce dumping investigation to consist of a single product from a single country, recognizing that, in general, a single product from a single country will be produced by more than a single firm. The second and third columns present the country-product pairs that define each dumping determination. As can be seen from the final row of Table 1, during our 12-year sample 1979–1990, a total of 119 determinations of dumping of finished manufactures were issued by the Commerce Department. This works out to just under 10 determinations

Table 1
Department of Commerce Dumping Determinations, Finished Manufactures, 1979–1990

			Basis of Investigation			
Year	Country	Product	Home Sales	Constructed Value	Third-Country Sales	Surrogate Sales
1979	Japan	Motors	h	c	t	
1979	Japan	Ovens	h			
1979	Japan	Typewriters	h			
1981	Taiwan	Batteries	h		t	
1981	Hungary	Brakes			t	
1981	Taiwan	Fireplaces		c		
1981	Japan	Microwave amplifers		c		
1981	Germany	Valves	h			
1982	Taiwan	Bicycles	h		t	
1982	China	Cloth				s
1982	Japan	Fabric	h			
1982	Korea	Fabric	h	c		
1982	Japan	Pagers			t	
1982	Sweden	Staples	h			
1982	Taiwan	Tires	h		t	
1982	China	Towels		c		
1983	Germany	Bearings			t	
1983	Japan	Bearings			t	
1983	Italy	Bearings			t	
1983	Italy	Chassis			t	
1983	Taiwan	Film	h		t	
1983	Italy	Pads	h	c		
1983	Korea	Tires	h			
1983	Korea	TVs	h	c	t	
1984	Argentina	Barbed wire		c		
1984	Poland	Barded wire				s
1984	Brazil	Barded wire		c		
1984	Canada	Boxes	h			
1984	Japan	Cellular telephone receivers		c		
1984	Japan	Cellular telephones	h	c	t	
1984	Korea	Pianos	h			
1984	Italy	Valves			t	
1985	Korea	Albums		c	t	
1985	Hong Kong	Albums		c	t	

Table 1 (continued)

Year	Country	Product	Home Sales	Constructed Value	Third-Country Sales	Surrogate Sales
1985	China	Brushes				s
1985	Mexico	Cookware	h			
1985	Spain	Cookware	h			
1985	China	Cookware				s
1985	Taiwan	Cookware	h	c	t	
1985	New Zealand	Copper wire	h			
1985	South Africa	Copper wire	h	c		
1985	Japan	DRAMs	h	c		
1985	Japan	DRAMs	h	c		
1985	Japan	EPROMs	h	c		
1985	Korea	Oil platforms		c		
1985	Japan	Oil platforms		c		
1985	Taiwan	Pipefittings	h	c	t	
1985	Korea	Pipefittings	h			
1985	Brazil	Pipefittings	h			
1985	Thailand	Pipefittings	h			
1985	Japan	Pipefittings	h			
1986	ElSalvador	Awnings	h			
1986	Hong Kong	Bearings			t	
1986	Japan	Bearings	h	c		
1986	China	Bearings		c		
1986	Italy	Bearings			t	
1986	Hungary	Bearings		c		s
1986	Yugoslavia	Bearings		c		
1986	Romania	Bearings		c		s
1986	China	Candles				s
1986	Japan	DRAMs	h	c		
1986	Japan	Fabric	h			
1986	Brazil	Filters			t	
1986	Poland	Mirrors	h			
1986	Germany	Mirrors	h	c		
1986	Britain	Mirrors	h			
1986	Italy	Mirrors		c		
1986	Japan	Mirrors	h			
1986	Belgium	Mirrors			t	
1986	Korea	TV tubes	h			
1986	Japan	TV tubes	h		t	

Table 1 (continued)

			Basis of Investigation			
Year	Country	Product	Home Sales	Constructed Value	Third-Country Sales	Surrogate Sales
1986	Canada	TV tubes	h		t	
1986	Singapore	TV tubes	h		t	
1987	Japan	Cylinders	h			
1987	Japan	Forklifts		c		
1987	Japan	Forklifts	h			
1988	Japan	All-terrain vehicles			t	
1988	Taiwan	Batteries	h		t	
1988	Thailand	Bearings		c		
1988	Italy	Bearings	h	c	t	
1988	Germany	Bearings	h			
1988	Romania	Bearings		c		
1988	Japan	Bearings	h	c		
1988	Britain	Bearings	h			
1988	Sweden	Bearings	h		t	
1988	Singapore	Bearings	h			
1988	France	Bearings	h			
1988	Italy	Belts	h			
1988	Japan	Belts	h			
1988	Britain	Belts	h			
1988	Taiwan	Belts	h			
1988	Germany	Belts	h			
1988	Singapore	Belts			t	
1988	Israel	Belts	h			
1988	Korea	Belts	h			
1988	Japan	Digital reading devices	h			
1988	Japan	Disks	h			
1988	China	Headware	h			s
1988	Korea	Telephone systems	h	c	t	
1988	Japan	Telephone systems	h			
1988	Taiwan	Telephone systems			t	
1988	Canada	Thermostatically controlled appliance plugs	h			

Table 1 (continued)

			Basis of Investigation			
Year	Country	Product	Home Sales	Constructed Value	Third-Country Sales	Surrogate Sales
1988	Taiwan	Thermostatically controlled appliance plugs		c		
1988	Hong Kong	Thermostatically controlled appliance plugs	h			
1988	Japan	Thermostatically controlled appliance plugs		c		
1988	Malaysia	Thermostatically controlled appliance plugs		c		
1988	Taiwan	Uniforms	h			
1989	Japan	Drafting machines	h			
1989	Japan	Drafting machines	h			
1989	Canada	Limos	h			
1989	Taiwan	Locks	h	c	t	
1989	Japan	Mechanical presses	h	c		
1989	Korea	Sweaters		c		
1989	Taiwan	Sweaters	h	c	t	
1989	Hong Kong	Sweaters		c	t	
1990	Japan	Film	h			
1990	Korea	Film	h			
1990	China	Hand tools		c		
1990	Japan	Lighting installations	h			
Totals		119	76	44	35	8

Source: "Preliminary Determinations of Dumping Issued by the U.S. Department of Commerce," *Federal Register*, various issues, and author's calculations.

per year. The final four columns of the table present information on the basis employed by the Commerce Department to reach each dumping determination. As discussed earlier, if sufficient data on sales in the home market are available, the Commerce Department is required to use this information to determine whether or not the importer is selling the merchandise in the United States for less than the home sales price. However, in making this calculation, the Commerce Department ignores all home-market sales that are made at prices that are less than constructed value: the department's estimate of the variable cost of production plus an 18 percent markup (of which 10 percent is to represent general and administrative expenses and 8 percent is a "reasonable" profit margin). If home-market sales are insufficient, the department either compares the constructed value of the imports with the U.S. sales price or compares the sales price in a third country with the U.S. sales price.[6] The last column in Table 1 records those cases in which a surrogate market price is used to determine if a command economy such as China or Poland is dumping exports in the United States.

As can be seen in Table 1, in the typical dumping case, the Commerce Department employs more than one basis for its finding. Indeed, the most common dumping finding for finished manufactures employs all three of the relevant benchmarks, home-market sales, third-country sales, and constructed value.[7] How can this be? As mentioned previously, we follow the standard convention and define a single dumping investigation to consist of a single product from a single country, recognizing that, in general, a single product from a single country can be produced by many firms. In practice, the Commerce Department often applies different benchmarks to the exports from different companies of the same product from the same country. As shown in Table 1, 76 of the 119 dumping determinations (64 percent) relied at least in part on the benchmark of home-country sales, 44 (37 percent) relied at least in part on the constructed-value standard, and 35 (29 percent) relied at least in part on third-country sales. Notice that this finding implies that, notwithstanding the fact that the Commerce Department is directed by statute to select home-country sales as the "first-choice" basis for determining dumping, a full 36 percent of Commerce Department determinations of dumping finished manufactures do not rely on any information about the home-country sales price!

Over the 1979–1990 sample covered by this study, finished-manufactures imports from just 12 countries accounted for more than three-quarters of the dumping cases investigated by the Commerce Department. These countries were Japan; the Asian newly industrialized countries (NICs)—Taiwan, Korea, Singapore, Hong Kong, Malaysia, and Thailand; and the major industrial countries other than Japan—Germany, France, Italy, Britain, and Canada. Over the entire 1979–1990 sample, the Commerce Department issued 34 determinations on the dumping of finished-manufactures imports from Japan. The products that were alleged to have been dumped from Japan ranged from forklift trucks to fan belts, and included such high-tech products as DRAM computer chips and cellular telephones. Of the 34 determinations of dumping finished manufactures from Japan, 14 were based, at least in part, on the constructed-value benchmark. We also note that several investigations of imports from Japan of such products as paging devices and all-terrain vehicles relied exclusively on third-country sales as the basis for determining dumping.

Between 1979 and 1990, the Commerce Department issued a full 36 determinations on the dumping of finished-manufactures imports from the Asian NICs, two more determinations than were issued on the dumping of finished manufactures from Japan. The bulk of these cases, 28, investigated dumping that was alleged to have taken place since 1985. The range of products that were alleged to have been dumped from the Asian NICs exhibit at least as much variety as do those from Japan. This range of products includes photo albums from Hong Kong, color televisions from Korea, business telephone systems from Taiwan, ball bearings from Singapore and Thailand, and electrical appliance plugs from Malaysia. Of the 36 determinations of dumping finished manufactures from Japan, a full 16 were based, at least in part, on the constructed-value definition of dumping.

Consider now findings of dumping from the major industrial countries other than Japan. There are two striking facts evident in the data. First, notwithstanding the fact that imports from these "Atlantic Five" industrial countries have accounted for nearly 40 percent of total U.S. imports in recent years, only 21 dumping investigations, fewer than two determinations per year since 1979 and less than one-fifth of the 119 total, have been launched by the Commerce Department against finished manufactures imports from these countries. The second noteworthy fact is that it was actually rare for the Commerce Department to employ the constructed-value definition of dumping in its investigation of manufactures imports from Canada and Europe. In particular, in only four of these 21 investigations was the determination of dumping based, at least in part, on constructed value. We note however that in five of these 21 cases, the Commerce Department was forced to rely on a third-country sales price as a basis for comparison with the U.S. sales price because of insufficient sales in the home countries. It will be recalled that, by statute, in determining whether or not home sales are sufficient the Commerce Department must ignore home-market sales made at less than constructed value. One final aspect of the data on the dumping of finished manufactures imports from the major industrial countries other than Japan is worth noting: the bulk of these 21 cases, at least 15, involve relatively simple, low-tech manufactures such as ball bearings, mirrors, industrial belts, boxes, and electrical appliance plugs. Table 2 summarizes this discussion.

9.2.3   Summary

Data compiled from Commerce Department reports document 119 determinations of dumping finished-manufactures products over the 12 years 1979–1990, or slightly fewer than 10 determinations per year. Products that were found to be dumped ranged from the lowest of low-tech—electrical appliance plugs from Malaysia, photo albums from Hong Kong, mirrors from Italy—to the highest of high-tech—telephone switching systems from Taiwan, DRAM chips from Japan, color televisions from Korea. The dumping of finished manufactures was actually much more prevalent during the "boom years" between 1984 and 1989, years during which more than 15 cases per year were investigated, than during the recession years, in which fewer than six cases per year were investigated. The data show clearly that Commerce Department findings of pricing below average cost are not limited to investigations of the steel, chemical, and other such heavy industries, but instead are also quite common in investigations of finished-manufactures imports. In particular, we find that more than one in three determinations of dumping finished manufactures during these years were based at least in part on the constructed-value definition of dumping. Finally, perhaps the most surprising facts revealed by the data are the very large number of cases finding the dumping of finished manufacturers from the Asian NICs, over 30 percent of the total and 36 percent of all cases in which the constructed-value standard was employed, and the relatively small number of cases finding the dumping of finished manufacturers from Europe and Canada, only 17 percent of the total and just 9 percent of all cases in which the constructed-value standard was employed.

9.3   Dumping: In Theory

The early literature on dumping was concerned with explaining price discrimination between home and export markets that were segmented

Table 2
Dumping Determinations, Finished Manufactures

Bloc	Year 1979	1981	1982	1983	1984	1985	1986	1987	1988	1989	1990	Total
Major industrial	0	1	0	4	2	0	5	0	8	1	0	21
Japan	3	1	2	1	2	5	5	3	7	3	2	34
Asian NICs	0	2	3	3	1	7	3	0	12	4	1	36
Other	0	1	3	0	3	7	9	0	4	0	1	28
Total	3	5	8	8	8	19	22	3	31	8	4	119

Summary Statistics

	Major Industrial	Japan	Asian NICs	Other	Total
Dumping determinations	21	34	36	28	119
Of which, constructed value	4	14	16	10	44
Fraction of determinations	0.19	0.41	0.44	0.36	0.37

(because of tariffs or quotas) in favor of consumers in the export market.[8] If it is just assumed that market demand is more elastic in the export market, a price-discriminating monopolist will of course choose to charge a lower price in the export market and thus dump under the U.S. trade laws. It is not necessary to assume the dumping result, however. Suppose instead that the trade pattern is unilateral, and that market structure differs across the home and export markets. In particular, suppose that the export firm is a monopolist at home but faces local competition in the export market. Thus, even if the market elasticity of demand is the same in both markets, the elasticity of demand facing each firm will be greater in the importing country because more firms compete there. In such a world the sheltered, monopoly exporter will choose to charge a lower price in the export market and thus dump (Eichengreen and van der Ven, 1984).

Over the past 15 years, at least six theoretical approaches to modeling dumping have appeared in the economics literature: Brander and Krugman (1983), Ethier (1982), Gruenspecht (1988), Staiger and Wolak (1991), Clarida (1993), and Hartigan (1994). Three of these papers, by Brander and Krugman (1983), Staiger and Wolak (1991), and Hartigan (1994), present models of dumping as international price discrimination between segmented markets by oligopolistic rivals. The other three papers, by Ethier (1982), Gruenspecht (1988), and Clarida (1993), present models of dumping as selling below the cost of production in a world in which the law of one price holds. In Ethier (1982) and Clarida (1993), the market structure is competitive; in Gruenspecht, it is duopolistic.

In five of these six papers, no firm takes into account that its actions may influence the number of its competitors. In four of these five papers, the actual number of firms is exogenous. This is true of the oligopolistic models of Brander and Krugman (1983), Staiger and Wolak (1991), and Gruenspecht (1988), and it is also true of the competitive model of Ethier (1982). Obviously, none of these four models can be used to study or make predictions about predatory dumping. By "predatory dumping," we refer to actions that would, under the Supreme Court's 1986 ruling in Zenith v. Matsushita, be in violation of the Antidumping Duty Act of 1916. That is, predatory dumping is an act of setting prices in the home market by a foreign rival with the intent of driving home firms out of business, leaving all of the home market to the foreign rival and allowing the rival to recoup its losses—and thus injure competition, not just competitors—from the monopoly profits that will be earned after the home firms have exited. Clarida (1993) does present a competitive model (in the spirit of Jovanovic, 1982) of industry selection, international trade, and dumping in which the number of firms is endogenous, although no firm takes into account that its actions have any influence on either price or the number of its competitors. In Clarida's model, the dynamics of industry selection and the determination of comparative advantage appear to result in "ruinous competition." Exporters lose money, on average, and drive established producers out of business. However, in the context of this model, firms can only learn of their production cost by actually producing. High-cost firms eventually exit, and this process of entry, dumping, and shakeout is shown to be a constrained Pareto optimum.

In one of these six papers, Hartigan (1994), dumping is modeled as the outcome of a rivalry between an incumbent foreign "predator" and a home market "prey" producer in which the foreign "predator" takes into account the entry and exit decision of the "prey," and thus chooses whether or not the market structure will be duopolistic or monopolistic in the future. If the predator foreign firm chooses to price so as to drive the home firm out of business, profits will be low initially but will be high in the future when the predator has the home market to himself. In Hartigan's model, this strategy may not be possible, and if it is possible, it may not be optimal. When it is both possible and optimal, the effects of antidumping policies on welfare are not unambiguous, and depend upon whether a sorting or separating equilibrium would arise in the absence of these policies.

Thus, as a matter of economics, dumping—defined either as international price discrimination or pricing below cost by the Antidumping Act of 1921 and its successor statutes the Trade Reform Act of 1974 and the Trade Agreements Act of 1979—is easily understood within the context of a variety of modern theoretical models (Brander and Krugman, 1983; Ethier, 1982; Gruenspecht, 1988; Staiger and Wolak, 1991; Clarida, 1993) in which neither predation nor predatory intent plays any role by assumption. Of course, it is possible that foreign firms, as in Hartigan's (1994) model, do dump as part of a long-term predation strategy aimed at eliminating competitors in the United States. The point is that a finding of dumping consistent with the Antidumping Act of 1921 and its successor statutes conveys no information about the presence or absence of predatory behavior on the part of the dumping firms. Moreover, the theoretical models imply that the absence of predatory behavior on the part of a firm that exports to the United States at a price that is less than the Commerce Department's definition of fair value is perfectly consistent with both (1) international price discrimination by oligopolistic rivals across segmented national markets, as originally shown in Brander and Krugman (1983) and generalized recently by Weinstein (1992), and (2) sales at less than average cost in an industry in which the law of one price holds, as in the competitive models of Ethier (1982) and Clarida (1993) and the duopolistic model of forward pricing by Gruenspecht (1988). Thus the basis upon which the Commerce Department determines that sales at less than fair value have occurred—either international price discrimination or sales at less than constructed value—does not appear to be informative about the presence or absence of predatory dumping.

9.4   Antidumping Administration: In Practice

Imagine a system of civil litigation in which a party serves a massive discovery request, consisting of interrogatories and requests for production of documents. Imagine further that the serving party has the sole authority to prescribe the time within which responses must be made and the format.... Imagine still further that the serving party is the sole judge of the adequacy of the response and of the merits of all objections as to relevancy or burdensomeness of the request; that the serving party also is the imposer of sanctions for failure to comply, and the ultimate decision maker in the underlying matter for which the information is sought.

Such a system would be intolerable in the state or federal courts of the United States. It would raise serious question of due process in a system of administrative law that separates the investigative from the judicial functions within a single agency. But this is the inquisitorial system that was ordained by Congress for the administration of the antidumping [laws]. Torquemada, no doubt, would be right at home with it. But this is hardly a recommendation for the system. (McGee, 1993, p. 496)

In this section of the chapter, we review the administration of the antidumping laws—the 1921 Antidumping Act and its successor statues the Trade Reform Act of 1974 and the Trade Agreements Act of 1979— by the Department of Commerce and in the International Trade Commission. The administration of the antidumping laws has been subjected to a number of criticisms from a variety of sources in recent years (Murray, 1991; Palmeter, 1991; Cass and Narkin, 1991; Bovard, 1991; McGee, 1993). These criticisms fall into two broad categories.

The first criticism of the administration of the antidumping laws is that the methods used by the Commerce Department to investigate claims of dumping can, and often do, result in a determination of dumping where none actually takes place. That is, according to this critique, the Commerce Department employs accounting and investigative methods that indicate that goods are being sold in the United States at less than the price charged in the exporter's country or at less than the average costs of production. These false determinations can be made for a variety of reasons. The Commerce Department often uses the "method of averaging" to compare the *average* selling price in the exporter's country to the price at which each sale is made in the United States. When sales in the United States are below the average foreign price, these transactions are recorded as dumped for the purpose of calculating the dumping margin. However, when sales in the United States are above the average foreign price, the transactions are not used to offset the "dumped" sales. Thus, even if the average U.S. price is equal to the average price (expressed in dollars) charged in the exporter's country, the Commerce Department will determine that dumping has taken place.

The Commerce Department also employs the "constructed-value" method to determine whether or not the U.S. sales price fails to cover the average cost of production. As discussed in section 9.1 and as documented in section 9.2, even though the constructed-value method is supposed to be used only as "a last resort," it has over the past decade become a common benchmark for assessing dumping duties. There are several frequent complaints with the constructed-value definition. First, the average variable cost of production is extremely difficult to estimate in practice, requiring many arbitrary assumptions and allocations of costs across shipments and products (Murray, 1991, p. 47). Second, on top of the estimated average variable cost of production is added a 10 percent markup for general, sales, and administrative expenses, and an additional 8 percent margin for profit. Any exporting firm that is efficient enough to keep its overhead expenses under 10 percent of variable cost will be found dumping under this standard, as will any competitive firm with a markup of less than 8 percent over average total cost. This practice is especially important in light of the fact that "a meeting of competition" defense is not allowed under the 1921 Antidumping Act and its successor statutes (Victor, 1983, p. 349). Thus a foreign exporter that merely meets the prevailing U.S. price and in the process earns less than 18 percent *above* his average variable cost is dumping under the administration of the U.S. antidumping laws. Under the so-called Areeda-Turner (1975) doctrine, a widely employed standard in U.S. predatory pricing cases, a firm that sets prices at or above average variable cost cannot, other things being equal, be found guilty of selling at predatory prices.

Fluctuations in exchange rates introduce additional complications in investigations of dumping.[9] Consider a foreign firm that contracts with buyers in the United States and its home market to sell its output at a specified price for the coming year, and suppose that on the contract date the home price expressed in dollars and the U.S. price are the same. If over the year the dollar depreciates, each dollar received from exports to the United States will buy fewer units of domestic currency than on the date the contract was signed, and the firm would be dumping under the U.S. statutes. Yet any firm that signs such a fixed-price contract has no choice but to dump when the dollar depreciates, or else be in violation of the original contract! Moreover, to the extent that the exporter hedges his dollar accounts receivable by selling them in the forward market or by buying dollar put options, he will not suffer any domestic currency loss on his fixed-price export contract when the dollar depreciates. That loss will be borne by any speculator who took the other side of the forward or option contract.

In sum, according to this criticism of the administration of the anti-dumping laws,

the antidumping regime in the United States rarely answers accurately the basic question it asks: are prices to the United States from a particular exporter really below fair value? The standards of the law, the procedures it uses, and the implementation of these standards and procedures by the Department of Commerce increasingly ensure that, at the end of the day, an exporter determined to have been selling in the United States below fair value has probably been doing no such thing in any meaningful sense of the word "fair". On the contrary, rather than being a price discriminator, a dumper is more likely the victim of an anti-dumping process that has become a legal and administrative nontariff barrier. (Palmeter, 1991, p. 66)

The second criticism of the administration of the antidumping laws is that, even when goods really are exported at less than the home market price or the variable cost of production, the International Trade Commission need only find just more than *de minimis* injury to support an affirmative finding of dumping (Victor, 1983, p. 349). Under the statutes, the ITC is to determine if dumping has caused "harm which is not inconsequential, immaterial, or unimportant" (19 U.S.C. 1677(7)(A)(Supp. V 1981), and whether this harm has injured a domestic industry, has threatened to injure a domestic industry, or is retarding the growth of a domestic industry. The ITC typically considers a number of indicators to determine whether or not sales at less than fair value are the source of injury to a domestic industry, including import penetration and recent changes in the employment, shipments, profits, and the capacity of the domestic industry. According to Baldwin and Steagall (1993), since 1980 a full 66 percent of all dumping investigations in which a final determination was rendered by the ITC resulted in a finding of injury.

Implicit in this criticism is the view that *de minimis* injury to U.S. producers that is meant to be reversed by the imposition of dumping duties is more than outweighed by the reduction in household welfare that results from the imposition of dumping duties. Of course, the 1921 Antidumping Act and its successor statutes do not specifically require the ITC to trade off domestic producer interests against consumer surplus; that is, the statutes instruct the ITC to investigate injury to domestic competitors, not to domestic competition. Such a standard might be defensible if the motive for any dumping that does in fact occur were predatory dumping or if the Commerce Department and the International Trade Commission, as part of their parallel investigations into an allegation of dumping, sought to determine if any sales at less than fair value that were made in the United States were in fact part of a predatory strategy to eliminate competition by U.S. producers and to recoup the losses incurred by pushing prices charged in the United States above competitive levels once the U.S. competition was eliminated.

This is most assuredly *not* the way in which the Commerce Department and the ITC administer the U.S. antidumping laws that they are charged with administering. With regards to the ITC, Applebaum (1974) argues,

There is a real economic distinction between the use of dumping as a predatory pricing practice to injure U.S. companies, and as a reaction by the foreign producer to meet the prevailing U.S. price or to go slightly under the U.S. price to gain a foothold. The predatory dumping action more closely resembles the practice feared at the time of the enactment of both antidumping laws [in 1916 and 1921]; that is, a foreign producer's decision to charge a high, cartel price in the home market, and dump any excess capacity in other markets.... The Commission has focused on the impact of the practice on the U.S. industry; *it has generally not considered the distinction, made by many commentators, between predatory and more benign forms of dumping* [emphasis added]. (Applebaum, 1974, pp. 600–601)

Moreover, Victor notes, "The Commission has consistently rejected such traditional antitrust defenses as the meeting of competition defense, and the absence of predatory intent is irrelevant to a determination of dumping under the law" (Victor, 1983, p. 349).

With regard to the Commerce Department administration of the antidumping statutes, Murray (1991) points out that Commerce has two separate responsibilities explicitly set forth in the Trade Agreements Act of 1979 (section 733[b]): (1) to determine whether imports are being sold in the United States at less than fair value and, if so, (2) to estimate the margin of dumping. He notes that, in practice, the Commerce Department begins the investigation by collecting the information needed to quantify the U.S. price of imports and the foreign market value of like merchandise in order to estimate the margin of dumping. If the estimated margin of dumping exceeds the threshold value [.005], a positive dumping determination will be issued. *The DOC does not conduct an independent investigation to reveal whether the allegation makes sense from the foreign producer's point of view.* . . . [If such an investigation were to be conducted by DOC], it might reveal such motives as the exploitation of market power (that is, traditional profit maximizing price discrimination), predation, market share objectives, and hidden subsidies. Or [said hypothetical] investigation into the pricing policies of the foreign producer might produce evidence that the foreign firm is not engaged in dumping. (Murray, 1991, p. 30)

Murray goes on to recommend that, in contrast to the current practice, the "DOC should (1) determine whether dumping exists and, if so, (2) estimate the margin of dumping. Both questions could be investigated concurrently, but separate determinations should be made" (Murray, 1991, p. 30). Even the most ardent defenders of the current administration of the antidumping laws by the Commerce Department and the ITC acknowledge this "fundamental conflict" between these laws, which seek to protect *competitors not competition*, and the antitrust laws, which seek to protect *competition not competitors*. For example, Stewart (1991) in his defense of the current administration of the antidumping laws by the Commerce Department and the ITC, states that critics just don't understand the coverage of the Antidumping Act, which

is not limited to "predatory" conduct. The law is designed to protect businesses and workers from being harmed by conduct that does not flow from comparative advantage. . . . [Critics argue that the absence of] predatory intent [should be a defense against dumping], but that is not the purpose of the antidumping law. [While] variable costs are used as a benchmark to show predatory intent in the context of antitrust law, [i]n the remedial context of the antidumping law . . . there is no justification for such a low threshold. (Stewart, 1991, p. 309)

Since the Antidumping Act of 1921 expressly does not require that predatory intent or the likely success of a predatory strategy be established, it is not surprising that the administration of the antidumping laws by the Commerce Department and the International Trade Commission does not, as a rule, include any investigation into whether or not a lack of access by a U.S. firm to the alleged dumper's home market has made sales at less than fair value possible. This is not to say that such a lack of access is never cited, at least for public consumption, by U.S. firms making dumping allegations against foreign exporters. Indeed, in two of the most famous dumping cases involving Japan, those alleging the dumping of semiconductors and color televisions, a lack of access by U.S. producers to the Japanese market was cited by U.S. firms as a trade barrier that made dumping possible. Nonetheless, it is clear that the Commerce Department is content to rely on rather mechanical and conceptually flawed accounting studies that use imperfect and often misleading data on prices and costs to determine whether or not goods are exported to the United States at "less than fair value". Based upon such a finding, bureaucrats, domestic producers, politicians, and sometimes even special trade representatives, merely *infer* and, based only upon the inference, then publicly proclaim that foreign exporters must be engaging in predatory dumping. We now evaluate whether or not such an inference has any merit.

9.5   An Assessment in Light of Theory

We now provide an assessment of the administration of the antidumping laws in the United States by the Department of Commerce and the International Trade Commission. A frequent justification for the administration of the antidumping laws in the United States is that it serves to protect domestic firms and workers against the ever-present threat of foreign predation. We argued in section 9.4 that neither the ITC nor the Commerce Department conducts, as part of the typical antidumping inquiry, an independent investigation to determine whether or not sales at less than fair value are part of a forward-looking predatory strategy first to drive out U.S. competition and then second to raise U.S. prices enough so as to recoup the losses incurred while dumping. Rather, predation is merely just *inferred* from a determination of dumping by the Commerce Department and the ITC. We will argue in this section that such an inference is, in general, without any substantial basis in either economics or the law.

As a matter of economics, dumping—defined either as international price discrimination or pricing below cost by the Antidumping Act of 1921 and its successor statutes the Trade Reform Act of 1974 and the Trade Agreements Act of 1979—is easily understood within the context of a variety of modern theoretical models surveyed in section 9.3 (Brander and Krugman, 1983; Ethier, 1982; Gruenspecht, 1988; Staiger and Wolak, 1991; Clarida, 1993) *in which neither predation nor predatory intent plays any role by assumption.* Of course, it is possible that foreign firms, as in Hartigan's (1994) model, do dump as part of a long-term predation strategy aimed at eliminating competitors in the United States. If so, a U.S. firm can petition the Department of Commerce and the International Trade Commission to investigate the allegation of dumping and to impose dumping duties if dumping is found. The point is that a finding of dumping consistent with the Antidumping Act of 1921 and its successor statutes conveys no information about the presence or absence of predatory behavior on the part of the dumping firms. Moreover, the absence of predatory behavior on the part of a firm that exports to the United States at a price that is less than the Commerce Department's definition of fair value is perfectly consistent with international price discrimination by oligopolistic rivals across segmented national markets, as in Brander and Krugman (1983) and Weinstein (1992), but is also fully consistent with sales at less than average cost in an industry in which the law of one price holds, as in the competitive models of Ethier (1982) and Clarida (1993) and the duopolistic model of forward pricing by Gruenspecht (1988). Thus the basis upon which the Commerce Department determines that sales at less than fair value have occurred is not in itself informative about predatory dumping.

Firms in the United States that believe themselves to be injured by the predatory dumping of foreign exporters may, of course, also bring a treble-damages civil suit against these foreign firms under the 1916 Antidumping Duty Act. This was the path pursued by U.S. television producers in *Zenith* v. *Matsushita*, one of the very few dumping cases brought under the 1916 act. In its 1986 decision upholding the district's court grant of summary judgment for the defendants, the Supreme Court made clear that a plaintiff in such a treble-damages predatory-dumping case faces a significant burden in resisting a motion for summary judgment by the defendant (Liebeler, 1986), since "there is a consensus among commentators that predatory pricing schemes are rarely tried, and even more rarely successful" (*Matsushita Electric Industries* v. *Zenith Radio Corporation*, 106 Supreme Court 1348, 1357–1358, 1986). Following *Zenith* v. *Matsushita*, "whenever predatory intent must be shown inferentially, as is almost always the case, the competing hypothesis of vigorous competition will ordinarily overcome an inference of predatory behavior" (Liebeler, 1986, p. 1053).

Thus, in the wake of *Zenith* v. *Matsushita*, merely demonstrating that price discrimination or sales at less than average total cost have taken place would not appear to be enough for a U.S. plaintiff to win a civil treble-damages judgment against a foreign firm that sells at less than fair value in the United States. By contrast, a Commerce Department finding that price discrimination or sales at less than average cost have taken place will most likely result in the imposition of a dumping duty on the importer. Why the difference? Because, the 1921 "dumping law has consistently been interpreted to protect competitors rather than competition, a goal directly at odds with ... the antitrust laws [which] were enacted for the 'protection of competition not competitors'" (Victor, 1983, p. 350).

The 1981 district court decision in *Zenith* v. *Matsushita* made clear that the 1916 Antidumping Duty Act was "intended to complement the antitrust laws by imposing on importers substantially the same legal strictures relating to price discrimination as those which had already been imposed on domestic business by the Clayton Antitrust Act of 1914" (*Zenith Radio Corporation* v. *Matsushita Electric Industries*, 494 F. Supp. 1197, E.D.Pa. 1980). In this regard, Victor (1983) writes:

Having reviewed the case law under the 1916 Act, certain conclusions may be drawn regarding the character and utility of this statute. At the very least it is clear that despite its partial use of customs terminology, courts have applied the 1916 Act as an antitrust-type statute, and have concluded that it must not be used in a manner inconsistent with the overall antitrust policy of promoting aggressive price competition at all levels of commerce. Thus, although the statute does not provide so by its terms, ... it seems likely that ... "cost justification" or "meeting competition" will be permitted as a defense against allegedly predatory price discrimination when this issue arises. Absent such defenses [which are not permitted under the current administration of the antidumping laws based upon the 1921 Antidumping Act (author)], the [1916] Act would have a chilling effect on price competition in the international arena, and could hardly be construed in a pro-competitive fashion. At a minimum, one would think that the courts will consider evidence of "cost justification" or "meeting competition" as evidence that tends to negate claims of predatory intent. (Victor, 1983, pp. 345–346)

According to Liebeler (1986, pp. 1055–56), a plaintiff must establish that three conditions are satisfied in order to prove predatory pricing under the Sherman Act:

1. Predatory or anticompetitive conduct directed to accomplishing the unlawful purpose of controlling prices or destroying competition in a market.

2. A dangerous probability that this conduct will succeed and that any losses sustained while cutting prices to predatory levels can be recouped once competition has been reduced.

3. Antitrust injury.

Liebeler (1986) argues that, while in a Sherman case a plaintiff could establish predatory conduct according to the Areeda-Turner test by proving that a rival charged a price that failed to cover average variable cost, this proof, in and of itself, would not be sufficient. The plaintiff would also have to show that the defendant has a "dangerous" probability of monopolizing sales in the United States as well as a "dangerous" probability of recouping his predatory losses. This point has been emphasized by Areeda and Hovenkamp (1992) and Klevorick (1993) and played an important role in Judge Easterbrook's 1989 decision in the key recent predatory pricing case *A.A. Poultry Farms, Inc.* v. *Rose Acre Farms, Inc.* 881 F.2d 1396 (7th Cir. 1989). In this case, according to Klevorick,

> the *Rose Acre court* adopts the analysis of market structure and the possibility of future recoupment as a filter to separate those cases that need careful consideration of the pricing behavior of the firm—and particularly inquiry into the relationship between price and cost—from those that do not. . . . Since Judge Easterbrook and his colleagues conclude that recoupment was not possible in the *Rose Acre* market and hence that predation was not a rational strategy there . . . "antitrust inquiry [into the relationship between prices and cost] could not be justified." (Klevorick, 1993, pp. 163–164)

Finally, a plaintiff must prove antitrust injury in a predatory pricing case. According to Page (1980), "Antitrust injury can consistently be seen as narrowing the standard for recoverable damages from all those suffered by the plaintiff as a result of an antitrust violation to those that actually flow from the aspect of the violation that causes market inefficiency" (quoted in Liebeler, 1986, p. 1070). According to the precedents established in such cases as *Brunswick Corporation* v. *Pueblo Bowl-O-Mat* and *California Computer Products, Inc.* v. *IBM*, "antitrust injury in a predatory pricing case must be defined independently of a plaintiff's loss of business and the number of competitors in the market. . . . An act can injure competition and thereby create an antitrust injury only when it creates a market inefficiency" (Liebeler, 1986, p. 1069–1070).

Based upon the state of play in the antitrust case law pertaining to predatory pricing following *Zenith* v. *Matsushita*, we would surmise that only a *very* few allegations of dumping that are supported by final determinations of dumping and injury by the Commerce Department and the ITC under the 1921 act and its successor statutes would have any chance to clear all four of the hurdles required to win a treble-damages civil judgment against a defendant if the standards of the Sherman Act were required to be met. In particular, even a cursory examination of the products that have been found to have been dumped in the United States since 1979 reveals that it is laughable to even ponder the probability that a foreign cartel could successfully monopolize the markets for ball bearings, barbed wire, cookware, pipe fittings, mirrors, television tubes, fan belts, telephone systems, appliance plugs, sweaters, and a host of other products listed in Table 1.

9.6 Conclusion

We have shown in sections 9.4 and 9.5 that the 1921 Antidumping Act and its successor statutes have consistently been interpreted by the Commerce Department and the ITC as the Congress, in recent decades, has intended: as a means to protect U.S. companies against "unfair" foreign competition. Although the original justification for these laws may well have been a belief that the predominant source of unfair foreign competition was the predatory dumping of foreign cartels, it is clear that very few of the cases brought since 1979 would stand under the scrutiny of the *Zenith v. Matsushita* requirements for establishing a predatory pricing scheme that injures competition. From the perspective of the goals of antitrust policy, this proclivity of the Commerce Department and the ITC to punish eminently reasonable and nonpredatory business pricing practices with antidumping duties is costly. The potentially large cost of these "type I" (Joskow and Klevorick, 1979) errors has been acknowledged and emphasized by the Antitrust Division of the Justice department in a number of dumping cases. According to Applebaum (1974):

The Division has, basically, advocated that the Commission reconcile the Antidumping Act with the antitrust laws. It has urged the Commission to apply antitrust concepts in weighing injury, and has also urged the Commission to take consumer interests into account. The Division has been especially concerned where it has concluded that the U.S. industry utilizing the antidumping statute was itself non-competitive or "concentrated". The Justice Department lawyers have vigorously attacked application of the Antidumping Act when the importers were simply meeting the prevailing U.S. price, or, in the view of the Department, providing a significant source of competition.... The Division does not appear to have been well received by the Commissioners, perhaps, in part, because it has not appeared as a neutral arm of the executive branch but rather as an advocate of the importer's viewpoint. (Applebaum, 1974, pp. 602–603)

Victor (1983) states well the inherent friction between the objectives of the antitrust laws and the objectives of the administrative dumping laws:

The dumping law has consistently been interpreted to protect competitors rather than competition, a goal directly at odds with fundamental antitrust policy. While this may be lamentable from a competition policy standpoint, and while it may be troublesome to some that the administrative dumping law does not distinguish between truly predatory dumping and such arguably procompetitive forms of dumping as price-cutting to meet a lower U.S. price, and short-term dumping by a new entrant below the prevailing U.S. price level in an effort to gain a foothold in the U.S. market, the administrative antidumping statute does not purport to concern itself with such objectives. A different national policy is sought to be served by that law—the protection of U.S. industries from supposedly unfair competition.... [I]t seems reasonable to conclude that dumping law enforcement officials should not be so quick to scoff at the concerns of competition policy when put before them, but should instead administer the dumping law with a sensitivity to the delicate balance that exists between two important, but inconsistent, national policies—the protection of our industries and the promotion of competition. (Victor, 1983, p. 350)

This chapter has confirmed that the antidumping laws have become the battleground of the new protectionism; in many cases, the battles fought have no doubt inflicted a not insubstantial cost on U.S. consumers and downstream producers. Whatever the original motivation for their passage, the antidumping laws as administered by the Commerce Department and the International Trade Commission are an extremely clumsy, blunt, and inaccurate instrument for protecting U.S. producers against that rare foreign predator who seeks to destroy a U.S. industry and to reap large monopoly profits as the reward of his intertemporal predatory strategy. Moreover, it is even difficult in light of the facts and the available alternatives to make an equity or fairness case in favor of the continuation of the current antidumping laws as administered by the Commerce Department and the International Trade Commission.

If there is to be U.S. policy to protect industries against the rigors of foreign competition—whether it be "fair" or "unfair"—then why not, as suggested by Hemmendinger (1991), scrap the Commerce Department investigation into dumping altogether, and let all U.S. industries petition for relief under the "Escape Clause," Section 201 of the U.S. trade laws? This approach would have a number of advantages. It would increase the likelihood of White House involvement—as well as Treasury, the Council of Economic Advisers, and the Justice Department—in making the decision to protect an industry against "unfair" foreign competition. Such involvement is most certainly not typical under the existing regime. This approach would also have the advantage of delinking the tariff imposed to protect a U.S. industry needing relief from the Commerce Department's flawed calculation of the dumping margin. If the Commerce Department is put out of the business of imposing dumping duties, predation by foreign firms selling in the United States can be deterred by either civil or criminal action brought under the 1916 Antidumping Duty Act. Yes, it is true that after *Zenith* v. *Matsushita*, it will be quite difficult to find an exporter guilty of predatory dumping. But this is as it should be, since, in international as in domestic commerce, "predatory pricing schemes are rarely tried, and even more rarely successful."

NOTES

I would like to thank Jagdish Bhagwati, Robert Hudec, and Al Klevorick for their many constructive comments on earlier drafts. Any errors that remain are those of the author.

1. Viner (1923) remains the classic reference on dumping as international price discrimination.

2. The next three paragraphs draw upon Applebaum (1974), pp. 591–593; Victor (1983), pp. 339–350; and McGee (1993), pp. 492–496.

3. Until 1954, the Treasury also determined whether dumping had injured U.S. industry. As a result of the Customs Simplification Act of 1954, the determination of injury was shifted to the International Trade Commission.

4. This discussion draws on Murray (1991), pp. 31–32.

5. The dumping margin calculated by the Commerce Department in the preliminary determination is actually the maximum margin for which the importer is potentially liable. If the dumping margin ultimately calculated as part of the final determination is lower, the importer is liable for this lesser margin.

6. According to Cass and Narkin (1991, p. 212), "Commerce's practice is to view the home market as inadequate for purposes of price comparisons if sales in the home market are less than 5 percent of sales to third countries."

7. Recall that surrogate market comparisons are only used for imports from nonmarket, command economies.

8. This paragraph draws liberally from Ethier's (1987) article "Dumping" in the *New Palgrave Dictionary of Economics*.

9. This paragraph draws heavily from Murray (1991), pp. 49–50.

REFERENCES

Applebaum, H. 1974. "The antidumping laws—Impact on the competitive process." *Antitrust Law Journal*, 43, 590–600.

Areeda, P., and H. Hovenkamp. 1992. *Antitrust law: An analysis of antitrust principles and their application*. Boston: Little Brown.

Areeda, P., and D. Turner. 1975. "Predatory pricing and related practices under Section 2 of the Sherman Act." *Harvard Law Review*, 88 (February): 697–733.

Baldwin, R., and M. Moore. 1991. "Political aspects of the trade remedy laws." In R. Boltuck and R. Litan, eds., *Down in the dumps*. Washington, DC: Brookings Press.

Baldwin, R., and J. Steagall. 1993. "An analysis of factors influencing ITC decisions in antidumping, countervailing duty, and safeguard cases." NBER Working Paper.

Bhagwati, Jagdish. 1986. *Protectionism*. London: Basil Blackwell.

Boltuck, R., and R. Litan. *Down in the Dumps*. Washington: Brookings, 1991.

Bovard, J. 1991. *The fair trade fraud*. New York: St. Martins Press.

Brander, J., and P. Krugman. 1983. "A reciprocal dumping model of international trade." *Journal of International Economics*, 15.

Cass, R., and S. Narkin. 1991. "Antidumping and countervailing duty law: The United States and the GATT." In R. Boltuck and R. Litan, eds., *Down in the dumps*.

Clarida, R. 1993. "Entry, dumping, and shakeout." *The American Economic Review*, 83.

Eichengreen, B., and H. van der Ven. 1984. "US antidumping policies: The case of steel." In *The structure and evolution of recent US trade policy*, ed. R. Baldwin and A. Kreuger. Chicago: University of Chicago Press.

Ethier, W. 1982. "Dumping." *Journal of Political Economy*, 90, 487–506.

Ethier, W. 1987. "Dumping." *New Palgrave Dictionary of Economics*. New York: Stockton.

Gruenspecht, Howard. 1988. "Dumping and dynamic competition." *Journal of International Economics*, 25, 225–248.

Hartigan, J. 1994. "Dumping and signaling." *Journal of Economic Behavior and Organization*, 23, 69–81.

Hemmendinger, N. 1991. "Comment on Murray." In R. Boltuck and R. Litan, eds., *Down in the dumps*. Washington: Brookings.

Horlick, G. 1989. "The United States antidumping system." In J. Jackson and E. Vermulst, eds., *Antidumping law and practice: A comparative study*. Ann Arbor: University of Michigan Press.

Joskow, P., and A. Klevorick. 1979. "A framework for analyzing predatory pricing policy." *Yale Law Journal*, 89 (December): 213–270.

Jovanovic, Boyan. 1982. "Selection and the evolution of industry." *Econometrica*, 50, 699–670.

Kaplan, G., L. Kamarck, and M. Parker. 1988. "Cost analysis under the antidumping law." *George Washington Journal of International Law and Economics*, 21, 351–409.

Klevorick, A. 1993. "The current state of the law and economics of predatory pricing." *AEA Papers and Proceedings*, 83 (May): 162–167.

Liebeler, W. 1986. "Wither predatory pricing? From Areeda and Turner to Matsushita." *Notre Dame Law Review*, 61:1052–76.

Lloyd, P. 1977. *Antidumping actions and the GATT system*. Thames Essay No. 9. London: Trade Policy Research Center.

McGee, R. 1993. "The case to repeal the antidumping laws." *Northwestern Journal of International Law and Business*, 13, 991–1062.

Murray, T. 1996. "The administration of the antidumping duty law by the Department of Commerce." In R. Boltuck and R. Litan, eds., *Down in the dumps*. Washington DC: Brookings.

Palmeter, N. D. 1991. "The antidumping law: A legal and administrative non-tariff barrier." In R. Boltuck and R. Litan, eds., *Down in the dumps*. Washington, DC: Brookings.

Staiger, R., and F. Wolak. 1991. "Strategic use of antidumping law to enforce tacit international collusion" (mimeo). Stanford University.

Stewart, T. 1991. "Administration of the antidumping law: A different perspective." In R. Boltuck and R. Litan, eds., *Down in the Dumps.*

Victor, P. 1983. "Antidumping and antitrust: Can the inconsistencies be resolved?" *Journal of International Law and Politics,* 15.

Viner, J. 1923. *Dumping.* Chicago: University of Chicago Press.

Wares, W. 1977. *The theory of dumping, and American commercial policy.* Lexington, MA: Heath.

Weinstein, D. 1992. "Competition and unilateral dumping." *Journal of International Economics,* 32, 379–388.

VI

Race to the Bottom

10

Capital Mobility and Environmental Standards: Is There a Theoretical Basis for a Race to the Bottom?

John Douglas Wilson

10.1 Introduction

With the increasing integration of world capital markets, there has emerged a heightened concern about the effects of this integration on the environmental policies pursued by national governments. Specifically, the ability of investors to freely locate their capital in the region where it can earn the highest return is said to produce a "race to the bottom," by which it is meant that independent governments compete for scarce investment through reductions in environmental standards to levels that are inefficient for the entire system of regions.[1] Within the United States, a similar concern has provided a justification for locating environmental regulation at the federal level, rather than at the state and local level.

There is little empirical evidence of any such "race." Levinson (Chapter 11 of this volume) and Cropper and Oates (1993) review this lack of evidence, but the latter authors then write, "This, of course, does not preclude the possibility that state and local officials, in *fear* of such effects, will scale down standards for environmental quality" (p. 695). In the absence of clear empirical evidence, it appears particularly worthwhile to carefully assess the theoretical case for a race to the bottom.

This chapter examines the theoretical literature that has something to say about a possible "race." Much of this literature lies in the area of local public economics, where the efficiency properties of systems of independent governments have been a key concern. Some recent contributions have explicitly modeled environmental problems, whereas other contributions omit any explicit treatment of such problems but nevertheless can be extended in this direction. I shall discuss both. The international trade literature has had less to say about a potential race, in part because it often focuses on the welfare of a single country, rather than a system of countries. But I shall discuss a couple of important recent contributions by international trade economists. My review of the literature is not meant to be exhaustive, but I do cover several major modeling approaches to the problem, hopefully in a way that suggests possible avenues for future research. Throughout the chapter, I consider pollution emissions that harm only the environment of the jurisdiction where they occur, because the case of "spillover effects" has not been a major component of arguments favoring a race to the bottom.

A basic message that emerges from the first part of this study is that there can be no race to the bottom if there are no constraints on available tax instruments and the economy is competitive and distortion free. The basic idea is an old one, particularly for economists familiar with the literature on local public economics. In that literature, jurisdictions compete for people, not firms, and the result is an efficient sorting of people across jurisdictions. It has been long recognized that the same type of efficiency properties hold in the case of interjurisdictional competition for firms. Two studies that make this point are described in section 10.3. A critical condition for efficiency is that each firm pays a tax equal to the costs that its operations impose on the jurisdiction. These costs can consist of the costs incurred in providing public goods and services to the firm, plus environmental costs. Given that governments are able to use taxes as "user fees" in this manner, considerations involving capital mobility do not enter into the benefit-cost rules governments use to choose environmental standards. These rules are discussed in section 10.2. I am not arguing here that weaker standards will not attract more capital investment. Rather, any additional capital investment will not benefit or harm the jurisdiction, because firms effectively compensate the jurisdiction for any environmental costs associated with this investment. Moreover, this efficiency argument can be extended to the case where jurisdictions are large enough to exercise monopoly power on world capital markets or product markets. In these cases, jurisdictions face incentives to use their tax systems to exploit this power, leaving them free to set environmental standards efficiently.

The rest of the chapter explores cases in which this benchmark efficiency result breaks down. In the first set of cases, governments do not optimally tax capital. If the tax on capital exceeds the environmental and other social costs associated with this capital, then these governments face incentives to attract capital by means of inefficiently lax environmental standards; that is, there is a race to the bottom. For example, section 10.4 discusses a study by Oates and Schwab (1988), in which production activities reduce environmental quality but this reduction is not tied directly to the use of capital inputs. They find that a race to the bottom does indeed occur if capital is taxed at a positive rate, since the optimal rate is zero. In cases where capital is taxed at inefficiently low rates, however, there is a "race to the top," or, to use a popular phrase, the phenomenon known as "not in my backyard" (NIMBY). This relation between capital taxation and environmental standards extends to situations involving market failures. For example, section 10.6 deals with the case of unemployment. Additional capital investment reduces unemployment, suggesting that capital investment should be subsidized. In the absence of such a subsidy, jurisdictions may face incentives to weaken environmental standards to attract capital.

Thus the existence of a race to the bottom is very dependent on assumptions about what taxes or subsidies are available, and what types of market imperfections exist. Sections 10.5 and 10.6 describe a few approaches to endogenizing the taxation of capital in a way that explains inefficient environmental standards. One approach is to model the costs involved in collecting and administering taxes. If such costs lead to the absence of particular tax instruments or the suboptimal use of others, then there may exist a role for environmental standards as a means of influencing capital investment. An alternative type of approach may be labeled "political market failures," meaning that the political process produces an inefficient tax treatment of capital and, consequently, the possibility of a race to the bottom. For example, section 10.6 discusses a theory of "optimal obfuscation," under which weaker environmental regulations may be used to attract scarce capital and therefore increase employment if the costs of such employment-generating activities are less transparent to general voters than more direct employment-generating methods. On the other hand, section 10.5 describes how heterogeneity in the voter population can lead to the NIMBY phenomenon. The current state of the literature does not allow us to say confidently which of these two possibilities is more likely.

The remainder of this chapter considers what might be called "small-numbers" cases, where there is some type of strategic interaction between a small number of governments, or between these governments and firms. These cases provide more evidence that a race to the bottom need not occur. Section 10.7 shows that NIMBY is possible when investments are "lumpy," meaning that the investment projects available to a jurisdiction cannot be subdivided into small units. Section 10.8 discusses Markusen, Morey, and Olewiler's (1993) analysis of imperfect competition, a problem that is often associated with large-scale production, including "lumpy investments." Their numerical examples show that either NIMBY or a race to the bottom can occur, depending on the level of "disutility" from pollution. For the cases where a race occurs, however, I argue that environmental taxes are too high when the locations of production facilities cannot be changed; mobility merely reduces these taxes toward more efficient levels. Two alternative specifications of the model are considered, including one suggested by Janeba (1995), but neither supports a race.

The next two sections explicitly introduce intertemporal considerations into the analysis through the use of two-period models. Section 10.9 shows how the Bond-Samuelson (1989) model of country-firm bargaining over taxes can be extended to include the environmental concerns of the present chapter. It turns out that a race to the bottom can occur in the absence of capital taxation. Section 10.10 discusses a model developed by King, McAfee, and Welling (1993) in which two jurisdictions use an auction mechanism to compete for firms. A nice feature of this model is that its investment in "infrastructure" may be readily interpreted as investment in environmental quality. But these authors show that the equilibrium levels of such investment are fully efficient, even though they *must* differ across jurisdictions. Their paper, therefore, provides a nice counterexample to the view that a "level playing field" in environmental regulations should serve as a general goal.

To conclude, this chapter shows that the theoretical case for a race to the bottom is mixed at best. High on the agenda for future research is a better understanding of why governments might choose to substitute less stringent environmental standards for more effective tax and subsidy policies. Progress on this issue will probably require a better understanding of the sources of political market failures. Section 10.11 discusses some additional issues that need to be addressed.

10.2 Rules for Optimal Public Good Provision

In the present study, a local government's environmental policies have the attributes of "local public goods," in the sense that they affect the well-being of all residents residing in the jurisdiction (but not outsiders). Thus a "race to the bottom" may be largely viewed as a problem involving deviations from the "first-best" rules for the optimal provision of local public goods. I therefore begin with a quick description of these rules, followed by a discussion of how a "race" leads to their violation.

A "first-best economy" contains none of the many possible sources of inefficient behavior by consumers, firms, and factor owners: government-imposed taxes and subsidies, distortions arising from imperfect market structures, and the many possible external benefits and costs associated

with private decision making ("externalities"). Income distribution problems are also absent. Under these circumstances, the famous "Samuelson
rule" determines the optimal level of a "public good." Specifically, the sum
of each person's willingness to pay for another unit of the good, MB^i for
person i's "marginal benefit," should equal the resource cost of another
unit, MC:

$$\Sigma_i MB^i = MC \tag{1}$$

A critical aspect of this rule is that it contains no "behavioral responses" by
firms or individuals to either the additional supply of the public good or
the manner in which it is financed.

Unfortunately, this state of affairs ignores the fact that benefit-cost
analysis is practiced, if at all, in a "second-best economy," where the
decisions of firms and individuals are distorted. Given these distortions,
policy-induced behavioral changes have welfare effects that should enter
the rules for optimal public good determination.

The race to the bottom concerns one such policy-induced behavioral
effect for the case where the public good in question may be viewed as
either some measure of "environmental quality" or one of the regulations
that affects this quality, that is, "emissions standards." For the appropriate
measure of these standards, we may continue to define the marginal benefit and marginal cost terms in equation 1. There are no behavioral changes
here: MB^i gives individual i's willingness to pay for the environmental
improvements associated with a marginal rise in emissions standards, and
MC depends only on production technologies and market prices. However, race-to-the-bottom advocates would argue that there is another cost
involved here: the cost associated with the behavioral response of investors to the disincentive effects created by tighter emissions standards. This
additional cost may be measured by the decline in the capital supply from
a marginal tightening of standards, $-\Delta K$, multiplied by the net value of an
additional unit of capital to the given jurisdiction, t. Equation 1 is then
modified as follows:

$$\Sigma_i MB^i = MC - t \cdot \Delta K \tag{2}$$

With capital outflows being treated as a cost of raising environmental
standards, we may expect the jurisdiction's optimal environmental quality
to decline. We will see that the existence of this positive net value on a
marginal unit of capital is due to an unwillingness or inability of jurisdictions to use their tax systems to achieve an optimal supply of capital.

The presence of the behavioral response in equation 2 would not be a problem if this response were indeed a cost from the viewpoint of the system of jurisdictions under consideration. But a central feature of the "race" argument is that the "watering down" of environmental standards results from competition among jurisdictions for scarce capital. Under this view, activities that discourage capital investment in one jurisdiction provide other jurisdictions with more capital. As a result, the term $-t \cdot \Delta K$ overestimates the cost of investment disincentives to the entire system of jurisdictions. In fact, a model is presented below in which no portion of $-t \cdot \Delta K$ should be treated as a cost, because the total supply of capital is fixed for the entire system of jurisdictions. In any case, we may say that a race to the bottom exists if environmental standards are tightened only to the point where the direct benefits of tighter standards, $\Sigma_i MB^i$, still exceed the sum of the direct costs, MC, and whatever portion of $-t \cdot \Delta K$ represents a social cost for the entire system of jurisdictions. This discrepancy between benefits and costs implies that a "central government" should be able to make all jurisdictions better off by simultaneously raising standards in all of them, because no single jurisdiction would then be put at a competitive disadvantage with respect to its attractiveness to investors. In other words, a race to the bottom leads to an "inefficiently" low level of environmental quality, where the economist's definition of "inefficiency" is that it is technologically possible to make some group of individuals better off without making anyone worse off.

In some of the cases discussed in this paper, the framework represented by equations 1 and 2 either does not apply or must be significantly modified. In particular, equations 1 and 2 assume that environmental quality can be varied continuously within a jurisdiction. For the case of "lumpy investments" considered in section 10.7, or for the competition among two jurisdictions for a single firm discussed in section 10.10, the jurisdiction must choose between either a large reduction in environmental quality or none. The present study also concentrates mainly on cases in which governments do not attach "welfare weights" to the benefit or cost terms in equations 1 and 2. Such weights might arise from a government's desire to take into account income distribution problems by placing more weight on the net benefits received by low-income residents. Alternatively, the weighting of benefits and costs might reflect a political process. In either case, the use of welfare weights can lead to inefficient outcomes independently of whether capital is mobile, thereby weakening the possible link between competition for scarce capital and lax environmental standards.

The present chapter avoids this complexity, allowing us to rely on the efficiency condition given by equation 1 as a benchmark from which to study the effects of competition for scarce capital.

10.3 The Tiebout Hypothesis

As originally formulated by Tiebout (1956), the "Tiebout hypothesis" states that the ability of individuals to "vote with their feet" leads to an efficient provision of local public goods. The conditions under which this claim is valid are now well understood. Specifically, there must be many "competitive" jurisdictions, each "competing" for new residents through its choices of tax and expenditure policies. Much of this literature assumes that the goal of local governments is to maximize land values, an objective that has been found to possess desirable efficiency properties.

It is less well known that the Tiebout hypothesis also applies to competition for firms by local governments and, therefore, offers a counterargument to race-to-the-bottom claims. In this section, I discuss two early articles that not only undertake this extension, but also explicitly consider the adverse environmental effects associated with firm location: Fischel (1975) and White (1975).

These two papers contain important differences, but we may still give a set of assumptions that captures the essence of the basic models in both papers. First, the number of jurisdictions is sufficiently large for no single jurisdiction to possess forms of "market power" that might allow it to "exploit" firms. Second, a large number of firms exist and are perfectly mobile across jurisdictions. Thus, firms also do not possess "market power." White and Fischel consider different ways in which the firms might differ, which I will describe subsequently.

Third, each firm emits a fixed amount of pollution, and the environmental quality in a particular jurisdiction is determined by the total number of firms located there. Issues involving firm location are the main focus of the Fischel and White papers, rather than the optimal control of a given firm's emissions. But we may still define a race to the bottom as occurring when local governments choose tax and zoning policies that are "inefficiently favorable," so that too many pollution-generating firms occupy the jurisdictions under consideration. In contrast, the "pollution-intensity" of production processes is a major focus of the Oates-Schwab (1988) analysis, which I discuss in section 10.4.

Fourth, each jurisdiction chooses its level of environmental quality to maximize the well-being, or "utility," of the "representative resident."

Thus differences across residents in preferences for environmental quality are not explicitly considered. Fischel explains that Tiebout migration ("voting with feet") should eliminate such differences, resulting in a distribution of individuals across jurisdictions that reflects differences in tastes for both environmental quality and other "public goods." However, labor migration is not an explicit feature of either paper, nor will it be given much attention in the current study.

Finally, there are no "spillover effects" involving environmental quality. In other words, the pollution generated by firms in one jurisdiction does not affect environmental quality in another jurisdiction. I ignore these spillover effects throughout this chapter because they have not been a major aspect of arguments in favor of a race to the bottom.

Given these assumptions, the efficiency properties of the equilibrium turn critically on the ability of local governments to collect cash payments from firms residing in their jurisdictions, either directly or indirectly through the appropriate tax and zoning policies. Fischel first investigates the use of "direct cash payments," which are collected by a "zoning board" and may then be distributed to residents through reductions in local taxes. The representative resident then faces an effective unit price of environmental quality, defined by the cash payment per firm multiplied by the impact of a unit increase in environmental quality on the number of firms. Given this effective price, the local government can decide how many firms to allow into the jurisdiction so as to maximize the resident's utility.

The ability of a local government to increase the required cash payments from firms is limited by the ability of firms to "shop around" among jurisdictions, in the same manner that mobile residents are able to "vote with their feet." The resulting equilibrium is fully efficient; there is no race to the bottom or any other form of inefficiency. Fischel explains:

The problem of external effects of firms is solved in a Pareto efficient way. Firms must pay residents exactly the value the latter put on their environment. Zoning insures that firms do not pay too little, and interjurisdiction competition insures that residents of any jurisdiction are not paid too much. Payments go only to those affected by the externalities, so the least-cost input combinations of firms and the choice of goods by residents are not affected. (Fischel, 1975, p. 129)

Of course, firms typically impose other costs on jurisdictions through their use of local public goods and services. But local governments possess incentives to adjust the cash payments they collect from firms to reflect these additional costs.

With firms paying fees that directly reflect the costs they impose on the community, including costs to the environment, the local government will effectively be indifferent about the entry of another firm at the margin. In terms of the optimality conditions in the previous section, this indifference means that the net value of another unit of investment, denoted t in equation 2, equals zero. There can be no race to the bottom.

Turn now to the issue of whether the commonly employed local property tax can serve the same role as a direct cash payment. White and Fischel approach this issue in different ways, but each builds on Hamilton's (1975) work concerning the residential property tax. He shows that such a tax is equivalent to an efficient "user fee" for public goods, provided the appropriate zoning restrictions are employed to prevent the property tax from reducing housing consumption to inefficiently low levels. White and Fischel extend this basic idea to cases where there are two types of property, residential and business. It is not surprising, then, that the property tax on business property acts like a "user fee" for public goods, including "use" of the environment, if local governments are able to tax business property at rates that differ from those on residential property, while employing zoning policies to prevent any tax-induced distortion to the ratios of inputs used by firms.

However, both White and Fischel concentrate on the case where residential and business property are taxed identically. Given this constraint, they then offer different methods for achieving an efficient equilibrium, both of which are based on the existence of heterogeneous firms. The common key insight is that this heterogeneity enables local governments to vary the effective pollution payment without varying the property tax. In Fischel's paper, this variation is achieved by assuming that firms differ in their pollution emissions. As a result of such differences, local governments can select the firms allowed to operate in their jurisdictions so that the environmental costs associated with each firm's emissions equal its tax payments. In White's paper, firms differ in the amounts of property they must employ to produce their products. With property serving as the tax base, local governments can again select those firms that pay taxes equal to environmental costs. Neither solution is complete, however, because each relies on the existence of a sufficiently large amount of heterogeneity in firms.

The requirement that residential and business property be taxed identically is open to question, despite the attention given to this case by White and Fischel. Many states in the United States utilize "classification systems" under which residential and business property are taxed at different rates. This differential treatment has been the subject of both theoretical and empirical studies. Wilson (1986) shows that localities have an incentive to tax residential property more heavily than business property, given the relatively high tax elasticities of the latter. On the other hand, it is often the case that tax systems impose higher effective tax rates on business property than on residential property. Wilson conjectures that this common practice may reflect attempts to "export" a region's tax burden to nonresidents, a possibility that is omitted from the theoretical model. In line with this conjecture, Sonstelie's (1978) interesting empirical analysis of the District of Columbia property tax system concludes that "[tax] classification has substantial power to change the distribution of the property tax burden." An alternative explanation suggested by the concerns of this chapter is that relatively high tax rates reflect payments for various environmental costs firms may impose on the jurisdictions where they locate. Fischel recognizes this possibility (1975, p. 135) but concludes that there is no evidence that differences in residential and business tax burdens are motivated by the existence of environmental costs. It is difficult to dismiss this motivation in the absence of strong evidence that jurisdictions are unable or unwilling to act on it.

The ability of local governments to differentiate between the tax treatment of firms and residents is further enhanced by their increasing use of policy instruments other than the property tax to attract new investment. One such instrument is the use of "tax holidays," that provide firms with a zero or substantially reduced tax burden for a limited period of time after they locate in a jurisdiction. Subsidized improvements in the public infrastructure are another method of attracting new investment. Given these developments, a literature has begun to emerge on "bidding for firms" by local governments. One particularly relevant contribution to this literature is discussed in section 10.10.

To conclude, local governments appear to have considerable ability to use tax instruments to effectively collect efficient cash payments from firms, thereby precluding a race to the bottom. But I shall argue in the next section that in some cases the capitalization of environmental policies into the values of the factors held by residents may substitute for these tax instruments as a mechanism by which firms are effectively forced to pay for the costs they impose on jurisdictions.

10.4   The Oates-Schwab Model

Oates and Schwab (1988) explicitly analyze the possibility of a race to the bottom in a property-tax model. They treat the property tax as a tax on the capital used in industrial production, and they do not explicitly include a housing sector in their model. No other tax instruments are considered. Nevertheless, their analysis effectively demonstrates that a race to the bottom will not occur in the absence of capital taxation. Unlike the White-Fischel analysis, cash payments or taxes are not used to compensate residents for the environmental costs associated with industrial production. Instead, this compensation effectively occurs because the appropriately designed environmental regulations lead to higher prices for the factors supplied by residents. In other words, compensation in the Oates-Schwab model occurs through "capitalization." I first describe this model, and then I use it to examine the role of capitalization. Finally, I discuss why a "race" does occur under a positive property tax. My analysis emphasizes a shortcoming of this explanation for a race: local governments possess incentives not to tax mobile capital.

10.4.1   Wage Capitalization and Efficiency

A distinguishing feature of the Oates-Schwab model is that pollution emissions enter a firm's production function as a separate argument. Specifically, a firm's output is a function of the capital and labor it employs plus the amount of emissions it creates: $Q = F(K, L, E)$, where Q denotes output and K, L, and E denote capital, labor, and emissions. This function exhibits the normal properties of "well-behaved" production functions in economic theory, including "constant returns to scale." In other words, a proportional increase in the capital, labor, and emissions employed by firms raises output by the same proportion. But if only capital and labor are increased by a given proportion, say, 1 percent, then output will rise by less than 1 percent. This property reflects the idea that some amounts of capital and labor must be diverted from the production of output in order to prevent emissions from increasing as output rises.

Oates and Schwab assume that each local government can regulate emissions by controlling the emissions-labor ratio:

$$E = \alpha \cdot L \tag{3}$$

for some number α set by the government. To concentrate on the issue of capital mobility, Oates and Schwab treat a jurisdiction's supply of labor as fixed, while assuming that its firms can obtain as much capital as desired by paying investors an after-tax return determined on "world" or "national" capital markets. With environmental regulations taking the form given by equation 3, we shall see that the assumption of a fixed labor supply enables capitalization to substitute for taxes as a means of assessing firms for environmental costs.

Observe first that capital taxation serves no useful role in this model. To elaborate, note that each firm maximizes profits by setting the revenue from another unit of capital, or VMP_K for "value of the marginal product," equal to the unit cost of capital:

$$VMP_K = r + t_K \tag{4}$$

where r is the after-tax return on capital facing the jurisdiction, and t_K is the effective tax imposed on a unit of capital, if any. From equation 4, it is apparent that the tax on capital is purely distortionary. Because the firm is able to vary its capital supply independently of emissions, any capital tax will reduce capital investment without optimally controlling emissions. In fact, emissions will be completely unaffected by this tax under the regulated emissions-labor ratio described by equation 3. For this reason, Oates and Schwab are able to demonstrate that this tax should be reduced to zero. It should not be negative either, because the cost of a capital subsidy would outweigh the benefits from additional investment. If emissions were unregulated, then there might be a "second-best" role for capital taxation as a means of indirectly reducing emissions, but this would come at the cost of inefficient disincentives to investment. For now, I assume that the emissions-labor ratio is regulated and that local governments optimally set the capital tax equal to zero.

In contrast to equation 4, firms hire labor beyond the point where its value of marginal product, denoted VMP_L, equals the unit cost of labor. The reason is that there is an extra benefit to hiring a unit of labor: the firm is allowed to raise emissions by α units. Letting w denote the after-tax wage rate and t_L the effective tax rate on a unit of labor, we may sum these two contributions to revenue to get the following condition for the profit-maximizing demand for labor:

$$VMP_L + VMP_E \cdot \alpha = w + t_L \tag{5}$$

where VMP_E is the additional value of output from a unit rise in emissions, or the "value of the marginal product of emissions."

Unlike the capital tax, this tax on labor is nondistortionary. In fact, it has no allocative effects in the Oates-Schwab model, because labor is assumed to be fixed in supply. A central law of tax incidence is that a tax on a "fixed factor" is borne entirely by that factor and does not distort the allocation of goods and resources. Thus a rise in t_L in equation 5 will merely cause the equilibrium w to fall by the same amount, leaving the cost of a unit of labor unchanged. The local government may want to set t_L at a positive level to finance public goods and services, but it cannot use this tax as a means of influencing firm behavior. In fact, the only policy that optimally influences firm behavior in this model is the regulation of emissions.

Turn now to the capitalization effect discussed at the start of this section. This effect is evident from equation 5. Given the tax rate t_L, the presence of $VMP_E \cdot \alpha$ on the left side must increase the wage rate on the right side by

$$\Delta w = VMP_E \cdot \alpha \tag{6}$$

In other words, the benefit a firm receives from being allowed to raise emissions as it hires more labor is fully "capitalized" into a higher wage rate. Through their local governments, therefore, residents have an incentive to reduce α to the level where the marginal value they place on the cleaner environment equals marginal loss in output, as measured by VMP_E. In other words, the equilibrium level of emissions will satisfy the optimality condition given by equation 1. No considerations involving capital flows enter into this decision-making rule, so there is no race to the bottom.

The assumption of a fixed labor supply is critical for this result. Suppose instead that there is an upward-sloping supply curve for labor. Then efficiency requires that the tax on labor be set equal to $VMP_E \cdot \alpha$ so that workers receive a wage rate equal to the value of marginal product of labor. In the absence of such a tax, equation 5 shows that the wage rate will exceed VMP_L, implying that workers supply too much labor in equilibrium. The problem here is that the local government effectively subsidizes labor through its policy of allowing firms to increase total emissions by α for each unit increase in the labor supply. Since a reduction in α from its first-best optimum reduces this distortionary subsidy, the government has an incentive to set α inefficiently low.

This is an argument in favor of NIMBY, however. Moreover, it relies on the unexplained absence of an optimal tax on labor. In any case, it seems odd that allowable emissions should be tied to firms' labor decisions, when restrictions on land use are a natural means of controlling production activities, including pollution emissions. We turn next to the role of land capitalization.

10.4.2   Land Capitalization

Let us now replace labor with land as the fixed factor in the Oates-Schwab model. Using the appropriate land-use controls, the government can control the emissions-land ratio, rather than the emissions-labor ratio. As a result, a rise in emissions is now capitalized into higher land rents. Thus a cleaner environment is again efficiently priced, and residents continue to face incentives to limit emissions efficiently, provided that they own the land used in production activities. If, however, there exist absentee landowners who can influence their land rents through changes in environmental quality, then political conflicts may arise. Some examples are discussed in the following paragraphs.

The ability of land-value capitalization to bring about efficient results calls into question whether equality between the tax treatment of residential and business property is really a problem, despite the focus given to this restriction by White and Fischel. These authors ignore capitalization as a means of compensating residents for the environmental costs firms impose on residents. For land-value capitalization to work, it must be accompanied by the appropriate land-use controls. In the White-Fischel framework, where jurisdictions contain both residential and business property, these controls must restrict the division of a jurisdiction's land between business and residential uses.

This recognition of the power of capitalization to achieve efficient results is not entirely new. Indeed, Hamilton (1976) has already constructed a similar type of argument for the case where the same tax rate is imposed on two types of housing to finance congestible public goods. Among the conditions he gives for "efficient supplies of all possible housing plus public service bundles" is the requirement that "in mixed-house value jurisdictions, land value differentials exactly reflect the present value of fiscal surplus differentials." Here, a "fiscal surplus differential" is the excess of the cost of providing a homeowner with public goods over the homeowner's property-tax payments. Hamilton's condition works against the common perception that the relatively low tax burdens faced by owners of low-value housing imply that their consumption of public goods is subsidized by owners of high-value housing. Land-value differentials compensate for such "fiscal surplus differentials," thereby bringing each homeowner's total burden in line with the cost of providing him or her with public goods. The same type of argument applies to the "fiscal surplus differentials" that might arise between residential and business property under a uniform property tax. As a result, residents are fully compensated for environmental costs even when the property tax fails to distinguish between different uses of property.

Consider now the types of political conflicts that might arise if some land available for industrial development is owned by absentee landowners, who are not harmed by the emissions from firms located there. Assume that there exist no mechanisms for transferring the land rents received by these owners to the local government, other than a uniform property tax on both residential and business property. These owners will obviously favor inefficiently lax environmental standards because they bear none of the resulting costs associated with a decline in environmental quality. In contrast, residents will favor inefficiently restrictive standards, because they do not fully bear the costs that stricter standards impose on landowners in the form of lower land rents. (To the extent that wages fall, residents will bear some of the costs, however.) In a jurisdiction with majority rule, the residents will win. On the other hand, the absentee landowners can exercise power by means of lobbying activities. Moreover, their incentive and ability to lobby should exceed that of residents in the likely case where the potential benefits from lobbying are concentrated among relatively few absentee landowners, in comparison to the more diffuse benefits of a cleaner environment. The final political equilibrium will depend on the importance of lobbying activities in determining policy decisions. None of these potential inefficiencies are directly tied to competition for scarce capital, however.

10.4.3   Capital Taxation and the Race to the Bottom

Section 10.4.1 observed that efficiency requires that mobile capital not be taxed. Let us now suppose that local governments do tax mobile capital for some unexplained reason. It follows that a reduction in the allowable emissions-labor ratio will carry a cost in addition to the wage reduction identified in section 10.4.1: Tax revenue falls because the tighter emission standards contract the capital supply, which serves as the tax base. This additional cost is represented by the second term on the right side of the benefit-cost rule (equation 2), with the net value of a unit of capital now equal to the unit tax rate on capital, t_K:

$$\Sigma_i MB^i = MC - t_K \cdot \Delta K \tag{7}$$

Thus the willingness to pay for tighter standards, given by the left side of equation 7, exceeds the direct resource cost, given by MC. In other words, there now exists a race to the bottom.

This result depends critically on the manner in which emissions are regulated in the Oates-Schwab model: a specified ratio of emissions to the quantity of a fixed factor ("labor" in the Oates-Schwab model). Capital taxes would emerge as efficiency enhancing if instead the government set a permissible ratio of emissions to capital supply. Under this regulation, the net value of capital at the margin (t in equation 2) would be negative in the absence of taxes, reflecting the additional emissions associated with another unit of capital. As a result, jurisdictions would possess incentives to discourage capital investment indirectly, including the use of stricter environmental regulations. To restore efficiency, it would be necessary to tax capital at a rate equal to the environmental damage associated with another unit of capital. In this manner, a jurisdiction would be fully compensated for the environmental costs associated with production within its borders. The local government would then have an incentive to choose an emissions level that is efficient from the viewpoint of the entire system of jurisdictions.

More generally, there may exist a variety of costs associated directly with capital inflows. Some may be government mandated, such as the emissions-capital ratio just discussed, while others may be technologically related to capital inflows, such as the need for additional utility hookups to service a given amount of capital. To the extent that direct "user fees" are not paid for these capital-related costs, a positive tax on capital will be desirable. If the tax exceeds the marginal value of these costs, however, then a race to the bottom will occur: Governments will view capital as being undersupplied because of the tax distortion, and they will possess incentives to lower environmental quality to inefficiently low levels to attract scarce capital.

This critical relation between capital taxes and capital-related costs is recognized by Revesz (1992) in his discussion of the race to the bottom. His reading of the literature leads to a negative conclusion about the race to the bottom:

There is an extensive literature on whether local property taxes are nondistortionary benefit taxes or user fees on public services received by the property owners or, whether, instead they are distortionary taxes on capital that are borne primarily by the owners of capital. But neither the theoretical nor the empirical work points clearly in one direction.... the fact remains that race-to-the-bottom arguments in the environmental area have been made for the last two decades with essentially no theoretical foundation.

Although Revesz's final conclusion is a bit strong, I agree that "neither the theoretical nor empirical work points clearly in one direction." Some theoretical approaches to endogenizing the taxation of capital are discussed in the next section.

10.5   Endogenous Capital Taxation

In the previous section, a positive tax rate on capital was shown to produce a race to the bottom, because capital then had a positive net value at the margin (a positive t in equation 2). But there is clearly no role for capital taxation in this model. More generally, if a government is concerned with attracting capital, then the least-cost way to do so would appear to be through either capital subsidies or reductions in existing taxes on capital, rather than through inefficiently lax environmental standards. This section discusses a few reasons why we might observe nonoptimalities in the tax treatment of capital, thereby creating a role for environmental policy as a means of influencing capital investment.

10.5.1   Productive and Unproductive Public Expenditures

One way to endogenize the tax rate on capital is to explicitly model the use of the tax revenue, and then treat the tax rate as a "control variable" in each local government's optimization problem.[2] The literature contains two ways to proceed. First, we can follow the approach of the optimal taxation literature by assuming that capital is taxed to finance public goods that directly benefit residents (see Zodrow and Mieszkowski, 1986, and Wilson, 1986). Alternatively, we could follow Oates and Schwab's extension of their basic model to account for the self-interested behavior of government officials. Specifically, they consider the implications of Niskanen's (1971) revenue-maximization hypothesis for the race to the bottom, under which government officials benefit from increasing the "size of government." Revenue maximization would have rather extreme implications, if there were not some type of constraint on this behavior. Rather than directly model such constraints, Oates and Schwab consider a model in which government officials maximize not just government revenue, but rather a function that has both government revenue and resident utilities as arguments. But tax revenue also enters the objective function in the tax competition literature. The difference is that the use of tax revenue is treated as socially unproductive in the Niskanen model, whereas it finances public goods that benefit the voters in the tax competition model. Because this is just a difference of interpretation, the two models must yield similar results about the tax system.

Two main results emerge. First, the existence of tax revenue in the government objective function implies that the optimal tax on capital is positive. Second, government officials choose inefficiently lax environmental standards. Given the positive tax rate, weaker standards are beneficial because they expand the tax base.

This model may explain the rate at which capital is taxed, given the assumption that capital taxation is needed to raise revenue, but it does not explain why local governments do not rely on less distortionary revenue sources. One approach to correcting this deficiency is to use Bucovetsky and Wilson's (1991) extension of the tax competition model to include wage taxation. They prove that a tax on wage income dominates a tax on capital income, although their model contains labor-leisure distortions.[3] Despite the absence of capital taxation, they reach the same conclusion as the tax competition literature: public goods are underprovided. Their argument basically consists of showing that a rise in one jurisdiction's tax-financed public-good supply benefits other jurisdictions by providing them with more capital. In other words, public-good provision creates a "positive externality," which implies that local governments underprovide the public good.

This underprovision result can be extended to the case of environmental quality. When a single jurisdiction strengthens its environmental standards, capital investment is redirected into other jurisdictions, thereby depressing the equilibrium return on capital. The wage rates offered to workers in other jurisdictions are then bid up to maintain zero profits, as required for a competitive equilibrium. But higher wage rates encourage workers to supply more labor, thereby counteracting the distortionary effect of wage taxation on the supply of labor.[4] This reduction in labor-supply distortions represents a "positive externality" from the stricter environmental standards. Thus we find that there is a race to the bottom here, despite the absence of capital taxation.

10.5.2   Heterogeneous Voters

Another approach is to assume that jurisdictions contain individuals with different factor endowments, thereby creating a political conflict with respect to the determination of environmental quality. Oates and Schwab investigate this approach by amending their basic model to include a group of residents who do not supply labor. If wage earners control the government, then they will desire to subsidize mobile capital, because attracting additional capital increases wage rates, while non-wage earners are assumed to pay part of the cost of the subsidy. With capital subsidized, however, the capital outflow that results from tighter environmental standards will now enter the optimality condition as a benefit (t is negative in equation 2). This consideration produces the NIMBY possibility, but the failure of wage earners to account for the benefits non-wage earners receive from improved environmental quality works in the direction of overly lax standards. Oates and Schwab are also unable to determine whether non-wage earners prefer more or less environmental quality than do wage earners. It is clear that heterogeneity in the residential population cannot be expected to produce firm conclusions for or against a race to the bottom.

10.5.3   Tax Evasion

The collection of taxes is not a costless activity. Governments face administrative and collection costs, and the individual taxpayers face compliance costs. In part, these costs are caused by the incentives taxpayers face to try to avoid paying taxes, either through legal tax-avoidance schemes or through illegal tax evasion. Much of the literature reviewed in this paper makes assumptions about which tax instruments are available to governments, but then it assumes that the available tax instruments may be used at no cost, whereas presumably those tax instruments not employed possess prohibitive costs. It would be far more satisfying to analyze the possibility of a race to the bottom when the costs of taxation are more explicitly recognized in the analysis. This section briefly discusses how the Oates-Schwab model can be amended to include the costs associated with tax evasion.

To create a role for capital taxation, assume now that the use of capital requires public services, at a constant cost c per unit of capital. If the taxation of capital were costless, as in Oates-Schwab, governments would have an incentive to levy a tax on firms equal to c dollars per unit of capital employed, thereby forcing these firms to take into account the costs they impose on the community when they employ additional capital. With capital optimally taxed, there would be no reason for governments to manipulate environmental policies to achieve a desirable change in the capital supply. Assume, however, that firms can evade this tax by failing to report the full amount of capital that they employ, and let g be the cost of failing to report a unit of capital. Following the specification of Cremer and Gahvari (1993), assume that the evasion cost g is positively related to the percentage of capital that is unreported. The firm has knowledge of this evasion cost, along with the statutory tax rate and the probability that it will be audited and thereby caught evading taxes (in which case it is fined). Given these variables, the firm chooses the profit-maximizing level of tax evasion, thereby determining the expected tax rate on a unit of capital, denoted t^e. (Firms are assumed to be risk neutral.) Following the arguments of Cremer and Gahvari, it is possible to show that a rise in the statutory tax rate induces the firm to evade taxes on a greater percentage of its capital stock. Thus, the evasion cost g is also positively related to this tax rate.

This model produces a discrepancy between t^e and public-service costs c that would not be present if a higher tax rate did not raise evasion costs. The basic intuition may be briefly stated. Since capital investors demand the equilibrium after-tax return r, regardless of the level of evasion, the capital costs facing domestic firms fully reflect all evasion costs. Since these firms are competitive and therefore always receive zero economic profits, the burden of these evasion costs must be passed on to residents in the form of lower wages. In an effort to induce firms to lower costly evasion activities, the government will lower the statutory tax rate to a level where t^e falls short of c.

This discrepancy implies that the government no longer follows the first-best rule for environmental standards, given by equation 1. Rather it follows the second-best rule given by equation 2, where the net value of capital, t, is given by the negative quantity, $t^e - c$. In other words, the undertaxation of capital leaves the government with an incentive to deviate from the first-best rule in a way that causes a capital *outflow*. We therefore come to the conclusion that there is a NIMBY problem, rather than a race to the bottom.

10.5.4   Monopoly Power on Capital Markets

Another way to generate nonzero tax rates on capital is to modify the Oates-Schwab model by assuming that the individual jurisdictions are sufficiently large demanders of capital to have some influence over the equilibrium after-tax return that investors are able to receive for their capital (r). In this case, standard arguments show that a jurisdiction that imports capital has an incentive to tax it at a positive rate; doing so drives down r by discouraging domestic firms from employing capital. The fall in r represents a favorable change in the "terms of trade" for a capital-importing jurisdiction. By symmetrical arguments, a jurisdiction that exports capital has an incentive to subsidize capital.

If these capital taxes and subsidies can be costlessly chosen, however, then a jurisdiction can achieve its optimal capital supply without any need to deviate from the rules for a first-best environmental policy. On the other hand, the existence of costs in the collection and administration of capital taxes, such as the evasion costs discussed earlier, will again lead to inefficient choices of environmental policies, as these policies are now used to influence the location of capital. Thus market power alone does not create a race or NIMBY. Rather, it creates a role for capital taxes (or subsidies) and, as a result, the possibility that environmental policies will be used to compensate for nonoptimalities in these taxes.

10.6   Unemployment

To this point, I have considered models where the only potential sources of inefficiency in the private sector are government imposed, most notably capital taxation. Two alternative sources of inefficiency are imperfect competition and unemployment. The current section discusses the implications of unemployment for the possibility of a race to the bottom.

Huang (1992) provides an extensive analysis of unemployment in the context of a tax-competition model. As described in the previous section, a common feature of tax-competition models is that local governments provide public goods to their residents and finance them with a tax on mobile capital. Huang considers two types of unemployment: fixed-wage unemployment, which results from wage rates being exogenously fixed at levels above those that equate supply with demand; and efficiency-wage unemployment, where firms endogenously choose to offer wage rates above their market-clearing levels because worker productivity is positively related to these wage rates. (Huang assumes that higher wage rates lessen "shirking" among workers, but the efficiency-wage literature contains several justifications for the positive relation between wages and productivity.) These two specifications yield similar results. Specifically, the presence of unemployment aggravates the basic inefficiency associated with tax competition, this being inefficiently low public-good levels. It does so by adding another cost to public-good provision: the positive effect of a higher tax rate on unemployment, which is present because a tax-induced outflow of capital causes firms to reduce their employment levels.

By adding pollution emissions to Huang's model, it is possible to demonstrate the existence of a race to the bottom in the presence of unemployment. Specifically, consider his fixed-wage model, which contains land, capital, and labor. Emissions can be added to this model as a fourth "factor of production." As in section 10.4.2, suppose that environmental regulations take the form of a fixed emissions-land ratio. Then the rule used by a local government for determining this ratio takes the form of equation 2, in which the capital outflow associated with a decrease in allowable emissions represents an additional cost. In other words, an additional unit of capital has a positive net value to the jurisdiction, denoted t in equation 2. To describe this value, let $\Delta L/\Delta K$ denote the employment change from a unit rise in the supply of capital, let w denote the wage rate, and let e denote the opportunity cost of work. In other words, e is the value of a worker's time in activities while unemployed.[5] It is then easy to see that a unit of capital has the following value:

$$t = (w - e) \cdot (\Delta L/\Delta K) \tag{8}$$

Given that unemployment is involuntary, the wage rate will exceed the opportunity cost. Thus any employment reduction associated with a tax-induced capital outflow will represent a social cost of higher standards. As defined in section 10.2, there is a race to the bottom.

This argument does not require the use of capital taxation, which also leads to a race to the bottom (see section 10.4.3). Thus this explanation for a race to the bottom is not weakened by the presence of an unexplained tax. (If capital is taxed, then the presence of unemployment can aggravate an existing race.) However, the use of environmental policies to influence unemployment raises a common question about unemployment models: Why do governments not employ subsidies that might eliminate or reduce unemployment at a far lower social cost than would be incurred by manipulating regulatory or expenditure policies? Wage subsidies are an obvious candidate, and capital subsidies would indirectly raise employment by encouraging firms to employ more capital, thereby making labor more productive.

A couple of explanations can be given for the limited use of subsidies as an employment-increasing device, but each has its shortcomings. First, the taxes needed to finance these subsidies distort other consumption and production decisions. The problem with this explanation is that tax distortions are typically viewed as small relative to the inefficiencies associated with unemployment. Alternatively, a political-economy explanation could be constructed. One approach is Magee, Brock, and Young's (1989) theory of "optimal obfuscation," which they use to explain the choice of trade policy instruments. Direct production subsidies may be more efficient than tariffs (because the latter distort both production decisions and consumption decisions), but tariffs achieve their desired goals—protecting specific industries from import competition—at a cost that is less transparent to most voters. Similarly, one might try to argue that the costs involved in competing for capital through complex manipulations in environmental regulations are less transparent than those associated with wage or investment subsidies. On the other hand, the increasing focus of voters on environmental concerns makes such arguments less compelling.

10.7 Lumpy Investments

An important feature of the analysis so far is that investment decisions may be made in small increments. Suppose, instead, that investments come in only large increments. Then the minimum investment required in a jurisdiction may be too large to be beneficial for that jurisdiction. Whether this is the case may depend on whether similar types of investment have already been undertaken in other jurisdictions. Specifically, an investment in one jurisdiction may benefit other jurisdictions by supplying them with goods while allowing them to escape the environmental costs associated with the production of these goods.

This type of situation is considered by Markusen, Morey, and Olewiler (1995, hereafter MMO), using a model with two jurisdictions and one imperfectly competitive firm. An important decision facing the firm is whether to locate its entire production activities in one jurisdiction or to split these activities between jurisdictions. Investment is lumpy, because the operation of a plant requires a "plant-specific fixed cost." For this reason, the firm can lower total production costs by operating only a single plant in one of the two jurisdictions. The trade-off here is that the firm must then incur the "export costs" needed to export its output to consumers in the other jurisdiction. MMO emphasize imperfectly competitive markets by assuming that the firm faces a downward-sloping demand curve for its product, but the lumpy-investment aspect of the model creates its own problems for efficient investment decisions, independently of imperfect competition.

To see this, consider instead a competitive industry that finds it desirable to locate operations in only one jurisdiction, because of the "agglomeration effects" that come from the firms in the industry operating in close proximity to each other. (Thus perfect competition is maintained despite advantages to large-scale production, because there exist increasing returns to scale that are "external" to the firms within the industry but "internal" to the industry itself.) Suppose finally that the industry produces a fixed amount of pollution, which has an income-equivalent value of P to the residents of the given jurisdiction; that is, they are willing to pay P to forgo this pollution.

Given this setup, it is easy to identify cases where neither jurisdiction finds it worthwhile for the industry to operate within its borders, although the industry should operate in one of the two jurisdictions from the viewpoint of their combined welfare. Let CS^i denote the "consumers' surplus" generated by the sale of output at the competitive price in jurisdiction i—that is, the excess of the maximum amount that consumers are willing to pay for the good over what they actually pay. CS^i is positive under the assumption of downward-sloping demand curves. Following MMO, assume for simplicity that industry operations do not alter factor prices or other product prices. Then the total value of the industry's production activities to the two jurisdictions is

$$CS^1 + CS^2 - P \tag{9}$$

If this quantity is positive, then it is efficient for the industry to operate. (Economic profits do not enter equation 9 because they are zero under the assumption of perfect competition.) Specifically, the operation of the industry would make both jurisdictions better off, at least in the case where a central government could use intergovernmental transfers to distribute the gains.

However, a single jurisdiction acting unilaterally may find it desirable to disallow industry operations within its borders, even when the total value of industry operations, given by equation 9, is positive. For jurisdiction i, this case occurs when

$$CS^i - P < 0 \tag{10}$$

Thus, rather than producing a race to the bottom, lumpy investment has the potential to produce the case of NIMBY, or "not in my backyard."

This problem seems to justify central government intervention. Specifically, the central government could distribute the gains from a lumpy investment project by announcing that a subsidy would be provided to the jurisdiction that agreed to allow the polluting firm to locate there. Alternatively, the jurisdictions might enter into a cooperative agreement by engaging in similar interjurisdictional transfers themselves.

Myers (1990) and Mansoorian and Myers (1993) argue that the role for central government intervention in the form of a transfer policy may be more limited than previously supposed. In particular, local governments may have an incentive to voluntarily implement the interjurisdictional transfers needed to achieve an efficient equilibrium. These authors consider the use of transfers to achieve an efficient allocation of labor across jurisdictions, but the same idea can be applied to capital mobility. Specifically, suppose that each jurisdiction chooses one of the following courses of action: impose a positive pollution tax on the industry but allow it to enter, or bar entry but subsidize the industry's activities elsewhere. Then there exists a noncooperative "Nash equilibrium" under which jurisdiction 1 allows entry and collects tax payments of, say, aP for some fraction a, whereas jurisdiction 2 provides the industry with a subsidy of aP (which the firms in the industry then use to pay the tax). In this case, industry profits remain equal to zero, but the appropriate choice of a enables both jurisdictions to benefit from the industry's operations, provided the total net benefits (measured by equation 9) are positive. For this to be a Nash equilibrium, each jurisdiction must be choosing its optimal tax or subsidy, given that levied by the other jurisdiction. This condition is met here: Jurisdiction 2 wants to provide the minimum subsidy needed to induce the industry to operate in 1, and this minimum subsidy equals the tax that jurisdiction 1 is levying, aP. Any lower subsidy would leave the competitive industry with negative profits, which is impossible in equilibrium. Likewise, jurisdiction 1 wants to levy the maximum tax, which equals the subsidy jurisdiction 1 is levying. The combination of tax and subsidy leaves the industry with zero profits. Note that this Nash equilibrium is not unique: there clearly exists a range of tax-subsidy combinations that are consistent with zero profits and positive benefits for both jurisdictions.

The assumption of two jurisdictions is not critical. A similar Nash equilibrium could be defined for a system of many jurisdictions. As the number of jurisdictions rises, however, the assumption that jurisdictions possess perfect information about the industry's profit opportunities, pollution emissions, and the strategies of all other jurisdictions is likely to become increasingly troublesome. Central government intervention might be used here to facilitate an investment allocation that the jurisdictions would like to achieve. However, political conflicts are likely to arise with regard to the distribution of intergovernmental transfers.

10.8   Imperfect Competition

This section uses the Markusen et al. (MMO) model to investigate the implications of imperfect competition for a possible race to the bottom. Little support is found for such a race, and two alternative specifications of the model also fail to generate support.

We might expect the presence of imperfect competition to lead to inefficient government behavior, regardless of the presence of environmental externalities. The problem is that each jurisdiction possesses incentives to engage in profit-shifting activities, by which the profits associated with imperfect competition are shifted into the hands of the jurisdiction's residents. This problem has long been recognized in the international trade literature, and it is also evident in the MMO analysis, because the authors assume that the firm is owned by nonresidents, or "absentee owners." Under their assumption that each unit of output produces pollution with an income-equivalent cost of b, the efficient pollution tax would be levied at the unit rate b on all output. This policy would "internalize" the cost of pollution, causing the firm to efficiently account for pollution in its output decisions. Local governments choose not to adhere to this optimal policy, regardless of whether plant location is endogenous. The reason is that taxes on output serve a profit-shifting role in addition to their pollution-control role. In fact, MMO's numerical calculations for the exogenous-location case show that the equilibrium tax rates chosen by local governments significantly exceed b. If plant location is endogenous, then either the NIMBY case discussed earlier arises, where taxes drive the firm out of both jurisdictions, or a "race to the bottom" occurs, with taxes being significantly reduced through interjurisdictional competition for plants. However, this competition brings the output taxes *closer* to b, because it takes away a local government's ability to tax away a sizable share of the profits going to absentee owners.[6]

Is this a race to the bottom? The answer depends on how we view welfare. If the absentee owners of the firm do not "count" in the measure of welfare, then the lower output taxes that result from competition for plants may be viewed as undesirable. Indeed, MMO show that this competition does reduce the total welfare of the two jurisdictions. On the other hand, it seems sensible to recognize the distributional implications of this competition by placing some weight on firm profits. In this case, the drop in output taxes is not necessarily bad.

One way to eliminate profit shifting as a central motivation behind the taxation of output is to introduce a nondistortionary profits tax. This change allows local governments to compete for plants through lower profits taxes, rather than lower taxes on plant outputs. Whether the equilibrium is efficient from the combined viewpoints of jurisdictions and firm owners depends on the level of export costs. If these costs are high enough to induce the firm to locate a plant in each jurisdiction, then the equilibrium is efficient. Note, however, that the tax rates on output must be less than the efficient pollution tax, b, in order to raise outputs above their inefficiently low monopoly levels. The taxes may even be negative if b is small relative to the exercise of monopoly power. These relatively low taxes may look like a race to the bottom, but this conclusion ignores the role of these taxes in controlling monopoly power.

Efficiency is not possible when export costs are low enough to induce the firm to locate all production activities in only one jurisdiction. In this case, the host jurisdiction's local government taxes exports at the rate b, because it has no incentive to raise the consumers' surplus received by the residents in the importing jurisdiction.[7] But the result is an inefficiently low level of exports, implying too little pollution, not too much.

Another direction to go with the analysis of imperfect competition is to use Janeba's (1995) alternative specification of tax competition under imperfect competition, where there are no absentee landowners. He assumes that there exist two firms, "home" and "foreign," as distinguished by the jurisdiction in which the owners reside. A key feature of the model is that the two firms compete with each other in a third country, where they sell all of their output. The two local governments play a Nash game in "profits taxes," with profits calculated with less than full deductibility of costs. These taxes are equivalent to the taxes on output in the MMO model. Local governments choose the rates of taxation prior to the locational and output decisions of firms, and welfare in a jurisdiction is the sum of tax revenue and the profits of its firm, where the former is negative in the case of negative tax rates (a profits subsidy). This model contains no pollution externalities, but they could be added by using the MMO specification, under which a unit of output generates pollution with an income-equivalent cost equal to b.

Janeba shows that local governments subsidize production when firm locations are fixed, the motivation being to encourage firms to grab a larger share of the market and thereby increase profits. When pollution is added to the model, production is still effectively subsidized, in the sense that it is taxed at a rate (possibly negative) that lies below pollution cost b. This effective subsidy disappears once firms become mobile. The two jurisdictions essentially compete for firms by bidding the tax rate up to b (zero in Janeba's model), at which point they are indifferent about where firms locate. If the tax rate were lower than b, each jurisdiction would have an incentive to "overcut" the other in order to prevent the firms from locating there. This process of "overcutting" would then lead to the tax rate b, at which point all production costs, including pollution externalities, are fully "internalized." Similarly, a tax rate greater than b would lead to undercutting.

To conclude, allowing firms to be interjurisdictionally mobile in Janeba's model *raises* the equilibrium pollution tax. This is certainly not a race to the bottom, but it is not NIMBY either, because the equilibrium pollution taxes are efficient. We may add Janeba's model to the growing list of models that fail to produce a race to the bottom.

10.9   Bargaining: The Bond-Samuelson Model

The models discussed to this point have assumed that local governments confront potential firms with taxes and environmental standards. An alternative approach would be for each local government to bargain with individual firms over these two variables. Can any type of "race" result from such a model? The answer is again found to depend on assumptions about the available tax instruments.

I consider the two-period model developed by Bond and Samuelson (1989). They assume that a single "host country" negotiates with a firm over tax rates. The firm has the option of serving the "world market" from the "host country" in both periods. Alternatively, it can operate in the "source country" both periods, or it can enter the host country in the first period but then return to the source country in the second period. The model is partial equilibrium in the sense that the firm's presence in the host country is assumed not to affect product or factor prices. Thus the host government cares only about the tax revenue it can obtain over the two periods. The tax under consideration is a "profits tax," with the tax base equaling revenue minus an exogenously determined percentage of costs. The authors do not consider pollution externalities, but their model has important implications for a race to the bottom once pollution is added to the model.

Two bargaining situations are compared. First, the host country initially commits to a tax policy for both periods. In this case, it is not allowed to renege on a previously announced tax policy once the second period arrives. The second case assumes that commitment is not possible; that is, the host country is free to renegotiate taxes once the second period arrives. A major result of the paper, however, is that this freedom to renegotiate generally harms the host country: The firm will anticipate that if it enters in the first period, the host country will raise taxes in the second period. As a result, the firm will insist on significantly lower first-period taxes than it would accept if commitment were possible. (In both cases, the authors employ the "Nash bargaining solution," under which the two parties split the gains that can be obtained over the noncooperative outcome, which here consists of the firm locating in the source country.)

The way in which Bond and Samuelson handle capital investment suggests a natural way to model bargaining over environmental standards. Specifically, they assume that the firm makes its investment decisions after first-period tax rates have been determined. Having chosen its level of capital, however, the firm is unable to alter this level during the two periods under consideration. In other words, the presence of significant adjustment costs turns capital into a fixed factor. By similar reasoning, it seems reasonable to interpret pollution emissions as a fixed factor for a firm. Once the firm and government have bargained over emission levels in the first period, the firm will have to invest in the type of production process needed to achieve these levels. If the government were to insist on a change in these levels in the second period, then the firm would likely encounter significant adjustment costs in making the required change. On the other hand, taxes can be changed with little cost, making it relatively difficult for a government to commit to particular rates of taxation over a significant period of time. Indeed, this lack of commitment is reflected in the popular use of tax holidays, by which governments typically guarantee a firm little or no tax liabilities over an *initial* period of time.

Thus, assume that the first-period bargaining between the firm and government is over first-period taxes *and* environmental standards for both periods. Second-period bargaining is then over second-period taxes alone. Following Oates and Schwab, assume that the firm's output is a function of its labor, capital, and pollution emissions. Capital is fixed once first-period decisions are made.[8] Finally, amend the government's objective function by assuming not only that it depends positively on tax payments, but also that it depends negatively on the pollution emissions generated over the two periods.

Based on the analysis of capital taxation in the Oates-Schwab model (see section 10.4.3), it seems reasonable to expect this framework to produce a race to the bottom, if the firm and government choose a tax rate that distorts the firm's subsequent capital investment decision. This is indeed the case. Lower emission standards will attract additional investment, which will raise tax revenue, and this additional tax revenue represents an added benefit that would not be present if the tax base were fixed.

The surprising conclusion, however, is that a race will occur even in the case where a pure profits tax is employed, under which all costs are tax deductible. In this case, no race would occur in the Oates-Schwab model, because an additional unit of capital would fail to benefit the jurisdiction by increasing tax revenue. In the current model, tax revenue does rise, even with full deductibility. The reason is that the investment raises second-period profits by increasing the firm's revenue; all investment costs are incurred in the first period. Under the Nash bargaining solution, the government and firm split the gains from the higher second-period profits when they negotiate the tax burden in the second period. Consequently, any additional investment that can be attracted to the country by means of lower environmental standards will generate additional tax revenue, even if production costs are fully tax deductible. It follows that a race to the bottom will occur. In terms of our benchmark equation (2), the net value of investment, t, can be positive even if capital is not directly taxed at the margin.

The existence of a race to the bottom under pure profits taxation leads to the same type of question asked throughout this study: Are other policy instruments available that might preclude this race? The answer is clearly yes. In particular, the government would benefit from being able to commit to a definition of taxable profits that includes more than 100 percent deduction of costs. (Various accelerated depreciation rules have this effect.) At a given positive tax rate on these profits, this would produce a subsidy to capital investment at the margin, and the appropriate subsidy rate could be used to offset the positive relation between investment and the tax burden negotiated in the second period. In this way, the government might be able to eliminate capital market distortions and, by so doing, get rid of the race to the bottom. On the other hand, an argument in defense of Bond and Samuelson's exogenously fixed deduction rate is that this rate is set with objectives in mind other than those involving the bargaining process under consideration. Thus there may be some justification for the assumptions that produce a race to the bottom in this bargaining framework.

10.10   Auctions: The King-McAfee-Welling Model

I now consider interjurisdictional competition for capital by means of an auction mechanism. This approach is investigated by King, McAfee, and Welling (1993), using a model with two jurisdictions competing for a single firm. As in Bond and Samuelson, there are two periods, and the firm is free to relocate (at a cost) in the second period. The local governments use an ascending-bid auction in each period to determine the firm's location. This auction has the property that the "winner" allows the firm to keep income equal to the "surplus" that it would have received by locating in the other jurisdiction. The surpluses are exogenously fixed in the first part of the paper (i.e., no public or private investment decisions are modeled), but the surplus earned in a given jurisdiction becomes known only after the firm locates there. The authors show that, in each period, the firm locates where its expected surplus is highest.

The second part of the paper allows each jurisdiction to invest in "infrastructure," which increases the surplus available in both periods. What makes this analysis particularly intriguing for the environmental concerns of the present chapter is the authors' reinterpretation of "infrastructure" as environmental standards: "Thus the infrastructure game in our model can be reinterpreted as one in which regions compete by, for instance, setting environmental standards with which firms must comply" (pp. 605–606). Before the auction takes place, the two jurisdictions play a Nash game in investment levels, under which each jurisdiction sets its investment level optimally, given the level chosen by the other jurisdiction. The authors show that only an asymmetric Nash equilibrium exists, where the equilibrium investment levels differ. In the first period, the firm locates where investment is highest. However, the losing jurisdiction may still choose a positive (but lower) investment level, because this raises the probability that the firm will switch locations in the second period. This possibility of relocation implies that the losing jurisdiction's investment is not socially wasteful. In fact, the authors show that the equilibrium is efficient.

With regard to environmental policy, then, the analysis shows that a bidding process between jurisdictions for a firm need not lead to a race to the bottom, and that the asymmetric environmental standards that result from this bidding may be an efficient outcome. Thus the paper provides a nice counterexample to arguments that environmental standards should be equalized to "level the playing field."

10.11   Concluding Remarks

The local-public-economics literature has uncovered many ways in which decentralized decision making by local governments is inefficient and therefore requires some type of central government intervention. However, the results reported in this paper suggest that a "race" is not a generic feature of systems of independent governments. Models of a "race" tend to be incomplete, because they fail to justify the absence of more direct means of attracting capital to a jurisdiction, most notably direct subsidies or at least reduced tax rates on capital. Other models give rise to the opposite problem, NIMBY, where environmental standards are inefficiently restrictive. Throughout this study, I have emphasized the need for a better understanding of why governments choose to use some tax or subsidy instruments but not others, particularly those that might substitute for the use of environmental policy to influence capital investment. A priority for future research should be better models of the "political market failures" that may cause governments to bypass efficient tax and subsidy policies in favor of inefficient environmental policies.

The analysis of environmental policies in a system of independent governments raises other special problems that have been insufficiently studied in the local-public-economics literature. I close by mentioning a few:

Enforcement Problems
This chapter has largely ignored imperfections in a government's ability to implement environmental regulations. For the concerns of the present study, an important question is whether such imperfections affect the role of capital mobility in environmental decisions. Among the many ways to approach this question, one can think of the particular problems associated with "adverse selection," whereby firms possess different abilities to evade standards, forcing jurisdictions to give special attention to designing their standards in a way that does not attract the "more able evaders."

Uncertainty and Durability
Environmental regulations are a good example of a durable public good, because the production decisions that firms must make to satisfy these regulations are not easily undone. Uncertainty about future costs and benefits is an inherent feature of projects with a long life. There are major uncertainties concerning the long-run impacts of particular pollutants on the environment, and future technologies for controlling pollution are also highly uncertain. It is not clear whether these uncertainties favor local governments or the central government as the appropriate decision makers on environmental issues. To the extent that environmental costs are localized in the area where production occurs, an argument in favor of local governments is that they possess well-known informational advantages over a central government with regard to activities occurring within their boundaries. On the other hand, firms themselves may possess information that is superior to that of local or central governments, at least in the area of technological capabilities for reducing pollution emissions. It would be useful to examine how mobile firms might exploit this advantage

in their negotiations with competing local governments, and whether this advantage might provide a role for central government intervention.

Labor Mobility and Durability
Given that some effects of environmental regulations are long-lived, many of the existing residents of a jurisdiction are likely to be absent from that jurisdiction before the benefits and costs of these regulations have been fully realized. Oates and Schwab claim that this is not a problem, because these existing benefits and costs will accrue to residents who leave jurisdictions in the form of reduced property values: "Capitalization of future streams of benefits and costs can thus compel even myopic decision-makers to take cognizance of the future" (1988, p. 352). But this gets us back to the problems of uncertainty in future benefits and costs. To the extent that such uncertainties cause the expected net benefits of specific regulatory programs to be undercapitalized, there will exist incentives to weaken these programs. Recent work by Sprunger and Wilson (1994) has identified conditions for both under- and overcapitalization of the net benefits of durable public goods. It would be useful to investigate the environmental standards chosen by local governments in a model with both capital mobility and the type of labor mobility examined by Sprunger and Wilson.

NOTES

I would like to thank Jagdish Bhagwati, Alvin Klevorick, Ray Riezman, and T. N. Srinavasan for helpful comments and suggestions. Partial research support was provided by the National Science Foundation under Grant No. SES 9209168.

1. Thus it is more accurate to use the term "race toward the bottom," but I will stick with the more popular terminology.

2. In Oates and Schwab's main model, the tax revenue is returned to residents as a lump-sum payment. In other words, the government has no revenue needs.

3. This result assumes that the jurisdiction has a negligible influence over the after-tax return on capital. Bucovetsky and Wilson also consider the case where jurisdictions possess market power on the capital market.

4. This argument assumes that government revenue requirements are sufficiently high for the chosen labor tax to exceed the efficient rate. As noted in Section 10.4.1, this rate will be positive under the Oates-Schwab assumption that the labor-emissions ratio is fixed by the government. Details are available upon request.

5. In Huang's fixed-wage model, e equals zero because workers have no uses of time outside of labor. But the analysis may be easily extended to the case of a positive e.

6. Rauscher (1994) identifies an intermediate case where plant mobility raises the equilibrium taxes, but not enough to eliminate production. By restricting the firm to operate only a single plant and assuming zero export costs, he is able to obtain analytical results that help clarify the numerical examples described by MMO.

7. Rauscher (1994) has independently made the same point.

8. Unlike Oates and Schwab, who assume a fixed supply of labor for a jurisdiction, Bond and Samuelson allow a perfectly elastic supply of labor, in keeping with their analysis of the choices confronting a single firm.

REFERENCES

Bond, Eric W., and Larry Samuelson. 1989. "Bargaining with commitment, choice of techniques, and direct foreign investment." *Journal of International Economics*, 26:77–98.

Bucovetsky, S., and J. D. Wilson. 1991. "Tax competition with two tax instruments." *Regional Science and Urban Economics*, 21:333–350.

Cremer, Helmuth, and Firouz Gahvari. 1993. "Tax evasion and optimal commodity taxation." *Journal of Public Economics*, 50:261–276.

Cropper, Maureen L., and Wallace E. Oates. 1992. "Environmental economics: A survey." *Journal of Economic Literature*, 30:675–740.

Fischel, William A. 1975. "Fiscal and environmental considerations in the location of firms in suburban communities." In E. Mills and W. Oates, eds., *Fiscal zoning and land use controls*, 119–174. Lexington, MA: D. C. Heath.

Hamilton, Bruce W. 1975. "Zoning and property taxation in a system of local governments." *Urban Studies*, 12:205–211.

Hamilton, Bruce W. 1976. "Capitalization of intrajurisdictional differences in local tax prices." *American Economic Review*, 66:743–753.

Huang, Yophy. 1992. "Tax competition with involuntary unemployment." Ph.D. thesis, Indiana University.

Janeba, Eckhard. 1995. "Tax competition in imperfectly competitive markets" (unpublished manuscript). Indiana University.

King, Ian, R. Preston McAfee, and Linda Welling. "Industrial blackmail: Dynamic tax competition and public investment." *Canadian Journal of Economics*, 26:590–608.

Magee, Stephen P., William A. Brock, and Leslie Young. 1989. *Black hole tariffs and endogenous policy theory*. Cambridge: Cambridge University Press.

Mansoorian, Arman, and Gordon M. Myers. 1993. "Attachment to home and efficient purchases of population in a fiscal externality economy." *Journal of Public Economics*, 52: 117–132.

Markusen, James R., Edward R. Morey, and Nancy Olewiler. 1995. "Competition in regional environmental policies when plant locations are endogenous. *Journal of Public Economics*, 56:55–77.

Myers, Gordon M. 1990. "Optimality, free mobility, and the regional authority in a federation." *Journal of Public Economics*, 43:107–122.

Niskanen, W. 1971. *Bureaucracy and representative government.* Chicago: Aldine.

Oates, Wallace E., and Robert M. Schwab. 1988. "Economic competition among jurisdictions: Efficiency enhancing or distortion inducing." *Journal of Public Economics*, 35:333–354.

Rauscher, Michael, 1994. "Environmental regulation and the location of polluting industries" (unpublished manuscript). University of Kiel.

Revesz, Richard L. 1992. "Rehabilitating interstate competition: Rethinking the "race-to-the-bottom" rationale for federal environmental regulation." *New York University Law Review*, 67:1220–54.

Sonstelie, Jon. 1978. "Classified property tax." In *Technical aspects of the district's tax system: Studies and papers prepared for the District of Columbia Tax Revision Commission.* Washington, DC: U.S. Government Printing Office.

Sprunger, Philip, and John Douglas Wilson. 1994. "Imperfectly mobile households and durable local public goods: Does the capitalization mechanism work?" (unpublished manuscript). Indiana University.

Tiebout, Charles M. 1956. "A pure theory of local expenditures." *Journal of Political Economy*, 64:416–424.

White, Michelle J. 1975. "Firm location in a zoned metropolitan area." In Edwin S. Mills and Wallace E. Oates, eds., *Fiscal zoning and land use controls.* Lexington, MA: D. C. Heath.

Wilson, John Douglas. 1986. "A theory of interregional tax competition." *Journal of Urban Economics*, 19:296–315.

Zodrow, G. R., and P. Mieszkowski. 1986. "Pigou, Tiebout, property taxation, and the underprovision of local public goods." *Journal of Urban Economics*, 19:356–370.

11

Environmental Regulations and Industry Location: International and Domestic Evidence

Arik Levinson

All my life I've seen the lads leaving ... for the big smoke in London, Pittsburgh, Birmingham, and Chicago. It'd be better....if they stayed here and we imported the smoke.[1]

For nearly a quarter century, since industrialized nations began legislating and enforcing environmental laws with substantial compliance costs, critics of those regulations have protested that stringent environmental regulations force manufacturers of pollution-intensive products overseas. Jargon such as "eco-dumping," "race to the bottom," and "competition in laxity" have been used to describe a feared consequence of this phenomenon, that different jurisdictions competing to attract international businesses would create pollution havens by lowering their environmental standards below socially efficient levels. Most of the theoretical economics literature on interjurisdictional competition concludes that without a long and somewhat unrealistic list of assumptions concerning the nature of the jurisdictions involved, such competition will indeed lead to inefficient outcomes.[2] However, in contrast to the fears of environmentalists and the models of economic theorists, such competition does not seem to have occurred on a large scale. While there is some anecdotal evidence that political jurisdictions (national or sub-national) pass environmental laws with an eye toward attracting (or retaining) industry, there is no evidence that industry responds to differences in these laws in significant ways.

The literature on trade and the environment has evolved in two waves. The first set of research peaked during the late 1970s and seems to have been inspired by the growth of environmental regulations in industrialized nations during the early to mid-1970s. The second set has come more recently, apparently motivated by the debate over international trade agreements such as the North American Free Trade Agreement (NAFTA) and the Uruguay Round of the General Agreement on Tariffs and Trade (GATT). The theory involved combines basic Heckscher-Ohlin trade theory with environmental economic theory and predicts that countries with lower environmental compliance costs have a competitive advantage in the production of pollution-intensive products and will export those goods.

The papers discussed in this chapter examine competitiveness from two different angles: trade patterns and industry-location choice. These represent two ways of asking the same question. If an industry selling a product on a world market relocates from one country to another, the former country's net exports of that product will decline while the latter's will rise, all else being equal. Trade patterns, therefore, are merely the visible manifestation of industry relocation. Because trade data are more frequently and consistently available than industry-location data, the trade-pattern approach is more prevalent. One advantage of using trade data comes in helping to differentiate between economic growth based on the internal dynamics of each nation's economy and growth that comes at the expense of other nations. If the trade-off between economics and the environment is purely internal, there may be no cause for international concern. However, if economic growth within one country can be enhanced at other countries' expense by lowering environmental standards and attracting export industries, the result may be a "race to the bottom" in environmental standards. This is the fear that motivates much of the rhetoric surrounding environmental regulations and competitiveness.

11.1   International Environmental Regulations and Fear of Industrial Flight

Whether some nations actively seek foreign investment by allowing themselves to become pollution havens is a question addressed by Leonard (1988). Leonard presents case studies of development strategies in four countries, of which only Ireland seems to have explicitly attempted to attract polluting industry. One official is quoted as saying, "The permission to pollute may well be more valuable in economics terms than any Industrial Development Authority grants." In its defense, Ireland's high tolerance for pollution may come not only from its relative poverty, but also from its geography—an island with high winds and ample rain. Nevertheless, it is this type of interjurisdictional regulatory competition that advocates of harmonization of pollution regulations would like to prevent.

An early attempt to harmonize international environmental regulations took place at the 1972 Stockholm Conference on the Human Environment. Industrialized countries looked to the United Nations to unify environmental rules to prevent industrial flight from nations with stringent standards, but developing countries argued that it was their turn to industrialize and that industrialized growth necessarily leads to pollution (Leonard, 1988). That same year, OECD countries passed the Polluter Pays Principle, which has an element of regulatory harmonization. It states that "the polluter should bear the cost of measures to reduce pollution." In a partial equilibrium framework, it does not really matter to efficiency whether the polluter pays to pollute or the state subsidizes pollution abatement.[3] But without such an international agreement, pollution cleanup subsidies might provide a way to circumvent trade agreements and subsidize domestic industries. As Daly and Goodland (1994) argue, "Nations that do not count the full environmental costs in the prices of their exports are in effect subsidizing those exports as surely as if they taxed their citizens and transferred the money to the exporters." The Polluter Pays Principle is merely an agreement among nations not to subsidize export industries in this way.

More recently, the debate over the United Nations Code of Conduct of Transnational Corporations focused on establishing a set of minimum standards for the treatment of multinational corporations (UN, 1988), although the section on environmental protection that was eventually passed contained little more than an insubstantial statement that they shall obey local laws. Even more recently, the debate over NAFTA has illustrated the dual fears that environmentalists and free trade advocates have about trade and the environment. Environmentalists worry that trade agreements will restrict domestic environmental laws, while free traders worry that environmental laws will serve as barriers to trade. The treaty, with its environmental side agreement, includes an affirmation of the right of each country to choose its own level of environmental protection and a general statement that NAFTA countries should not lower their health, safety, or environment standards to attract foreign investment.

Nations are not the only group that promulgates international guidelines. Industry associations have also done so. The International Chamber of Commerce passed its own environmental guidelines in 1981 and supported harmonizing pollution regulations worldwide (Leonard, 1988). One explanation for industries' interest in this issue is that "it is important for industry to keep a level playing field to avoid detrimental competition among its members as regards environmental standards" (UNCTAD,

1993). Presumably this form of collusion reduces the ill will an industry could generate by competing to pollute. An alternate explanation is that these associations may be controlled by companies wishing to protect existing plants in countries with stringent regulations. Most firms, however, seem to ignore the guidelines set by international political or industrial associations. Less than 20 percent of chemical companies surveyed adhere to the Chemical Manufacturers Association's "Responsible CARE Program," while less than 10 percent of all surveyed firms say that they follow guidelines set by international organizations such as UNEP and OECD (UNCTAD, 1993). Still, the existence of these types of rules provides evidence that industry associations believe that international competition in pollution regulations is important.

In the United States, the concern over international industrial flight dates back to some of the earliest national environmental legislation. The U.S. Federal Water Pollution Control Act of 1970 requires the Commerce Department to conduct a study of the competitive effect of environmental regulations on U.S. firms and requires the president to seek international agreements harmonizing water pollution standards.[4]

In fact, the United States has entered into many international environmental treaties since 1970.[5] But because these treaties generally lack enforcement mechanisms, individual nations are often tempted to take unilateral action, often in the form of an environmental trade barrier. Walter Cronkite advocated a ban on products from any country with environmental standards less strict than those of the United States in a 1980 letter to the New York Times, claiming that it would "protect both American industry and the environment."[6] Senator David Boren's (D-OK) proposed International Pollution Deterrence Act of 1991 would have imposed a tariff on imports of products from countries without "effective pollution controls." Had it passed, the proposed tariff was to be equal to the costs that a foreign producer would have had to incur in order to comply with U.S. environmental standards. Representative Morris Udall's (D-AZ) Copper Environmental Equalization Act, similar in intent, was defeated in 1977 and 1979.

The concern in the United States also crosses political-party boundaries. In 1978, President Jimmy Carter's chief trade negotiator, Robert Strauss, said that "we do not want the U.S. willingness to protect the environment and our workers to disadvantage the various U.S. producers."[7] President Ronald Reagan's administration established the Task Force on Regulatory Relief, chaired by Vice President George Bush, who when he became president then established the Council on Competitiveness, chaired by

Vice President Dan Quayle. Both groups' goals included limiting the extent to which domestic regulations reduced U.S. trade competitiveness. The Council on Competitiveness succeeded in blocking a number of environmentally oriented regulations, including a plan requiring municipal waste recycling, a regulation discouraging lead-battery incineration, and a proposal limiting sulfur-dioxide emissions from a power plant near the Grand Canyon (GATT, 1992). Most recently, President Bill Clinton's support for the NAFTA came with the caveat that environmental side agreements be negotiated with Mexico, and former California governor and presidential candidate Edmund G. Brown, Jr., opposed NAFTA, claiming that it would "create a race to the bottom in . . . environmental standards."[8]

The evidence outlined here illustrates that many different interest groups, including politicians of various ideologies, environmental groups, and industry organizations, have expressed concern that industry location will be sensitive to environmental regulations. Some of these groups have even taken steps toward thwarting industry migration, such as proposing legislation, opposing free trade agreements, and promoting harmonization of international standards. The next section examines the empirical evidence to see how well founded their concerns may be.

11.2 Industry Location and International Environmental Regulations: Empirical Evidence

Although there seems to be plenty of anecdotal evidence that policy makers and industry representatives take industrial flight seriously, there is only a limited amount of empirical evidence that industrial flight exists. For example, one of the most vocal opponents of NAFTA has been U.S. businessman-politician Ross Perot, whose opposition has been couched largely in terms of U.S. competitiveness. His organization catalyzed fears that free trade with Mexico could not be fair trade, given Mexico's lower wages and weaker standards for working conditions and pollution. In a now notorious remark, Perot likened the aftereffect of the trade agreement to a "giant sucking sound" as U.S. jobs would disappear across the border. Yet six months after the agreement's start date, the Perot organization's newsletter, *Afta-NAFTA Update*, found meager evidence of disruptions caused by NAFTA. The newsletter documents fewer than a dozen cases of firms expanding operations in Mexico while simultaneously contracting them in the United States. The largest of these involves the glass maker PPG, which closed two plants in Pennsylvania, eliminating 560 jobs, hardly noticeable to the U.S. economy as a whole. In contrast, the newsletter also reports the incredible results of a survey conducted by the National Association of Purchasing Management: "17.1 percent of large U.S. companies plan to move operations to Mexico because of the NAFTA."[9]

More objective evidence comes from the U.S. General Accounting Office, which in April 1991 reported on the relocation of wood-furniture firms from Los Angeles to Mexico. Their survey found that from 1988 to 1990 between 11 and 28 of the 2,675 wood-furniture manufacturers in Los Angeles relocated at least some part of their operations to Mexico, affecting somewhere between 950 and 2,500 jobs. In addition, between three and 100 firms relocated to other areas within the United States. Of those relocating to Mexico, 83 percent identified labor costs as a significant factor, while 78 percent identified pollution control costs.[10] Although the number relocating appears quite small, the proportion of those that did move that acknowledged doing so for environmental reasons is surprisingly large. Examining corporate records, it is generally difficult to find evidence that manufacturing facilities located to take advantage of lax environmental policies. While industrialists are quick to blame plant closures on tough regulations, nobody would want to poison community relations by saying that a new factory will be polluting more heavily than would be allowed elsewhere.

Direct evidence of this paradox was provided by Knögden (1979), who surveyed West German firms known to have made significant investments in developing countries (presumed to have less stringent environmental standards) since the early 1970s, when West Germany began to enforce strict environmental laws. In response to an open-ended question as to the companies' investment motives, only one company (a chemical manufacturer) volunteered that environmental regulations played a role, and only as the least important of the seven considerations it mentioned. Table 1 reproduces responses to two of Knögden's survey questions. Respondents rated the importance of various investment motives on a scale from 1 (very important) to 5 (totally unimportant). The vast majority responded that environmental regulations are totally unimportant to the location of investment.

Knögden then looked further at the firms that answered these two questions with a 1 or a 2. These firms belonged primarily to the chemicals and primary and fabricated metals industries, and they tended to rate all cost factors higher than the rest of the sample. Of those firms rating environmental factors "very important," the majority rated all other investment motives at 1, 2, or 3. The pattern of responses suggests that

Table 1
West German Firms' Rating of the Importance of Environmental Regulations to Investment
(percent responding)

| Investment Motive | Very Important | | | | Totally Unimportant |
	1	2	3	4	5
Strict environmental regulations in West Germany	2	3	7	18	70
Especially lax environmental regulations in the host country	2*	4	6	20	68

Source: Knögden (1979).
*Best estimate, because of an apparent typographic error in the source.

these industries are more sensitive to all types of local characteristics, perhaps because they are more geographically footloose.

A more recent survey of multinational corporations was conducted by the UN Conference on Trade and Development Program on Transnational Corporations. The UN surveyed 794 corporations with sales over $1 billion during the summer of 1990. Of these, 169 had responded by the end of 1991. Of the 169, most claimed that environmental, health, and safety practices overseas are determined by environmental regulations in their home countries. In general, differences across plants in their environmental practices seem to be affected more by home-country regulations than host-country regulations. Many of the companies surveyed claimed that they would not only comply with all local laws, but would write their own company policies if local laws were thought to be inadequate.

No matter how expertly assembled, survey evidence cannot prove that environmental regulations cause industrial flight or that their absence creates pollution havens, because there can be a large difference between what people (or firms) say they do in response to a survey and what they actually do. The difference may come about through intent or ignorance, but it means that convincing proof must come from analyzing data on what firms do rather than say.

Robison (1988) examines the evidence provided by trade patterns in an update of a study initially done by Walter (1973).[11] He compares U.S. pollution-abatement costs by industry for U.S. imports and exports, and finds that the ratio of abatement costs per dollar of value added for imports relative to exports rose from 1.15 in 1973 to 1.39 in 1982. In other words, goods imported into the United States are increasingly those goods that face high pollution-abatement costs in the United States. For trade with Canada, which has similarly strict laws, the abatement cost ratio has not changed over this period. Robison infers that environmental regulations are causing the United States to become less competitive in pollution-intensive products relative to countries with less stringent regulations. He goes so far as to estimate that an increase in U.S. environmental compliance costs that led to a 1 percent increase in U.S. total costs would reduce the net value of U.S. trade by 0.67 percent. (This would have to be a very large increase in compliance costs, since they make up a small fraction of total costs.) The estimate represents an upper bound, since it assumes that all of the environmental control costs pass through to the product price, and it abstracts away from any general equilibrium effects. So even if Robison is correct that the United States is losing competitive advantage in pollution-intensive products, the trade effects he reports appear negligible.

Many of the papers in this literature begin with the assumption (often implicit) that developing nations have a competitive advantage in production of pollution-intensive products.[12] Their advantage could come from several sources. They may have greater physical capacities to absorb or assimilate pollution, or they may have environmental regulations with compliance costs that are lower than those of industrialized countries. Pearson (1987) suggests that "sketchy evidence on physical attributes such as level and seasonal distribution of rainfall, river discharge per unit of land surface, and variability of river flows ... as well as on soil types and structures, suggests that developing countries have a lower inherent physical capacity ... to tolerate environmental stress." Thus it is more likely that developing countries' environmental competitive advantage, if they have one, stems from their weaker environmental laws. These weaker regulations may be a result of the fact that developing countries' citizens value the environment less, are poorer and cannot afford as much environmental quality as their wealthier counterparts, or simply do not have the administrative ability to monitor and enforce sophisticated regulations.

Leonard (1988) assumes that developing countries have lower standards and defines pollution-intensive industries in terms of spending on pollution-abatement capital by U.S. plants. Of the four costliest industries, Leonard focuses on two in particular, the mineral-processing and chemical industries. If U.S. pollution regulations are pushing these industries overseas, Leonard argues, there are four effects that should be discernible in aggregate international data: (1) the polluting sectors will be increasing their foreign direct investment (FDI) faster than other sectors; (2) developing countries will be receiving an increasing fraction of FDI in these industries; (3) U.S. imports of these products will be increasing faster than imports of other products; and (4) an increasing fraction of these imports will be coming from developing countries. Leonard finds little or no evidence that any of these changes has taken place. The closest he comes is to show that U.S. capital expenditures in the chemicals and mineral-processing industries have increased more in developing countries than in industrialized countries during the 1970s. However, the vast majority of these industries' capital expenditures abroad still occur in other industrialized countries.

A previous study by the same author (Leonard, 1984), asks the same set of questions using more disaggregate industry definitions. He finds that for three specific sets of industries, stringent U.S. laws seem to have pushed new investment overseas. The three are (1) manufacturers of very toxic, dangerous, or carcinogenic products such as asbestos, arsenic trioxide, benzidine-based dyes, and some pesticides; (2) some metal-processing industries such as copper, zinc, and lead (though this shift may be due to a combination of changes in mineral availability and some countries' requirements that minerals mined there be processed domestically); and (3) manufacturers of some organic chemicals that are intermediate products. Never, however, was Leonard able to find evidence that a healthy domestic industry, for which domestic demand was growing and U.S. producers maintained technological competitiveness, was pushed abroad by stringent domestic environmental regulations.

Low and Yeats (1992) also use developing countries as a proxy for the set of countries with weak environmental regulations and examine trade in pollution-intensive industries (iron and steel, nonferrous metals, refined petroleum, metal manufactures, and paper goods). Their data, presented in Table 2, show that developing countries, roughly categorized, have gained

Table 2
"Dirty" Products as a Percent of Total Exports

	1965	1988
World	18.9	15.7
EEC(10)	19.9	16.1
North America	18.5	14.2
Eastern Europe	21.6	27.6
Latin America	17.0	20.9
Southeast Asia	11.4	10.8
Western Asia	9.2	13.4

Source: Low and Yeats (1992).

a greater share of total world exports of pollution-intensive products, relative to other products and relative to industrialized countries. This finding provides rough empirical evidence of a pollution-haven effect, but it does not prove its existence. In fact, industrialized countries continue to be the largest exporters of these polluting goods, by far. Of the top 25 exporters of Low and Yeats' "dirty" products, accounting for 85 percent of world trade in those products, only eight are not OECD nations. It is also true that Low and Yeats make no claims as to the cause of the shift they describe, which could well be due to changes in labor costs, natural resource availability, or different phases of the cycle of industrialization. Low and Yeats acknowledge that the observed patterns are "unlikely to be adequately explained by environmental policy" alone.

In a related piece, Low (1992) examines U.S.–Mexican trade for evidence that increases in U.S. environmental standards have caused industry to relocate to Mexico. He looks at the 48 industries that spend the most on pollution abatement in the United States. These 48 industries accounted for 12 percent of Mexico's exports to the United States, but these exports were growing at 9 percent annually compared to 3 percent for all exports. Although this result may provide evidence of industrial flight, Low calculates that raising Mexico's pollution-abatement costs to the level of the United States would add 0.6 percent to the costs of the imported products, and would result in at most a 2 percent drop in Mexican export earnings. So Low concludes, like Robison, that even if these environmental trade effects exist, they are very small.

Grossman and Krueger (1991) also look at U.S.–Mexico trade patterns. They model U.S. imports from Mexico by industry as a function of factor shares, U.S. effective tariff rates, and U.S. pollution abatement costs:

$$\left(\frac{\text{U.S. imports from Mexico}}{\text{Total U.S. shipments}}\right) = \underset{(.008)}{.028^*} - \underset{(.016)}{.053^*} \cdot (\text{Skilled labor})$$

$$- \underset{(.010)}{.024^*} \cdot (\text{Capital}) - \underset{(.028)}{.002} \cdot (\text{Tariff})$$

$$+ \underset{(.060)}{.014} \cdot (\text{Pollution abatement costs})$$

$n = 135$

$R^2 = .127$

*Significant at 5%

The results indicate that the United States imports from Mexico goods that use fewer skilled workers and less physical capital. Although the coefficient on U.S. pollution abatement costs is positive, as would be predicted by industrial flight from pollution regulations, it is both quantitatively and statistically insignificant. Based on this result, and those from similar specifications, Grossman and Krueger conclude that differences between the United States' and Mexico's environmental regulations "play at most a minor role in guiding intersectoral resource allocations."

Several economists at the World Bank (Lucas, Wheeler, and Hettige, 1992; Birdsall and Wheeler, 1992) have taken a different approach to examining industrial flight to pollution havens, using data from the U.S. Environmental Protection Agency's Toxics Release Inventory (TRI) merged with the Census of Manufactures. The TRI has, since 1987, reported plant-level emissions of each of over 300 toxic chemicals into various environmental media. Lucas, Wheeler, and Hettige used human risk-weighted indices of the various chemicals to compile a general index of "toxic intensity" for each of 37 industries. Birdsall and Wheeler note that the toxic intensity of a country as a whole can be described by the following simple equation:

$$\left(\frac{\text{Industrial pollution}}{\text{GDP}}\right) = \left(\frac{\text{Value added by all industry}}{\text{GDP}}\right)$$

$$\times \left(\frac{\text{Value added by polluting industry}}{\text{Value added by all industry}}\right)$$

$$\times \left(\frac{\text{Industrial pollution}}{\text{Value added by polluting industry}}\right)$$

The first term on the right-hand side is probably a function of a country's stage of economic development, and the third term may depend on the country's pollution regulations. The second term on the right-hand side is Lucas, Wheeler, and Hettige's index of national toxic intensity and is of principal interest to Birdsall and Wheeler. It measures the amount of pollution-intensive industry that a given country attracts, as measured by its toxic intensity in the United States, as a fraction of that country's total industry. It is a weak measure of overall national toxic intensity, as it ignores the other two terms and is purely a product of the country's mix of industry, not its pollution standards. Nevertheless, it remains a decent measure of the type of industry that forms each country's industrial base.

The primary question asked by Birdsall and Wheeler is whether developing countries with more open trade policies attract more pollution-intensive industry. They regress the change in their toxic intensity measure on per capita income, the growth in per capita income, and an interaction between per capita income growth and an index of trade policy openness,[13] all in logs, for each of the 25 Latin American countries from 1960 to 1988. The results include negative and statistically significant coefficients on the log of per capita income and the change in per capita income. The findings suggest that wealthier countries, as well as those that are growing faster, have cleaner industries, and this result is consistent with many economists' expectations regarding development paths. Two dummy variables for the 1970s and 1980s, interacted with the logarithm of income growth, turn out to be positive and significant. Birdsall and Wheeler argue that this result shows that "Latin American growth rates of toxic intensity were generally higher (at each income level) after OECD environmental regulation became stricter." This appears to be a strong conclusion to draw from a simple dummy variable. The coefficient on the interaction between the 1980s dummy variable and the Dollar index of openness is positive and marginally statistically significant ($t = 1.87$), suggesting that more open economies attract less pollution-intensive industry and that more closed economies (with higher values of the Dollar index) have dirtier industries. The conclusions drawn by Birdsall and Wheeler are thus the opposite of those claimed by many environmentalists, who worry that open trade leads to environmental degradation overseas, and by the representatives of labor and manufacturing interests in industrialized nations, who worry that open trade leads to the creation of pollution havens abroad and industrial flight from more stringent regulations. Birdsall and Wheeler found that it is the more protectionist economies of Latin America whose industries are most pollution intensive.

All the studies discussed use aggregate trade or FDI data to attempt to discern evidence of industrial flight from pollution regulations and acknowledge that they merely seek support for the effect. Proof of the effect would require controlling for all of the other factors that are likely to alter international patterns of trade and investment. The general lack of a shift of polluting industries toward developing countries does not prove the absence of a deterring effect of environmental regulations any more than evidence of such a shift would have proved the existence of a deterring effect. As Leonard (1988) puts it, "The real-world environment in which firms make long-term trade and investment decisions is not a Heckscher-Ohlin world, and all other things are never equal." Although statistical techniques for holding "all else equal" have been readily available for a long time, and although these techniques have been applied in the search for domestic evidence of interjurisdictional effects of environmental regulations (see section 11.3), few studies have attempted to do so on an international level, largely because of the difficulty inherent in comparing regulations and factor costs across international boundaries.

Of the recent studies of the effects of environmental regulations on trade patterns, Tobey (1990) is unique in attempting to control for other factors that may explain changes in these patterns. Tobey examines trade in 24 products (three-digit SIC codes) for which pollution-abatement costs in 1977 in the United States exceeded 1.85 percent of total costs. These pollution-intensive industries included subsets of five commodity groups: mining, primary iron and steel, primary nonferrous metals, paper and pulp, and chemicals. To measure environmental regulatory stringency across countries, Tobey uses a 1976 study conducted by the United Nations Conference on Trade and Development (UNCTAD) cited by Walter and Ugelow (1979) that rates the environmental policies of about 40 countries on a scale from 1 (strict) to 7 (tolerant).[14] He then estimates the following regression across countries for each of the five commodity groups separately:

Net exports $= \alpha + \beta V + \gamma E + \mu$

where V is a vector of 11 country-specific factor endowments (labor, capital, minerals, etc.) and E is the UNCTAD index of regulatory stringency. The resulting estimates of the coefficient γ are never statistically significant in any of the specifications that Tobey tests. Tobey's interpretation is that "the magnitude of environmental expenditures in countries with stringent environmental policies [is] not sufficiently large to cause a noticeable effect." However the coefficients of V, the resource endowments of the countries, do not have a sensible pattern either (though perhaps the absence of a logical pattern is due to the fact that the *quantities* of those factors may be less important than their *prices* in determining business locations). Of the 55 coefficients presented (11 resources and five commodity groups) five of the resource coefficients are negative, seven are positive, and the remaining 43 are statistically insignificant. An alternative explanation for this model's estimated zero effect of regulations may be that the data are insufficient to answer the question.

All of the international studies of environmental regulations and competitiveness suffer from one or both of two major problems. They lack information about relative environmental compliance costs, or they rely on aggregate data. The dearth of information on relative compliance costs is partly because there are no good data on these costs, especially outside the OECD. As a result, most of the studies simply look for patterns in foreign direct investment, trade flows, or economic growth that would indicate sensitivity to environmental regulations, without trying to isolate the effect of environmental regulations by controlling for other factors that would affect those patterns. Only Tobey (1990) uses a ranking of countries' environmental-standard stringency to try to control for other country characteristics. And even Tobey's results are unsatisfactory because the UNCTAD ranking is subjective and ordinal, and because Tobey finds that environmental endowments are no worse predictors of net exports than are other factors.

The problem faced by all of the international studies using aggregate trade or FDI data to measure competitiveness is that the aggregate data represent the net changes caused by the births of new plants, the expansions and contractions of existing plants, and plant closures, some of which are due to changes in countries' own consumption patterns, and each of which can be expected to react differently to various environmental regulations. Many environmental regulations, for example, consist of "new source performance standards" that only apply to new firms. These standards effectively raise barriers to entry that favor existing older, often more labor-intensive plants. Using data that include all investment in a study of the consequences of regulations may conceal effects that work in opposite directions. Consequently, to isolate the effects of regulation on location, it is necessary to use establishment-level data. One solution for the lack of international data on specific industrial-location decisions and on relative pollution-abatement costs is to study industrial location within a given country. An obvious choice for such an empirical test is the United States, because of the data available, the stringency of its regulations, and the high degree of variation in those regulations across the 50 states.

11.3   Domestic Environmental Regulations in the United States and Fear of Industrial Flight

Before 1970 local governments in the United States (states, counties, and municipalities) were primarily responsible for environmental regulations (Portney, 1990). The situation changed in 1970, with the passage of the National Environmental Protection Act and the Clean Air Act, and the establishment of the Environmental Protection Agency and the Council on Environmental Quality. This federal involvement was motivated in part by congressional impatience over the lack of local progress, by public activism (notably the first Earth Day, in 1970), and by the fear that local jurisdictions would compete among themselves to attract industry by delaying the implementation of pollution-control measures. Grounds for this last fear can be found in the statements of Louisiana Governor Edwin Edwards:

We have ... taken the position that the need for ... stimulation to our economy justified ... serious tradeoffs, where the environment became either totally or partially damaged. None of us ... in positions of authority in the state apologize for that. We did what we thought was best for the people and the economy of Louisiana. We accommodated industry where we thought we could in order to get the jobs and the development, and in some instances we knowingly and advisedly accepted environmental tradeoffs.[15]

More systematic evidence that states use environmental regulations as competitive tools was provided by Pashigian (1985), who examined the congressional vote on the 1977 Prevention of Significant Deterioration (PSD) amendment to the Clean Air Act. The PSD amendment modified the national ambient-air-quality rules to prevent the air quality of many clean jurisdictions from deteriorating to the level of the minimum national standards. The amendment was most popular among representatives from northeastern states whose air quality failed to attain the national standards. Pashigian surmised that these representatives hoped that the PSD amendment would prevent industry from relocating to attainment regions to avoid compliance costs necessary in nonattainment areas. In addition, both the 1970 Clean Air Act and the 1977 Clean Water Act were designed, in part, to mitigate the chance that interjurisdictional competition would create pollution havens in states with lenient standards or cause industrial flight from states with stringent standards (Portney, 1990).

As with the international situation, there is ample evidence that policy makers and various interest groups take seriously the threat that environmental regulations will cause industry to locate in jurisdictions with the least stringent regulations. The next section reviews the empirical evidence as to the importance of this threat from a domestic perspective.

11.4   Industry Location and U.S. State Environmental Regulations: Empirical Evidence

Direct evidence of firms relocating within the United States to avoid environmental regulations is, like the international evidence, difficult to find. Again, however, there are plenty of anecdotes. The California Business

Roundtable claims that because of California's high business taxes and stringent environmental regulations, one-fourth of the state's manufacturers plan to relocate.[16] Commenting on New Jersey's (now amended) version of the federal "Superfund" law, the chief of a large manufacturing firm threatened "we just won't ever open a plant in New Jersey again" (Lyne, 1985).

Early surveys (before 1970) of U.S. factory managers involved in plant-site choice neglected even to ask about environmental regulations (Mueller and Morgan, 1969; Greenhut and Colberg, 1969; U.S. Census, 1973). Most of the more recent surveys concluded that environmental regulations matter little to the locations of manufacturing plants, yet a few did find numerous respondents who claimed that environmental regulations affected their location choice (Wintner, 1982; Lyne, 1990). Comparing responses across these studies is difficult because they differ in scope and methodology. Some ask open-ended questions about factors potentially influencing location, while others ask respondents to rank a preselected list of factors. A sampling of such surveys is presented in Table 3. One survey was performed fairly consistently during the early 1980s by Alexander Grant and Company, a consulting firm specializing in manufacturing plant siting. Their annually published survey of business climates in the 48 contiguous U.S. states relies on interviews with several dozen state manufacturing associations. The associations rate more than 20 state characteristics as to their importance in determining a state's attractiveness to business. The ratings are expressed as percentages, summing to 100 percent. Environmental-control costs consistently appear two-thirds of the way down the list, at approximately 4 percent. Leaders include energy costs at 8 percent and wages at 7 percent.[17]

Potentially more satisfying are the empirical studies that examine the statistical evidence using data on state characteristics. Because of the limited availability of establishment-level data on new plant locations, most such work has used aggregate data on economic growth, employment changes, and so on. One of the largest such studies was conducted by the Conservation Foundation (Duerksen, 1983) and was motivated by several well-publicized cases of interstate industry movement allegedly provoked by environmental regulations (Chapman and Walker, 1991). The study examined changes in industrial employment among states during the 1970s. States that gained employment relative to the national average had more-lax environmental standards than states that lost employment, though this difference was statistically insignificant and even smaller for pollution-intensive industries.

Table 3
Surveys of the Importance of Environmental Regulations to Plant Location in the United
States

Survey	Sample	Result
Epping (1986)	Survey of manufacturers (late 1970s) that located facilities 1958–1977	"Favorable pollution laws" ranked 43rd to 47th, out of 84 location factors presented.
Fortune (1977)	Fortune's 1977 survey of 1,000 largest U.S. corporations	11% ranked state or local environmental regulations among top 5 factors.
Schmenner (1982)	Sample of Dun & Bradstreet data for new Fortune 500 branch plants opening 1972–1978	Environmental concerns not among the top 6 items mentioned.
Wintner (1982)	Conference Board survey of 68 urban manufacturing firms	29 (43%) mentioned environmental and pollution control regulations as a factor in location choice.
Stafford (1985)	Interviews and questionnaire responses of 162 branch plants built in the late 1970s and early 1980s	"Environmental regulations are not a major factor," but more important than in 1970. When only self-described "less clean" plants were examined, environmental regulations were "of mid-level importance."
Alexander Grant (various years)	Surveys of industry associations	Environmental compliance costs given an average weight of below 4%, though growing slightly over time.
Lyne (1990)	Site Selection magazine's 1990 survey of corporate real estate executives	Asked to pick 3 of 12 factors affecting location choice, 42% of executives selected "state clean air legislation."

Duffy-Deno (1992) regresses total employment and total earnings (for all manufacturing industries) on a list of regional characteristics, including total pollution-abatement costs, for 63 metropolitan areas from 1974 through 1982. Not surprisingly, given that he looks at aggregate employment and earnings for all industries, he finds that the coefficient on abatement costs per dollar of value added has statistically and economically insignificant coefficients. The exception appears when Duffy-Deno divides the sample into sun-belt and frost-belt cities, and runs the models separately for the two samples. Then the coefficients on abatement costs are statistically significant and negative for the frost-belt sample, and remain insignificant for the sun belt. Yet even the frost-belt coefficient remains tiny. The frost-belt locations that have 10 percent higher pollution-abatement costs are predicted to have manufacturing employment that is 1.05 percent lower, or overall employment that is 0.27 percent lower.

Crandall (1993) obtains a similar result using data on states rather than SMSAs. Crandall regresses employment growth on state characteristics, including annual statewide pollution abatement operating costs divided by gross state manufacturing output. He concludes from the statistically insignificant coefficients on this measure that compliance costs do not have a "measurable effect on the regional distribution of manufacturing employment."

For the same reasons as in the international studies, using aggregate data may mask the true effects of environmental regulations on industry location. The primary obstacle to studying plant location decisions directly has been the inaccessibility of high-quality establishment-level data. Three studies have used extracts of the Dun & Bradstreet data[18] to examine this relationship between industry growth and environmental regulations: Bartik (1988), McConnell and Schwab (1990), and Crandall (1993). None found significant or strong effects of variations in environmental regulations on location choice.

The Bartik paper uses McFadden's (1974) conditional logit model to predict the locations chosen by branch plants of *Fortune* 500 companies between 1972 and 1978. Its conclusion supports "the prevailing wisdom that environmental variables have only small effects on business locations." The McConnell and Schwab paper uses the conditional logit model and Dun & Bradstreet data on SIC code 3711, vehicle assembly. These plants, while painting cars and trucks, emit volatile organic compounds that contribute to urban ozone (smog). As a measure of regional environmental stringency, McConnell and Schwab use a series of dummy variables for whether or not the county chosen meets federal ambient ozone standards.[19] They find significant coefficients only for those counties that are extremely far out of compliance: at the time Houston, Los Angeles, and Milwaukee. This finding is closer in spirit to an anecdote than a general conclusion: A particular industry, with a particular pollution problem, appears deterred from three specific cities.[20]

Crandall uses the Dun & Bradstreet data to disaggregate employment changes that result from new plants, plant expansions, plant contractions, and plant closures. As a measure of regulatory stringency, Crandall uses total statewide pollution-abatement operating costs, divided by gross state manufacturing output. He finds that plant start-ups and closures are unresponsive to compliance costs, but warns against the conclusion that environmental policy does not affect plant openings, because compliance costs from plants deterred from opening are by definition zero. In other words, Crandall is justifiably concerned about the nature of his proxy for environmental stringency: States may have low pollution-abatement costs because they have stringent regulations and polluting industries choose to locate elsewhere.

A common theme running through much of the previous work is that studying location choice in detail requires access to establishment-level microeconomic data, and that such data are either expensive, of poor quality, or not publicly available. Schmenner (1982), Bartik (1988), and Crandall (1993) noted the suitability of the Census of Manufactures, which is used by Levinson (forthcoming) to examine the location decisions of U.S. manufacturing establishments between 1982 and 1987. Levinson tests a number of measures of state environmental-standard stringency, including subjective indices composed by environmental groups, a measure of state monitoring and enforcement effort, and an index created from plant-level pollution-abatement expenditure data. He uses the conditional logit model used by Bartik and by McConnell and Schwab, and concludes similarly that environmental regulatory stringency does not have a significant effect, either statistically or economically, on manufacturer locations.

Finally, in a paper that links this domestic literature to the international papers discussed earlier, Freidman, Gerlowski, and Silberman (1992) use establishment-level data on the planned plant locations by foreign-owned firms within the United States. Like Bartik, McConnell and Schwab, and Levinson, they use McFadden's conditional logit model to fit the choice of state on various state characteristics. In one of their specifications, they include total pollution-abatement capital expenditure per dollar of gross state product from manufacturing. Although the estimated coefficient is statistically insignificant, that result may be a product of the fact that the measure of stringency is its nominal incidence, includes only direct capital expenditures, and does not control for the industrial composition of the state. Nevertheless, their conclusion supports that made by the literature on domestic firms, that plant locations appear unaffected by environmental compliance costs.

Table 4 presents representative specifications from each of the four studies that use establishment-level data and McFadden's conditional logit model to study the effect of local characteristics, including environmental regulations, on plant-site choice. Although the results are not directly comparable, because they use different samples of plants, independent variables, and measures of environmental-standard stringency, they consistently conclude that environmental regulations do not significantly affect site choice.

Table 4
Studies of Industrial Location and Environmental Regulations in the United States Using Establishment-Level Data and the Conditional Logit Model

Independent Variables	Bartik (1988)—Fortune 500 Branches by State	McConnell and Schwab (1990)—Vehicle Assembly Plants by County	Freidman, Gerlowski, and Silberman (1992)—Foreign MNCs by State	Levinson (forthcoming)—Branch Plants of Large Firms by State
Environmental stringency	State air pollution spending 0.150[†] (0.088)	County below national air quality stds. 0.512 (0.492)	Aggregate pollution abatement \$/state GDP −0.018 (0.055)	Number of regulations −0.009[†] (0.005)
	State water pollution spending 0.007 (0.085)			State monitoring effort −0.099 (0.073)
				Industry-specific abatement costs −0.501* (0.252)
Taxes	1 − corporate tax** 6.21* (1.89)	State tax −0.157[†] (0.084)	Tax receipts/population −1.448* (0.225)	1 − corporate tax** 0.797 (1.699)
	Property tax −0.578 (0.378)	County property tax −4.367 (5.132)	Promotional \$ 0.440* (0.044)	
Labor	Wage −0.161 (0.350)	Wage 0.056 (0.145)	Wage −1.854* (0.449)	Wage 0.122 (0.350)
	Percent union −4.10* (0.795)	Percent union −0.025 (0.042)	Percent union 0.390* (0.126)	Percent union −1.058* (0.377)
	Education −1.21 (1.00)		Productivity 0.722* (0.352)	
	UI tax rate 5.14 (13.89)		Unemployment 0.570* (0.183)	
	Workers compensation 0.992 (2.36)			

Category	Model 1 (N = 1,607)	Model 2 (N = 50)	Model 3 (N = 884)	Model 4 (N = 1,648)
Market access/size	Roads 0.566* (0.202)	Urban 1.344* (0.422)	Port 0.819* (0.107)	Roads 0.364* (0.127)
	Population density −0.303 (0.205)	Demand 2.169 (4.725)	Demand 0.423* (0.040)	Existing manufacturing 1.028* (0.052)
	Existing manufacturing 0.956* (0.181)	State production workers 0.005† (0.003)		
	Land area 1.02* (0.07)	County production workers 0.017* (0.006)		
Other costs	Energy prices −0.208 (0.254)	Energy prices 0.091 (0.276)		Energy prices −0.013 (0.281)
	Construction costs 3.11* (1.07)			
Region	West 0.621* (0.202)	West 1.262 (1.319)		West 0.547* (0.108)
	South 0.297 (0.188)	South −0.011 (0.883)		South 0.818* (0.120)
	Northeast −0.047 (0.124)	Midwest 0.257 (0.943)		Midwest 0.603* (0.097)
Number of plants	1,607	50	884	1,648

Standard errors in parentheses.
*Statistically significant at 5%.
†Statistically significant at 10%.
**The corporate tax is measured as $\log(1 - \text{tax rate})$. See Bartik (1985).

The conclusions of both the international and domestic studies of industry location are that environmental regulations do not deter investment to any statistically or economically significant degree. Most authors are careful to note the limitations of their individual research and to place caveats on their counterintuitive conclusions that stringent regulations do not deter plants, nor do lax regulations attract them. But the literature as a whole presents fairly compelling evidence across a broad range of industries, time periods, and econometric specifications, that regulations do not matter to site choice. The natural follow-up question is why not?

11.5 Explanations for the Absence of Evidence of Industrial Flight

The literature surveyed is almost unanimous in its conclusion that environmental regulations have not affected interjurisdictional trade or the location decisions of manufacturers. Where studies have found statistically significant effects of these regulations, the effects are always quite small. Yet, despite more than 20 years of these types of empirical studies, politicians and interest groups of various types continue to debate the issue of "jobs versus the environment." The fear of industrial flight has been and continues to be used by coalitions within both industrialized and developing nations as an argument in favor of postponing the imposition of stringent pollution regulations (Pearson, 1987). The explanations for this gap between the evidence and the anecdotes take two forms: (1) reasons why the empirical studies to date have been done incorrectly, and (2) reasons why one should not expect to find a significant effect of those regulations.

Some have suggested that regulations are not nearly as important to industrial location decisions as local public opposition to new plants (Gladwin and Welles, 1976). Few U.S. oil companies expanded their East Coast refining capacity in the 1970s, and Dow Chemical dropped plans to build a large petrochemical plant in Solano, California, in 1977, in large part because of local public protests and the resulting delays (Chapman and Walker, 1991). This information implies that the empirical studies of industrial flight have mistakenly focused on the regulations and their compliance costs, when they should have concentrated on public environmental sentiment as a determinant of industry location. Hamilton (1993) included voting participation in a model of hazardous-waste-dump siting, and found that communities with higher participation were less likely to have dumps located there. Perhaps a similar variable is missing from the models of industrial site choice reviewed here. On the other hand,

Gladwin and Welles (1976) discuss a sample of 50 cases of conflict between local environmental activists and multinational corporations seeking to open a new facility and find that most projects are merely delayed, not canceled, as a result of public protest. A spokesperson for one U.S.–based oil refinery claimed that its policy was to fight for its chosen location despite local opposition, and that it usually won such battles. When it did not, the firm's response was to search for another site within the same country because market proximity, transport costs, and political risks outweigh environmental considerations (Walter, 1982a).

Others have suggested that corporations doing business in a variety of jurisdictions find it most cost effective to operate according to the most stringent regulations. This policy eliminates the necessity of designing different production processes for each location. Gladwin and Welles (1976) examine many environmental policies of multinational corporations. Most then merely vowed to obey local standards. Even those few companies claiming to have global policies, such as Dow Chemical's "Global Pollution Control Guidelines," modified their policies in the face of different local situations. Yet, as Gladwin and Welles note, in several cases companies use worldwide processes or technologies that meet the most stringent standards, despite local laws, and that in those cases cost savings rather than corporate environmental policy generated the uniformity. Knögden (1979) found that 90 percent of the West German firms she surveyed claimed to use the same environmental protection measures in developing countries as they did in West Germany, mostly for efficiency reasons. In a similar vein, *The Economist* notes that the number of American chemical manufacturers following procedures more strict than those required by local legislation increased significantly after the Union Carbide accident in Bhopal, India. If it is true that multinational corporations comply with company-wide environmental practices, it would explain their lack of sensitivity to local regulations and would weaken the arguments of those advocating international harmonization of environmental laws.

Cropper and Oates (1992) conclude that there has been no measurable industrial flight because environmental compliance costs are too small, relative to other costs, and too similar across countries to weigh heavily in location decisions. They conclude that "from an environmental perspective, this is a comforting finding, for it means that there is little force to the argument that we need to relax environmental policies to preserve international competitiveness." Yet the U.S. EPA (1990) has estimated that environmental-control costs amount to 2 percent of U.S. GNP, and expects them to grow much larger in the future. It seems feasible that these growing costs could divert investment abroad unless they are similar across countries. This latter argument takes several forms. Environmentalists have expressed fears that free trade agreements will "homogenize the world's laws at the common denominators which gigantic transnational corporations find comfortable."[21] Others believe that most countries are just a few short years (less than the lifetime of a factory) behind the United States in environmental-standard stringency, and that multinational corporations would rather invest now than be forced to retrofit later. Globerman (1993) claims, for example, that "the experience of the EC suggests that when environmental standards differ across countries, convergence of standards will ultimately take place in the direction of the more restrictive set of standards." And one New York bank's chemical-industry analyst claimed that "everywhere the clock is ticking; even countries that seem not to care about pollution control now probably will have very strict rules long before [a new] plant has been on line for even half its 30 or 40 years lifetime" (Leonard and Duerksen, 1980). If it is correct that national environmental standards are naturally harmonizing at a stringent level, then one would expect that foresighted multinational corporations might not seek short-term gains from locating in temporarily less stringent jurisdictions.

Various other explanations for the discrepancy between public rhetoric and the lack of economic evidence abound. Pearson (1987) suggests that environmental regulations in developing countries promote, rather than deter, foreign direct investment. Multinational corporations have a superior ability to comply with those regulations than do domestic corporations, as a result of their experience in jurisdictions with more stringent laws. As an example, he suggests that multinational corporations have more expertise and ability in preventing and containing oil spills than domestic producers. Walter (1982b) suggests that one reason there may be no effect of environmental compliance costs on location of industry is that large pollution-intensive industry tends to exist in oligopolistic markets. If one believes that oligopolistic firms are not as sensitive to competitive pressures, then this argument makes sense. It may also be that industries that are pollution intensive also happen to be relatively less footloose. Such industries are often more energy, transportation, capital, and technology intensive, and if any of these considerations dominates the environmental compliance costs, then firms will appear insensitive to such costs. Finally, I would argue that there is a cynical but compelling explanation for public officials' concern about the link between environmental regulations and competitiveness despite the dearth of evidence for such a link.

Politicians receive support from many sources, including industry groups using pollution-intensive production processes. One convenient and inherently credible way of justifying favorable treatment for these polluting industries is to argue that regulations threaten their competitive position and that those industries might be forced to relocate.

Whatever the reason, there remains a large gap between the popular perception that environmental regulations harm competitiveness and the lack of economic evidence to support that perception. I suspect that the existing literature cannot convince policy makers or the public that links between environmental regulations and industrial location are insignificant, and that the gap between this literature and the conventional wisdom will continue to foster attempts to measure those links empirically.

NOTES

The author acknowledges invaluable counsel and research assistance provided by Bill Harbaugh.

1. David Byrne, environmental officer of Dublin Corporation, quoted in Leonard (1988).

2. See Wilson's contribution to this volume (Chapter 10) for a summary of this literature. Wilson shows that interjurisdictional competition does not necessarily result in a "race to the bottom" with inefficiently lax standards. In theory, it can just as easily lead to the "NIMBY" phenomenon, with inefficiently stringent standards.

3. It only matters in a general equilibrium sense, because if the state subsidizes cleanup, then being a member of a polluting industry becomes more profitable, firms will enter the industry, and the long-run equilibrium can include more pollution than before subsidization.

4. *Selected environmental law statutes* (St. Paul, MN: West Publishing, 1994).

5. The United States signed two multilateral environmental treaties between 1940 and 1959, ten from 1960 to 1979, and 11 during the 1980s (*The Economist*, May 30, 1992).

6. *New York Times*, October 8, 1980, cited in Leonard (1988).

7. *Environment Reporter*, vol. 9, no. 10 (July 7, 1978), p. 451, cited in Leonard and Duerksen (1980).

8. *New York Times*, May 23, 1993.

9. Not to be outdone, the U.S. Commerce Department publishes a biweekly newsletter called *NAFTA News* full of stories about U.S. companies increasing their exports to Mexico.

10. The process of painting or staining wood furniture releases volatile organic compounds (VOCs), precursors to ozone (smog). Los Angeles has been steadily tightening its control of VOC sources in an attempt to meet national ambient-air-quality standards. Wood-furniture manufacturers have been required to reduce emissions by 93 percent, incrementally as of 1989, 1990, 1994, and 1996. Manufacturers claim to be uncertain that they can meet the most stringent requirements.

11. Walter's study relied on data from the late 1960s, which may have been too soon to pick up the effect of early U.S. environmental regulations. Robison examines data from 1973, 1977, and 1982.

12. The only attempt to quantify countries' environmental stringency has shown it to be roughly inversely related to per capita income (Walter and Ugelow, 1979).

13. The trade policy index is due to Dollar (1990), and was developed for the World Bank's 1991 *World Development Report*. It simply ranks countries from 1 (open) to 7 (closed).

14. Clearly any such index has its faults, but the UNCTAD index is the only international index of environmental regulatory stringency I have located. Senator Boren's Pollution Deterrence Act of 1991, had it passed, would have required the U.S. EPA to construct an "International Pollution Control Index" for the top 50 trading partners of the United States. This index would compare each country's pollution control standards to those in the United States. Although the bill failed to indicate how the EPA was to accomplish this difficult task, many of the empirical studies discussed here would have found such an index extremely useful.

15. ABC documentary "The Killing Grounds," 1979.

16. "Raising business costs," *Journal of Commerce*, October 16, 1991.

17. Unfortunately, by the late 1980s Alexander Grant had stopped including environmental-control costs on its list of location influences.

18. There are many acknowledged problems with these data. Both Schmenner (1982) and McConnell and Schwab (1990) cross-checked their extracts of the Dun & Bradstreet data carefully, and found problems with many of the observations. Crandall (1993) notes that the Dun & Bradstreet data have difficulty distinguishing plant births and deaths from sales and acquisitions.

19. Their explanation of this regulatory stringency variable is that out-of-compliance counties will enforce stricter standards in an effort to comply. It is possible, of course, that the effect works in the other direction, that cities with lax regulations exceed federal ambient-air-quality standards.

20. McConnell and Schwab's choice of industry may have been unfortunate, if vehicle assembly plants are not geographically footloose.

21. Sierra Club advertisement in the *New York Times*, June 20, 1994, p. A5.

REFERENCES

Alexander Grant and Company. Various years. *Annual study of general manufacturing climates of the forty-eight contiguous states of America*. Chicago: Alexander Grant and Company.

Bartik, Timothy J. 1985. "Business location decisions in the United States: Estimates of the effects of unionization, taxes, and other characteristics of states." *Journal of Business and Economic Statistics* 3:14–22.

Bartik, Timothy J. 1988. "The effects of environmental regulation on business location in the United States." *Growth and Change*, Summer, pp. 22–44.

Birdsall, Nancy, and David Wheeler. 1992. "Trade policy and industrial pollution in Latin America: Where are the pollution havens?" In Patrick Low, ed., *International trade and the environment*. Washington, DC: World Bank.

Chapman, Keith, and David F. Walker. 1991. *Industrial location: Principles and policies*. Cambridge, MA: Basil Blackwell.

Crandall, Robert W. 1993. *Manufacturing on the move*. Washington, DC: Brookings Institution.

Cropper, Maureen, and Wallace Oates. 1992. "Environmental economics: A survey." *Journal of Economic Literature*, 30 (June): 675–740.

Daly, Herman, and Robert Goodland. 1994. An ecological-economic assessment of deregulation of international commerce under GATT. *Ecological Economics*, 9:73–92.

Dollar, David. 1990. *Outward orientation and growth: An empirical study using a price-based measure of openness*, Washington, DC: World Bank.

Duerksen, Christopher J. 1983. *Environmental regulation of industrial plant siting*. Washington, DC: Conservation Foundation.

Duffy-Deno, Kevin T. 1992. "Pollution abatement expenditures and regional manufacturing activity." *Journal of Regional Science*, 32(4):419–436.

Epping, Michael G. 1986. "Tradition in transition: The emergence of new categories in plant location." *Arkansas Business and Economic Review*, 19(3):16–25.

Friedman, Joseph, Daniel A. Gerlowski, and Johnathan Silberman. 1992. "What attracts foreign multinational corporations? Evidence from branch plant location in the United States." *Journal of Regional Science*, 32(4):403–418.

General Agreement on Tariffs and Trade (GATT). 1992. *International trade 90–91*. Geneva: GATT.

Gladwin, Thomas N., and John G. Welles. 1976. "Environmental policy and multinational corporate strategy." In Ingo Walter, ed., *Studies in international environmental economics*. New York: John Wiley & Sons.

Globerman, Steven. 1993. "Trade liberalization and the environment." In Steven Globerman and Michael Walker, eds., *Assessing NAFTA: A trinational analysis*. Vancouver, BC: Fraser Institute.

Greenhut, Melvin L., and Marshall R. Colberg. 1969. "Factors in the location of Florida industry." In Gerald J. Karaska and David F. Bramhall, eds., *Locational analysis for manufacturing*. Cambridge, MA: MIT Press.

Grossman, Gene M., and Alan B. Krueger. 1991. "Environmental impacts of a North American free trade agreement." Woodrow Wilson School Discussion Papers in Economics No. 158, November.

Hamilton, James. 1993. "Politics and social costs: Estimating the impact of collective action on hazardous waste facilities." *Rand Journal of Economics*, 24, no. 1 (Spring): 101–125.

Knögden, Gabriele. 1979. "Environment and industrial siting." *Zeitschrift für Umweltpolitik*, December.

Leonard, H. Jeffrey. 1984. *Are environmental regulations driving U.S. industry overseas?* Washington, DC: Conservation Foundation.

Leonard, H. Jeffrey. 1988. *Pollution and the struggle for the world product.* Cambridge: Cambridge University Press.

Leonard, H. Jeffrey, and Christopher J. Duerksen. 1980. "Environmental regulations and the location of industry: An international perspective." *Columbia Journal of World Business,* Summer, pp. 52–68.

Levinson, Arik M. Forthcoming. "Environmental regulations and manufacturers' location choices: Evidence from the Census of Manufactures" *Journal of Public Economics.*

Low, Patrick. 1992. "Trade measures and environmental quality: The implications for Mexico's exports." In Patrick Low, ed., *International trade and the environment.* Washington, DC: World Bank.

Low, Patrick, and Alexander Yeats. 1992. "Do 'dirty' industries migrate?" In Patrick Low, ed., *International trade and the environment.* Washington, DC: World Bank.

Lucas, Robert E.B., David Wheeler, and Hemamala Hettige. 1992. "Economic development, environmental regulation and the international migration of toxic industrial pollution, 1960–1988." In Patrick Low, ed., *International trade and the environment.* Washington, DC: World Bank.

Lyne, Jack. 1985. "Survey suggests laws on reuse of industrial sites toughening in many states." *Site selection handbook.* Atlanta, GA: Conway Data, October.

Lyne, Jack. 1990. "Service taxes, international site selection and the 'green' movement dominate executives' political focus." *Site Selection,* October.

McConnell, Virginia D., and Robert M. Schwab. 1990. "The impact of environmental regulation on industry location decisions: The motor vehicle industry." *Land Economics,* 66, no. 1 (February): 67–81.

McFadden, Daniel. 1974. "Conditional logit analysis of qualitative choice behavior." In P. Zarembka, *Frontiers in econometrics,* 105–142. New York: Academic Press.

Mueller, Eva, and James N. Morgan. 1969. "Location decisions of manufacturers." In Gerald J. Karaska and David F. Bramhall, eds., *Locational analysis for manufacturing.* Cambridge, MA: MIT Press.

Pashigian, Peter. 1985. "Environmental regulations: Whose self interests are being protected?" *Economic Inquiry,* October, pp. 551–584.

Pearson, Charles S. 1987. "Environmental standards, industrial relocation, and pollution havens." In Charles S. Pearson, ed., *Multinational corporations, environment, and the third world.* Durham, NC: Duke University Press.

Portney, Paul R., ed. 1990. *Public policies for environmental protection.* Washington, DC: Resources for the Future.

Robison, H. David. 1988. "Industrial pollution abatement: The impact on the balance of trade." *Canadian Journal of Economics,* 21, no. 1 (February).

Schmenner, R. 1982. *Making business location decisions.* Englewood Cliffs, NJ: Prentice-Hall.

Stafford, Howard A. 1985. "Environmental protection and industrial location." *Annals of the Association of American Geographers,* 75(2):227–240.

Tobey, James A. 1990. "The impact of domestic environmental policies on patterns of world trade: An empirical test." *Kyklos,* 43:191–209.

United Nations Center on Transnational Corporations. 1988. *The United Nations Code of Conduct on Transnational Corporations*. Boston: Graham and Trotman.

United Nations Conference on Trade and Development (UNCTAD): Program on Transnational Corporations. 1993. *Environmental management in transnational corporations: Report on the Benchmark Environmental Survey*. New York: UN.

United States Census Bureau. 1973. *Industrial location determinants, 1971–75*. Washington, DC: U.S. Census Bureau, February.

United States Environmental Protection Agency. 1990. *Environmental investments: The cost of a clean environment*. Washington, DC: EPA, December.

United States General Accounting Office (GAO). 1991. *U.S.–Mexico trade: Some U.S. wood furniture firms relocated from Los Angeles area to Mexico* (GAO/NSIAD-91-191). Washington, DC: GAO, April.

Walter, Ingo. 1973. "The pollution content of American trade." *Western Economic Journal*, 11:61–70.

Walter, Ingo. 1982a. "Environmentally induced industrial relocation to developing countries." In Seymour J. Rubin and James R. Graham, eds., *Environment and trade*. Totawa, NJ: Allanheld, Osmun.

Walter, Ingo. 1982b. "International economic repercussions of environmental policy: An economist's perspective." In Seymour J. Rubin and James R. Graham, eds., *Environment and trade*. Totawa, NJ: Allanheld, Osmun.

Walter, Ingo, and Judith L. Ugelow. 1979. "Environmental policies in developing countries." *Ambio*, 8:102–109.

Wintner, Linda. 1982. *Urban plant siting*. New York: Conference Board.

12

Reflections on the Race to the Bottom

Alvin K. Klevorick

The rhetoric of many recent discussions of international trade policy centers on a mixed metaphor. Countries, whether actual or potential trading partners, are characterized as participating in "a race to the bottom," and the remedy urged upon them is "harmonization." The vision evoked is of a group of misguided athletes who have run off in the wrong direction and who need, to make things right, only to transform themselves into a smooth-sounding a cappella singing group. The problem with the characterization, however, runs deeper (no pun intended) than a matter of expositional style. The question is whether the common formulation accurately identifies an important problem, and if it does, whether the proposed solution is appropriate. In this chapter I shall argue that the putative problem of "a race to the bottom" may or may not be a serious and substantial concern, but that even if it is, "harmonization," as often described in these discussions, is not the elixir it is held out to be. The case for uniformity of standards is not nearly as compelling as its proponents believe.

What is the concern that motivates the "race to the bottom" literature and discussion of trade policy? It is that to attract mobile resources, especially firms, governments will choose policies—for example, environmental standards, occupational health and safety standards, competition policy—that entail suboptimal requirements, which afford their citizens too little protection—whether from environmental hazards, unsafe or unhealthy working conditions, or cartel behavior. The idea is that to make its country a hospitable location in which to do business, a government would establish lax standards to be imposed upon those it wishes to draw. The result, it is argued, is that all countries will impose standards that are much more lax than those they would set if they did not have to compete with one another for the mobile resources. In short, they will race to the bottom of the domain of standards, and the contest will be to no avail because with all countries choosing the same standard, mobile resources will have no incremental incentive to move. If only these countries could agree not to compete in the dimensions of these standards, the argument concludes, each government would choose the socially optimal level of the relevant standard, and all their populations would be better served.

At the heart of the race-to-the-bottom argument is the view that the competitive process among countries is imperfect. The market failure upon which the argument is premised is distinct from the typical spillover argument commonly identified with global environmental concerns. Indeed, the concern about countries racing to the bottom is seen most distinctly when the typical environmental externalities are eliminated by assumption, and for ease of exposition I shall make that assumption. The defect upon which adherents of the view that nations race to the bottom focus actually sounds much more like the complaint of "ruinous competition" or "destructive competition" that one firm in an industry makes about another when the second has won the battle of the marketplace or the claim that competitors in an industry make when trying to justify agreements among themselves as to prices, quantities, qualities, and so on. In each case the claim is that the competitive process itself is harmful to the interests of one or more competitors and to those they serve, consumers of the product. These are claims about which most antitrust laws and competition laws are highly and justifiably skeptical.

The reference to a race to the bottom that results from competition among countries suggests that the problematic outcomes are due to failures in the interactions among states, to failures *external* to any one country. This interpretation suggests that repairing the market in which these countries compete would eliminate the detrimental effects, in a manner analogous, for example, to the way in which domestic antitrust policy is meant to preserve the competitive process or regulation in the public interest is intended to remove a market failure. I shall argue, however, that the concern that motivates critics of the race to the bottom is quite frequently not a problem with the character of the international competition but rather the failure of a state to attain a particular standard, an *internal* failure. The critic's position is that from a normative perspective, the particular state is not setting the appropriate standard, is not fulfilling the obligations that the critic believes the state has to its population.

But since, at least nominally, at the center of the concern about a race to the bottom is a criticism of the quality or caliber of competition among countries, it should come as no surprise that whether or not there is a theoretical basis for the argument is bound to be highly contextual. The very careful review of the literature on local public goods competition that John D. Wilson (1996) discusses in Chapter 10 of this volume makes that point in a very compelling way.

Consider but two extremes. The appropriate first-cut formulation of the race-to-the-bottom argument, as set out cogently by Richard L. Revesz (1992), posits two countries for whom the payoffs to competing in the choice of environmental policies have the structure of a prisoner's dilemma game. If that is an accurate picture of competition among governments, then those who argue that there is a race to the bottom are on firm ground. The governments playing noncooperative strategies in their self-interest will choose strategies that leave both countries' populations with lower environmental quality than they want and could have.

On the other hand, if the competition among governments is perfect, as it is in the first model of competition among jurisdictions presented by Wallace E. Oates and Robert M. Schwab (1988), then the failure underlying the argument that overly lax standards will result is absent. In the first Oates-Schwab model, competition among jurisdictions results in socially optimal levels of environmental quality all around. They go on to show, however, that the need to use distortionary taxation of capital as an instrument or the existence of considerable divergences in the preferences of constituents in the same jurisdiction can shatter this wonderful world of socially optimizing jurisdictions.

Moreover, the Oates-Schwab optimality-producing equilibrium is, naturally enough, founded on specific assumptions about production technologies—for example, constant returns to scale. As the article by James R. Markusen, Edward R. Morey, and Nancy Olewiler (1995) demonstrates in a somewhat different context, where two jurisdictions are competing for the plants of a single firm with market power, the character of the production technology will affect whether the location pattern that results yields too much pollution, too little, or the optimal amount. More generally, to the extent that models of Tiebout-like competition are critical to arguments that interjurisdictional competition will yield optimal levels of public goods—including environmental quality, labor standards, and the like—it is important to recall Truman F. Bewley's (1981) critique of Tiebout models. As he demonstrated, the conditions under which competition among jurisdictions can be shown, in general, to yield an equilibrium that is Pareto optimal are very restrictive.

Since the existence of a race to the bottom among national governments depends so much on the character of the competition among them, it is striking that there is so little evidence beyond the anecdotal about the relevant market. How do countries compete with one another with regard to environmental controls, labor safety standards, consumer product safety standards? How effective is lax environmental regulation as an instrument for attracting firms? The few empirical studies of the impact of environmental regulation on firm location in the U.S. domestic context that Revesz (1992) cites yield mixed results about whether this is an effective tool. Arik Levinson's (1996) study (see Chapter 11 of this volume) also leads one to wonder how much of a race there really is. Finally, in a recent article, "Free Trade, Regulatory Competition, and the Autonomous Market Fallacy," Joel R. Paul (1994/95) provides an excellent case study of competition among European countries in the regulation of packaging waste. He describes the rich texture of the political economy of the regulatory choices each country has made so far, and he shows, in this story, how cooperation may lead to less stringent rather than stricter controls.

But suppose the race to the bottom is a reality, and consider the remedy proposed—harmonization of national standards or, to pursue the athletic metaphor, leveling the playing field. Note first that if those who argue there is a race to the bottom are correct, and if the participants succeed in reaching bottom (and not just racing toward it), then the outcome is actually a harmonized one and the playing field is level—all standards are at the bottom. The proposal that harmonization of national standards is the beneficial alternative to the race carries with it more freight than harmonization alone suggests. The idea must be not only that there be uniformity among standards but uniformity at the "appropriate" or "correct" level. I intentionally use quotation marks on the modifiers *appropriate* and *correct* because it is not clear how either one, though I use them synonymously here, would be defined. Furthermore, who would define them—that is, what agency, organization, or other governing body would decide the standard to which all nations should conform? And remember that this is a standard for the environment *fully within* the country (no spillovers) or a standard for health and safety standards of workers *fully within* the country.

In some instances of international cooperation—for example, NAFTA or the formation of the new World Trade Organization (WTO)—a multilateral agreement explicitly specifies how a standard should be set and adherence to it enforced. This is, of course, a positive, descriptive answer, not a normative response, to the question posed here about the selection of the harmonized standard.

To be sure, citizens of one country may well be—they undoubtedly are—concerned about the well-being of their fellow human beings in other countries; this is a set of externalities that surely must be weighed. (Guido Calabresi and A. Douglas Melamed, 1972, use the term "moralisms" to refer to the class of externalities of which these are examples.) But recall that such direct spillovers are put to the side in the sharpest of the cases for a race to the bottom and the need to cope with it.

Second, if the citizens of one country are concerned about the well-being of populations elsewhere—if the condition of distant populations enters the utility functions of citizens of a given country—why should that concern manifest itself with respect to specific aspects of the distant folks' lives and not with their overall well-being, the utility or welfare they perceive themselves as achieving? One can make an argument that some goods or living conditions satisfy what Richard A. Musgrave (1959) called "merit wants" or that they constitute elements of living with respect to which James Tobin (1970) would argue that we believe in "specific egalitarianism." But who is the "one" in the first clause and the "we" in the second, and what if the people whom we (or one) would have adopt these standards do not agree? Again, this merit want or specific egalitarianism argument does not seem to be at the heart of the concern of those who would end the race to the bottom with harmonization.

Supposing, then, that there is a race to the bottom, is the fixing of a uniform standard in each area of concern—environment, labor, competition policy, and so on—the optimal response? Put the opposite way, what is the optimal diversity of standards, and is the answer none? There is no doubt that uniformity of laws or standards has its virtues. If all units of the zidget part of each widget conform to the same specifications, such standardization facilitates trade, enables widget manufacturers in any one country to meet their need for zidgets from any one of a number of sources, and presumably satisfies consumers' preferences more efficiently. The recently developed literature on standards that are adopted to ensure compatibility in goods or services with network externalities highlights the importance of uniformity. The continuing debates and discussions about worldwide adherence to the metric system provide another example of a context in which uniformity's virtues seem real and have been extolled.

Note, however, that in each of these cases there is a spillover effect or externality to any one participant's adoption of the standard. Indeed, in the network externalities case, an innovative firm with a superior product might depart from a previously uniform standard to gain a competitive advantage. Another way of putting the point is to observe that in each of the cases mentioned, there are economies of scale in the adoption of the standard.

In analyzing the level of environmental quality in a particular country where, by assumption, there is no spillover to any other country's environment or population, what is the argument for requiring the same standard that has been adopted in another country? What is the positive force pressing for uniformity? It is difficult to see one. Rather it is the argument *against* imposing uniformity and for allowing diversity that is compelling. First, we know that if the international trading system is functioning effectively, economies with different resource endowments, preferences, and technologies will use different input combinations, produce different output vectors, and consume different quantities of goods and services. This well-known result is nicely reviewed by Jagdish Bhagwati and T. N. Srinivasan (1996) in Chapter 4 of this volume. Allowing diversity in standards simply allows the tailoring to local circumstances that emerges in the standard trade equilibrium.

Moreover, even in models that allow strategic behavior with regard to choice of legal and capital infrastructure to attract firms to a region, the equilibrium can entail diverse levels of infrastructure—for example, environmental standards—and yet be efficient. That is, coordination would not enhance the aggregate well-being of the two competing regions. Such is the conclusion that Ian King, R. Preston McAfee, and Linda Welling (1993) reach in their analysis of two governments competing to have a firm locate in their respective regions. Similarly, in a model of tax competition between two countries—where favorable tax treatment is intended to induce consumers to shop in the home country and hence cause domestic businesses to thrive—Ravi Kanbur and Michael Keen (1993) demonstrate that joint revenue maximization by the two competing governments does not generally require uniform tax rates.

A second reason for permitting diverse standards to coexist and for not imposing uniformity on all countries derives from our collective uncertainty about what the correct standard is. In the face of such uncertainty, imposing a uniform standard risks subjecting all countries to the wrong requirement. It also removes the possibility of learning, from experimentation with diverse standards, both what the immediate effects of different standards are and how economic agents respond to them. In the presence of uncertainty about the optimal standard, caution and flexibility are desirable. Imposing a uniform standard seems to be a move in precisely the wrong direction.

Finally, the imposition of uniform standards, whether with regard to the environment, working conditions, or the like, effectively redistributes wealth among countries. Suppose, for example, that the population of one country, call it Precisia, was by nature—by genetic endowment alone—extraordinarily careful when working with complex machinery. Then imposing on the people of Precisia the same occupational safety standards as were imposed on all other countries would diminish the value of their resource endowment. They would be forced to bear costs of production that they need not incur, and the value attached to their supercareful approach would be diminished. In short, because of the imposition of a uniform occupational safety standard, wealth would be effectively redistributed from Precisians to citizens of other countries. To be sure, this may be an extreme example, but the point is general: imposing a uniform standard diminishes the wealth of those countries that have the capacity—because of either the technology they possess or their predilection—to do perfectly well with a lower standard.

The argument for uniformity is stronger, though still not entirely unproblematic, at the level of the decision-making process. That is, the case is stronger for harmonizing the process by which standards are set. What one wants to try to assure is that all the relevant information and values are weighed when a government decides on an environmental standard, an occupational health and safety standard, a competition policy. If the process is flawed, if relevant information is not considered, or if particular views are deliberately ignored, then an argument can be made that the government is intentionally tilting the playing field.

Even at this process level, however, there is a potential problem in imposing uniformity because the differences in process may reflect differences in the values of different populations. But this observation rapidly takes us into the domain of moral philosophy and out of the realm where economists and lawyers have any comparative advantage. Attempting to reach agreement on harmonized decision processes for setting environmental and labor standards will serve, however, to isolate and identify the more fundamental disagreements that need to be understood, whether or not they can be resolved. The irreducible minimum of harmonization that is required, and that seems justifiable, relates to characteristics of the standard-setting process. In particular, the process must be sufficiently transparent that such disagreements can be identified.

Having said that, however, there are problems even with imposing and enforcing a uniform process-oriented value of transparency. Making difficult choices nontransparent may be valuable—to some societies all the time, to some just when they are faced with particular choices. The point is made effectively in the discussion of tragic choices by Guido Calabresi and Philip Bobbitt (1978). But even if there were a shared appreciation of the value of transparency, how effectively could that element of uniformity be achieved and monitored in the face of disparate political systems—some unitary, some federal; some democratic, some nondemocratic; some two-party, some with more diffuse centers of power? How would the entity assigned the task of assessing the process ascertain what interests and whose interests had been represented and effectively voiced? How would this discussion be disentangled if the society relied on a noisy, broadly participatory process rather than a systematic, univocal bureaucratic approach where expertise is more valued?

Perhaps the difficulty of assuring clear, deliberate decision-making processes leads those who worry about a race to the bottom, as well as its consequences, to advocate harmonization of standards themselves rather than of processes. But then we are brought back to the earlier question, Are critics of putative races to the bottom in the international setting principally concerned with failures of *external* markets in which countries participate or with perceived shortcomings in the *internal* political systems of those countries?

NOTE

I am indebted to Bruce Ackerman, Joel Paul, Roberta Romano, Alan Schwartz, and T. N. Srinivasan for their comments on an earlier version of this paper.

REFERENCES

Bewley, Truman F. 1981. "A critique of Tiebout's theory of local public expenditures." *Econometrica*, 49:713.

Bhagwati, Jagdish, and T. N. Srinivasan. 1996. "Trade and the environment: Does environmental diversity detract from the case for free trade?" See Chapter 4 of this volume.

Calabresi, Guido, and Philip Bobbitt. 1978. *Tragic choices*. New York: W. W. Norton.

Calabresi, Guido, and A. Douglas Melamed. 1972. "Property rules, liability rules, and inalienability: One view of the cathedral." *Harvard Law Review*, 88:1089.

Kanbur, Ravi, and Michael Keen. 1993. "Jeux sans frontières: Tax competition and tax coordination when countries differ in size." *American Economic Review*, 83:877.

King, Ian, R. Preston McAfee, and Linda Welling. 1993. "Industrial blackmail: Dynamic tax competition and public investment." *Canadian Journal of Economics*, 26:590.

Levinson, Arik. 1996. "Environmental regulation and industry location: International and domestic evidence." See Chapter 11 of this volume.

Markusen, James R., Edward R. Morey, and Nancy Olewiler. 1995. "Competition in regional environmental policies when plant locations are endogenous." *Journal of Public Economics*, 56:55.

Musgrave, Richard A. 1959. *The theory of public finance.* New York: McGraw-Hill.

Oates, Wallace E., and Robert M. Schwab. 1988. "Economic competition among jurisdictions: Efficiency enhancing or distortion inducing?" *Journal of Public Economics,* 35:333.

Paul, Joel R. 1994/95. "Free trade, regulatory competition and the autonomous market fallacy." *Columbia Journal of European Law,* 1:29.

Revesz, Richard L. 1992. "Rehabilitating interstate competition: Rethinking the 'race-to-the-bottom' rationale for federal environmental regulation." *New York University Law Review,* 67:1210.

Tobin, James. 1970. "Limiting the domain of inequality." *Journal of Law and Economics,* 13:263.

Wilson, John D. 1996. "Capital mobility and environmental standards: Is there a theoretical basis for a race to the bottom?" See Chapter 10 of this volume.

VII

Japan and Europe: Fair
Trade and Harmonization

13

A Short Summary of the Long History of Unfair Trade Allegations against Japan

Gary R. Saxonhouse

13.1 Introduction

In the absence of differences between countries, no gains accrue from international trade. Putting aside government policy for the present, international trade will be based largely on differences between countries in the supply of labor, capital, skill, land, and minerals, differences in technology, and differences in taste. These differences, in turn, are the product of differences between countries in historical experience and geographic inheritance.

Not all differences between countries are regarded as legitimate bases for a system of international trade. The social policy debates that have raged in liberal democracies in Europe and in North America in the 19th and 20th centuries have not always looked kindly on competitive outcomes shaped by history and geography.[1] The intertemporal (in particular, the intergenerational) transmission of economic and social status resulting from outcomes determined by such factors has long been considered illegitimate by influential segments of public opinion. Such concerns have resulted in domestic social policies (such as equal access to education, equal access to childhood nutrition, and even progressive income and wealth taxation) whose ideal is to equalize the terms under which competition takes place on first entry to the labor market.

While shaping a domestic economy to make competitive outcomes more independent of antecedent conditions appears to help the disadvantaged both relatively and absolutely, the opposite appears to be the case when these same concerns have been transmitted to the international economic system. For the better part of the past 150 years, an equal-opportunity international economic system has meant that economic competition between nations should take place solely on the basis of individual ingenuity and individual tastes with trade policy working to equalize the costs of inputs such as labor, capital, and minerals. As F. W. Taussig noted in 1910,

The vogue of the plan of basing the tariff on differences in costs of production is a curious phenomenon and a significant one.... The doctrine has an engaging appearance of fairness. It seems to say, no favors, no undue rates. Offset the higher expenses of the American producer, put him in a position to meet the foreign competitor without being under a disadvantage, and then let the best man win. Conditions being thus equalized, the competition will become a fair one.[2]

Still earlier, in 1888, William Graham Sumner, under the heading "Rules for Knowing When It Is Safe to Trade," observed:

It has been affirmed that we can not safely trade unless we have taxes to exactly offset the lower wages of foreign countries
...
It has been said that two nations can not trade if the rate of interest in the two differs by more than two per cent[3]

However skillfully Taussig and Sumner may have dispatched such arguments three-quarters of a century ago and a century ago, respectively, they continue to have great appeal even today. During the debate surrounding the ratification of the NAFTA agreement in the fall of 1993, Ross Perot, the former presidential candidate and a NAFTA opponent, set among necessary conditions before he could support ratification a border tax designed to equalize the cost of labor between the United States and Mexico.[4]

Neither the rules for fair trade of long ago nor Perot's border tax helps equalize the terms under which labor competes in global markets. Such policies, while benefiting relatively unskilled workers in skill-abundant, capital-abundant, and natural-resource-abundant economies, will constrict opportunities for workers in poorer economies. Export industries in these economies will diminish in importance, while workers there are likely to face higher unemployment and lower wages or both as they are pushed toward producing nontradable goods and services.

While wealthy-country policies aiming at creating an equal-opportunity international economic system are likely to accomplish just the opposite, the interest in thwarting outcomes based on differences in geography and history has generalized. Increasingly over the course of the 20th century, but particularly accelerating in recent years, almost any difference between countries that has an impact on foreign trade has come to be seen by many as illegitimate. This increasing intolerance of diversity among nations has culminated in efforts not just to remove the influence of geographic, historical, cultural, and institutional differences that might influence foreign trade, but also in efforts that remove differences in foreign-trade outcomes directly. Enter managed trade.

The history of Japan's foreign-trade relations best exemplifies the changing attitudes in North America and Europe regarding the legitimate range of differences among trading partners. For more than a century, allegations of unfairness against Japan have almost always been framed as complaints about the fundamental structure and operation of the Japanese economy. Over the course of the past 100 years, rapid economic progress has gone hand in hand with marked changes in Japan's most basic economic institutions and conditions. As rapid institutional changes have undermined the premise of an allegation of unfair trade practice, invariably new complaints have arisen premised on the new circumstances. First, Japanese competition was illegitimate because it was based on labor cheaper in cost than labor in its trading partners. When labor was no longer cheap, competition was unfair because capital was cheaper in Japan. First, it was argued, Japan's dumping abroad was done at the expense of its exploited labor. Later it was argued Japan had to dump because by giving its labor force job security it was treating it rather too well. First it was argued that Japan's tariffs were high and its quotas numerous. When tariffs and quotas were largely harmonized with practices in the other advanced industrialized economies, it was then argued that it was Japan's unique economic institutions and their attendant informal barriers that were really keeping foreign products out. Finally, even as Japan's informal barriers were melting under continued structural change in the Japanese economy, demands came to be made for guaranteed market shares for foreign products in Japan. In what follows the evolution of these complaints will be traced. Throughout the long history of these complaints, Japan's trading partners have rarely been prepared to concede that Japan's participation in the international economic system is legitimate.

13.2   Differential Factor Endowments as Unfair Trade

13.2.1   Labor

No other country has yet been criticized as long or as severely for the low wages paid its workers. Ironically, the worldwide condemnation in the late 1890s of the low wages paid Japanese workers in export industries was stimulated by the Japanese government's seemingly innocent dissemination of what would be later seized upon as incriminating evidence.

With the growth of factory work in Japan in the late 1880s and early 1890s, leaders of Japan's nascent socialist movement working in concert with foreign missionaries were successful in making the issue of regulating factory working conditions part of the Japanese government's social welfare agenda. Japanese industry, particularly Japan's rapidly growing textile industry, resisted government interference with their affairs. As part of a persistent effort to head off government regulation, in 1897, at the suggestion of their allies in the Japanese Diet, the All Japan Cotton Spinners Association conducted a landmark survey on working conditions in the industry. Included as part of this survey was unprecedentedly detailed information regarding wages and fringe benefits paid the industry's workers.

Shortly after its completion, full results of the survey were published.[5] Japan's cotton spinners apparently believed that the survey and its publication would persuade the Japanese government and social critics alike that the allegedly idyllic, if paternalistic, Lowell system, the wonder of the early factory age, had been resurrected in late-19th-century Japan.[6] The industry's expectations were not realized. In short order, the dissemination of the survey's results provoked an avalanche of new criticism.[7] Rather than focusing on what the industry believed was a praiseworthy effort to prevent the disruption of traditional social institutions by avoiding the creation of a permanent proletariat, journalists such as Gennosuke Yokoyama highlighted what he felt were the extremely low wages paid to young female workers. Rather than throwbacks to the Lowell system, the textile industry's company dormitories and worker welfare programs were viewed as cruel prisons. Within six months of the survey's publication, Yokoyama had published his best-selling expose *Nihon no shakai kasō*, a significant portion of which drew heavily on the survey.[8] Soon all of literate Japan was talking about the textile industry.

Nihon no shakai kasō was not the only book published in 1898 that drew heavily on the survey. Half a world away in Paris, Kashiro Saito, an official from Noshomusho, the government ministry from which both Japan's Ministry of International Trade and Industry (MITI) and Ministry of Agriculture, Forestries, and Fisheries claim descent, published *La protection ouvrière du Japon*.[9] Saito's intent was to publish a sober, detailed, and numerate account of conditions in the industry together with a discussion of future Japanese government plans to regulate the terms of factory employment. Saito hoped to show that the Japanese government, in common with governments in the West, was sensitive to the problems of factory labor. Had Saito's book been published even a few months later, the enormous success of *Nihon no shakai kasō* might have forewarned him of the reception awaiting his work.

The quality and candor of Saito's volume won him high praise from professional social scientists. Ernest Foxwell, an eminent English economist, wrote a detailed and appreciative review article for the *Economic Journal* in 1901.[10] Long before Foxwell's review appeared, however, *La protection ouvrière du Japon* had stimulated a still greater outrage and concern in Europe than had *Nihon no shakai kasō* in Japan. Note that 1898 was also the year Japanese cotton-textile-industry exports first exceeded imports. For the first time since Japan had been forcibly opened to foreign trade 40 years earlier, Japanese cotton spinners succeeded in wresting a significant share of their own home market from Indian and British yarn and cloth imports. At the very same time they were beginning to export in very large volume to China and Korea.[11]

Government officials, churchmen, and, particularly, British and continental European textile industry representatives and union leaders all condemned the wages paid Japanese textile industry workers ($0.11 an hour at 1990 prices) as not simply unconscionably low but also as a threat to European living standards.[12] Japanese wages were characterized as low even by poverty-stricken Asian standards. Ignoring the very different skill levels of mature Indian mule spinners and teenage and subteen Japanese ring spinners, as well as the free housing, medical care, and food subsidies provided to Japanese workers, European commentators regularly observed that Japanese wages were one-third the level paid by the Indian textile industry.[13] Small wonder that Saito was soon recalled to Tokyo.

Having once acquired the reputation as a country whose economic success was driven by the payment of extremely low wages, another seven decades were to pass before this perception would change. For example, in 1915, when Japanese government officials and industry leaders protested that 80 years earlier, when poorer, Europe and the United States were paying wage rates of the sort they were now condemning in Japan, Sidney Gulick, the celebrated American missionary to Japan, replied,

Before condemning Japan unduly, it is true Occidentals should remember their own record is none too bright. . . . If comparison is to be made, however, between Japan and the West, it may be made along other lines. The West fell into its paltry treatment of workers with no example from which to learn. But this is not true of Japan: She can easily learn the lesson of a century of Western experience; but she seems slow to do it.

In explanation, Gulick observed,

In the West, the great movements of industrial reform are movements of the
peoples themselves ... led by enlightened humanists and Christian popular opinion. In the West, the Churches are fairly in line with forward social movements,
whereas in Japan, Shintoism, Confucianism and even Buddhism are apparently
wholly indifferent to the economic and even ethical condition of the nation's
toilers.[14]

The criticism of the cultural basis of Japan's economic organization made
by Gulick reappears in many guises throughout the 20th century.[15]

The criticism by Yokoyama and Gulick of Japanese low wages is echoed
in succeeding decades. In 1934, Fernand Maurette of the International
Labor Office wrote:

[Japan's] workers ... have to work harder than those of other nations in order to
maintain a living for themselves and their families, even at great sacrifice in
comfort, for they are placed in a situation where they are forced to choose
between living in such a way and dying.[16]

As late as 1961, Takejiro Shindo could still observe,

The labor problem in Japan's cotton industry has long been the target of severe
criticism from abroad. After Japan's cotton industry became an export industry
and its products began appearing in world markets, questions began to be raised
about the so-called low wages ... in the industry. These matters have since been
the focal point of comments and criticisms. Because of this Japan's cotton products
have been subjected to discriminatory treatment. Japan is still considered one of
the so-called "rice wage countries" or low wage countries.[17]

Four years later, John W. Hall, the leading historian of Japan of his generation, noted,

In the final analysis, a dense population has been a major resource for Japan's
economic growth. It has often been claimed that Japan's serious "overpopulation
problem" has been a drag on the economy. It is true it has delayed increases in per
capita income. On the other hand, an abundant labor force remains the country's
main asset for international competitiveness.... Japan's advantage by contrast
with other overpopulated, underdeveloped countries lies in the industriousness of
its labor force.[18]

Curiously, between the time Yokoyama wrote and Gulick's time, and
then between the time Gulick wrote and Maurette wrote, and finally
between the times Maurette and Shindo and Hall all wrote (wartime excluded), Japan's wages rose persistently. In real terms, Japanese wages rose
40 percent between 1898 and 1915, 80 percent between 1915 and 1934,
and finally 385 percent between 1934 and 1965. These wage increases

resulted in an enormous improvement in the standard of living of Japanese workers both absolutely and relative to workers abroad.[19] For almost the entire period, his enormous improvement in conditions in Japan appears not to have resulted in any lessening of the foreign complaints about Japanese worker compensation.

The relentless closing of the gap between Japanese wages and wages in the West went hand in hand with the increasing presence of Japanese goods in global markets. Japanese exports as a percentage of global exports increased from 1.2 percent in 1900, to 1.9 percent in 1913, to 3.6 percent in 1929, and finally to 7.0 percent in 1965.[20] The speed with which Japanese exports increased their share of global markets imposed unwanted structural adjustment on major industries in Japan's trading partners. No matter that economy-wide levels of Japanese wages went from $\frac{1}{7}$ to $\frac{3}{5}$ of the average of the advanced industrialized countries. As Shindo commented, the representatives of factors of production with specialized skills in all the affected industries were all too ready to seize on wage differences of any size in their efforts to secure protection from Japanese competition.

13.2.2 Capital

No sooner had Japanese wages finally converged with those in the West than Japan's financial system in general, and its reputedly low-cost capital in particular, came to be viewed by many as the new and unfair basis for Japanese success in global markets. Echoing arguments that Sumner had strenuously criticized a century ago, this issue was first raised by the Semiconductor Industry Association in 1980 and has continued to attract considerable attention since that time.[21] Foreign commentators have viewed Japan's cost of capital as unfairly low because of the character of Japanese financial regulation. It is argued that government regulation, by constraining the Japanese household's arranging of its assets and liabilities, elicits more savings for a given rate of time preference than would otherwise be the case. This same regulation puts these high household savings at the exclusive disposal of the Japanese banking and insurance system to allocate to Japanese industry. It accomplishes this purpose by imposing controls on capital outflows at the same time that equity financing of new investment is restricted.[22] By unfairly coercing both Japanese households and Japanese industry, Japan's economy overcomes important problems of asymmetric information and incentive incompatibility in financing.[23]

As is so often the case when discussing Japanese institutions, the regime that attracts attention has virtually collapsed by the time foreign observers begin to take notice of it.[24] As Georg W.F. Hegel put it, "The Owl of Minerva flies only at dusk." With the revision of the administration of the Foreign Exchange Control Law in 1980, whatever nominal interest-rate differential has continued to exist in favor of Japan has been exactly equal to the discount on the dollar (or other currency) in the forward exchange market. Contrary to what was widely believed in the early 1980s when complaints of Japan's unfairly low cost of capital were first made, Japan was then and is now highly integrated into global financial markets.

The integration of Japan into global financial markets has not only linked nominal interest rates in Japan to interest rates abroad, but it has also undermined the centrality of Japanese banks and related financial institutions. The much greater freedom that Japanese households and corporations have had since the late 1970s to arrange their assets and liabilities has led to a relative decline in the role of indirect finance. Whatever problems of asymmetric information and incentive incompatibility Japan's financial system may have overcome, large numbers of Japanese companies have opted out of financial intimacy in favor of arm's-length, American-style relationships with their main bank.

While the complaints about capital controls, low nominal interest rates, and Japan's main bank system might better have been raised not during the 1980s but, if at all, 20 years earlier when critics of Japanese economic policies were busy complaining about cheap Japanese labor, the real interest rate (defined as the inflation-corrected long-term bond rate) in Japan was low in the 1980s and, excepting a brief interlude in the early 1990s, has remained low to this day. Japan is integrated into global financial markets, and if nominal interest rates in Japan and abroad are the same when correction is made for expectations about exchange-rate changes, how is it possible that the real interest rate is low? Is the very real advantage of a low real interest rate the result of some unfair public or private action in Japan? On this question, Frankel notes that differentials in real interest rates across countries can occur for much the same reason that differentials in nominal interest rates occur.

Expectations that the dollar may depreciate against the yen in real terms may certainly explain why the yen real interest rate was less than the dollar real interest rate. ... real interest rates are not necessarily equalized internationally and changes in savings (even if truly exogenous) need not be offset by borrowing from or lending abroad and thus may be heavily reflected as changes in investment ... and yet the explanation may be the imperfect international goods markets that allows failures of purchasing power parity rather than the imperfect international integration of financial markets. If there is no way of arbitraging directly among countries' goods or among their plant and equipment, and if plant and equipment are imperfect substitutes for bonds *within* each country, then perfect international arbitrage among countries' bonds is not sufficient to equalize real rates of return among countries' plant and equipment.[25]

Since the worldwide failure of purchasing power parity can hardly be attributed to uniquely unfair Japanese government policy, low real interest rates more likely reflect Japan's abundant savings.[26]

If Japan's undeniably low real interest rates reflect abundant savings, is there something unfair about how Japan's high rate of household savings has been achieved? Before the early 1980s, when Japan's low real interest rate and its low cost of capital were not issues, Japanese government policies did effectively limit many Japanese households to no better a financial instrument than a low-yielding passbook savings account, while consumer credit was nonexistent and banks were encouraged to discriminate against single-unit residential housing investment.[27] These policies undoubtedly lowered household welfare, but it does not appear that they did much to raise the rate of Japanese household savings by more than a very small amount.[28] Regardless, such strict controls were long since abandoned as part of Japan's financial deregulation program in the early 1980s. Quite apart from clearly legitimate differences in demography, geography, history, and taste, if the Japanese savings rate has been high, it is because the Japanese government budget deficit is low.

13.3   Social Dumping

During the first six decades of the 20th century, concern about the low wages received by Japanese workers and the poor conditions under which they labored regularly merged with more traditional concerns about trade practices such as dumping. While many firms in many countries have been the object of dumping complaints, dumping complaints aimed at Japan have had a special edge. Japan was the first country to be accused not just of dumping, but of social dumping. Foreign competitors claimed that Japanese firms intermittently forced their workers to accept extraordinarily sharp reductions in real wages and working conditions to support the predatory acquisition of markets overseas. Japanese firms were not accused of selling their products below cost or even of practicing price discrimination. Rather they were accused of obtaining their labor at a cost even below what would be indicated by competitive market conditions in labor-abundant Japan.[29]

Japan is promoting the export of national products by decreasing their cost of production as the result of depressing conditions of labour in the undertakings which produce them, or keeping those conditions at an artificially low level if they are already at such a level.[30]

At the depths of the Great Depression accusations of social dumping by Japan became so widespread as to trigger a special investigation by the League of Nations' International Labor Office. The investigation, while noting Japan's extremely low wages, strenuously rejected the claim that Japan was engaging in social dumping.[31]

Once again, no sooner had complaints ceased that Japanese firms were dumping at the expense of their workers than complaints arose that Japanese firms were dumping precisely because they were treating their workers rather too well by offering them permanent employment.

Take an industrial sector (such as steel) in two economies (such as Japan and the United States). Suppose [Japan] is characterized by ... worker tenure (no layoffs of workers) ... and [the United States] is characterized by ... no worker tenure (wages for workers are therefore variable costs).... [Because variable costs will differ markedly in Japan and the United States] ... in a period of falling prices and demand, the producers in [Japan] can be expected to garner, through exports to [the United States], an increasing share of [the United States'] market.... Are [Japan]'s exports to [the United States] unfair?[32]

13.4   Shoddy Goods as Unfair Trade

Cheap labor and social dumping are not the only unfair trade charges that economic growth and structural adjustment in Japan have made undeniably incorrect, whatever the original merits of the charges may have been. In the early decades of the 20th century, Japanese manufacturers were also bitterly criticized for the poor quality of their products.[33] While Japanese exploration of the trade-off between price and quality was itself criticized as an unfair practice, Japanese manufacturers were also accused of misrepresenting the quality (in particular, the durability) of their products, in a predatory attempt to capture markets at home and abroad.

There are no limitations placed on Japanese efforts to take control of the Manchurian market. Cloth is increasingly less densely woven and starch very heavily applied so that prices may be kept unfairly low.[34]

... a wide complaint of Occidental importers is that goods are not made according to contract or sample.... for as soon as a large demand has arisen in foreign lands for any article, its quality as a rule has rapidly deteriorated. It is this ... that makes so difficult direct exportation without the supervision of Occidental middlemen.[35]

Ironically, in the last quarter century, the standard of quality set by many Japanese products has become so high as to almost erase past memories of shoddy Japanese-made goods. At the same time, while there may be criticisms that Japan's provision of a high-quality employment environment has led to unfair trading practices, no such charges have been made concerning the high quality of Japanese products. Envy and attempted emulation have been the response of producers abroad.

13.5   The Recent Origin of Complaints about Japanese Trade Barriers

Charges of unfair competition abroad have been leveled against Japanese manufacturers for the better part of the 20th century. In contrast, complaints by Japan's trading partners about lack of access to the Japanese market are really of very recent origin. Surprisingly, charges that the Japanese market is unfairly closed to foreign competition only began to surface in the mid-1960s. Herman Kahn's widely read *The Emerging Japanese Superstate*, published in 1970, which provides extended treatment of the structure and operation of the Japanese economy and Japan's international economic relations, does not mention the issue at all.[36] Nor is the issue mentioned in Zbigniew Brzezinski's *The Fragile Blossom*, published two years later in 1972, which also contains a substantial number of chapters focusing on Japan's international economic relations.[37]

13.5.1   Japan Not Out of Step with the Protectionist Policies of Other Countries

Why is it only very lately that there are such forceful allegations that access to Japan's market is unfairly out of step with the conditions of access to the world's other major markets? Given a century of complaints about unfair Japanese competition, it is not that such charges could not have arisen earlier because Japan has only recently become a major factor in the global economy. It also cannot be because Japan has erected major new barriers to international trade over the past 20 to 25 years. No one accuses Japan of doing so. Certainly, for much of the 20th century, Japan did maintain a wide array of clearly identifiable formal trade barriers.[38] In this practice, however, it did not differ from most of its major trading partners. With the United Kingdom during the early decades of the 20th century excluded, few industrialized economies would have been able to credibly argue that their policies were not protectionist.[39] For example, in 1913 Japan's average tariff level of 12 percent, while similar to that of the continental European countries, was only one-third the American average tariff level of 32.5 percent.

The rough equivalence of Japan's nominal tariffs with those of its major trading partners for much of the 20th century does not mean that the level of effective tariffs was necessarily equivalent. In fact, what little systematic evidence is available on this question suggests that while trade policy may have substantially altered the allocation of resources in at least some of the trading partners, it is much less clear that Japan's substantial barriers provided it with much protection at all. Price studies in the 1950s found that Japan's highest duties were on those products whose prices in Japan were cheap by comparison with prices of similar products abroad. Apparently, high tariffs on finished Japanese products were ineffective in raising domestic Japanese prices.[40] In contrast, during the same period, American protection so distorted price signals that resources were allocated as if the United States were a labor-abundant country.[41]

13.5.2   Trade Balances as a Measure of Fair Trade

In addition to the equivalence of nominal tariffs with those of its trading partners, six and one-half decades of Japanese trade deficits were quite successful in helping to inoculate Japan against the perception abroad that its home market was uniquely closed. Surprising as it may seem from the perspective of the last 25 years, for most of the 20th century, the yen was a very weak currency. Japan was usually in global trade deficit, and with the exception of its bilateral trade relations with the United States in the years before the Great Depression, Japan ran a trade deficit with all of its major, politically significant trading partners.[42]

It was only in the mid-1960s, when a large, persistent Japanese global trade surplus in general, and a large persistent bilateral trade surplus with the United States in particular, emerged, that the now-familiar complaints about foreign access to the Japanese market finally became a major issue in international economic relations. In the mid-1960s as today trade balances were viewed as a summary measure of the extent to which a country participates fairly in its international economic transactions.[43] Economists in both Japan and the United States were quick to argue that such a view of the trade balance is wrong as a matter of both fact and economic logic. As the 1983 *Economic Report of the President* noted in describing Japan's bilateral surplus with the United States,

Japan runs a huge surplus in its manufactures trade, while the United States runs only a small one, and Japan also has a large bilateral surplus with the United States.... The main explanation of Japan's surplus in manufactures and in trade with the United States is that Japan, with few natural resources incurs huge deficits in its trade in primary products, especially oil and with primary producers.... looking at Japanese trade in isolation is misleading. The Japanese surplus in trade is largely a response to the rise of OPEC.[44]

The 1983 *Report* also rejected the view that Japan was responsible for the U.S. trade deficit.

Large trade deficits are not the result of unfair trade competition. Large projected US deficits are a result of macroeconomic forces, particularly large budget deficits. The main sources of the US trade deficit are not to be found in Paris or Tokyo but in Washington.[45]

This important point has been emphasized over and over again in subsequent *Economic Reports*. For example, the 1994 *Economic Report of the President* observes,

If private saving is insufficient to cover ... private investment and the combined deficit of all levels of government we must borrow the difference from abroad. Such a shortage of savings has characterized the United States for about a decade now.

When Americans borrow from foreigners we run a surplus in our international capital account ... the mirror image of this capital account surplus is an equally large current account deficit. Thus a country that saves less than it invests and runs a budget deficit is bound to have a large current account deficit. Indeed, chronic, large current account deficits date from precisely the time that the United States started running huge budget deficits.[46]

For all the efforts at public education that the President's Council of Economic Advisers, not to mention the Japanese, attempted in the 1980s and early 1990s, when the U.S.–Japan Framework talks broke down February 11, 1994, President Bill Clinton himself denounced "the unfair $60 billion bilateral trade deficit with Japan."[47]

13.5.3   Harmonization of Japan's Formal Barriers against Imports

Unhappily, at just the same time that Japan's trade balance was moving into structural surplus in the mid-1960s, it lagged its major trading partners in lowering its formal trade barriers. As a result of the Kennedy Round agreements, Japan was left, for the first time in the 20th century, maintaining substantially higher tariffs on its industrial products and many more quotas on both industrial and agricultural products than all of its major trading partners.[48] Still more embarrassing, while it was not an active participant in the diplomacy of the Kennedy Round, Japan, standardized for size (whether measured in welfare or trade terms), received a disproportionate share of its benefits.[49]

The embarrassment stemming from both Japan's high formal trade barriers and its newly emerging structural surplus was still further exacerbated by the new international economic status Japan was achieving. In the mid-1960s, Japan joined the Organization of Economic Cooperation and Development and achieved Article 8 status within the International Monetary Fund. In the view of its trading partners, such status encumbered Japan with new responsibilities. For the first time since the end of the Pacific War, Japan was seen as a pillar of the international economic system. Japan's evident tariffs and quotas, its equally widely publicized barriers to foreign investment, and its large structural trade surpluses were viewed as manifestly inconsistent with Japan's new status and responsibilities.

The simultaneous emergence of Japan's large structural trade surplus with its relatively high formal trade barriers led to the widespread misconception that these two phenomena were intimately related, a misconception that remains to this day. Once again, economists working in the U.S. government were quick to attack this misconception. The 1983 *Economic Report of the President* argued,

Trade restrictions probably do not lead to an overall large trade surplus. If they were removed, the yen would depreciate and increased Japanese imports in the currently protected sectors would be offset by reduced deficits or increased surpluses elsewhere.[50]

Whether because the actual impact of Japan's high nominal barriers was small or because the cost in international economic goodwill of maintaining them was just too high, in the face of mounting criticism Japan moved to bring down its formal barriers. Central to its strategy was the active promotion of a new set of multilateral trade negotiations, which came to be rather aptly known as the Tokyo Round. Complementing its efforts at lowering trade barriers, Japan moved to bring its regulations on inward foreign investment into conformity with OECD codes.[51] By the early 1980s, there was little substance to the complaint that Japanese formal trade barriers on industrial products were higher than those of its trading partners or that Japan maintained more formal barriers to inward or outward direct investment than those of its trading partners.[52]

13.6   The Original Informal Barrier: The Government-Business Relationship, Industrial Policy, and Fair Access to the Japanese Market

The substantial steps that Japan took to bring its formal trade and investment barriers into line with those of its major trading partners did little to change perceptions abroad that its home market was closed to foreign manufactures. While it was comparatively easy to harmonize the barriers at Japan's borders with those of its trading partners, other complaints that surfaced in the late 1960s were less easy to resolve. Along with criticism of the very evident barriers at Japan's borders, came foreign complaints about the role the government played in Japan's economy. The Japanese government was not just maintaining barriers at its borders. Unlike American or European trade policy, which too often served the interests of those industries using disproportionate amounts of unskilled labor, it was alleged that Japanese trade policy was embedded in a much broader set of Japanese policies aimed at continually upgrading Japan's industrial structure.[53]

If Japanese industrial policy had just been viewed from abroad as protective trade policies laced with subsidies and special tax preferences, harmonization of Japanese practices with foreign practices would have presented no special, uniquely Japanese problem. Article VI of the GATT identifies such policies as unfair trading practices and allows the imposition of countervailing duties when injury can be shown.[54] By 1980, however, Japanese industrial subsidies were negligible, and special tax preferences were extremely small by any reasonable standard.[55] Almost from the very beginning of complaints about the government's role in the Japanese economy, however, it was alleged that the relationship between government and business was too intimate to be characterized by tax, subsidy, or tariff policies. Labeling Japanese government's role as *gyōsei shidō* (administrative guidance) and Japan, Inc., to convey both its subtlety and its comprehensiveness suggested that any measurement of its unfair impact on the welfare of Japan's trading partners was impossible.

In the early 1980s, the terminology used to complain about the government role in the Japanese economy changed. Complaints of *gyōsei shidō* and Japan, Inc. gave way to complaints about industrial targeting.[56] A deputy U.S. trade representative testified before Congress that industrial targeting, as practiced, gives selected firms in the targeted industry a privileged position in the home market. Once a firm is so identified, it benefits from specific government programs. Perhaps more important, the firm's welfare becomes a national goal, leading to less explicit benefits, such as preferential status with creditors and buyer preferences. The total effect can be to give the chosen firm in the identified sector protection from foreign competition (in the past explicit through quotas, now less transparent).[57]

Such complaints about Japanese industrial targeting, like earlier complaints about *gyōsei shidō* and Japan, Inc., presented a particular quandary for traditional international trade law.[58] The explicit government aid given any Japanese industry was so small, that, even by the most generous of standards, only a trivially small countervailing duty could result from any complaint initiated under existing trade law. Nonetheless, it was argued that even such a small amount of aid, particularly for research and development, could often be decisive for the successful development of an industry at the expense of actual or potential foreign competition.[59]

Concern about Japanese government targeting and the seemingly new challenge it represented to the international economic system prompted both a major investigation of Japanese practices by the U.S. International Trade Commission and calls in Congress for new legislation.[60] In early 1984, Sam Gibbons, the chair of the House Ways and Means Subcommittee on Trade, proposed the Trade Remedies Reform Act, singling out industrial targeting and mandating government action to counter it.[61] The Gibbons bill would have required that countervailing duties be placed on imports that were the beneficiaries of foreign government targeting. Left unresolved was just how the benefits of targeting might be quantified so that the appropriate countervailing duty could be imposed. Clearly, if such benefits had been readily quantifiable, targeting would never have been raised as a special issue in the first place. For this reason, and most importantly because many groups wanted to emulate and not outlaw Japanese targeting practices, the Gibbons bill was never passed.

Early interest in emulating Japanese industrial restructuring policies found popular expression in Robert Reich's *The Next American Frontier*, a book endorsed by both leading candidates for the Democratic nomination for president in 1984.[62] At the same time that Reich's overview was being published, calls were also being made to match Japanese efforts in particular industries. For example, specialists in artificial intelligence announced:

The Japanese have seen gold on distant hills … and have audaciously made it a national goal to become number one in this industry by the latter half of the 1990s. They aim not only to dominate the traditional forms of the computer industry but also to establish a "knowledge industry" in which knowledge itself will be a salable commodity like food and oil. Knowledge itself will become the new wealth of nations. . . .

To implement this vision the Japanese have both strategy and tactics. . . . The tactics are set forth in a major and impressive national plans of the Ministry of International Trade and Industry (MITI) called Fifth Generation Computer Systems. The plan documents a carefully staged ten-year research and development program on Knowledge Information Processing Systems.[63]

Nor did interest in emulating Japanese industrial policy subside in the early 1980s. A decade later, after noting that "Unlike . . . Japan, the United States does not have a commercially oriented industrial policy," Laura Tyson, the chair-designate of the President's Council of Economic Advisers, called for the U.S. government to develop "an institutional capability to fund research on precompetitive generic technologies that are likely to be underfunded by individual private companies."[64] Tyson urged the U.S. government to begin the

development of an institutional mechanism for assessing competitive and technological trends in global high-technology industries on an ongoing and timely basis. The government should either designate an existing agency or construct a new one to perform several related tasks, including evaluating the likely course of key American industries, comparing these baseline projections with visions of industry paths that would be compatible with a prosperous and competitive economy; and monitoring the activities of foreign governments and firms in these industries to provide an early warning of potential competitive problems in the future.[65]

Whatever visions of Japan American proponents of industrial policy may have, there is little more substance to such views than to observations that Japanese government policy in the 1980s and 1990s has kept the cost of capital low for Japanese firms at the unfair expense of Japan's foreign competitors. Indeed, these two incorrect views about the unique character of the Japanese economy are linked. Once again American views were quite out of date. In the 1950s, 1960s, and 1970s, Japan did need an industrial policy. With Japan's financial system highly concentrated and heavily regulated, its equity markets played too marginal a role in the allocation of resources to serve as the ultimate arbiter of future prospects. High concentration and heavy regulation provided a framework within which the Japanese government, through the financial system, could influence the allocation of resources. High concentration of capital made a government presence not only possible but necessary prior to 1980. Moreover, as long as Japan was far from the global economy's technological frontier, fathoming what structural change the Japanese economy required was not difficult. At the same time, however, the complicated pressures of politics within *keiretsu* bank groups often meant that in the absence of government pressure, it was too easy for established industries to divert badly needed resources from emerging industries.

The institutions of Japan during the 1950s, 1960, and 1970s that allowed the Japanese government to work through Japan's private financial system to shape Japan's industrial structure no longer exist today. As noted, since 1980 financial deregulation has allowed Japanese firms to draw on far more diverse sources of finance, both domestic and overseas, than had once been the case. Today's Japanese firms seeking to promote new industries no longer need the Japanese government as an ally to force a bank to turn on its financial spigot. The same deregulation that removes the need for the government to intervene removes the means by which the government might intervene. The Japanese banking system, now forced to compete with many other financial institutions both at home and abroad, and burdened with a staggering overhang of loans gone bad, is not a fit instrument to shape Japan's industrial structure. Rather than giving Japanese firms an unfair competitive advantage, industrial policy is better viewed as a Japanese substitute for well-functioning capital markets. With financial deregulation, its rationale has been lost.[66]

Even if financial deregulation had not taken place, almost certainly cues from the government would not be taken as seriously as was once the case. Consider the highly uncertain environment within which the Japanese economy now operates. With Japan at the technological frontier, unlike the 1950s, 1960s, and 1970s, the precise direction structural change should follow is by no means clear. And there's certainly little reason to believe that the government might be better informed than the private sector.

There is no better illustration of the fate of Japanese industrial policy after 1980 than the Ministry of International Trade and Industry's Fifth Generation Computer System Project. Despite the alarmist reactions of American specialists in artificial intelligence, this project was actually created over the strenuous objections of Japan's computer manufacturers. The Fifth Generation Project sought to change the traditional structure of computer architecture. It was planned that the older von Neumann architecture would be replaced by a new distinctive Japanese approach that would allow the parallel processing of data. The Fifth Generation project was intended to provide for a great Japanese leap forward not only in computers but also in computer software. In particular, it was hoped that the great increases in speed permitted by parallel processing would allow all Fifth Generation computers to self-generate software for new applications. With one well-targeted stroke, the competitive disadvantage of Japan's software industry might be eliminated.

With a self-confidence that would have been lacking a decade or two earlier, Japan's computer manufacturers characterized the Fifth Generation project as unrealistic. If there was to be a MITI-sponsored project, computer manufacturers hoped for something that would support their efforts to develop technologies and products for newly emerging markets in personal computers. Japan's computer manufacturers were loath to have precious human resources siphoned off for years into what was believed to be, contrary to America's artificial intelligence experts, a largely academic project with a highly uncertain outcome. Japan's major computer manufacturers ultimately succumbed to MITI pressure to participate, but unlike earlier MITI projects, they refused to contribute a single yen to its finance.

The results of the decade-long Fifth Generation project now show quite clearly that Japanese private-sector skepticism was well merited. Japan's computer manufacturers had accurately forecast the trends in their industry for the 1980s and 1990s. The leading edge of the computer industry as promoted by American innovation was miniaturization, ease of user interface and specific dedication. To the extent that Japanese manufacturers were able to keep up with these extraordinary changes in their industry, they did it without MITI's help.

While a continuing stream of innovation was changing the global computer industry, MITI remained wedded to its original Fifth Generation concepts. In the absence of corporate funding and remote from market pressure, the Fifth Generation project's bureaucratic leaders were too insulated to acknowledge mistakes and dramatically change course. After a decade, large numbers of computers embodying the fruits of Fifth Generation research had been built, but all were highly experimental in character and provided little the private sector could build upon. Even the experimental machines met none of the goals originally proferred for the Fifth Generation project.

13.7 Other Distinctive Institutions and Fair Access to the Japanese Market

Though the government-business relationship was the first seemingly distinctive Japanese institution that attracted foreign attention in connection with trade problems, the persistence of a structural surplus in Japan's balance of trade led in the 1980s to complaints about a much broader and more detailed array of allegedly distinctive Japanese institutions. In particular, it was alleged that the character of government regulation of the Japanese economy permitted the development of a wide variety of collusive private-sector institutions and structural impediments that frustrated foreign access to the Japanese market. Such complaints were made within Japan as well and reflected the same kinds of frustration with government interference that made Japanese industrial policy so ineffective in the 1980s. These complaints were sufficiently persistent and sufficiently detailed and so politically salient as to elicit two extremely detailed Japanese government reports in the mid-1980s.[67]

13.7.1 The Maekawa Commission

The so-called Maekawa Commission, officially known as the Advisory Committee on Economic Structural Adjustment for International Harmony, included many of Japan's most distinguished economic and financial leaders. While not dealing directly with foreign allegations about lack of access to the Japanese market, the Maekawa Reports explicitly accepted the premise that the harmonization of many important Japanese institutions with Western practices can both substantially increase the role imports play in the Japanese economy and substantially improve Japanese welfare. Among many other recommendations, the Maekawa Reports called for (1) removal of government restrictions on Japan's distribution system; (2) strict enforcement of Japan's Antimonopoly Law; (3) strengthened domestic protection of foreign intellectual property; (4) increased overseas investment in the interest of both improving the global division of labor and increasing the imports of intermediate manufactures into Japan; (5) increasing agricultural imports (excepting basic foodstuffs) in the interest of removing differentials between Japanese and world market prices; (6) abolition of tariffs on industrial products; (7) improving foreign access to Japanese government procurement; (8) increased taxation of urban agriculture and the modification of urban zoning regulations in the interest of better allocating resources; (9) reduction of the Japanese workweek; (10) large expansion of public works programs to improve Japan's social capital stock, including in particular the expansion of leisure industry infrastructure; and (11) better structural balance between Japanese savings and investment. Despite the Maekawa Reports' extraparliamentary and extrabureaucratic auspices, their recommendations have set the agenda for Japanese structural change since the mid-1980s.

The Maekawa Reports whetted the appetite of Japan's foreign critics for structural change in the interest of promoting access to the Japanese market. Following the issue of the first Maekawa Report, the Japanese government agreed to meet with U.S. government officials on a regular basis for what was formally called the Structural Adjustment Dialogue. The stated purpose of this negotiation was to monitor implementation of the Maekawa Report from the perspective of foreign interests and to discuss what further institutional change might be helpful in promoting the access of foreign goods and services to the Japanese market.[68]

13.7.2   Structural Adjustment and the Exchange Rate Mechanism

At the same time that the more broadly based Structural Adjustment Dialogue was ongoing, in other quarters considerable attention began to focus on the exchange rate mechanism and structural issues. In the three years following the beginning of the yen-dollar realignment in 1985, the pace of adjustment of the external payments imbalance of the United States and Japan was frustratingly slow. The slow pace of adjustment reflected, in considerable measure, the failure of the United States to adopt restrictive macroeconomic demand-management policies supporting this exchange rate realignment. Nonetheless, during these years considerable surprise was expressed that exchange rate adjustment had relatively little impact on the prices of Japanese exports when denominated in foreign currencies or for that matter on the prices on Japanese imports when denominated in yen. Ignoring the role foreign barriers to Japanese exports might have played in frustrating the adjustment process, the U.S. Department of the Treasury took its cue from the Maekawa Report and concluded that impediments in the domestic structure of the Japanese economy were to blame.[69]

13.8   The Structural Impediments Initiative

The passage of the Omnibus Trade and Competitiveness Act of 1988 with its Super 301 provision dramatically changed the character of the discussion of structural issues between the United States and Japan. Faced with intense Congressional pressure that the entire structure and operation of the Japanese economy be negotiated under the deadlines and threats spelled out in Super 301, the market-access-focused Structural Adjustment Dialogue fused with the U.S. Treasury's interest in the structural barriers to macroeconomic adjustment to give rise to the Structural Impediments

Initiative (SII). Outside the Super 301 framework, it was generally imagined, particularly on the Japanese side, that SII would follow in form and substance the low-profile Structural Adjustment Dialogue. This forecast proved to be mistaken. Congress, together with their allies in the Bush Administration, kept SII, under tight deadlines, as the centerpiece of U.S.–Japanese economic relations for the better part of two years. The negotiations proved costly in the sense that they engaged the energies of American and Japanese government officials at the very highest levels (including President George Bush and Prime Minister Toshiki Kaifu) over a considerable period of time.

In form, the SII negotiations were entirely symmetrical. Japan was encouraged to harmonize some of its institutions with U.S. practice, while for the first time in U.S.–Japanese economic relations there were discussions about harmonizing some U.S. institutions with Japanese practice. While Japan's Maekawa Reports formed the basis for all but one set (those pertaining to *keiretsu*) of the voluminous series of American recommendations for structural change in the Japanese economy, the equally voluminous set of Japanese recommendations for the American economy largely resembled the economic proposals that came to be made by the Clinton presidential campaign in 1992.[70] The features of the Japanese economy addressed by the American negotiating team included (1) saving and investment imbalances; (2) price differentials between Japan and elsewhere; (3) land use; (4) the distribution system; (5) *keiretsu*; and (6) exclusionary business practices. By contrast, Japan made its recommendations for the American economy concerning (1) the U.S. government budget deficit and low U.S. household savings; (2) corporate investment and supply capacity; (3) corporate planning horizons; (4) government regulations; (5) research and development; (6) export promotion; and (7) workforce education and training.

In practice, while equal time was carefully allowed for both U.S. and Japanese topics during formal negotiations, it would be difficult to characterize these negotiations as symmetrical. Japan was pressed continually and successfully for commitments. In contrast, it was understood by both U.S. and Japanese negotiators that only Congress could deal with most of the issues being raised by the Japanese. While negotiating sessions dealing with the structure of the Japanese economy were well attended by senior representatives on both sides, attendance on days devoted to discussions of the American economy was sparse.[71]

The use of the Maekawa Reports as the basis of the American negotiating position came to be a double-edged sword. Initially, this helped generate considerable favorable publicity in Japan for SII. After all, Japan was largely being asked to do what its own blue-ribbon commission had recommended.[72] What was helpful in Japan was not necessarily helpful in the United States. Many of the Maekawa Reports' proposals for the harmonization of Japanese institutions with foreign practices have a very direct connection with improving the quality of life in Japan, but only a rather indirect connection with more harmonious international economic relations. Many of the long list of points of interest tabled by the United States, such as changes in the regulations on credit card use or changes in the standards governing initial public equity offerings, seemed to many American observers as neither having much connection with improving foreign market access or with better legitimizing the character of Japan's participation in the international economic system.[73] To what extent were such complaints merited? Had American trade officials at long last adopted a realistic, up-to-date view of how the Japanese economy differed from advanced industrialized economies, only to have marginalized themselves in the process?

13.8.1 Savings-Investment Imbalances

The Bush-Uno Statement issued in July, 1989, at the Bonn summit authorizing the SII talks emphasized the importance of correcting disparities in national savings and investment patterns that create current-account imbalances.[74] At just about the same time that American and Japanese officials were organizing the talks, however, the World Bank issued an urgent call for more, not less, global savings. With this in mind, it was decided that SII should not ask the Japanese to save less, except in those few, remaining instances where Japanese savings appeared to be propped up by government policies that biased the choice between savings and consumption. While the U.S. government did not ask Japan to spend less, it urged Japan to spend more by increasing its public investment. From the World Bank perspective, however, the impact on international capital flows of Japan saving less or spending more would surely be similar.

The original outlook of American officials in raising the public investment issue was long-term. During the 1980s a succession of Japanese prime ministers worked to cut what had once been a very large Japanese government budget deficit by restraining public spending. With private savings continuing at a high level, the decline in the government deficit left Japan to generating a very large current-account surplus. American officials hoping to reverse Japanese government policies of the 1980s emphasized that the 1990s should be a time to harmonize many of Japan's long-neglected public amenities with those of its major trading partners. Americans regularly pointed out to their Japanese counterparts that Japanese government objectives from the mid-1970s to match European and American standards in housing, sewerage, parks, and waste disposal were still nowhere close to being met.[75]

For their part, Japanese officials complained that American participants in SII showed insufficient appreciation of the considerations that drove Japan's fiscal reconstruction in the 1980s. Among the advanced industrialized economies, Japan has had one of the youngest populations and with it correspondingly low expenditures on social security. However, more than in any other advanced industrialized economy, the average age of Japan's population is increasing rapidly. Before very long, Japan's population will be among the oldest in the advanced industrialized economies. In the absence of expenditure declines resulting from slower population growth, the heavy social security expenditures associated with an aging population, under current benefit levels, will force very significant deficits on Japan's public sector.[76] It was argued during SII that much of the Japanese government's continuing interest in fiscal austerity was geared to these long-term considerations and the need to delay as long as possible the politically unwelcome downward revision in the benefit levels available to future social security recipients.

While none of this was necessarily meant to suggest that real need did not exist for significantly larger Japanese expenditures for social infrastructure, in the view of many Japanese officials available Japanese public-sector surpluses were already committed for other purposes.[77] Japan may have resisted demands that it finally harmonize its social amenities and social infrastructure with those of other advanced industrialized economies in the interest of international goodwill, but Japanese officials regularly pointed out that the median quality of life has improved by a far greater extent in Japan than in any other major industrialized economy over the course of the past 45 years.

The SII talks began as something of a departure in U.S.–Japanese economic relations because of their emphasis on deep-rooted issues of Japan's economic structure. They ended, however, where negotiations between the United States and Japan had ended so often in the previous 20 years. Great pressure was brought to bear on Japan to increase its public spending, not for any long-term consideration, but rather in the interest of short-term, international macroeconomic coordination. In the spring of 1990 the Bush administration became preoccupied with forecasts that the

American current-account deficit would reverse course and begin increasing once again.[78] This concern led it to make obtaining a firm commitment from the Japanese government to expand domestic demand by increasing public spending one of the very highest priorities of the SII discussions.

Partially in response to requests at the SII talks, the Japanese government agreed to undertake 430 trillion yen in new public investment during the 1990s. By contrast 263 trillion yen was spent on public investment during the 1980s. Even assuming equivalent growth rates in 1990s and 1980s, the SII agreements called for an increasing share of Japanese GNP to be devoted to building up Japan's social capital stock.

13.8.2   Land Use

Even without the SII talks, land policy was almost certainly the foremost issue in Japan in the late 1980s. It was widely believed in Japan that the extraordinary bubble in Japan land prices was being fed by government regulations and policies that encouraged extremely inefficient use of Japan's scarcest resource. This was not the reason why U.S. government officials wished to discuss this issue with the Japanese government. Ending Japan's urban agriculture, by itself, would have little impact on Japan's agricultural imports. Rather, U.S. negotiators reasoned that better use and lower prices of land might reduce saving and release some spending for the purchase of imports.

The relationship between the high price of land, housing conditions, and Japan's high rate of personal savings is not so straightforward. As noted, housing-related saving is not a major cause of Japan's high savings rate. As might be expected, savings motivated by the desire to own residential real estate assets, in aggregate, are largely matched by dissaving for much the same purpose. High land prices increase the wealth of existing owners. It is not obvious that their increased consumption out of capital gains falls short of the increased savings of young families seeking housing.[79]

A decline in the price of land might stimulate a short-term boom in housing investment. Given the very large role that land plays in the Japanese household balance sheet, in the long run this new housing investment might be overwhelmed by increases in the household savings rate needed to compensate for losses in household wealth related to declines in land prices.[80] The net impact might well be to increase the household sector's financial surplus.

More important, if a goal of SII was to encourage an increase in Japanese imports of manufactured products, lower land prices could have just the opposite impact. Japanese land use policy keeps land cheap for Japanese farmers and expensive for everyone else. To the extent that SII sought to help American manufacturers compete with their Japanese counterparts, encouraging a change in Japanese land-use policies cannot be helpful. Better land-use policies only make Japanese manufacturers still more competitive.[81]

13.8.3   Financial *Keiretsu*

The strongly held belief in the United States and elsewhere that Japan's bank-centered industrial groups, or *keiretsu*, convey special competitive advantages, caused American trade officials to raise the widespread presence of this institution in Japan as an issue at the SII talks. Financial *keiretsu* was the only major issue raised in SII that did not come from the Maekawa Report.

In the 1950s, 1960s, and 1970s, only through membership in a financial *keiretsu* did a firm have regular, continuing access to bank finance. And during these years there were few alternatives to bank finance. Did the market power that Japanese banks possessed during these years also make it possible for the main bank to force their borrowers to buy from other members of its financial *keiretsu*? While it is difficult to answer this question with any precision, with increasing financial deregulation, these *keiretsu* by the 1980s were much less closely affiliated than is generally imagined. The six best-known financial *keiretsu* are Mitsui, Mitsubishi, Sumitomo, Fuyo, Dai-Ichi Kangyo, and Sanwa. Mitsui, Mitsubishi, and Sumitomo are directly descended from the prewar *zaibatsu* that the Supreme Command of the Allied Powers tried to break up during the American occupation of Japan. By contrast, the Fuyo, Dai-Ichi Kangyo, and Sanwa *keiretsu* have been formed largely in the years after 1945. Already in 1983 the member firms in *keiretsu* with strong prewar roots purchased only 14.8 percent of their procurement from fellow *keiretsu* members. For the more recently organized *keiretsu*, procurement from fellow *keiretsu* members was still less important, with only 8.9 percent of procurement being purchased from affiliated firms.[82]

While reciprocal purchasing seems to be too weak to tie *keiretsu* together, American government officials have been concerned that cross-shareholding among member firms allows the *keiretsu* as a whole effective control over individual member firms. In fact, cross-shareholding is not nearly as pervasive nor so exclusive among *keiretsu* members as is commonly believed. Among the six best-known *keiretsu*, the average individual firm equity held by all other members of its *keiretsu* is 17.9 percent.[83] While this is a relatively small amount of cross-holding, if ownership of the firm's remaining equity is widely dispersed, even this amount might be sufficient to give the *keiretsu* control of a member firm. In fact, for a typical member firm, control of the remaining equity is not widely dispersed. Large blocks of equity are often held by members of rival *keiretsu*.[84] Such holdings, if exercised in concert, can be sufficient to block effective *keiretsu* control of member firms.

Suppose *keiretsu* members do discriminate with each other against non-*keiretsu* products, and therefore against imported products; they would have to know with whom they are supposed to be colluding. This knowledge may not be easy to come by. Definitions of *keiretsu* vary so widely it is often difficult to tell who is inside and who is outside. For example, by some definitions only 9.4 percent of all firms listed as manufacturers on the Tokyo Stock Exchange are *keiretsu* affiliated. Other definitions have 79 percent of all Tokyo Stock Exchange–listed firms as *keiretsu* affiliates. Similarly, estimates of sales by *keiretsu* members can be as low as 40 percent of all sales by Tokyo Stock Exchange–listed firms by one definition or as high as 94 percent by another. None of the five most common definitions of *keiretsu* are correlated with each other at a rate higher than 0.32.[85]

Quite apart from arbitrary classification, which can lead to a misunderstanding of the role of the *keiretsu* in the Japanese economy, Japanese firms change their affiliations far more frequently than is generally believed. Between the mid-1970s and the early 1980s no less than 25 percent of the firms listed with the Tokyo Stock Exchange changed their main bank affiliation.[86] With the growth of equity financing and with the increasing equalization in the terms of access to capital between *keiretsu* and non-*keiretsu* firms, one of the main props of the *keiretsu* system is coming undone.[87] With the recovery in the Tokyo Stock Exchange, an acceleration of *keiretsu* hopping and disaffiliation should be part of the Japanese economy's future.

13.8.4   Distribution System

Even if the long-term relationships that Japanese firms maintain with other Japanese firms are a barrier against foreign access to the Japanese market, direct action against *keiretsu* may have little merit. As a general rule, there is little that can be done to force private firms to buy imports they do not desire. If SII and other bilateral and multilateral initiatives work to insure that there is competition in Japan's final goods markets, it may make little difference to foreign welfare that Japanese firms wish to continue to purchase imports from high-cost domestic suppliers. If Japanese firms wish to handicap themselves in this way, what foreign firms lose in intermediate goods markets, they will make up in final goods markets. In any event, experience has shown that Japanese producers when confronted with vigorous competition are quite prepared to shift from domestic to foreign suppliers in the interest of maintaining market shares and profits. For example, when Japan's tobacco market was finally opened to foreign competition in the mid- and late 1980s, the newly privatized Japan Tobacco Corporation discarded decades-old relationships with domestic cigarette paper suppliers and packagers in favor of imported goods and services in an effort to remain competitive.

While great concern with the procurement practices of Japanese private firms might not be warranted provided there is free entry into Japan's final goods market, at the time of SII the operation of Japan's Large-Scale Retail Store Law did call this premise into question. This law provides that a construction plan for any store of more than 500 square meters must be discussed by a committee of the local Chamber of Commerce and approved by the prefectural governor or the Ministry of International Trade and Industry. Throughout the 1980s, the administration of this law was such that it commonly took almost three years for a construction plan to receive final approval. Before final approval was granted, which effectively required the acquiescence of potential competitors, considerable adjustment typically had to be made in the floor space, the number of days the store would be open during a week, the store hours, and the total number of days the store would be open during the year.[88]

For all the nuisance value of this law, its actual impact on the character of Japanese commerce is difficult to establish. Contrary to its overseas reputation, the Japanese distribution system has not been inefficient. While there are many small stores in Japan, productivity is high and profit margins are not out of line with the experience of most other countries, including the United States.[89] Even in the absence of the Large-Scale Retail Store Law, Japan would have an abundance of small stores because the space in the average Japanese home is extremely limited and because Japanese retailers have very low reorder costs.[90]

Even if the Large-Scale Retail Store Law is effective in changing the size mix of retail establishments, should Japanese trading partners be concerned? To be sure, there is some reason to believe that the size distribution of retail and wholesale establishments can make a difference for the access of foreign products to the Japanese market. Japan's large department stores and supermarket chains import directly from overseas, while smaller retailers and wholesalers must typically rely on one of the giant general trading companies to stock their shelves and inventories. By relying on these general trading companies, which handle a majority of all Japanese imports, small-scale Japanese distributors' opportunities to stock foreign products may be limited. It was argued during SII that Japan's trading companies may restrict what they import, not so much to protect their own domestic production, of which they do little, but rather to protect the interests of other firms to which they are tied through their *keiretsu* affiliations. It remains an open question, however, whether *keiretsu* ties have been sufficiently strong to warrant any conclusion as to the impact trading companies might have on the level and structure of Japanese imports.

Under pressure from the SII negotiations, the Japanese government undertook to revise the administration of the Large-Scale Distribution Law. Under the new administrative guidelines that were implemented in 1990, neither MITI nor local governments could delay beyond a year and one-half the approval of building plans for retail stores.[91]

13.8.5   Exclusionary Business Practices

Japan's trading companies may restrict what they import and therefore what they supply to Japan's retailers, in order to protect the interests of other firms to which they are tied through their *keiretsu* affiliations, but this fact is not sufficient in and of itself to explain why Japan's imports in aggregate may be low. It is also necessary to assume either that trading companies through their *keiretsu* all have the same set of domestic interests or that there is collusion across *keiretsu*. In principle, Japan's Antimonopoly Law should prevent such collusion. In practice, American trade officials argued in SII that weak enforcement made the Antimonopoly Law almost irrelevant for Japanese corporate decision making.

Japan's Fair Trade Commission, which is in charge of enforcing the Antimonopoly Law, responded to American complaints by arguing that form was being confused with substance. The Fair Trade Commission prefers informal consultation with the parties concerned as opposed to any kind of formal proceeding. Since the Antimonopoly Law contains no private right of action, it is hardly surprising that by comparison with the United States or even European practices, there is very little litigation under this statute. When litigation does occur, the resulting penalties for violation of the Antimonopoly Law appear very modest.

It was ironic that at just the time when American officials were urging the Japanese government to remake their antitrust law in the American model, students of American productivity were arguing that it was America's antitrust law that was undermining American performance. As William Baumol noted at just the time the SII talks were commencing:

The United States may well not be suffering from a loss of entrepreneurial talent and initiative as has sometimes been suggested. Rather, if there is a problem in this arena (a conjecture that is in any event very difficult to test), much of the difficulty may be a misdirection of entrepreneurial talent rather than its disappearance. Moreover, whether conditions on the entrepreneurial front have or have not deteriorated, surely an injection of productive entrepreneurship should contribute to productivity. And this can be achieved by closing off, to the extent that is practical, the most attractive opportunities for rent seeking. The Japanese example shows how this can be done by suitable alteration in the economic "rules of the game." Even if we do not want to go as far as Japan has in discouraging private antitrust suits, for example, more moderate rules of a similar sort are easily formulated. And one can be quite sure that, once suitable measures have closed off or at least impeded access to the avenues for unproductive entrepreneurship, entrepreneurial energy and talent will automatically be redirected to the productive means that still remain open. Such measures can benefit other industrialized countries and not just the United States. However, as we have seen, there is reason to suspect that in this area it is the United States that has the most to gain.[92]

Regardless of whether Japan's postwar competition policies had kept unproductive rent seeking at bay, as part of the outcome of the SII talks, the Japanese government did agree to enhance the Antimonopoly Law and to significantly increase the resources devoted to its enforcement. The Fair Trade Commission's staff was increased by 20 percent. In 1991, the surcharge rate on illegal cartels was raised by up to four times, and in 1992 the maximum allowable rate on firms and trade associations for violations of the Antimonopoly Law was boosted from 5 million yen to 100 million yen.

13.9   From SII to the Framework Talks

The Structural Impediments Initiative was the culmination of more than one hundred years of complaints about differences between the Japanese economy and economies in the West. In this instance, however, the economic harmonization being proposed by American trade negotiators had broad support within Japan. In the years since SII, many of the changes agreed to at that time have been unilaterally augmented by the Japanese government. For example, where in 1990 the Japanese government agreed to undertake 430 trillion yen in new public investment during the 1980s, a newly announced ten-year plan for public investment now foresees a total expenditure of 630 trillion yen. This implies an increase in the nominal value of public investment on the order of 3 percent per year. Such growth will hold the share of public investment in real terms in Japanese GDP constant at about 8 percent. This is more than double the share of other OECD countries.[93] At this rate Japan's social capital stock per capita will reach the level of the wealthiest OECD countries by the end of the first decade of the 21st century.

The same macroeconomic forces that have encouraged a vast increase in Japan's public investment have also forced down the price of land by at least a third since the end of SII. From this new, lower plateau, and in cooperation with other advanced industrialized countries, the increase in the price of land in Japan over the past 20 years does not seem out of the ordinary. Notwithstanding, since SII, the Japanese government has both raised the effective inheritance tax on land and at the same time made it more costly for farmers to hold land while speculating on future increases in residential real estate prices. Both these steps were proposed by American negotiators at SII.

A rise in the yen in the early 1990s was certainly not a necessary concomitant of Japan's economic slump and collapsing land prices, but rise the yen did. Between 1990 and 1994 the yen rose in relation to the dollar by almost 50 percent. With economic distress at home, the possibility of substituting newly cheaper imports for more expensive domestically produced goods became irresistible. This new interest drove changes in Japanese government policies toward the distribution sector. The 18-month deadline for central government approval of new store plans established in 1990 as a product of SII was unilaterally shortened to one year in 1992. In addition steps were taken in 1992 to prevent local governments from overriding these new arrangements with their own approval process. These changes have had a real impact. Applications, which had previously taken an average of 35 months to be processed, now took only eight months on average. At the same time, regulations on the operating hours of large stores have been relaxed. Retailers have begun to respond to the new environment by increasing the number of department stores, supermarkets, and superstores. These large retailers, in particular, supermarkets and superstores, have taken the lead in discount retailing, which has grown increasingly popular during Japan's recession.[94]

The SII-related increase in the Fair Trade Commission staff and budget has allowed it to support Japanese government efforts to make the distribution sector more competitive. In 1994, for example, it published for the first time guidelines that identify the specific business practices related to distribution that may violate the Antimonopoly Law. Just the year before, the Fair Trade Commission ended the special exemptions that had allowed retail price maintenance of 23 medical and cosmetic products. At the same time its newly aggressive staff brought criminal charges against a group of construction companies accused of forming a cartel. This was the first such action by the Fair Trade Commission in almost 20 years.[95]

Among the major issues raised by American trade negotiators, financial *keiretsu* was the only one not drawn from the Maekawa Commission's recommendations. Unsurprisingly, it is the only major issue where Japanese policies were not influenced by the SII talks. Indeed, if anything, Japanese policy has been moving in the opposite direction—toward encouraging greater financial concentration and control. In particular, in the interest of shoring up the Japanese financial system and promoting economic recovery, the Ministry of Finance has proposed new legislation that would permit holding companies in Japan for the first time since 1945.[96]

That the SII process was consistent with ongoing structural change in Japan accounts for much of its success. While SII continued to be popular in many quarters in Japan, its popularity proved short-lived elsewhere. With the Clinton administration's arrival in Washington in January 1993, there occurred a radical change in U.S. trade policy. The success of SII made the century-old strategy of undermining the legitimacy of Japan's international trade success by pointing out fundamental economic differences between Japan and other advanced industrialized countries seem outmoded. Despite sometimes spirited bargaining, Japan seemed quite ready to make fundamental changes in its economic institutions. From the Clinton administration's point of view, however, it did not matter whether or not Japan had been changing for the past century, the past half century, or the past decade with conditions and institutions increasingly harmonized with those of other advanced industrialized economies. What mattered was that outcomes were not being harmonized. It was with this perspective that the Clinton administration commenced the United States–Japan Framework talks.

13.10   The Harmonization of Outcomes—Managed Trade

The Clinton administration's position that the harmonization of outcomes should be stressed over the harmonization of institutions and conditions in bilateral negotiations with Japan rested on the assumption that the character of Japan's participation in international trade was somehow illegitimate. Unlike earlier critics of Japan's role in international trade, the Clinton administration effectively took the position that either it did not know what it was that caused Japanese international trade outcomes to be illegitimate, or if it did know it could not directly negotiate a change in those determinants.

How did the Clinton administration know that Japanese trade outcomes were illegitimate? The *1994 Economic Report of the President* in discussing Japanese trade policy stressed the following:

Manufactured imports play a relatively small role in the Japanese economy with the share of manufactured imports in consumption less than half that of the other advanced industrialized economies.[97]

In drawing the conclusion from such evidence that the Japanese market remained closed, the Clinton administration ignored the results of the vast majority of studies on this subject which found that the unusual structure of Japanese trade could be explained by such perfectly legitimate factors as the paucity of natural resources and the distance from trading partners.[98] If Japan's unusual trade structure was neither the result of unusual economic institutions in Japan nor the result of illegitimate government policies, that it does not change when these institutions and policies change can hardly be surprising.

In the interest of furthering its goal of harmonizing Japan's trade structure with other advanced industrialized economies, the hallmark of the U.S.–Japan Framework Talks was the U.S. government's insistence that whatever new agreements were reached, the expected results of the agreements in terms of increased imports into the Japanese market must be specified. Japanese negotiators, however, although agreeing that structural and sectoral issues should be resolved in the interest of increasing market access and sales of foreign products, rejected any such benchmarks. Pointing to the history of U.S.–Japanese bilateral agreements on semiconductors, autos, and auto parts, they argued that no matter what diplomatic context surrounds the benchmarks, failing to meet a benchmark would be treated by the U.S. side as a broken promise.

Was the Clinton administration's position on benchmarks good public policy? If they work to restrain inefficient Japanese industries in their home market in favor of efficient U.S., European, and non-Japanese Asian producers, quantitative benchmarks might have some merit. Efficient industries expanding at the expense of inefficient industries improves welfare. How can it be determined, however, whether the U.S. government is trying to intervene on behalf of firms that are or are not competitive with their Japanese counterparts?

The Clinton administration answered this question by pointing to the share of the global market that Japan held for a particular product and comparing it with the share Japan held of the market for that product at home. Any discrepancies between the two shares became the degree to which Japan discriminates against particular foreign products. These same measures were also used to develop the benchmarks for evaluating the success of new agreements.

Such measures do not make as much sense as is too often glibly assumed. It is commonplace to find a substantial positive gap between domestic market share and global market share. For example, this is just as true for U.S. high-technology industries as it is for Japanese high-technology industries.[99] Does this mean that the U.S. market for high-technology products is closed in some illegitimate way? Probably not. It does mean, however, that using this criterion may make it very easy for U.S. industry trade groups to convince the U.S. government that open Japanese markets are closed. The net result of the quantitative benchmark approach in U.S.– Japan trade negotiations may be simply to create unholy alliances between favored American industries and their Japanese competitors, who are suddenly jointly licensed to jack up prices and reap windfall profits in the Japanese home market.

For this reason it is hardly surprising that, unlike SII, the Framework Talks have not been a success. At a time when there is great popular support within Japan for deregulation, Japanese government officials have little interest in agreeing to proposals that might well cartelize important parts of the Japanese economy for the benefit of both foreign and Japanese firms.

13.11   Finale

The Japanese economy has undergone extraordinary changes over the course of the 20th century. What has not changed, however, is the ingenuity with which Japan's trading partners have constructed arguments about the illegitimacy of Japan's competitive success to match each new set of circumstances in Japan. It is likely, however, that even these complaints will finally end not so much because of the harmonization of Japan's institutions and conditions with those in other advanced industrialized economies, as because of Japan's slowing economic growth. The maturation of the Japanese economy suggests it will impose no more unwanted structural changes on its trading partners than the median advanced industrialized economy. As a result, the legitimacy of Japan's participation in the international economic system should finally be fully accepted.

NOTES

1. The classic treatment of these debates is Karl Polanyi's *The Great Transformation* (1957).

2. Taussig (1920), p. 134.

3. Sumner (1888), pp. 67–68.

4. Perot with Choate (1993).

5. Dai nihon bōseki rengōkai (1897).

6. A number of articles appeared in the monthly report of the All Japan Cotton Spinners Association characterizing Japanese labor management methods as inspired by the Lowell system. *Rengō bōseki geppō*, No. 20 (December 1890), and *Dai nihon bōseki dōgyō rengōkai hokoku*, No. 110 (October 1898).

7. Unbeknownst to the Japanese cotton spinners, the Lowell system also had many contemporary critics. See the discussion in Ware (1931).

8. Yokoyama (1898).

9. Saito (1898).

10. Foxwell, "The protection of labour in Japan" (1901).

11. The Japanese cotton textile industry's competitive edge was greatly aided by the exemption in 1895 of raw cotton from the otherwise uniform 5% tariff on imports maintained by the Japanese government. See Kinugawa (1937).

12. *Textile Mercury*, October 18, 1898.

13. *The Textile Recorder*, November 1898. On the differing skill requirements of mule spinners and ring spinners, see Saxonhouse and Wright (1984).

14. Gulick (1915).

15. Ironically, in the United States, Gulick is best remembered as an eloquent opponent of the Oriental Exclusion Act. Gulick hoped emigration abroad might help alleviate the extreme poverty he observed in Japan. See Daniels (1962).

16. Maurette (1934).

17. Shindo (1961).

18. Hall (1965).

19. Ohkawa (1971); Ohkawa and Rosovsky (1973); Maddison (1989).

20. Maddison (1989).

21. Semiconductor Industry Association (1980). Other influential statements of this charge since that time include Hatsopoulos (1983), Hatsopoulos and Brooks (1986), and Hatsopoulos, Krugman, and Summers (1988).

22. See the discussion in Saxonhouse (1983a).

23. See Myers and Majluf (1984), pp. 187–222, on asymmetric information; and Jensen and Meckling (1976), pp. 305–360, on incentive compatibility.

24. Frankel (1993).

25. Ibid.

26. Saxonhouse (1993a).

27. In the 1970s, concern was first expressed about Japan's high rate of savings, not in connection with an unfairly low cost of capital, but because of its implications for Japan's current account imbalance. See Trezise (1980).

28. Hayashi, Ito, and Slemrod (1988).

29. American Council, Institute of Pacific Relations (1936).

30. *Textile Mercury*, February 23, 1934.

31. Maurette (1934).

32. Jackson (1989).

33. *Tōyō bōseki nanajūnen shi* (Osaka, 1953).

34. *Nichibō nanajūgōnen shi* (Osaka, 1966).

35. Gulick (1915).

36. Kahn (1970).

37. Brzezinski (1972).

38. Yamazawa (1984); Kojima and Komiya (1972).

39. Maddison (1989).

40. Watanabe and Komiya (1958).

41. Travis (1964).

42. Lockwood (1954); Saxonhouse and Patrick (1976). Before the Great Depression, Japan ran a trade surplus with the United States solely because of its exports of raw silk. Otherwise, Japan was a heavy net importer of American manufactures.

43. Fallows (1989).

44. *Economic Report of the President, 1983*, p. 56.

45. *Economic Report of the President, 1983*, p. 67.

46. *Economic Report of the President, 1994*, p. 29.

47. Footnote, "Remarks by Clinton and Hosokawa," *New York Times*, February 12, 1994, p. 8. In fact, President Clinton's Council of Economic Advisers seemed to be of two minds on the question of trade balances. The earlier quote in the text is taken from Chapter 1 of

the 1994 *Economic Report*. Chapter 6 of the same *Report*, however, takes the position that Japan's bilateral trade imbalance with the United States is unacceptably and unfairly large. This view is quite consistent with President Clinton's public statements at the time of the breakdown of the Framework talks. See Saxonhouse (1994a).

48. Hazumi and Ogura (1972).

49. Cline (1978).

50. *Economic Report of the President, 1983*, p. 56.

51. Stone (1969).

52. Saxonhouse (1983a).

53. Eugene J. Kaplan, *Japan: The government-business relationship* (1972). This study was prepared under U.S. Department of Commerce auspices . In this study, as in others prepared at this time, the government-business relationship by being characterized with terms such as *gyōsei shidō* and Japan, Inc., took on a decidedly exotic quality. The term "Japan, Inc.," seems to have been first introduced in Kahn (1970).

54. Jackson (1969).

55. Saxonhouse (1983b). While it would be difficult to infer it from his current public statements, Johnson (1982) argues Japanese industrial policy effectively ended in 1975.

56. Semiconductor Industry Association (1983).

57. David R. McDonald, Deputy U.S. Trade Representative, *Hearings before Committee on Foreign Affairs* (1982).

58. Jackson (1989), pp. 245, 253.

59. Tyson, Borrus, and Zysman (1986).

60. Destler (1986), p. 136. The U.S. International Trade Commission study was done at the request of the House Ways and Means Subcommittee on Trade.

61. U.S. International Trade Commission (1983).

62. Reich (1983).

63. Feigenbaum and McCorduck (1983).

64. Tyson (1992), pp. 292–293.

65. Ibid., p. 289.

66. This subject is taken up in more detail in Saxonhouse, "What's all this about Japanese technology policy?" (1993b).

67. *Report of the Advisory Committee on Economic Structural Adjustment for International Harmony* (Tokyo, 1986); *Outline of Procedures for the Promotion of Structural Adjustment* (Tokyo, 1986); *Policy Recommendations of the Economic Council* (Tokyo, 1987).

68. Wallis (1987).

69. The role that foreign barriers to Japanese exports might play in frustrating the adjustment process is laid out in Bhagwati (1991).

70. U.S. Department of Commerce (1989).

71. U.S. officials claim that at least the timing of President Bush's announcement that he was willing to raise taxes was much affected by SII. This announcement was made on June 28, 1990, the same day that the *Final Report and Assessment of the U.S.–Japan Working Group on the Structural Impediments Initiative* was issued.

72. *Nihon keizai shimbun*, September 5, 1989.

73. Dornbusch (1990); Summers (1993).

74. This and other SII issues are discussed in more detail in Saxonhouse, "Japan, SII and the international harmonization of domestic economic practices" (1991).

75. Boskin (1989).

76. Yukio Noguchi, "Japan's Fiscal Policy and External Balance" (September 1989) argues that aging of the Japanese population will leave Japan's fiscal balance unchanged.

77. Ishi (1989). Net social security liabilities as a proportion of gross domestic product are three times as great in Japan as in the United States. Still more significant from the point of view of Japanese government officials, these Japanese social security liabilities are as much as seven times as great, as a proportion of gross domestic product, as the seemingly politically unacceptable net accumulated non-social-security liabilities of the U.S. government: *OECD Economic Survey: Japan* (Paris, 1994).

78. Nomura Research Institute (1990).

79. Campbell (1994).

80. Sachs and Boone (1988).

81. Saxonhouse (1986).

82. Kōsei torihiki iinkai (1983), pp. 39–42. By including vertical as well as horizontal relationships, these studies overestimate distinctive *keiretsu* ties. On the other hand, these estimates do ignore transactions of *keiretsu* members with the *keiretsu* trading company. To the extent that Japanese companies have traditionally delegated distribution and purchasing-agent functions to Japanese trading companies, such an exclusion has a rationale. To the extent, however, that trading companies handle transactions between the nonvertically related members of a *keiretsu*, the conventional procurement estimates may be too low. As Okumura (1983) notes, overall trading companies handle between 15 and 30 percent of all transactions of the typical *keiretsu* member. In fact, there is good evidence that the markets in which *keiretsu* operate are highly competitive. As Weinstein and Yafeh (1992) show, the higher the proportion of *keiretsu* firms in an industry, the lower the price cost margin.

83. Toyo keizai (1989).

84. Imai (1989).

85. Weinstein and Yafeh (1992).

86. Horiuchi, Packer, and Fukuda (1988).

87. Frankel (1991).

88. Maruyama et al. (1989).

89. Ibid.

90. Flath (1990).

91. *OECD Economy Surveys: Japan, 1993–1994* (Paris, 1994).

92. Baumol, Blackman, and Wolff (1989), pp. 276–277.

93. OECD, *Economic Outlook*, No. 56 (December 1994), p. 60.

94. OECD, *Economic Survey: Japan*, p. 62.

95. OECD, *Economic Survey: Japan*, p. 61.

96. *Nihon keizai shimbun*, February 15, 1995.

97. *Economic Report of the President, 1994*, p. 216.

98. See the discussion in Saxonhouse (1994a), especially Table 4 listing studies that have been done on the structure and volume of Japanese trade, and Saxonhouse (1993a).

99. Bhagwati (1994); Saxonhouse (1994b).

REFERENCES

American Council, Institute of Pacific Relations. 1936. *Trade and trade rivalry between the United States and Japan*. New York.

Baumol, William J., Sue Anne Batey Blackman, and Edward N. Wolff. 1989. *Productivity and American leadership*. Cambridge, MA: MIT Press.

Bhagwati, Jagdish. 1991. *Political economy and international economics*. Cambridge, MA: MIT Press.

Bhagwati, Jagdish. 1994. "Samurai no more." *Foreign Affairs*, Spring.

Boskin, Michael. 1989. "Keynote address to the Symposium on the Structural Adjustment of the Asian Pacific Economies and the Role of the OECD." October 3.

Brzezinski, Zbigniew. 1972. *The fragile blossom*. New York: Harper & Row.

Campbell, David W. 1994. "Explaining Japan's savings rate." Nissan Occasional Paper Series No. 21.

Cline, William. 1978. *Trade negotiations in the Tokyo Round: A quantitative assessment*. Washington, DC: Brookings Institution.

Dai nihon bōseki dōgyō rengōkai hokoku, No. 110, October 1898.

Dai nihon bōseki rengōkai. 1897. *Bōseki shokkō jijō chōsa gaiyō*. Osaka.

Daniels, Roger. 1962. *The politics of prejudice*. Berkeley: University of California Press.

Destler, I. M. 1986. *American trade politics*. Washington, DC: Institute for International Economics; New York: Twentieth Century Fund.

Dornbusch, Rudiger. 1990. "Policy options for freer trade: The case for bilateralism." In Robert Lawrence and Charles Schultz, eds., *An American trade strategy*. Washington, DC: Brookings Institution.

Economic Report of the President, 1983. Washington, DC.

Economic Report of the President, 1994. Washington, DC.

Fallows, James. 1989. "Getting along with Japan." *Atlantic Monthly*, December, pp. 53−64.

Feigenbaum, Edward A., and Pamela McCorduck. 1983. *The fifth generation.* Reading, MA: Addison-Wesley.

Flath, David. 1990. "Why are there so many retail stores in Japan?" *Japan and the World Economy* 2(4): 365−386.

Foxwell, Ernest. 1901. "The protection of labour in Japan." *Economic Journal*, 11 (March).

Frankel, Jeffrey. 1991. "Japanese finance in the 1980's: A survey." In Paul R. Krugman, ed., *Trade with Japan*, 225−268. Chicago: University of Chicago Press for the National Bureau of Economic Research.

Frankel, Jeffrey A. 1993. "The cost of capital: A survey." In Shinji Takagi, ed., *Handbook of Japanese capital markets.* Cambridge, MA: Basil Blackwell.

Gulick, Sidney L. 1915. *The Working Women of Japan.* New York: Missionary Education Movement of the United States and Canada.

Hall, John Whitney. 1965. "Aspects of Japanese economic development." In John Whitney Hall and Richard K. Beardsley, eds., *Twelve doors to Japan.* New York: McGraw-Hill.

Hatsopoulos, George. 1983. *High cost of capital: Handicap of American industry.* Waltham, MA: American Business Conference.

Hatsopoulos, George, and Steven Brooks. 1986. "The gap in the cost of capital: Causes, effects and remedies." In Ralph Landau and Dale Jorgenson, eds., *Technology and economic policy.* Cambridge, MA: Ballinger.

Hatsopoulos, George, Paul Krugman, and Lawrence Summers. 1988. "U.S. competitiveness: Beyond the trade deficit." *Science*, July 15.

Hayashi, Fumio, Takatoshi Ito, and Joel Slemrod. 1988. "Housing finance imperfections, taxation and private savings: A comparative simulation analysis of the United States and Japan." *Journal of the Japanese and International Economies*, 2 (June).

Hazumi, Mitsuhiko, and Kazuo Ogura. 1972. "Tai-nichi sabetsu mondai no ippanteki haikei." In Kiyoshi Kojima and Ryutaro Komiya, eds., *Nihon no hikanzei boeki shoheki.* Tokyo: Nihon keizai shimbunsha.

Hearing before Committee on Foreign Affairs, House of Representatives and its subcommittees on International Economic Policy and Trade and on Asian and Pacific Affairs on United States−Japan Relations, March 1, 1982, pp. 939−943. Washington, DC.

Horiuchi, Akiyoshi, Frank Packer, and Shoichi Fukuda. 1988. "What role has the main bank played in Japan?" *Journal of the Japanese and International Economies*, 2(2): 159−180.

Imai, Ken-ichi. 1989. "Kigyō gurupu." In Ken-ichi Imai and Ryutaro Komiya, eds., *Nihon no kigyō.* Tōkyō: Tōkyō daigaku shuppankai.

Ishi, Hiromitsu. 1989. *The Japanese tax system.* Oxford: Oxford University Press.

Jackson, John H. 1969. *World trade and the law of GATT.* Indianapolis: Bobbs-Merrill.

Jackson, John H. 1989. *The world trading system.* Cambridge, MA: MIT Press.

Jensen, Michael, and William Meckling. 1976. "Theory of the firm: managerial behavior, agency costs and ownership structure." *Journal of Financial Economics,* 3(3): 305–360.

Johnson, Chalmers. 1982. *MITI and the Japanese miracle.* Stanford, CA: Stanford University Press.

Kahn, Herman. 1970. *The emerging Japanese superstate.* Englewood Cliffs, NJ: Prentice Hall.

Kaplan, Eugene J. 1972. *Japan: The government-business relationship.* Washington, DC: U.S. Government Printing Office.

Kinugawa, Eiichi. 1937. *Hompō menshi bōseki shi,* vol. 2. Osaka: Nippon mengyō kurubu.

Kojima, Kiyoshi, and Ryutaro Komiya. 1972. *Nihon no hikanzei boeki shoheki.* Tokyo: Nihon keizai shimbunsha.

Kōsei torihiki iinkai. 1983. *Kigyō shudan no jittai ni tsuite.* Tokyo: Kōsei torohiki kyokai.

Lockwood, William W. 1954. *The economic development of Japan.* Princeton, NJ: Princeton University Press.

Maddison, Angus. 1989. *The world economy in the 20th century.* Paris: Organization for Economic Cooperation and Development.

Maruyama, Masayoshi, Yoko Togawa, Kyohei Sakai, Nobuo Sakamoto, and Masaharu Arakawa. 1989. "Distribution system and business practices in Japan." EPA International Symposium, October 12–13.

Maurette, Fernand. 1934. *Social aspects of industrial development in Japan.* London: P. S. King & Son for the International Labor Office.

Myers, Stewart, and N. Majluf. 1984. "Corporate financing and investment decisions when firms have information that investors do not have." *Journal of Financial Economics,* 13(2): 187–222.

Nichibō nanajūgōnen shi. Osaka, 1966.

Nihon keizai shimbun, September 5, 1989.

Nihon keizai shimbun, February 15, 1995.

New York Times, February 12, 1994, p. 8.

Nomura Research Institute. 1990. *Nomura Investment Review,* 3 (February).

OECD, *Economic Outlook,* No. 56, December 1994.

OECD *Economy Surveys: Japan, 1993–1994.* Paris, 1994.

Ohkawa, Kazushi, ed. 1971. *Nihon keizai no chōki bunseki chūkan hōkoku.* Tokyo: Tokei kenkyu kai.

Ohkawa, Kazushi, and Henry Rosovsky. 1973. *Japanese economic growth.* Stanford, CA: Stanford University Press.

Okumura, Hiroshi. 1983. *Shin-nihon no koku dai—kōgyō shudan.* Tokyo: Diamond.

Perot, Ross, with Pat Choate. 1993. *Save your job, save our country.* Washington, DC: Hyperion.

Polanyi, Karl. 1957. *The great transformation.* Boston: Beacon Press.

Reich, Robert. 1983. *The next American frontier.* New York: Times Books.

Rengō bōseki geppō, No. 20. December 1890.

Sachs, Jeffrey, and Peter Boone. 1988. "Japanese structural adjustment and the balance of payments." *Journal of the Japanese and International Economies,* September, pp. 286–327.

Saito, Kashiro. 1898. *La protection ouvrière du Japon.* Paris: Hachette.

Saxonhouse, Gary R. 1983a. "The micro- and macroeconomics of foreign sales to Japan." In William R. Cline, ed., *Trade policy for the 1980s,* 259–304. Cambridge, MA: MIT Press for the Institute of International Economics.

Saxonhouse, Gary R. 1983b. "What is all this about industrial targeting in Japan?" *The World Economy,* 6(3).

Saxonhouse, Gary. 1986. "Japan's intractable trade balances." *World Economy* 9(3): 239–257.

Saxonhouse, Gary R. 1991. "Japan, SII and the international harmonization of domestic economic practices." *Michigan Journal of International Law,* 12(2): 450–469.

Saxonhouse, Gary R. 1993a. "What does Japanese trade structure tell us about Japanese trade policy." *Journal of Economic Perspectives,* 7(3).

Saxonhouse, Gary R. 1993b. "What's all this about Japanese technology policy?" *Regulation,* 16(4): 38–47.

Saxonhouse, Gary R. 1994a. "Japan and the 1994 Economic Report of the President." Research Forum in international Economics Discussion Paper No. 372, December.

Saxonhouse, Gary R. 1994b. "The economics of the U.S.–Japan Framework talks." Hoover Essays in Public Policy No. 53.

Saxonhouse, Gary, and Hugh Patrick. 1976. "Japan and the United States: Bilateral tensions and multilateral issues in the economic relationship." In Donald C. Hellman, ed., *China and Japan: A new balance of power.* Lexington, MA: D. C. Heath.

Saxonhouse, Gary, and Gavin Wright. 1984. "Two forms of cheap labor." In Gary Saxonhouse and Gavin Wright, eds., *Technique, spirit and form and the making of the modern economies.* Greenwich, CT: JAI Press.

Semiconductor Industry Association. 1980. *U.S. and Japanese semiconductor industries: A financial comparison.* Cupertino, CA.

Semiconductor Industry Association. 1983. *The effect of government targeting on world semiconductor competition.* Cupertino, CA.

Shindo, Takejiro. 1961. *Labor in the Japanese cotton industry.* Tokyo: Japanese Society for the Promotion of Science.

Stone, P. B. 1969. *Japan surges ahead.* London: Weidenfeld and Nicolson.

Summers, Lawrence. 1993. "Speech to the Japan Society of New York." May 27.

Sumner, William Graham. 1888. *Protectionism.* New York: Henry Holt.

Taussig, F. W. 1920. *Free trade, the tariff, and reciprocity.* New York: Macmillan.

Textile Mercury, October 18, 1898.

Textile Mercury, February 23, 1934.

The Textile Recorder, November 1898.

Tōyō bōseki nanajūnen shi. Osaka, 1953.

Toyo keizai. 1989. *Kigyō keiretsu sōran.* Tokyo.

Travis, William P. 1964. *The theory of trade and protection.* Cambridge, MA: Harvard University Press.

Trezise, Phillip H. 1980. "The evolution of United States–Japan relations." In Leon Hollerman, ed., *Japan and the United States: Economic and political adversaries.* Boulder, CO: Westview Press.

Tyson, Laura D. 1992. *Who's bashing whom?* Washington, DC: Institute for International Economics.

Tyson, Laura D'Andrea, Michael Borrus, and John Zysman. 1986. "Creating advantage: How government policies shape international trade in the semiconductor industry." In Paul R. Krugman, ed., *Strategic trade policy and the new international economics.* Cambridge, MA: MIT Press.

U.S. Department of Commerce. 1989. "Reporting cables on the November 6–7 SII meetings." Washington, DC.

U.S. International Trade Commission. 1983. *Foreign industrial targeting and its effects on U.S. industries phase I: Japan.* Washington, DC.

Wallis, W. A. 1987. "The structural adjustment dialogue and U.S.–Japan economic relations." Address before the Annual Executive Committee Meeting of the U.S.–Japan Business Council, February 16.

Ware, Caroline. 1931. *The early New England cotton manufacture: A study in industrial origins.* Cambridge, MA: Harvard University Press.

Watanabe, Tsunehiko, and Ryutaro Komiya. 1958. "Findings from price comparisons, principally Japan vs. the United States." *Weltwirtschaftliches Archiv,* 81(2).

Weinstein, David, and Yishay Yafeh. 1992. "Japan's corporate groups: Collusive or competitive? An empirical investigation of *keiretsu* behavior." Harvard University.

Yamazawa, Ippei. 1984. *Boeki nihon no katsuro.* Tokyo: Yukikaku.

Yokoyama, Gennosuke. 1898. *Nihon no shakai kasō.* Tokyo: Maruzen.

14

Why Does Japan Resist Foreign Market-Opening Pressure?

John McMillan

14.1 The Level Playing Field

Fairness is in the eye of the beholder. Whether or not the playing field looks level depends on the angle of the observer. Trade-policy partisans do not necessarily have an upright stance. The advent of fairness as a criterion has had the virtue of enlivening trade-policy debates with some unintended irony. A European Community agriculture representative, rejecting U.S. demands for a reduction in Common Agricultural Policy subsidies, said that acceding to the U.S. demands would unduly favor U.S. producers. European farmers, said the spokesperson plaintively, merely want a level playing field. This was said with apparent sincerity, even though anyone other than a French peasant would find it bizarre.[1]

Unintended irony arose also when the case against intervention in other countries' affairs, and for multilateral rather than bilateral trade-policy initiatives, was made by none other than the U.S. trade representative, Mickey Kantor. In response to a 1993 Japanese government report accusing the United States and the European Community of engaging in unfair trading practices—many of the practices named in the report are indeed distortionary, like the misuse of antidumping laws and discrimination in government procurement—Kantor said, apparently without a trace of recognition that his words could be turned back against himself, "We believe it would be better for Japan to take a leadership role in the Uruguay Round, instead of criticizing other countries' practices."[2]

When is criticism of other countries' trading practices justified? Economic analysis offers tools to help judge whether in any particular case foreign market-opening pressure is justified: techniques for measuring the costs and benefits of any given intervention. The implications for economic welfare of changing existing practices can be analyzed from the point of view of the plaintiff country, the target country, or the world as a whole.[3] Identifying the welfare effects of a market-opening initiative requires a different, more micro-level analysis than is usually done in empirical trade studies, because the benefits from a successful market opening typically include such gains as a reduction in domestic monopoly pricing, an increase in foreign firms' profits, and an improvement in the technical efficiency of the domestic industry.

When are outside interventions in the name of fair trade likely to succeed? Implicitly underlying fairness claims is the assumption that it is feasible for politicians or bureaucrats to carry out the requested changes: someone has the power to do what is demanded. When the demanded changes go deeply into the country's domestic institutions, however, this assumption is often false. Lowering a country's tariffs can be done with the stroke of a pen. Changing a country's industrial structure is of a different order. Any well-functioning economy has considerable inertia: the ability of politicians and bureaucrats to change an economy is limited. The economy, being a complicated and reasonably stable system, does impose limits on what the state can do. It would be absurd—and empirically false—to claim that foreign pressure for change can never be successful in Japan or anywhere else. But any such proposed change will always be met with resistance, generated by systemic interactions.

If implemented, the change would have a string of direct and indirect consequences, with the indirect consequences often being much larger than the direct consequences. Because the economy is a system, the indirect consequences of a change are usually important. The indirect consequences are difficult to foresee and as a result are usually overlooked by the proponents of the foreign intervention. To the extent that these consequences, direct and indirect, impose losses on people, the change will be resisted. Sometimes this resistance will be weak and easily overcome; but often it will be powerful and will overrule the foreign pressure, regardless of what the country's trade negotiators may have promised.

Depending on your point of view, the leading perpetrator of unfair trading practices, or the main victim of unjustified complaints about unfair trade, has been Japan. For this reason I shall draw my examples from Japan. Japan does seem to be an extreme case: its institutions seem to be more resistant to change than those of other countries. (Former U.S. Commerce Secretary Malcolm Baldrige, in one of the stronger statements of this view, once told the Japanese: "You will have to change your culture.")[4] Japan's economic and political institutions are in many ways different from those of other countries. But I suggest that Japan's propensity to resist foreign pressure is not fundamentally different from any other country's, and that what is learned from the study of Japan can be applied elsewhere.

To help clarify the general issues, I shall examine three Japanese business practices involving cooperative relationships among firms, each of which has generated accusations from the United States of unfair trade: collusion in public-construction bidding, subcontracting in manufacturing, and the regulation of large retail stores.[5] All three involve exclusionary practices. But they are not as simple as they seem; they are far from being straightforward cases of protectionism. In each case the U.S. pressure was met with resistance from within Japan. Two questions will be asked of each case, one normative, the other positive. Was the change the United States demanded justified on economic-welfare grounds? Was it feasible, within the relevant time span, for Japan to make the demanded change? I shall conclude that the subcontracting case was unjustified and infeasible; the public-construction case was justified but infeasible; and the retail-stores case was both justified and feasible.

Is Japan victim or villain? I come down on both sides. It depends on the issue. In some cases, such as public construction, Japan's practices damage the global trading system (as well as Japan's own citizens), and foreign intervention is justified. In others, such as subcontracting, Japan has been unjustly maligned. The point is that any broad, uncontingent statement about the rightness or wrongness in general of foreign market-opening demands is likely to be an oversimplification. Whether a foreign intervention is justified can be answered only after empirically examining the details of the particular issue, estimating the size of the costs and benefits of the proposed changes and calculating whether their net effect is positive or negative.

I shall analyze the three cases of U.S. pressure on Japan not for their own sake but to try to extract some general lessons. How should fair trade claims be evaluated? When is outside intervention in the micro-details of a nation's economy justified, when is it not? What is the link between domestic market organization and the rules of international trade?

14.2   Winners and Losers from Market Opening

Restrictions on the entry of foreign competitors in many cases are designed not to exclude foreign firms in particular, but simply to exclude new entrants in general. Preventing foreign competition is often just part of a broader phenomenon of inhibiting competition overall for the sake of some favored firms. This statement is true, as will be seen, of Japan's restrictions in public construction and retail stores. Other cases of U.S. market-opening initiatives against barriers to competition include Guatemala's law that goods being shipped to Guatemala be carried in Guatemalan ships (the first use by the United States of its Section 301 legislation); South Korea's restrictions on its insurance markets; and Brazil's regulation of its computer industry. In these cases, as in many others, it is government policies that generate the restrictions on entry and competition.

Regulatory restrictions exist, according to George Stigler's notion of capture, because the regulatory body that oversees the industry has been lured by the incumbent firms into being their advocate. Regulation, Stigler said, is "designed and operated primarily for [the industry's] benefit." As a result, regulation often harms consumers. In the United States, according to Alfred Kahn, a former regulator himself, regulation "has consisted largely in the imposition and administration of restrictions on entry and on what might otherwise have been independent and competitive price and output decisions." In Japan, as Chalmers Johnson has eloquently documented, official policies in public construction, retailing, and elsewhere cause considerable harm to ordinary Japanese people, generating the phenomenon of "rich Japan, poor Japanese."[6]

Whether Stigler was right and regulation is anticompetitive, or whether it is procompetitive, depends on the circumstances of the particular case, according to the deepest existing analysis of the logic of cartelization by regulation, that of Laffont and Tirole (1993, ch. 13). The regulator will tend to favor the incumbent firms at the expense of consumers and outside firms if (a) the incumbent firms are well organized and consumers and potential entrants are not; (b) information about the size of the potential gains from competition is not readily and widely available; and (c) supervision by politicians of the bureaucrats in the regulatory agency is weak. Given these circumstances, the political-economic equilibrium has regulators and industry comfortably cohabiting at the expense of the consumers and potential entrants.

Foreign intervention adds a new player to the political-economic game. If the domestic interests that benefit from the status quo are sufficiently well organized relative to the domestic interests that are harmed by it, the foreign intervention will be unsuccessful. If not, the foreign pressure could change the nature of the political-economic equilibrium so as to induce the regulatory body to permit entry and competition. A foreign attack on anticompetitive regulation, if successful, will actually help the target country, in that it will make domestic consumers better off through reducing monopoly pricing (as in the cases of Japan's public-construction market and large retail stores law). The Australian political scientist Aurelia George says: "U.S. pressure has become a powerful catalyst for change in the Japanese economy, polity, and society.... In many respects the United States is itself an actor in the Japanese policy process: as a surrogate opposition party presenting the only true set of alternative policies to the government's, as an interest group representing the voice of Japanese consumers, and as an alternative power base for Japanese prime ministers seeking to overcome both shortfalls in their factional strength and domestic resistance to change."[7]

A standard prescription in international economics says that free trade works as an effective antitrust device: allowing imports is an easy way to remove the market power of a domestic monopolist (Bhagwati, 1965). The use of antitrust policies to promote free trade outcomes reverses this prescription: the entry restrictions that permit domestic monopoly are broken down for the sake of international trade.

A market-opening initiative against an entrenched monopoly position, if successful, creates both welfare gains and welfare losses. Consumers, powerless to affect the outcome in the absence of the foreign intervention, are made better off by the increased competition. The incumbent domestic firms are harmed, and foreign firms, and often some formerly excluded domestic firms, gain. Beyond these straightforward direct gains and losses is a range of indirect gains and losses, as the effects of the change work their way through the political-economic system. The increase in competition generated by a successful foreign intervention has not only direct benefits to the economy—such as lower prices and more choice for buyers—but also indirect benefits and, perhaps, costs.

In a large firm, with separated ownership and management, product-market competition generates discipline on managers. When competition is strong, a firm must be efficient to survive; whereas when competition is weak, managers, and perhaps workers, are able to extract rents for themselves to the detriment of the efficient operation of the firm. ("The best of all monopoly profits is a quiet life," as Sir John Hicks said.) As the firms respond to the extra competition that they now face, managers and workers will be given more high-powered incentives, making their pay and promotion prospects depend more sensitively on both short-run and long-run performance measures, according to the model of Gates, Milgrom, and Roberts (1996). As a consequence, a further welfare gain from eliminating monopoly comes in the form of increases in the firms' technical efficiency: production is organized less wastefully, so that more output is achieved from a given amount of inputs.

If the gains from market opening come in the form of increased competition, lower prices, and higher technical efficiency, then measuring those gains requires a different, more micro-level method of analysis than is usual in empirical trade studies. It is necessary to look at the industry or the firm. Examples of studies that quantify the gains from the removal of monopoly price distortions following an opening to foreign competition include the simulation by Harris and Cox (1983) of the effects of free trade on Canadian manufacturing industry, the study by Krause (1962) of the effects of import quotas on the U.S. steel industry, and the analysis by Levinsohn (1991) of Turkey's trade liberalization. Studies that go to a still more micro level, looking at the consequences for firms' technical efficiency of market opening in the United States, the United Kingdom, Canada, South Korea, and Australia, are collected in Caves et al. (1992). Partial equilibrium modeling is not enough, however, for that assumes away any systemic interactions; the sectoral studies must be extended to incorporate some general equilibrium effects (as in Harris and Cox, 1983).

The test to be applied to any given attempt to open a country's market in the name of fair trade, then, is this: Would the net effect of the foreign intervention be to raise technical and/or allocative efficiency, in both the target country and the rest of the world?

In the following analysis of the effects of U.S. pressure on Japan for market opening in public construction, subcontracting, and retailing, I shall try to list the potential or actual gainers and losers, inside and outside Japan. I shall look for both direct and indirect effects. The systemic interactions, as will be seen, are such that the indirect effects often outweigh the direct effects, although they are harder to predict and as a result are often overlooked.

I shall try to identify the gainers and losers from two points of view, economic welfare and political power, corresponding to the two questions, normative and positive. Is the foreign intervention justified on economic-welfare grounds? Is it likely to be successful? What is attempted in what follows is a quantitative analysis, measuring the gains and losses. These effects can in principle be measured, but in many cases the numbers needed for such a computation are not yet available. I shall offer guesses or rough estimates of the relative magnitudes of the various effects. Although in most cases it is easy to guess at the relative sizes of the various effects, the analysis is incomplete: my purpose is to suggest a method of approach to an accounting of the gains and losses from the various market-opening initiatives, rather than to offer definitive answers.

To address the normative question of whether the foreign intervention is justified on economic-welfare grounds, it is enough to identify the gainers and losers and to measure the sizes of their gains and losses. To address the positive question of whether the intervention will be successful, it is necessary to go one step further and ask how the gains and losses translate into political action. How effectively can the gainers and losers compete with each other in the political arena? As is illustrated by innumerable examples of bad policies, it is possible for a policy that generates a net loss to society to be enacted. A small number of agents with concentrated stakes in the outcome, according to the standard argument, can beat a large number with diffuse stakes. Thus it is necessary to ask how well organized the groups affected by the prospective market opening are, and how the political institutions, like the electoral system and the political-funding process, determine the relative effectiveness of the different groups.

One potential benefit of foreign intervention is information provision. People within the target country who are harmed by the restrictive practice, such as consumers, may be unaware of the size of their losses. The foreign intervention might be effective merely because it induces the domestic groups to start exerting pressure on politicians in their own interest.

14.3 *Dango*

Dango is a negotiation among bidders for a Japanese public-works contract in which it is decided which firm will get the job. The designated firm submits a high bid and its "rivals" bid still higher, maintaining the illusion of competition. Under *dango*, each firm knows it will eventually "win" a contract, without having to go to the trouble of competing; and *dango* spares the firms the discomfort of low prices.

Collusion in the public-construction market does not occur only in Japan: it is common in Europe and the United States. The Ronald Reagan administration's antitrust chief, Charles F. Rule, said of bid-rigging: "The cost of building roads in this country was increased by 10 percent or more as a result of these crimes." The main difference between Japan and the United States is the strength of the antitrust laws and the assiduity with which they are enforced. While *dango* is illegal in Japan under the Anti-monopoly Act, sanctions against bid-riggers are weak. The investigative capacity of the Japanese authorities is more limited than that of the U.S. authorities: the Japanese Fair Trade Commission secretariat has a staff less than one-fourth the number working in the U.S. Federal Trade Commission and the Justice Department's Antitrust Division. Administrative surcharges levied by the Fair Trade Commission against bid-riggers, before the U.S. intervention, amounted to only 0.5 to 2 percent of the contract value—far less than the amounts that could be earned from colluding (up to one-third of the contract value, according to the simulations in McMillan, 1991). The average fine levied by the Japanese antitrust authorities between 1985 and 1988 was $38,000, one-sixth the $224,000 average fine in the United States over the same period. Criminal cases are filed at a rate of about 80 a year in the United States. Convictions in the United States regularly result in prison sentences, about five per year, compared with none in Japan, although prison terms are provided for in Japanese law.

Even if the legal authorities can be evaded, collusion is—in any industry, in any country—difficult to achieve. Any bidding conspiracy must somehow overcome its natural tendency to self-destruct. Japanese government policies, advertently or inadvertently, help to sustain *dango*.[8]

A decision on how high to bid must be made by the bidding firms before the bidding. The scope for potentially damaging disagreement among the conspirators is removed by the official practice of setting a ceiling price, and the unofficial practice of leaking this ceiling price to the bidders (often via former Ministry of Construction officials now employed by the bidding firms). In many *dango* cases, according to a Japanese newspaper, "local government officials effectively have helped to hide the abuse by setting estimates that include generous profit margins for the contractors." Further aid to collusion comes from the policy of announcing all bids after the bids are opened, with the result that each bidding firm is aware that, if it deviates from its prespecified bid, the others learn of its deviation immediately.

Entry of new bidders, which if it were allowed to occur would undermine any collusion, is hindered by the designated-bidder policy, under which only selected firms are allowed to bid for any given contract. (This policy of selective tendering, incidentally, while rare in the United States, is common in many other OECD countries.) For a firm to be put on the list of qualified bidders, only work done in Japan is taken into account. This provision effectively prevents the entry into the market of foreign firms, for they do not have a history of work in Japan. The foreign firms are caught in a Catch-22: you cannot win a contract unless you bid; but you cannot bid unless you have won a contract.

The main victim of *dango* is the Japanese taxpayer. The Japanese government awards over $100 billion worth of construction contracts annually. The unduly high prices attributable to *dango* mean that many billions of dollars of taxpayers' money are wasted.

Why does *dango* persist, and why is the construction industry so hard to reform? Who benefits from *dango*? Reported profit data provide no evidence that the firms involved benefit greatly. Doubtless some of the profits from dango make their way into the pockets of the firms' owners and are hidden by creative accounting; but most do not. The firms are on a treadmill: they must try so hard to earn the monopoly profits that they end up with little net gain. Firms use up resources in competing for monopoly profits; and the entry of new firms into this rent-seeking competition results in the resources expended rising to become equal to the monopoly profits themselves (Posner, 1975; Bhagwati, 1982). Entry into the construction industry is relatively easy: the Japanese industry contains over half a million firms, and the number increases steadily over time. Any excess profits that *dango*'s high prices generate are bid away in the competition for political favor.

Much of the *dango* profits end up in the hands of the politicians. The construction industry is the largest single source of political contributions in Japan. The political funding process is so murky that it cannot be known how large the construction industry's contributions are; but they probably come to some billions of dollars. According to a Japanese newspaper report, the large construction companies distribute money to politicians according to how influential the individual politician is in the awarding of public contracts: twice a year each politician is assigned a letter grade that determines how large a contribution he receives. This money is used to cover the large costs in Japan of being a politician and running a political party. In March 1993, when Tokyo prosecuters arrested Shin Kanemaru, the deputy prime minister and Liberal Democratic Party power broker, on charges of income tax evasion, they found in his office safe more than $50 million worth of cash, bonds, and gold bars: donations mainly from the construction industry (intended, according to Kanemaru, not for his personal use but to realize his "cherished dream of political reform").

Construction Ministry bureacrats also benefit from *dango*. When top officials retire, they "descend from heaven" into well-paid jobs in construction firms. In return for hiring a former official, construction companies reportedly receive $88,000 worth of contracts.[9]

It is unlikely that, by publicizing the costs of *dango*, the U.S. pressure changed public opinion. The general public seem to have been well informed before the United States intervened: parts of the news media had been campaigning against *dango* for many years (in fact, colluders seemed to fear discovery and publicity by the media more than they feared official antitrust enforcement).

The U.S. government demanded that Japan strengthen its antitrust enforcement and replace the designated-bidder policy (which U.S. trade representative Carla Hills called "a hotbed of *dango* practices") with open competition. Japan was asked, in other words, to become more like the United States. The Japanese government response to the U.S. pressure was to increase the Fair Trade Commission's investigative capacity by hiring more staff, and to revise the Antimonopoly Law, with stronger penalties for collusive behavior: the administrative surcharge levied on participants in a cartel was raised from 2 percent of the value of sales to 6 percent; the maximum fine was raised from 5 million yen to 100 million yen; and a program under which the Fair Trade Commission would assist private plaintiffs to recover damages was instituted. A cartel that could not raise prices by more than 6 percent would be a notably incompetent group of conspirators;[10] so the U.S. complaints that the sanctions were still too low were probably correct. The Japanese government said that U.S. firms must form joint ventures with Japanese partners "in order to understand the particular demands of the Japanese construction and design market." The designated-bidder rule remained in place. Foreign firms were given permission to bid on some specified contracts, but there was little real opening to foreign firms: in 1992, U.S. firms received 0.02 percent of Japan's construction contracts. Thus, as of mid-1993, after seven years of negotiations, the market-opening pressure had had little effect. In January 1994, however, some opening occurred. In response to the U.S. threat of sanctions, the Japanese government announced that it would allow open bidding on large construction projects funded by the national government. On projects worth at least $6.4 million, any company meeting certain qualifications would be allowed to bid, instead of just the preset group of designated bidders. Furthermore, the government said that in qualifying foreign firms, it would consider work done outside Japan. This plan would open about 20 percent of Japan's public works to open bidding.[11] There was progress, therefore, though very slow.

What would have happened had there been faster and deeper response to the U.S. pressure? The direct effects would include harm to many, though not all, of the Japanese construction firms. Many of the firms currently operating, according to industry observers, survive only because the *dango* system guarantees them a share of the contracts. The introduction of genuine competition would be followed by a shakeout, with many firms, mainly small firms, going bankrupt. Construction workers would suffer from the unemployment that would follow reform. Some Japanese construction firms, however, would gain: the large, efficient firms would have a bigger market share once the inefficient firms were no longer being propped up. (By the early 1990s, some of the larger and more technologically advanced Japanese firms were in fact advocating an end to *dango*.) The technical efficiency of the Japanese industry would be improved, as the new competition generated extra discipline on the firms. Foreign firms would gain from access to the huge Japanese public-construction market. Japanese taxpayers would gain from the lower price of public-works projects: this gain is potentially huge, and doubtless outweighs any of the other considerations.

The indirect effects of removing *dango* would be on political funding: as noted, the political parties are dependent on construction-industry donations. This political side effect is not inconsequential, and it determined the Japanese stance in the negotiations with the United States. (As one of the Japanese trade negotiators said, public works expenditures "provide the necessary lubrication to the Japanese political process.")

It seems clear that the welfare effects of eliminating *dango* are large and positive, because of the overwhelming benefits to Japan's taxpayers, and because *dango* is inconsistent with an open global trading system. But the systemic resistance—the effects on political funding, and the political influence of the very many small firms that would be harmed—is strong enough to overwhelm any influence from the potential gainers. What looks at first glance to be a simple issue, a clear-cut case of some corrupt firms conspiring to earn illicit profits at the expense of the economy as a whole, turns out to be deeply rooted in Japanese society.

14.4   *Keiretsu*

Keiretsu have had a bad press outside Japan. According to the Office of the United States Trade Representative, "Japan's *keiretsu* system involves close intercompany linkages which impede the importation of many U.S. products into the Japanese market." According to Laura Tyson and John Zysman, "even when the government reduces policy barriers to market access in Japan, foreign firms continue to confront barriers that stem from the long-term contractual relationships among Japanese firms." According to Ronald Dore, "Imports penetrate into markets, and where there *are* no markets, only a network of 'established relationships,' it is hard for them to make headway."[12]

Are *keiretsu* simply a device to exclude foreign firms? Or do they have something else going for them? Entry restrictions raise the costs of the procuring firm: since these entry barriers are imposed by the procuring firm itself, they are not consistent with the procuring firm's acting in its own interest unless they bring some additional benefits. The *keiretsu* form of organization is, according to many observers, a source of efficiency. According to the Ministry of International Trade and Industry (MITI), "Japanese manufacturing industry owes its competitive advantage and strength to its subcontracting structure." A U.S. automobile executive has estimated that about a quarter of the cost advantage of Japanese automobile firms is due to the superior efficiency of their supplier networks.[13]

Evidence of the efficiency-promoting effects of subcontracting relationships comes from a series of studies that ask statistically whether *keiretsu* have a measurable impact on Japan's trade volumes: Fung (1991), Lawrence (1991), and Noland (1991). These studies find that vertical keiretsu—those involving subcontracting relationships—tend to increase exports, suggesting that the vertical *keiretsu* is associated with low-cost and high-quality production. These studies also find that a different kind of *keiretsu*, horizontal *keiretsu*—groups of firms operating in separate markets, often with common financial links—tend to decrease imports, and therefore seem to have a protectionist effect. In what follows I shall focus on vertical *keiretsu*, for they raise interesting issues about the relationship between domestic institutions and global trade.

Japanese-style subcontracting, involving deals among separate firms, actually makes more use of the market mechanism than the more vertically integrated form of organization traditionally used by U.S. firms. Subcontracting permits an efficient division of labor among firms. And decisions as to what gets produced and who produces it are guided not by internal accounting but by the price mechanism (although *keiretsu* involve a more subtle use of prices than that depicted in elementary economics textbooks).

Long-term relationships are essential to the workability of the Japanese subcontracting system, for several reasons. Buyer-seller interactions in general do not always work smoothly. As Williamson (1975) has pointed out, the manufacture of an item requiring specific investment cannot be successfully contracted to another firm unless shortsighted profit seeking can be curtailed. A subcontracting firm often has to retool in order to be able to manufacture a particular item. Having made this specific investment, not usable for anything else, the subcontracting firm is in a weak bargaining position; it is susceptible to a demand from the procuring firm for a renegotiation of the contract. Unless there is some assurance that the procuring firm will live up to its promises, the subcontracting firm will be reluctant to undertake the specific investment. Willamson concluded that production requiring specific investment can be undertaken only within a vertically integrated firm. The theory of repeated games suggests another resolution. If firms deal with each other repeatedly, they have incentives to act cooperatively. In an ongoing situation, firms cooperate because it is in their interest to do so. Concern for the future can prevent a firm from squeezing the last cent of profit out of its trading partner. The maintenance of these ongoing relationships is facilitated by Japanese firms' propensity to deal directly with a relatively small number of subcontracting firms— fewer than a typical U.S. firm.

As well as providing a way around the specific-capital problem, long-term relationships serve to generate incentives for the subcontractors. A subcontracting firm is motivated to do good work by the threat that, if it does not, when its contract expires it will not be renewed. Direct and immediate monitoring of a subcontractor's performance is often impossible; the procuring firm only accumulates information about performance slowly and imperfectly. In such circumstances contracts that base payment on current performance do not work well. The subcontracting firm is instead motivated by the promise that, should it do good work—producing high-quality parts or finding cost-lowering innovations—it will receive favorable consideration at contract-renewal time (Laffont and Tirole, 1993, ch. 8).

Incentives also come from the hierarchical nature of the Japanese subcontracting system. Subcontractors are organized in multiple tiers, with the procuring firm dealing directly only with a few first-tier subcontractors, who in turn control second-tier subcontractors, and so on down to third-tier and sometimes fourth-tier subcontractors. The size and complexity of this system is exemplified by Toyota, which in 1980 had about 170 first-tier subcontractors, 4,700 second-tier subcontractors, and 31,600 third-tier subcontractors. The benefit of the multitier hierarchy of separate firms is that the buyer at the top of the hierarchy need know less of the details of low-tier production than would be necessary in a hierarchy that was completely inside one firm (McAfee and McMillan, 1995). The classical benefit of decentralized systems is that they economize on the costly activities of acquiring and processing information. A huge amount of diverse information about production technologies, sources and prices of input supplies, and so on is needed in any reasonably complex modern manufacturing process. In a centralized system, all of this information must be collected at the top. In a decentralized hierarchy, by contrast, less information need be collected and collated, for control rights are closer to the source of the information. The hierarchy is a crucial part of Japan's subcontracting, viewed as an incentive system. High-tier subcontractors are awarded larger and more technologically sophisticated, and therefore more profitable, contracts. Low-tier subcontractors are promised promotion to a higher tier, and consequently higher profits, should they perform well over a series of contracts. Promotion to a higher tier, analogous to a worker's promotion within a firm, is explicitly part of the reward system in Japanese subcontracting.

The exchange of technological information between subcontractor and purchasing firm is a feature of Japanese subcontracting. Long-term relationships are needed for this: a subcontractor would be reluctant to reveal its innovations if it believed that its contract would not be renewed and so one of its competitors would reap the benefits of its discovery.

Long-term relationships, therefore, are crucial to the working of the subcontracting hierarchy. The corollary of ongoing relationships is that incumbents are favored when contracts are renewed, and it is hard, though not impossible, for outsiders to win contracts. Practices that look exclusionary in fact increase efficiency and therefore are ultimately procompetitive.

Although insiders are favored, the *keiretsu* system is not static: outsiders can, and do, win contracts. But entry is a much slower process than in a simple arms-length system in which the lowest bidder wins the contract. Relationships are built up slowly: a new firm typically is given small contracts, and only after proving itself is given larger and more technologically sophisticated work.

The U.S. case against *keiretsu* is different in nature from the public-construction and retail-stores interventions, where the barriers to entry were government-imposed and the United States wanted the Japanese government's involvement to be reduced. In the case of *keiretsu*, the barriers to entry are imposed by the firms themselves, and the U.S. demand was that the Japanese government strengthen its powers of oversight; the United States wanted the Japanese government's involvement to be increased rather than decreased.

The U.S. government's demand that Japan make its subcontracting practices more open—by limiting cross-shareholding, and requiring that managers publicly disclose the basis of their purchasing decisions—produced few concessions from the Japanese. The U.S. negotiators wanted to force "the Japanese firms to be more responsive to profit considerations" (Schoppa, 1993); though, if the preceding argument is correct, this position was based on a misunderstanding of the *keiretsu* system. The U.S. proposals were attacked by Japanese business representatives, academics, and bureacrats. The Japanese negotiators insisted that the United States recognize "certain aspects of economic rationality of the *keiretsu* relationships." The Japanese argued that it was the United States that should change its system (which, as will be discussed, had in fact been happening spontaneously—without government guidance—for over a decade).

The Japanese government agreed in 1990 to increase its monitoring of *keiretsu*, to check whether *keiretsu* restricted competition; but the 1992 Fair Trade Commission report that resulted from this agreement concluded that trade within *keiretsu* groups did not discriminate in favor of insiders. One of the U.S. arguments was that the lack of transparency of Japanese firms' decision making was a barrier to trade. In response to the U.S. pressure, the Ministry of Justice in 1993 proposed changes in Japan's commercial code designed to make executives more accountable for their decisions: giving shareholders greater access to confidential corporate documents, and making it easier for shareholders to file lawsuits against management.[14]

The trade friction has had the effect of encouraging Japanese car makers to buy some U.S.-made parts. Exports of U.S.-made car parts to Japan rose through the second half of the 1980s, though by 1992 they still amounted to only 1 percent of the Japanese car-parts market. In January 1992, during President George Bush's much publicized trip to Japan, the Japanese car companies announced what they called a voluntary plan to double their 1990 purchases of American-made auto parts by 1994. MITI officials are reported to have told the five major Japanese car makers in 1993 to increase their purchases from U.S. parts makers by 90 percent. Actual purchases rose 30 percent from 1992 to 1993. Toyota's 1993 purchases of U.S.-made parts amounted to $4.65 billion, more than four times the $1.1 billion of four years earlier: in response both to the threat of U.S. retaliation and to the rise in the value of the yen. Initially, simple mechanical parts and such items as carpets and aluminum were purchased, rather than more technologically complicated parts like electronic controls and engines. When the U.S. trade negotiators complained about this fact, the Japanese car makers said that high-technology parts must be designed into the car by a collaboration between purchaser and supplier, and so the purchase of such parts could not begin immediately. By 1993, some

U.S.-made parts were starting to be incorporated into the designs of new car models, and more complex parts were beginning to be purchased. In the meantime, Japanese parts makers were complaining that they were suffering from the new competition. Changes did occur, therefore, though only very gradually.[15]

What would have happened had Japan suddenly made the changes the United States demanded? The direct effects are straightforward: some Japanese supplier firms would lose, and some foreign supplier firms would gain. Ironically, the size of the potential gain to U.S. supplier-firms from opening the Japanese parts market is determined by the United States' own protectionist policies. Restrictions in the United States on car imports from Japan—euphemistically called voluntary export restraints—have the well-known effect, by creating a scarcity of Japanese cars in the United States, of generating extra profits for Japanese car manufacturers. A portion of these extra profits, according to the computations of Ries (1993), in turn go to some of the subcontractors within Japan, reflecting the fact that the larger subcontractors have some bargaining power in their dealings with the car manufacturers.[16] Thus a successful market opening, allowing U.S. firms to sell to the Japanese car manufacturers, might in turn transfer some of these profits, artificially created by U.S. protectionism, back home to the United States.

The indirect costs of forcing Japanese manufacturers to procure components from foreign firms would be huge, if the preceding analysis of the value of the subcontracting system, in promoting efficient production, is correct. Japanese procuring firms would lose, through having to pay higher prices and accept lower-quality parts. Technological innovation would be reduced. The technical efficiency with which production is carried out would fall. Japanese and foreign consumers would lose, paying higher prices and getting lower quality products. These indirect effects would seem to be sufficient to explain Japan's reluctance to change its subcontracting system in the way the United States demanded.

The U.S. pressure was intended to produce harmonization: to make Japanese practices more like U.S. practices. Oddly, this pressure came at a time when there was already a well-established trend for harmonization. But this was spontaneous harmonization, and it was working in the opposite direction: U.S. practices were becoming more like Japanese practices. There has been a kind of technology transfer from Japan to the United States, not of ordinary technology but of organizational technology. By their actions if not their words, U.S. businesspeople reject the negative interpretations of the Japanese subcontracting system.

During the 1980s many American firms began adopting *keiretsu*-like interfirm relationships. Increased use began to be made of subcontracting in place of vertically integrated production; subcontractors were given extra design and production responsibilities; and longer-term relationships between procuring firm and subcontractors were instituted. The U.S. automobile manufacturers, for example, began reassessing their relationships with their suppliers, shifting toward more work being subcontracted, longer-term relationships with suppliers, fewer suppliers, earlier involvement of suppliers in the design process, and more monitoring of suppliers' quality. The U.S. machine-tool industry made increased use of subcontracting. American textile firms began reducing the number of their suppliers and offering longer-term contracts; in exchange for the greater security, the subcontractors were expected to time their deliveries to minimize the textile firms' inventory holdings. Xerox reduced its pool of suppliers from over 5,000 companies to 400, trained the selected suppliers in quality control, and began involving them in the design of new products. Boeing began working with its suppliers to reduce their costs and improve their quality, and involving them earlier in the development processes.[17] The U.S. firms began using these *keiretsu*-like methods of organization as part of a quest for increased efficiency prompted by import competition, often from Japanese firms. Imitation, as they say, is the sincerest form of flattery. This imitation by U.S. firms of Japanese practices casts doubt on the basis for the U.S. government's complaints about *keiretsu*.

At the same time, Japan's subcontracting system began changing. In response to changed circumstances in 1993—increased costs relative to their foreign competitors' and falling sales—the Japanese car industry and computer industry introduced a new degree of "openness."[18] They reduced the usage of parts designed specifically for the particular model, and instead adopted the U.S. practice of using standardized parts, thus benefiting from economies of scale. They became more willing to dump inefficient parts makers, regardless of long-term relationships, in favor of lower-cost rivals, some of them overseas; as a result the efficient parts makers gained in market share, while smaller and less efficient parts makers went bankrupt. Large companies, taking advantage of the lack of formal contracts, canceled orders or slashed prices paid to subcontractors. In-house production increased. In some respects, however, the changes intensified the specifically Japanese features of the system. Honda began involving suppliers still earlier in the design process. Mazda cut its first-tier suppliers from 62 companies to 16. The system continues to evolve.

Are *keiretsu* exclusionary or efficiency enhancing? The paradoxical answer is that they are both. They restrict trade, at least in the short run, but in doing so they enhance welfare. The exclusionary practises are necessary to the functioning of the subcontracting system; and the subcontracting system promotes efficiency gains. Consumers benefit—there are trade gains—as production costs and therefore prices are lowered.

14.5   Large Retail Stores

The case of the large retail stores is the easiest of the three to analyze, for we have the benefit of hindsight: the U.S. pressure was successful, and the Japanese market was opened.

Japanese retailing in the 1970s and 1980s was, according to common belief, inefficient. The number of retail stores per capita was much higher than in the United States and Europe, and they were less efficient (by an OECD estimate, their value-added per employee was 28 percent lower than in the United States).[19] Under the large-scale retail sales law a retailer wishing to open a store of more than 1,500 square meters had to notify MITI, after which MITI was supposed to consult the existing small retailers and others, including consumer groups, before making a recommendation. In practice MITI, as described by Upham (1992), "privatized" the law, delegating its implementation to the retailers themselves. The prospective large store had to negotiate and reach an agreement with the local merchants, which MITI would then routinely ratify. The negotiations took up to a decade to complete. Since consumer groups were excluded from the negotiations, and their supposed representative, the government, chose not to involve itself, the resulting agreements were not notably consumer-friendly. The large stores, once admitted, earned profits from their privileged position. The local merchants were able to extract a considerable part of these profits from the veto power MITI had granted them. The agreements typically included requirements that a new large store "include specified local merchants as subtenants on favorable terms; make large 'donations' to local merchant groups; and maintain prices or services at the same level as surrounding merchants" (Upham, 1992, p. 16). Just as in Stigler's account of regulatory capture, MITI was administering a retailers' cartel.

The force of the restrictions on entry was demonstrated by the flood of entry that followed MITI's 1990 lowering of the barriers. "In the first six months following the measures, over nine hundred prospective new large stores were announced, more than double that of the previous year and

more than nine times the rate of 1982−85. The American toy retailer Toys
'R' Us in December 1991 became the first foreign store to be allowed to
open under the large-scale retail stores law, and announced that it planned
one hundred new stores within ten years."[20] Hundreds of new discount
stores opened, then began a price war against the established retailers. The
entry of the discounters was only partly in response to the dergulation,
however; it was also partly caused by consumers becoming more price-
conscious during recessionary times.

In a related development, the Fair Trade Commission began taking
action against manufacturers who set a "suggested retail price." Where
formerly manufacturers had threatened to stop shipments to retailers who
discounted their products, now they were forced to allow manufacturers to
set their own prices. In November 1993, some of the leading electronics
manufacturers stopped printing recommended prices on 1,500 products.[21]

The direct effects of relaxing the large-scale retail stores law are straightforward: a lowering in the profits of the incumbents, both the small stores
and the large stores that were already in place and therefore benefiting
from the entry restrictions; an improvement in the well-being of Japanese
consumers as a result of the lower prices and increased choice following
the increased competition in the retail market; and a gain to U.S. and other
foreign retailers and the manufacturers who supply them as a result of
having access to a market they were formerly excluded from. The new
discounters in particular purchased overseas, bypassing Japan's multiple-
layered wholesale distribution network. Foreign manufacturers gained to
the extent that the status quo had hindered imports. (The benefits to U.S.
manufacturers, however, turned out to be smaller than predicted: less than
a fifth of the toys sold by Toys 'R' Us in Japan are made in the United
States.)[22]

There would seem to be few indirect effects within Japan. One, probably small, is a gain to Japanese manufacturers. (The *Keidanren*, Japan's
big-business federation, in fact supported the change.) A manufacturer
with market power loses out if the retail market is imperfectly competitive,
in that some of the profits attributable to the manufacturer's monopoly
position stay with the retailers. Making the retail market more competitive
has the effect of transferring those profits back to the manufacturer. A
broader indirect effect was the effect of this market opening on the global
trading system: to the extent that the retailing restrictions served as a
nontariff barrier to trade, their removal strengthened the global trading
system. The net welfare gains from this particular market opening, therefore, were clearly positive.

Although the U.S. demands were at first strongly opposed by MITI, the Ministry of Home Affairs, and the ruling Liberal Democratic Party (responding to pressure from the very numerous owners of small stores),[23] the pressure from the United States ultimately met quite easily with success. The change caused, apparently, few indirect effects, and so the opposition it faced was weak. At the time of the U.S. intervention, forces had already been building up within Japan for a shift in policy: the Economic Planning Agency and the Fair Trade Commission were publicly in favor of change, and the news media were campaigning for reform. The American pressure helped move the opinion of the general public in favor of reform, according to Schoppa (1993). The internal political equilibrium seems to have been finely balanced, and some outside pressure was all that was needed to shift the equilibrium.

14.6   Restrictive Practices and Global Trade

Harmonization means reducing the diversity among countries' domestic institutions and policies. Calls for harmonization of different countries' business practices often seem to presume that the term "market economy" defines a unique and well-defined entity, departures from which are improper. This is, however, an oversimplified view of how markets work. Diversity among market economies is the norm. According to Albert Hirschman, "there is and always has been a large variety of 'really existing' market societies. This diversity helps to account for the shifting leadership of advanced industrial countries; it has also been a considerable, if somewhat hidden, element in the overall resilience of market societies" (Hirschman, 1992, p. vi). The market is not a unique organizational form; many different forms of organization are consistent with the label "market economy" and with efficient production and exchange. This obvious, even trite, point is often obscured in discussions of fair trade: the call for a level playing field is a call to eliminate organizational differences. I have argued that in some, but far from all, cases it is justified or feasible to ask a nation, in the interests of fair trade, to harmonize its industrial practices with international norms.

A market is a subtle and complex institution, which needs rules and customs in order to operate. Given the disparate goals of the market participants, and the uneven distribution of information among them, the rules of exchange must be craftily structured for a market to work smoothly. Market institutions facilitate the flow of information among market participants, and create appropriate incentives to shape their decisions. Moreover, market economies are systems; how exchange is organized in one part of the system affects how it is organized elsewhere. This markets-as-institutions view explains the empirical observation that quite different forms of market economy can coexist. Because markets are complex institutions, there is scope for institutional innovation, serving a similar purpose to technological innovation in the quest for improved methods of production. And because markets are systems, different choices about organizational structure in one area dictate different choices elsewhere, so market economies in their totality can look quite different from each other.

Japan's use of exclusionary practices cannot be explained as being the result of Japan's supposed cultural uniqueness. There is nothing inherently Japanese about attempts to shelter firms from competition. Each of the three forms of exclusionary practices that we have discussed has echoes elsewhere. European governments are as reluctant as the Japanese government to buy from foreign firms. Only 2 percent of European government contracts go to foreign firms; the European countries buy almost nothing abroad, even from their partners in the supposedly unified EC market. European Community restrictions on American sales of electrical-power generation equipment and telecommunications equipment were the subject of a 1993 trade dispute. Excluding large retail stores for the sake of small stores happens elsewhere than in Japan. French Prime Minister Edouard Balladur announced measures in 1993 to make it harder for new supermarkets to open, and ordered a six-month freeze on the opening of new supermarkets. The small shopkeepers, an influential constituency of Balladur's RPR Gaullist Party, were also offered subsidized loans.[24] Organizing production by means of long-term buyer-supplier relationships among firms is far from being uniquely Japanese: practices that are in many ways similar can be found in Italy and Germany, for example, as well as, to a smaller but increasing extent, in the United States. "Harmonization" is inappropriate terminology: to eliminate Japan's restrictive practices would be to move Japan away from what is commonly done in many other countries.

Are exclusionary practices consistent with mutually gainful trade among nations? It depends on the nature of the exclusionary practice. It is not the case that "exclusion is exclusion." Some forms of exclusion promote efficient production and therefore permit gains from international trade. The essential difference between vertical *keiretsu*, on the one hand, and large-retail-stores restrictions and *dango*, on the other, is in the effects on technical and allocative efficiency of the exclusionary practice. If, as with vertical *keiretsu*, a practice is efficiency enhancing, and if there is nothing to stop firms in other countries from adopting the practice, then it is analogous to technological progress and is consistent with liberal trade.

In other cases, harmonization of nations' regulatory standards is warranted (as exemplified by the *dango* and large-stores cases); international actions against such restrictive practices are justified. Such actions have up until now been unilateral, with one country, usually the United States, acting as prosecuting attorney, judge, and jury. Even when the unilateral action is justified, however, multilateral action, if feasible, can be expected in general to produce better results, for several reasons. First, unilateral action runs a greater risk than multilateral action of being applied with excessive force and leading to a contentious impasse, with harm to the global trading system as a whole (see McMillan, 1990a; Spier and Weinstein, 1992). Second, the response to U.S. pressure might take the form of leaving the restrictions on entry in place and including a few U.S. firms in the set of privileged incumbents, so that the selected U.S. firms share in the monopoly profits. From a global point of view this would be no improvement, as third-country firms, as well as other U.S. firms, would continue to be excluded. (European governments are for this reason wary of unilateral U.S. market-opening actions directed at Japan.) Third, trade negotiators being much subject to Stigler-style capture as domestic regulatory bodies—they often act as though what is good for General Motors is good for the country—a multilateral, rules-based approach might serve better than unilateral actions to protect the interests of consumers against well-organized producer lobbies. The co-opting of trade negotiators is illustrated by the 1985 Section 301 action over the South Korean insurance market. Negotiators from both sides "approached the case with the perception that the main issue was the sharing of profits in Korea's insurance markets. In the negotiations, both governments, especially that of the United States, basically represented the interests of their insurance industries. The effect of what was being sought in the negotiations on other activities, and on the efficiency of the economy as a whole, was not a major consideration" (Cho, 1987, p. 493).

Must actions against restrictive practices, because of the complexity of the issues, be unilateral? Or could the multilateral rules of international trade be extended to incorporate them? A precedent exists. GATT's still-born predecessor, the International Trade Organization (ITO), explicitly addressed restrictive practices, as John H. Jackson points out: its 1948 charter obliged member countries to enact laws against restraint of trade, price-fixing, and so on. Ironically, given its subsequent concern about other countries' competition policies, it was the United States itself that blocked this attempt, when the Congress rejected the ITO charter on the gounds of national sovereignty. The GATT treaty that replaced it omitted the ITO's competition-policy measures. The GATT subsequently made some attempts to address the issue, which produced little more than procrastination. A GATT study group recommended in 1960 that there be consultations whenever a member country felt harmed by restrictive practices in other member countries. But the group concluded that competition policy should not be written into GATT rules, arguing that any action "would involve the grave risk of retaliatory measures ... which would be taken on the basis of judgments which would have to be made without factual information about the restrictive practice in question, with consequent counterproductive effects on trade."[25]

This warning is justified. Not all exclusionary practices are equal. Some can be justified as enhancing efficiency. Careful, detailed empirical study is needed in order to distinguish whether a given exclusionary practice has some social benefits. A blanket prohibition on restrictive practices could be harmful (and in any case is probably not implementable). In the area of competition policy, there are few statements, analogous to "reducing tariffs will improve welfare," that are both simple and true. Trade-offs must be made in judging a nation's business practices. The absence of a clear, simple standard makes it difficult to write multilateral rules and difficult to conduct international negotiations. Clarification of what the issues are, however, is necessary before rational multilateral rules can even be contemplated.

NOTES

This chapter was begun while I was visiting the Center for Economic Studies at the University of Munich. I thank the members of CES for their hospitality, and Jagdish Bhagwati, Peter Gourevitch, Takeo Hoshi, Robert Hudec, and Miles Kahler for comments.

1. Quoted on the BBC World Service, June 11, 1993. By an OECD estimate, EC farmers in 1992 received a total of $132 billion in direct and indirect subsidies; this is equivalent to more than $15,000 for every full-time farmer in the community, or to $950 for each hectare of farmland, nearly four times the OECD average (*Sunday Times*, London, June 27, 1993, p. 8).

2. *New York Times*, May 12, 1993, p. C2.

3. The measure of welfare that will be used in what follows is the sum of consumers' surplus and firms' profits. This is oversimple, but workable. Noneconomists might argue

that the concept of economic welfare is limited and does not encompass all of the relevant costs and benefits. I do not deny this assertion, but in what follows I confine attention to what can be measured. Any additional effects that are thought to be important can be added, according to taste, into the policy accounting that follows.

4. Quoted by Johnson (1993, p. 26).

5. These are only some of the areas in which the United States has demanded changes of Japan. Others include land policy, rice pricing, satellite and computer procurement, cellular-phone services, financial-market deregulation, and macroeconomic and savings policies. Related analyses of U.S. market-opening pressure on Japan include Bhagwati (1994), Ito (1993), Johnson (1990), Kahler (1993), Saxonhouse (1993), Schoppa (1993), Sheard (1991, 1992), and Upham (1992).

6. Stigler (1971, p. 3); Kahn is quoted in Laffont and Tirole (1993, p. 537); Johnson (1990).

7. Quoted by Johnson (1991, p. 13). Schoppa makes the point that the effects of U.S. market-opening pressure on Japan can be understood only by looking at how the foreign pressure interacts with domestic politics: "The effectiveness of foreign pressure is not simply a function of the voracity of threats, it is also a function of how positively foreign demands resonate in the domestic politics of the target country" (Schoppa, 1993). Kahler says: "The principal prerequisite for success [in harmonization negotiations] seems to be the presence of powerful domestic allies in the target state, both to ensure effective implementation of agreed policy changes and to guard against nationalist backlash" (Kahler, 1993, p. 46).

8. For more on *dango*, and for the sources of the facts cited here, see McMillan (1991). On the incentives of colluding bidders, see McAfee and McMillan (1992).

9. The letter-grade practice is reported in the *New York Times*, March 28, 1993, p. A9; the story of Kanemaru comes from the *Financial Times*, July 23, 1993, p. 4; and the hiring of former ministry officials is reported in the *Far Eastern Economic Review*, April 15, 1993, p. 55. On the construction industry's political ties, see Coles (1989), Curtis (1988), and Hrebenar (1986).

10. Some elementary economics arithmetic illustrates this point. Suppose a cartel succeeds in raising the price from the perfectly competitive level (which is equal to c, the marginal cost, assumed to be constant and the same for all firms) to the monopolistic level (which, by the standard formula for marginal revenue, is equal to $c/[1 - (1/\eta)]$, where η is the price elasticity of demand). Then the price rise is less than 6 percent only if the market demand elasticity η exceeds 17.67, an implausibly high number.

11. *Financial Times*, June 21, 1993, p. 4; *The Economist*, May 22, 1993, p. 37; *New York Times*, January 17, 1994, p. C1, and January 19, 1994, p. C9.

12. These quotations were collected by Sheard (1991, pp. 32, 40).

13. For more on Japan's subcontracting networks, and for the sources of the facts cited here, see McMillan (1990b, 1995).

14. Schoppa (1993); *Far Eastern Economic Review*, March 11, 1993, p. 47.

15. *Financial Times*, June 16, 1993, p. 18, and June 16, 1994, p. 5; *The Economist*, January 11, 1993, p. 62; *New York Times*, July 1, 1993, p. C16.

16. Ries deduced his conclusion from looking at Tokyo stock-price data before and after the imposition of the voluntary export restrictions. He found that the VERs had a statistically significant effect in raising the stock-market values not only of the car makers, but also of some of the parts suppliers—the suppliers that were large or produced specialized components.

17. Alexander (1993), Burt (1989), Cole and Yakushiji (1984), Dertouzos, Lester, and Solow (1989), March (1989), McMillan (1990b, 1995).

18. According to *The Economist*, October 16, 1993, pp. 71–77; *Financial Times*, October 21, 1993, p. 15; and *Financial Times*, November 23, 1993, p. 14.

19. The facts cited in the section come from the fascinating analysis of Upham (1992). The common judgment about the inefficiency of Japanese retailing has been questioned by Ito (1992, ch. 13): according to Ito's estimates, the Japanese distribution system performs comparably to the American, as measured by value added, gross margin, and operating expenses; Nishimura (1993) finds a similar result.

20. The quote is from Upham (1992, p. 35).

21. Dick (1993); *Financial Times*, December 3, 1993, p. V; *Far Eastern Economic Review*, May 5, 1994, p. 63.

22. *New York Times*, June 2, 1993, p. C2; *Far Eastern Economic Review*, September 16, 1993, pp. 62–63.

23. Schoppa (1993).

24. *Financial Times*, June 29, 1993, pp. 1, 14.

25. Quoted by Jackson (1992, p. 114).

REFERENCES

Alexander, Arthur. 1993. "Adaptation to change in the U.S. machine tool industry." In *Troubled industries in the United States and Japan*, ed. H. Tan and H. Shimada.

Bhagwati, Jagdish. 1965. "On the equivalence of tariffs and quotas." In *Trade, growth, and the balance of payments*, ed. R. E. Baldwin et al. Chicago: Rand McNally.

Bhagwati, Jagdish. 1982. "Directly unproductive, profit-seeking (DUP) activities." *Journal of Political Economy*, 90 (October): 988–1002.

Bhagwati, Jagdish. 1994. "Samurai no more." *Foreign Affairs*, 73 (May/June): 7–12.

Burt, David N. 1989. "Managing suppliers up to speed." *Harvard Business Review*, pp. 127–135.

Caves, Richard, et al. 1992. *Industrial efficiency in six nations*. Cambridge, MA: MIT Press.

Cho, Yoon-je. 1987. "How the United States broke into Korea's insurance market." *The World Economy*, 10:483–496.

Cole, Robert E., and Taizo Yakushiji. 1984. *American and Japanese auto industries in transition*. Ann Arbor, MI: Center for Japanese Studies.

Coles, Isobel D. 1989. "The public works access dispute: Case study of a Japan–U.S. trade conflict." M.Phil. thesis, Oxford University.

Curtis, G. L. 1988. *The Japanese way of politics.* New York: Columbia University Press.

Dertouzos, Michael L., Richard K. Lester, and Robert M. Solow. 1989. *Made in America.* Cambridge, MA: MIT Press.

Dick, Andrew R. 1993. "Japanese antitrust: Reconciling theory and evidence." *Contemporary Policy Issues,* 11 (April): 50–61.

Fung, K. C. 1991. "Characteristics of Japanese industrial groups and their potential impact on U.S.-Japan trade." In *Empirical studies of commercial policy,* ed. Robert Baldwin. Chicago: University of Chicago Press.

Gates, Susan, Paul Milgrom, and John Roberts. 1996. "Complementarities in economic reform: A firm-level analysis." In *Reforming Asian socialism: The evolution of market institutions in transition economies,* ed. John McMillan and Barry Naughton. Ann Arbor: University of Michigan Press.

Harris, Richard G., and David Cox. 1983. *Trade, industrial policy, and Canadian manufacturing.* Toronto: Ontario Economic Council.

Hirschman, Albert. 1992. *Rival views of market society and other recent essays.* Cambridge, MA: Harvard University Press.

Hrebenar, Ronald J. 1986. "The money base of Japanese politics." In *The Japanese party system,* ed. R. J. Hrebenar. Boulder, CO: Westview Press.

Ito, Takatoshi. 1992. *The Japanese economy.* Cambridge, MA: MIT Press.

Ito, Takatoshi, 1993. "U.S. political pressure and economic liberalization in East Asia." In *Regionalism and rivalry: Japan and the U.S. in Pacific Asia,* ed. J. Frankel and M. Kahler. Chicago: University of Chicago Press.

Jackson, John H. 1992. "Statement on competition and trade policy before the U.S. Senate Committee on Judiciary." *Journal of World Trade,* 26 (October): 111–116.

Johnson, Chalmers. 1990. "Trade, revisionism, and the future of Japanese-American relations." In *Japan's economic structure: Should it change?* ed. K. Yamamura. Seattle: Society for Japanese Studies.

Johnson, Chalmers. 1991. "History Restarted: Japanese-American relations at the end of the century" (mimeo). University of California, San Diego, December.

Johnson, Chalmers. 1993. "Rethinking Asia." *The National Interest,* 32 (Summer): 20–28.

Kahler, Miles. 1993. "Trade and domestic differences" (mimeo). University of California, San Diego, January.

Krause, Lawrence B. 1962. "Import discipline: The case of the United States steel industry." *Journal of Industrial Economics,* 11:33–47.

Laffont, Jean-Jacques, and Jean Tirole. 1993. *A theory of incentives in procurement and regulation.* Cambridge, MA: MIT Press.

Lawrence, Robert Z. 1991. "Efficient or exclusionist? The import behavior of Japanese corporate groups." *Brookings Papers on Economic Activity,* 1.

Levinsohn, James. 1991. "Testing the imports-as-market-discipline hypothesis" (mimeo). University of Michigan, January.

March, Artemis. 1989. "The U.S. commercial aircraft industry and its foreign competitors." In *The working papers of the MIT Commission on Industrial Productivity*. Cambridge, MA: MIT Press.

McAfee, R. Preston, and John McMillan. 1992. "Bidding rings." *American Economic Review*, 82 (June): 579–599.

McAfee, R. Preston, and John McMillan. 1995. "Organizational diseconomies of scale" *Journal of Economics and Management Strategy*, 4 (Fall): 399–426.

McMillan, John. 1990a. "The economics of Section 301: A game-theoretic guide." *Economics and Politics*, 2 (March): 45–58; also chapter 6 of *Aggressive unilateralism*, ed. Jagdish Bhagwati and Hugh Patrick, 203–216. Ann Arbor: University of Michigan Press.

McMillan, John. 1990b. "Managing suppliers: Incentive systems in Japanese and U.S. industry." *California Management Review*, 32 (Summer): 38–55.

McMillan, John. 1991. "*Dango*: Japan's price-fixing conspiracies." *Economics and Politics*, 3 (November): 201–218.

McMillan, John. 1995. "Reorganizing vertical supply relationships" In *Trends in Business Organization*, ed. H. Siebert. Tübingen: J.C.B. Mohr.

Nishimura, Kiyohiko. 1993. "The distribution system of Japan and the United States: A comparative study from the viewpoint of final-goods buyers." *Japan and the World Economy*, 5:265–288.

Noland, Marcus. 1991. "Public policy, private preferences, and the Japanese trade pattern" (mimeo). Institute for International Economics, November.

Posner, Richard. 1975. "The social costs of monopoly and regulation." *Journal of Political Economy*, 83 (August): 807–827.

Ries, John C. 1993. "Windfall profits and vertical relationships: Who gained in the Japanese auto industry from VERs?" *Journal of Industrial Economics*, September.

Saxonhouse, Gary. 1993. "A short summary of the long history of unfair trade allegations against Japan" (mimeo).

Schoppa, Leonard J. 1993. "Two level games and bargaining outcomes: Why *gaiatsu* succeeds in Japan in some cases but not others." *International Organization*, 47(3): 353–386.

Sheard, Paul. 1991. "The economics of Japanese corporate organization and the 'structural impediments' debate: A critical review." *Japanese Economic Studies*, 19 (Summer): 30–78.

Sheard, Paul. 1992. "*Keiretsu* and the closedness of the Japanese market: An economic appraisal." Discussion Paper No. 273, Institute of Social and Economic Research, Osaka University, June.

Spier, Kathryn E., and David Weinstein. 1992. "Aggresive unilateralism vs. GATT cooperation: Optimal mechanisms for eliminating trade barriers" (mimeo). Harvard University, September.

Stigler, George. 1971. "The theory of economic regulation." *Bell Journal of Economics and Management Science*, 2 (Spring): 3–20.

Upham, Frank K. 1992. "Privatizing regulation: The implementation of the large-scale retail stores law in contemporary Japan" (mimeo). Boston College Law School.

Williamson, Oliver E. 1975. *Markets and hierarchies*. New York: Free Press.

15

Trade Liberalization and the Harmonization of Social Policies: Lessons from European Integration

André Sapir

15.1 Introduction

According to Balassa (1961), economic integration entails the elimination of various forms of discrimination between national economies. Furthermore, different levels of economic integration imply the elimination of different forms of discrimination. At the lowest level, a free trade area only requires abolishing tariffs and quantitative restrictions among member states. At the other extreme, total economic integration necessitates the unification of economic policies. In between these two polar cases, a common market or an economic union posits some degree of harmonization of national economic policies.

In the context of economic integration, harmonization of (some) economic policies is often considered as an essential complement to trade liberalization in the name of assuring "fair play" and of equalizing the conditions of competition. There are, however, two opposite views on the sequencing of trade liberalization and harmonization. Some regard harmonization as a consequence of trade liberalization, while others consider it a prerequisite.

The view that freedom of trade among a group of countries cannot go on for long without the harmonization of general economic policies—because disparities in economic conditions between countries would be intolerable to national producers—goes back to early discussions on European integration. In the political science literature this concept is known as the "spillover" effect. According to this concept, originally proposed by Haas (1958), once trade liberalization has been achieved, compelling interest-group pressure will arise to promote economic harmonization and, ultimately, even political unification. The spillover effect has always played an important role in the attitude of European political leaders toward harmonization of economic policies. Those wishing European political unification tend to be inclined in favor of economic harmonization, while those who oppose unification are generally suspicious of it. Hence, the debate on harmonization of economic policies in Europe is strongly tainted by political considerations.

Scholars of economic integration hold different views on the optimal sequencing of trade liberalization and harmonization, depending on the nature of the economic policies at issue. They generally share the opinion that harmonization of fiscal and monetary policies need only be envisioned much further down the road of trade liberalization. Equally, they tend to agree that some harmonization of competition rules should come prior to (or in parallel with) trade liberalization.

On the contrary, no broad consensus has ever existed with respect to social policies, by which is meant the set of rules that directly affect labor costs (such as wage policies, working conditions, and social benefits). One school holds that international differences in wages and other social conditions provide an "unfair" advantage to countries with lower labor standards. It recommends that social conditions be harmonized prior to or concurrently with trade liberalization. The other school regards differences in wages and social conditions as reflections of differences in productivity and social preferences. It rejects calls for measures of harmonization and argues that these differences will be reduced in any event as a result of trade liberalization.

The purpose of this chapter is to analyze the debate on the relationship between trade liberalization and the harmonization of social policies in the context of European integration and to draw lessons for world trade liberalization. The chapter is divided into two main parts. The first examines the debate that raged prior to the creation, and also in the early years, of the European Economic Community (EEC). It shows that harmonization of social policies was not imposed in the 1960s and 1970s as a precondition for trade liberalization inside the Community. The chapter argues that two elements were crucial in warding off, at that time, pressures in favor of harmonization: a high degree of homogeneity of economic and social conditions among the six original members of the EEC, and a rapid amelioration of living standards throughout the Community. The second part of the chapter examines the demand for and the actual measures in favor of harmonizing social policies that have increasingly occurred in the Community since the mid-1970s. The chapter contends that this new regime corresponds to a greater heterogeneity and a slower growth inside the Community. Renewed efforts to liberalize intra-EC trade in the mid-1980s also played a significant part in the shift toward harmonization.

15.2   The Early Years of European Integration

The debate on whether European integration calls for harmonization of social policies has a long and rich history. As far back as the 1950s, many prominent European economists took part in the debate, including three future Nobel prize winners. The first part of this section examines the discussion that took place in the early stages of European integration, before the EEC was established in 1958. The second part inspects the Treaty of Rome and assesses its potential impact on harmonization. The last part investigates the actual impact of the treaty on harmonization of social policies in the EEC.

15.2.1   The Debate Prior to the Treaty of Rome

The problem of harmonization of social policies was a subject of intense discussions in the framework of early European integration projects: the Benelux,[1] born in 1947; the Organization for European Economic Cooperation (OEEC),[2] established in 1948; and the European Coal and Steel Community (ECSC), created in 1953 by the Benelux, France, Germany, and Italy. It was not, however, until a little later that clear progress was made in sorting out the main issues.

The breakthrough occurred in 1956, with the publication of three influential volumes: a study on social policy and European integration by Albert Delpérée, a Belgian academic and civil servant who was chairman of OEEC's Manpower Committee; a report by the Group of Experts on Social Aspects of Problems of European Economic Cooperation (chaired by Bertil Ohlin) appointed by the International Labor Office (ILO); and a report to the Intergovernmental Committee (chaired by Paul-Henri Spaak, Belgium's foreign minister) created at the Messina Conference by governments of the six ECSC members with a view to preparing the EEC.

The Delpérée Study
In the discussion of social policies, it is customary to distinguish between wage costs, which comprise wages and social charges, and other labor costs, which relate to working conditions and industrial relations.

Delpérée (1956) began by noting that harmonization of wage costs is a central theme in the debate on European economic integration. He correctly stated that harmonization could mean either of two things: requiring equal wages for equal work throughout the common market; or simply encouraging, by setting up the common market, the rise of wages

toward the highest levels. The author rejected the first alternative as inde-
fensible and embraced the second as a sensible objective.

Delpérée further rejected the claim that harmonization was a prerequisite for liberalization inside the common market. "This thesis is defended
by those who believe that the economy of poor countries with low labor
productivity could never resist the competition from economies with high
productivity and by those who claim that high-wage countries could not
resist the competition from low-wage countries" (pp. 203–204, my translation). He pointed out that "both opinions are equally false" and, therefore, that "it seems incorrect to demand wage harmonization prior to the
common market" (p. 204). Instead, harmonization of wages toward the
highest levels had to be seen as "a commendable and justified long-term
objective. It will result from the international specialization of labor, the
decline of certain activities, and the development of others" (p. 205).

According to Delpérée, the fact that wage determination had to remain
outside the purview of public intervention was an argument in favor of
harmonizing working conditions, at least to the extent that one attached
greater importance to social than to economic conditions. He recognized
that such harmonization may "slow down certain changes that would have
been brought by the opening up of the common market" (p. 217). He
argued, however, that the harmonization of working conditions would
"prevent 'social dumping' and stimulate the generalized development of
social progress" (p. 217).

In order to harmonize working conditions, the author recommended
instituting European collective agreements. He noted that there had been
several unfruitful attempts in this direction since the 19th century but
attached great hopes to the ECSC Treaty. The latter, he believed, created a
new institutional environment, by calling for "the improvement of living
and working conditions, allowing their equalization, within each of the
industries covered by the Community" (Article 3).

Having reviewed the activities of OEEC and the ECSC in the field of
social policies, Delpérée (1956) concluded regretfully that the result was so
modest that it left employees and employers equally indifferent. The remedy, he suggested, should come in the form of a European Social Charter.
Delpérée warned that the charter should not be a simple repetition of
existing ILO conventions. Rather, "it should be a declaration of principles
and a declaration of obligations that [European] States are ready to assume
in the social field" (p. 238), granting a number of fundamental social rights
to each citizen in every European country.

The Council of Europe[3] initiated work in 1954 on a European Social Charter. The final text was signed in 1961 by the member states of the Council, but it was disappointing to many because it did not go beyond existing ILO conventions.[4]

In conclusion, the study by Delpérée represents an excellent exposition of the moderate continental view in the early debate on European integration and social policies. The author was strongly committed to an approach encompassing both social and economic dimensions of European integration. He argued forcefully in favor of a European social policy not only on moral grounds but also as a stimulus for economic progress. He rejected the harmonization of wage costs as a prerequisite for the common market, but endorsed the harmonization of working conditions to prevent "social dumping." Finally, he advocated a European Social Charter granting minimal social fundamental rights throughout Europe.

The Ohlin Report
The Ohlin Report is probably one of the most influential pieces of economic work on the subject of international differences in labor standards and international trade. The Report by a Group of Experts, commissioned and published by the International Labor Office, endeavored to answer two main questions, one mainly conceptual, the other relating specifically to European integration.[5]

The first question was whether international differences in labor costs, and especially in social charges, constitute an obstacle to trade liberalization. In order to answer this question, the report distinguished between "differences in general levels of wages and social charges" and "differences in wage structures."

The Group of Experts argued that international differences in the general level of remunerations, "far from being an obstacle to freer international trade, are, so long as differences in productivity persist, indispensable ... to ensure the [optimal] allocation of manpower and capital in each country" (p. 111). Concerning, therefore, differences in general labor costs, the experts did "not consider it necessary or practicable that special measures to 'harmonise' social policies or social conditions should precede or accompany measures to promote greater freedom of international trade" (p. 40).

Note that, contrary to Delpérée (1956), the Ohlin Report did not distinguish labor costs into wage costs and other costs (such as working conditions). Rather, it insisted that the various components of labor costs "constitute a finely balanced complex of interdependent elements. For this reason it seems highly doubtful whether it would be desirable or feasible to proceed to harmonization in respect to one particular element, such as working conditions" (p. 71), when harmonization of total labor costs is not deemed necessary.

The case was different "if the level of workers' remuneration (taking into account differences in skill, real effort, cost of living, etc.) in one industry ... were much lower than in other industries in the same country" (p. 112), due allowance being made for differences in economic conditions. In such an instance, branded as "unfair competition," the report recommended that the country in question adopt measures of harmonization, "in the sense of measures to bring wages and social conditions in [this] industry into line with those in other industries" (p. 42), prior to trade liberalization. The report noted, however, that it was obviously very difficult to assess at all precisely "whether wages and social benefits are or are not 'substandard' in any particular case" (p. 43).

The second main question examined by the Ohlin Report was whether some harmonization of social policies was required before or at the establishment of a European common market. Examining the differences in wage costs prevailing in the mid-1950s, the report found that "differences in the general level of wages are much more important in Europe than differences in the inter-industrial wage pattern" (p. 43). Hence, "the extent to which ... harmonization may be required ... seems to be smaller than is often thought" (p. 72).

Wages plus social charges were found to range from 58 (for Ireland) to 128 (for Sweden) among thirteen European countries,[6] and from 62 (for the Netherlands) to 92 (for France) among five of the six ECSC members.[7] However, in accordance with the previous discussion, the report argued that such differences in the general level of wage costs did not raise any special problem of international competition.

Regarding differences in interindustrial labor costs, the Group of Experts indicated that "while the statistical material that was at our disposal did not show that there are substantial inter-industrial differences in wages in European countries, we would agree that wages which are exceptionally low compared with wages paid in other industries (or regions) of a particular country may have a distorting effect on international competition and may therefore call for corrective action" (p. 62). The experts stressed repeatedly, however, that they had "not found practical examples in which such a situation is likely to arise" (p. 73).

Hence, the general message of the Ohlin Report was that the harmonization of labor costs across countries was not necessary as a precondition for trade liberalization. Whenever harmonization was useful, it was rather between industries within a country. In the case of the European common market, situations where harmonization of the latter, within-country variety would be necessary were deemed extremely rare.

The Spaak Report

The Spaak Report was the precursor of the Treaty of Rome. Its importance derives mainly from the fact that over the years it has been used regularly by the EC Commission to interpret certain passages of the treaty itself. In the part devoted to the common market, the report contains an entire chapter on "correction of distortions and approximation of laws."

The section on distortions distinguished between "general distortions" and "specific distortions," rather like the distinction made by the Ohlin Report between across-country and within-country differences. According to the Spaak Report, general distortions, including differences in wage levels, result from differences in general economic conditions. The report stated, "One cannot attempt to modify by decree an economy's fundamental conditions that result from natural resources, the level of productivity, and the importance of public charges. A part of what is generally referred to as harmonization will, therefore, result from the functioning itself of the market" (p. 61, my translation).[8]

On the other hand, the Spaak Report stated that "deliberate and concerted actions [are] necessary for the functioning of the common market ... in order to correct or eliminate the effect of specific distortions that are advantageous or disadvantageous to certain branches of activity" (p. 61).

The report specified that a specific distortion occurs when the following conditions prevail: (1) a branch of activity supports charges that are greater or lower than the national average; (2) the same (advantageous or disadvantageous) relative charges do not apply to the same branch in the other countries of the common market; and (3) these relative charges are not compensated by other charges. The report also indicates that specific distortions often have general causes. Among the distorting factors, it cited several examples, including disparities associated with "working conditions such as the relationship between male and female wages, working hours, overtime rates, or paid holidays" (p. 63).

The report recommended that the EC Commission monitor distortions within the common market and made proposals for their elimination. If its proposals are rejected by the member states, "the Commission has the right ... to grant a safeguard clause to disadvantaged industries" (p. 63). Such safeguard clauses were viewed as necessary incentives for the elimination of specific distortions by member states.

The report did not, however, regard safeguard clauses as the only solution for eliminating specific distortions. Thus, in the section on the approximation of laws, it discussed instances where harmonization of legal arrangements may be necessary.

In the case of working conditions, the report considered that "one can hardly conceive maintaining significantly different regimes inside the common market" (p. 65). Happily, "the spontaneous tendency toward harmonization of social systems and wage levels ... will be encouraged by the progressive creation of the common market" (p. 65).

Nonetheless, even if existing differences in working conditions did not create specific distortions, the report advocated a special effort by governments in favor of progressive harmonization in the following areas: (1) the principle of equality of male and female wages; (2) the conditions of overtime remuneration; and (3) the duration of paid holidays. At the same time, it proclaimed that "one cannot underestimate the difficulty of solving these problems through a purely governmental action and according to a rigidly predetermined calendar" (p. 65).

In conclusion, the Spaak Report generally took the view that differences in wages and social conditions reflected differences in productivity and social preferences. While maintaining, therefore, that the harmonization of wages across countries should be seen as a consequence of rather than a condition for the common market, the report defended measures aimed at eliminating specific distortions within countries. It also supported harmonizing working conditions throughout the common market, even in the absence of specific distortions.

15.2.2   The Treaty of Rome

The Treaty of Rome, which established the European Economic Community, contains several provisions related to the harmonization of social policies in the name of assuring "fair play" and of equalizing the conditions of competition. Some of these provisions deal with harmonization in general, while others address social policies specifically.

Approximation of Laws (Articles 100–102)
Article 101 of the Treaty of Rome deals with the approximation of laws that may be required for equalizing the conditions of competition. Its

application is rather stringent, being subject to several cumulative conditions: there must be a *difference* between national rules; this difference must be "distorting the conditions of competition"; and the "distortion" must be sufficiently severe that it "needs to be eliminated." The key is the notion of "distortion," which is defined nowhere in the treaty. It can only be understood with reference to the Spaak Report, distinguishing between "general" and "specific" distortions. There is a consensus among legal scholars that Article 101 only applies to specific distortions in the sense of the Spaak Report.[9]

Article 101 establishes a two-step procedure. During the first step, the Commission consults the member states concerned and seeks an agreement eliminating the distortion in question. In the absence of such agreement, the second step calls for the adoption of appropriate measures by the Community's Council of Ministers. The exact nature of these measures is not specified. The fact that Article 101 does not use the term "harmonization" implies that it contains no obligation of harmonization between all member states. At the same time, such harmonization is, obviously, not prohibited.

Article 101 applies to all national rules that distort the conditions of competition in the common market. It may, therefore, pertain to social policies, provided these are regarded as affecting the conditions of competition by introducing specific distortions.[10]

Social Provisions (Articles 117–122)
Article 117 defines the general objective of the EEC in the social area. It states that "Member States agree upon the need to promote improved working conditions and an improved standard of living for workers, so as to make possible their *harmonization* while the improvement is being maintained" (emphasis added). Article 117 defines a double approach for the harmonization of social policies: "naturally," through the functioning of the common market; and deliberately, through the approximation of national social legislation. The Treaty of Rome singles out two specific areas of action for the approximation of national social legislation: equal pay statutes (Article 119), and paid holiday schemes (Article 120).

Article 118 invites the Commission to promote close cooperation between member states in the area of social policies, including labor law and working conditions, social security, and industrial relations. Article 118, however, contains no enforcement mechanism.

Article 119 is probably the most debated social provision of the treaty. It declares that "Each Member State shall during the first stage ensure and subsequently maintain the application of the principle that men and women should receive equal pay for equal work."[11]

The principle of equal remuneration between men and women for equal work was introduced in the treaty at the demand of France, which feared the competition of other countries in sectors (such as textiles) employing a high proportion of female workers.[12]

The problem arose because France had introduced, before 1957, legislation imposing equal pay between men and women, while other countries had not. Consequently, the relative wage of women was higher in France than elsewhere. The liberalization of trade inside the common market would, therefore, have handicapped the French industry vis-à-vis its competitors in sectors (such as textiles) with a large female labor force.

There were two possible solutions to this problem. One was to abrogate the French legislation and allow supply-and-demand conditions to determine the relative wages of men and women in each member state. The other was to harmonize legislation by extending the French legislation to all the other member states of the common market.

The first solution was defended by Tinbergen (1958), who argued that Article 119 would "create female unemployment in countries where ... the natural female wage is low and create a shortage where it is high" (p. 201). Allais (1960) agreed that allowing relative wages to be determined by supply and demand would be best from the viewpoint of efficiency. Nonetheless, he opted in favor of harmonizing equal-wage statutes and other legislation, even though they introduced "specific institutional distortions" (p. 107), presumably on social or political grounds.[13]

France also insisted on including a provision on paid holidays in the treaty. Since it was found that paid holiday schemes were broadly comparable between member states, Article 120 only demanded that countries "endeavour to maintain the existing equivalence between ... schemes."

The French Protocol

Besides disparities in paid holiday schemes and unequal wages between men and women, France was also concerned during the negotiations on the Treaty of Rome with differences in overtime payments as a source of distortion.

The "protocol on certain provisions relating to France" indicates that member states were expecting working hours and overtime rates in the EEC to correspond, by the end of the first stage of the common market, to the levels prevailing in France in 1956. In the absence of such conformity, France would be authorized to adopt "protective measures" in the sectors of industry affected by the disparities in overtime payments.

Assessment

To conclude, "social harmonization" had been considered during the negotiations on the Treaty of Rome. This notion was largely rejected at that time, except by France, which feared that without harmonization of national social-protection systems its relatively advanced system would hurt its competitiveness.

The attitude of the treaty toward the harmonization of social policies is, therefore, rather similar to that of the Ohlin Report and the Spaak Report. The treaty proclaims that harmonization should, in general, be regarded as a corollary of rather than a requirement for the common market. Differences in social policies need not be addressed, provided they reflect differences in general economic conditions.

Differences in social policies that create specific distortions should, on the other hand, be eliminated. Harmonization is, however, only one of the possible methods that can be applied.

In certain circumstances the treaty calls for harmonization measures, even in the absence of specific distortions. These circumstances involve principally differences in legislation relating to working conditions, such as equal-pay statutes and paid holiday schemes. Moreover, in the case of equal-pay statutes, harmonization should be accomplished in the very first stage of the common market.

In conclusion, the Treaty of Rome never mandates that social policies be harmonized prior to or concurrently with trade liberalization inside the common market. The single exception to this rule concerns equal-pay statutes.

15.2.3 The Period of "Benign Neglect": 1958–1973

The first period of European integration has been described by some authors as one of "benign neglect" as far as social policies are concerned.[14] The main reason is that the Treaty of Rome does not, generally, advocate "social harmonization." In the few instances where it does promote harmonization, EC policy has remained largely dormant.

Article 101—which applies to all national rules that distort the conditions of competition in the common market—has been very rarely used since 1958, mainly because of restrictive conditions of its application. There have been a few instances of consultation by the Commission, but no case in which a measure was adopted by the Council. More importantly, it has never been applied to social policies because of the reluctance by the Commission and the member states to consider that social policies affect and distort the conditions of competition.[15]

Similarly, Article 118—which promotes cooperation in the area of social policies—has not been an effective basis for harmonization of national social legislations, owing to its lack of enforcement mechanisms.

The principle of equal pay between men and women should have been applied during the first stage of the common market. Its nonfulfillment by December 31, 1961, should have prevented transition from the first to the second stage. Instead, however, the member states decided on December 30, 1961, to enter phase two and to postpone the deadline for the application of Article 119 until December 31, 1964. In reality, even after this date, application of Article 119 continued to be blocked for a long time because of a lack of political agreement between member states on its compulsory nature. As a result, no directive based on Article 119 was adopted by the Council of Ministers until 1975.[16]

Nonetheless, Article 119 was not entirely absent from the scene during the period 1958–1973. In 1970, the European Court of Justice heard its first case (*Defrenne I*) involving Article 119.[17] On this occasion, Advocate-General Dutheillet de Lamothe attempted to clarify the meaning of this article. He argued that, during the negotiations on the treaty, the member states had agreed that Article 119 corresponded not only to a social but also to an economic objective. Therefore, "by blocking any attempt at 'social dumping' resulting from the employment of a female labor force paid less than a male labor force, [Article 119] favored the fulfillment of one of the fundamental objectives of the common market, the establishment of a regime ensuring that 'competition is not distorted'" (my translation).[18] In its decision, the court did not, however, pronounce a judgment on this interpretation of Article 119, so it remained without effect.[19]

The objective of maintaining equivalence between paid holiday schemes should also have been pursued by member states, in accordance with Article 120. In reality, no Community action was adopted in this area either during the period 1958–1973.[20]

At the end of the day, it clearly appears that the first phase of integration witnessed little or no measure of "social harmonization" on the part of member states. This absence of harmonization inside the common market can be traced back to two factors. One was lack of political consensus on the need for harmonization at the time of the negotiations on the Treaty of Rome. Essentially, France was the only country advocating harmonization, for fear that its relatively advanced social protection system would result in competitive disadvantage for its industries.

The other factor—which further weakened the case of those in favor of harmonization—was the highly favorable economic and social environment. During the period 1958–1973, the unemployment rate remained below 4 percent throughout the Community, while the real earnings of industrial workers rose steadily at an annual rate of nearly 5 percent. At the same time, differences in labor costs between member states were never very significant. Setting the cost in the country with highest level equal to 100, the level in the lowest-cost country was at 58 in 1958. By the end of the period, differences had further narrowed, the level in the lowest-cost country being already at 70 in 1972.[21]

15.3   The Social Dimension of European Integration

After 1973, the change of economic climate resulted in greater political interest in the "social dimension" of European integration. Two subperiods can be distinguished. During the first, from 1974 to 1984, the unemployment rate in the Community rose steadily from 3 to 10 percent, while the real earnings of industrial workers increased by less than 2 percent annually. On the other hand, differences in labor costs between member states further narrowed.[22] As a result, the pressure for "social harmonization" increased, but remained fairly moderate.

During the second subperiod, from 1985 to the present, the unemployment rate remained around 10 percent, while real earnings continued to increase at a slow pace. At the same time, differences in labor costs between member states widened considerably as a result of the entry of Portugal and Spain into the common market in 1986. Together with other events, this expansion led to strong demands for "social harmonization."

15.3.1   The Period of "Increased Social Activism": 1974–1984

In the beginning of the 1970s, a political consensus in favor of a Community-wide social policy emerged among the member states, which coincided with the Werner Plan on economic and monetary union. This led to the adoption by the Council in 1974 of the Social Action Program setting out precise actions in the social field.[23]

The impulse imparted by the Social Action Program led to the adoption, mainly between 1974 and 1980, of several important directives establishing the foundations for harmonization of national social legislation.[24] These concerned equal treatment for men and women as well as other social laws.

The key measure in the area of equal treatment for men and women is Council Directive 75/117/EEC of February 10, 1975, on the approximation of member states' laws relating to the application of the principle of equal pay between men and women. Together with Article 119, this directive constituted the skeleton for the harmonization of equal pay statutes.[25]

The Council also adopted important directives on labor law and working conditions: Directive 75/129/EEC on the approximation of national labor laws relating to collective redundancies; Directive 77/187/EEC regarding the safeguarding of employee's rights in the event of transfers of economic activities; and Directive 80/987/EEC on the protection of employees in the event of bankruptcy. A number of directives were also adopted in the area of occupational health and safety.

In addition to directives, a number of important decisions on sex discrimination in employment were adopted by the European Court of Justice.[26] In the landmark judgment of *Defrenne II*, the court stated that the Community "is not merely an economic union."[27] It confirmed that Article 119 pursues a double aim, economic as well as social. Regarding the former, the court considered that Article 119 "seeks to avoid that, in intra-Community competition, undertakings established in States which effectively implement the principle of equal pay suffer a competitive disadvantage as compared with undertakings established in States which have not yet eliminated wage discrimination against women."[28] It also confirmed that harmonization requires the leveling up of women's remunerations, rather than the leveling down of men's.

Moreover, the court ruled that "the application of Article 119 had to be fully implemented by the original Member States as of 1 January 1962 ... [regardless of] the decision of the Member States of 30 December 1961,"[29] therefore confirming that application of the principle of equal pay was a prerequisite for entering phase two of the common market.

Directive 75/117 and *Defrenne II* were important victories for the proponents of "social harmonization." But their success did no extend beyond equal treatment for men and women.[30]

The Community's reluctance to enlarge the scope of "social harmonization" beyond the explicit requirement of the Treaty of Rome in regard to equal pay for women and men was demonstrated in 1981, when the Commission presented its views on the interpretation and application of Article 101. In response to a question raised by a member of the European Parliament, the Commission confirmed its opinion that for the conditions of Article 101 to be fulfilled there should be a specific distortion to the conditions of competition. It accepted, however, that the notion of distortion in the sense of Article 101 could be revised.[31] There was an attempt to weaken the conditions for the application of Article 101 in 1983, but it failed. As a result, Article 101 has generally remained a sideshow.[32] In the field of social policy, it has played no role whatsoever.[33]

In conclusion, the period from the mid-1970s to the mid-1980s witnessed mixed results as far as "social harmonization" is concerned. There were some advances by the advocates of such harmonization, but, according to a close aide of President Jacques Delors, "the unanimity requirement within the Council for any measure concerning the harmonization of national social legislation [and other problems] halted this progress."[34]

15.3.2   The 1992 Program and the North/South Divide

In the mid-1980s, after ten years of slow growth and rising unemployment, the Community was suffering from severe "Eurosclerosis." To counter this disease, the European Commission, now led by President Delors, in June 1985 launched a bold program for completing the internal market by the end of 1992. The purpose was to regain economic dynamism by eliminating all barriers to free circulation of goods, services, labor, and capital between the member states.

A crucial step in fulfilling the "1992 objective" was the adoption of the Single European Act, which amended the Treaty of Rome in important ways. The Single Act, agreed in December 1985, took effect in July 1987. It greatly improved the decision-making process in the Community by introducing qualified majority voting for most internal market issues. Unanimity, however, continued to be required in sensitive matters relating to fiscal provisions, the free movement of persons, and "the rights and interest of employed persons" (Article 100A).

The Resurgence of the "Social Dumping" Argument
Liberalization of the European internal market offered the prospect of important economic gains. It also involved greater potential adjustment costs than the previous phase of integration. Before its successive enlargements, the Community was a fairly homogeneous group of countries in terms of factor endowments. Early integration, therefore, had resulted mainly in an increase of intra-industry trade, with few attendant adjustment costs. After the third enlargement in 1986, the Community was divided into a North and a South, the latter comprising Greece, Portugal, and Spain.[35] This action suggested that liberalization would increase inter-industry trade, thereby causing more adjustment problems than past integration.[36] The North-South divide also raised the specter of "social

dumping." In particular, unions in the North feared that trade liberalization coupled with free capital movements would weaken the social protection of their members.[37] To prevent such threats, union and political leaders demanded that the completion of the internal market be accompanied by Community action to harmonize social policies.

The European Commission, endorsing the view that the creation of an "economic space" should be supplemented by a "social space," sought to introduce new social legislation. The Single Act added two new articles to the Treaty of Rome in the area of social policy: Article 118A on occupational health and safety standards, and Article 118B on collective bargaining.

Article 118A declares that "Member States ... shall set as their objective the harmonization of conditions in th[e] area [of health and safety for workers]." In order to achieve this objective, the Council was invited to adopt, by a qualified majority, directives defining "minimum requirements for gradual implementation." Article 118A is not regarded by the proponents of "social harmonization" as an important addition to the treaty.[38] The main reason is that it contains several restrictive clauses, such as the need to "avoid imposing administrative, financial and legal constraints" on small and medium-sized enterprises.

Article 118B enshrines in the treaty the notion of "social dialogue" established in 1985 by President Delors. It invites the Commission "to develop the dialogue between management and labour at the European level which could, if the two sides consider it desirable, lend to relations based on agreement." Talks between representatives of employers, employees, and the Commission have become a regular feature of the European social arena, but remain fairly superficial. There is no sign of evolution toward EC-wide collective bargaining.

Plainly, the Single European Act reflected a wish to introduce a "social dimension" into the internal market program. At the same time, however, its actual provisions clearly demonstrated the lack of consensus between member states on social policies. The result was sufficiently ambiguous and imprecise to permit national governments to resist "social harmonization" at a European level.[39] It was also insufficient to silence the advocates of the "social dumping" argument.

In 1988 an interdepartmental working party appointed by the European Commission published a report entitled "The Social Dimension of the Internal Market."[40] The report noted that "the frontier-free area ... cannot be left to develop on its own without adequate management of the process of change, in short without commensurate economic and social regulation. Dynamic mechanisms must therefore be established to ensure the harmonization and convergence of economic and social forces" (p. 61).[41]

Two types of approach were identified by the working party: "(i) a 'normative' approach using a range of binding provisions ... and seeking to regulate the various social questions at Community level; (ii) a 'decentralized' approach rejecting ... any further social legislation at Community level, apart from minimum health and safety standards" (p. 61). Having rejected both approaches as unrealistic, the working party proposed a "middle, less simplistic way[:] the development of a European industrial relations area" (p. 61).

The creation of a "European industrial relations area" was deemed necessary in order to counter "three types of problem sometimes associated, rightly or wrongly, with the completion and success of the internal market: the threat of 'social dumping,' illicit work, and the question of wage costs" (p. 65).

On the question of "social dumping," the report began by stressing that "this concept is a vague one" (p. 65). The following definition was adopted: it is "the fear that national social progress will be blocked or, worse, that there will be downward pressure on social conditions (wages, level of social protection, fringe benefits, etc.) in the most advanced countries [of the EEC], simply because of th[e] competition ... [from] certain [EEC] countries, where average labour costs are significantly lower" (p. 65). Regarding the threat of "social dumping" linked to the completion of the internal market, the report concluded that "the risk ... exists and cannot therefore be discounted, but arises in specific sectors and cases which are at all events very much in the minority, although they should not be disregarded." The risk was said to concern mainly "labour intensive sectors involving relatively unskilled activities" (pp. 65–66).

To prevent "social dumping" and other "undesirable practices," the report recommended that a balance be struck between EC-wide labor standards and collective agreements. The aim of "establishing Community harmonization of employment and working conditions [would, therefore,] no longer [be] entrusted to regulations and directives alone: the social dialogue" would play an equally important role (p. 70). This approach should produce "a body of minimum social provisions," including the right of all workers to be covered by collective agreement and social security, the definition of employment contracts for all workers, and prior information and consultation of workers in the event of restructuring.

In conclusion, the working party appears somewhat ambiguous on the topic of "social harmonization." On one hand, its members considered it necessary to prevent "unfair competition." On the other, they recognized that the Community was marked by profound differences in social conditions and that it lacked the legal apparatus to adopt far-reaching social measures. In the eyes of the working party, the solution to this dilemma seems to have lain in the full implementation of Articles 118A and 118B. This would permit the adoption of EC-wide labor standards either on legal grounds (in the health and safety area, based on Article 118A) or on the basis of collective bargaining at European level (in other social areas, based on Article 118B). In practice, therefore, given that EC-wide collective negotiation appears a long way off, the working party does not seem to have seriously envisioned that "social harmonization" would go beyond the realm of health and safety standards in the near future.

The Social Charter
The ideas embodied in the report "The Social Dimension of the Internal Market" led the Commission to formulate the Community Charter of the Fundamental Social Rights of Workers, which was adopted by all member states (except the United Kingdom) in December 1989. The so-called Social Charter was explicitly linked to the "1992 objective," the Commission judging that "the construction of a dynamic and strong Europe depend[ed] on the recognition of a foundation of social rights. A political signal given at the highest level was crucial."[42]

The British government of Margaret Thatcher objected to what it considered an attempt at "social engineering" on the part of the Commission. The United Kingdom had a less regulated labor market than most other EC countries and did not intend changing this situation. Moreover, contrary to governments in continental member states that were more closely linked with labor unions, the British government did not regard "social dumping" as a potential problem requiring even minimum pan-EC labor standards. Instead, it argued for Community-wide labor market deregulation through "competition among rules."[43]

The Social Charter was a "solemn declaration," with no direct legally binding consequences. It represented a framework of principles proclaiming basic social rights of workers. In a sense, it was less ambitious than the European Social Charter adopted by the Council of Europe in 1961 (and signed by all its members, including the United Kingdom under the Conservative government of Harold Macmillan), that formally recognized and guaranteed basic social rights. On the other hand, the new charter was potentially much more far-reaching than the previous document because, contrary to the Council of Europe, the Community had at its disposal a legislative-cum-executive body. Hence, although the implementation of both charters was the responsibility of the respective member states, the Social Charter explicitly called upon the Commission to submit initiatives for the adoption of specific measures. It did so in 1989, by providing a very detailed action program for implementing the charter.

The action program contained almost 50 initiatives, of which about 30 would be binding on the member states if approved by the Council. At the end of 1993, half of these binding measures had been adopted, including ten directives that may be labeled as "social harmonization." Eight of these directives, based mostly on Article 118A and requiring a qualified majority, concern health and safety standards. The other two, requiring unanimity, relate to working conditions: Directive 91/533/EEC on an employer's obligation to inform employees of the conditions applicable to the contract on employment relationship; and Directive 92/56/EEC amending a directive of 1975 on the approximation of the member states pertaining to collective redundancies. The more contentious proposals of the action program, all requiring unanimity, have met difficulties in the Council. These pertain mostly to the equivalence of treatment between "atypical" workers (i.e., part-timers, agency and seasonal workers, and those on fixed-term contracts) and full-time workers, and the establishment of supranational European works councils in Community-scale enterprises (i.e., firms with 1,000 or more employees that operate in at least two member states) for the purposes of minimum information and consultation.

In conclusion, the Social Charter and the implementing action program do not appear to have added much in the way of "social harmonization"— except in the area of occupational health and safety. Besides, the harmonization measures that have been decided do not seem to reflect the fear of "social dumping." In fact, the Social Charter contains no reference to "social dumping." This expression appears twice in the action program, but in a way that was considered rather inoffensive even to critical British commentators.[44] Sections of the Social Charter introducing new harmonization have been blocked in the Council because of the unanimity requirement.

The Treaty of Maastricht
During the negotiations on the Treaty of Maastricht, the Commission had hoped to incorporate a "social chapter" in the treaty in order to reinforce the Community's "social dimension." This was vehemently opposed by the British government of John Major for fear that it would enhance public intervention in social matters.[45] In the end, despite a substantial dilution of

the original project, the chapter was removed from the main text of the Treaty on European Union signed at Maastricht in February 1992.[46] The Protocol on Social Policy annexed to the treaty states that the 12 High Contracting Parties, "noting that eleven Member States ... wish to continue along the path laid down in the 1989 Social Charter," agree to authorize the Community's members with the exception of the United Kingdom to sign an Agreement on Social Policy.

Article 2 of the agreement declares that "the Community shall support and complement" the activities of the member states in the social field, including occupational health and safety, working conditions, informing and consulting workers, and equality between men and women in the labor market. To this end, it authorizes the Council (except for the United Kingdom) to adopt, by means of directives approved by a qualified majority, "minimum requirements for gradual implementation."[47] The United Kingdom's opt-out from the agreement implies that it will not be affected by measures decided under the agreement's provisions.

The agreement clearly extends, for 11 member states, the scope of Article 118A beyond health and safety. It does not, however, much enhance the possibility of "social harmonization," since Article 2 requires that directives "hav[e] regard to the conditions and technical rules obtaining in each of the Member States ... [and] avoid imposing administrative, financial and legal constraints" on small and medium-sized enterprises. Interestingly, the text of the agreement contains no reference to the term "harmonization," which is present in Article 118A. The main effect of the agreement was to unblock the adoption of parts of the Social Charter's action program that previously required unanimity among the Twelve.[48]

The United Kingdom's opt-out from the Maastricht treaty's Agreement on Social Policy immediately renewed the fear of "social dumping" within the Community. This possibility was well summarized by two British authors who wondered whether "Britain [would] gain an unfair advantage in the single market by being able to pull in Japanese and US capital attracted by very liberal employment legislation."[49,50]

The Hoover Case
A vivid example of the fear expressed at Maastricht occurred in January 1993, when U.S.-owned Hoover Europe announced the closure of the company's factory in Burgundy, France, and its relocation to an existing site in Scotland, United Kingdom.[51] The Hoover decision was motivated by a new collective agreement at the Scottish plant, where unions agreed

on various social conditions (regarding flexibility, union representation, and pay) that were clearly inferior to those prevailing at the Burgundy factory.[52]

The Hoover affair rapidly became the symbol of the debate on the danger of "social dumping" inside the integrated European market. It was probably the first instance of enterprise relocation inside the Community that attracted massive media and political attention. It was the perfect case, pitting France, the champion of "social harmonization" and the Social Charter, against the United Kingdom, the champion of "competition among rules" and opponent of the Social Charter. The political climate was also ripe. Unemployment had reached record levels in France and the United Kingdom, the debate on the ratification of the Maastricht treaty was raging in Europe, and the general election was only a few weeks away in France.

In France, the prime minister stated—the day after the announcement—that Hoover's decision was blatant "social dumping," and the minister of labor explicitly linked the decision with the United Kingdom's opt-out from the Agreement on Social Policy. The British government not only accepted the connection, but even claimed it, the prime minister insisting that the Social Charter was destroying jobs and competitiveness.

In reality, neither the Social Charter nor the Protocol and Agreement on Social Policy annexed to the Treaty of Maastricht, even if they had been ratified by the United Kingdom, could have prevented Hoover from adopting the decision to relocate from France to the United Kingdom in order to reduce labor costs. The fact of the matter is simply that neither eliminates differences in labor costs between member states. The only impact of fully implementing these texts would have been to set up European works councils that would have informed and consulted Hoover's employees throughout the Community. Assuming—a big "if" in times of recession—international union solidarity, this approach could perhaps have prevented the relocation.[53] At the same time, this was by no means the first case of enterprise relocation inside the EC, nor has France been systematically on the losing end of relocation.[54]

The Commission found itself in a somewhat awkward position. On one hand, it regarded the process of enterprise relocation as a normal, even desirable, phenomenon inside the single market inaugurated barely weeks earlier on January 1, 1993. On the other, it had fought hard to introduce a "social dimension" into the internal market program, but it turned out that EC social legislation was irrelevant in the Hoover case. In the end, therefore, despite the sympathy expressed by President Delors when he received a delegation of workers from Hoover France at the peak of the crisis, the Commission adopted a low profile throughout the affair.

The Commission's view on "social dumping" came as part of the green paper *European Social Policy* presented in November 1993. There the Commission (1993) stated that "competition within the Community on the basis of unacceptably low social standards ... will undermine the economic objectives of the Union" (pp. 59–60). To prevent "social dumping," common minimum social standards were required. Their purpose was "not one of limiting the competition from countries and regions with lower labour costs, but of ensuring that their competitive power contributes to raising the standards for the workers who contribute to rising national income" (pp. 60–61). At the same time, "it has to be recognized that, under the present conditions of high unemployment, *the social rules may need to be strengthened* (for example, *with regard to the problem of the delocalization of production units within the Union)*" (p. 61, emphasis added). The Commission did not specify what form these reinforced social rules should take, but it insisted that Community legislation should not be the only approach. On the contrary, EC-wide social standards resulting from collective agreements at European level should play "a most important" role.

In conclusion, there seems to be a consensus that "social dumping" in the sense of the Hoover case (a) could not have been prevented by existing EC social legislation, (b) would not have been prevented by currently envisaged EC legislation, and (c) could only be avoided by trans-European union coordination and collective agreements. However, since the latter is probably a long way off, the real question is whether the European Union will witness more outcries of "social dumping" in periods of high unemployment, and if so, what will be the response from the member states.

15.4   Conclusion

This paper has attempted to carefully analyze 40 years of debate on the relationship between European integration and the harmonization of social policies. A certain number of conclusions emerge from the study.

First, it is fascinating to note that the nature and the tenets of the debate have remained almost constant throughout the entire period. The dividing line has always been between the "pessimists" and the "optimists." The former have insisted on the dangers of trade liberalization in the presence of differences in social conditions between the member states. They have tended to regard such differences as "unfair" and call for "social harmoniza-

tion" in order to prevent "social dumping." The latter have viewed differences in social conditions as natural consequences of differences in the
underlying economic conditions. They have held the belief that the common market will gradually reduce differences in economic conditions and,
therefore, lead to the harmonization of social conditions.

Second, the Treaty of Rome clearly sided with the "optimists." Apart
from equal-pay statutes, it never prescribed that social policies be harmonized prior to trade liberalization inside the common market. This view
was generally accepted throughout the Community until the mid-1970s.
After a decade of hesitation prompted largely by rising unemployment, a
clear shift in the direction of "social harmonization" occurred in the mid-
1980s. Several factors contributed to the shift: the enlargement of the
Community, creating wide differences in labor costs between member
states; high unemployment and stagnating real wages; the 1992 program,
increasing competition inside the common market; and the "social activism" of the Delors Commission. The new disposition culminated with the
Social Charter and the Maastricht treaty's Agreement on Social Policy.

Third, in spite of the Social Charter and Maastricht, "social harmonization" remains a distant reality inside the European Union. Differences in
labor standards between member states remain substantial. The OECD
Secretariat has recently constructed a synthetic index of labor standards
that measures the stringency of government regulations on working time,
employment contracts, minimum wages, and workers' representation
rights. Its scale ranges from 0 to 10. According to this index, regulations
are rather light in the United Kingdom and Denmark, but stringent in
Greece, Italy, and Spain.[55]

Fourth, it is likely that progress toward the harmonization of national
social legislation will be considerably slowed down in coming years. The
main reason is that the unprecedented unemployment levels have incited
governments throughout Europe to adopt more flexible labor-market rules.
Reduced social regulation in the member states can be expected to decrease the demand for harmonization.

Finally, it should be stressed that for the proponents of a European
"social dimension," the harmonization of social policies has always been
only one of two facets of the problem. The other is a redistributive mechanism inside the Community. As a matter of fact, this two-pronged approach was already enshrined in the Treaty of Rome. Thus, besides the
social provisions contained in Articles 117–122, the treaty established a
European Social Fund in order to improve employment opportunities for
workers in the common market. This and other so-called Structural Funds

in favor of low-income regions were greatly extended after the enlargement of the Community in the mid-1980s. At the same time, the Single European Act introduced the notion of "economic and social cohesion" into the treaty, whereby the Community pledged to reduce economic disparities between regions. Clearly, whatever harmonization of social policies has actually taken place in he EC, it would not have been possible in the absence of such redistributive mechanisms. Without similar devices, the harmonization of social policies cannot be contemplated in other regional integration schemes such as NAFTA.

NOTES

I am grateful to Jagdish Bhagwati for many helpful suggestions on an earlier draft and to other participants of the project for useful comments. I am also indebted to several officials of the European Commission for their careful observations.

1. The three members of Benelux are Belgium, Luxembourg, and the Netherlands.

2. The members of the OEEC were the United States and 16 European countries: Austria, Belgium, Denmark, France, Greece, Iceland, Ireland, Italy, Luxembourg, the Netherlands, Norway, Portugal, Sweden, Switzerland, Turkey, and the United Kingdom.

3. The members of the Council of Europe were Belgium, Denmark, France, Germany, Greece, Iceland, Ireland, Italy, Luxembourg, the Netherlands, Norway, Saarland, Sweden, Turkey, and the United Kingdom.

4. See Council of Europe (1991), International Labor Office (1961), and Hansson (1983), p. 24.

5. International Labor Office (1956).

6. Roughly the European members of OEEC, plus Germany minus Turkey. The figures are indices, with Switzerland = 100.

7. Excluding Luxembourg.

8. Comité Intergouvernemental Créé par la Conférence de Messine (1956).

9. See, for instance, Simon (1992).

10. See Lyon-Caen (1993), p. 10.

11. The first stage of the common market was supposed to be completed by December 31, 1961.

12. See Philip (1992a). Many French authors strongly defended this argument. Philip (1957) insisted that "France is one of the few European countries that have ratified and apply the Equal Remuneration Convention, 1951. If a common market is established without corresponding action on the part of the other countries the French textile industry, which uses a great deal of female labour, will be placed in a position of inferiority as compared with that of other countries" (p. 250). Allais (1960) also argued that "in the current state of affairs trade liberalization would *artificially* handicap the French textile industry vis-à-vis the Italian textile industry" (p. 88, my translation).

13. The reasons underlying this choice by Allais remained unspecified.

14. See Mosley (1990).

15. See Lyon-Caen (1993), p. 12.

16. See Philip (1992a).

17. Case 80/70 (*Defrenne* v. *Belgian State*) of May 25, 1970.

18. Cour de Justice des Communautés européennes (1970), p. 456. The advocate-general also confirmed that Article 119 was introduced at the request of France and that it gave rise to lengthy negotiations.

19. The court only addressed the question relating to whether contributions paid to a state social security scheme by an employer on behalf of his employees constituted a "pay" in the sense of Article 119.

20. See Philip (1992b).

21. Labor costs in industry (workers only). In 1958, the costs were 100 for Luxembourg, 76 for Belgium, 70 for Germany, 68 for France, 60 for the Netherlands, and 58 for Italy. In 1972, the costs were 100 for Germany, 95 for the Netherlands, 92 for Belgium and Luxembourg, 78 for Italy, and 70 for France.

22. This trend was reversed in 1981 with the entry of Greece into the Common Market. However, the size of this country was too small to have a significant effect.

23. See Venturini (1988).

24. Articles of the treaty are binding on all member states. However, their implementation often requires the adoption of regulations, directives, or decisions by the Council (or, to a lesser extent, by the Commission). Both regulations and directives are binding in all member states. Regulations apply as such throughout the Community. Directives need to be translated into national laws, therefore leaving national authorities the choice of form and methods of execution. Decisions are binding only upon those to whom they are addressed. The Council may also make recommendations or deliver opinions, neither of which is binding.

25. Two other directives on equality of treatment between women and men were adopted during this period.

26. Decisions by the European Court are binding on member states. They can be used *inter alia* to ensure that directives are properly translated into national laws. For instance, on June 8, 1994, the court ruled that the translation of directives 75/129/EEC and 77/187/EEC into British law was not in conformity with the directives. The *Financial Times* of June 9 reported that the British government was expected to introduce the required changes to legislation in the next few months.

27. Case 43/75 (*Defrenne* v. *Sabena*) of April 8, 1976. Cour de Justice des Communautés européennes (1976), p. 473.

28. Ibid., p. 472.

29. Ibid., p. 483.

30. In spite of the Community's directives and court rulings, differences in the pay of men and women have persisted.

31. Official Journal C222 of September 2, 1981.

32. This point is demonstrated, for instance, by the fact that Wyatt and Dashwood (1993) devote only two footnotes to Article 101. By contrast, 20 pages are dedicated to Article 119.

33. Lyon-Caen (1993) doubts whether the member states would ever accept the use of Article 101 in the social field.

34. Venturini (1988), p. 25.

35. Ireland, with a per capita GDP below the EC-12 average, is generally also classified in the "South."

36. See Sapir (1992).

37. See Teague (1989) and the literature cited therein.

38. See, for instance, Vogel-Polski and Vogel (1990), pp. 131–133.

39. See, for instance, Wise and Gibb (1993), ch. 5.

40. Despite a disclaimer stating the report does not necessarily reflect the views of the Commission, it clearly mirrors the position of President Delors. Indeed, both the vice chairman and one of the two rapporteurs of the working party were members of his personal staff.

41. Commission of the European Communities (1988).

42. Commission of the European Communities (1990), p. 5.

43. See Addison and Siebert (1993) and Wise and Gibb (1993).

44. See Knox (1990), pp. 67–68.

45. See, for instance, Wise and Gibb (1993).

46. The treaty entered into force on November 1, 1993.

47. In some instances, the Council must act unanimously.

48. The *Financial Times* of May 20, 1994, reported that, by the end of the year, the Council (with the exception of the United Kingdom) should adopt a directive providing for minimum requirements on consultation with elected trans-European works councils in cases where companies fail to agree to a voluntary arrangement sought by 100 employees or their representatives in at least two member states.

49. Wise and Gibb (1993), p. 307.

50. As a matter of fact, the Financial Times Survey on Relocation in the United Kingdom, published as a supplement to the *Financial Times* of May 27, 1994, notes that the United Kingdom has recently been attracting a disproportionate share of the EC's inward investment. Among other factors, it attributes this situation to "a relatively cheap and flexible workforce, factors that are reinforced by the UK's opt-out from the EU's 'social chapter'" (p. I).

51. For details on the Hoover case, see anonymous (1993), Lefresne (1993), and Sohlberg (1993).

52. According to anonymous (1993), there was relatively little in the Scottish agreement that could not, in theory, have been agreed in France. Two provisions, however, would not been possible: a "peace clause" and the exclusion of new employees from the company's pension scheme for two years.

53. The *Financial Times* of February 15, 1993, doubted whether a works council would have made much difference in the Hoover case. At the same time, it noted that compulsory work councils would horrify many U.S. multinationals and prompt them even more to concentrate their EC investment in the United Kingdom. Pochet (1993) also expresses doubts as to the efficacy of works councils in situations like the Hoover affair.

54. Paradoxically, in February 1993, Nestlé Rowntree announced its decision to relocate some activities from Scotland to Burgundy.

55. The scores are as follows: Belgium 5, Denmark 2, France 6, Germany 6, Greece 8, Ireland 4, Italy 7, Netherlands 5, Portugal 4, Spain 7, and United Kingdom 0. This index only covers legal as opposed to conventional regulations. As such it provides a rather biased view of labor standards across member states because some tend to rely mostly on legal regulations while others (such as Denmark) prefer the conventional approach.

REFERENCES

Addison, J. T., and W. S. Siebert. 1993. "The EC social charter: The nature of the beast." *National Westminster Quarterly Review*, pp. 13–28.

Allais, M. 1960. *L'Europe unie, Route de la prosperité*. Paris: Calmann-Lévy.

Anonymous. 1993. "The Hoover affair and social dumping." *European Industrial Relations Review*, 230:14–20.

Balassa, B. 1961. *The theory of economic integration*. Homewood, IL: Richard D. Irwin.

Comité Intergouvernemental Créé par la Conférence de Messine. 1956. *Rapport de Chefs de Délégation aux Ministres des Affaires Etrangères* (Rapport Spaak). Brussels.

Commission of the European Communities. 1988. "The social dimension of the internal market." *Social Europe*, special issue. Luxembourg: Office for Official Publications of the European Communities.

Commission of the European Communities. 1990. Community Charter of the Fundamental Social Rights of Workers. Luxembourg: Office for Official Publications of the European Communities.

Commission of the European Communities. 1993. *European social policy: Options for the union, green paper*. Luxembourg: Office for Official Publications of the European Communities.

Constantinesco, V., J.-P. Jacqué, R. Kovar, and D. Simon, eds. 1992. *Traité instituant la CEE: Commentaire article par article*. Paris: Economica.

Council of Europe. 1991. *The European Social Charter and its protocol*. Strasbourg: Council of Europe.

Cour de Justice des Communautés européennes. 1970. *Recueil de la jurisprudence de la cour*. Luxembourg.

Cour de Justice des Communautés européennes. 1976. *Recueil de la jurisprudence de la cour,* vol. 1. Luxembourg.

Delpérée, A. 1956. *Politique sociale et intégration economique.* Liège: Georges Thone.

Haas, E. 1958. *The uniting of Europe.* London: Stevens and Sons.

Hansson, G. 1983. *Social clauses and international trade.* London: Croom Helm.

International Labor Office. 1956. *Social aspects of European economic co-operation,* Report by a Group of Experts (Ohlin Report). Geneva.

International Labor Office. 1961. "The European Social Charter and international labour standards." *International Labour Review,* 84.

Knox, F. 1990. *1992: The social dimension.* London: Trade and Tariffs Research.

Lefresne, F. 1993. "Europe sociale: L'affaire Hoover." *Chronique Internationale de l'IRES* 21. Reprinted in *Problèmes Economiques,* no. 2329, June 9, 1993.

Lyon-Caen, A. 1993. "Les conditions de travail face au dumping social dans le contexte international et communautaire." *Social Papers.* Brussels: Commission of the European Communities, Directorate-General for Employment, Industrial Relations and Social Affairs.

Mosley, H. G. 1990. "The social dimension of European integration." *International Labour Review,* 129:147−164.

Philip, A. 1957. "Social aspects of European economic co-operation." *International Labor Review,* 76:244−256.

Philip, C. 1992a. "Article 119." In Constantinesco et al.

Philip, C. 1992b. "Article 120." In Constantinesco et al.

Pochet, P. 1993. "1993, faut-il une dimension sociale au marché intérieur?" *Nota Bene,* 72:9−11.

Sapir, A. 1992. "Regional integration in Europe." *Economic Journal,* 102:1491−1506.

Simon, D. 1992. "Article 101." In Constantinesco et al.

Sohlberg, P. 1993. "Les leçons de l'affaire Hoover." *Alternatives Economiques,* pp. 22−26.

Teague, P. 1989. *The European Community: The social dimension.* London: Kogan Page.

Tinbergen, J. 1958. "Les distorsions et leurs corrections." *Revue d'Economie Politique,* 68: 256−263.

Venturini, P. 1988. *1992: The European social dimension.* Luxembourg: Office for Official Publications of the European Communities.

Vogel-Polsky, E., and J. Vogel. 1990. *L'Europe sociale 1993: Illusion, alibi ou réalité?* Brussels: Editions de l'Université de Bruxelles.

Wise, M., and R. Gibb. 1993. *Single market to social Europe: The European Community in the 1990s.* London: Longman.

Wyatt, D., and A. Dashwood. 1993. *European Community law.* London: Sweet & Maxwell.

Index